Pro Windows Phone App Development

Falafel Software

Apress®

Pro Windows Phone App Development

ISBN-13 (pbk): 978-1-4302-4782-1

ISBN-13 (electronic): 978-1-4302-4783-8

President and Publisher: Paul Manning
Lead Editor: Jonathan Hassell
Technical Reviewer: Ken Cenerelli

Coordinating Editor: Christine Ricketts
Copy Editor: Lori Cavanaugh
Compositor: SPi Global
Indexer: SPi Global
Artist: SPi Global
Cover Designer: Anna Ishchenko

Distributed to the book trade worldwide by Springer Science+Business Media New York, 233 Spring Street, 6th Floor, New York, NY 10013. Phone 1-800-SPRINGER, fax (201) 348-4505, e-mail `orders-ny@springer-sbm.com`, or visit `www.springeronline.com`. Apress Media, LLC is a California LLC and the sole member (owner) is Springer Science + Business Media Finance Inc (SSBM Finance Inc). SSBM Finance Inc is a Delaware corporation.

For information on translations, please e-mail `rights@apress.com`, or visit `www.apress.com`.

Apress and friends of ED books may be purchased in bulk for academic, corporate, or promotional use. eBook versions and licenses are also available for most titles. For more information, reference our Special Bulk Sales–eBook Licensing web page at `www.apress.com/bulk-sales`.

Any source code or other supplementary materials referenced by the author in this text is available to readers at `www.apress.com`. For detailed information about how to locate your book's source code, go to `www.apress.com/source-code/`.

For my wife Kathy

Contents at a Glance

Contents

About the Author

Falafel Software Inc., an 8-time Microsoft Gold Certified partner, has been providing custom software development, consultation, and training services worldwide since 2003. For over a decade, both large and small businesses have worked with our dynamic team of Microsoft MVPs, Microsoft Certified Professionals, and Nokia Developer Champions to deliver cutting-edge custom solutions.

We began consulting in the early days of .NET and have evolved with technology, self-publishing over a dozen books along the way and speaking at events all over the world, including the Windows Phone 7 Developer Launch in 2010. In 2011, Falafel Software won the "Best of the Bay" award given to the best Software Design Company in the Bay Area, and a year later was featured on the nationally televised "Today in America" with Terry Bradshaw.

Today, we're focusing heavily on the latest cloud, mobile, and web development trends. Technologies for our current consulting customers range from simple ASP.NET MVC implementations to complex Windows Azure backed mobile solutions, complete with native mobile applications for Windows Phone, Windows 8, iOS, and Android.

Whether your organization needs help moving to the cloud, a suite of mobile applications, or assistance with a particular Microsoft technology, the Falafel family is here to help. Visit `www.falafel.com` for more information.

Noel Rice has been with Falafel Software since its inception in 2003. Noel has over 20 years of experience in the software industry including numerous successful projects in the industries of medical, telecom, financial, and manufacturing. Noel has authored over ten books on diverse subjects ranging over ASP.NET, ASP.NET AJAX, Silverlight, Android development, CMS, Reporting, automated testing, Winforms, and ORM.

About the Technical Reviewer

Ken Cenerelli is a developer specializing in designing and creating effective solutions for both the web and desktop environments. With over 12 years of experience in software design, development, and support, he has engineered strong, data-driven web applications using the Microsoft .NET Framework for large and small companies throughout North America. Ken also works with mobile technologies and has built apps for both the Windows Phone and the Android OS.

He currently lives in Guelph, Ontario, Canada with his wife Renée.

Ken blogs regularly at `kencenerelli.wordpress.com` and can be found on Twitter via `@KenCenerelli`.

CHAPTER 1

Introduction

This chapter describes the groundwork you need to perform before writing Windows Phone 8 applications including:

- The particular skill sets in Windows 8, Visual Studio, and Windows Phone 8 that you need to have to get the most from this book.
- PC and phone hardware requirements to support the development environment.
- Software requirements for the operating system and the Visual Studio development environment.

Why Upgrade to Windows Phone 8?

Microsoft's intent is to lead and not follow in the race to create a superior phone operating system. Windows Phone 8 takes advantages of all the latest hardware features, such as Near Field Communications (NFC), while Windows Phone 7.x applications will still run "out of the box." The clean user interface favors content over "chrome" and is easy to learn. From the developer's perspective, Windows Phone 8 is simply a lot of fun to develop on and is quite productive. Having worked with the Android platform and having a nodding aquintanceship with iOS, Windows Phone 8 is clearly my platform of choice.

What You Need to Know

You should be able to navigate the Windows 8 environment, at least to the point where you can get to the Start screen, search for applications on the PC, and run applications.

You should be familiar with the Visual Studio environment, be able to create projects, add project items, and assembly references. You should know how to code in either Visual Basic .NET or C#. The code for this book is presented in C#. If you already use XAML, you will have a good head start learning Windows Phone 8 development.

In particular, this book will not specifically include `using` statements in code listings except for unusual circumstances. When Visual Studio encounters a member that it cannot resolve, the editor underlines the member with a wavy red line. You should right-click the member and choose the `Resolve` context menu option to add the `using` statement automatically. In cases where the namespace includes extensions, such as `System.Linq`, Visual Studio will not offer the Resolve context menu. In these cases, the instructions or code listings will include the specific `using` statements.

Spend some time learning the features and operation of Windows Phone 8 devices, including unlocking the screen, navigating from the Start screen, and "pinning" tiles. The link below should get you started:

`www.windowsphone.com/en-us/how-to/wp8/start/get-started-with-windows-phone-8`

What You Need to Have

To get started with Windows Phone 8 development, you will need some specific hardware and software. In this section, we'll cover the requirements for:

- PC Hardware requirements
- Phone Hardware Requirements
- Operating system requirements
- The Windows Phone 8 SDK
- Visual Studio

PC Hardware Requirements

Your PC must have *Hyper V* and *SLAT* support. Hyper V is required to run virtual machines, namely the Windows Phone 8 emulator. SLAT (Second Level Address Translation) is used by Hyper V to translate virtualized guest addresses to real physical addresses. The bottom line is that you need to enable virtualization in your PC BIOS settings for Hyper V and SLAT. The specific settings will vary according to your PC's BIOS setup. Older machines may not have these settings available.

How do you know if you're good to go? There are a number of software utilities that assess hardware and firmware. Microsoft offers a command line tool, Coreinfo, that lists virtualization capabilities. Find Coreinfo for download at Technet:

```
http://technet.microsoft.com/en-us/sysinternals/cc835722.aspx
```

Run CoreInfo from the developer command line as an administrator:

1. Navigate to the Windows 8 Start screen.
2. Type "Command" to search on and select the available command line applications.
3. Locate the "Developer Command Prompt for VS2012" application in the results list, right-click, and select Run as administrator from the app bar.
4. Change your directory (`cd`) to the folder that contains `Coreinfo.exe`.
5. Run the command `coreinfo -v`.

The command will list information relating to virtualization capabilities. The output below shows a sample run of Coreinfo on a laptop that is ready for Windows Phone 8 development. The hyphen in the HYPERVISOR line indicates that the Hypervisor is present but not enabled. Asterisks in the VMX and EPT lines indicate that hardware-assisted virtualization and SLAT support are supported.

```
C:\WINDOWS\system32>cd C:\Download\Coreinfo

C:\Download\Coreinfo>coreinfo -v

Coreinfo v3.2 - Dump information on system CPU and memory topology
Copyright (C) 2008-2012 Mark Russinovich
Sysinternals - www.sysinternals.com
```

```
Intel(R) Core(TM) i7 CPU       Q 720  @ 1.60GHz
Intel64 Family 6 Model 30 Stepping 5, GenuineIntel
HYPERVISOR      -       Hypervisor is present
VMX             *       Supports Intel hardware-assisted virtualization
EPT             *       Supports Intel extended page tables (SLAT)
```

The *Microsoft Assessment and Planning Toolkit* (http://technet.microsoft.com/en-us/library/bb977556.aspx) verifies that your machine supports Hyper V. The Microsoft Assessment and Planning Toolkit may be overkill compared with CoreInfo. This toolkit is a complete planning utility that checks for capabilities over cloud, desktop, server, and more. In Figure 1-1, the Microsoft Assessment and Planning tool indicates support for Hyper V support and Windows 8 readiness.

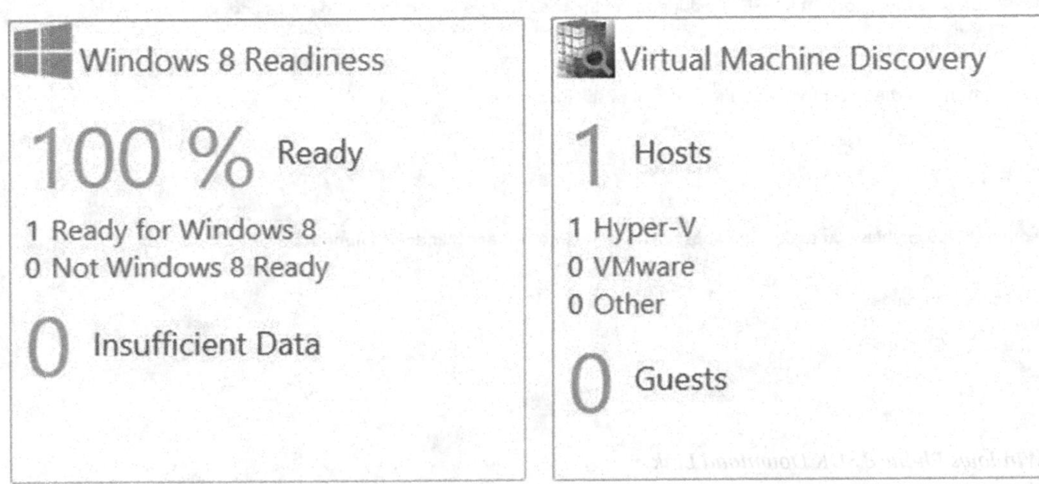

Figure 1-1. *Microsoft Assessment and Planning Toolkit Output*

Phone Hardware Requirements

Windows Phone 8 development does not actually require a phone. You can get by using the Emulator application until you require specific device capabilities operating in a physical environment (e.g., the Accelerometer or geographic location). While the Emulator is convenient for initial testing, you should run your application against one or more phone devices for final testing. When choosing a phone, be sure that it runs the Windows Phone 8 operating system, such as the Nokia 92x, HTC Windows Phone 8x, or Samsung ATIV S. *Legacy phones intended for Windows Phone 7.x are not upgradable to Windows Phone 8.* For more information on using a Windows Phone 8 device, see the section "Creating, Configuring, and Testing an Application" in Chapter 2.

Operating System Requirements

Windows Phone 8 development requires the 64-bit version of *Windows 8 Pro or greater.* You can still install and run using only Windows 8, but the emulator will not work.

The Windows Phone 8 SDK

The Windows Phone 8 SDK allows you to create Windows Phone 8 applications in Visual Studio and to test your applications on your PC using an emulator. The most important download is located at the *Windows Phone Dev Center* (`https://dev.windowsphone.com`). Here you'll find a link to the SDK 8 download, as shown in Figure 1-2, and a full list of requirements for install (`www.microsoft.com/download/details.aspx?id=35471`).

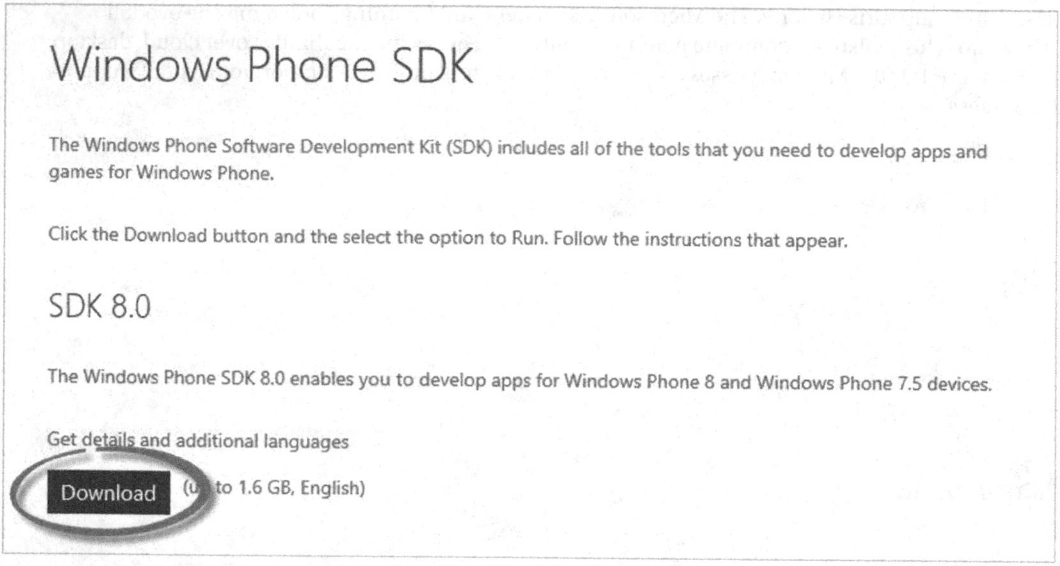

Windows Phone SDK

The Windows Phone Software Development Kit (SDK) includes all of the tools that you need to develop apps and games for Windows Phone.

Click the Download button and the select the option to Run. Follow the instructions that appear.

SDK 8.0

The Windows Phone SDK 8.0 enables you to develop apps for Windows Phone 8 and Windows Phone 7.5 devices.

Get details and additional languages

Download (u to 1.6 GB, English)

Figure 1-2. *The Windows Phone 8 SDK Download Link*

The download consists of `Wpexpress_full.exe` that installs to the `\Program Files (x86)\Windows Phone Kits\8.0` directory by default. Here are some of the goodies that are installed:

- SDK Windows Phone 8 Assemblies
- Windows Phone 8 Emulator
- Visual Studio Express 2012 for Windows Phone
- Adds project and item templates to Visual Studio 2012
- Development Kit Tools for Windows Store Apps
- MS C++ 2012 Compilers and Core Libraries for Windows Phone 8
- Direct X Libraries
- XNA Game Studio 40
- Windows Phone 7.1 Support
- Blend SDK for Windows Phone 8 and 7.1
- Microsoft Advertising SDK

■ **Note** "If you install the Windows Phone SDK 8.0 on a computer with a Gigabyte motherboard and the USB 3.0 host controller enabled in the BIOS, the computer might stop responding when it boots (for details on impacted Gigabyte motherboard models, see Installing Hyper-V on Gigabyte systems). To resolve this, disable USB 3.0 support in computer's BIOS." Source: Windows Phone SDK 8 Install Notes (`www.microsoft.com/en-us/download/details.aspx?id=35471`).

Visual Studio

A stand-alone version of *Visual Studio Express 2012 for Windows Phone* is included as part of the Windows Phone 8 SDK install. If you already have Visual Studio Professional, Premium, or Ultimate installed, the SDK will install as an add-in to your existing version. Be aware that the Express version of Visual Studio 2012 will be missing some features you may be expecting—that do appear in the non-express versions—such as the ability to switch between Windows Phone and Web development within the same IDE, the ability to use Add-ins (such as JetBrains' ReSharper), and some architectural tools.

The screenshots in this book are taken from Visual Studio 2012 Professional.

Summary

The list of prerequisites may look daunting. In fact, if your hardware is too old, you may need to go shopping for new hardware to satisfy the requirements. Try scanning this chapter to get an idea of the overall process, and then work through each item in order. Once you are able to open Visual Studio 2012, open a new project and see Windows Phone 8 templates, you're good to go!

CHAPTER 2

Getting Started

This chapter focuses on learning your way around a Windows Phone 8 application project, including:

- How to create a basic "hello world" Windows Phone 8 project.
- How to navigate the Visual Studio solution, particularly the location and purpose of key files.
- How to run the application in Visual Studio.
- Running your application in the emulator.
- Running your application on your phone device.

Creating a Windows Phone 8 Project

To create Windows Phone 8 projects, select `File` ➤ `New` ➤ `Project` from the Visual Studio menu and choose one of the `Windows Phone` templates (see Figure 2-1). Windows Phone templates can be found under both the Visual Basic and Visual C# nodes; this book will be using C# as the default language. The `Windows Phone App` template creates a "Hello World" type application by default. Click `OK` to have Visual Studio begin creating the new Windows Phone App.

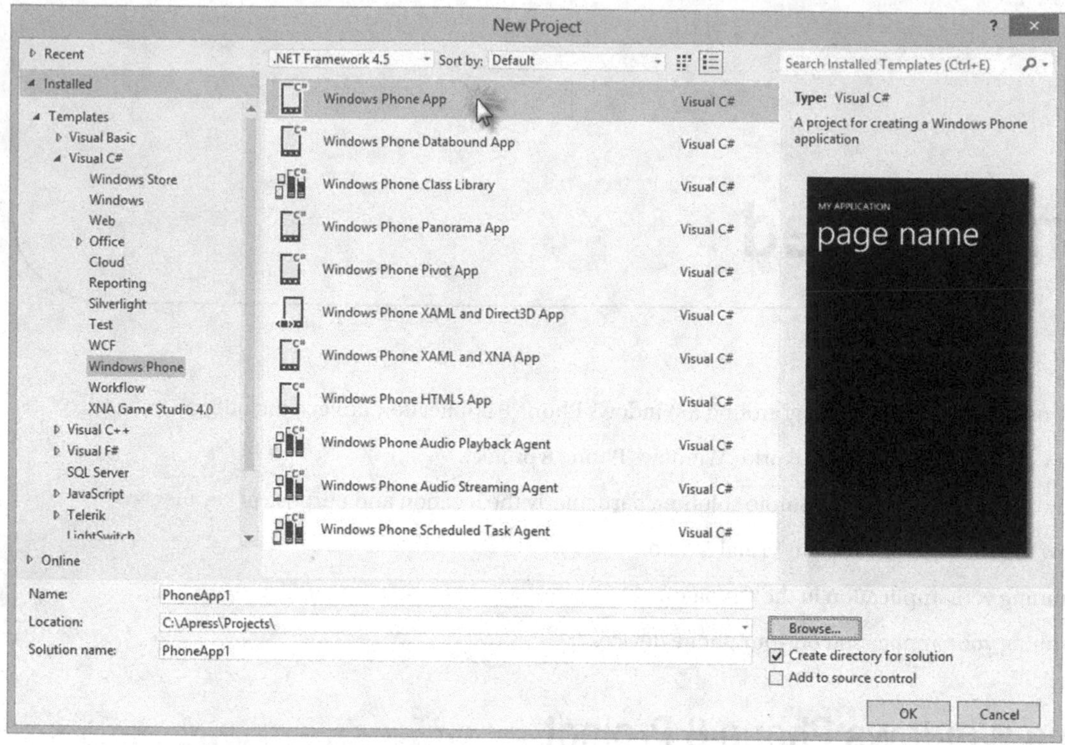

Figure 2-1. *Using the Windows Phone App Project Template*

Next, choose the Windows Phone OS version (see Figure 2-2). For the purposes of this book we will choose the `Windows Phone OS 8.0` default exclusively.

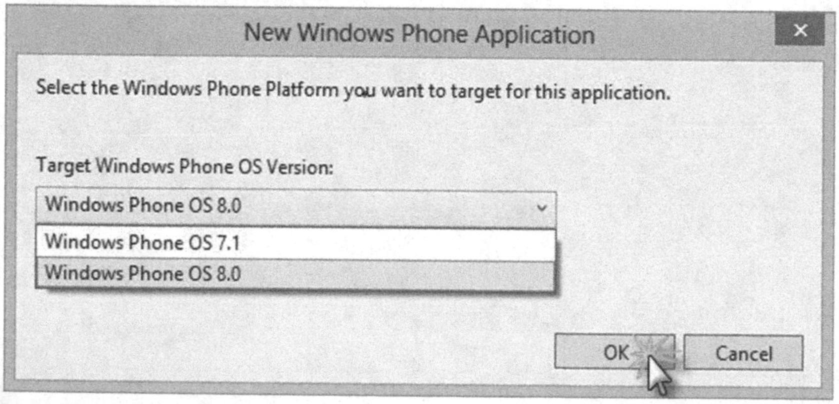

Figure 2-2. *Choosing the OS Version*

You can run the application by pressing F5 or clicking the green Run arrow to display the application and page titles in the emulator, as shown in Figure 2-3.

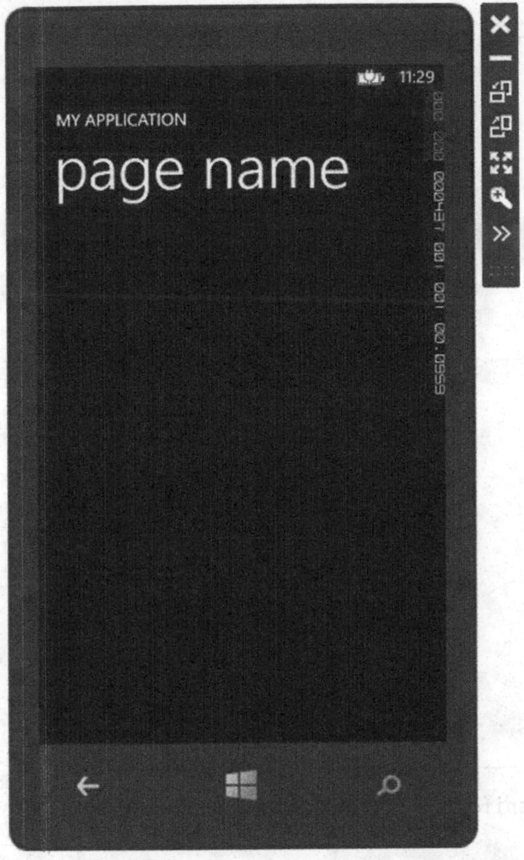

Figure 2-3. Default Application Running in the Emulator

Windows Phone 8 Solution Anatomy

When you create a new Windows Phone 8 application in Visual Studio, a single project is created. The key elements are:

- `AppManifest.xml` lists resources to include when deploying the application. Visual Studio takes care of maintaining this file for you. The `AppManifest.xml` file is located in the Properties folder of the project.
- `WMAppManifest.xml` describes the application in more detail including the `Display Name`, starting `Navigation Page`, `App Icon`, a list of `Capabilities` and hardware `Requirements`. The `WMAppManifest.xml` file is located in the Properties folder of the project. The values from the manifest are used by the device and by the Windows Phone Store application submission process. Double-click `WMAppManifest.xml` to see the Visual Studio designer. Figure 2-4 shows the visual tabbed interface where you can tweak settings without having to edit XML directly.

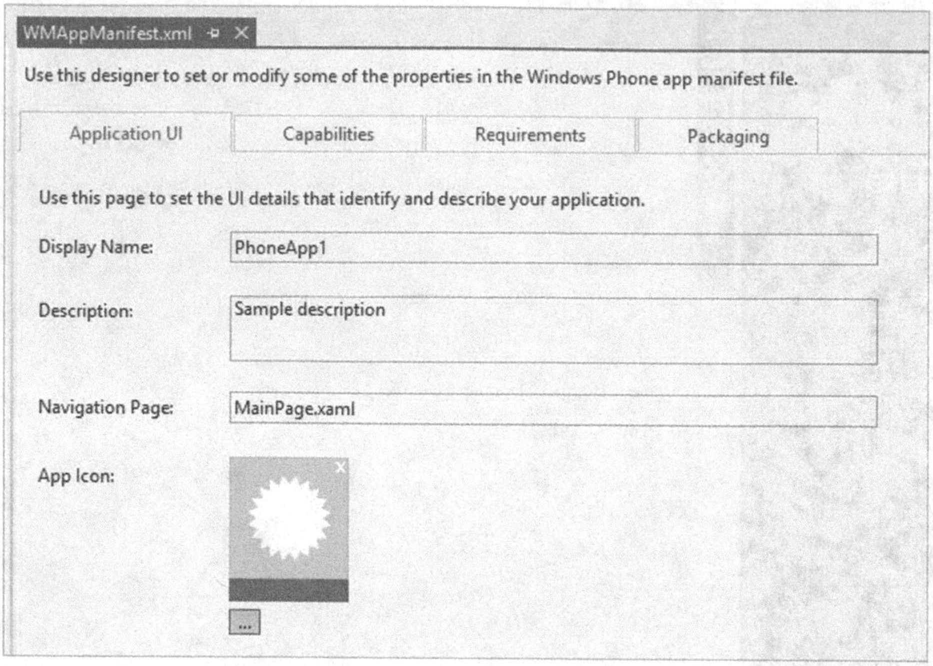

Figure 2-4. The WMAppManifest Designer

■ **Tip** If you prefer to work with the XML directly, right-click `WMAppManifest.xml` (located in the Properties folder of the project) and select `View Code` from the context menu.

- The `Assets` folder contains the images for the application icon and the tile images that display in the Windows Phone 8 Start screen.
- The `Resources` folder allows your application to be localized for particular languages and cultures.
- The `LocalizedStrings` class provides access to language resources and can be referenced in your application's user interface.
- The `App` class is defined in files `App.xaml` and `App.xaml.cs` located in the root directory of the project. It is the entry point for the application and handles application startup/shutdown, phone life-cycle events (launching, moving the application to the foreground or background), exceptions and navigation failure. The snippet below shows a small sample of the `App` class.

```
public App()
{
    // Global handler for uncaught exceptions.
    UnhandledException += Application_UnhandledException;

    // Standard XAML initialization
    InitializeComponent();
```

```
    // Phone-specific initialization
    InitializePhoneApplication();

    // Language display initialization
    InitializeLanguage();
...
```

- The initial main page is created automatically and contains a .XAML (Extensible Application Markup Language) file to describe the user interface and a .XAML.CS code-behind file to define client logic. Your application will typically have multiple page classes. The Figure 2-5 shows the editors for code behind, the XAML, and the design view of the XAML.

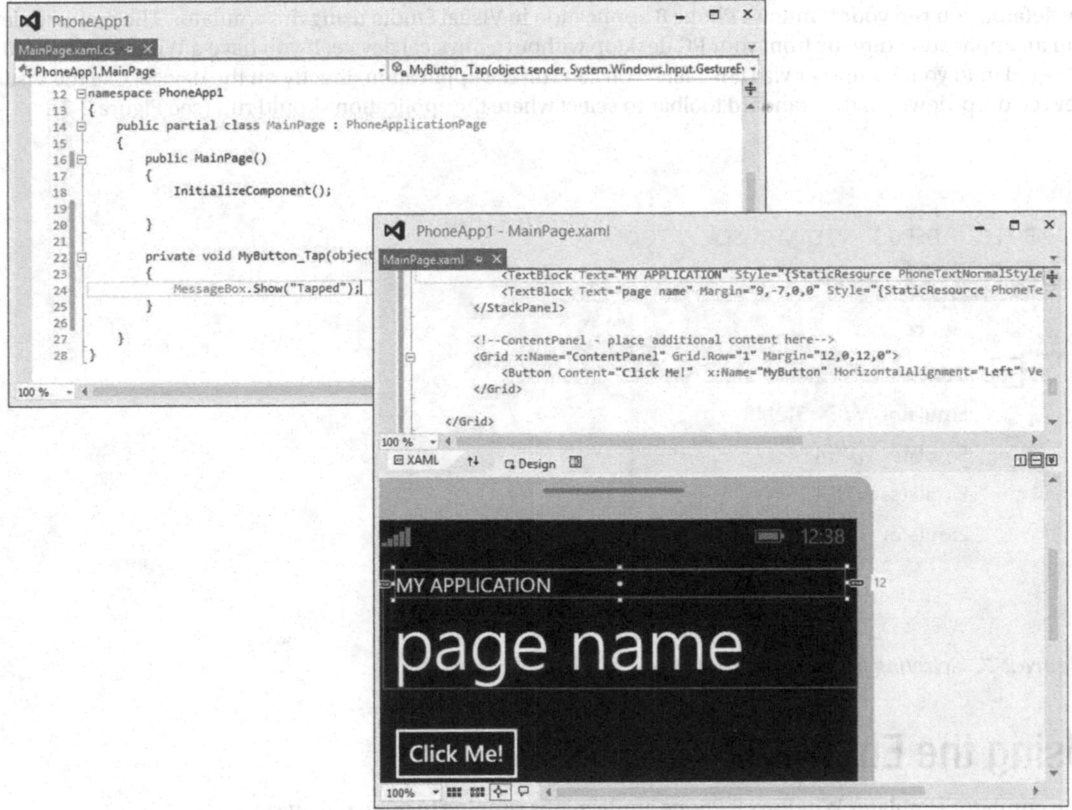

Figure 2-5. The MainPage XAML, Designer, and Code Behind

- The XAP file is simply a compressed file, like a ZIP file, that contains all the files needed to execute the application. This file is created automatically by Visual Studio and placed under the \bin directory. To see this file, you need to depress the "Show All Files" button in the Solution Explorer. It is the XAP file that is deployed to the device or to the Windows Phone Store (see Chapter 11 for more information). Figure 2-6 shows the unzipped contents of the XAP file.

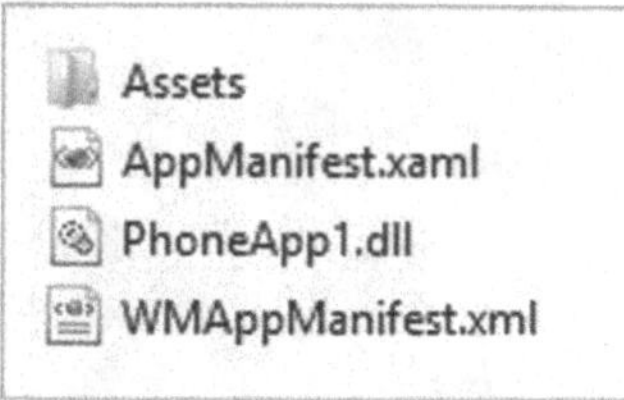

Figure 2-6. *XAP File Contents*

Running Applications from Visual Studio

By default, you run your Windows Phone 8 application in Visual Studio using the emulator. The emulator lets you run an application directly from your PC desktop without a physical device. If you have a Windows Phone 8 device plugged in to your computer via USB cable, you can run the application directly on the device. Use the Visual Studio `Device` drop-down on the Standard toolbar to select where the application should run (see Figure 2-7).

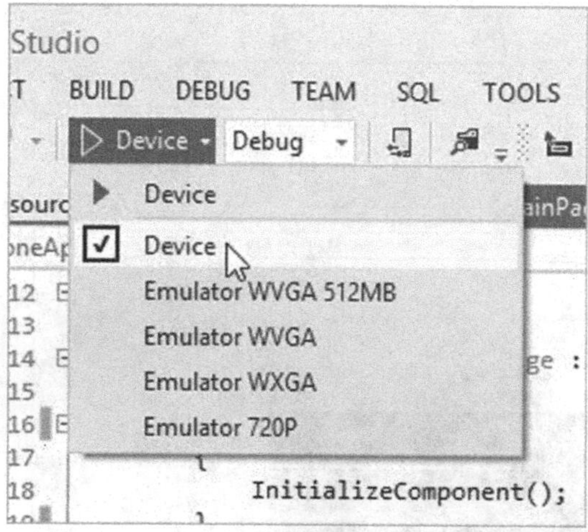

Figure 2-7. *Selecting from the Device Menu*

Using the Emulator

The emulator simulates Windows 8 Phone applications running in three screen sizes:

- WVGA - *800 × 480* pixels. An additional 512MB RAM version of WVGA allows you to emulate memory-constrained devices.
- WXGA - *1280 × 768* pixels.
- 720p - *1280 × 720* pixels.

The Emulator user interface allows you to try your application in various orientations (e.g., portrait, landscape, portrait up, etc.), and use additional tools that mimic phone interaction with the external world like Accelerometer and Location. The Emulator also has tools to take screenshots of the current phone screen image and a Network tab that describes the Emulator's connectivity.

The Emulator User Interface

The emulator lets you run your application directly from your PC without needing a physical device. You can use your mouse to "tap" items onscreen, or click the Back, Start, and Search buttons at the bottom of the emulator window (see Figure 2-8). The toolbar to the right of the emulator has commands that manipulate the window. To test your application in each basic orientation, use the Rotate Left and Rotate Right buttons.

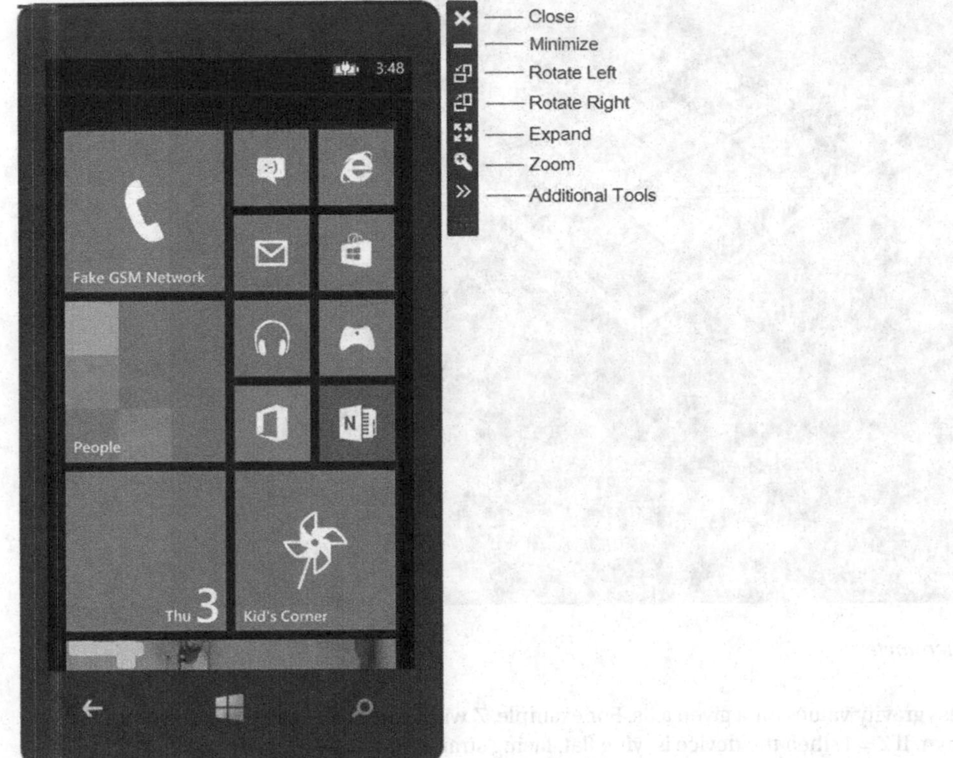

Figure 2-8. *The Emulator User Interface*

Additional Tools

Click the double angle (>>) button on the toolbar of the Emulator to open the `Additional Tools` dialog. This dialog lets you test several real-world scenarios without having an actual phone device, including moving the phone in space and geographically.

Emulator Accelerometer Tab

On the `Accelerometer` tab (see Figure 2-9), drag the red dot and observe the changes to the phone graphic and the X-Y-Z coordinates. Use the `Orientation` drop-down list to set the device to `Portrait Standing,` `Landscape Standing,` `Portrait Flat,` or `Landscape Flat` positions.

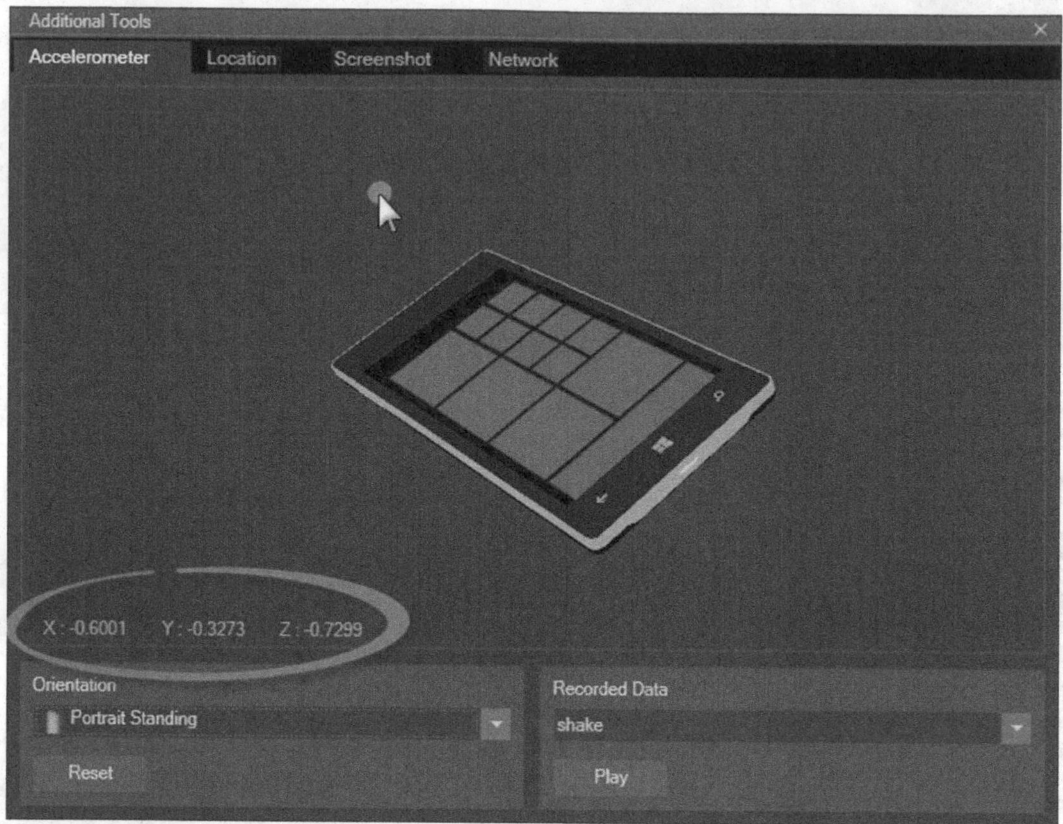

Figure 2-9. *Using the Accelerometer*

The coordinates express gravity values for a given axis. For example, Z will be negative when the device is faced up, positive when faced down. If Z = 1, then the device is lying flat, facing straight down (see Figure 2-10).

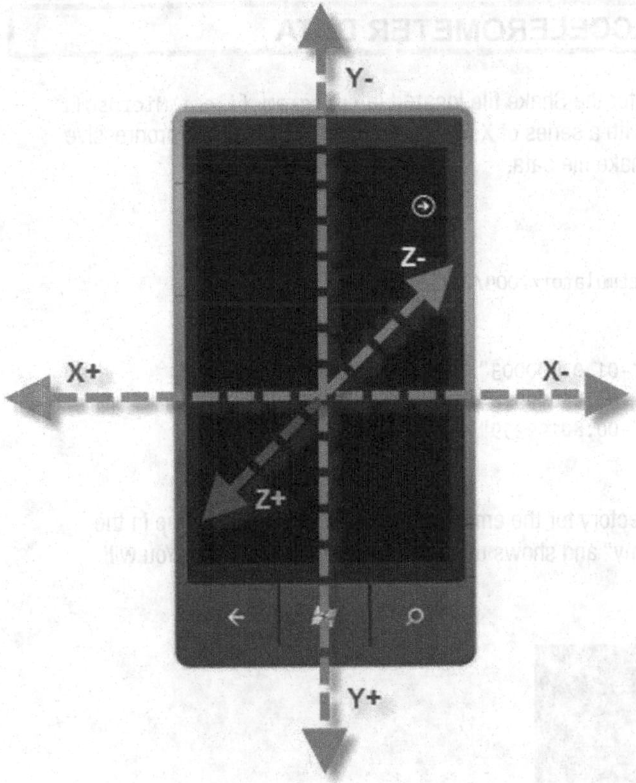

Figure 2-10. Coordinate Orientation in the Accelerometer

Select from the `Recorded Data` drop-down and click the `Play` button to play back some set of Accelerometer X-Y-Z settings in a series. The Shake option moves the X, then Y coordinates between negative and positive, back and forth, to simulate the physical shaking of a device (see Figure 2-11).

Figure 2-11. Playing Accelerometer Data from a File

CREATE CUSTOM ACCELEROMETER DATA

You can actually create your own recorded data. Look for the Shake file located in `<program files>\Microsoft XDE\8.0\sensordata\acc`. The file is in XML format with a series of X-Y-Z coordinates that occur at progressive offsets in time. The snippet below is a subset of the Shake file data.

```
<?xml version="1.0" encoding="utf-8"?>
<WindowsPhoneEmulator
xmlns="http://schemas.microsoft.com/WindowsPhoneEmulator/2009/08/SensorData">
  <SensorData>
    <Header version="1"/>
    <AccData offset="21" x="-00.08400000" y="-01.02100003" z="-00.41700000" />
    <AccData offset="42" x="-00.14200000" y="-00.95099998" z="-00.39700001" />
    <AccData offset="63" x="-00.29400000" y="-00.80199999" z="-00.30399999" />
    ...
```

Copy this file to another name, leave it in the same directory for the emulator to find and it will show up in the drop-down list. The example below is renamed "Shimmy" and shows up in the list (see Figure 2-12). You will need to restart the emulator for the file to display.

***Figure 2-12.** Showing the Custom Recorded Accelerometer Data*

Emulator Location Tab

The `Location` tab lets you mimic geographic position changes. Click anywhere on the map to set a point. Each point will show up in a list of `Latitude/Longitude` at the lower left of the screen. Click the `Live` button and then the Play button to "move" between each location (see Figure 2-13). The map will animate to show each point as the center of the world (which is Redmond, Washington, according to this map).

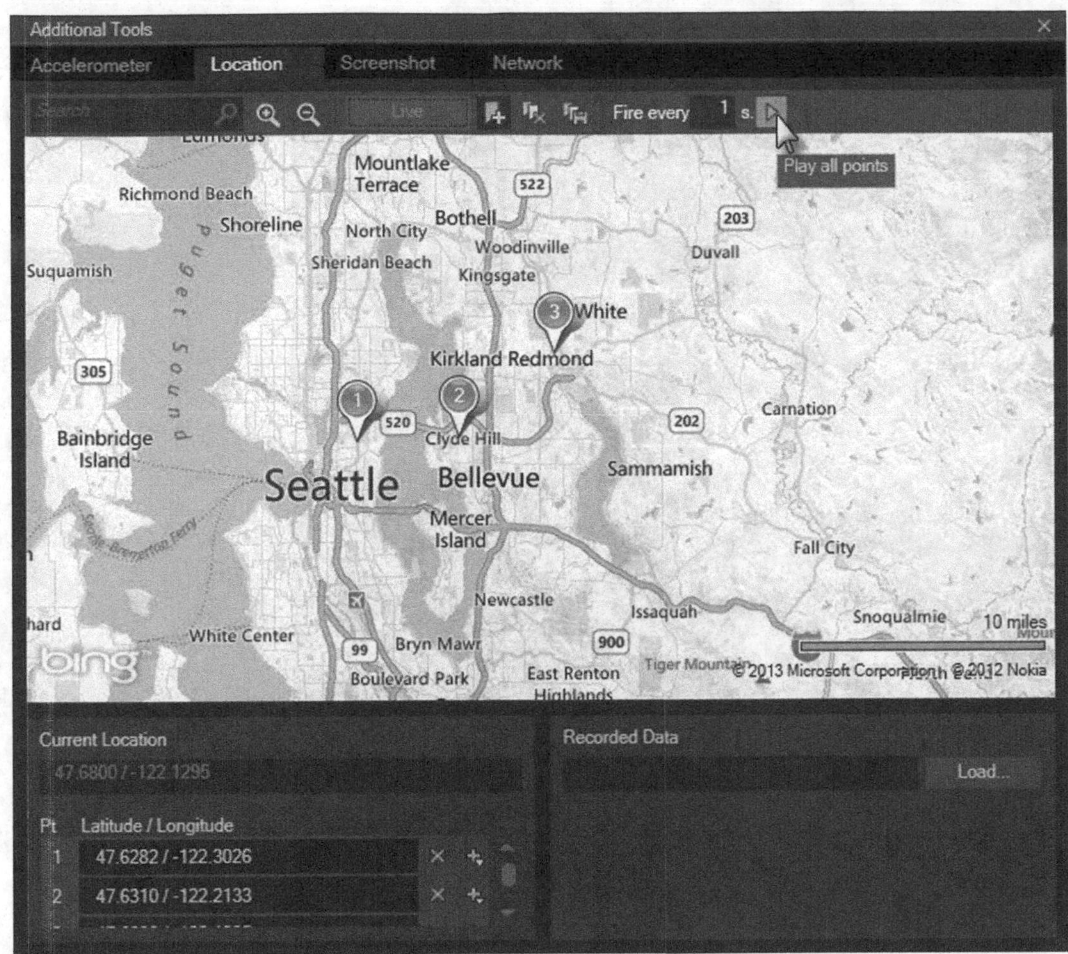

***Figure 2-13.** Simulating Location Changes*

If you need to restore a set of location points later, click the Save Map Points button (disk icon) from the toolbar at the top of the dialog (see Figure 2-13). The points are saved in `Locations.XML` at \Users\<user name>\Documents\WindowsPhoneEmulator\Location. The points are saved as XML and can be restored using the Recorded Data Load... button.

Emulator Screenshot Tab

The `Screenshot` tab makes it easy to capture the current emulator image in a size and format perfect for the Windows Phone Store. The `Capture` button saves the current emulator image without the chrome. That is, the hardware buttons and trim are left out of the image in accordance with requirements for App submissions for Windows Phone Store. Click the Save button to persist the image to disk (see Figure 2-14). See "App submission requirements for Windows Phone" – 4.6 – App Screenshots for more information (`http://msdn.microsoft.com/en-us/library/windowsphone/develop/hh184844(v=vs.105).aspx`). See Chapter 11 for directions on how to get your application published in the Windows Phone Store.

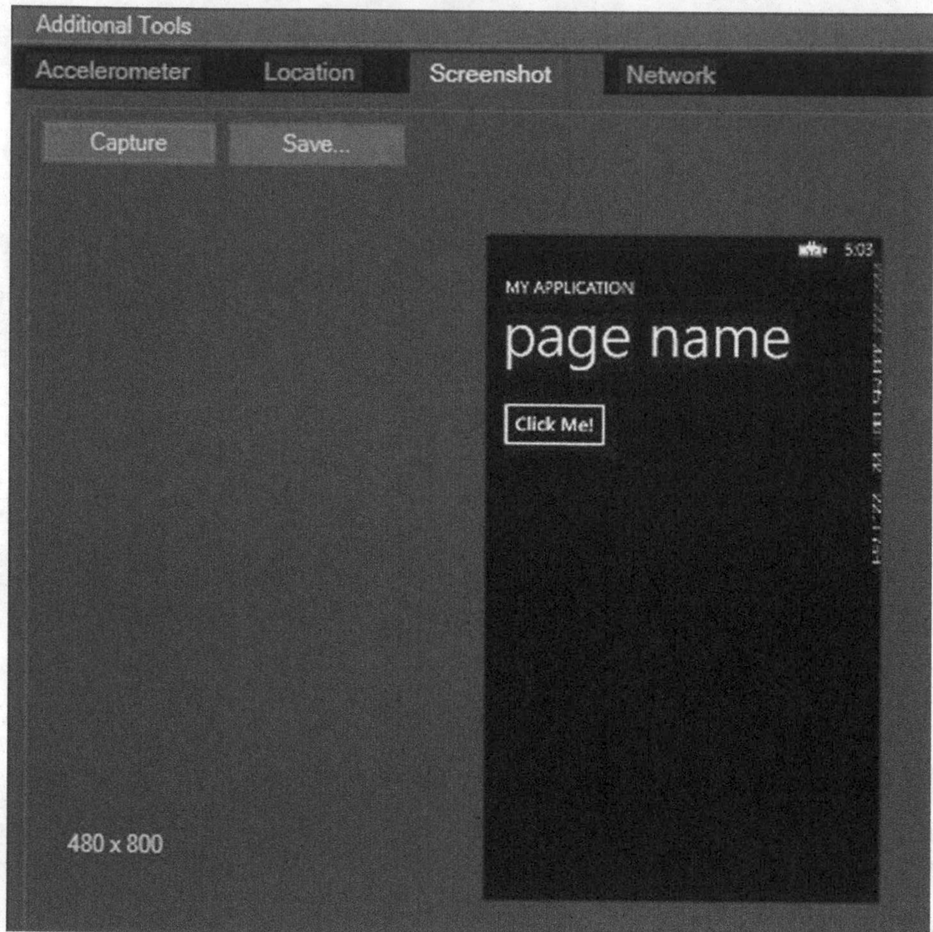

Figure 2-14. *Emulator Screen Capture*

Emulator Network Tab

The `Network` tab lists connections used by the emulator. The emulator comes with network support out-of-the-box. The emulator shows up on the network as a separate device with its own IP address. You don't need to install additional software (other than Windows 8) to get the emulator network connection. The connection will *not* be joined to a Windows domain, so if your development computer must log in to a domain or requires special client networking software, the emulator won't reach those network resources. Figure 2-15 shows the emulator's connection and IP address (the network address can be "pinged" from the command line).

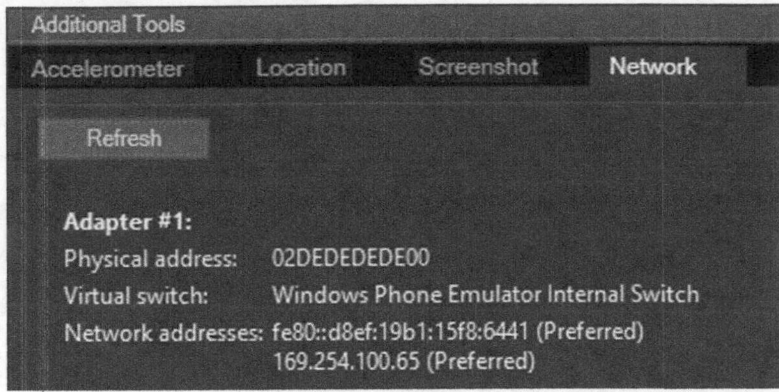

Figure 2-15. *List of Network Connections*

If your phone can access network resources over Wi-Fi, the emulator should be able to access those same resources. Figure 2-16 shows the emulator with a live internet connection to Google.

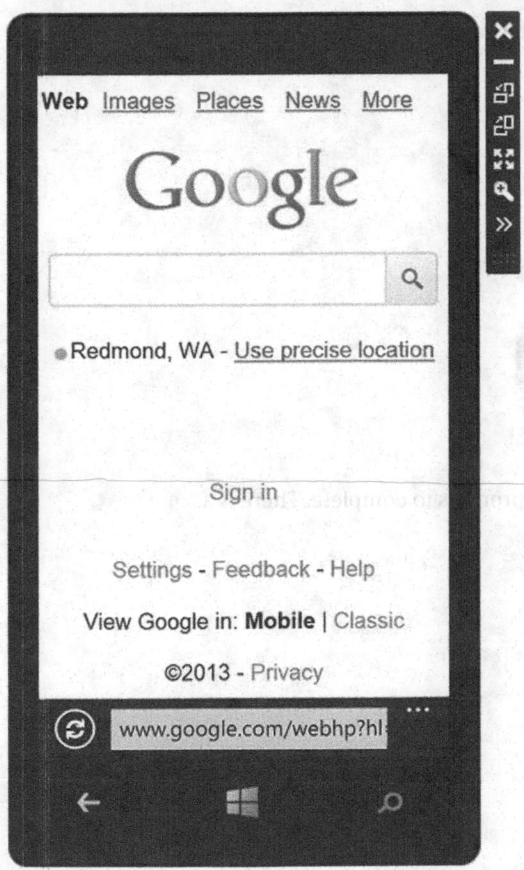

Figure 2-16. *The Emulator with Live Internet Connection*

Creating, Configuring, and Testing an Application

The following series of walk-throughs demonstrate:

- How to satisfy the prerequisites of deploying Windows Phone 8 applications to a phone, such as registering as a developer and unlocking the phone for development.
- How to build a simple Windows Phone 8 application and run the application in the Emulator.
- How to customize the application title and icons.
- How to customize elements on the page.

Prerequisites

There are a handful of prerequisites to deploying Windows Phone 8 applications to your phone device. The first is registering as a developer at `dev.windowsphone.com`. This step will require you to have a Microsoft (Windows Live ID) account.

1. Click the `Sign in` link to enter your existing Microsoft account credentials or follow the links to create a new Microsoft account.
2. Click the `Dashboard` link (see Figure 2-17) at the top of the page (`https://dev.windowsphone.com/join`).

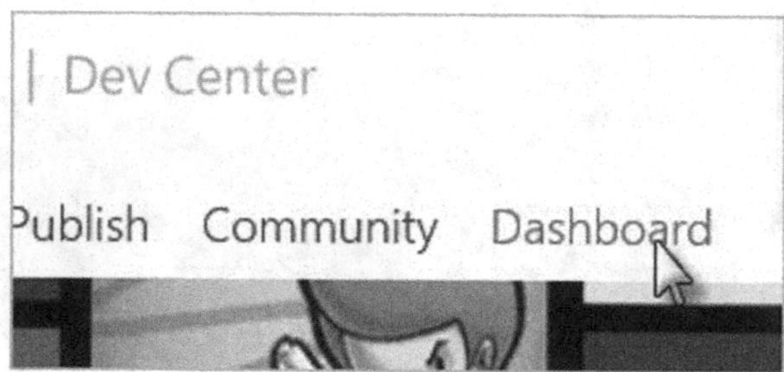

Figure 2-17. *Navigating to the Dashboard*

3. Click `Join Now`, as shown in Figure 2-18, and follow the prompts to complete. There is a subscription cost of $99 USD at the time of this writing.

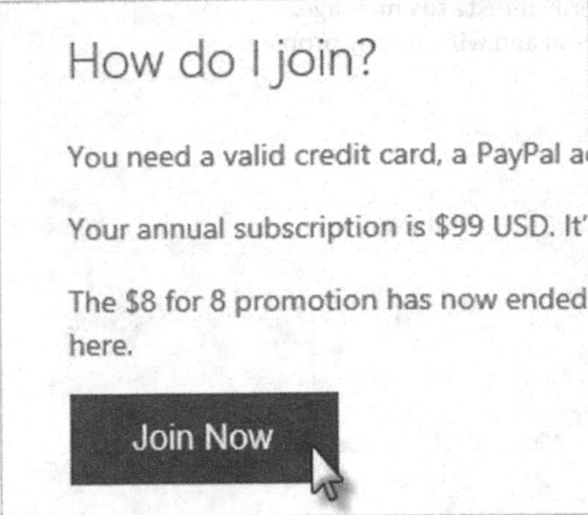

Figure 2-18. Creating a developer account

Next, register your phone device to "unlock" the phone for development. The phone must have a cell or Wi-Fi connection. The USB connection alone is not enough.

1. Turn on the phone and unlock the screen.
2. Verify the date and time on the phone. The `Settings` app lets you configure the date and time for the phone. Typically, this will be synced automatically with the correct date and time.
3. Connect the phone device USB to the development PC.
4. On the development PC, navigate to the `Start` screen, type "Windows Phone Developer Registration" to search for the registration application, and click the entry in the Apps list to run it (see Figure 2-19).

Figure 2-19. Running the Windows Phone Developer Registration Application

5. In the Windows Phone Developer Registration screen, verify the `Status` message. The Status will indicate if the phone is ready to be registered and will flag any problems, such as your device is unconnected, before continuing.

6. Click the `Register` button (see Figure 2-20).

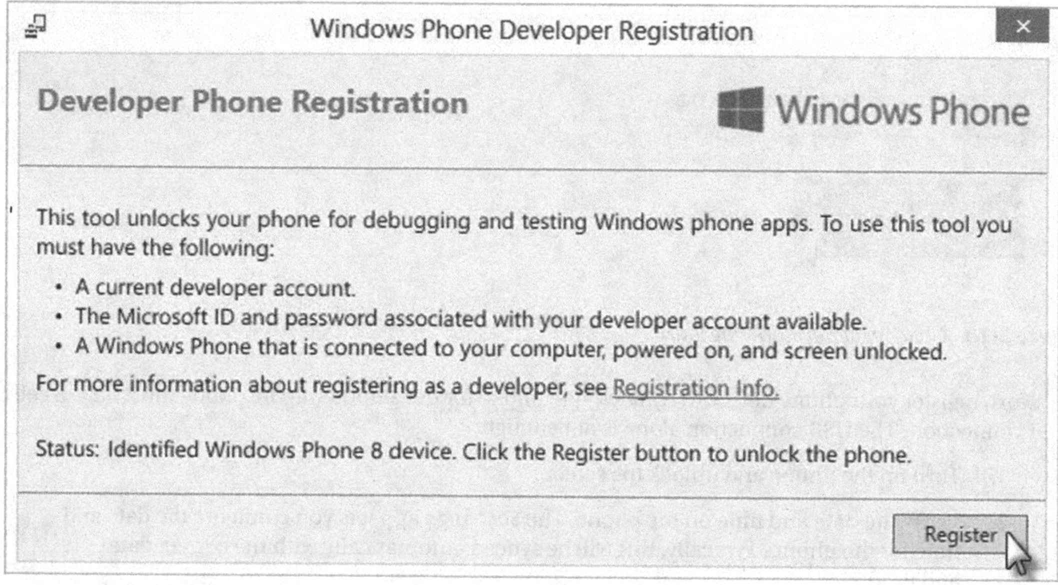

Figure 2-20. *Registering the Phone Device*

7. Sign in with your Windows Live ID connected to your registered developer's account.

8. Check the `Status` again to verify you have successfully unlocked your Windows Phone, as shown in Figure 2-21.

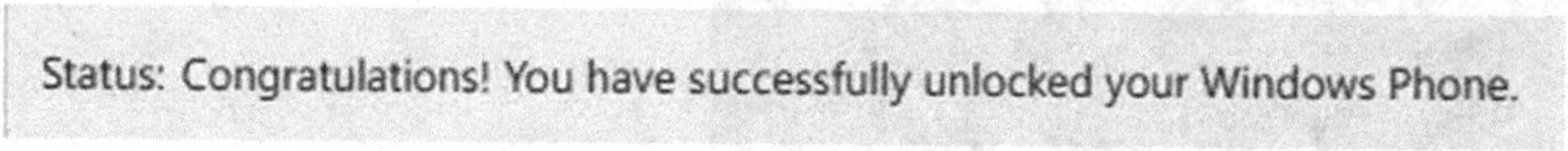

Status: Congratulations! You have successfully unlocked your Windows Phone.

Figure 2-21. *Success Status Message*

Well done, now you can deploy Windows Phone 8 applications directly onto the phone!

■ **Note** If you receive an error message "Not registered with the marketplace 80043001," this means that the Windows Live ID you used is not associated with an active developer account. You need to go to the Dashboard at `dev.windowsphone.com` and join to get a developer account.

Building the Example Application

The steps that follow demonstrate building and running a simple "hello world" application. In the process, we will change some superficial things like the application icon, tile icon, and titling.

1. From the Visual Studio menu select `File` ➤ `New` ➤ `Project`. In the `New Project` dialog, shown in Figure 2-22, select `Windows Phone` from the Installed Templates list. Select the `Windows Phone App` template. Set the Name of the project to "Getting Started." Click the `OK` button to continue.

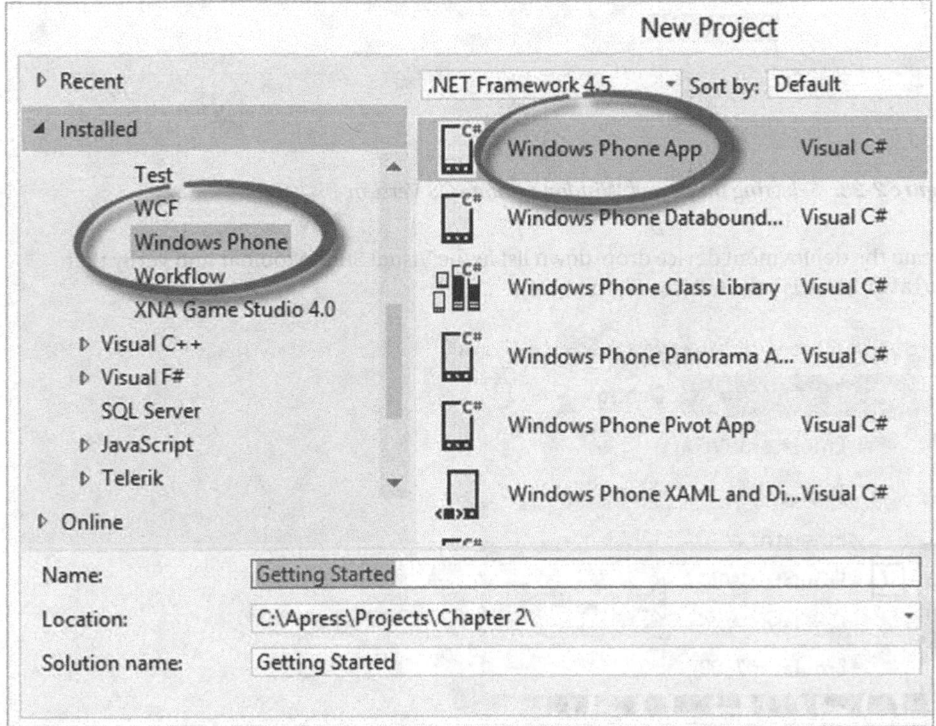

***Figure 2-22.** Creating a new Windows Phone App*

2. Next, the New Windows Phone Application dialog prompts for the `Target Windows Phone OS Version`. Leave the default Windows Phone OS 8.0 selected and click the OK button to continue (see Figure 2-23).

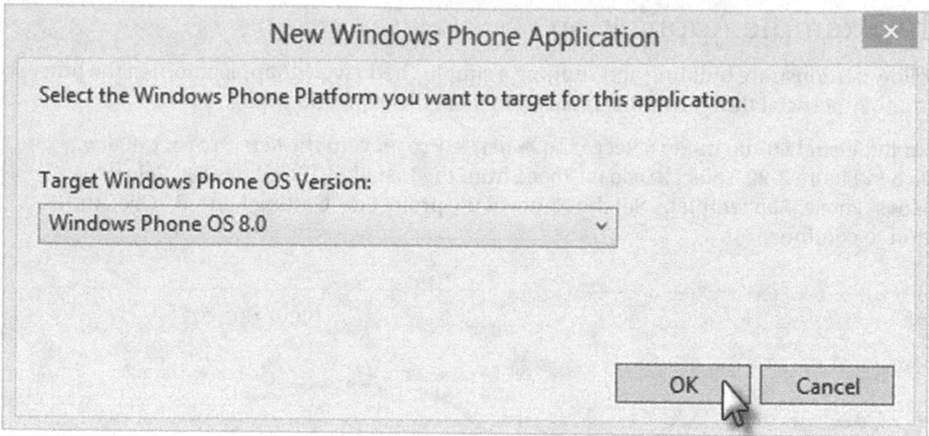

Figure 2-23. *Selecting the Target Windows Phone OS Version*

3. Locate the deployment device drop-down list in the Visual Studio toolbar and verify that `Emulator WVGA` is selected (see Figure 2-24).

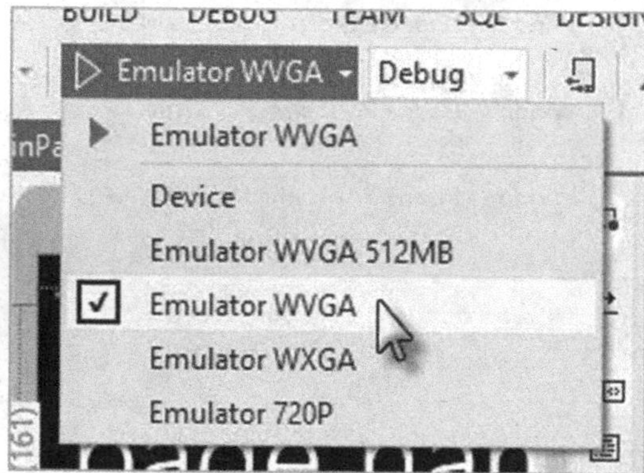

Figure 2-24. *Selecting the Deployment Device*

4. Click the green play button to run the emulator. The emulator should display and then load your application. By default, the application title reads "MY APPLICATION" and the page title is "page name" as shown in Figure 2-25.

***Figure 2-25.** The Default Page Running in the Emulator*

5. Click the back button shown in Figure 2-26 to return to the home page. The emulator will stay open.

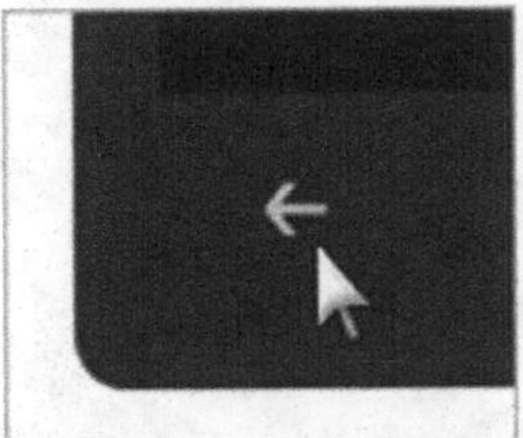

***Figure 2-26.** Navigating with the Back Button*

6. The Start screen displays *tiles* that display important live information and allow direct navigation to run your favorite apps. Scroll to the bottom of the Start screen and click the forward button shown in Figure 2-27 to display the *App List*.

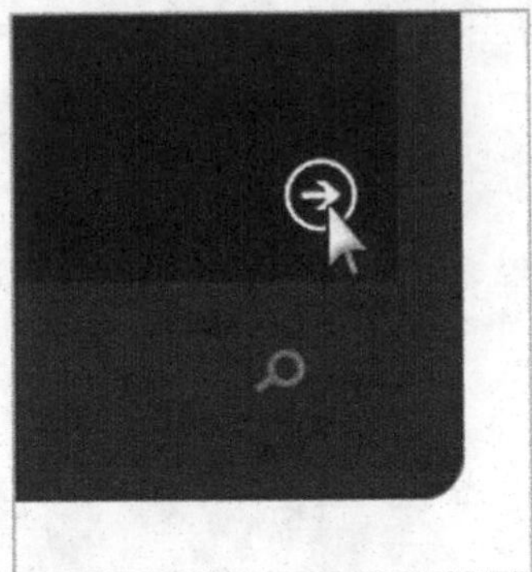

***Figure 2-27.** Navigating with the Forward Button*

7. The App List shows "Getting_Started" is listed along with the other applications available on the emulator. Click and hold the "Getting_Started" item. This is equivalent to a right-click on a PC and displays a context menu. Click the `pin to start` item from the menu (see Figure 2-28).

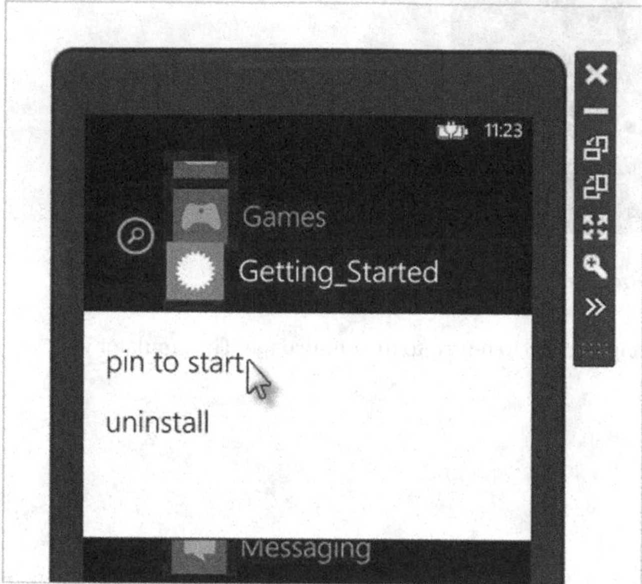

Figure 2-28. *Pinning the Application to the Start Screen*

8. The "Getting_Started" application now has a tile on the Start screen (see Figure 2-29).

Figure 2-29. *The Application Pinned in the Start Screen*

Click and hold the tile and select the "unpin" icon to remove the app tile. You will need it unpinned for the next exercise.

Customizing Application Settings

This extends the previous set of steps by customizing the title and icons for the application and tile graphics.

The initial Windows Phone 8 project created by default in Visual Studio uses three icons:

- `IconicTileSmall.png` and `IconicTileMediumLarge.png`, in the `\Assets\Tiles` directory, are displayed on the Start screen in two sizes the user can configure.
- `ApplicationIcon.png`, in the `\Assets` directory, shows up on the App List.

The following steps assign these icons and provide titling and captions:

1. Open the project from the previous exercise in Visual Studio.
2. In the Solution Explorer copy the three image files mentioned above and rename them. Figure 2-30 shows the three new files in the Solution Explorer.

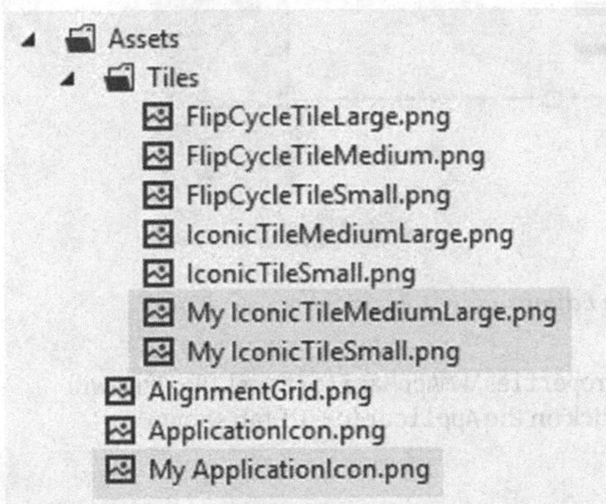

Figure 2-30. *Copied and Renamed Graphics in the Solution Explorer*

3. In the Solution Explorer, double-click each of the three images and edit each image using the Visual Studio 2012 icon editor. You can also use any other drawing tools you are familiar with. The point is to simply tweak the image enough that you will recognize the change when it's displayed in the running application. Figure 2-31 shows the addition of text using the icon editor.

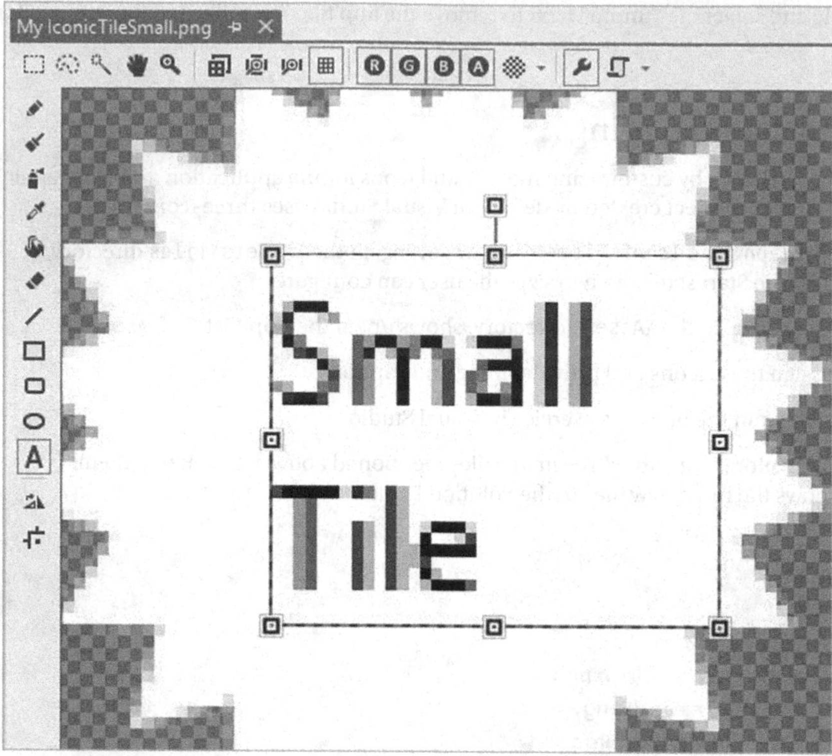

Figure 2-31. *Editing Tile Graphic in the Icon Editor*

4. In the Solution Explorer, double-click the `\Properties\WMAppManifest.xml` file. This will open up the editor for the project settings. Click on the `Application UI` tab shown in Figure 2-32.

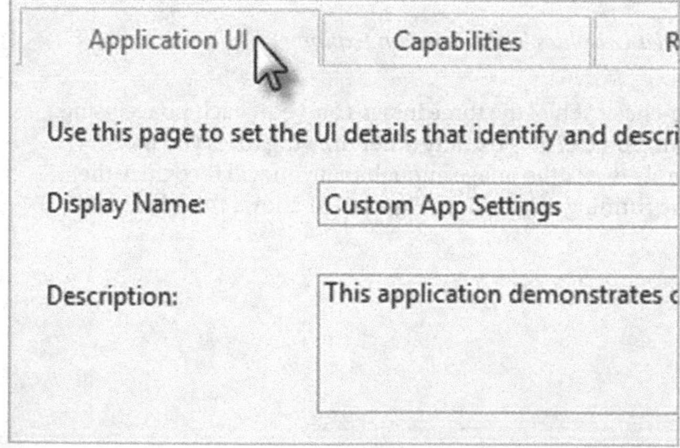

Figure 2-32. *Selecting the Application UI tab*

5. In the Application UI tab, change the following options:
    a. ***Display Name***: Custom App Settings
    b. ***Description***: This application demonstrates changing titling and icons.
    c. ***App Icon***: Click the ellipses and select the new image you created in the `\Assets` folder.
    d. ***Tile Title***: App Settings.
    e. ***Tile Images***: Click the ellipses for Small and Medium and select the new images you created in the `\Assets\Tiles` folder.

The WMAppManifest screen should now look something like Figure 2-33. Note that some portions of the screen have been omitted for brevity.

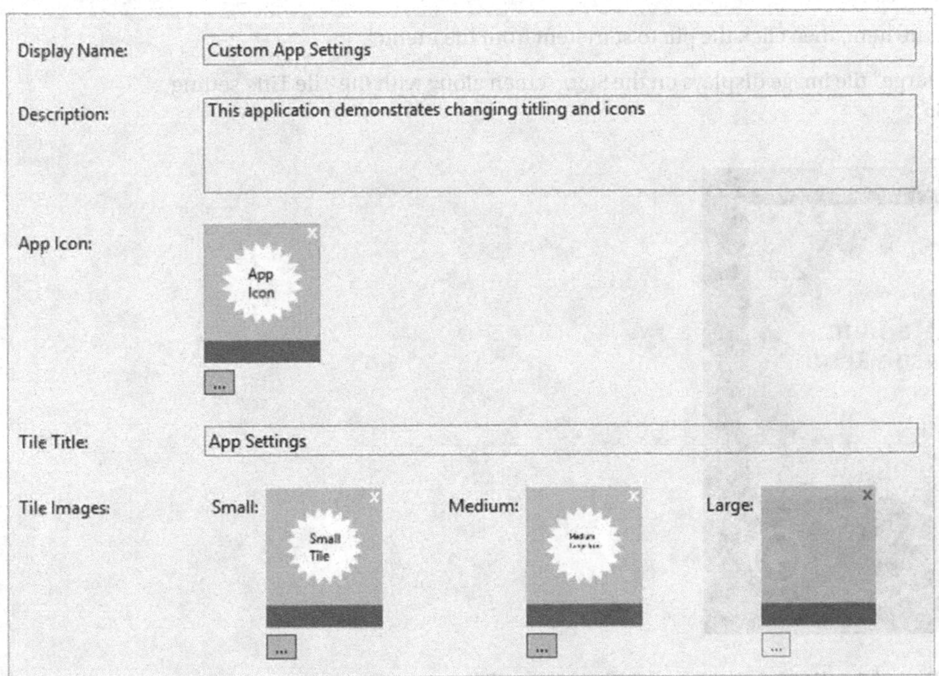

Figure 2-33. *Edited WMAppManifest Settings*

6. Run the application in the emulator or on your mobile device.
7. Click the back button to return to the Start screen.
8. Click the forward button to display the App List.
9. The "Display Name" and new application icon settings are reflected in the App List (see Figure 2-34).

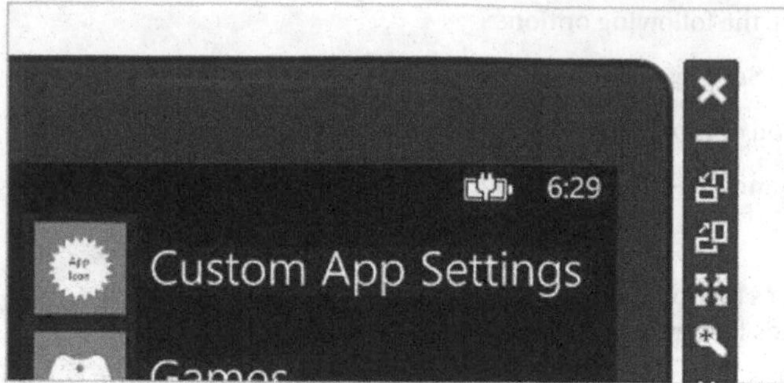

Figure 2-34. *App with Custom Settings Showing in the App List*

10. Click and hold the item, then click the pin to start item from the menu.
11. The "medium-large" tile image displays on the Start screen along with the Tile Title setting (see Figure 2-35).

Figure 2-35. *Pinned Application Showing Medium-Large Tile*

12. Click and hold the tile, then click the arrow that points up and left. This will display the "small" tile image as shown in Figure 2-36.

Figure 2-36. *Resizing the Pinned Tile*

Customizing Page Elements

The following steps demonstrate adding a button, click event and event handler to the main page. This example extends the preceding "Customizing Application Settings" set of steps.

1. Open the project in Visual Studio.
2. In the Solution Explorer, double-click `MainPage.xaml` to open the page for editing.
3. In the design view of `MainPage.xaml`, locate the TextBlock element with Text "MY APPLICATION," right-click it, and select Properties from the context menu. In the Properties Window, change the `Text` property to "GETTING STARTED DEMO" (see Figure 2-37).

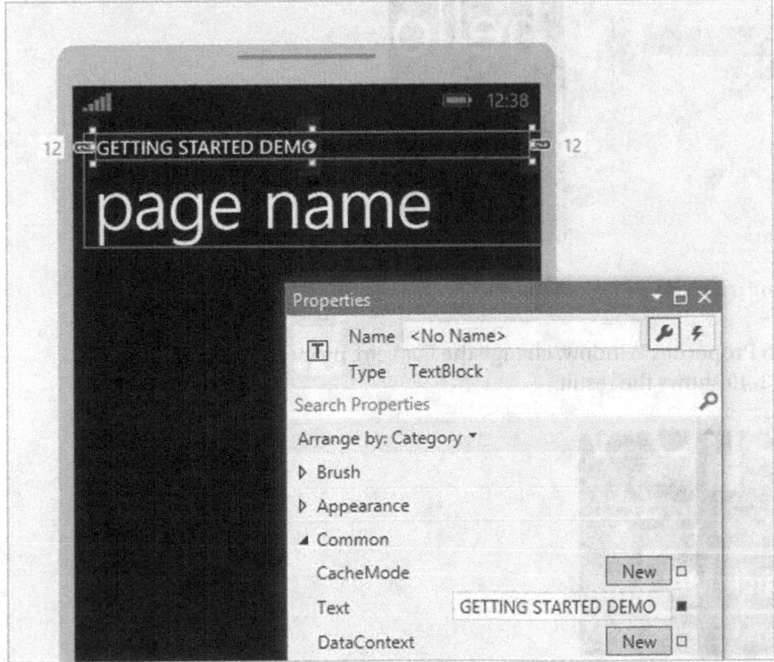

Figure 2-37. *Changing the Application Title*

4. Select the PageTitle element, i.e., "page name" with the mouse. In the Properties window, change the `Text` property to "hello world." Figure 2-38 shows the result.

Figure 2-38. *Changing the Page Title*

5. From the `Common Windows Phone Controls` section of the Toolbox, drag a `Button` element to the ContentPanel area below the PageTitle (see Figure 2-39).

Figure 2-39. *Adding a Button*

6. In the Visual Studio Properties Window, change the `Content` property of the button to "Click Me!" Figure 2-40 shows the result.

Figure 2-40. *Setting the Button Content Property*

7. In the Visual Studio designer, double-click the button to create a `Click` event handler in the code behind. Add the code below to the `Click` event handler.

```
private void button1_Click(object sender, RoutedEventArgs e)
{
    MessageBox.Show("The time is " + DateTime.Now.ToLongTimeString());
}
```

8. Run the application.

9. Click the button to display the message box (see Figure 2-41).

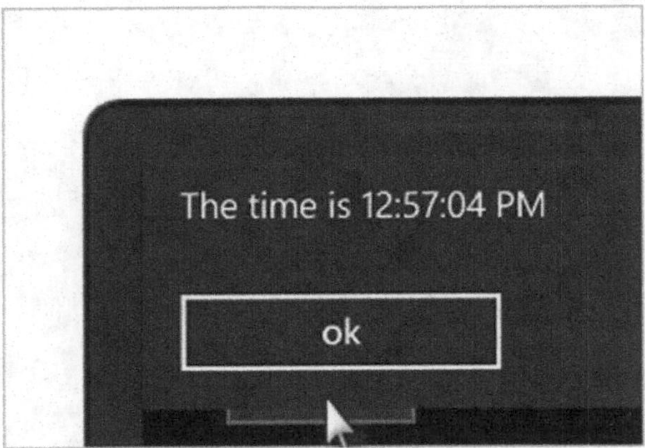

***Figure 2-41.** Testing the Application*

Summary

To "Get Started" you need to create a new Windows Phone 8 project, deploy the project in the emulator and on your device and make basic tweaks to both the application settings and the default page. Along the way, you've also learned how to sign up for a development account, unlock the phone for development, and navigate through the emulator.

Put these skills to work in the next chapter "Building the UI with XAML" where you will create your application's user interface with XAML markup and the Visual Studio Designer. In this next chapter you'll learn how to bind data to elements in your XAML, create styles, handle notification from the user interface, create resources, and use the power of the MVVM pattern.

CHAPTER 3

Building the UI with XAML

This chapter explains the basic syntax used to describe Windows Phone 8 user interfaces and then describes the key techniques used to construct responsive phone applications including:

- How to use resources and styles to control the look-and-feel of the application in an organized, scalable way.
- How templates are used to build new layouts on top of existing controls.
- How data is bound to elements of the page.
- How data binding allows changes in the data to be reflected automatically in the user interface and how changes made by the user are returned automatically to the data source.
- How the MVVM pattern helps structure your application in a way that is easy to maintain.

Working with XAML

XAML (Extended Application Markup Language) is a declarative markup language used to create user interfaces. Each XAML element represents an instantiated object. XAML elements are typically visual but can also represent data sources or custom objects.

You can define XAML directly in the XAML editor or use the designer. Although the Visual Studio designer improves constantly, some tasks can only be done directly in XAML. You should become familiar with both approaches and use the most convenient route for each situation.

Your typical starting point will be the `MainPage.xaml` file that defines the initial user interface. The root element is `PhoneApplicationPage`. The `x:Class` attribute points to the name of the underlying `PhoneApplicationPage` class defined in the code-behind (see Listing 3-1).

Listing 3-1. Basic Page XAML Structure

```
<phone:PhoneApplicationPage
    x:Class="WorkingWithXAML.MainPage"
    xmlns="http://schemas.microsoft.com/winfx/2006/xaml/presentation"
    xmlns:x="http://schemas.microsoft.com/winfx/2006/xaml"
    xmlns:phone="clr-namespace:Microsoft.Phone.Controls;assembly=Microsoft.Phone"
    xmlns:shell="clr-namespace:Microsoft.Phone.Shell;assembly=Microsoft.Phone"
    xmlns:d="http://schemas.microsoft.com/expression/blend/2008"
    xmlns:mc="http://schemas.openxmlformats.org/markup-compatibility/2006"
    mc:Ignorable="d"
    FontFamily="{StaticResource PhoneFontFamilyNormal}"
    FontSize="{StaticResource PhoneFontSizeNormal}"
```

```
    Foreground="{StaticResource PhoneForegroundBrush}"
    SupportedOrientations="Portrait" Orientation="Portrait"
    shell:SystemTray.IsVisible="True">

    <!--LayoutRoot is the root grid where all page content is placed-->
    <Grid x:Name="LayoutRoot" Background="Transparent">
        <!--...-->
    </Grid>

</phone:PhoneApplicationPage>
```

Namespaces

Inside the class declaration you will see a series of XML namespaces that start with xmlns followed by a colon, then the name of the namespace, an equal sign and a path to the assembly that the namespace represents. For example:

```
xmlns:phone="clr-namespace:Microsoft.Phone.Controls;assembly=Microsoft.Phone"
```

Here, the phone XML namespace represents the Microsoft.Phone.Controls namespace in the Microsoft.Phone assembly. With the namespace declared, you can use any of the namespace objects inside the XAML. For example you can use the WebBrowser control from the phone namespace by creating this tag:

```
<phone:WebBrowser />
```

You may also have noticed that one XML namespace in Listing 3-1 has no name. This is the default XML namespace and applies to all elements that don't specify an XML namespace. For example, the Grid element is in the default namespace and is declared like this:

```
<Grid x:Name="LayoutRoot" Background="Transparent">...
```

Namespaces are usually created automatically as controls are dragged from the toolbox to the XAML editor or designer. What if you want to reference an assembly that is not available from the toolbox? To declare a new XML namespace type **xmlns:**, add a unique name and type the equal sign. IntelliSense will drop down a list of assemblies referenced in the project for you to choose from. Figure 3-1 shows an XML namespace my and the list of assemblies from IntelliSense.

```
<phone:PhoneApplicationPage
    x:Class="WorkingWithXAML.MainPage"
    xmlns:my="work"
    xmlns="htt      System.Xml (System.Xml.ReaderWriter)
    xmlns:x="h      System.Xml.Linq (System.Xml.XDocument)
    xmlns:phon
    xmlns:shel      System.Xml.Schema (System.Xml.ReaderWriter)
    xmlns:d="h      System.Xml.Serialization (system.xml.serialization)
    xmlns:mc="      System.Xml.Serialization (System.Xml.XmlSerializer)
    mc:Ignorab      Windows.Foundation (System.Runtime.WindowsRuntime)
    FontFamily      Windows.UI (System.Runtime.WindowsRuntime)
    FontSize="      WorkingWithXAML (WorkingWithXAML)
    Foreground
    SupportedO      WorkingWithXAML.Resources (WorkingWithXAML)
    shell:SystemTray.IsVisible="True">
```

Figure 3-1. *Declaring an XML Namespace*

If you create a public class `MyClass` in code-behind and add a XML namespace, then you can use the XML namespace in the markup (see Figure 3-2). Once you type the colon, IntelliSense will display a list of objects that can be used.

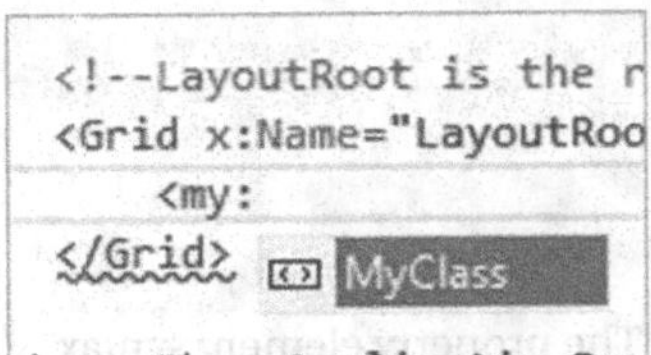

Figure 3-2. *Referencing Namespaces in the XAML Markup*

■ **Note** The referenced class must be a type that is valid in the markup. The example `MyClass` descends from `FrameworkElement`, a type that can be used in XAML layout.

XAML Syntax

To understand XAML syntax, it's best to start simple and build up. As you read this, copy snippets into the XAML and observe how they behave in the designer.

You can declare instances of a class in XAML using start and end elements or using "self closing" syntax as shown in Listing 3-2.

Listing 3-2. Using Start/End Elements and Self Closing Syntax

```
<!--start and end tags...-->
<Button></Button>

<!--self closing-->
<Button />
```

■ **Tip** Get comfortable with both the Design and XAML views. XAML is the most complete representation of the page design, while the Design view is usually (but not always) quicker and easier to use.

Object properties are defined through XAML attributes. The snippet below defines a button with Background property of "Red".

```
<Button Background="Red" />
```

What if the property is more complex than a simple attribute assignment can handle? "Property element" syntax allows each property to be expressed as a separate element. The Background example is trivial but shows the basic property element syntax.

```
<Button Content="Update">
    <Button.Background>Red</Button.Background>
</Button>
```

Property element syntax can handle nested objects such as this SolidColorBrush used for the button background in Listing 3-3.

Listing 3-3. Nested Objects

```
<Button Content="Update">
    <Button.Background>
        <SolidColorBrush Color="Red" />
    </Button.Background>
</Button>
```

The last few examples evaluate to the same result, a button with a red background. The property element syntax becomes really useful when the property can't be expressed in a simple string value. The example in Listing 3-4 defines a LinearGradientBrush background that fades from black to red.

Listing 3-4. Syntax Defining a LinearGradientBrush

```
<Button>
    <Button.Background>
        <LinearGradientBrush>
            <LinearGradientBrush.GradientStops>
                <GradientStopCollection>
                    <GradientStop Color="Black"
                                  Offset="0" />
                    <GradientStop Color="Red"
                                  Offset="1" />
                </GradientStopCollection>
            </LinearGradientBrush.GradientStops>
        </LinearGradientBrush>
    </Button.Background>
</Button>
```

Fortunately, the parser is quite good at optimizing, so the markup can be shortened to the markup in Listing 3-5. GradientStops is the default content for the element, so the tag can be left out. Likewise, the parser understands that GradientStop elements form a collection, so the GradientStopCollection element is not necessary.

Listing 3-5. Shorted Syntax Using Defaults

```
<Button>
    <Button.Background>
        <LinearGradientBrush>
            <GradientStop Color="Black"
                          Offset="0" />
            <GradientStop Color="Red"
                          Offset="1" />
        </LinearGradientBrush>
    </Button.Background>
</Button>
```

Attached Properties

Attached properties are properties that can be used by other classes. The syntax is basically "owner object.property". In listing 3-6, the StackPanel and "ContentPanel" Grid use the Grid.Row attached property to define where they will display in the grid.

Listing 3-6. Attached Row Property From the Grid

```
<Grid>
    <Grid.RowDefinitions>
        <RowDefinition Height="Auto" />
        <RowDefinition Height="*" />
    </Grid.RowDefinitions>

    <StackPanel x:Name="TitlePanel"
                Grid.Row="0">
    </StackPanel>

    <Grid x:Name="ContentPanel"
          Grid.Row="1">
    </Grid>
</Grid>
```

From the designer, you can access attached properties through the Properties Window. Figure 3-3 shows the Row property of the "TitlePanel" element. Notice the tool tip for Row uses dot notation to indicate that this is an attached property of the Grid class.

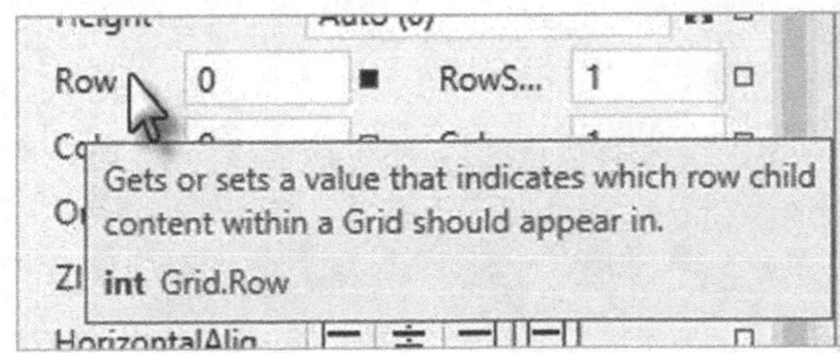

Figure 3-3. *Tooltip for an Attached Property*

Markup Extensions

Markup Extensions are expressions surrounded by curly braces to denote syntax that is different from standard XAML. Typically, markup extensions refer to resources or binding expressions. Listing 3-7 shows a sample that binds a TextBlock's Text property to data named "MyTitle" and also binds the style to the built-in resource PhoneTextNormalStyle.

Listing 3-7. Markup Extensions for Binding and StaticResources

```
<TextBlock x:Name="ApplicationTitle"
           Text="{Binding MyTitle}"
           Style="{StaticResource PhoneTextNormalStyle}" />
```

Resources and Styles

Resources are named containers of objects that allow you to define markup in a separate location from where that markup is being used. You can define classes, styles, properties, and so on in a resource and reuse these resources in multiple locations. This provides a great opportunity to refactor by moving commonly used chunks of markup to a resource.

■ **Caution** There is a second resource file type with extension "resx" that contains localized strings. The resource file we're working with here has a "xaml" extension.

Styles are collections of properties commonly stored in resource dictionaries. To see how this works, let's start with a Button having a set of related appearance properties (see Listing 3-8).

Listing 3-8. Button Properties

```
<Button Content="Update"
        Background="Red"
        BorderBrush="Maroon"
        BorderThickness="5" />
```

You can move a set of properties to a style using the property element syntax. The markup in Listing 3-9 moves the Background, BorderBrush, and BorderThickness properties inside the Style property.

Listing 3-9. Button Properties Moved into a Style

```
<Button Content="Update">
    <Button.Style>
        <Style TargetType="Button">
            <Setter Property="Background"
                    Value="Red" />
            <Setter Property="BorderBrush"
                    Value="Maroon" />
            <Setter Property="BorderThickness"
                    Value="5" />
        </Style>
    </Button.Style>
</Button>
```

So what did we get out of that? In itself, nothing. The code is more verbose and includes a new Style property called TargetType. The advantage comes into focus when you move the style out into a resource. Any element that can be part of the XAML layout has a Resources collection. In Listing 3-10, the Style is contained in the Resources collection of the Grid.

Listing 3-10. Style Defined in a Resource

```
<Grid>
    <Grid.Resources>
        <Style x:Key="MyButtonStyle"
                TargetType="Button">
            <Setter Property="Background"
                    Value="Red" />
            <Setter Property="BorderBrush"
                    Value="Maroon" />
            <Setter Property="BorderThickness"
                    Value="5" />
        </Style>
    </Grid.Resources>

    <Button Content="Update"
            Style="{StaticResource MyButtonStyle}" />
</Grid>
```

There are three key changes to make this work:

- Name the style using the x:Key property and assign a unique name. In this example the style is named "MyButtonStyle".
- The style must have a TargetType property assigned. In this example, the style applies to a Button element.
- The Style property of the button is assigned using the markup extension syntax (i.e., curly braces "{ }"), surrounding the StaticResource markup extension and the key of the resource MyButtonStyle. MyButtonStyle in the markup extension points back to the Style of the same name in the Grid's resources. Figure 3-4 shows the relationship.

```
<Grid>
    <Grid.Resources>
        <Style x:Key="MyButtonStyle" TargetType="Button" >
            <Setter Property="Background" Value="Red" />
            <Setter Property="BorderBrush" Value="Maroon" />
            <Setter Property="BorderThickness" Value="5" />
        </Style>
    </Grid.Resources>

    <Button Content="Update" Style="{StaticResource MyButtonStyle}" />
</Grid>
```

Figure 3-4. *Style Pointing Back to Resource*

Once the Style is moved into the resource, we can use the style in other buttons. Plus, the button syntax is cleaned up in the process. Bonus!

Listing 3-11 defines three buttons with different content, but all have the same MyButtonStyle applied. Each button displays with a red background and a five-pixel maroon border (see Figure 3-5).

Listing 3-11. Style Reused by Multiple Button Elements

```
<Button Content="Update"  Style="{StaticResource MyButtonStyle}" Grid.Row="0" />
<Button Content="Refresh" Style="{StaticResource MyButtonStyle}" Grid.Row="1"/>
<Button Content="Delete"  Style="{StaticResource MyButtonStyle}" Grid.Row="2"/>
```

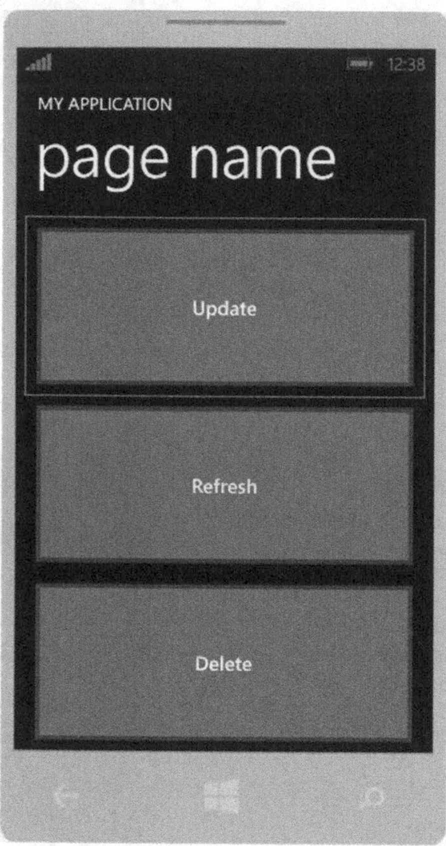

Figure 3-5. *Identically Styled Buttons*

Figure 3-5 shows the result in the designer where each button is styled identically.

Once styles are created, either in XAML or by hand, use the Visual Studio Properties Window context menu to set the Style property. To do this, click the box to the right of the button's Style property to show the context menu, click to expand the Local Resource option and select a resource from the list (see Figure 3-6).

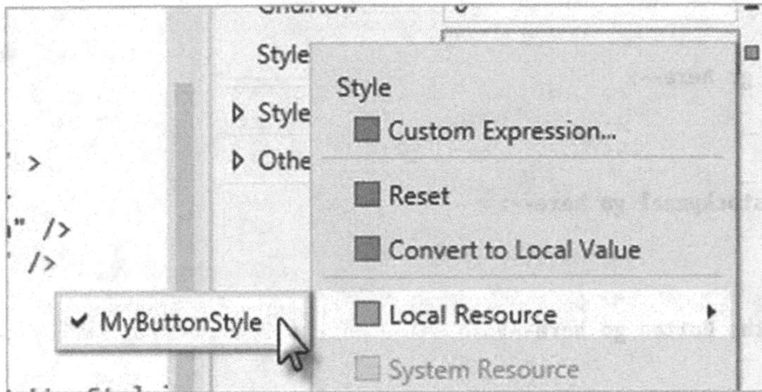

Figure 3-6. *Setting the Style from the Properties Pane*

Resource Scope

Where a resource is placed, determines scope. All `FrameworkElement` objects (i.e., all objects that can be in a XAML layout), have a `Resources` collection. Also, the application object itself has its own `Resources` collection. If you open `App.xaml`, you will find an `Application.Resources` element where you can add resources, just as we did for the grid (see Listing 3-12). These resources are available throughout the entire application scope.

Listing 3-12. Application Level Resources

```
<Application
    x:Class="WorkingWithXAML.App"
    xmlns="http://schemas.microsoft.com/winfx/2006/xaml/presentation"
    xmlns:x="http://schemas.microsoft.com/winfx/2006/xaml"
    xmlns:phone="clr-namespace:Microsoft.Phone.Controls;assembly=Microsoft.Phone"
    xmlns:shell="clr-namespace:Microsoft.Phone.Shell;assembly=Microsoft.Phone">

    <!--Application Resources-->
    <Application.Resources>

    </Application.Resources>

...

</Application>
```

You can have resources in the `PhoneApplicationPage` available to objects on the page (but not other pages), within a `Grid`, a `Button`, and so on. Listing 3-13 shows Resource elements defined at various levels within the page.

Listing 3-13. Resources at Various Levels

```
<phone:PhoneApplicationPage >
    <phone:PhoneApplicationPage.Resources>
        <!--Resources for the entire page go here-->
    </phone:PhoneApplicationPage.Resources>
```

```
    <Grid>
        <Grid.Resources>
            <!--Resources used in the grid go here-->
        </Grid.Resources>
        <StackPanel>
            <StackPanel.Resources>
                <!--Resources used in the stackpanel go here-->
            </StackPanel.Resources>
            <Button>
                <Button.Resources>
                    <!--Resources used in the Button go here-->
                </Button.Resources>
            </Button>
        </StackPanel>
    </Grid>

</phone:PhoneApplicationPage>
```

To illustrate a scoping problem you might run into, what's wrong with the XAML in Figure 3-7? The `Button`'s `Style` assignment is underlined and the design-time error is "The resource 'MyButtonStyle' could not be resolved."

```
<Grid>
    <Grid.Resources>
        <Style x:Key="MyButtonStyle" TargetType="Button">
            <Setter Property="Background" Value="Red" />
            <Setter Property="BorderBrush" Value="Maroon" />
            <Setter Property="BorderThickness" Value="5" />
        </Style>
    </Grid.Resources>
 </Grid>

<Button Content="Update"
            Style="{StaticResource MyButtonStyle}" />
            The resource "MyButtonStyle" could not be resolved.
```

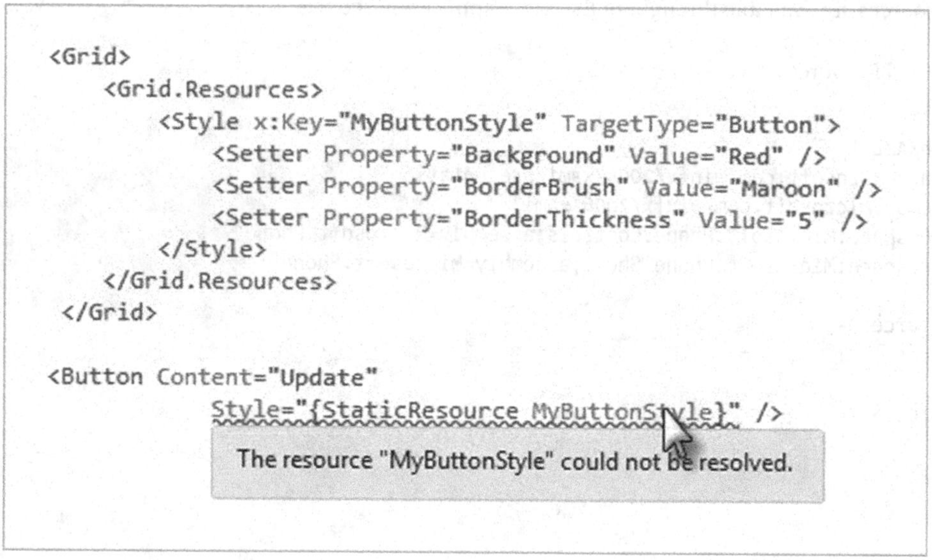

Figure 3-7. *Resource Out of Scope*

The answer: `"MyButtonStyle"` is defined inside the scope of a `Grid` and the `Button` is outside that grid. By moving the `Button` inside the grid, the resource is now in-scope and the error is resolved (see Figure 3-8).

```
<Grid>
    <Grid.Resources>
        <Style x:Key="MyButtonStyle" TargetType="Button">
            <Setter Property="Background" Value="Red" />
            <Setter Property="BorderBrush" Value="Maroon" />
            <Setter Property="BorderThickness" Value="5" />
        </Style>
    </Grid.Resources>
    <Button Content="Update"
            Style="{StaticResource MyButtonStyle}" />
</Grid>
```

***Figure 3-8.** Resource In Scope*

Style Inheritance

You may want to tweak a particular style without starting from scratch. Use the `BasedOn` property to reference another style. Figure 3-9 shows `"MyBigBorderStyle"` using the `BasedOn` attribute to refer to `"MyButtonStyle"`. The Delete button uses the `MyBigBorderStyle` style.

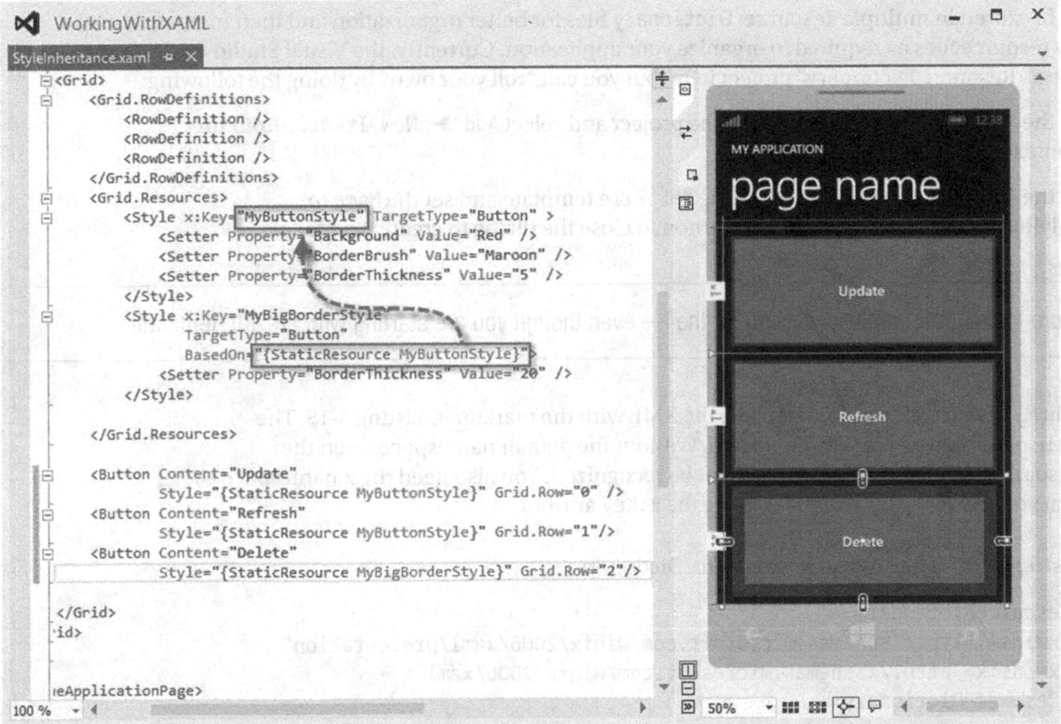

***Figure 3-9.** Inheriting Styles using the BasedOn Attribute*

Implicit Styles

Using the x:Key property to name the style and then using the {StaticResource keyname} syntax is an example of an *explicit* style. By leaving off the x:Key, the style applies *implicitly* to all instances of TargetType. In Listing 3-14, the style applies to all Button types automatically. Use this technique to set styles globally without needing to explicitly define a style name for each element.

Listing 3-14. Implicit Style Applies to All Buttons

```
<StackPanel>
    <StackPanel.Resources>
        <Style TargetType="Button">
            <Setter Property="Background" Value="Red" />
            <Setter Property="BorderBrush" Value="Maroon" />
            <Setter Property="BorderThickness" Value="5" />
        </Style>
    </StackPanel.Resources>

    <Button Content="Update" />
    <Button Content="Refresh" />
    <Button Content="Delete" />
</StackPanel>
```

Merging Resources

Resources can be stored in multiple Resource Dictionary files for better organization and then merged. You can create as many resource files as required to organize your application. Currently, the Visual Studio environment doesn't include a "Resource Dictionary" project item, but you can "roll your own" by doing the following:

1. In the Solution Explorer, right-click the project and select Add ➤ New Item... from the context menu.
2. In the Add New Item dialog, select the XML File template and set the Name to "MyResources.xaml". Click the Add button to close the dialog to create the file.

■ **Note** Be sure to use the ".xaml" extension for the file even though you are starting with an XML template.

---

3. Edit MyResources.xaml and replace the XML with the markup in Listing 3-15. The XML namespaces are very important. Without the default namespace, even the ResourceDictionary element will not be recognized. You also need the x namespace so that you can key your resources using the x:Key attribute.

   Listing 3-15. The Shell of the ResourceDictionary

   ```
   <ResourceDictionary
     xmlns="http://schemas.microsoft.com/winfx/2006/xaml/presentation"
     xmlns:x="http://schemas.microsoft.com/winfx/2006/xaml">
   </ResourceDictionary>
   ```

4. Add styles to the `ResourceDictionary`. This example uses `"MyButtonStyle"` and `"MyBigBorderStyle"` as a test (see Listing 3-16).

Listing 3-16. The ResourceDictionary Populated with Styles

```
<ResourceDictionary xmlns="http://schemas.microsoft.com/winfx/2006/xaml/presentation"
                    xmlns:x="http://schemas.microsoft.com/winfx/2006/xaml">
    <Style x:Key="MyButtonStyle"
           TargetType="Button">
        <Setter Property="Background"
                Value="Red" />
        <Setter Property="BorderBrush"
                Value="Maroon" />
        <Setter Property="BorderThickness"
                Value="5" />
    </Style>

    <Style x:Key="MyBigBorderStyle"
           TargetType="Button"
           BasedOn="{StaticResource MyButtonStyle}">
        <Setter Property="BorderThickness"
                Value="20" />
    </Style>
</ResourceDictionary>
```

5. In the Solution Explorer, double-click `App.xaml` to open the application XAML file.
6. Locate the `<Application.Resources>` element and add the markup in Listing 3-17.

Listing 3-17. ResourceDictionary inside the Application Resources Element

```
<Application.Resources>
    <ResourceDictionary>
        <ResourceDictionary.MergedDictionaries>
            <ResourceDictionary Source="MyResources.xaml" />
        </ResourceDictionary.MergedDictionaries>
        <local:LocalizedStrings xmlns:local="clr-namespace:WorkingWithXAML"
            x:Key="LocalizedStrings"/>
    </ResourceDictionary>
</Application.Resources>
```

7. The styles in `MyResources.xaml` are now available throughout the application.

■ **Note** The existing `LocalizedStrings` reference (included when you first create a Windows Phone 8 project) is moved inside the top level `ResourceDictionary`.

Themes

The user has the option of setting a theme on the device to change the background color between dark and light, and to set the accent color. Figure 3-10 shows the theme Settings screen.

Figure 3-10. *Theme Settings*

While a resource is a named set of properties, a theme is a named set of resources. These built-in collections help provide a consistent visual styling. Windows Phone 8 supplies a full set of resources including styles, fonts and brushes to support themes. Some of these are already set by default in the phone application page (see Listing 3-18).

Listing 3-18. Theme Resources in the Default Page

```
FontFamily="{StaticResource PhoneFontFamilyNormal}"
FontSize="{StaticResource PhoneFontSizeNormal}"
Foreground="{StaticResource PhoneForegroundBrush}"
```

The standard controls for Windows Phone 8 are all styled using these themes, so you should use these built-in styles wherever possible instead of creating new styles from scratch. You can find a full list and descriptions of these styles in the MSDN article Theme Resources for Windows Phone (bookmark this one, you'll use it daily):

`http://msdn.microsoft.com/en-us/library/windowsphone/develop/ff769552(v=vs.105).aspx`

You can find the XAML that defines these styles in the Microsoft SDK installation directory at `<program files>\Microsoft SDKs\Windows Phone\<version>\Design\` (see Figure 3-11).

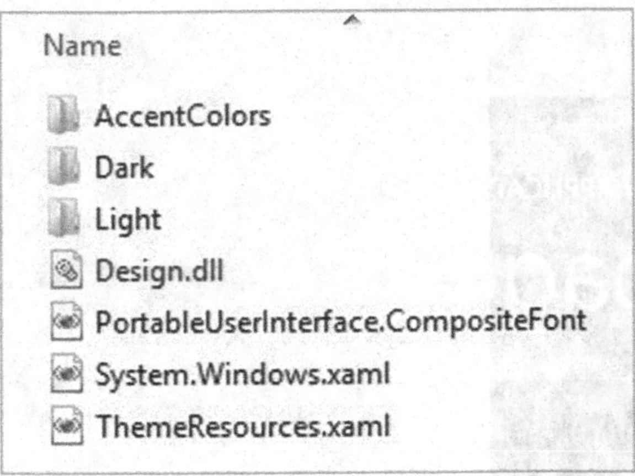

***Figure 3-11.** The Design Folder*

The two files to notice are `ThemeResources.xaml` and `System.Windows.xaml`. Each theme has its own folder, each with its own `ThemeResources.xaml` and `System.Windows.xaml`. `ThemeResources.xaml` is a resource dictionary that defines colors and styles for light and dark themes. `System.Windows.xaml` defines layout for common Windows Phone 8 controls, such as slider, textbox, and toggle button.

Define and Use a Style

This exercise demonstrates creating a style, storing the style in a resource and applying the style to multiple objects.

1. Create a new Windows Phone App.
2. In the Solution Explorer, open the `MainPage.xaml` file for editing. Switch to the Design view.
3. Drag a `StackPanel` from the `Common Windows Phone Controls` section of the Toolbox. Drop the `StackPanel` in the area below the application and page titles, as shown in Figure 3-12.

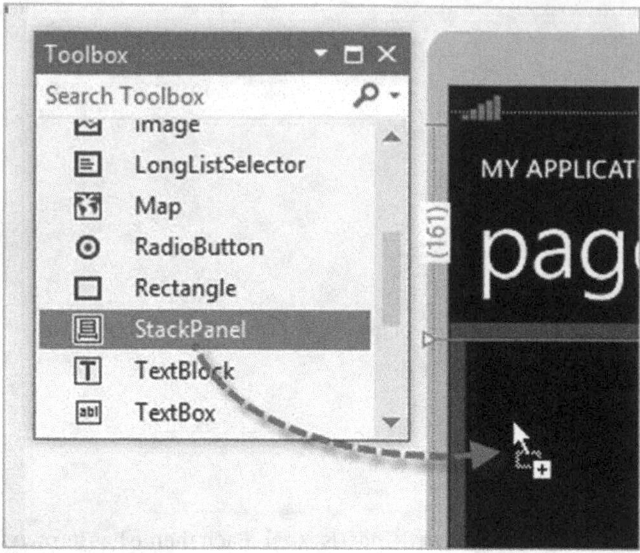

***Figure 3-12.** Adding a StackPanel*

4. In the Visual Studio Properties pane, locate the `Margin` property for the `StackPanel`. Notice that the property has values set already and that the small box to the right is selected. Click the small box to display a menu and select the `Reset` option (see Figure 3-13). Repeat this step for the `Width`, `Height`, and `HorizontalAlignment` properties.

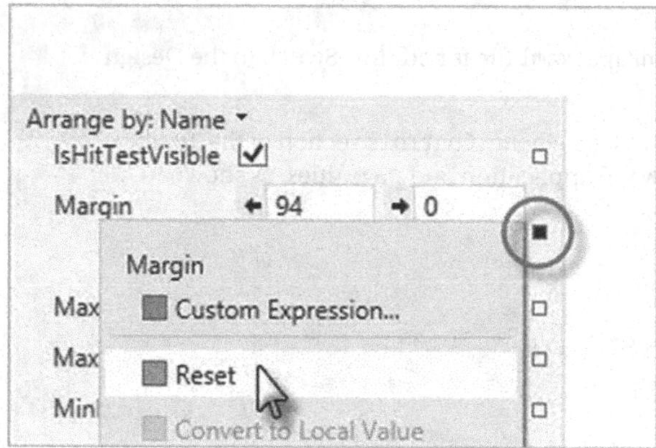

***Figure 3-13.** Resetting Property Values*

■ **Note** The designer will automatically place elements right where you drop them, using the `Margin` property to move the element in from the top and left edges. In this case, the `StackPanel` will take up all the empty space below the page and application titles.

---

5. Set the StackPanel Orientation property to Horizontal. The StackPanel automatically arranges child elements vertically in a stack (the default) or in a horizontal row.

6. From the Common Windows Phone Controls in the Toolbox, drag three Button controls out on top of the StackPanel.

7. Select each button in turn and set the Content property for each to "Hide", "Spam", and "Remove".

8. Switch from the Design view to the XAML view. Add a Resources element to <phone:PhoneApplicationPage>. Place the Resources tags shown in below to a spot just underneath the <phone:PhoneApplicationPage> start tag.

```
<phone:PhoneApplicationPage ...>

    <phone:PhoneApplicationPage.Resources>

    </phone:PhoneApplicationPage.Resources>
```

9. Inside the Resources tag, add a Style tag. Set the TargetType attribute to "Button". Set the x:Name attribute to "ButtonStyle".

```
<phone:PhoneApplicationPage.Resources>

    <Style TargetType="Button"  x:Name="ButtonStyle">

    </Style>

</phone:PhoneApplicationPage.Resources>
```

10. Inside the Style tag, add a Setter for the BorderThickness property with a Value of "0".

```
<phone:PhoneApplicationPage.Resources>

    <Style TargetType="Button" x:Name="ButtonStyle">
        <Setter Property="BorderThickness" Value="0" />
    </Style>

</phone:PhoneApplicationPage.Resources>
```

11. Inside the Style tag, add a second Setter for the VerticalAlignment property with a Value of "Top".

```
<phone:PhoneApplicationPage.Resources>

    <Style TargetType="Button" x:Name="ButtonStyle">
        <Setter Property="BorderThickness" Value="0" />
        <Setter Property="VerticalAlignment" Value="Top" />
    </Style>

</phone:PhoneApplicationPage.Resources>
```

12. Inside the Style tag, add a second Setter for the Background property. The Setter.Value will use the property element syntax to define a LinearGradientBrush.

```
<Style TargetType="Button" x:Name="ButtonStyle">
    <Setter Property="BorderThickness" Value="0" />
    <Setter Property="VerticalAlignment" Value="Top" />
    <Setter Property="Background">
        <Setter.Value>
            <LinearGradientBrush EndPoint="0.5,1" StartPoint="0.5,0">
                <GradientStop Color="#FFAAD3E6" Offset="0" />
                <GradientStop Color="#FF198BD3" Offset="1" />
            </LinearGradientBrush>
        </Setter.Value>
    </Setter>
</Style>
```

13. The style is defined, but hasn't been applied to the button yet. Assign the Style property explicitly for each of the buttons.

```
<Button Content="Hide" Style="{StaticResource ButtonStyle}" />
<Button Content="Spam" Style="{StaticResource ButtonStyle}" />
<Button Content="Remove" Style="{StaticResource ButtonStyle}" />
```

The buttons should now look like Figure 3-14.

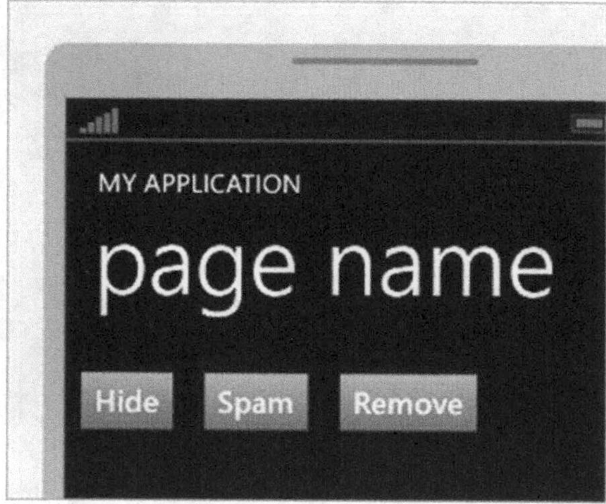

Figure 3-14. The Styled Buttons

■ **Note** To use implicit styles remove the Style property for each button. Also, remove the x:Name="ButtonStyle" from the resource. All the buttons with the TargetType of "Button" will be styled the same.

Templates

A *template* is a pattern expressed in XAML that describes a tree of elements. Use templates to customize an entire control, particular areas of a control, or the control in different states, such as portrait and landscape.

The beauty of templates is that the appearance of the control is not bolted directly to the behavior of the control. For example, a ListBox can be displayed as the typical scrolling series of text, or it can be customized to look like a "cover flow", displaying items moving in a three-dimensional arc across the screen or even as a book where items appear as pages that seem to "flip" across the screen.

Two common types of templates are ControlTemplate and DataTemplate. A ControlTemplate is used to customize the look of the entire control without affecting the control's behavior. While a ControlTemplate allows you to completely gut a control and build it up from scratch, a DataTemplate is used to display content inside some area of a control. The DataTemplate displays the content based on data bound to the template. The DataTemplate is dependent on data binding and is discussed in the "Binding the DataTemplate" section.

ControlTemplate

In a style, you can only set the properties available to the TargetType control. For example, in the section titled "Define and Use a Style", we were able to style a button extensively, but we couldn't have rounded the button corners because Button does not have a Radius property. Using a ControlTemplate, you can access all the primitive parts that make up a control. Elements that inherit from Control have a Template property of type ControlTemplate. Listing 3-19 shows a Template in action that replaces a Button's innards with a simple Border and TextBlock. Figure 3-15 shows the button in the designer.

Listing 3-19. A Simple ControlTemplate

```
<Button HorizontalAlignment="Left"
        VerticalAlignment="Top">
    <Button.Template>
        <ControlTemplate>
            <Border CornerRadius="10"
                    BorderThickness="3"
                    BorderBrush="White"
                    Margin="5"
                    Padding="5">
                <TextBlock Text="Hide" />
            </Border>
        </ControlTemplate>
    </Button.Template>
</Button>
```

Figure 3-15. *The Button in the Designer*

Notice that the button now has rounded corners. The examples that follow display identically, but the XAML is progressively refined to be more flexible and robust.

To move the template to a resource, create a `ControlTemplate`, then use the button's `Template` property to reference the resource. In Listing 3-20, `Resources` are stored in the `Grid` that contains the `Button`.

Listing 3-20. ControlTemplate Defined in a Resource

```
<Grid x:Name="ContentPanel"
      Grid.Row="1"
      Margin="12,0,12,0">
    <Grid.Resources>
        <ControlTemplate x:Key="ButtonTemplate"
                         TargetType="Button">
            <Border CornerRadius="10"
                    BorderThickness="3"
                    BorderBrush="White"
                    Margin="5"
                    Padding="5">
                <TextBlock Text="Hide" />
            </Border>
        </ControlTemplate>
    </Grid.Resources>

    <Button HorizontalAlignment="Left"
            VerticalAlignment="Top"
            Template="{StaticResource ButtonTemplate}">
    </Button>
</Grid>
```

What about the `TextBlock` with text `"Hide"`? Hard coded content in the template just won't cut it. You can fix the problem by using the `Button Content` property.

The markup extension syntax in the `TextBlock Text` property in Listing 3-21 uses `TemplateBinding` and references the `Content` property. `TemplateBinding` "links the value of a property in the control template to the value of some other exposed property on the templated control". In other words, the `Button`'s `Content` property value `"Hide"` gets plugged into the `ControlTemplate` where the `TemplateBinding` references `Content`.

Listing 3-21. Using TemplateBinding to Softcode Properties

```
<Grid x:Name="ContentPanel"
      Grid.Row="1"
      Margin="12,0,12,0">
    <Grid.Resources>
        <ControlTemplate x:Key="ButtonTemplate"
                         TargetType="Button">
            <Border CornerRadius="10"
                    BorderThickness="3"
                    BorderBrush="White"
                    Margin="5"
                    Padding="5">
                <TextBlock Text="{TemplateBinding Content}" />
            </Border>
        </ControlTemplate>
    </Grid.Resources>
```

```
    <Button Content="Hide" HorizontalAlignment="Left"
            VerticalAlignment="Top"
            Template="{StaticResource ButtonTemplate}">
    </Button>
</Grid>
```

You can test the effect of TemplateBinding by changing the Content property of the Button to see the text reflected in the Designer. Figure 3-16 shows the Content property changed to New Content and that the Button in the designer shows the new text.

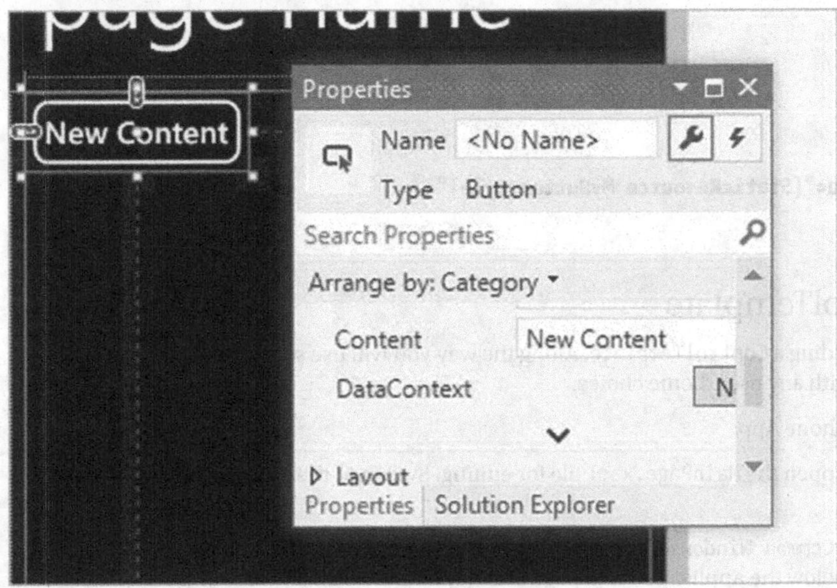

***Figure 3-16.** Content Changes Reflected in the Control via TemplateBinding*

Instead of referencing the Button Template property directly, use the Button Style property and place the Template inside the style. The advantage is that you can add, subtract, or change properties in the style. None of the controls referencing the style need to be changed. Ideally, the only properties assigned in the markup for a control are the properties that change (e.g., Content) and the Style. Listing 3-22 reduces the Button markup to only the Style property reference and the Content property.

Listing 3-22. Placing the Template into a Style

```
<Grid x:Name="ContentPanel"
      Grid.Row="1"
      Margin="12,0,12,0">
    <Grid.Resources>
        <Style x:Key="MyButtonStyle"
               TargetType="Button">
            <Setter Property="HorizontalAlignment"
                    Value="Left" />
            <Setter Property="VerticalAlignment"
                    Value="Top" />
            <Setter Property="Template">
```

```
                <Setter.Value>
                    <ControlTemplate TargetType="Button">
                        <Border CornerRadius="10"
                                BorderThickness="3"
                                BorderBrush="White"
                                Margin="5"
                                Padding="5">
                            <TextBlock Text="{TemplateBinding Content}" />
                        </Border>
                    </ControlTemplate>
                </Setter.Value>
            </Setter>
        </Style>

    </Grid.Resources>

    <Button Content="Hide" Style="{StaticResource MyButtonStyle}" />
</Grid>
```

Define and Use a ControlTemplate

The following steps demonstrate building a `ControlTemplate`. Along the way you will use some of the built-in styles to set appearance in a way that works with any user theme choice.

1. Create a new Windows Phone App.
2. In the Solution Explorer, open the `MainPage.xaml` file for editing. Switch to the Design view.
3. Drag a `TextBox` from the `Common Windows Phone Controls` section of the Toolbox. Drop the `TextBox` in the area below the application and page titles (see Figure 3-17).

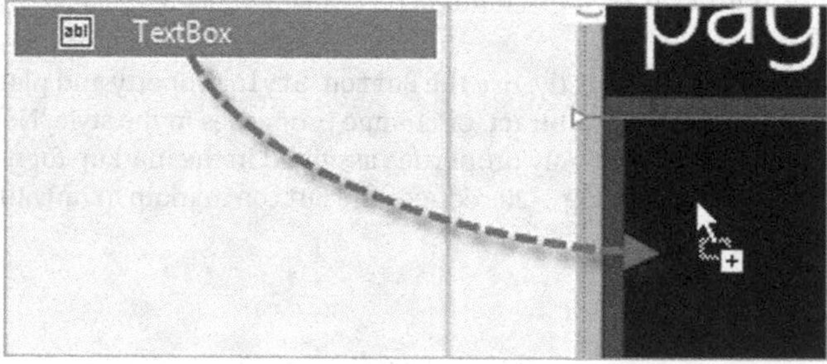

Figure 3-17. *Adding a TextBox to the Page*

4. In the Visual Studio Properties window, right-click the `Margin` property and select the `Reset` item from the context menu, as shown in Figure 3-18. Repeat this step for the `Width`, `Height`, and `HorizontalAlignment` properties.

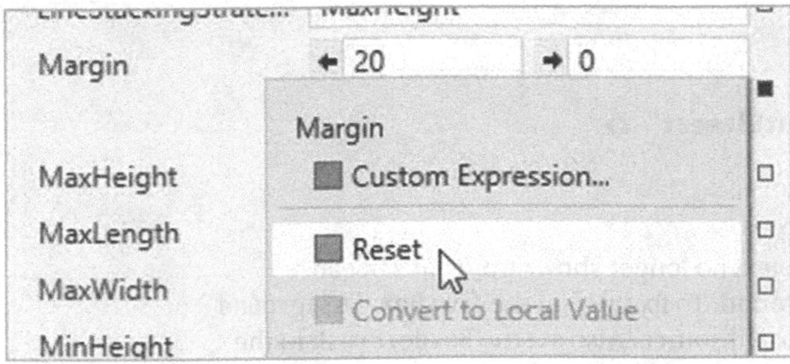

***Figure 3-18.** Resetting the Margin*

The Visual Studio designer should look like Figure 3-19.

***Figure 3-19.** TextBox in the Designer*

5. Using property element syntax, add tags for the `TextBox.Template` and `ControlTemplate` inside the `TextBox` tag. The code below shows how the markup should look. This sets up the shell of the `ControlTemplate` so you can fill it with new inner workings.

```
<TextBox Name="textBox1" Text="TextBox" VerticalAlignment="Top">
    <TextBox.Template>
        <ControlTemplate>

        </ControlTemplate>
    </TextBox.Template>
</TextBox>
```

6. Add a `Border` element to the `ControlTemplate` and a `ContentControl` inside the border. The `ContentControl` must be named `"ContentElement"` for the `TextBox` to interact correctly with it.

```
...
<ControlTemplate>
    <Border>
        <ContentControl x:Name="ContentElement" />
    </Border>
</ControlTemplate>
```

7. If you look at the designer, you'll see that the text no longer shows up. That's because we're displaying black text on a black background. To fix this, set the TextBox Foreground property to the built-in PhoneForegroundBrush resource. Also set the BorderBrush to the PhoneBorderBrush resource. While you're at it, set the TextWrapping property to Wrap and add longer Text content to test against.

```
<TextBox Name="textBox1"
    VerticalAlignment="Top"
    Foreground="{StaticResource PhoneForegroundBrush}"
    BorderBrush="{StaticResource PhoneBorderBrush}"
    Text="Silva quantum poterat woodchuck chuck si posset woodchuck chuck lignum."
    TextWrapping="Wrap">
```

At this point, the designer should look something like Figure 3-20.

12:38
MY APPLICATION
page name
Silva quantum poterat woodchuck chuck
si posset woodchuck chuck lignum.

Figure 3-20. *Unfinished Template*

8. Add a BorderBrush, BorderThickness, and CornerRadius to dress up the Border. Notice in the example below that we use TemplateBinding to get the BorderBrush passed down from the TextBox. TemplateBinding allows you to soft-code values that you want to cascade down from the control.

```
<Border BorderBrush="{TemplateBinding BorderBrush}"
        BorderThickness="1"
        CornerRadius="10">
    <ContentControl x:Name="ContentElement" />
</Border>
```

Figure 3-21 shows the rounded borders resulting from the new `CornerRadius` setting.

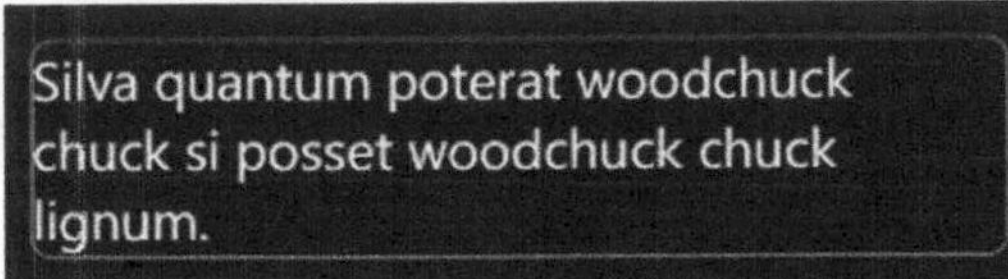

***Figure 3-21.** New Border Properties*

9. Typically, you'll want to store the template in a resource. Switch to the Visual Studio design view and select the TextBox. In the Properties pane, click the options button to the right of the `Template` property and select `Convert to New Resource` from the context menu (see Figure 3-22). Note that older versions of Visual Studio will have slightly different wording in the context menu.

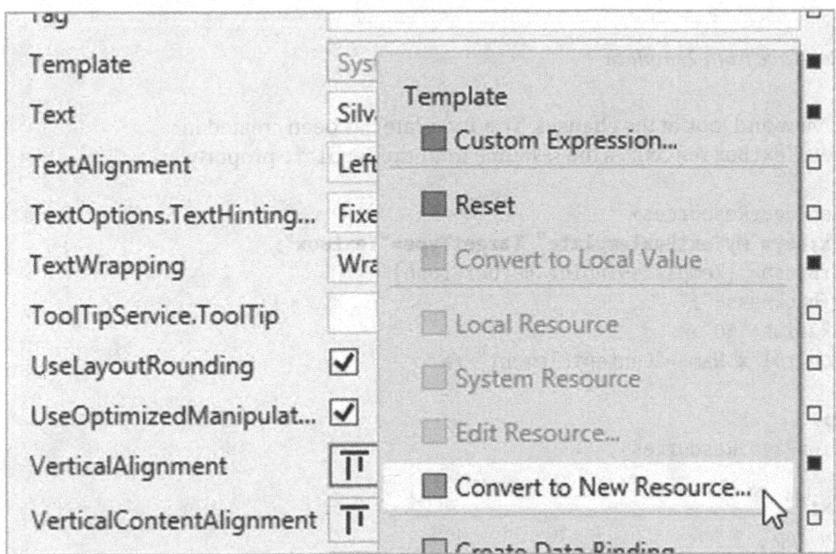

***Figure 3-22.** Converting to New Resource*

10. In the dialog that displays, set Key to `MyTextBoxTemplate`. Leave the defaults and click the `OK` button to close the dialog and create the resource (see Figure 3-23).

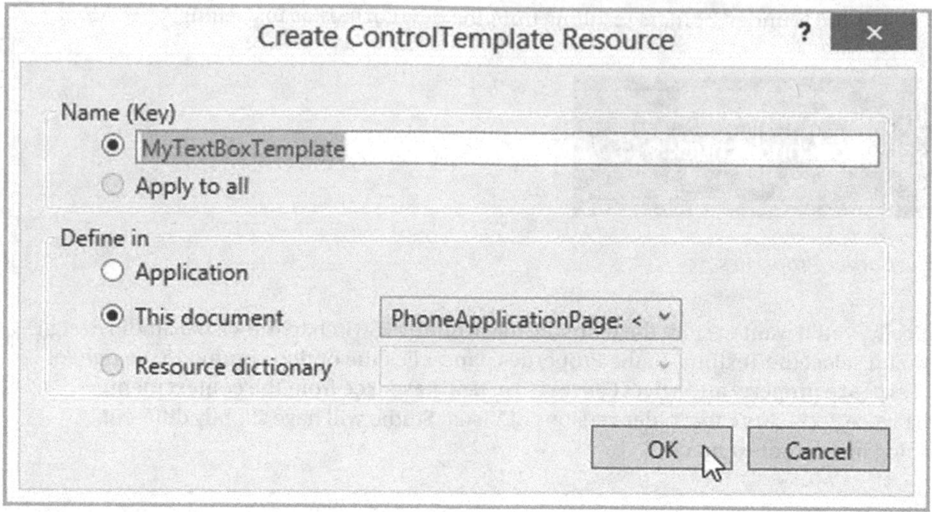

***Figure 3-23.** Making a Resource from Template*

11. Switch back to the XAML view and look at the changes. The Template has been created in the page `Resources` and the `TextBox` references the resource from the `Template` property.

```
<phone:PhoneApplicationPage.Resources>
    <ControlTemplate x:Key="MyTextBoxTemplate" TargetType="TextBox">
        <Border BorderBrush="{TemplateBinding BorderBrush}"
               BorderThickness="1"
               CornerRadius="10">
            <ContentControl x:Name="ContentElement" />
        </Border>
    </ControlTemplate>
</phone:PhoneApplicationPage.Resources>
...
<TextBox Name="textBox1"
    VerticalAlignment="Top"
    Foreground="{StaticResource PhoneForegroundBrush}"
    BorderBrush="{StaticResource PhoneBorderBrush}"
    Text="Silva quantum poterat woodchuck chuck si posset woodchuck chuck lignum."
    TextWrapping="Wrap"
    Template="{StaticResource MyTextBoxTemplate}"/>
```

12. Test that the application works in light and dark theme backgrounds.
13. Run the application.
14. Click the emulator Back button.
15. Click the Forward arrow.
16. Start the Settings Application.
17. Select Theme.
18. Drop down the Background list and select `light` (see Figure 3-24).

Figure 3-24. Changing the Theme Background

19. Back out of the Settings application and re-start the application. The text and border should both display using the light or dark background. Figure 3-25 shows both themes in play.

Figure 3-25. Showing in Light and Dark Theme Backgrounds

Key Classes and Dependency Properties

Here are some of the important stops on the way up the Windows Phone class tree (see Figure 3-26). You'll be working with these objects directly or indirectly every time you open Visual Studio. In particular, notice how `DependencyObject` is involved with the Windows Phone *dependency property system,* a critical mechanism that affects how Windows Phone user interfaces behave.

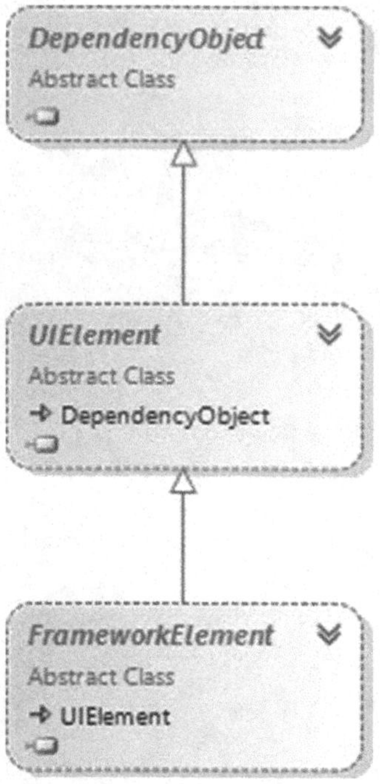

Figure 3-26. *Key Classes*

- **`DependencyObject`**: The base class for representing objects that participate in the Windows Phone dependency property system. `DependencyObject` is the immediate base class for several important Windows Phone classes including `UIElement`, `FrameworkTemplate`, `Style`, and `ResourceDictionary`.
- **`UIElement`**: The base class for objects with visual appearance and that can process basic input.
- **`FrameworkElement`**: The base class for objects that participate in layout. `FrameworkElement` also defines functionality for data binding, object tree and object lifetime features in Windows Phone.

So far, we have spent our time in XAML without having to resort to any code. And why should we? Resources, styles, and templates can be defined declaratively, have little to do with business logic, and shouldn't need any code behind.

The problem: Standard `CLR (Common Language Runtime)` object properties are hard-coded right within the single object. For example, take a WinForms `Panel` object with a `BackColor` property. The color can only be set from the `Panel`'s `BackColor` property and nowhere else. But in Windows Phone 8, we need to set properties from other parts of the XAML, such as bind properties to data, bind properties to other properties, set properties from animation, apply styles, and apply templates.

The Solution: `Dependency properties` are the key to making the magic happen. Dependency properties get values dynamically from different inputs. Windows Phone 8 recognizes this input in the following order of precedence:

1. Animation
2. Local values (CLR setters, binding and static resources go here)
3. Templated Values (Control or data templates)
4. Style values
5. Default value

In Figure 3-27, notice that the public properties of the `FrameworkElement` all participate in the dependency property system.

```
public abstract class FrameworkElement : UIElement
{
    ...public static readonly DependencyProperty ActualHeightProperty;
    ...public static readonly DependencyProperty ActualWidthProperty;
    ...public static readonly DependencyProperty CursorProperty;
    ...public static readonly DependencyProperty DataContextProperty;
    ...public static readonly DependencyProperty FlowDirectionProperty;
    ...public static readonly DependencyProperty HeightProperty;
```

Figure 3-27. *Dependency Properties in FrameworkElement*

You may not need to create dependency properties but be aware that property values can come from a number of different sources (particularly during debugging). For example, the `HeightProperty` of a FrameworkElement could be set by another element in the XAML, such as a `Slider` control. The HeightProperty could also be set by an animation, to gradually grow the height of the element.

Data Binding

Data binding is essentially a conversation between a Windows Phone element and a standard CLR object. `FrameworkElement` introduces the `DataContext` property and is the base class for elements that can be data bound. `DataContext` can be assigned any CLR object using XAML or directly in code. Listing 3-23 shows a simple CLR object `MyData`.

Listing 3-23. Simple CLR Object

```
public class MyData
{
    public int ID { get; set; }
    public string AppTitle { get; set; }
    public string PageName { get; set; }
}
```

You can create an instance of the CLR object and assign it to any `FrameworkElement` on the page. For example, a `TextBlock` with the text "MY APPLICATION" is on the page by default when a Windows Phone project is first created. To access this element in code, you need to assign the `x:Name` property. The code in Listing 3-24 creates the `MyData` object and assigns the initialized object to the `ApplicationTitle DataContext`.

Listing 3-24. Setting the Element DataContext

```
// Constructor
public MainPage()
{
    InitializeComponent();
```

```
    this.ApplicationTitle.DataContext = new MyData()
    {
        ID = 1,
        AppTitle = "Real Estate Explorer",
        PageName = "explorer"
    };
}
```

MyData is now available to ApplicationTitle, but nothing can display until a property of the FrameworkElement ApplicationTitle is bound to a property of the CLR object MyData. Because we're working with dependency properties, the binding can take place right in the XAML. Listing 3-25 shows a Binding markup extension to establish a relationship between MyData and a Windows Phone element on the page. The Path points to the AppTitle property of MyData. To show the AppTitle defined in Listing 3-24, replace the hard-coded text with the binding expression shown in Listing 3-25.

Listing 3-25. Binding the Text DependencyProperty

```
<TextBlock x:Name="ApplicationTitle" Text="{Binding Path=AppTitle}"
  Style="{StaticResource PhoneTextNormalStyle}" />
```

Running the application in the emulator displays the AppTitle in the Text dependency property of the TextBlock "ApplicationTitle" (see Figure 3-28).

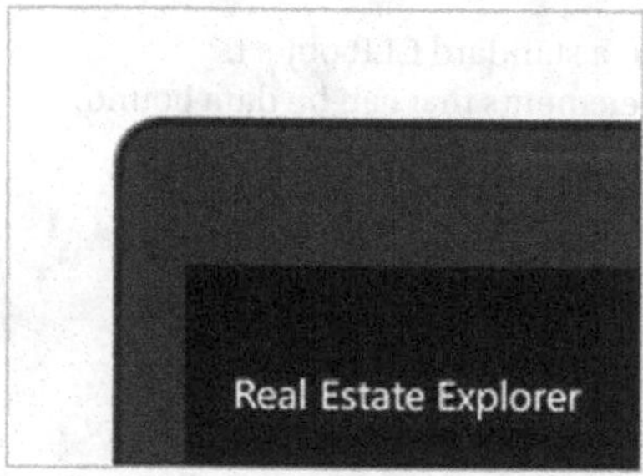

Figure 3-28. *Data Displaying in a Bound TextBlock*

Binding Basics

The key properties in a {Binding} statement are:

- ***Source:*** The CLR object that provides the data. This object is assigned to the DataContext of the target framework element we're binding to.
- ***Path:*** The name of the property in the source CLR object.
- ***Mode:*** The data's direction of travel. The values can be OneTime, where the target framework element is set initially from the source object, OneWay (the default), where the target framework element is updated by the source object, and TwoWay where the target framework element also updates the source object.

Listing 3-26 defines the MyData object directly in XAML as a resource. Notice that the page resources include a "MyData" declaration with properties defined inside the tag. In the TextBlock binding, the Source attribute points to the MyData resource, Path points to MyData.AppTitle and MyData.PageTitle properties, and Mode is OneTime.

Listing 3-26. Assigning the Source per Element

```
<phone:PhoneApplicationPage ...>
    <phone:PhoneApplicationPage.Resources>
    <local:MyData x:Key="MyData"
                  ID="1"
                  AppTitle="Real Estate Explorer"
                  PageName="Commercial Real Estate" />
    </phone:PhoneApplicationPage.Resources>

      ...
      <TextBlock x:Name="ApplicationTitle"
        Text="{Binding Path=AppTitle, Source={StaticResource MyData}, Mode=OneTime}" ... />
      <TextBlock x:Name="PageTitle"
        Text="{Binding Path=PageName, Source={StaticResource MyData}, Mode=OneTime}"... />
    ...

    </Grid>

</phone:PhoneApplicationPage>
```

To bind multiple properties in the same object, assign the DataContext to a source object, and then bind each of the properties, leaving out the Source attribute. The example below sets the DataContext to MyData, and then the Text and Tag are bound to properties in the source object. Listing 3-27 shows the key property settings.

Listing 3-27. Binding Multiple Properties

```
<TextBlock  DataContext="{StaticResource MyData}"
            Text="{Binding Path=AppTitle}"
            Tag="{Binding Path=ID}" .../>
```

The DataContext is available to child elements, so you can assign data to a Grid or other parent container and have it used "for free" by all child elements in the container. Listing 3-28 shows data is hooked up to a Grid. Only the source data properties need to be explicitly bound to the target elements "ApplicationTitle" and "PageTitle".

Listing 3-28. Assigning Parent Container DataContext

```
<phone:PhoneApplicationPage ...>
    <phone:PhoneApplicationPage.Resources>
        <local:MyData x:Key="MyData"
                      ID="1"
                      AppTitle="Real Estate Explorer"
                      PageName="Commercial Real Estate" />
    </phone:PhoneApplicationPage.Resources>

   <Grid x:Name="LayoutRoot"
         DataContext="{StaticResource MyData}">
           ...
           <TextBlock x:Name="ApplicationTitle"
                      Text="{Binding Path=AppTitle}"
                      Tag="{Binding Path=ID}" />
```

```
            <TextBlock x:Name="PageTitle"
                       Text="{Binding Path=PageName" />
            ...
    </Grid>

</phone:PhoneApplicationPage>
```

Binding in Code

Binding requires three objects: the `FrameworkElement` to display the data, a CLR object to contain the data and a `Binding` object to manage the conversation between the two. The XAML binding expression obscures the existence of the binding object, but the `Binding` object is more apparent when binding in code. The example in Listing 3-29 demonstrates creating a `Binding` object and populating it with a CLR object reference, a path to the CLR object property to be bound, and the direction of data travel.

Listing 3-29. Binding a CLR Object in Code

```
// create a CLR object instance
BikeType bikeType = new BikeType()
{
    TypeName = "Touring",
    TypeDescription = "Durable and comfortable bikes for long journeys."
};

// create a Binding object
Binding binding = new Binding()
{
    Source = bikeType,
    Path = new PropertyPath("TypeName"),
    Mode = BindingMode.OneTime
};

// assign the binding object to the FrameworkElement
BindInCodeTextBox.SetBinding(TextBox.TextProperty, binding);
```

Binding Collections

`ItemsSource` (or its descendant `ListBox`) can be assigned any `IEnumerable` implementation such as generic lists or arrays. By changing the `MyData` example and descending from a generic `List<>`, we can represent a list of `Item` types. Take a moment to examine the `MyData` and `Item` objects in Listing 3-30 before moving on to see *how* they're bound.

Listing 3-30. Binding a CLR Object in Code

```
public class MyData : List<Item>
{
    public int ID { get; set; }
    public string AppTitle { get; set; }
    public string PageName { get; set; }
```

```
    public MyData()
    {
        this.ID = 1;
        this.AppTitle = "Real Estate Explorer";
        this.PageName = "Explorer";
        this.Add(new Item {
            Title = "Open House",
            Description = "Open Houses in your area"
        });
        this.Add(new Item {
            Title = "Price Reduction",
            Description = "New deals this week"
        });
        this.Add(new Item {
            Title = "Recently Sold",
            Description = "What's moving in the market"
        });
    }
}
```

The collection binding in Listing 3-31 has three key sections. First, the "MyData" resource is defined. The new code initializes the data in the MyData constructor code-behind instead of the XAML. Second, the DataContext of the "LayoutRoot" Grid is assigned. Finally, an ItemsControl is added to the Grid "ContentPanel", the ItemsControl ItemsSource is assigned to the MyData static resource and DisplayMemberPath is "Title". Figure 3-29 shows the result.

Listing 3-31. Binding a CLR Object in Code

```
<phone:PhoneApplicationPage ...
    xmlns:local="clr-namespace:BindingCollections">
    <phone:PhoneApplicationPage.Resources>
        <!--define the resource-->
        <local:MyData x:Key="MyData" />
    </phone:PhoneApplicationPage.Resources>

    <!--assign the DataContext-->
    <Grid x:Name="LayoutRoot" Background="Transparent" DataContext="{StaticResource MyData}">
        <Grid.RowDefinitions>
            <RowDefinition Height="Auto"/>
            <RowDefinition Height="*"/>
        </Grid.RowDefinitions>

        <StackPanel x:Name="TitlePanel" Grid.Row="0" Margin="12,17,0,28">
            <TextBlock x:Name="ApplicationTitle"
                       Text="{Binding Path=AppTitle}"
                       Style="{StaticResource PhoneTextNormalStyle}" />
            <TextBlock x:Name="PageTitle"
                       Text="{Binding Path=PageName}"
                       Margin="9,-7,0,0"
                       Style="{StaticResource PhoneTextTitle1Style}" />
        </StackPanel>
```

```
        <Grid x:Name="ContentPanel" Grid.Row="1" Margin="12,0,12,0">
            <!--bind the collection here-->
            <ItemsControl ItemsSource="{StaticResource MyData}" DisplayMemberPath="Title" />

        </Grid>

    </Grid>

</phone:PhoneApplicationPage>
```

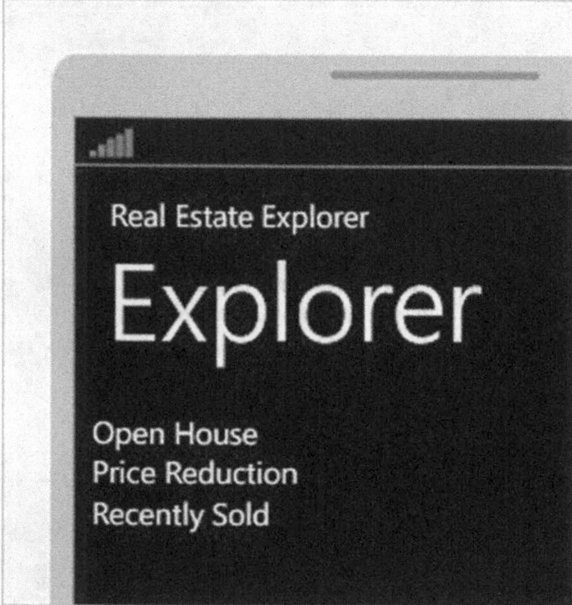

***Figure 3-29.** The list of items bound to the ItemsControl*

Bind Objects

This exercise demonstrates binding objects and collections of objects to framework elements.

1. Create a new Windows Phone Application.
2. In the Solution Explorer, right-click the project and select `Add > Class...` from the context menu. In the `Add New Item` dialog, set the `Name` of the class to `MyData.cs`. Then click the `Add` button to create the class and close the dialog.
3. In the code-behind, replace the `MyData` class with the code below.

```
public class Item
{
    public string Title { get; set; }
    public string Description { get; set; }
}
```

```
public class MyData : List<Item>
{
    public string AppTitle { get; set; }
    public string PageName { get; set; }

    public MyData()
    {
        this.AppTitle = "Real Estate Explorer";
        this.PageName = "explorer";
        this.Add(new Item {
            Title = "Open House",
            Description = "Open Houses in your area"
        });
        this.Add(new Item {
            Title = "Price Reduction",
            Description ="New deals this week"
        });
        this.Add(new Item {
            Title = "Recently Sold",
            Description = "What's moving in the market"
        });
    }
}
```

4. Open the XAML view for `MainPage.xaml`.

5. Add an XML namespace named `local` that points to the current project where `MyData` is stored. Now the page has all objects in the project available to the XAML on the page. Figure 3-30 shows the XML namespace declaration `local` for the assembly named `BindObjects`.

```
shell:SystemTray.IsVisible="True"
xmlns:local="clr-namespace:BindObjects" >

<Grid x:Name="LayoutRoot" Background="Transp
```

Figure 3-30. *Declaring the Namespace for the Project*

6. Add a `Resources` element under the `PhoneApplicationPage` element. Inside the `Resources` element, add a `MyData` tag with `Key = "MyData"`. Now you can refer to `MyData` as a static resource.

```
<phone:PhoneApplicationPage.Resources>
    <local:MyData x:Key="MyData" />
</phone:PhoneApplicationPage.Resources>
```

7. Find the `Grid` element named `"LayoutRoot"`. Add a `DataContext` attribute and assign the `MyData` static resource to it. `MyData` is now available to the `Grid` element and every child element inside the grid.

```
<Grid x:Name="LayoutRoot"
  DataContext="{StaticResource MyData}">
```

8. Locate the "TitlePanel" element in the XAML. Locate the TextBlock with Text "MY APPLICATION". Change the Text property to "{Binding Path=AppTitle}".
   Locate the TextBlock element with text "page name". Change the Text property to "{Binding Path=PageName}".

```
<StackPanel x:Name="TitlePanel" Grid.Row="0" Margin="12,17,0,28">
    <TextBlock Text="{Binding Path=AppTitle}"
               Margin="12,0"
               Style="{StaticResource PhoneTextNormalStyle}"/>
    <TextBlock Text="{Binding Path=PageName}"
               Margin="9,-7,0,0"
               Style="{StaticResource PhoneTextTitle1Style}"/>
</StackPanel>
```

9. Locate the Grid element named "ContentPanel". Add an ItemsControl with the ItemsSource property assigned the MyData static resource and set the DisplayMemberPath to "Title".

```
<Grid x:Name="ContentPanel" Grid.Row="1" Margin="12,0,12,0">
    <ItemsControl ItemsSource="{StaticResource MyData}"
                  DisplayMemberPath="Title" />
</Grid>
```

10. The application and page titles should now display the AppTitle and PageTitle properties from MyData. The ItemsControl should display the collection fed in from MyData items (see Figure 3-31).

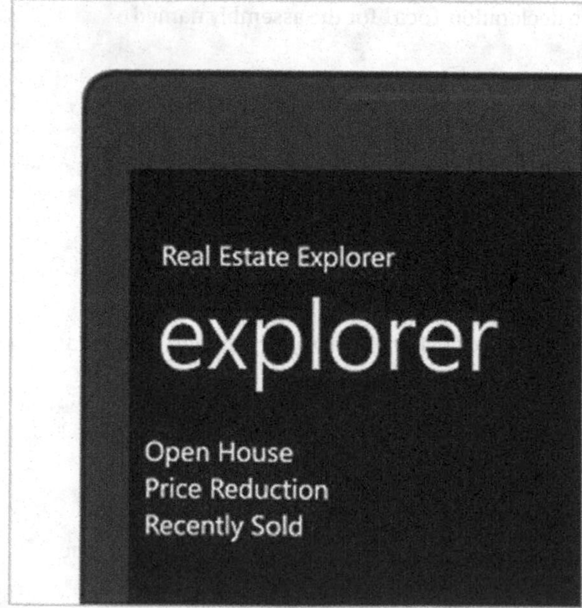

Figure 3-31. Bound Data Showing in the Running Application

Binding to Other Elements

You can use another element on the page as a binding source. For example, if you have a Slider that should update a TextBlock, you can bind the Text to the Slider value.

This next example uses an ItemsControl descendant, ListBox. ListBox can be used just like ItemsControl except that items can be selected and highlighted. ListBox doesn't show up in Toolbox, but is still available to use in the markup. We will bind the ListBox selection content to the Text in a TextBox.

In the Binding expression for the target element that will be updated, set the ElementName attribute to the name of the source element and the Path to a property on the source element. Notice in the example below that the Path property uses dot syntax, that is Selected.Content, to drill down to the data needed by the target TextBox element (see Listing 3-32).

Listing 3-32. Binding the TextBox to the ListBox SelectedItem

```
<Grid x:Name="ContentPanel" Grid.Row="1" Margin="12,0,12,0">
    <Grid.RowDefinitions>
        <RowDefinition Height="Auto"/>
        <RowDefinition Height="*"/>
    </Grid.RowDefinitions>
    <ListBox x:Name="PriorityList"
             Height="100"
             HorizontalAlignment="Stretch"
             VerticalAlignment="Top"
             SelectedIndex="0">
        <ListBoxItem Content="High" />
        <ListBoxItem Content="Medium" />
        <ListBoxItem Content="Low" />
    </ListBox>
    <TextBox
        Text="{Binding ElementName=PriorityList, Path=SelectedItem.Content}"
        HorizontalAlignment="Stretch"
        VerticalAlignment="Top"
        Grid.Row="1" />
</Grid>
```

■ **Note** ListBox is deprecated and no longer shows up in the Toolbox. Instead, the LongListSelector is recommended by Microsoft, even for displaying simple flat lists. LongListSelector is performant, very flexible, and can display lists in various groupings. Unfortunately, at the time of this writing, the LongListSelector SelectedItem property is not a dependency property and so can not be bound in XAML. ListBox is used here for the sake of showing the element binding as simply as possible.

Converters

Converters are adapters that sit between the data coming from the source and the data going out to the target element. Converters are a good choice when you need a versatile, reusable, general purpose tool that can be placed directly in XAML.

For example, a converter can take enumeration values "Stop", "Slow", and "Go" and convert to corresponding color values "Red", "Yellow", and "Green". Or, you can convert Boolean values into `Visibility` enumeration values. Or, you can convert a `DateTime` to a formatted date and time string. You get the idea. Whenever the underlying data is of one type and you need to display that data differently, think about using a converter. Using a converter requires three steps:

1. Create a converter class that implements `IValueConverter`. `IValueConverter` has just two methods, `Convert()` and `ConvertBack()`. The `Convert()` method takes an object as a parameter and returns an object of some other type.
2. Surface the converter as a resource that can be used in the XAML markup.
3. Add a `Converter` attribute to a Binding markup extension.

Listing 3-33 shows a simplified Converter that returns a `Visibility` enumeration value based on a Boolean input. The Boolean is passed in the "value" parameter. The value is assumed to be a Boolean and cast as such. You can optionally use the "targetType" parameter to perform type checking before allowing a conversion. If "value" is true, then the Visibility.Visible parameter is returned, otherwise, Visibility.Collapsed is returned.

Listing 3-33. Defining a Converter

```
public class BoolToVisibilityConverter : IValueConverter
{

    public object Convert(object value, Type targetType, object parameter,
System.Globalization.CultureInfo culture)
    {
        return (bool)value ? Visibility.Visible : Visibility.Collapsed;
    }

    public object ConvertBack(object value, Type targetType, object parameter,
        System.Globalization.CultureInfo culture)
    {
        throw new NotImplementedException();
    }
}
```

The resource need only have an `x:Key` so that it can be referred to in the `Binding` expression. In the example in Listing 3-34, our custom `BoolToVisibilityConverter` has a key of `"VisibilityConverter"` that will be referenced later in binding expressions. A second resource `"MyData"` has properties for a string `Title` and a Boolean `IsFavorite`.

Listing 3-34. Defining the Converter as a Resource

```
<phone:PhoneApplicationPage.Resources>
    <local:BoolToVisibilityConverter x:Key="VisibilityConverter" />
    <local:MyData x:Key="MyData" Title="Hot Chocolate" IsFavorite="true" />
</phone:PhoneApplicationPage.Resources>
```

The `Binding` expression for the `TextBlock Visibility` property in Listing 3-35 includes the path to a Boolean property `IsFavorite` and the `Converter` attribute that points to the `VisibilityConverter` static resource.

***Listing* 3-35.** Using a Converter in a Binding Expression

```
<TextBlock
    DataContext="{StaticResource MyData}"
    Text="{Binding Path=Title}"
    Visibility="{Binding Path=IsFavorite,
        Converter={StaticResource VisibilityConverter}}" />
```

Implement and Bind a Converter

The following steps demonstrate how to bind objects using a converter. The converter adapts an enumeration value (High, Medium, and Low) to a `Brush` object used to color an `Ellipse` element (Red, Yellow, and Green).

1. Create a new Windows Phone Application

2. In the Solution Explorer, right-click the project and select Add ➤ `Class...` from the context menu. In the `Add New Item` dialog, set the Name of the class to `Project.cs`, and then click the Add button to create the class and close the dialog.

3. Replace the code-behind for the `Project` class with the code below.

```
public enum Status { NotStarted, Deferred, InProgress, Complete };

public class Project
{
    public Status ProjectStatus { get; set; }
    public string ProjectTitle { get; set; }
}
```

4. Add the following using statements to the page:

```
using System.Windows.Data;
using System.Windows.Media;
```

5. Add a second class to the project and name it "StatusToBrushConverter". Replace the code with the code listed below. `StatusToBrushConverter` takes a `Status` enumeration and returns a `Brush` object. Each `Status` will have a corresponding color brush.

```
public class StatusToBrushConverter : IValueConverter
{

    public object Convert(object value, Type targetType, object parameter,
        System.Globalization.CultureInfo culture)
    {
        switch ((Status)value)
        {
            case Status.Complete: return new SolidColorBrush(Colors.Black);
            case Status.Deferred: return new SolidColorBrush(Colors.LightGray);
            case Status.InProgress: return new SolidColorBrush(Colors.Green);
            case Status.NotStarted: return new SolidColorBrush(Colors.Red);
            default: return Colors.Transparent;
        }
    }
```

```
    public object ConvertBack(object value, Type targetType, object parameter,
        System.Globalization.CultureInfo culture)
    {
        throw new NotImplementedException();
    }
}
```

6. In the Solution Explorer locate the `MainPage.xaml` file, and then double-click to open the XAML for editing.
7. Add an XML namespace named `local` that points back to the current project.
8. Create a `Resources` element for the page using the code below. The first resource creates a `Project` object with data and is keyed `"Project1"` for later reference. The second resource creates an instance of the `StatusToBrushConverter`.

```
<phone:PhoneApplicationPage.Resources>
    <local:Project x:Key="Project1"
                ProjectTitle="Implement TPS Reports"
                ProjectStatus="InProgress" />
    <local:StatusToBrushConverter x:Key="StatusToBrushConverter" />
</phone:PhoneApplicationPage.Resources>
```

9. Locate the `Grid` named `"ContentPanel"` and place the bolded XAML markup below inside the Grid tags.

```
<Grid x:Name="ContentPanel"
    Grid.Row="1"
    Margin="12,0,12,0">

    <StackPanel Orientation="Horizontal"
        HorizontalAlignment="Stretch"
        VerticalAlignment="Top" DataContext="{StaticResource Project1}">
        <Ellipse
            Fill="{Binding Path=ProjectStatus,
                Converter={StaticResource StatusToBrushConverter}}"
            Width="25"
            Height="25"
            VerticalAlignment="Top"
            Margin="5" />
                    <TextBlock Text="{Binding Path=ProjectTitle}"
            VerticalAlignment="top"
            Margin="5" />

    </StackPanel>

</Grid>
```

10. Switch to the Design view. The `ContentPanel` should look something like Figure 3-32.

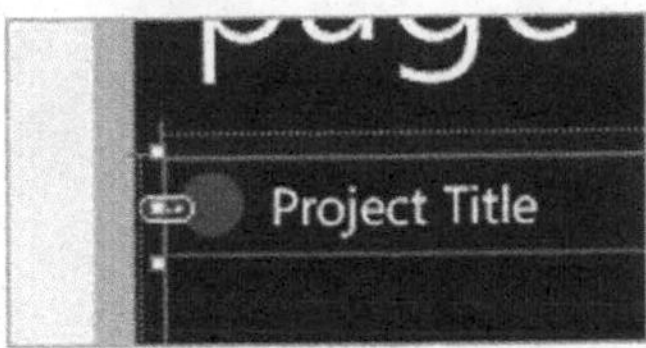

Figure 3-32. Unbound Ellipse

11. Add a `DataContext` attribute to the `StackPanel`. Assign the `Project1 StaticResource` to the `StackPanel DataContext`.

```
<StackPanel Orientation="Horizontal"
    HorizontalAlignment="Stretch"
    VerticalAlignment="Top"
    DataContext="{StaticResource Project1}">
```

12. Change the `Ellipse Fill` property to bind to the `ProjectStatus` property of the `Project` object. In the `Binding` expression, the `Converter` attribute should point to the `StatusToBrushConverter` static resource.

```
<Ellipse
    Fill="{Binding Path=ProjectStatus,
        Converter={StaticResource StatusToBrushConverter}}"
    Width="25"
    Height="25"
    VerticalAlignment="Top"
    Margin="5" />
```

■ **Note** While the `StatusToBrushConverter` is a valid use of a `Converter` and helps demonstrate how a `Converter` works, this example converter is not general purpose and therefore not particularly reusable. The conversion is between a business-specific "Status" to another type. For this kind of situation, consider using a ViewModel as described in the MVVM topic. The earlier example, "`BoolToVisibility`" is a better example of the best use for a Converter, namely a standard CLR type converted to another CLR type that can be reused for multiple projects, regardless of the business content.

---

13. Bind the `TextBlock Text` property to the `ProjectTitle` property of the `Project` object.

```
<TextBlock Text="{Binding Path=ProjectTitle}"
    VerticalAlignment="top"
    Margin="5" />
```

14. Switch to the Design view to see the results. The `Ellipse Fill` property is bound to the `ProjectStatus` property and has a value of `"InProgress"`. The Converter takes the `"InProgress"` value and returns the corresponding Green color brush (see Figure 3-33).

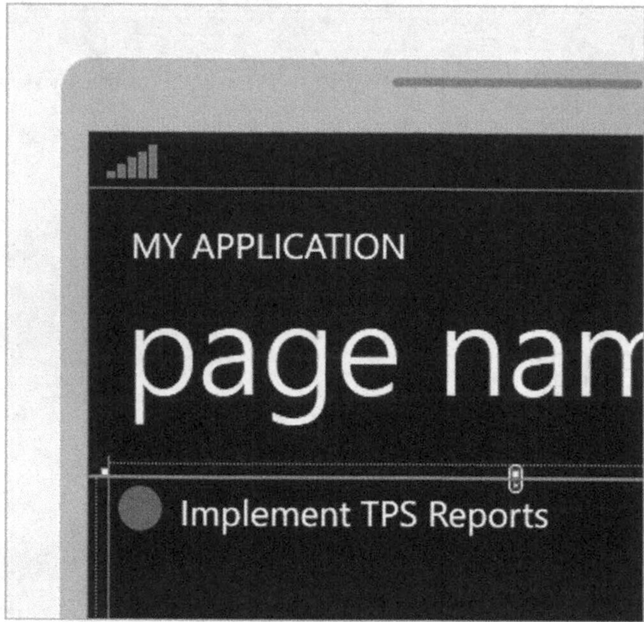

Figure 3-33. Bound Ellipse Using Converter

15. Navigate to the `MainPage.xaml.cs` code-behind file to view the application code. The naming of the class may be different from the example here, but the point is that there is *no added application-level code to get all this functionality*. Without Binding expressions and converters, you would be forced to write some conditional statement to map the status values to the brushes, assign the brushes, and make sure that code was called whenever the status values changed. You get that for free using `Binding` expressions and converters. Very clean.

```
namespace ImplementAndBindAConverter
{
    public partial class MainPage : PhoneApplicationPage
    {
        public MainPage()
        {
            InitializeComponent();
        }
    }
}
```

Binding the DataTemplate

When you need to bind a collection, but need a free-form layout with multiple elements, use the `DataTemplate`. The `ItemsControl`, `ListBox`, and `LongListSelector` all have an `ItemTemplate` property of type `DataTemplate` just for this purpose. The template is used for every item in the list. The basic XAML markup syntax looks something like the minimal example in Listing 3-36.

Listing 3-36. Defining a DataTemplate

```
<phone:LongListSelector >
    <phone:LongListSelector.ItemTemplate>
        <DataTemplate>
         <!--put any content here-->
        </DataTemplate>
    </phone:LongListSelector.ItemTemplate>
</phone:LongListSelector>
```

Instead of using the `DisplayMemberPath` to bind to only one specific property, you can bind as many properties and elements as you like inside of the `DataTemplate`, and in any visual arrangement. Notice that each line in the `LongListSelector` has multiple elements and where each element is bound to a separate property. For an example of what `DataTemplate` can do, take a look at the example in Figure 3-34.

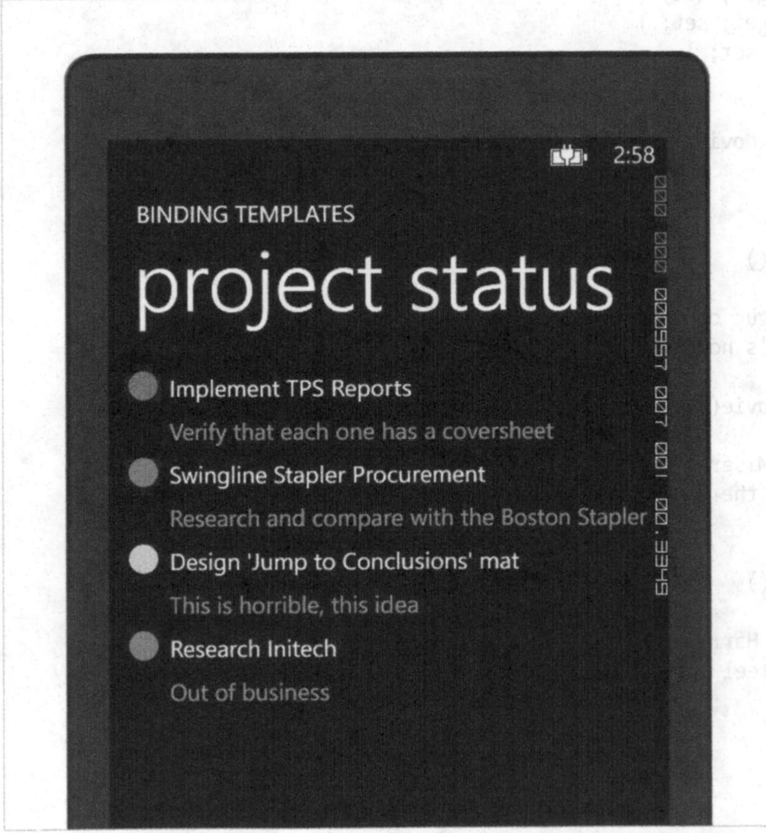

Figure 3-34. *ItemTemplate DataTemplate Layout*

■ **Note** See the "BindingTemplates" project for the complete listing.

Bind a Template

The following steps demonstrate using a DataTemplate to arrange, bind, and display multiple properties of an object.

1. Create a new Windows Phone Application.
2. In the Solution Explorer, right-click the project and select Add ➤ Class... from the context menu. In the Add New Item dialog, set the Name of the class to Movie.cs, and then click the Add button to create the class and close the dialog.
3. Replace the code-behind for Movie class with the code below. The Movie object defines a single movie Title, Quote, and Year. The Movies class is a generic List of Movie that creates and initializes several movies in the constructor.

```
public class Movie
{
    public string Title { get; set; }
    public string Quote { get; set; }
    public int Year { get; set; }
}

public class Movies : List<Movie>
{
    public Movies()
    {
        this.Add(new Movie()
        {
            Title = "A League of Their Own",
            Quote = "There's no crying in baseball!",
            Year = 1992
        }); this.Add(new Movie()
        {
            Title = " Les Misérables",
            Quote = " Even the darkest night will end and the sun will rise.",
            Year = 2012
        });
        this.Add(new Movie()
        {
            Title = "Dirty Harry",
            Quote = "Do I feel lucky?' Well, do ya, punk?",
            Year = 1971
        });
    }
}
```

4. Open MainPage.xaml file for editing.
5. Add an XML namespace named local that references your current project. The example below declares the XML namespace local for the project named BindATemplate.

```
<phone:PhoneApplicationPage xmlns:local="clr-namespace:BindATemplate" ...">
```

6. Create a Resources element for the page using the code below. The resource creates a Movies collection object and is keyed "Movies" for later reference.

```
<phone:PhoneApplicationPage.Resources>
    <local:Movies x:Key="Movies" />
</phone:PhoneApplicationPage.Resources>
```

7. Locate the Grid named "ContentPanel" and add the LongListSelector markup below inside the Grid. This XAML just sets up the shell of the LongListSelector ItemTemplate, ready to receive whatever content you place in it.

```
<phone:LongListSelector
    Height="100"
    HorizontalAlignment="Stretch"
    VerticalAlignment="Stretch">
    <phone:LongListSelector.ItemTemplate>
        <DataTemplate>

            <!--add content here-->

        </DataTemplate>
    </phone:LongListSelector.ItemTemplate>
</phone:LongListSelector >
```

8. Add a Grid element inside the DataTemplate. Set up definitions for two rows and two columns in the Grid. Hook up the Movies static resource to the ItemsSource of the LongListSelector.

```
<phone:LongListSelector
    ItemsSource="{StaticResource Movies}"
    HorizontalAlignment="Stretch"
    VerticalAlignment="Stretch">
    <phone:LongListSelector.ItemTemplate>
        <DataTemplate>

            <Grid>
                <Grid.RowDefinitions>
                    <RowDefinition Height="Auto" />
                    <RowDefinition Height="*" />
                </Grid.RowDefinitions>
                <Grid.ColumnDefinitions>
                    <ColumnDefinition Width="Auto" />
                    <ColumnDefinition Width="*" />
                </Grid.ColumnDefinitions>

                <!--add content to Grid here-->

            </Grid>

        </DataTemplate>
    </phone:LongListSelector.ItemTemplate>
</phone:LongListSelector>
```

9. Inside the Grid, add three TextBlock elements and bind them to the Year, Title, and Quote properties. Notice that the example uses built-in phone styles and that each element is placed in a particular part of the Grid using the Grid Row and Column attached properties.

```
<TextBlock Text="{Binding Path=Year}"
    Style="{StaticResource PhoneTextSmallStyle}"
    Grid.Column="0"
    Grid.Row="0"
    VerticalAlignment="top"
    Margin="5" />

<TextBlock Text="{Binding Path=Title}"
    Style="{StaticResource PhoneTextNormalStyle}"
    Grid.Column="1"
    Grid.Row="0"
    VerticalAlignment="top"
    Margin="5" />

<TextBlock Text="{Binding Path=Quote}"
    Style="{StaticResource PhoneTextAccentStyle}"
    Grid.Column="1"
    Grid.Row="1"
    VerticalAlignment="top"
    Margin="5" />
```

10. Run the application. Each row of "Movie" data is displayed in its own instance of the bound Grid inside the ItemTemplate (see Figure 3-35).

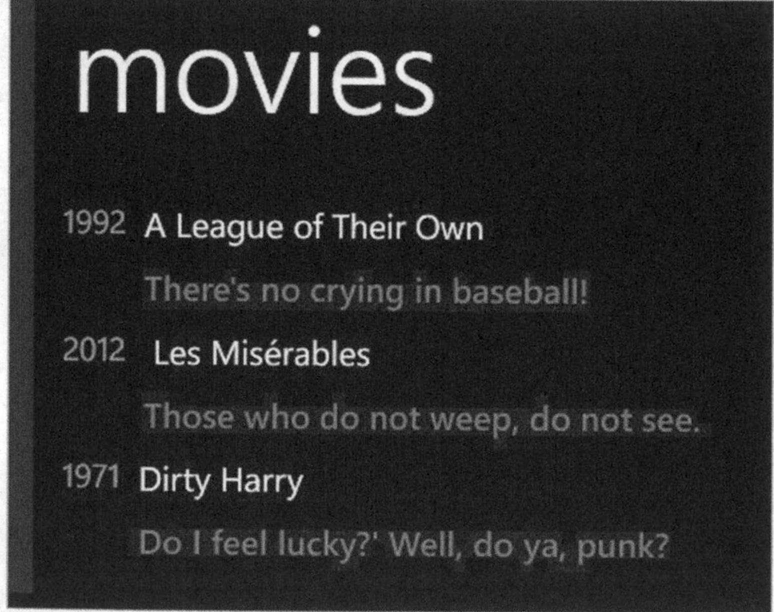

Figure 3-35. *Bound DataTemplate*

Change Notification

If binding is made possible with Windows Phone elements in XAML using dependency properties, how does a plain old CLR object let the element know what's going on? If I change a Movie object description, or add a new "Movie" to a list, how is the XAML element notified that something has changed? Three key classes handle property change notification:

- Classes that implement INotifyPropertyChanged allow communication between data source and Windows Phone 8 elements. By implementing the INotifyPropertyChanged interface, client objects are notified when property values change.
- Classes that implement INotifyCollectionChanged notify when collections are changed.
- ObservableCollection<T> implements INotifyCollectionChanged for you. ObservableCollection<T> is commonly used instead of implementing your own INotifyCollectionChanged.

Property Change Notification

To demonstrate INotifyPropertyChanged, start with the Movie object from the "Bind a Template" exercise. First implement the INotifyPropertyChanged interface. INotifyPropertyChanged has a single event called PropertyChanged. Wrap the event in a convenience method to make it easy to call from each property setter. For each property assignment, call the convenience method and pass the name of the property. See the NotifyPropertyChanged method in Listing 3-37.

Listing 3-37. Implementing INotifyPropertyChanged

```
public class Movie : INotifyPropertyChanged
{
    private string _title;
    public string Title
    {
        get { return _title; }
        set
        {
            _title = value;
            NotifyPropertyChanged("Title");
        }
    }

    private string _quote;
    public string Quote
    {
        get { return _quote; }
        set
        {
            _quote = value;
            NotifyPropertyChanged("Quote");
        }
    }

    private int _year;
    public int Year
```

```
    {
        get { return _year; }
        set
        {
            _year = value;
            NotifyPropertyChanged("Year");
        }
    }

    public event PropertyChangedEventHandler PropertyChanged;

    public void NotifyPropertyChanged(string propertyName)
    {
        if (PropertyChanged != null)
        {
            PropertyChanged(this, new PropertyChangedEventArgs(propertyName));
        }
    }
}
```

For demonstration purposes, the code-behind creates and binds a `Movie` object in the page's constructor. Later, when the user clicks a button, the underlying data is changed. Notice that the bound `TextBlock` element properties are not changed directly, only the data (see Figure 3-36).

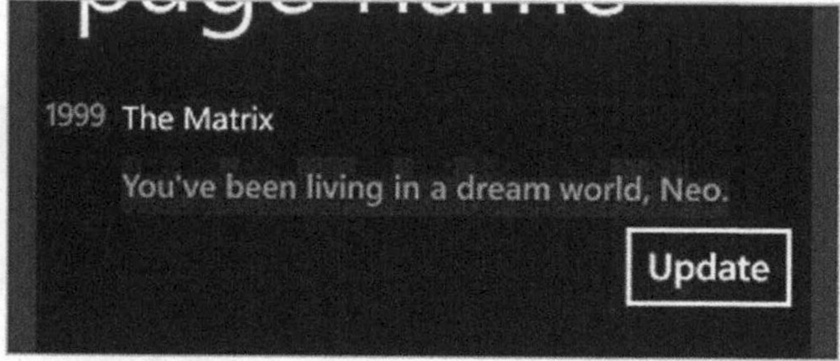

Figure 3-36. *Updating an Object Property*

Collection Change Notification

As items in a collection are added and deleted, the elements need notification to know when to refresh their display. Descend your collections from `ObservableCollection<T>` to get this behavior automatically. For example, the earlier "Movies" example from the "Bind a Template" topic is defined as a generic list (see Listing 3-38):

Listing 3-38. Descending from List<>

```
public class Movies : List<Movie>
```

You only need to change `List<>` to `ObservableCollection` as shown in Listing 3-39:

Listing 3-39. Descending from ObservableCollection<>

```
public class Movies : ObservableCollection<Movie>
```

Nothing else needs to happen to the class except use it. The example in Listing 3-40 is entirely in code to demonstrate altering the collection without acting on the LongListSelector element directly.

Listing 3-40. Using the ObservableCollection

```
private Movies movies = new Movies();

public MainPage()
{
    InitializeComponent();
    this.MoviesList.ItemsSource = movies;
}

private void ChangeCollectionButton_Click(object sender, RoutedEventArgs e)
{
    this.movies.Add(new Movie()
    {
        Title = "New Movie",
        Quote = "Have you seen it?",
        Year = DateTime.Today.Year
    });
}
```

The running application shows the "Add Movie" button click, adding a new Movie object to the collection. The new "Movie" is displayed instantly in the list without any other explicit code (see Figure 3-37).

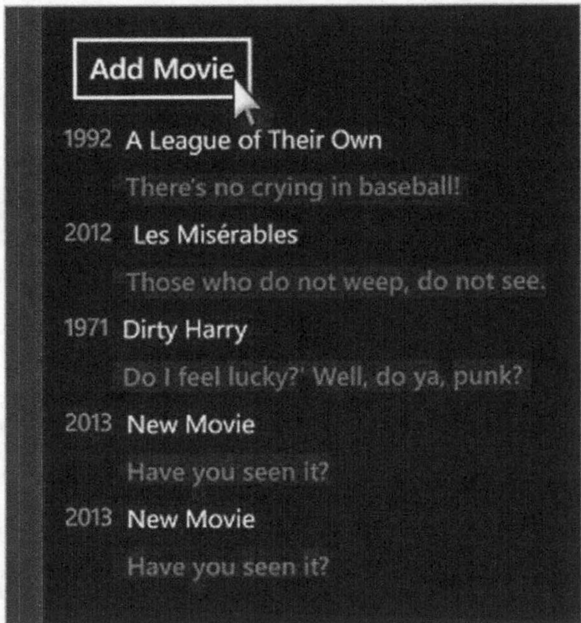

Figure 3-37. *Adding to the Collection*

MVVM

Model-View-ViewModel or MVVM is a pattern that helps you cleanly architect applications with a clear "separation of concerns". MVVM has three conceptual components:

- The ***View*** represents the user interface and presents data for the end user.
- The ***Model*** contains, but does not manipulate, the data.
- The ***ViewModel*** is an adapter between the View and the Model. The ViewModel gets raw data from the Model and transforms it to View-friendly form. The ViewModel has also been described as "the model for the view", that is the View connects to the ViewModel as if it were the model.

The journey from Model ➤ ViewModel ➤ View is a one way trip, where the Model is independent, the ViewModel only knows about the Model and the View only knows about the ViewModel.

Why should you go to the trouble of implementing your application with MVVM in mind? Here are a few selling points:

- The View can be built separately (and nearly simultaneously) with the development of the Model and ViewModel.
- The component parts of MVVM can be tested easily. The View will be smaller for not dragging along code to handle data and business logic. The ViewModel can be more easily tested because it has no user interface. The Model is easily testable because it is completely independent of the other two layers.
- Developers who are familiar with MVVM can join new projects, understand the project structure, and work on their parts of the job without conflict.
- You can change the user interface without refactoring the other layers.
- The separation of concerns makes it easier to reuse the pieces.
- It ain't that hard. Once you start working from the MVVM pattern, it becomes second nature.

Keep in mind that MVVM is a *pattern*, not a religion. The point is to organize your application in a way that is easy to develop, maintain, and extend. The highly simplified solution structure and naming examples that follow show an interpretation of the MVVM pattern, but not the only possible version.

Create and Bind a ViewModel

The following steps create a solution containing a `Model`, `View`, and `ViewModel`. The application displays a list of retail categories and binds the title and description at the top of the page.

1. Create a new Windows Phone App. Set the project `Name` to "View" and the `Solution` name to "MVVM". The `Create directory for solution` option should be checked (see Figure 3-38).

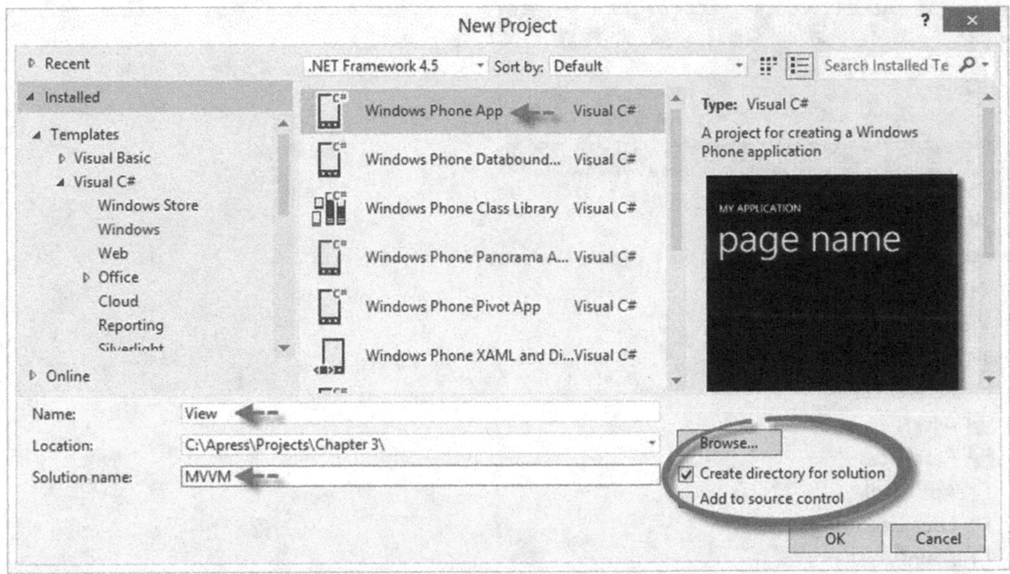

Figure 3-38. Creating the MVVM Solution

2. Add a new project to the solution. Select the `Windows Phone Class Library` template and name the project "Model" (see Figure 3-39).

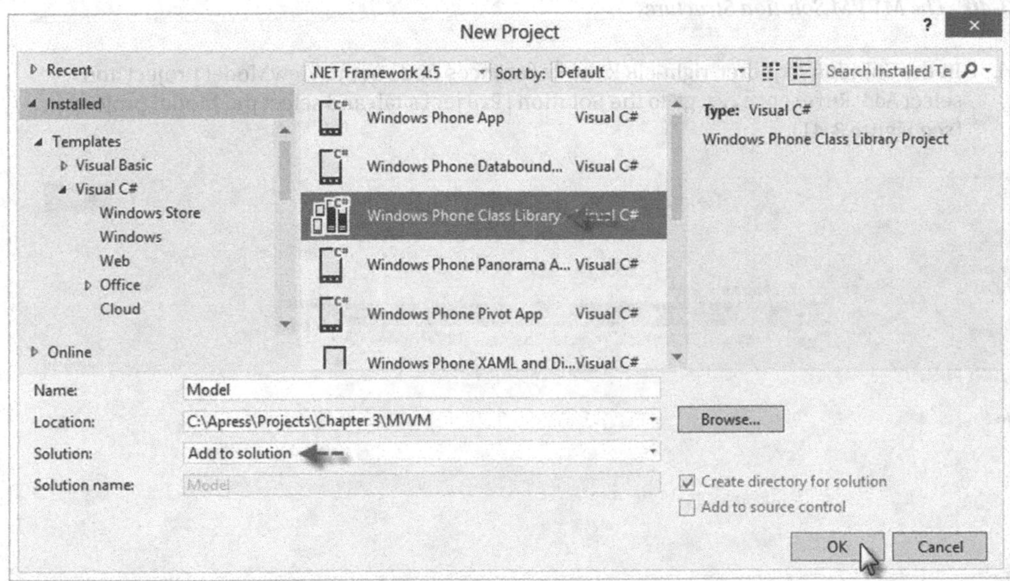

Figure 3-39. Adding a Windows Phone Class Library to the Solution

3. Add a third new project to the MVVM solution. Select the `Windows Phone Class Library` template and name the project "ViewModel".

The solution should now look something like Figure 3-40.

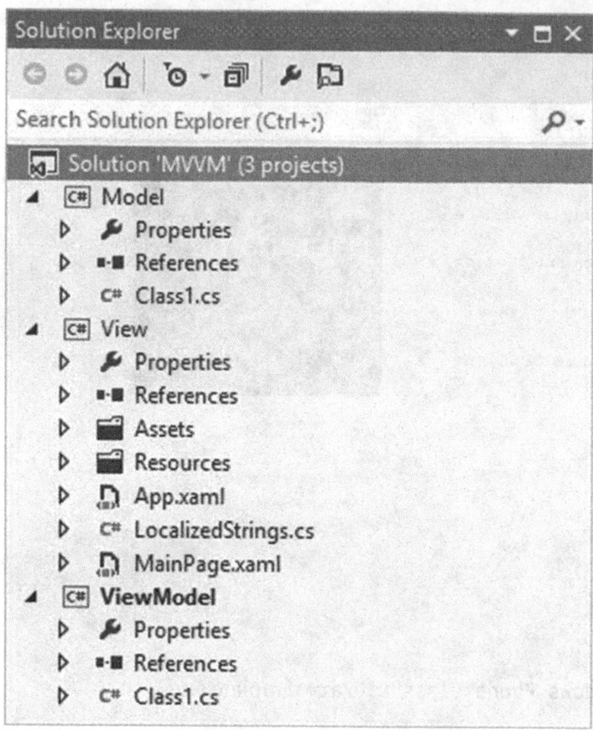

Figure 3-40. *The MVVM Solution Structure*

4. In the Solution Explorer, right-click the `References` node of the ViewModel project and select `Add Reference...`, go to the Solution | `Projects` tab and select the Model project (see Figure 3-41).

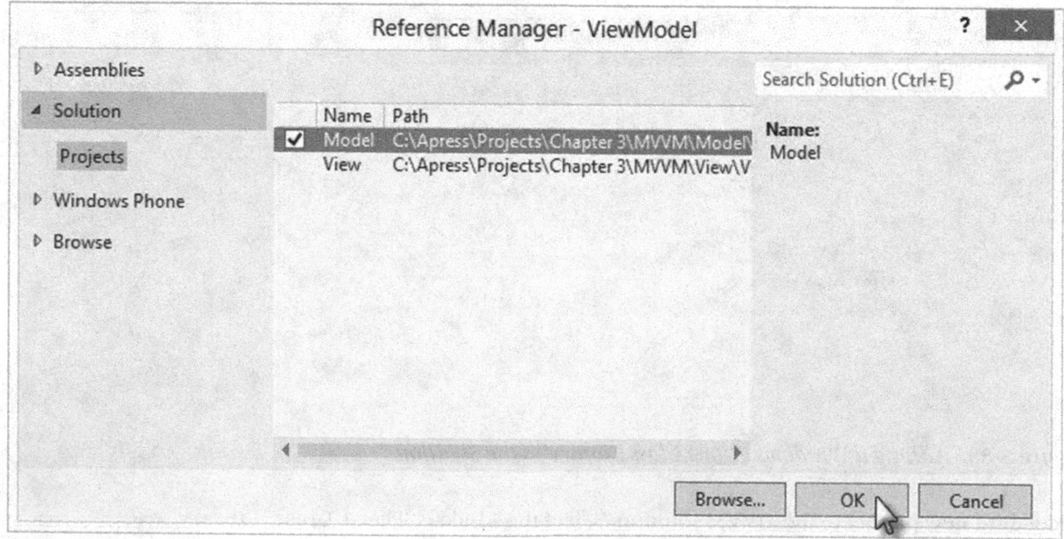

Figure 3-41. *Referencing the Model from the ViewModel*

5. In the Solution Explorer, right-click the `References` node for the View project and select `Add Reference...`, go to the `Solution | Projects` tab and select the ViewModel project.

6. The projects are now referenced so that View can see the ViewModel and the ViewModel can see the Model, that is View ➤ ViewModel ➤ Model, as shown in Figure 3-42.

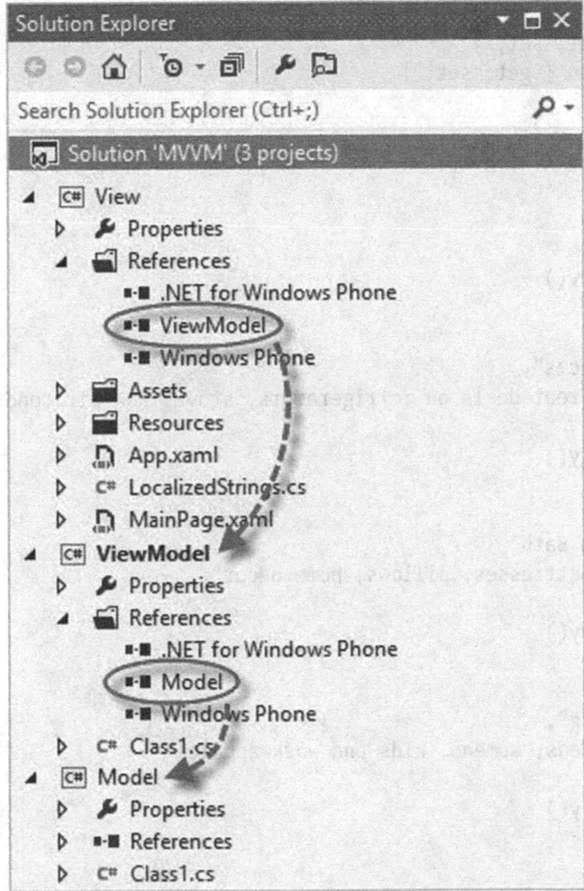

***Figure 3-42.** Referencing Order in the MVVM Project*

7. Locate the Model project in Solution Explorer and rename the default `Class1.cs` file to `Category.cs`.

8. Open `Category.cs` up for editing. Replace the code with the code below.

   This very simple `Category` class does not implement `INotifyPropertyChanged`. Likewise, the `Categories` collection is a generic `List` of `Category`, not an `ObservableCollection`. These mechanisms are good for the View, but not needed in the Model.

```
using System.Collections.Generic;

namespace Model
{
    public class Category
    {
        public int ID { get; set; }
        public string Title { get; set; }
        public string Description { get; set; }
    }

    public class Categories : List<Category>
    {
        public Categories()
        {
            this.Add(new Category()
            {
                ID = 1,
                Title = "Appliances",
                Description = "Great deals on refrigerators, stoves and air conditioners"
            });
            this.Add(new Category()
            {
                ID = 2,
                Title = "Bed and Bath",
                Description = "Mattresses, pillows, home decor"
            });
            this.Add(new Category()
            {
                ID = 3,
                Title = "Clothing",
                Description = "Mens, womens, kids and work apparel"
            });
            this.Add(new Category()
            {
                ID = 4,
                Title = "Electronics",
                Description = "Home theater, home office, phone accessories"
            });
        }
    }
}
```

9. Locate the ViewModel project in Solution Explorer and rename the default `Class1.cs` file to `CategoryViewModel.cs`.

10. Open `CategoryViewModel.cs` up for editing. Replace the code with the code below.

    This roughs out the shell of the `CategoryViewModel` class and implements the `INotifyPropertyChanged` interface.

```
using System.Collections.ObjectModel;
using System.ComponentModel;
using Model;

namespace ViewModel
{
    public class CategoryViewModel : INotifyPropertyChanged
    {

        public CategoryViewModel() { }

        public void NotifyPropertyChanged(string propertyName)
        {
            if (PropertyChanged != null)
            {
                PropertyChanged(this, new PropertyChangedEventArgs(propertyName));
            }
        }

        public event PropertyChangedEventHandler PropertyChanged;
    }
}
```

11. Add the properties below to the CategoryViewModel class.

```
private string title;
public string CategoryTitle
{
    get { return this.title; }
    set
    {
        this.title = value;
        NotifyPropertyChanged("Title");
    }
}

private string description;
public string CategoryDescription
{
    get { return this.description; }
    set
    {
        this.description = value;
        NotifyPropertyChanged("Description");
    }
}

public ObservableCollection<Category> CategoriesCollection { get; set; }
```

12. In the CategoryViewModel class definition, replace the constructor with the code below.

    This new constructor code initializes the CategoriesCollection ObservableCollection using the generic List<Category> defined in the Model. New properties CategoryTitle and CategoryDescription are also initialized here.

```
public CategoryViewModel()
{
    this.CategoriesCollection = new ObservableCollection<Category>(new Categories());
    this.CategoryTitle = "categories";
    this.CategoryDescription = "store departments";
}
```

13. Open App.xaml from the View project. Add an xml namespace reference to the ViewModel. In the example below, the namespace is named vm for the ViewModel it represents.

```
<Application ...
             xmlns:vm="clr-namespace:ViewModel;assembly=ViewModel">
```

14. Add a resource that points to the CategoriesViewModel object.

```
<Application.Resources>
    <vm:CategoryViewModel x:Key="CategoryViewModel" />
</Application.Resources>
```

15. In the View project, open MainPage.xaml for editing. Bind the CategoriesViewModel resource to the page's DataContext property. This step makes the ViewModel available to every element on the page.

```
<phone:PhoneApplicationPage ...
                            DataContext="{StaticResource CategoryViewModel}">
```

16. Locate the StackPanel element with the Name attribute "TitlePanel". Bind the first TextBlock Text property inside the StackPanel to the CategoryTitle of the ViewModel. Bind the second TextBlock Text property to the CategoryDescription of the ViewModel.

```
<StackPanel x:Name="TitlePanel" ...>
    <TextBlock Text="{Binding Path=CategoryDescription}"
               Style="{StaticResource PhoneTextNormalStyle}"
               Margin="12,0"/>
    <TextBlock Text="{Binding Path=CategoryTitle}"
               Style="{StaticResource PhoneTextTitle1Style}"
               Margin="9,-7,0,0" />
</StackPanel>
```

17. Drag a LongListSelector from the Toolbox to the Grid with Name "ContentPanel".

18. Locate the Grid with Name "ContentPanel". Bind the ItemsSource property to the CategoriesCollection property of the ViewModel. Bind the Title to the DisplayMemberPath property. Name the LongListSelector "CategoryList".

```
<Grid x:Name="ContentPanel" ...>
    <phone:LongListSelector x:Name="CategoryList"
      ItemsSource="{Binding Path=CategoriesCollection}" >
        <phone:LongListSelector.ItemTemplate>
            <DataTemplate>
                <TextBlock Text="{Binding Title}" />
            </DataTemplate>
        </phone:LongListSelector.ItemTemplate>
    </phone:LongListSelector>
</Grid>
```

19. Run the application. The View displays using data from the ViewModel (see Figure 3-43).

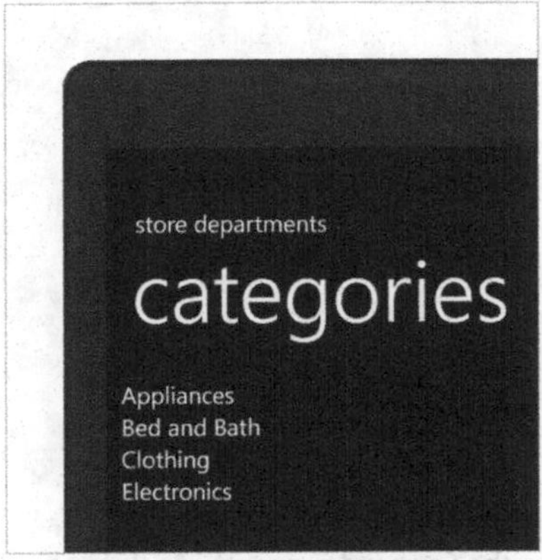

***Figure 3-43.** The View Displaying ViewModel Properties*

Binding Commands

Commands encapsulate logic for some business action, such as "Update", that can be bound declaratively in XAML. Commands also fit neatly into the MVVM pattern where the command itself lives in the ViewModel. To create and use a command:

1. Create a class that implements the ICommand interface.
2. Implement a ViewModel that contains the command.
3. Bind the ViewModel object to the View.
4. Bind the command to a command source, namely a button or menu item.

ICommand has only two methods, CanExecute (controls if the button is enabled) and Execute (your command logic goes here). See Listing 3-41 for an example implementation of ICommand. Command source controls such as Button or HyperlinkButton have their Enabled properties toggled automatically based on what CanExecute() returns. CanExecute() de-clutters application code by removing all those "if x, then ButtonSaveItem.Enabled = true" blocks of code that litter traditional, non-MVVM, applications. In the example below, the command can execute at any time and the button is always enabled. The other bit of code here, CanExecuteChanged, is an event used to signal the command source (i.e., the button, hyperlink button) to re-read the CanExecute state.

Listing 3-41. Implementing an ICommand Interface

```
public class MyCommand : ICommand{
    public bool CanExecute(object parameter)
    {
        return true;
    }

    public event EventHandler CanExecuteChanged;

    public void Execute(object parameter)
    {
        MessageBox.Show("Executing command...");
    }
}
```

In Listing 3-42, the ViewModel only has a single property, the command object itself.

Listing 3-42. Defining the Command in the ViewModel

```
public class MyViewModel{
    public MyCommand MessageCommand { get; set; }
    public MyViewModel()
    {
        this.MessageCommand = new MyCommand();
    }
}
```

Finally, in Listing 3-43, the ViewModel command is hooked up to the `Command` property of a `Button`.

Listing 3-43. Binding the Command

```
<Button Command="{Binding MessageCommand}" Content="Run MyCommand" />
```

Implement and Bind a Command

The following steps demonstrate how to add a command to the ViewModel and bind the command to a `Button` element. This example uses the *Create and Bind a ViewModel* project as a starting point. The command displays a message whenever text is passed to it as a parameter.

1. In the Solution Explorer right-click the ViewModel project, select `Add` ➤ `Class...`, and then set the class file `Name` to `DisplayCommand.cs`.

2. Add `ICommand` to the `DisplayCommand` declaration as shown in Figure 3-44. Set the scope of the class to `public` and implement the interface (you can use the context menu option or use the drop-down options tag to add the implementation methods automatically).

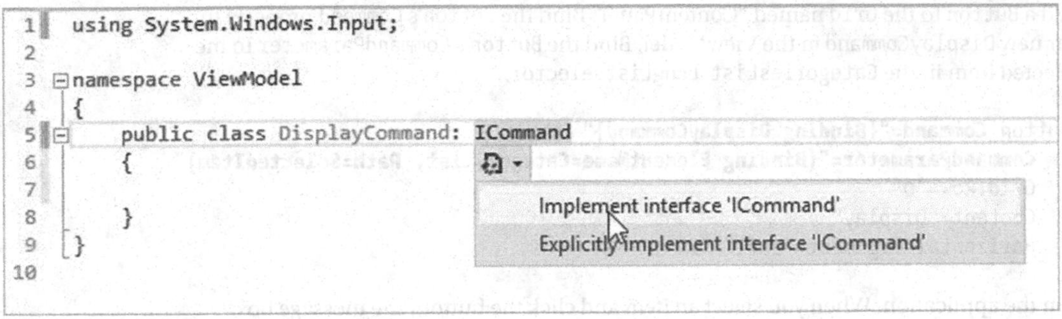

```
using System.Windows.Input;

namespace ViewModel
{
    public class DisplayCommand: ICommand
    {

    }
}
```

Implement interface 'ICommand'
Explicitly implement interface 'ICommand'

Figure 3-44. Implementing ICommand

3. Replace the command's implementation with the code below. The `CanExecute()` method returns false if the title contains "Clothing", disabling the button when the user selects the clothing item in the list. The `Execute()` method checks that there is something in parameter, casts it to a `Category` class object, and displays the `Title` as the message.

```
public class DisplayCommand : ICommand
{
    public bool CanExecute(object parameter)
    {
        if (parameter == null)
            return false;
        else
            return ! (parameter as Category).Title.Contains("Clothing");
    }

    public event EventHandler CanExecuteChanged;

    public void Execute(object parameter)
    {
        if (parameter != null)
            MessageBox.Show((parameter as Category).Title);
    }
}
```

4. Open `CategoryViewModel.cs` class file for editing. Add a `DisplayCommand` property to the class. Initialize the `DisplayCommand` property in the `CategoryViewModel` constructor.

```
public DisplayCommand DisplayCommand { get; set; }

public CategoryViewModel()
{
    //...
    this.DisplayCommand = new DisplayCommand();
}
```

5. Add a Button to the Grid named "ContentPanel". Bind the Button's Command property to our new DisplayCommand in the ViewModel. Bind the Button's CommandParameter to the selected item in the CategoriesList LongListSelector.

```
<Button Command="{Binding DisplayCommand}"
    CommandParameter="{Binding ElementName=CategoryList, Path=SelectedItem}"
    Grid.Row="0"
    Content="Display"
    HorizontalAlignment="Left" />
```

6. Run the application. When you select an item and click the button, the message box displays the description for the Category object. When the user selects "Clothing" from the list, the button is disabled.

7. Open the View MainPage.xaml.cs file and notice that there is still no application level code.

Summary

XAML is a rich, flexible syntax for building responsive user interfaces that incorporate best practices: maintainability, extensibility, reusability, scalability, and good separation of concerns. Resources store important application building blocks at any scope and lend themselves to easy refactoring and reuse. Templates establish a visual pattern for user interface components that can be extended from existing templates. Data binding brings live information to the user interface with minimal code. The MVVM pattern helps pull these features together in a structure that is easy to build now and will hold together in the future.

CHAPTER 4

Phone Controls

Phone Controls are the building blocks for your user interface. Windows Phone 8 includes a full set of layout controls to arrange elements on the page, buttons to initiate actions, input controls to collect information in a user-friendly way, performant lists, menus, and media presentation. To make life easy for the user, these controls are tailored to the Windows Phone 8 environment, with features like built-in gesture support and pop-up keyboards for text input. Performance is essential to the Windows Phone experience and each control is designed from the ground up to respond quickly while maintaining a small resource footprint.

Layout Controls

Phone controls that inherit from `Panel` are used to position and arrange child objects. The three key objects that handle layout are `Grid`, `StackPanel`, and `Canvas`:

- ***Grid*** positions elements in rows and columns of cells.
- ***StackPanel*** positions elements in a horizontal or vertical series.
- ***Canvas*** positions elements at absolute coordinates.

The `PhoneApplicationPage` is designed to accept a single element of content. This means that you can only have one layout control added directly to the page. Once the layout control is added, you can include as many child controls in the layout as you like.

Canvas

`Canvas` is a container for applications where elements are drawn at arbitrary locations and may overlap. `Canvas` is a likely candidate for simple games or other graphic-intensive applications. The attached properties `Canvas.Left` and `Canvas.Top` place elements at offsets from the left and top of the Canvas. Listing 4-1 defines a single `Ellipse` element placed 120 pixels from the top and 278 pixels from the left of the Canvas (see Figure 4-1).

Listing 4-1. Drawing on the Canvas

```
<Canvas x:Name="LayoutRoot">
    <Ellipse Canvas.Left="278"
             Canvas.Top="120"
             Width="100"
             Height="100"
             Fill="LawnGreen" />
</Canvas>
```

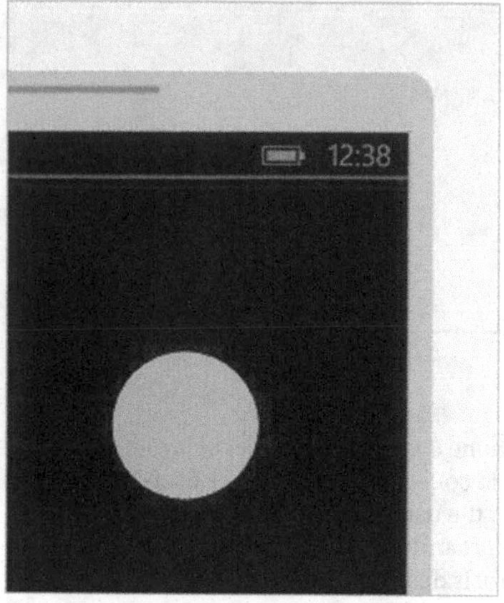

Figure 4-1. Ellipse on Canvas

This example shows several Ellipse elements stacked on top of each other. The Canvas class has a third property, "Z-Index" that places the element in front or back of other elements. By default, Z-Index is implied from the order the elements are declared, with the first elements being in the back and the following elements appearing in front of previous elements, as shown in Listing 4-2 and Figure 4-2. You can use the Canvas ZIndex property to override this behavior and specifically place an element in the stack.

Listing 4-2. Setting the Z-Order

```
<Canvas x:Name="LayoutRoot">
    <Ellipse Canvas.Left="278"
      Canvas.Top="120"
      Canvas.ZIndex="0"
      Style="{StaticResource BlueEllipseStyle}" />
    <Ellipse Canvas.Left="340"
      Canvas.Top="100"
      Style="{StaticResource GreenEllipseStyle}" />
    <Ellipse Canvas.Left="278"
      Canvas.Top="52"
      Style="{StaticResource RedEllipseStyle}" />
</Canvas>
```

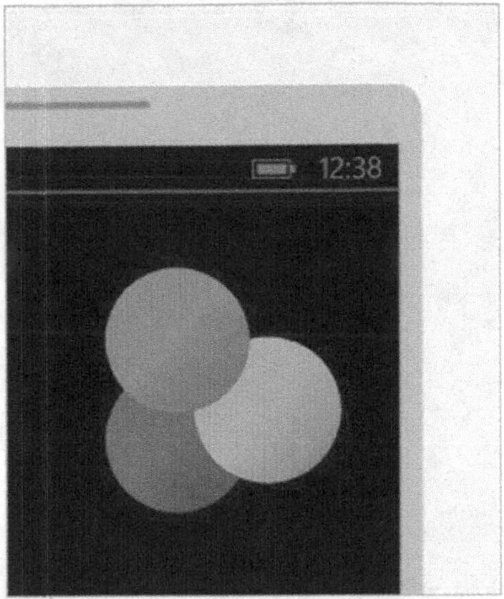

Figure 4-2. *Z-Index Order*

To exclude graphics outside of a given area, use the Canvas Clip property. Clip is actually a property of UIElement that Canvas descends from. The clip area is defined by a Geometry class, such as RectangleGeometry, as shown in Listing 4-3 and Figure 4-3.

Listing 4-3. Defining Clipping Geometry

```
<Canvas x:Name="LayoutRoot">
    <Canvas.Clip>
        <RectangleGeometry Rect="200, 100, 200, 300" />
    </Canvas.Clip>

    <Ellipse Canvas.Left="278"
             Canvas.Top="120"
             Canvas.ZIndex="0"
             Style="{StaticResource BlueEllipseStyle}" />
    <Ellipse Canvas.Left="340"
             Canvas.Top="100"
             Style="{StaticResource GreenEllipseStyle}" />
    <Ellipse Canvas.Left="278"
             Canvas.Top="52"
             Style="{StaticResource RedEllipseStyle}" />
</Canvas>
```

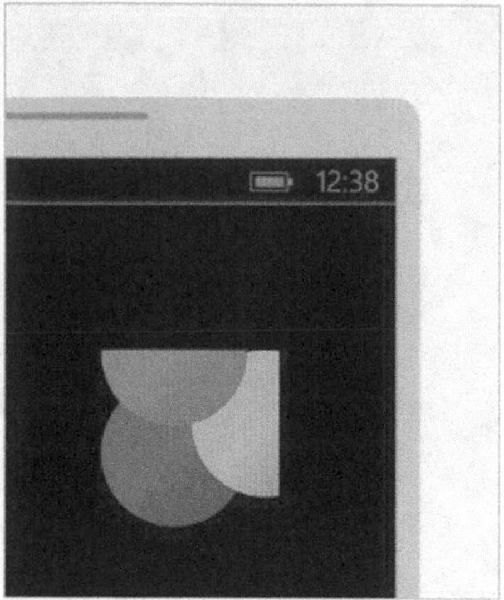

Figure 4-3. *Clipping Rectangle*

Instead of defining a rectangle, `EllipseGeometry` clips a curved area that starts from an X and Y center and defines a radius distance from the X and Y coordinates, as shown in Listing 4-4 and Figure 4-4.

Listing 4-4. Clipping to an Ellipse

```
<Canvas.Clip>
    <EllipseGeometry Center="200, 200"
                     RadiusX="200"
                     RadiusY="150" />
</Canvas.Clip>
```

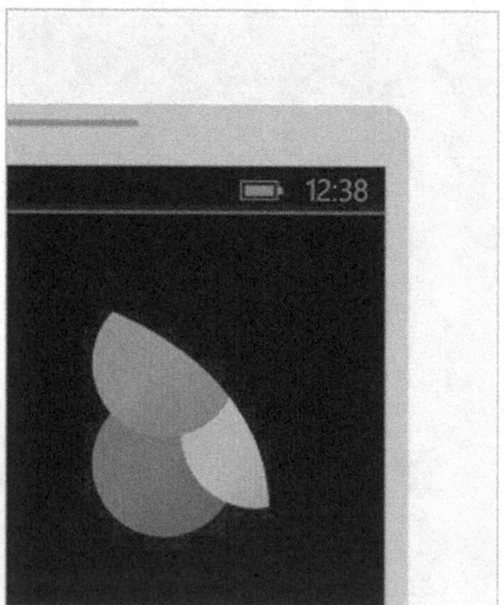

Figure 4-4. *Clipping Ellipse*

InkPresenter

InkPresenter is a canvas that captures "ink" pen "strokes" used in freehand drawing. The InkPresenter element is a Canvas descendant that includes a StrokeCollection. Each Stroke in the collection represents a single pass of the pen or stylus to record stylus location, stylus pressure, and drawing attributes such as stroke color and dimensions.

■ **Note** The device's touch-sensitive "capacitive" screen reacts to the small electrical charge in your finger and is not designed for non-conducive materials such as pen or stylus. Third-party products allow a stylus or pen to support signature capture and accurate menu navigation when using gloves in adverse conditions. The InkPresenter does not support handwriting recognition.

MouseEventArgs and descendants passed to mouse events include a StylusDevice object that will let you know if you're using a TabletDeviceType of Mouse, Stylus, or Touch screen, and a GetStylusPoints() method that returns a StylusPointsCollection. The example below records a new Stroke when the MouseLeftButtonDown event fires. As the mouse moves, StylusPoints are added to the collection in the Stroke. When the pointer is removed from the surface (MouseLeftButtonUp), the Stroke is nulled out and a new Stroke must be created on the next MouseLeftButtonDown. Finally, the DoubleTap event clears the collection and erases the drawing. You will need to add the System.Windows.Ink namespace to your using statements to support the Stroke object, as shown in Listing 4-5.

Listing 4-5. Tracking InkPresenter Strokes

```
private Stroke _stroke;
public InkPresenterDemo()
{
    InitializeComponent();
}

private void InkCanvas_MouseLeftButtonDown(object sender, MouseButtonEventArgs e)
{
    _stroke = new Stroke();
    _stroke.StylusPoints.Add(e.StylusDevice.GetStylusPoints(InkCanvas));
    InkCanvas.Strokes.Add(_stroke);
}

private void InkCanvas_MouseMove(object sender, MouseEventArgs e)
{
    if (_stroke != null)
    {
        _stroke.StylusPoints.Add(e.StylusDevice.GetStylusPoints(InkCanvas));
    }
}

private void InkCanvas_MouseLeftButtonUp(object sender, MouseButtonEventArgs e)
{
    _stroke = null;
}
```

```
private void InkCanvas_DoubleTap(object sender, GestureEventArgs e)
{
    InkCanvas.Strokes.Clear();
}
```

The simple XAML in Listing 4-6 uses a white rectangle to contain a signature.

Listing 4-6. Defining an InkPresenter in XAML

```
<InkPresenter x:Name="InkCanvas"
    Background="White"
    MouseLeftButtonDown="InkCanvas_MouseLeftButtonDown"
    MouseMove="InkCanvas_MouseMove"
    MouseLeftButtonUp="InkCanvas_MouseLeftButtonUp"
    DoubleTap="InkCanvas_DoubleTap">
    <Rectangle
        Canvas.Left="34" Canvas.Top="649"
        Height="74" Width="402"
        Stroke="Black" StrokeThickness="1" />
</InkPresenter>
```

The running example (see Figure 4-5) lets you use the mouse in the emulator or trace with your finger on a phone device screen.

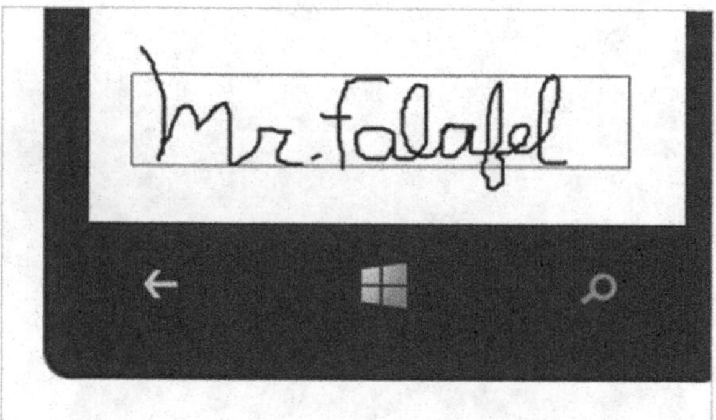

Figure 4-5. *The Running InkPresenter Application*

StackPanel

`StackPanel` arranges child objects in a horizontal or vertical series. By default, the `StackPanel Orientation` is `Vertical` and places child elements from top to bottom. Listing 4-7 and Figure 4-6 show the same `Ellipse` elements used in the `Canvas` example, with the `Canvas` attached properties removed.

Listing 4-7. Displaying a StackPanel

```
<StackPanel x:Name="LayoutRoot">
    <Ellipse Style="{StaticResource BlueEllipseStyle}" />
    <Ellipse Style="{StaticResource GreenEllipseStyle}" />
    <Ellipse Style="{StaticResource RedEllipseStyle}" />
</StackPanel>
```

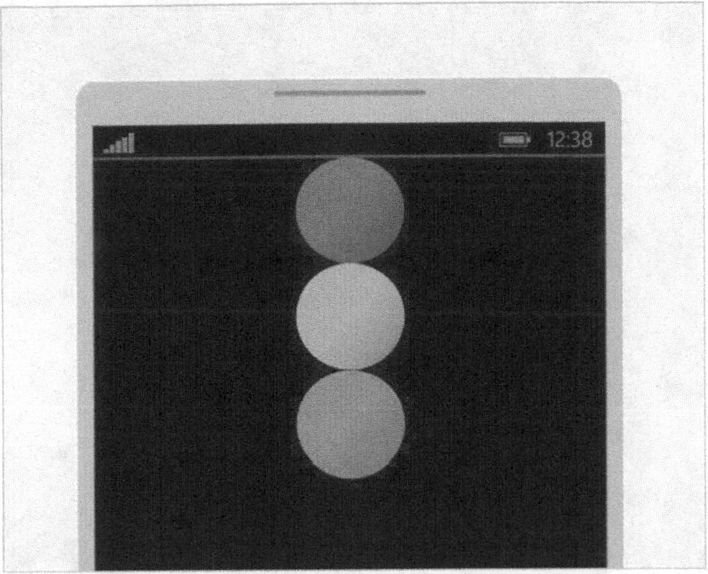

Figure 4-6. *Ellipses Arranged Vertically in a StackPanel*

WrapPanel

`WrapPanel` is similar to `StackPanel`, but adds the ability to wrap overflowing content to the next row or column. `WrapPanel` can arrange child items in `Vertical` or `Horizontal Orientation`. `WrapPanel` is currently included in the Windows Phone 8 Toolkit, available for download from CodePlex (`http://phone.codeplex.com/`), as shown in Listing 4-8.

Listing 4-8. Elements in a WrapPanel

```
<toolkit:WrapPanel x:Name="LayoutRoot"  Orientation="Vertical"
                  ItemHeight="130"  ItemWidth="130">
    <Button Content="1"  Style="{StaticResource BlueButtonStyle}" />
    <Button Content="2" Style="{StaticResource GreenButtonStyle}" />
    <Button Content="3" Style="{StaticResource RedButtonStyle}" />
    <Button Content="4" Style="{StaticResource BlueButtonStyle}" />
    <Button Content="5" Style="{StaticResource GreenButtonStyle}" />
    <Button Content="6" Style="{StaticResource RedButtonStyle}" />
    <Button Content="7" Style="{StaticResource BlueButtonStyle}" />
    <Button Content="8" Style="{StaticResource GreenButtonStyle}" />
    <Button Content="9" Style="{StaticResource RedButtonStyle}" />
    <Button Content="10"  Style="{StaticResource BlueButtonStyle}" />
    <Button Content="11" Style="{StaticResource GreenButtonStyle}" />
    <Button Content="12" Style="{StaticResource RedButtonStyle}" />
</toolkit:WrapPanel>
```

Figure 4-7 displays 12 ellipse-shaped buttons that overflow the vertical orientation of the panel. You can see that after number "5", the next column wraps and displays number "6". `ItemWidth` and `ItemHeight` properties determine element dimensions for each child element.

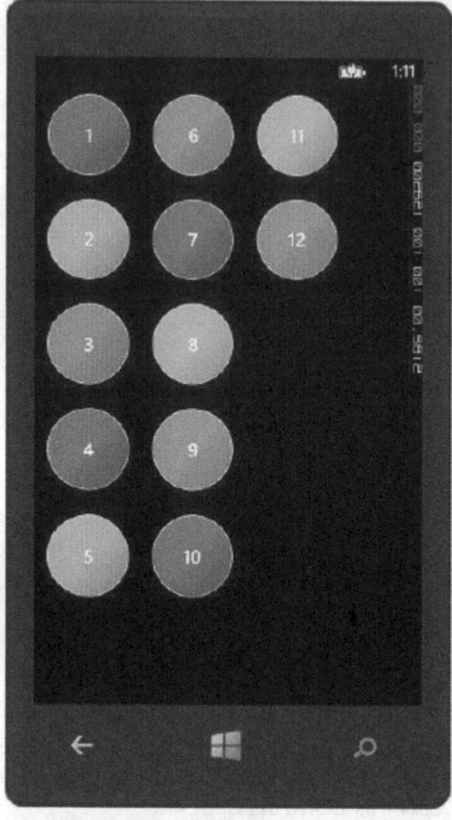

Figure 4-7. *Ellipses Arranged Vertically in a WrapPanel*

Installing the Windows Phone 8 Toolkit

Windows phone toolkit is packed with new controls and effects. The toolkit is available at `http://phone.codeplex.com/` where you can download source and examples. You can install the toolkit for a given project through the NuGet Package Manager using an option off the Solution Explorer (see Figure 4-8):

1. In the Solution Explorer, right-click the References node and select `Manage NuGet Packages...` from the context menu.
2. In the Manage NuGet Packages dialog that displays, select the `Online` ➤ `NuGet official package source` from the outline on the left.
3. In the Search Online box on the right, enter Windows Phone Toolkit.
4. Select the package in the center list and click the `Install` button. When the install completes, close the dialog.

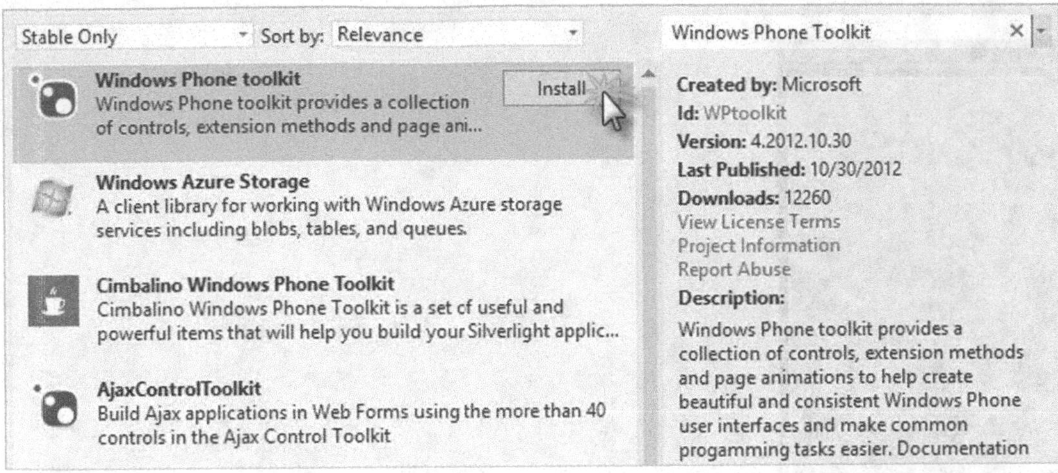

Figure 4-8. *Installing Windows Phone Toolkit*

You can also install the toolkit from the Package Manager Console. Select from the Visual Studio menu `Tools` ➤ `Library Package Manager` ➤ `Package Manager Console`. Run the following command in the Package Manager Console window:

```
Install-Package Wptoolkit
```

The installation adds the `Microsoft.Phone.Controls.Toolkit` to the solution. You must have a Windows Phone application open to install the package.

To use the referenced controls at design time, add an XML namespace that points to `Microsoft.Phone.Controls.Toolkit`.

Grid

The `Grid` arranges elements in rows and columns. By default, the `Grid` is used for new pages. `Grid` is easy to extend when you need to add new elements and is conceptually similar to an HTML table. Without setting any `RowDefinition` and `ColumnDefinition` properties, each element in the `Grid` takes up the same amount of space, as shown in Listing 4-9.

Listing 4-9. Defining a Grid

```
<Grid x:Name="LayoutRoot" >
    <Button Content="Click Me!" Background="BlueViolet" />
</Grid>
```

Figure 4-9 shows the `Grid` in the design view of Visual Studio. The grid here has a single cell. A single button placed inside the grid takes up the entire area.

Figure 4-9. *One Element in the Default Grid*

Row and Column Definitions

To get any mileage out of the Grid you need to define columns and rows. `ColumnDefinitions` and `RowDefinitions` collections are somewhat similar to HTML row `<tr>` and cell `<td>` elements. Listing 4-10 shows how attached properties `Grid.Row` and `Grid.Column` are used to associate each element to a position in the grid.

Listing 4-10. Defining a Grid

```
<Grid x:Name="LayoutRoot" >
    <Grid.ColumnDefinitions>
        <ColumnDefinition />
        <ColumnDefinition  />
        <ColumnDefinition  />
    </Grid.ColumnDefinitions>
    <Grid.RowDefinitions>
        <RowDefinition  />
        <RowDefinition  />
        <RowDefinition  />
    </Grid.RowDefinitions>
```

```
    <Button Content="0,0" Grid.Row="0" Grid.Column="0" Style="{StaticResource ButtonStyle}"/>
    <Button Content="0,1" Grid.Row="0" Grid.Column="1" Style="{StaticResource ButtonStyle}"/>
    <Button Content="0,2" Grid.Row="0" Grid.Column="2" Style="{StaticResource ButtonStyle}"/>
    <Button Content="1,0" Grid.Row="1" Grid.Column="0" Style="{StaticResource ButtonStyle}"/>
    <Button Content="1,1" Grid.Row="1" Grid.Column="1" Style="{StaticResource ButtonStyle}"/>
    <Button Content="1,2" Grid.Row="1" Grid.Column="2" Style="{StaticResource ButtonStyle}"/>
    <Button Content="2,0" Grid.Row="2" Grid.Column="0" Style="{StaticResource ButtonStyle}"/>
    <Button Content="2,1" Grid.Row="2" Grid.Column="1" Style="{StaticResource ButtonStyle}"/>
    <Button Content="2,2" Grid.Row="2" Grid.Column="2" Style="{StaticResource ButtonStyle}"/>
</Grid>
```

Figure 4-10 shows the resulting grid divided into a series of nine buttons placed in a 3 x 3 cell grid.

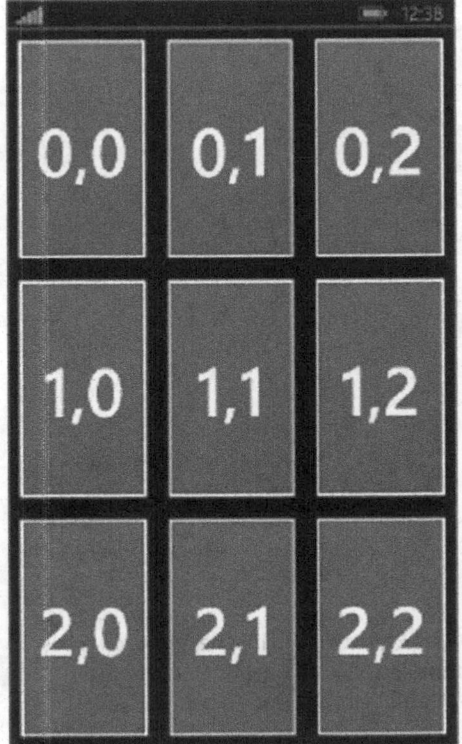

Figure 4-10. *Row and Column Definitions in the Grid*

Set the `ColumnDefinition Width` to assign an absolute width for the column and the `RowDefinition Height` to assign an absolute, fixed height for the row (see Listing 4-11). Notice that while content inside each may be truncated, the remaining horizontal and vertical space outside the cells is left blank (see Figure 4-11).

Listing 4-11. Assigning Fixed Dimensions

```
<Grid.ColumnDefinitions>
    <ColumnDefinition Width="150" />
    <ColumnDefinition Width="200" />
    <ColumnDefinition Width="130" />
```

```
</Grid.ColumnDefinitions>
<Grid.RowDefinitions>
    <RowDefinition Height="150" />
    <RowDefinition Height="250" />
    <RowDefinition Height="150" />
</Grid.RowDefinitions>
```

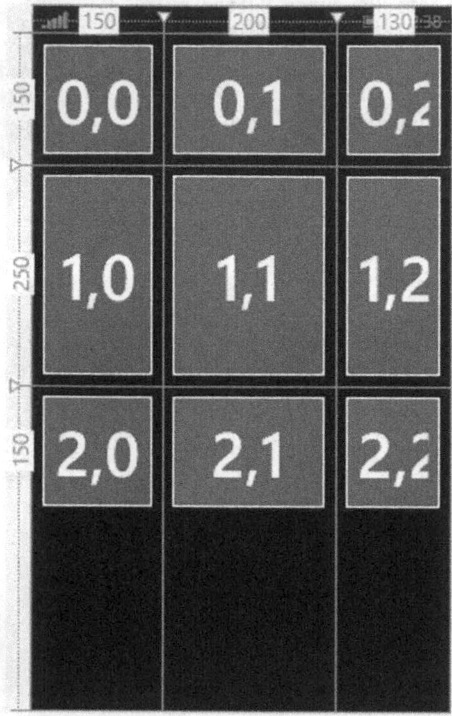

Figure 4-11. *Row and Column Definitions in the Grid*

What if I want each column to be just wide enough to fit the content? Assign Auto to Width or Height properties to have the content width automatically calculated. To use all available remaining space, assign "*". One common strategy is to have all columns but the last size automatically (see Listing 4-12 and Figure 4-12).

Listing 4-12. Auto and "*" Width and Height

```
<Grid.ColumnDefinitions>
    <ColumnDefinition Width="Auto" />
    <ColumnDefinition Width="Auto" />
    <ColumnDefinition Width="*" />
</Grid.ColumnDefinitions>
<Grid.RowDefinitions>
    <RowDefinition Height="Auto"  />
    <RowDefinition Height="Auto" />
    <RowDefinition Height="*" />
</Grid.RowDefinitions>
```

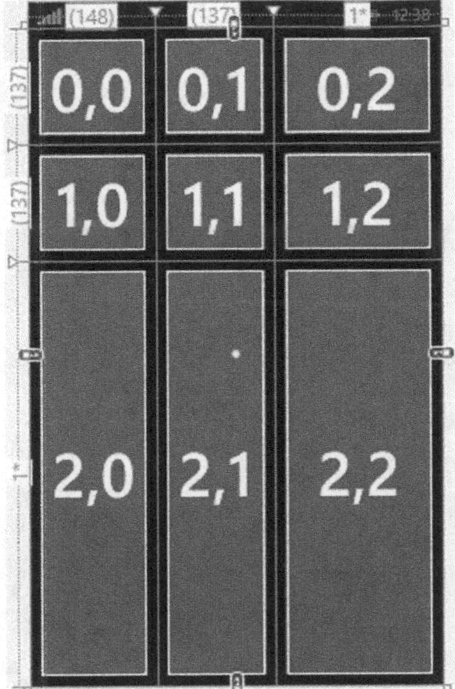

Figure 4-12. Auto and "" Dimensions*

The star "*" `Width` setting causes that remaining space to be divided equally. Placing a number before the star "*" signals a proportion of the remaining space. Listing 4-13 sets column widths divided equally and the row heights with proportions of 1:2:3 (see Figure 4-13).

Listing 4-13. Auto and "*" Width and Height

```
<Grid.ColumnDefinitions>
    <ColumnDefinition Width="*" />
    <ColumnDefinition Width="*" />
    <ColumnDefinition Width="*" />
</Grid.ColumnDefinitions>
<Grid.RowDefinitions>
    <RowDefinition Height="1*"  />
    <RowDefinition Height="2*" />
    <RowDefinition Height="3*" />
</Grid.RowDefinitions>
```

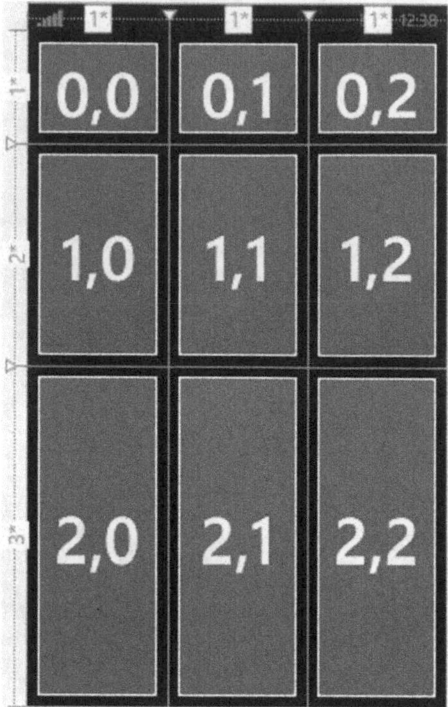

Figure 4-13. *Proportional Dimensions*

Use the MinWidth, MaxWidth, MinHeight, and MaxHeight properties to constrain widths and heights to a range. The cells defined in Listing 4-14 can be no larger than 100 pixels. Note that setting Width or Height to Auto will override these constraints (see Figure 4-14).

Listing 4-14. Configuring Min and Max Width and Height

```
<Grid.ColumnDefinitions>
    <ColumnDefinition MaxWidth="100" />
    <ColumnDefinition MaxWidth="100" />
    <ColumnDefinition MaxWidth="100" />
</Grid.ColumnDefinitions>
<Grid.RowDefinitions>
    <RowDefinition MaxHeight="100" />
    <RowDefinition MaxHeight="100" />
    <RowDefinition MaxHeight="100" />
</Grid.RowDefinitions>
```

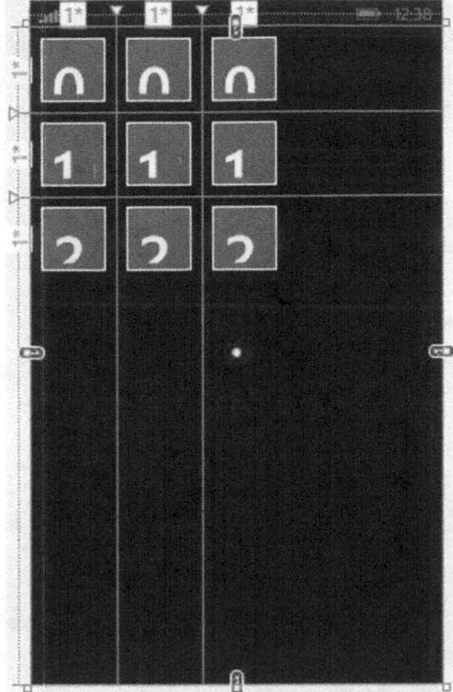

Figure 4-14. *Min and Max Width and Height*

Row and Column Spans

The attached properties Grid.ColumnSpan and Grid.RowSpan work much like their HTML counterparts where elements can stretch over multiple columns or rows. In Listing 4-15, the upper left cell "0,0" spans three columns. The centermost column "1,1" spans two rows and two columns (see Figure 4-15).

Listing 4-15. Configuring Min and Max Width and Height

```
<Grid x:Name="LayoutRoot" >
    <Grid.ColumnDefinitions>
        <ColumnDefinition />
        <ColumnDefinition />
        <ColumnDefinition />
    </Grid.ColumnDefinitions>
    <Grid.RowDefinitions>
        <RowDefinition />
        <RowDefinition />
        <RowDefinition />
    </Grid.RowDefinitions>
        <Button Content="0,0" Grid.Row="0" Grid.Column="0"
                Grid.ColumnSpan="3"
                Style="{StaticResource ButtonStyle}"/>
        <Button Content="1,0" Grid.Row="1" Grid.Column="0"
                Style="{StaticResource ButtonStyle}"/>
```

```
        <Button Content="1,1" Grid.Row="1" Grid.Column="1"
                Grid.RowSpan="2" Grid.ColumnSpan="2"
                Style="{StaticResource ButtonStyle}"/>
        <Button Content="2,0" Grid.Row="2" Grid.Column="0"
                Style="{StaticResource ButtonStyle}"/>
</Grid>
```

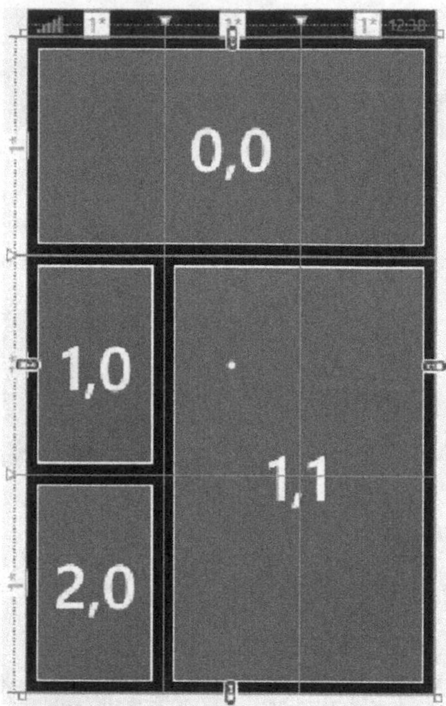

Figure 4-15. RowSpan and ColumnSpan

Grid Designer

Now that you're familiar with XAML syntax, you can use the Visual Studio designer to edit XAML visually. The Visual Studio designer has a number of visual cues and tools to help you work with a `Grid`.

Select the Grid (in either the Designer or in the XAML) to display the visual cues. Let the mouse rest over an edge of a row or column to display a menu for choosing between fixed sizes, Star "*" or "Auto." Figure 4-16 shows the "*" size selection for the first row. You can also add, move, and delete rows and columns from this menu. The gutter to the left of each row and on top of each column will display the unit of measure and current setting.

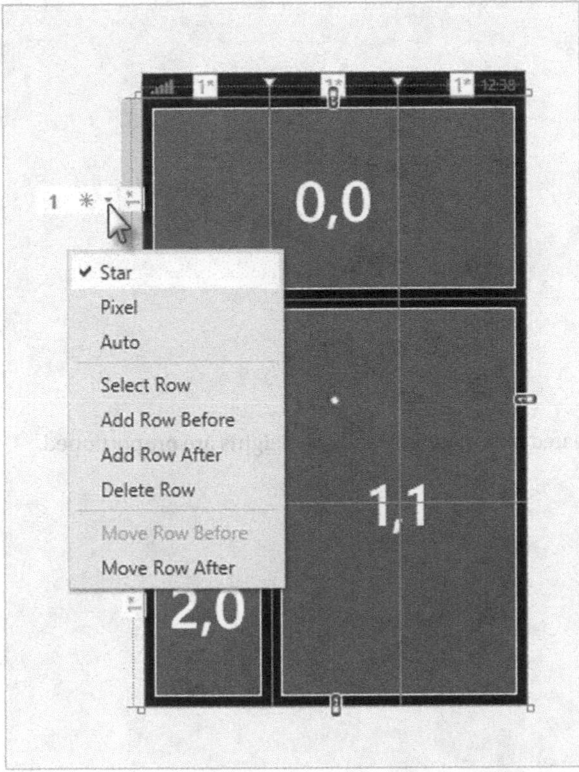

***Figure 4-16.** Setting Row Height*

Clicking the left or top divides the current row or column in two. In the process, the Width for the other rows or columns is converted to the size type selected from the menu, that is, if you select the Star "*" sizing from the menu, the row definitions are converted to the nearest proportions. For example, with XAML that defines three rows as shown in Listing 4-16.

Listing 4-16. Three Row Definitions

```
<Grid.RowDefinitions>
    <RowDefinition  Height="*" />
    <RowDefinition />
    <RowDefinition />
</Grid.RowDefinitions>
```

Create a new row by moving the mouse into the gutter until the cursor highlights where the border of the new row will appear and the plus sign appears next to the cursor. Left click to create the row (see Figure 4-17).

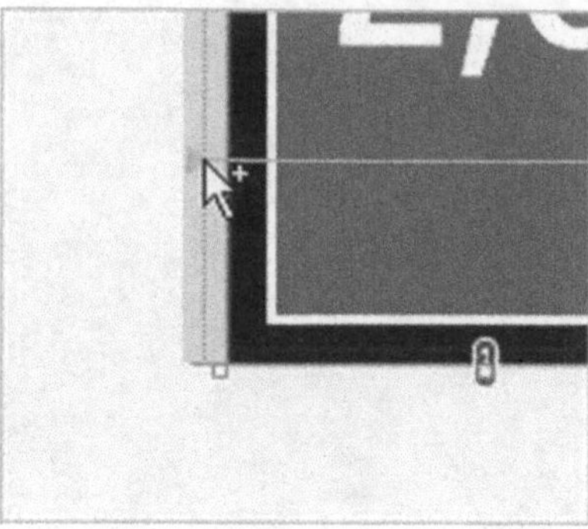

Figure 4-17. *Creating a new Row*

When the row is clicked in the designer, a fourth row is created automatically and the heights are proportioned automatically (see Listing 4-17).

Listing 4-17. Four Rows Automatically Proportioned

```
<Grid.RowDefinitions>
    <RowDefinition Height="64*" />
    <RowDefinition Height="64*" />
    <RowDefinition Height="51*" />
    <RowDefinition Height="13*"/>
</Grid.RowDefinitions>
```

Use the drag handles to change row and column widths and heights (see Figure 4-18). Again, this causes the widths or heights to be converted to the current selected size type.

Figure 4-18. *Adjusting Column Width*

Border

`Border` is not a layout control itself, but is used to create a border and background for a single element (see Figure 4-19). `Border` is often used to surround a `Grid` or `StackPanel`. Listing 4-18 defines a border that surrounds a `StackPanel`.

Listing 4-18. Border around a StackPanel

```
<phone:PhoneApplicationPage.Resources>
    <LinearGradientBrush x:Key="MyBackgroundBrush"
           EndPoint="0.5,1" StartPoint="0.5,0">
```

```
        <GradientStop Color="Black" Offset="0" />
        <GradientStop Color="White" Offset="1" />
    </LinearGradientBrush>
    <LinearGradientBrush x:Key="MyBorderBrush"
          EndPoint="0.5,1" StartPoint="0.5,0">
        <GradientStop Color="#FF2C36F5" Offset="0.081" />
        <GradientStop Color="Black" Offset="0.523" />
        <GradientStop Color="#FF7BFB00" Offset="0.221" />
        <GradientStop Color="#FFF03232" Offset="0.424" />
    </LinearGradientBrush>
</phone:PhoneApplicationPage.Resources>

<Border BorderThickness="10" CornerRadius="50" Margin="10" Padding="10"
    Background="{StaticResource MyBackgroundBrush}"
    BorderBrush="{StaticResource MyBorderBrush}">
    <StackPanel>
        <Ellipse Style="{StaticResource BlueEllipseStyle}" />
        <Ellipse Style="{StaticResource GreenEllipseStyle}" />
        <Ellipse Style="{StaticResource RedEllipseStyle}" />
    </StackPanel>
</Border>
```

Figure 4-19. *Border Surrounding StackPanel*

■ **Caution** Typically, it's best to use the built-in resource `PhoneBorderBrush` for the `BorderBrush` property and `PhoneBackgroundBrush` for the `Background` property. Built-in resources provide consistency across applications; consistency with other applications produced in the industry for the Windows Phone 8 platform, and will help your application display nicely in both light and dark themes.

ScrollViewer

The `ScrollViewer` is not really a layout control but a `ContentControl` descendant designed to contain a layout control. Figure 4-20 shows a ScrollViewer that contains primitive elements. As the user swipes the ScrollViewer area, the scrollbar on the right shows up and the client area moves to display the entire contents. The ScrollViewer background is transparent by default but set to a light yellow here.

Figure 4-20. *Using the ScrollViewer at Runtime*

The ScrollViewer scrolls content exceeding the dimensions of the "view port." The `VerticalScrollBarVisibility` and `HorizontalScrollBarVisibility` properties control scrolling behavior:

- ***Disabled*** hides the scrollbars and prevents scrolling content.
- ***Auto*** displays the scrollbars when the content overflows the view port dimensions.
- ***Hidden*** hides the scrollbars but still allows the content to be scrolled.
- ***Visible*** shows the scrollbars and scrolls the content.

The ScrollViewer in Listing 4-19 wraps a StackPanel. The StackPanel contains multiple TextBlocks.

Listing 4-19. Using Scrollbars

```
<phone:PhoneApplicationPage.Resources>
    <Style x:Name="MyTextBlockStyle" TargetType="TextBlock">
        <Setter Property="TextWrapping" Value="Wrap" />
        <Setter Property="Margin" Value="0,10,0,10" />
    </Style>
</phone:PhoneApplicationPage.Resources>

<ScrollViewer Margin="20" Height="400" VerticalAlignment="Top">
    <StackPanel Orientation="Vertical"  >
        <TextBlock HorizontalAlignment="Center" Margin="5"
                   Style="{StaticResource PhoneTextTitle2Style}">
        Through The Looking-Glass</TextBlock>
        <TextBlock HorizontalAlignment="Center" Margin="5"
               Foreground="{StaticResource PhoneAccentBrush}"
               Style="{StaticResource PhoneTextTitle3Style}">
            By Lewis Carroll</TextBlock>

        <TextBlock Style="{StaticResource MyTextBlockStyle}" >
        One thing was certain, that the WHITE kitten had nothing to do with
        it:-it was the black kitten's fault entirely. For the white kitten had
        been having its face washed by the old cat for the last quarter of an
        hour (and bearing it pretty well, considering); so you see that it COULDN'T
        have had any hand in the mischief.</TextBlock>

        <TextBlock Style="{StaticResource MyTextBlockStyle}" >
        The way Dinah washed her children's faces was this: first she held the poor
        thing down by its ear with one paw, and then with the other paw she rubbed
        its face all over, the wrong way, beginning at the nose: and just now, as I
        said, she was hard at work on the white kitten, which was lying quite still
        and trying to purr—no doubt feeling that it was all meant for its good.</TextBlock>

    </StackPanel>
</ScrollViewer>
```

Figure 4-21 shows the vertical scrollbar in the emulator. Be aware that the scrollbar doesn't show up right away, but only as the content is scrolled.

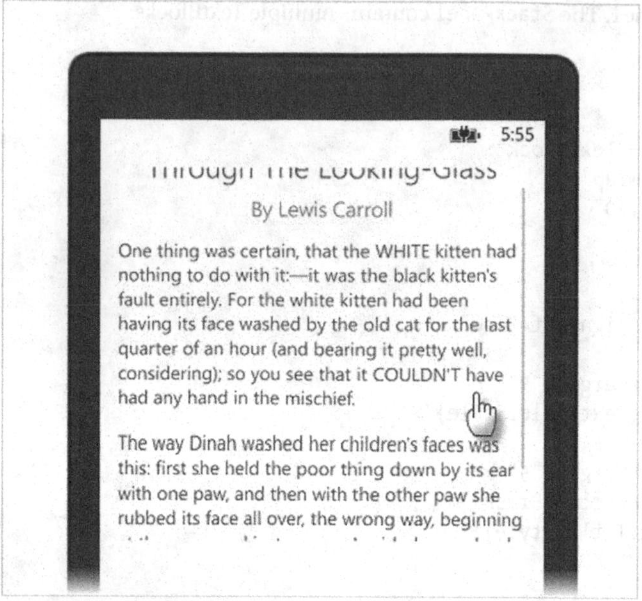

Figure 4-21. *Scrollbars in the Scrollviewer*

Scrolling Programmatically

To scroll to the top or bottom of the ScrollViewer programmatically, use the `ScrollToVerticalOffset()` and `ScrollToHorizontalOffset()` methods, passing a position offset in both cases (see Listing 4-20). The `ScrollViewer` in this example wraps a `StackPanel` that contains multiple TextBlocks (see Figure 4-22). Scrolling to the top can be done using `ScrollToVerticalOffset()` and passing zero as the offset. Scrolling to the bottom uses `ScrollToVerticalOffset()`, passing the client area height of the `ScrollViewer`.

Listing 4-20. Scrolling Programmatically

```
private void ScrollTopButton_Click(object sender, RoutedEventArgs e)
{
    TextScrollViewer.ScrollToVerticalOffset(0);
}

private void ScrollBottomButton_Click(object sender, RoutedEventArgs e)
{
    TextScrollViewer.ScrollToVerticalOffset(TextScrollViewer.ExtentHeight);
}
```

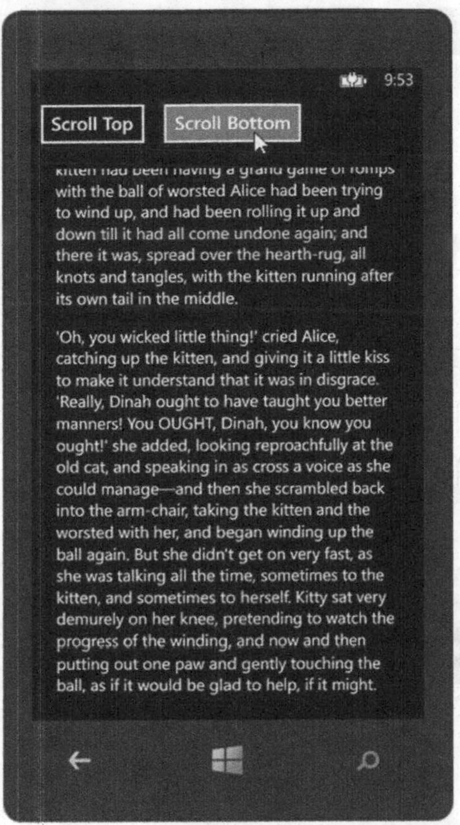

***Figure 4-22.** Content Scrolled Programmatically*

Viewbox

The `Viewbox` control scales child controls automatically as its `Width` and `Height` are changed. The `Viewbox Stretch` and `StretchDirection` properties govern scaling, particularly in regards to aspect ratio. `Stretch` values can be:

- ***None***: The child elements appear in the original sizes.
- ***Fill***: The child elements stretch to fill the parent container and ignore aspect ratio. Depending on the dimensions of the `Viewbox`, this option can distort the child elements.
- ***Uniform***: Stretches child elements proportionally without distortion, always staying inside the bounds of the `Viewbox`.
- ***UniformToFill***: Stretches child elements proportionally but may exceed the dimensions of the `Viewbox`.

`StretchDirection` can be `UpOnly`, `DownOnly`, or `Both`. Figure 4-23 shows the Viewbox with the same child elements but different `Stretch`, `StretchDirection`, `Width`, and `Height` settings. This example uses a slider control that is bound to both the `Viewbox Width` and `Height`.

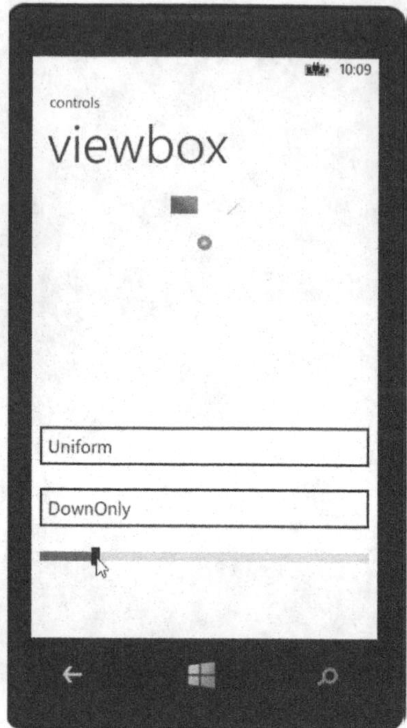

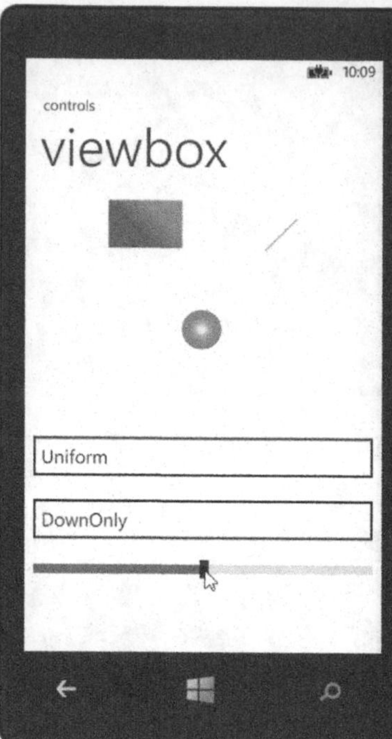

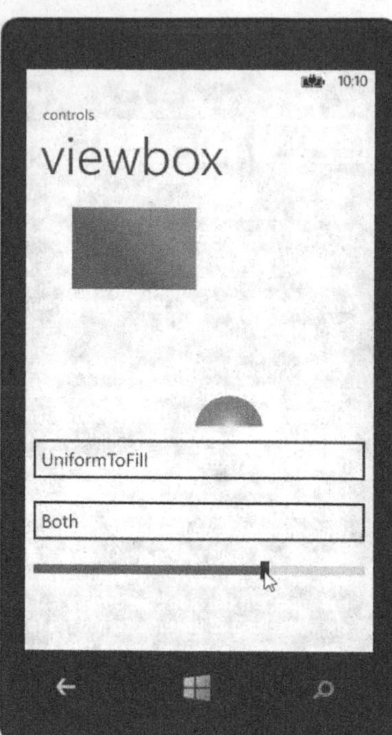

Figure 4-23. *Bound ViewBox*

Button Controls

Windows Phone 8 buttons include all the "usual suspects:" radio buttons, check boxes, and also a ToggleSwitch control (a mobile version of the checkbox available from the Windows Phone 8 Toolkit). The class diagram in Figure 4-24 shows that most buttons, except the ToggleSwitch, descend from ButtonBase.

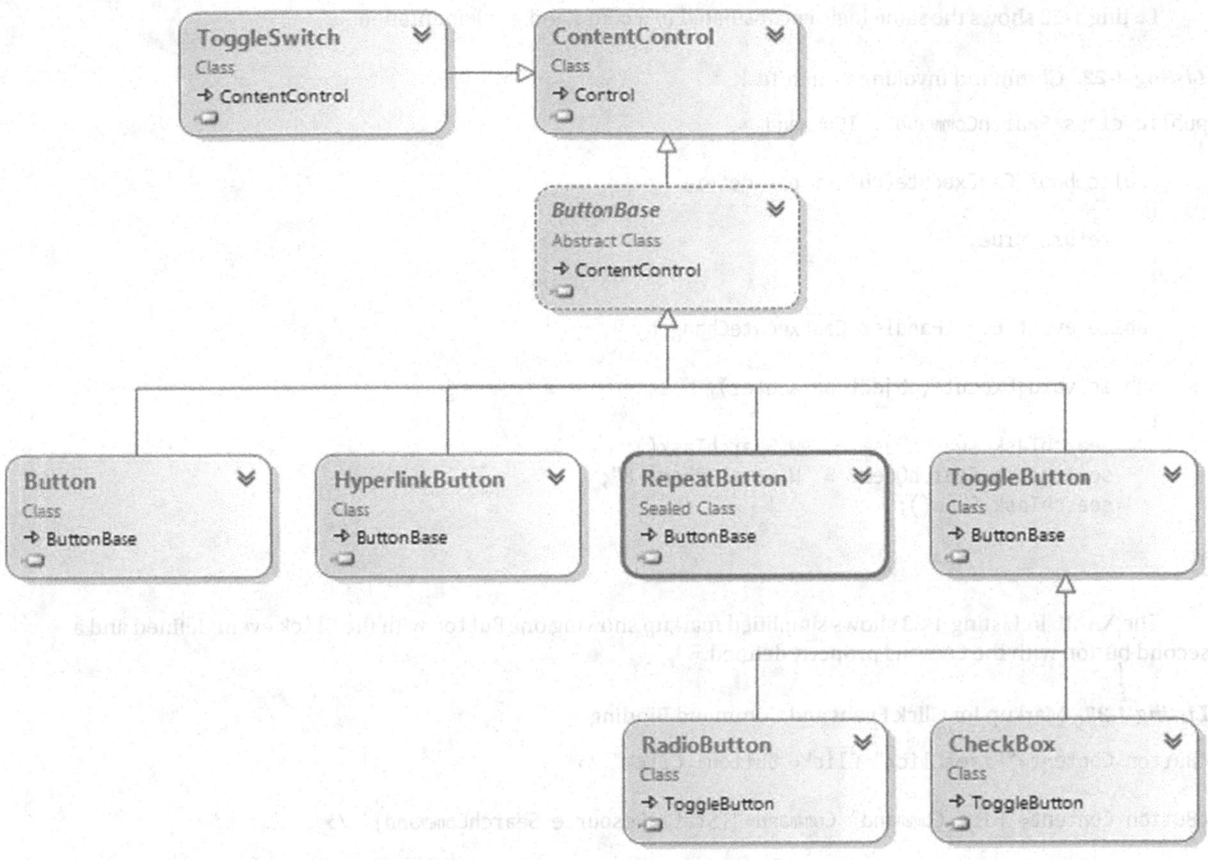

Figure 4-24. *Class Diagram of Button Classes*

The abstract ButtonBase class introduces basic button functionality through its Click and Tap event or through its ability to invoke commands using the Command and CommandParameter properties. Set the ClickMode enumeration property to determine if the Click event is fired on Release, Press, or Hover. Boolean properties IsFocused, IsMouseOver, and IsPressed help bind the state of the button with the state of your view model.

The concrete Button class surfaces the abilities of ButtonBase and can be used to trigger the Click event or trigger a bound Command. Listing 4-21 shows a search task triggered directly from a Button Click event.

Listing 4-21. Click Event Invoking Search Task

```
private void ClickButton_Click(object sender, RoutedEventArgs e)
{
    SearchTask searchTask = new SearchTask();
    searchTask.SearchQuery = "Windows Phone 8";
    searchTask.Show();
}
```

Listing 4-22 shows the same logic encapsulated in a command implementation.

Listing 4-22. Command Invoking Search Task

```
public class SearchCommand : ICommand
{
    public bool CanExecute(object parameter)
    {
        return true;
    }

    public event EventHandler CanExecuteChanged;

    public void Execute(object parameter)
    {
        SearchTask searchTask = new SearchTask();
        searchTask.SearchQuery = "Windows Phone 8";
        searchTask.Show();
    }
}
```

The XAML in Listing 4-23 shows simplified markup showing one `Button` with the `Click` event defined and a second button with the `Command` property defined.

Listing 4-23. Markup for Click Event and Command Binding

```
<Button Content="Fire Click" Click="button1_Click" />

<Button Content="Fire Command" Command="{StaticResource SearchCommand}" />
```

Figure 4-25 shows an assortment of buttons including a search task triggered by both a button click event and using a command.

Figure 4-25. *Button Elements*

- ***RepeatButton*** fires the `Click` event continually while pressed. The `Delay` property controls the initial wait in milliseconds before the first `Click` event fires. The `Interval` property controls the pause between `Click` events.
- ***HyperlinkButton*** navigates to URLs set in the `NavigateUri` property. Set the `TargetName` to the target window or frame that the page should open in. To use external URLs, set the `TargetName` property to `"_blank"` (this will trigger the Browser task). `HyperlinkButton` is intended for use within text where a Button would be too large and obtrusive.
- ***ToggleButton*** is the base class for buttons that can switch states. The `Checked` and `Unchecked` events fire as the state of the `ToggleButton` changes. If the `IsThreeState` property is "true", then the `ToggleButton` also fires the `Indeterminate` event.
- ***RadioButton*** is a `ToggleButton` descendant that uses the `GroupName` property to work in concert with other `RadioButtons` in the user interface.
- ***CheckBox*** is also a ToggleButton descendant with the standard check box appearance.
- While most buttons descend from `ButtonBase`, ***ToggleSwitch*** descends directly from `ContentControl`. `ToggleSwitch` fires `Checked`, `Unchecked`, and `Indeterminate` events. The Indeterminate event will fire when the `IsChecked` property is assigned null. Place any object content to the `Header` property; likewise, any object can be placed in the `Content` property. `SwitchForeground` is a brush property for the highlight color in the switch graphic and can be changed on any `ToggleSwitch` event.

Binding ThreeState Buttons

The IsChecked property of ToggleButton is a type "null?," a nullable Boolean with possible values true, false, and null. You can bind these states from a view model or a converter. Consider a view model with project status enumeration values, Unknown, Started, and NotStarted, as shown in Listing 4-24. Instead of binding directly to a project status, this example binds to the public nullable Boolean property Started and the setter for this property distributes changes to related properties like StatusCaption.

Listing 4-24. View Model Containing Project Status

```
public class ProjectViewModel : INotifyPropertyChanged
{
    public enum ProjectStatus { Unknown = 0, Started = 1, NotStarted = 2 };

    private ProjectStatus _status;

    public bool? Started
    {
        get
        {
            switch (this._status)
            {
                case ProjectStatus.Started: return true;
                case ProjectStatus.NotStarted: return false;
                default: return null; // unknown
            }
        }
        set
        {
            switch (value)
            {
                case true: { _status = ProjectStatus.Started; break; }
                case false: { _status = ProjectStatus.NotStarted; break; }
                case null: { _status = ProjectStatus.Unknown; break; }
            }
            OnPropertyChanged("Started");
            OnPropertyChanged("StatusCaption");
        }
    }

    public string StatusCaption
    {
        get
        {
            return Enum.GetName(typeof(ProjectStatus), this._status);
        }
    }

    private void OnPropertyChanged(string propertyName)
    {
        if (PropertyChanged != null)
        {
```

```
            PropertyChanged(this, new PropertyChangedEventArgs(propertyName));
        }
    }

    public event PropertyChangedEventHandler PropertyChanged;
}
```

Most of the work happens in the view model, leaving simple binding to hook up the buttons (see Listing 4-25). Both the CheckBox and ToggleButton are configured identically with the IsChecked property bound to the Started property in the view model.

Listing 4-25. Binding IsChecked to the View Model

```
<CheckBox Content="{Binding StatusCaption}"
          IsChecked="{Binding Started, Mode=TwoWay}"
          VerticalAlignment="Top"/>
<ToggleButton Content="{Binding StatusCaption}"
          IsChecked="{Binding Started, Mode=TwoWay}"
          VerticalAlignment="Top" HorizontalAlignment="left"/>
```

The binding is TwoWay so that selecting the CheckBox or ToggleButton will change the status and the caption for both (see Figure 4-26).

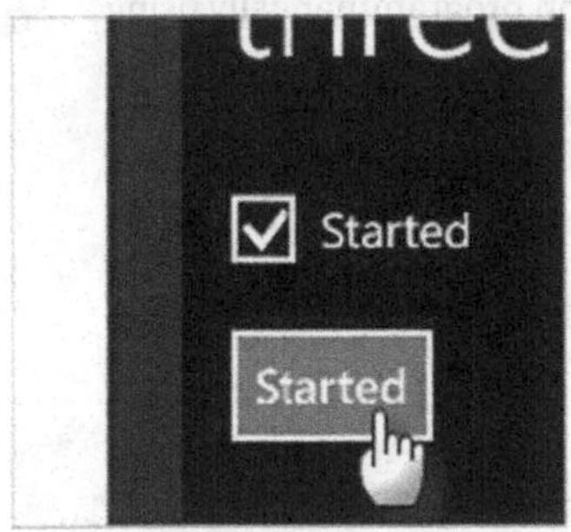

Figure 4-26. *Binding ThreeState Controls*

Input Controls

The controls in this section are grouped somewhat arbitrarily under the heading “input” controls. They all descend from Control, the class that introduces ControlTemplate to define appearance.

TextBox

TextBox is a one-size-fits-all data input control where the pop-up keyboard characteristics are controlled by the InputScope property. The primary property is simply Text. If you’re not binding directly to the Text or SelectedText properties, subscribe to the TextChanged event to react programmatically when text is updated. You can prevent input by turning on the IsReadOnly property, setting the MaxLength property to the maximum number of characters allowed and by using TextAlignment to place text Center|Left | Right | Justify within the control.

Windows Phone 8 doesn’t have a “text area” or a control with a multi-line property. Instead, increase the Height of the control, turn on AcceptsReturn and TextWrapping properties (see Listing 4-26).

Listing 4-26. Configuring the TextBox for Multiple Lines

```
<TextBox  AcceptsReturn="True" TextWrapping="Wrap" Height="150"
  Text="This is text that will appear on several lines. This will also handle carriage returns." />
```

Figure 4-27 shows the `TextBox` with `AcceptsReturn` set to `True` and `TextWrapping` to `Wrap`.

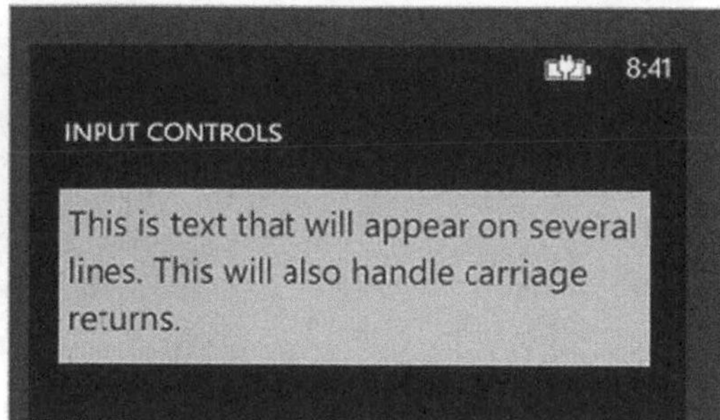

Figure 4-27. *TextBox With Multiple Lines of Text*

If the user selects some set of words in a `TextBox` (see Figure 4-28), you can retrieve the `SelectedText` property programmatically or through binding. `SelectedText` is positioned at `SelectionStart` number of characters within the `Text` and extends for SelectionLength number of characters. You can set the selection programmatically using methods `Select(start, length)` or `SelectAll()`.

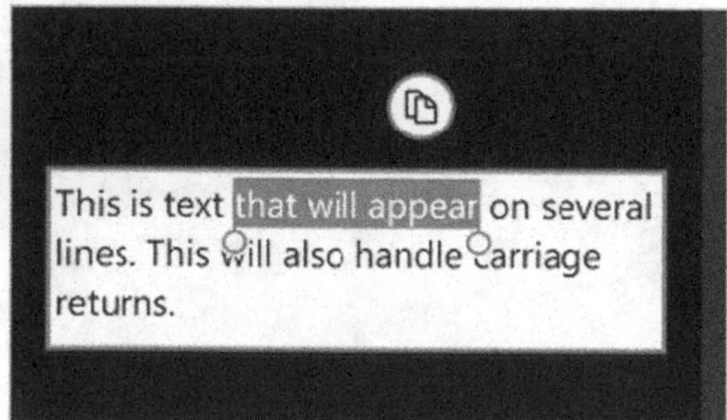

Figure 4-28. *Selected Text*

Input Keyboards

Users on a phone device need all the help they can get to enter data efficiently. The `InputScope` property sets the onscreen keyboard display to show "smiley faces" for chat, .com/.net for URLs and numeric input for currency. If you know the correct enumeration value, `InputScope` will show correctly, but will not give you any IntelliSense help. Use the full property element syntax to get IntelliSense with a full List of `InputScopeNameValue` enumeration values as shown in Figure 4-29.

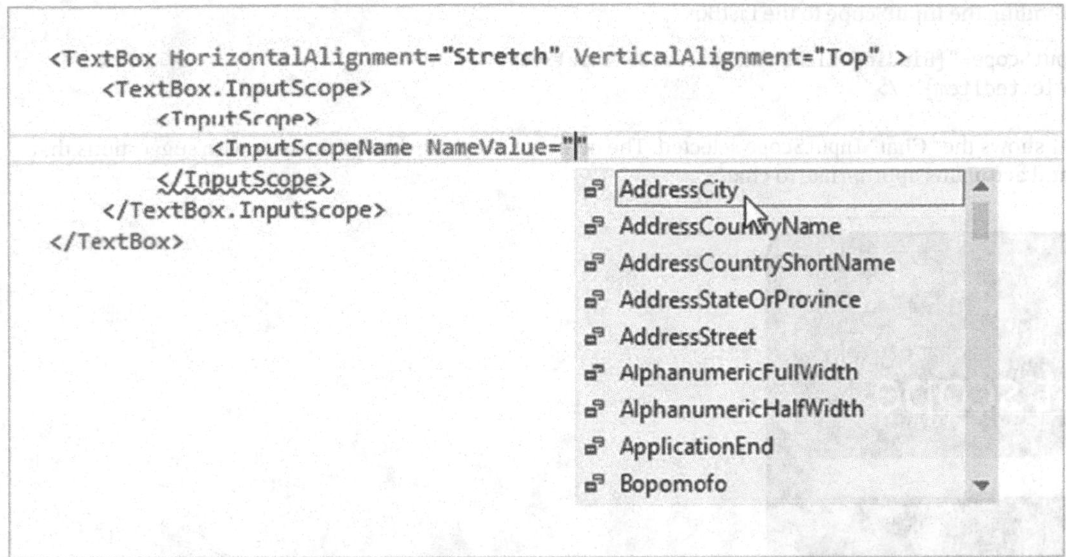

Figure 4-29. *InputScopeName Property Element Syntax*

A few examples of `InputScope` in action in Figure 4-30 show keyboards for Default, URL, and TelephoneNumber.

Figure 4-30. *Keyboards for Default, URL, and TelephoneNumber*

For "grins", try using the `GetFields()` method against the `InputScopeNameValue` type. This will return a collection that you can "massage" with LINQ and assign to a `ListBox ItemsSource`, as shown in Listing 4-27.

Listing 4-27. Assigning InputScopeNameValues to a ListBox

```
var fields = typeof(InputScopeNameValue)
    .GetFields()
    .Where(f => f.IsLiteral)
    .Select(f => f.Name);

ListBoxInputScope.ItemsSource = fields;
```

Then, to assign the `InputScope` in the list to a `TextBox`, use element binding as shown in Listing 4-28.

Listing 4-28. Binding the InputScope to the ListBox

```
<TextBox  InputScope="{Binding ElementName=ListBoxInputScope,
     Path=SelectedItem}" />
```

Figure 4-31 shows the "Chat" InputScope selected. The on-screen keyboard helps the user with suggestions that include slang and acronyms appropriate to chat.

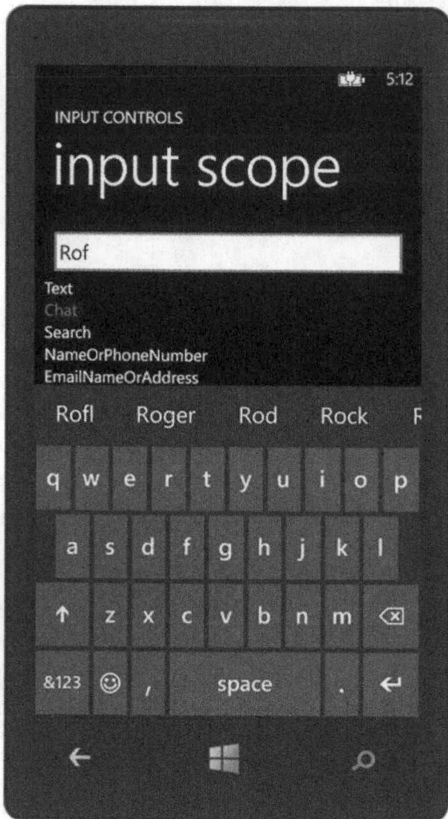

Figure 4-31. *Using the Chat Keyboard*

PasswordBox

PasswordBox is a simple control that does not have an InputScope property and shows the default keyboard layout, as shown in Figure 4-32. Each letter entered displays briefly until replaced by the PasswordChar property value.

Figure 4-32. *PasswordBox*

The TextBox InputScope property does include a "Password" value, but this has no effect and does not cause TextBox to behave like a PasswordBox.

RichTextBox

RichTextBox holds formatted text, hyperlinks, inline images, and other rich content. The Paragraphs element contains Runs of Text, Hyperlink, and InlineUIContainer (this last one can hold any UIElement), as shown in Listing 4-29.

Listing 4-29. Paragraph Structure and Key Elements

```
<RichTextBox >
    <Paragraph>
        <InlineUIContainer>
            <Image Stretch="None">
                <Image.Source>
                    <BitmapImage
         UriSource="http://a3.twimg.com/profile_images/728337241/conan_4cred_normal.jpg" />
                </Image.Source>
            </Image>
        </InlineUIContainer>
        <Hyperlink  NavigateUri="http://twitter.com/#!/ConanOBrien">
            <Span Foreground="Blue" TextDecorations="Underline">
                <Run Text="Conan O'Brien" />
            </Span>
        </Hyperlink>
    </Paragraph>
    <Paragraph>
        <Run Text="A publisher just asked me to write my autobiography, but they want it to be
         about Johnny Depp." />
    </Paragraph>
</RichTextBox>
```

Figure 4-33 shows an image, link, and text for a Conan O'Brien tweet.

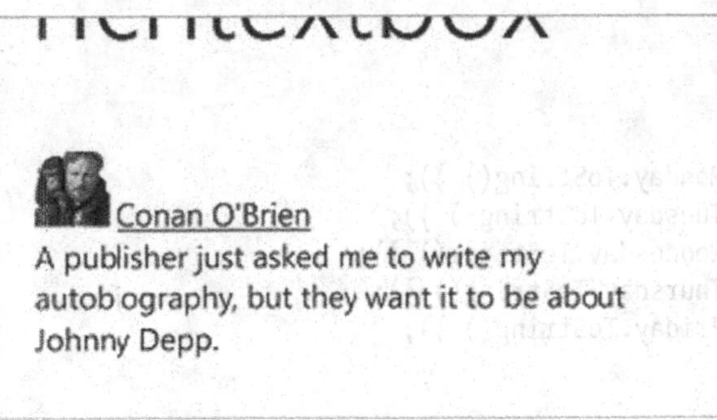

Figure 4-33. *RichTextBox*

AutoCompleteBox

AutoCompleteBox is like the TextBox, but has a list of possible values that display automatically. AutoCompleteBox is currently included in the Toolkit download, as shown in Figure 4-34.

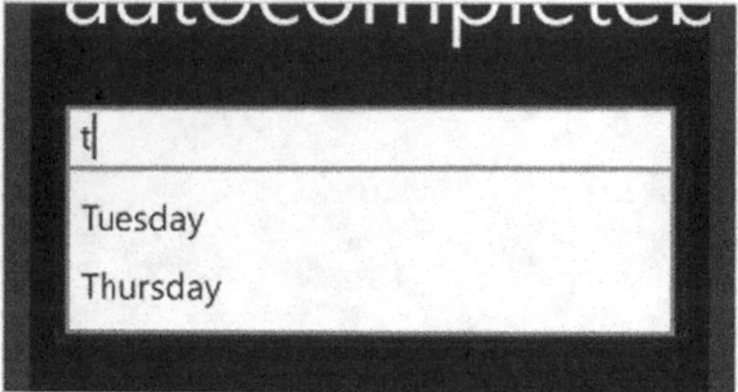

Figure 4-34. *AutoCompleteBox List of Items*

Populating the AutoCompleteBox

To populate the list, assign a collection to the ItemsSource property.

```
autoCompleteBox1.ItemsSource = new List<string>()  { "Monday",  "Tuesday",
    "Wednesday",  "Thursday", "Friday", "Saturday", "Sunday" };
```

If the ItemsSource is a complex object, assign the property to display in the ValueMemberPath. For example, Listing 4-30 shows a simple collection of AppointmentDays.

Listing 4-30. AppointmentDays Collection

```
public class Appointment
{
    public string Day { get; set; }
}

public class AppointmentDays : List<Appointment>
{
    public AppointmentDays()
    {
        this.Add(new Appointment() { Day = DayOfWeek.Monday.ToString() });
        this.Add(new Appointment() { Day = DayOfWeek.Tuesday.ToString() });
        this.Add(new Appointment() { Day = DayOfWeek.Wednesday.ToString() });
        this.Add(new Appointment() { Day = DayOfWeek.Thursday.ToString() });
        this.Add(new Appointment() { Day = DayOfWeek.Friday.ToString() });
    }
}
```

The AppointmentDays object is assigned to ItemsSource and the ValueMemberPath is assigned the Day property of an Appointment, as shown in Listing 4-31.

Listing 4-31. Assigning the AppointmentDays Data

```
autoCompleteBox1.ItemsSource = new AppointmentDays();
autoCompleteBox1.ValueMemberPath = "Day";
```

The tricky part here is that there is no corresponding `DisplayMemberPath` for `AutoCompleteBox`, so the list will only display the object name, such as `MyProject.Appointment`. You will have to define a template to get control of the list display. The example in Listing 4-32 binds within the `ItemTemplate`.

Listing 4-32. Defining the AutoCompleteBox ItemTemplate

```
<toolkit:AutoCompleteBox x:Name="autoCompleteBox1" VerticalAlignment="Top">
    <toolkit:AutoCompleteBox.ItemTemplate>
        <DataTemplate>
            <StackPanel Orientation="Horizontal">
                <Image Source="/Assets/Icons/Light/check.png"
                    Width="32" Height="32" Stretch="Uniform" />
                <TextBlock Text="{Binding Path=Day}" />
            </StackPanel>
        </DataTemplate>
    </toolkit:AutoCompleteBox.ItemTemplate>
</toolkit:AutoCompleteBox>
```

Figure 4-35 shows the running application. The single matching item in the list shows as an image and a `TextBlock` bound to the `Day` property of the `Appointment` object.

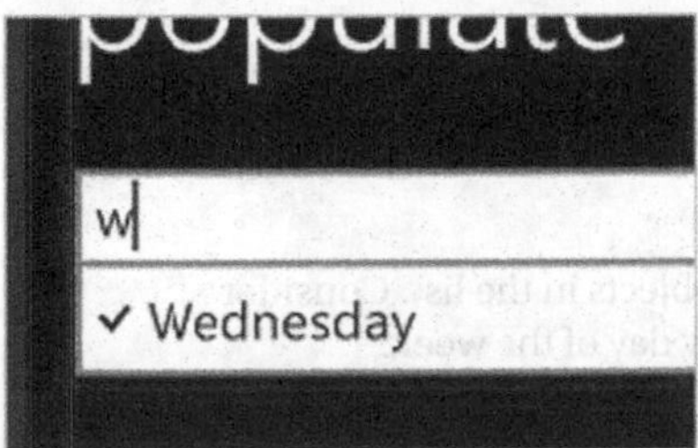

Figure 4-35. *Templated Items*

■ **Note** Windows Phone 8 comes with a standard set of icons (e.g., Play, Back, Check, Folder, etc.) located at `\Program Files (x86)\Microsoft SDKs\Windows Phone\v8.0\Icons`.

Filtering the AutoCompleteBox

`FilterMode` controls how comparisons to the list are performed and includes `StartsWith`, `StartsWithOrdinal`, `Contains`, `ContainsOrdinal`, `Equals`, `EqualsOrdinal`, and `Custom`. All of these except `Custom` have case-sensitive counterparts, such as `StartsWithCaseSensitive`. The snippet in Listing 4-33 only displays items in the list that match the starting characters of the entered text exactly. For example, the entry "Fri" will display "Friday," but not "fri."

Listing 4-33. Defining the AutoCompleteBox FilterMode

```
autoCompleteBox1.FilterMode = AutoCompleteFilterMode.StartsWithCaseSensitive;
```

AutoCompleteBox Custom Filters

For greater control over filtering, set `FilterMode` to `Custom` and assign either `ItemFilter` or `TextFilter`. Assign only one (the last one defined takes precedence). `TextFilter` compares based on the string representation of the items list while `ItemFilter` compares against objects in the items list. Both `ItemFilter` and `TextFilter` follow the signature shown in Listing 4-35.

Listing 4-35. Defining the AutoCompleteBox FilterMode

```
public delegate bool AutoCompleteFilterPredicate<T>(string search, T item);
```

The `TextFilter` example in Listing 4-36 shows a custom predicate that takes two string parameters and returns a Boolean. You can put any custom logic that suits your requirements in the method as long as it returns a bool. The `search` parameter represents user entry and the `item` parameter represents one of the items in the list. `WeekendFilter` fires for every entry defined in `ItemsSource`, verifies that the user entry matches an item in the list and checks that the item is not a weekend day.

Listing 4-36. Assigning a Custom TextFilter

```
autoCompleteBox1.TextFilter = WeekendFilter;
//. . .
public bool WeekendFilter(string search, string item)
{
    bool isWeekend = item.Equals("Saturday") || item.Equals("Sunday");
    return item.StartsWith(search, StringComparison.OrdinalIgnoreCase) && !isWeekend;
}
```

`ItemFilter` follows the same pattern as `TextFilter` but allows you to filter objects in the list. Consider `AppointmentDays` class in Listing 4-37 that includes `Appointment` objects for every day of the week.

Listing 4-37. The Appointments Collection

```
public class Appointment
{
    public string Day { get; set; }
}

public class AppointmentDays : List<Appointment>
{
    public AppointmentDays()
    {
        foreach (DayOfWeek dayOfWeek in Enum.GetValues(typeof(DayOfWeek)))
        {
            this.Add(new Appointment() { Day = dayOfWeek.ToString() });
        }
    }
}
```

The item filter defined in Listing 4-38, passes an object parameter named `item`. `item` is cast to the underlying `Appointment` type and used to make the comparison.

Listing 4-38. The Appointments Collection

```
autoCompleteBox1.ItemFilter = AppointmentFilter;
//. . .
public bool AppointmentFilter(string search, object item)
{
    Appointment appointment = item as Appointment;
    return appointment.Day.StartsWith(search, StringComparison.OrdinalIgnoreCase);
}
```

AutoCompleteBox Type Ahead

Enable `IsTextCompletionEnabled` to get "type ahead" assistance as the user enters new characters. To ensure that at least a certain number of characters are entered, set the `MinimumPrefixLength` to a value greater than zero. Figure 4-36 shows that "Tue" is automatically completed to "Tuesday." Also notice that the remaining letters ("sday") are selected and bracketed by the selection adorners, and that the "Copy" icon is displayed.

Figure 4-36. *AutoCompleteBox with IsTextCompletionEnabled*

Slider

Use the `Slider` sparingly in your user interface for quickly roughing in approximate values, not precision adjustments. Mice are good at hitting small targets like the slider, but fingers, not so much. Also, don't add a `Slider` to a parent that drags in the same orientation, such as `Panorama`, `Pivot`, or `LongListSelector`.

`Value` is the key `Slider` property that controls the position of the slider within `Minimum` and `Maximum` property values. The `Orientation` property displays the Slider `Vertical` or `Horizontal` positioning. Listing 4-39 hooks the `TextBlock.Text` property to the `Slider` element `Value`. The `StringFormat` presents the text as currency.

Listing 4-39. The Appointments Collection

```
<StackPanel Orientation="Horizontal">
    <Slider x:Name="MySlider"
        Orientation="Horizontal"
        Minimum="0"
        Maximum="100"
        Width="150"
        VerticalAlignment="Top"
```

```
        HorizontalAlignment="Stretch">
    </Slider>
    <TextBlock
        VerticalAlignment="Top"
        Text="{Binding ElementName=MySlider, Path=Value, StringFormat=C}"
        Style="{StaticResource PhoneTextAccentStyle}" />
</StackPanel>
```

The running example in Figure 4-37 shows the text responding to the bound slider value.

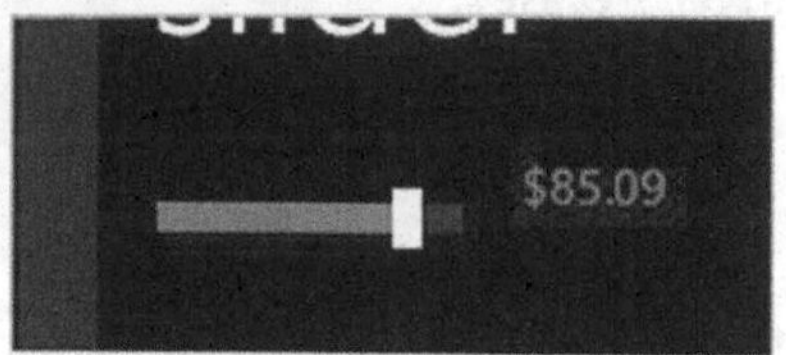

***Figure 4-37.** Bound Slider*

DatePicker and TimePicker

Using TextBox with Date input values is not particularly visual and a weak substitute for DatePicker and TimePicker controls, as shown in Figure 4-38. The picker controls display the standard date and time for the current culture. Both DatePicker and TimePicker are in the Windows Phone Toolkit available at CodePlex.

***Figure 4-38.** DatePicker and TimePicker*

Once selected, both picker controls display a page with three columns of "rolling" elements that can be dragged to select values, as shown Figure 4-39. Clicking the OK or Cancel buttons sets the Value and returns to the original picker display.

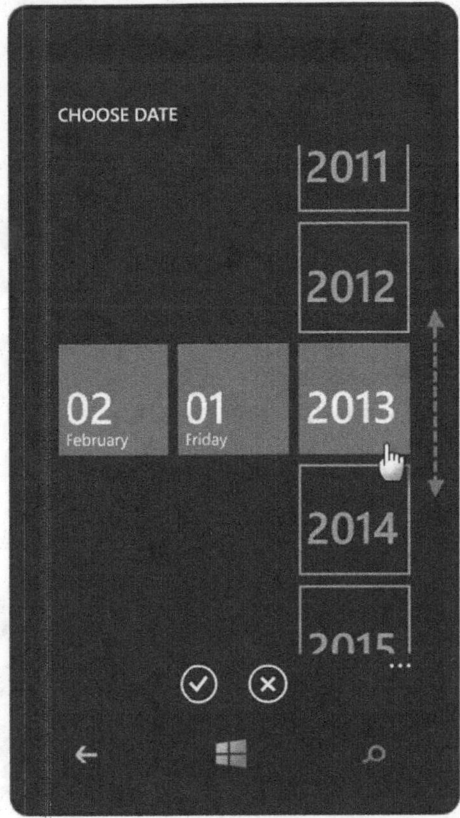

Figure 4-39. *Selecting the Value*

DateTimePickerBase

Both DatePicker and TimePicker are just thin veneers over the ancestor DateTimePickerBase. The key DateTimePickerBase properties are Value and ValueString (a string representation of the Value property).

The ValueStringFormat property sets the date or time display using date and time format strings. These industry standard formats may look familiar, but there's one little twist: the formats all use curly brackets "{}," the same characters used by XAML markup extensions. Use an additional pair of brackets to escape the starting format bracket. The example in Listing 4-40 displays a date in long format.

Listing 4-40. Using the ValueStringFormat

```
<toolkit:DatePicker
    Value="01/01/2011"
    ValueStringFormat="{}{0:D}" />
```

■ **Note** See the Microsoft Developer Network article "Formatting Types" for more details on predefined and custom formats.

■ http://msdn.microsoft.com/en-us/library/26etazsy.aspx

The Header content appears just above the date or time entry. You can assign text directly to the Header attribute or use the full property element syntax to define a custom layout. The snippet in Listing 4-41 assigns text directly to the DatePicker Header, but the TimePicker Header includes both an Image and TextBlock, as shown in Figure 4-40.

Listing 4-41. Defining the Header

```
<toolkit:DatePicker
    Header="Project Start Date"
    Value="01/01/2013"
    ValueStringFormat="{}{0:D}" />

<toolkit:TimePicker>
    <toolkit:TimePicker.Header>
        <StackPanel Orientation="Horizontal">
            <Rectangle Fill="{StaticResource PhoneForegroundBrush}" Width="32" Height="32" >
                <Rectangle.OpacityMask>
                    <ImageBrush ImageSource="/Assets/Icons/Light/feature.alarm.png"  />
                </Rectangle.OpacityMask>
            </Rectangle>
            <TextBlock Text="Project Start Time" Margin="5" />
        </StackPanel>
    </toolkit:TimePicker.Header>
</toolkit:TimePicker>
```

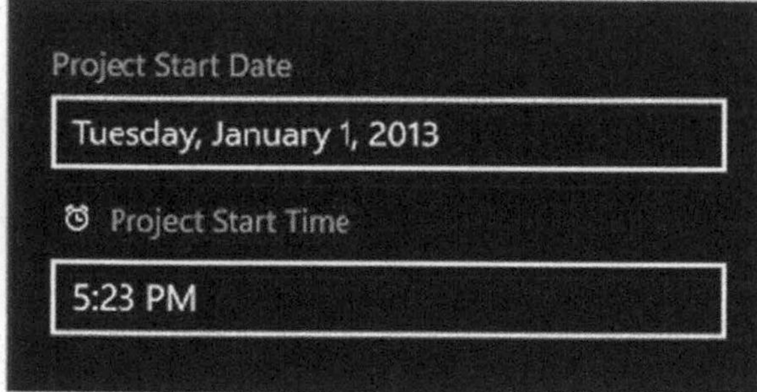

Figure 4-40. *Selecting the Value*

List Controls

List controls display a series of data vertically in an open list or in a drop-down control. These lists allow binding data and the ability to setup a template for each item in the list.

LongListSelector

LongListSelector displays lengthy lists of data as flat lists or displayed in grouped sections "jump list" style, similar to the standard "People" contacts application. LongListSelector allows your users to easily navigate between sections in the list and to scroll with great performance.

LongListSelector really shows its power presenting large amounts of data that can be categorized in some way, such as contacts organized alphabetically, pictures taken by date, or movies by genre, as shown in Figure 4-41.

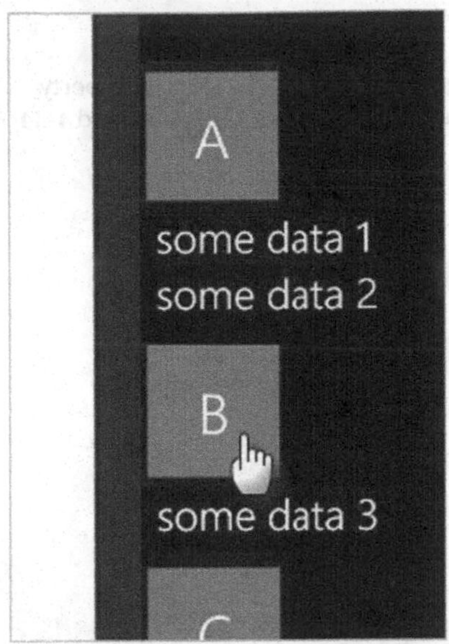

Figure 4-41. *Selecting a Group Header*

Tapping one of the group headers displays the jump list (see Figure 4-42). Touching an entry in the jump list displays the initial list, but with the selected category in view.

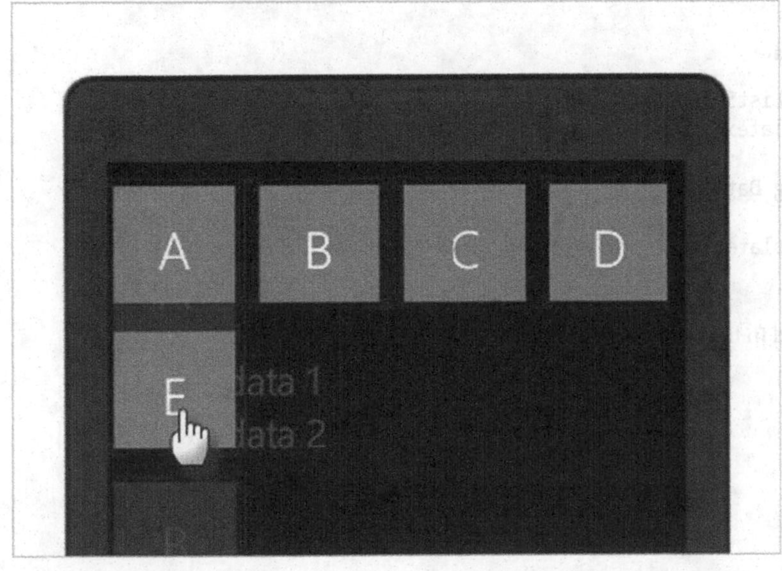

Figure 4-42. *The Jump List*

Bind a Simple List

To use `LongListSelector` without grouping, in a "flat" list, you only need to assign data to the `ItemsSource` property and an `ItemTemplate` to tell `LongListSelector` where to display the data. The example in Listings 4-42, 4-43, and 4-44 display a flat list of the `Data` property of the `MyObject` class.

Listing 4-42. The Detail Object

```
public class MyObject
{
    public string Category { get; set; }
    public string Data { get; set; }
}
```

Listing 4-43. Assigning a List to the LongListSelector

```
var flatList = new List<MyObject>()
{
    new MyObject() { Category = "A", Data = "some data 1" },
    new MyObject() { Category = "A", Data = "some data 2" },
    new MyObject() { Category = "B", Data = "some data 3" },
    new MyObject() { Category = "C", Data = "some data 4" },
    new MyObject() { Category = "C", Data = "some data 5" },
    new MyObject() { Category = "C", Data = "some data 6" }
};

LongListSelector1.ItemsSource = flatList;
```

Listing 4-44. LongListSelector ItemTemplate

```
<phone:LongListSelector x:Name="LongListSelector1">
    <phone:LongListSelector.ItemTemplate>
        <DataTemplate>
            <TextBlock Text="{Binding Data}"/>
        </DataTemplate>
    </phone:LongListSelector.ItemTemplate>
</phone:LongListSelector>
```

Figure 4-43 shows the flat list displayed in the LongListSelector.

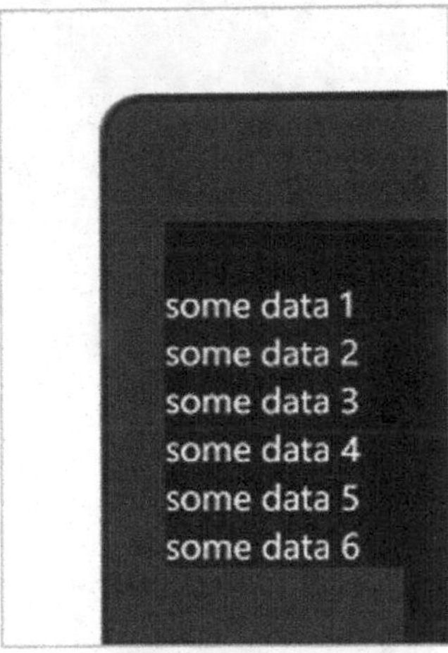

Figure 4-43. *Bound Flat List in LongListSelector*

Grouping

At a minimum, grouped lists require that you configure and bind grouped data, assign templates, and set group-related properties. Here are the steps that need to be performed:

- Arrange the data to form a *list of groups of objects*. Massaging this data is the most involved part of setting up `LongListSelector`, so we'll discuss this in detail.
- Bind the grouped data to the `LongListSelector ItemsSource`.
- Assign the `ItemTemplate` to define layout for each data item: `GroupHeaderTemplate` for the layout that appears above groups of items and `JumpListStyle` that configures the jump list.
- Set group-related properties.

`LongListSelector` is looking for a ***list of groups of object***. We already have a `MyObject` class used to store the detail for every item in the list (see "Bind a Simple List"). Next we need a `Group` object that has a list and also a key property to group on. The example in Listing 4-45 defines a generic List of T and also passes in a title to the constructor to be used as a key for grouping.

Listing 4-45. The Group Object

```
public class Group<TKey, T> : List<T>
{
    public Group(TKey key, IEnumerable<T> items) :
        base(items)
    {
        this.Key = key;
    }
    public TKey Key { get; set; }
}
```

The list of grouped objects are populated from a LINQ statement (see Listing 4-46) where the flat list of objects is grouped and ordered by the `Category` property of `MyObject`. The `ToList()` method returns a list of groups expected by `LongListSelector`. Finally, the prepared data is assigned to the `LongListSelector ItemsSource`.

Listing 4-46 Preparing the Grouped Data

```
var flatList = new List<MyObject>()
    {
        new MyObject() { Category = "A", Data = "some data 1" },
        new MyObject() { Category = "A", Data = "some data 2" },
        new MyObject() { Category = "B", Data = "some data 3" },
        new MyObject() { Category = "C", Data = "some data 4" },
        new MyObject() { Category = "C", Data = "some data 5" },
        new MyObject() { Category = "C", Data = "some data 6" },
        new MyObject() { Category = "D", Data = "some data 7" },
        new MyObject() { Category = "E", Data = "some data 8" },
        new MyObject() { Category = "E", Data = "some data 9" },
        new MyObject() { Category = "E", Data = "some data 10" },
    };

var groups =
    (from obj in flatList
        group obj by obj.Category into g
        orderby g.Key
        select new Group<string, MyObject>(g.Key, g));

LongListSelector1.ItemsSource = groups.ToList();
```

If we debug the application and break after the “groups” variable is assigned, the QuickWatch window shows that we have a List of Group, where each Group has a Title and a list of MyObject, as shown in Figure 4-44.

Name	Value	Type
⊟ groups	Count = 5	System.Collections.Generic.List<LongListSelector.Group>
⊟ [0]	Count = 2	LongListSelector.Group
⊞ [0]	{LongListSelector.MyObject}	LongListSelector.MyObject
⊞ [1]	{LongListSelector.MyObject}	LongListSelector.MyObject
⊟ Raw View		
⊞ base	Count = 2	System.Collections.Generic.List<LongListSelector.MyObject>
Title	"A"	string
⊞ [1]	Count = 1	LongListSelector.Group
⊞ [2]	Count = 3	LongListSelector.Group
⊞ [3]	Count = 1	LongListSelector.Group
⊞ [4]	Count = 3	LongListSelector.Group
⊞ Raw View		

Figure 4-44. *List of Groups in QuickWatch Window*

To display this data, you need to create template resources for ItemTemplate, GroupHeaderTemplate, and JumpListStyle. There are other templates that you can define, but these three are the minimum.

The ItemTemplate can be as simple as a single TextBlock (see Listing 4-47).

Listing 4-47. The Template for Items

```
<DataTemplate x:Key="MyObjectItemTemplate">
    <TextBlock Text="{Binding Data}" Style="{StaticResource PhoneTextLargeStyle}"/>
</DataTemplate>
```

For the group header and jump list, we can share the same "GroupTile" DataTemplate (see Listing 4-48) to show a square of accent color overlaid with the category text in a contrasting color. Notice the `JumpListItemBackgroundConverter` and `JumpListItemForegroundConverter` from the SDK that makes it easy to handle the background and foreground colors so that they show distinctly in light or dark themes of any color.

Listing 4-48. The Template for Group Header and the Jump List

```
<phone:JumpListItemBackgroundConverter x:Key="BackgroundConverter"/>
<phone:JumpListItemForegroundConverter x:Key="ForegroundConverter"/>

<DataTemplate x:Key="GroupTile">
    <Grid HorizontalAlignment="Left" Width="100" Height="100" Margin="5,20,5,5"
        Background="{Binding Converter={StaticResource BackgroundConverter}}">

        <TextBlock HorizontalAlignment="Center" VerticalAlignment="Center" Margin="5"
            Text="{Binding Title}"
            Style="{StaticResource PhoneTextExtraLargeStyle}"
            Foreground="{Binding Converter={StaticResource ForegroundConverter}}" />
    </Grid>
</DataTemplate>
```

Create a style to set the jump list `GridCellSize`, `LayoutMode`, and `ItemTemplate` attributes as shown in Listing 4-49. The `GridCellSize` should be large enough to fit the contents of the ItemTemplate. Set the `LayoutMode` to `Grid` or `List`. The ItemTemplate can reuse the `GroupTile` resource.

Listing 4-49. The Style for the Jump List

```
<Style x:Key="MyObjectJumpListStyle" TargetType="phone:LongListSelector">
    <Setter Property="GridCellSize"  Value="120,120"/>
    <Setter Property="LayoutMode" Value="Grid" />
    <Setter Property="ItemTemplate" Value="{StaticResource GroupTile}" />
</Style>
```

Now that resources are prepared, assign the template and style properties (see Listing 4-50). Be sure to set the `IsGroupingEnabled attribute` to true or the grouped data will not show up, even though you have done the previous steps correctly.

Listing 4-50. Setting LongListSelector Properties

```
<phone:LongListSelector x:Name="LongListSelector1"
        ItemTemplate="{StaticResource MyObjectItemTemplate}"
        GroupHeaderTemplate="{StaticResource GroupTile}"
        JumpListStyle="{StaticResource MyObjectJumpListStyle}"
        IsGroupingEnabled="true" />
```

Run the application and test that headers, items, and jump list display and that you can navigate using the jump list.

Grouping Complex Objects

If we play it right, we shouldn't have to touch the `Group` class (see Listing 4-45) to group where both key and list items are objects. This next example uses a playing card deck as a familiar data model that has categories to group on, namely, "Suit" that contains "Clubs," "Spades," "Hearts," and "Diamonds" and where each card has a value from two through nine and that includes "Jack," "Queen," "King," and "Ace." The cards appear in the `LongListSelector` with the Suit in the heading for each group and the value for each card making up the details in the list. Figure 4-45 shows one possible formatting of the data.

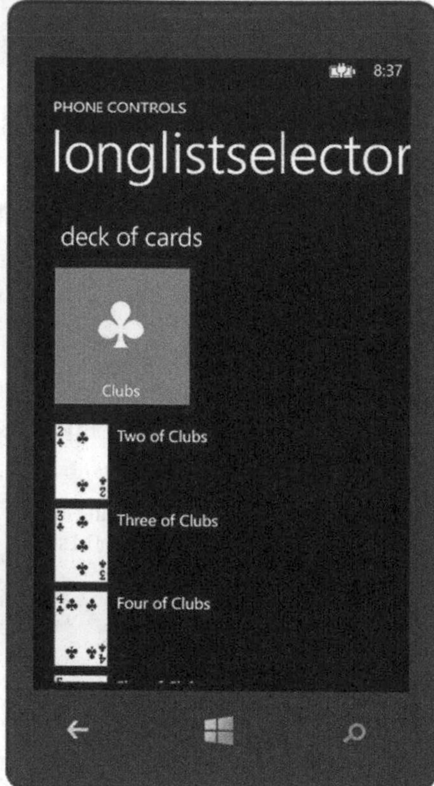

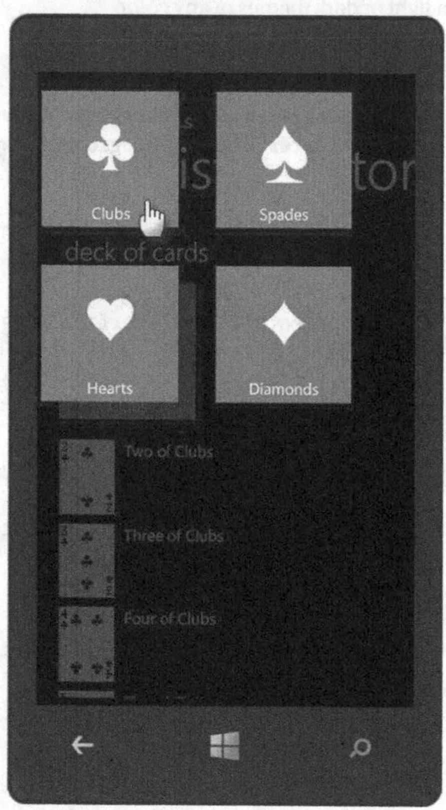

***Figure 4-45.** LongListSelector Items and Jump List Bound to Cards*

The `Deck` object in the snippet below will be the `ViewModel` for our purposes. We want to end up with an `IList` of `Group<>`, named "GroupedCards." Take a look at the logic flow in Listing 4-51. We start with a list of group, "Suit," objects using the `Enum.GetValues()` method to produce a "SuitType" collection ("Clubs," "Spades," etc.). Then we get a flat list of detail objects using both a collection of card values and suits. Each card in this flat list has a group (suit) and detail data (card type). Finally, the detail data is grouped by "suit" and placed in the list of custom `Group` objects.

Listing 4-51 The Deck Object

```
public class Deck
{
    public IList<Group<Suit, Card>> GroupedCards { get; private set; }

    public int Count { get; private set; }
```

```
    public Deck()
    {
        // get list of group objects
        var suits =
            from SuitType suitType in Enum.GetValues(typeof(SuitType))
            select new Suit() { SuitType = suitType };

        // get a flat list of detail objects that include the group data
        IEnumerable<Card> cards =
            from suit in suits
            from CardType cardType in Enum.GetValues(typeof(CardType))
            select new Card()
            {
                CardType = cardType,
                Suit = suit
            };

        // save the total card count
        this.Count = cards.Count();

        // group the detail
        this.GroupedCards =
            (from card in cards
                group card by card.Suit into grouped
                select new Group<Suit, Card>(grouped.Key, grouped)).ToList();
    }
}
```

The values used to drive the LINQ statements are simple enumerations, as shown in Listing 4-52.

Listing 4-52. Suit and Card Enumerations

```
public enum SuitType { Clubs, Spades, Hearts, Diamonds }
public enum CardType
{
    Two = 2, Three = 3, Four = 4, Five = 5, Six = 6,
    Seven = 7, Eight = 8, Nine = 9, Ten = 10,
    Jack = 11, Queen = 12, King = 13, Ace = 14
}
```

The `Suit` class uses `SuitType` to group card detail items, a `BitmapImage` to represent the `Suit` visually and an override of `ToString()` to format `SuitType` as the actual name of the enumeration value, as shown in Listing 4-53.

Listing 4-53. The Suit Class

```
public class Suit
{
    public SuitType SuitType { get; set; }

    public BitmapImage Image
    {
        get
```

```
        {
            const string pathFormat = "/Assets/Suits/tile_suit_{0}.png";
            string path = string.Format(pathFormat, this.ToString());
            return new BitmapImage(new System.Uri(path, System.UriKind.Relative));
        }
    }

    public override string ToString()
    {
        // For display as "Hearts", "Spades", etc.
        return this.SuitType.ToString("G");
    }
}
```

The Card class contains similar information but includes a reference to the Suit, as shown in Listing 4-54.

Listing 4-54. The Card Class

```
public class Card
{
    public Suit Suit { get; internal set; }
    public CardType CardType { get; internal set; }
    public BitmapImage Image
    {
        get
        {
            const string pathFormat = "/Assets/Cards/{0:d}_{1}.png";
            string path = string.Format(pathFormat, CardType, Suit.ToString());
            return new BitmapImage(new System.Uri(path, System.UriKind.Relative));
        }
    }

    public override string ToString()
    {
        // for display as "Two of Hearts", etc.
        return CardType.ToString("G") + " of " + this.Suit.ToString();
    }
}
```

The Group object stays clean and generic without needing to know anything about Suit or Card.

ListPicker

The ListPicker is the Windows Phone Toolkit answer to the combo box (see Figure 4-46). Use the Header property to provide a label above the picker. Header is a Content property, so you are not restricted to text only. The SelectionMode controls if the selected item is visible (Normal), all items are visible on the original page (Expanded) or all items display in a separate Popup (Full). ItemCountThreshold is the maximum number of items for the Expanded mode.

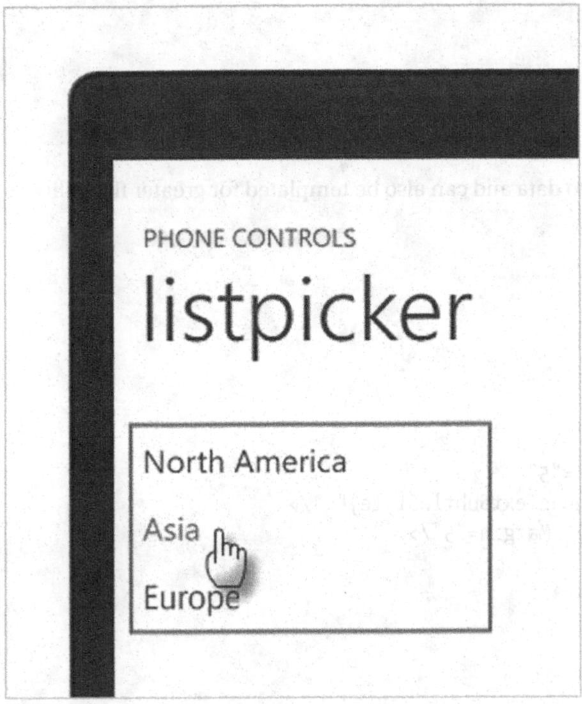

Figure 4-46. *Selecting from the ListPicker*

This `ListPicker` is another `ItemsControl` descendant that can be loaded with `ListPickerItem` objects at design-time as shown in Listing 4-55.

Listing 4-55. Defining ListPickerItems in XAML

```
<toolkit:ListPicker x:Name="RegionPicker">
    <toolkit:ListPickerItem Content="North America" />
    <toolkit:ListPickerItem Content="Asia" />
    <toolkit:ListPickerItem Content="Europe" />
</toolkit:ListPicker>
```

ListPickerItems can be added in code as shown in Listing 4-56. `ListPickerItem` is a `ContentControl` descendant that will accept a `Content` object.

Listing 4-56. Defining ListPickerItems in Code

```
RegionPicker.Items.Add(new ListPickerItem()
{
    Content = "North America",
    Tag = 123
});
RegionPicker.Items.Add(new ListPickerItem()
{
    Content = "Asia",
    Tag = 456
});
```

```
RegionPicker.Items.Add(new ListPickerItem()
{
    Content = "Europe",
    Tag = 789
});
```

Like any other ItemsControl, ListPicker can be bound to data and can also be templated for greater flexibility (Listing 4-57).

Listing 4-57. Binding ListPicker to Data

```
<toolkit:ListPicker x:Name="RegionPicker"
        ItemsSource="{StaticResource Regions}" >
    <toolkit:ListPicker.ItemTemplate>
        <DataTemplate>
            <StackPanel Orientation="Horizontal">
                <TextBlock Text="{Binding Id}" Margin="5"
                            Style="{StaticResource PhoneTextSubtleStyle}"  />
                <TextBlock Text="{Binding RegionName}" Margin="5"/>
            </StackPanel>
        </DataTemplate>
    </toolkit:ListPicker.ItemTemplate>
</toolkit:ListPicker>
```

Menu Controls

Menu controls display a series of items where each item has text that describes some action, an icon, and an event handler used to execute the action. Menus typically appear in the ApplicationBar or as context menu that can appear above any element.

ApplicationBar

The ApplicationBar is defined in the Microsoft.Phone.Shell namespace and is available to any new page using the "shell" XML namespace. The ApplicationBar is a subset of PhoneApplicationPage and can be defined directly in XAML as shown in Listing 4-58. ApplicationBar has two collections, the Buttons collection of ApplicationBarIconButton objects and the MenuItems collection of ApplicationBarMenuItem.

Listing 4-58. Declaring the ApplicationBar

```
<phone:PhoneApplicationPage.ApplicationBar>
    <shell:ApplicationBar>
        <shell:ApplicationBarIconButton IconUri="/assets/icons/dark/save.png" Text="save" />
        <shell:ApplicationBarIconButton IconUri="/assets/icons/dark/cancel.png" Text="cancel" />
        <shell:ApplicationBar.MenuItems>
            <shell:ApplicationBarMenuItem Text="menu item 1" />
            <shell:ApplicationBarMenuItem Text="menu item 2" />
            <shell:ApplicationBarMenuItem Text="menu item 3" />
        </shell:ApplicationBar.MenuItems>
    </shell:ApplicationBar>
</phone:PhoneApplicationPage.ApplicationBar>
```

You can define up to four buttons and five menu items. More than four buttons generates a XAML parse exception. Only five menu items are visible initially when the menu pops up. Clicking the ellipses causes the `ApplicationBar` to slide upwards and display an unlimited number of menu items in a scrolling list (see Figure 4-47).

Figure 4-47. *Invoking the ApplicationBar Menu*

WHY CAN'T I BIND THE APPLICATIONBAR?

The current *ApplicationBar is not a FrameworkElement* and does not participate in the dependency property system. This is a major problem for anyone hoping to use element naming, binding, commanding, and other XAML and MVVM related techniques with `ApplicationBar` button and menu items.

There are a number of Google-able workarounds like custom wrappers for `ApplicationBar`, calling commands from code behind or moving the `ApplicationBar` inside a view model and calling commands from there. One technique may work in a specific application, but none appear to be solutions to the general problem. Here is an abbreviated version of Peter Torr's (Microsoft) reply to this issue that summarizes it nicely:

> *...'Why can't I databind to the AppBar' or 'Why are my named AppBar objects always null in the code-behind?'...*

...the ApplicationBar is not a Silverlight element and thus not all Silverlight concepts apply to it. For example, you would expect that the Background could be set to any kind of brush - SolidColorBrush, LinearGradientBrush, and so on - but because the AppBar is actually rendered by the Windows Phone shell, it only supports a solid colour. You might also expect to be able to put arbitrary Content inside the buttons, or to apply RenderTransforms to the menu items, and so on. And you should be able to put it anywhere on the screen with HorizontalAlignment/VerticalAlignment, right? Again, none of these things are supported by the underlying shell UX, so they would all have to throw exceptions or no-op when called. And where's the fun in that?

...

That said, it is possible to make some FrameworkElement-derived wrappers for the AppBar if you're willing to do a bunch of work and be diligent about not relying on all the unsupported features or violating rules about what things can go in what collection. It's not something we'd like to ship in the core product though due to all the caveats.

Peter Torr, from his blog "Why are the ApplicationBar objects not FrameworkElements?"

(`http://blogs.msdn.com/b/ptorr/archive/2010/06/18/why-are-the-applicationbar-objects-not-frameworkelements.aspx`)

The ground rules for using `ApplicationBar` in your project are:

- A maximum of four buttons can be defined. Buttons will always display, but the text will be hidden until the menu items slide up.
- Any number of menu items can be defined, but only five will be visible at one time. The user can scroll to view all menu items. Menu items display text but not icons.
- To execute an action from a button or menu item, implement the `Click` event handler.
- Images for icons should be 48 x 48 pixels. Assign the image to the button `IconUri` property. Make sure that the `Build Action` property for each image file is set to "Content".
- Check out the Windows Phone 8 SDK icons for common tasks in `\Program Files (x86)\Microsoft SDKs\Windows Phone\<version>\Icons\`, in both light and dark styles (see Figure 4-48). The `Icons` directory also includes a vector, *.ai version.

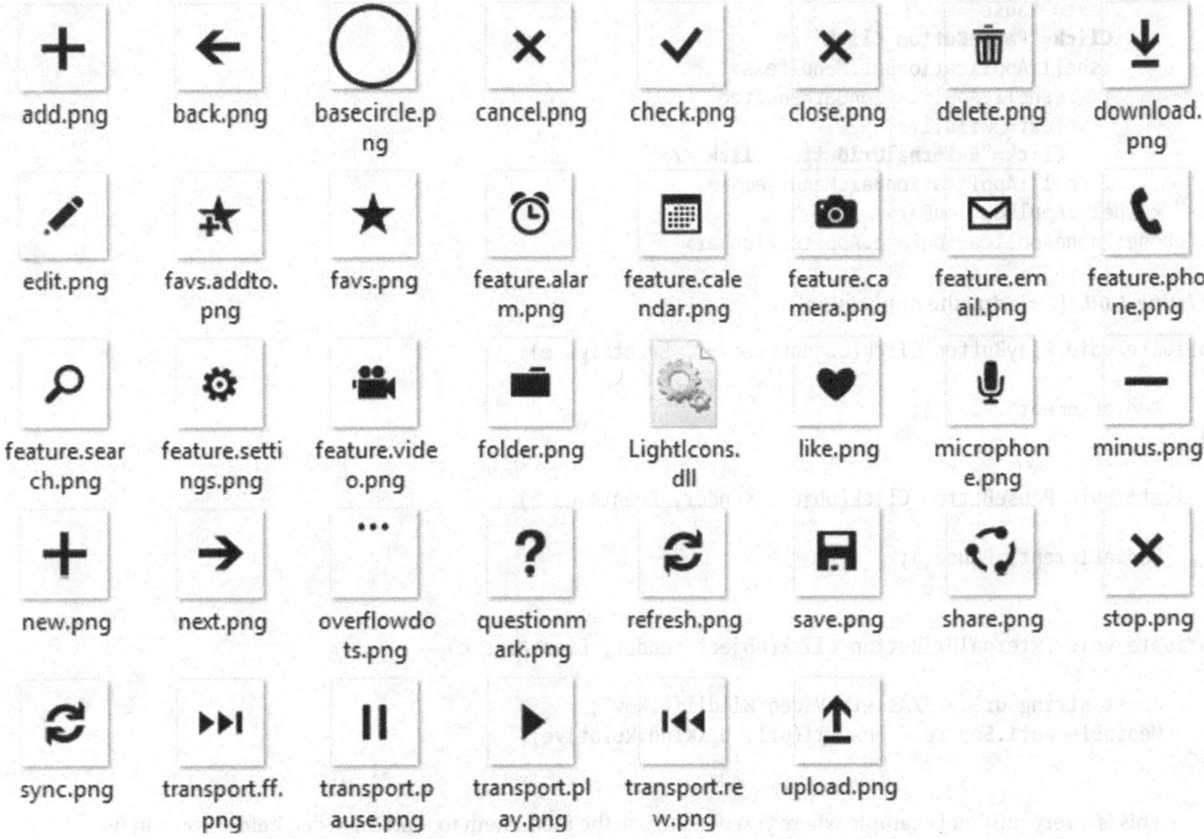

Figure 4-48. *SDK Icon Set*

Handling ApplicationBar Events

The user interacts with the `ApplicationBar` through the `Click` events triggered off the button and menu items. There is no ability to execute commands (see the "Why Can't I Bind the ApplicationBar?" sidebar). Listing 4-59 configures play and pause buttons and a menu item that loads a video to a `MediaElement`. The event handlers described in Listing 4-60 execute `MediaElement` methods.

Listing 4-59. Declaring Click Event Handlers

```
<phone:PhoneApplicationPage.ApplicationBar>
    <shell:ApplicationBar IsVisible="True" IsMenuEnabled="True">
        <shell:ApplicationBarIconButton
        IconUri="/Assets/Icons/Dark/transport.play.png"
        Text="Play"
        Click="PlayButton_Click" />
        <shell:ApplicationBarIconButton
        IconUri="/Assets/Icons/Dark/transport.pause.png"
```

```
        Text="Pause"
        Click="PauseButton_Click" />
        <shell:ApplicationBar.MenuItems>
            <shell:ApplicationBarMenuItem
            Text="wildlife"
            Click="ExternalUrlButton_Click" />
        </shell:ApplicationBar.MenuItems>
    </shell:ApplicationBar>
</phone:PhoneApplicationPage.ApplicationBar>
```

Listing 4-60. Declaring the ApplicationBar

```
private void PlayButton_Click(object sender, EventArgs e)
{
    MediaElement1.Play();
}

private void PauseButton_Click(object sender, EventArgs e)
{
    MediaElement1.Pause();
}

private void ExternalUrlButton_Click(object sender, EventArgs e)
{
    const string url = "/Assets/Video/Wildlife.wmv";
    MediaElement1.Source = new Uri(url, UriKind.Relative);
}
```

This is a very minimal example where you need to use the menu item to load the video before you can use the play and pause buttons (see Figure 4-49). There are no visual cues that enable and disable buttons based on MediaElement state. For a more complete example, see the "Media Controls" section of this chapter.

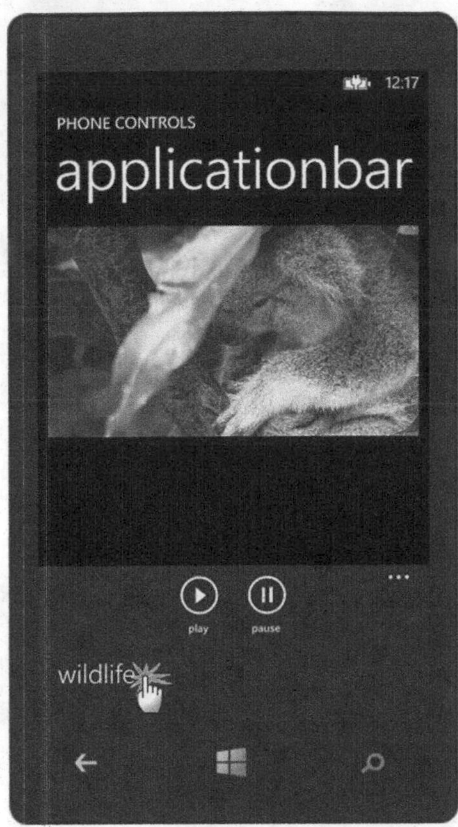

Figure 4-49. Running a Menu Item

Configure ApplicationBar in Code

Sample code for setting up the ApplicationBar is already embedded for you as comments in the MainPage.xaml.cs file. You will need to uncomment the call to BuildLocalizedApplicationBar() and its corresponding method. You will also need to add an icon graphic for the sample button and change the button's path to point back to the icon graphic, as shown in Listing 4-61.

Listing 4-61. Configuring the ApplicationBar in Code

```
// Sample code for building a localized ApplicationBar
private void BuildLocalizedApplicationBar()
{
    // Set the page's ApplicationBar to a new instance of ApplicationBar.
    ApplicationBar = new ApplicationBar();

    // Create a new button and set the text value to the localized string from AppResources.
    ApplicationBarIconButton appBarButton =
        new ApplicationBarIconButton(new Uri("/Assets/Icons/Dark/add.png", UriKind.Relative));
    appBarButton.Text = AppResources.AppBarButtonText;
    ApplicationBar.Buttons.Add(appBarButton);
```

```
    // Create a new menu item with the localized string from AppResources.
    ApplicationBarMenuItem appBarMenuItem = new
        ApplicationBarMenuItem(AppResources.AppBarMenuItemText);
    ApplicationBar.MenuItems.Add(appBarMenuItem);
}
```

Context Menus

Use the `ContextMenu` attached property of `ContextMenuService` from the Windows Phone 8 toolkit to create menus that respond to tap-and-hold gestures on a given element. `ContextMenu` can be attached to any `DependencyObject`. Figure 4-50 shows an example that attaches the `ContextMenu` to a `TextBox` element.

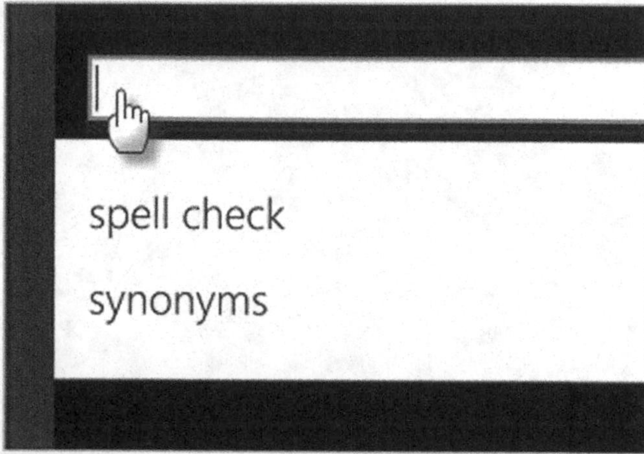

Figure 4-50. *Invoking the ContextMenu*

The XAML in Listing 4-62 defines a `ContextMenu` and its menu items inside the `TextBox` element tag. To use this XAML, you will need to first install the toolkit (see "Installing the Windows Phone 8 Toolkit" instructions in this chapter) and add a XML namespace named "toolkit" to the page.

Listing 4-62. Defining a ContextMenu for a TextBox

```
<TextBox VerticalAlignment="Top" HorizontalAlignment="Stretch">
    <toolkit:ContextMenuService.ContextMenu>
        <toolkit:ContextMenu>
            <toolkit:MenuItem Header="spell check"
                              Tag="spellcheck"
                              Click="Context_Menu_Click">
            </toolkit:MenuItem>
            <toolkit:MenuItem Header="synonyms"
                              Tag="synonyms"
                              Click="Context_Menu_Click">
            </toolkit:MenuItem>

        </toolkit:ContextMenu>
    </toolkit:ContextMenuService.ContextMenu>
</TextBox>
```

ContextMenu is an ItemsControl and can have a collection of items. ContextMenu can also be bound or templated. ContextMenu has a few unique properties that control behavior and positioning:

- **IsOpen** can be set programmatically or through binding to open or close the menu.
- **IsZoomEnabled** controls a zoom effect on the background when a menu item is open.
- **VerticalOffset** controls the distance between the target origin and the menu popup.
- **OnClosed** and **OnOpen** events fire as the user toggles the menu.

Each MenuItem has a Command property for MVVM-friendly support or you can go "old-school" and use the Click event handler. Assign content to the Header property to represent the menu item visually. All FrameworkElement descendants have an object Tag property that can store arbitrary data. The code snippet in Listing 4-63 shows the Click event handler retrieving the MenuItem from the sender parameter and displaying the Tag contents.

Listing 4-63. Handling the Menu Click Event

```
private void Context_Menu_Click(object sender, RoutedEventArgs e)
{
    MenuItem item = sender as MenuItem;
    MessageBox.Show(item.Tag.ToString());
}
```

To include images or other elements in a MenuItem, expand the Header property from a simple attribute assignment to the full element property syntax (see Figure 4-51). Inside the Header, add a container (e.g., StackPanel, Grid), then add your Image and TextBlock elements.

Figure 4-51. *Context Menu items with Images*

The example in Listing 4-64 replaces the ContextMenu defined in Listing 4-64 and replaces it with XAML that fills the MenuItem.Header with an icon and text. The Rectangle with OpacityMask displays the icon in either light or dark theme. To use this XAML, you will need to first install the toolkit (see "Installing the Windows Phone 8 Toolkit" instructions in this chapter) and add a XML namespace named "toolkit" to the page. You will also need to add icons to the project \assets folder.

Listing 4-64. Handling the Menu Click Event

```
<toolkit:ContextMenuService.ContextMenu>
    <toolkit:ContextMenu>

        <toolkit:MenuItem Tag="spellcheck" Click="Context_Menu_Click">
            <toolkit:MenuItem.Header>
                <StackPanel Orientation="Horizontal">
                    <Rectangle Fill="{StaticResource PhoneBackgroundBrush}"
                               Width="32" Height="32" >
                        <Rectangle.OpacityMask>
                            <ImageBrush ImageSource="/Assets/Icons/light/questionmark.png" />
                        </Rectangle.OpacityMask>
                    </Rectangle>

                    <TextBlock Text="spell check" />
                </StackPanel>
            </toolkit:MenuItem.Header>
        </toolkit:MenuItem>

        <toolkit:MenuItem Tag="synonyms" Click="Context_Menu_Click">
            <toolkit:MenuItem.Header>
                <StackPanel Orientation="Horizontal">
                    <Rectangle Fill="{StaticResource PhoneBackgroundBrush}"
                               Width="32" Height="32" >
                        <Rectangle.OpacityMask>
                            <ImageBrush ImageSource="/Assets/Icons/light/refresh.png" />
                        </Rectangle.OpacityMask>
                    </Rectangle>
                    <TextBlock Text="synonyms" />
                </StackPanel>
            </toolkit:MenuItem.Header>
        </toolkit:MenuItem>

    </toolkit:ContextMenu>
</toolkit:ContextMenuService.ContextMenu>
```

■ **Note** Windows Phone 8 comes with a standard set of icons (e.g., Play, Back, Check, Folder, etc.) located at `\Program Files (x86)\Microsoft SDKs\Windows Phone\v8.0\Icons`.

Using Commands with MenuItem

`ContextMenu` items support `Command` and `CommandParameter` properties, making the `ContextMenu` control ideal for binding to view model data and commands. The example in Figure 4-52 displays a series of subjects in a `LongListSelector`. Invoking the context menu displays a caption that searches on the current subject and if clicked, invokes a command that runs a search task (More on built-in Windows Phone 8 tasks in the Windows Phone 8 API chapter).

Figure 4-52. Context Menu Invoking Command

Listings 4-65 through 4-67 describe the command, the command's place in the ViewModel and the ViewModel binding to the LongListSelector. The list of subjects is not shown here, but consists of a Subject object with Title and Description properties, and a List<Subject>.

Listing 4-65. The Search Command

```
public class SearchCommand : ICommand
{
    public bool CanExecute(object parameter)
    {
        return (parameter != null) && (parameter is string);
    }

    public event EventHandler CanExecuteChanged;

    public void Execute(object parameter)
    {
        SearchTask searchTask = new SearchTask();
        searchTask.SearchQuery = parameter as string;
        searchTask.Show();
    }
}
```

Listing 4-66. The ViewModel

```
public class SubjectViewModel
{
    public Subjects Subjects { get; set;  }
    public SearchCommand SearchCommand { get; set; }
    public SubjectViewModel()
    {
        this.Subjects = new Subjects();
        this.SearchCommand = new SearchCommand();
    }
}
```

Listing 4-67. ContextMenu Command Binding

```
<phone:PhoneApplicationPage.Resources>
    <local:SubjectViewModel x:Key="SubjectViewModel" />

    <DataTemplate x:Key="SubjectTemplate">
        <TextBlock Text="{Binding Description}" >
            <toolkit:ContextMenuService.ContextMenu>
                <toolkit:ContextMenu>
                    <toolkit:MenuItem
                        Command="{Binding Source={StaticResource SubjectViewModel},
                            Path=SearchCommand}"
                            CommandParameter="{Binding Path=Title}">
                        <toolkit:MenuItem.Header>
                            <StackPanel Orientation="Horizontal">
                                <TextBlock Text="{Binding Path=Title,
                                    StringFormat='search on {0}'}" />
                            </StackPanel>
                        </toolkit:MenuItem.Header>
                    </toolkit:MenuItem>
                </toolkit:ContextMenu>
            </toolkit:ContextMenuService.ContextMenu>
        </TextBlock>
    </DataTemplate>
</phone:PhoneApplicationPage.Resources
<!-- . . . -->

<Grid x:Name="LayoutRoot" Background="Transparent"
    DataContext="{StaticResource SubjectViewModel}">

<!-- . . . -->

<phone:LongListSelector
    x:Name="LongListSelector1"
    VerticalAlignment="Stretch" HorizontalAlignment="Stretch"
    ItemTemplate="{StaticResource SubjectTemplate}"
    ItemsSource="{Binding Subjects}" >
</phone:LongListSelector>
```

CONTEXT MENU BINDING ISSUES

Context menu items binding can get out of sync when used with list controls that are heavily virtualized, such as `LongListSelector`. Changes to the `DataContext` of the parent, that is, the `LongListSelector` are not propagated to the `ContextMenu`. You can work around this by assigning the `ContextMenu Unloaded` event to clear the `DataContext` property and force a rebinding.

```
private void ContextMenu_Unloaded_1(object sender, RoutedEventArgs e)
{
    var contextMenu = sender as ContextMenu;
    contextMenu.ClearValue(FrameworkElement.DataContextProperty);
}
```

Media Controls

Media controls present images, multi-scale images, sound, or video files. The `Image`, `MultiScaleImage`, and `MediaElement` controls allow you to incorporate rich media directly into your own application without having to invoke some other process.

Resources vs. Content

The Properties pane `Build Action` must be set to `Resource` or `Content` for images and other media files. There are plenty of other options, but they don't apply for our purposes.

When you add an image or drag an image from the Windows Explorer, the `Build Action` of the image file is Content by default. When the `Build Action` is Content, you point to files in the project using a relative path (i.e., preceded with a slash). Instead of being loaded from the assembly, the file is loaded alongside the assembly, as a sibling. If you build the application and unzip the XAP file, you can see that the files marked Content are placed at the same level with the application assembly. By contrast, the paths for files marked Resource are not preceded with a slash and are contained inside the assembly.

What are the performance implications? Windows Phone 8 is optimized for files and network streams (but not in-memory streams). When the file `Build Action` is Resource, the file has to be streamed, which decreases performance. For videos, the resource is copied to the phone before playback, another performance hit. In contrast, Content files are available immediately, and are played back directly for videos. The short story is to leave the `Build Action` setting to Content for all your media files.

Image

The `Image Source` property knows how to convert data from multiple sources: external URLs, paths to images in your DLL, or paths within the project. The `Stretch` property controls image proportions along with the standard `Height` and `Width` properties. The example in Listing 4-68 points the `Source` to an icon at the Twitter logo download site and applies a `Uniform Stretch` to keep the image proportional, as shown in Figure 4-53.

Listing 4-68. Image with Source and Stretch Properties

```
<Image
Source="http://a0.twimg.com/a/1312493385/images/logos/logo_twitter_wordmark_1000.png"
Stretch="Uniform" Height="200" Width="250" />
```

Figure 4-53. *Image with Uniform Stretch*

The example in Figure 4-54 shows the effect of the `Stretch` property on a given image. The example here uses the Twitter logo. A three-pixel red border around each Image makes it easy to see the `Image` boundaries.

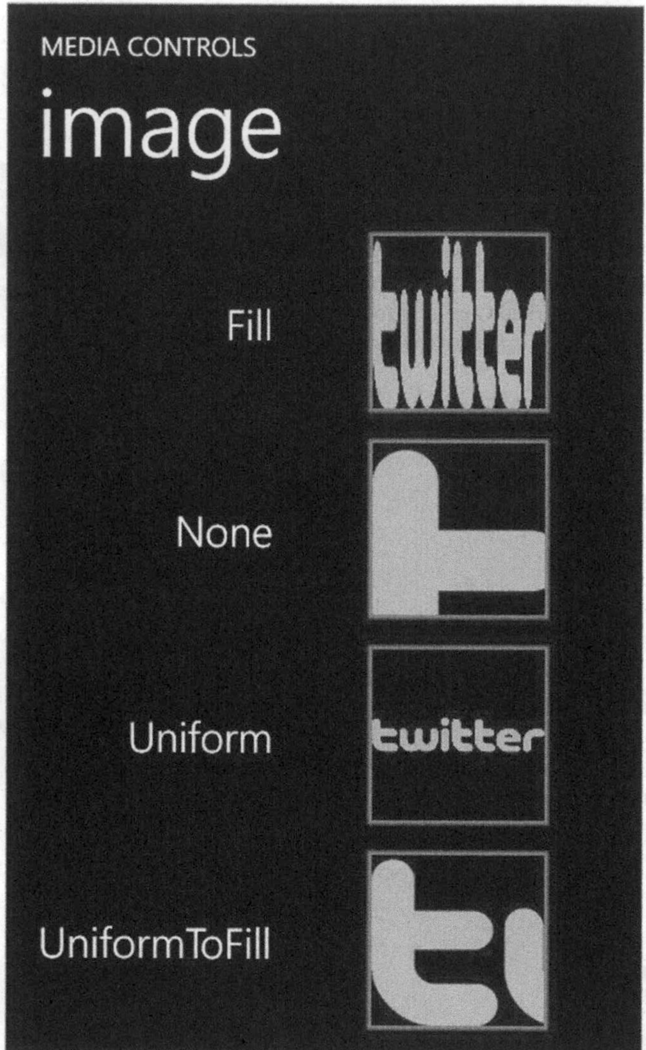

***Figure 4-54.** Image Stretch Settings*

- The `Fill` setting causes the Image to adopt the exact width and height dimensions of the Image, while ignoring proportion.
- `None` displays the image in its original dimensions. This option retains the proportion and fidelity of the original image but clips the `Image Width` and `Height` boundaries.
- `Uniform` displays the entire graphic within `Image` boundaries while preserving proportions.
- `UniformToFill` also preserves proportions, fills to the dimensions of the `Image`, but may extend past the `Image` boundaries.

MultiScaleImage

Images have a 2000 x 2000 limit in Windows Phone 8, but there are circumstances that need larger images or that require "Deep Zoom" capability:

- High-resolution images over 2000 x 2000.
- Panoramas where a set of overlapping photographs form a wide banner.
- Collections of images, such as photo albums or large sets of tiles that represent business entities.

The `MultiScaleImage` control allows the user to zoom in on a particular part of the image while maintaining sharp clarity. `MultiScaleImage` uses an XML file with a specific *Deep Zoom* format (see `http://msdn.microsoft.com/en-us/library/cc645077(v=vs.95).aspx` for details on the Deep Zoom format). The Deep Zoom format describes an image "pyramid" where the picture is divided into progressively higher resolution sub images (see Figure 4-55).

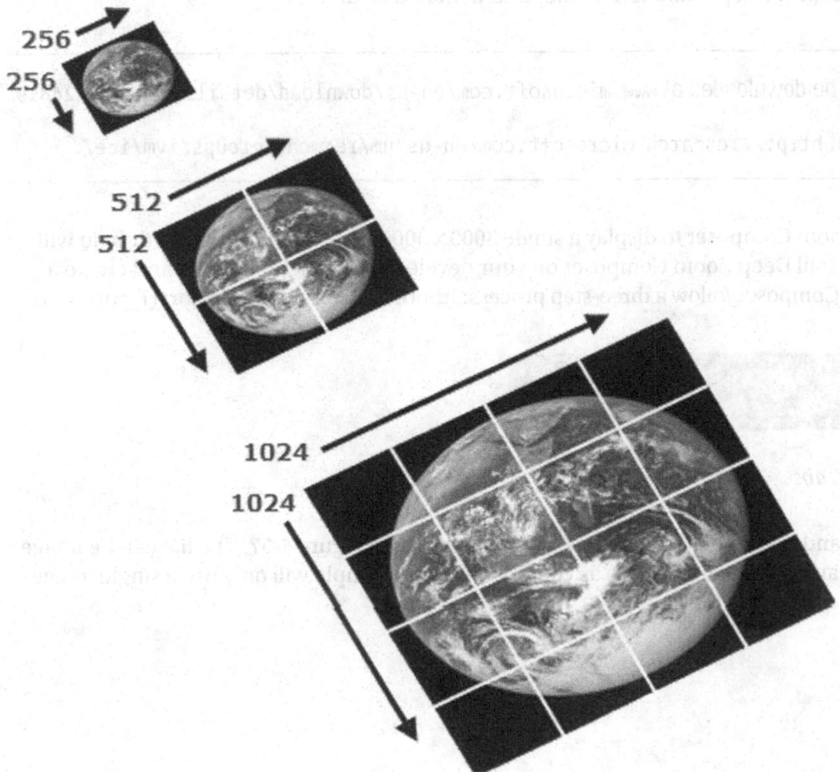

Figure 4-55. *Deep Zoom "Pyramid"*

■ **Note** Be aware that `MultiScaleImage` makes it possible to perform pinch-to-zoom, flicking and panning but does not actually supply these behaviors. You need to code these behaviors yourself. See the Windows Phone API chapter section on "Gestures" to learn how to implement these behaviors. In the example that follows, we will add ApplicationBar buttons to zoom in and out.

The steps to creating a Deep Zoom application are:

1. Create a Deep Zoom XML file and associated folders and images. We will discuss utilities that automate this step.
2. Deploy the Deep Zoom format files and folders to a web site. You will need to provide a host site that can be accessed through HTTP.
3. Assign the XML file to the `MultiScaleImage Source` property. You should be able to see the image in the Visual Studio design view if the path to the `Source` is valid.
4. Add behaviors through code or XAML for zooming and panning.

Create Deep Zoom Source Files

To slice the images into Deep Zoom format, use one of the utilities from Microsoft such as *Deep Zoom Composer* or *Image Composite Editor*. Both tools export Deep Zoom format files and folder structure.

■ **Note** *Deep Zoom Composer* can be downloaded at `www.microsoft.com/en-us/download/details.aspx?id=24819`. *Image Composite Editor* is available at `http://research.microsoft.com/en-us/um/redmond/groups/ivm/ice/`.

This next example uses Deep Zoom Composer to display a single 3000 x 3000 JPEG image of the Earth (you will need to obtain your own images). Install Deep Zoom Composer on your development machine, run it and create a new project. The tabs in Deep Zoom Composer follow a three-step process: Import ➤ Compose ➤ Export (Figure 4-56).

Figure 4-56. *Deep Zoom Composer Tabs*

Click the `Add image...` button and open a high-resolution image, as shown in Figure 4-57. The file can be image types TIFF, JPG, BMP, or PNG. You can add as many images as you like, but this example will only use a single image.

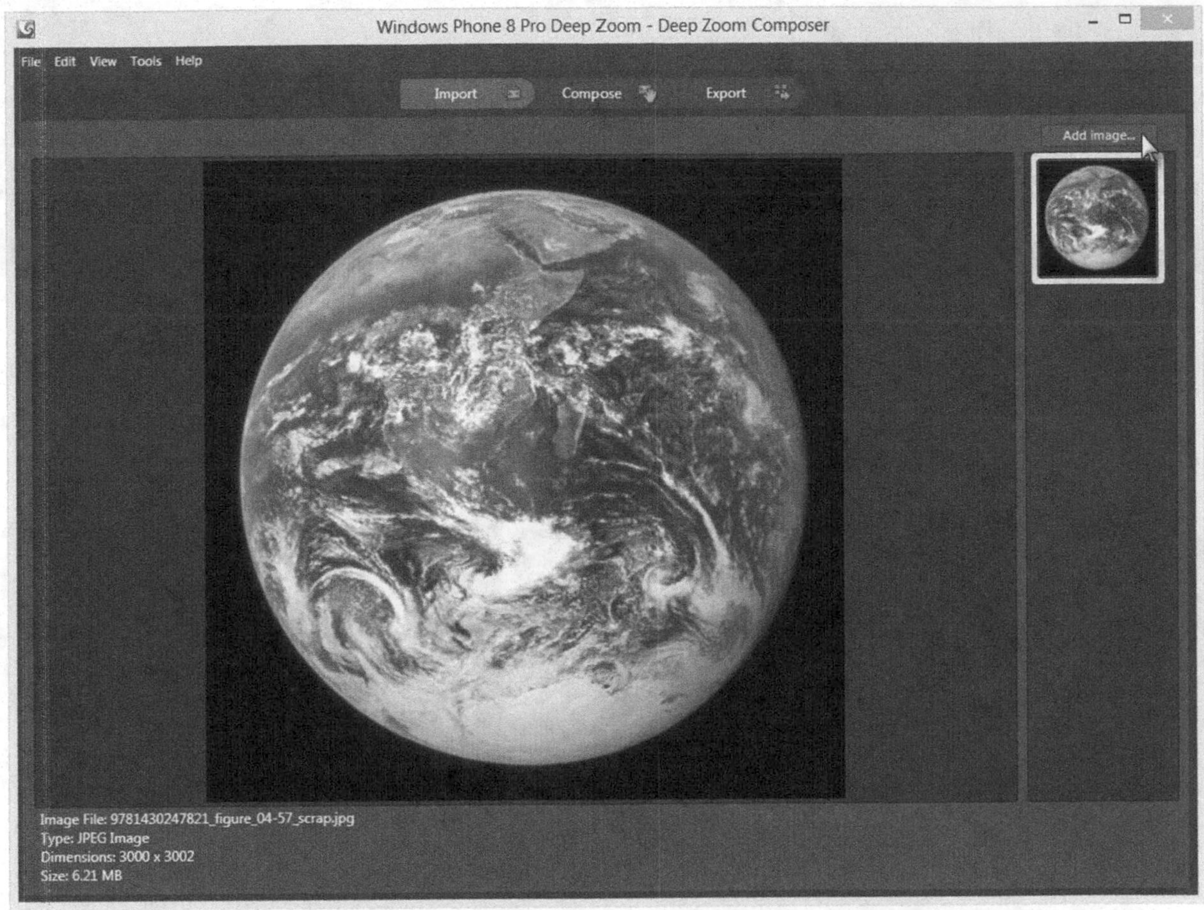

***Figure 4-57.** Imported Image in Deep Zoom Composer*

Click on the `Compose` tab to arrange imported images. Drag your images from the tray at the bottom of the screen onto the Artboard.

Click the `Export` tab to output the images in Deep Zoom format. Set the `Output type` to `Images`. You can also use the Silverlight Deep Zoom option if you want a Visual Studio or Expression Blend project that you can run in a browser. In this example, we only need the XML file and folders with images. Provide a `Name` that will be used for the folder that contains the output. Set the `Export Options` to `Export as a composition (single image)`. Click the `Export` button. When the Export Completed dialog displays, click the `View Image Folders` option (Figure 4-58).

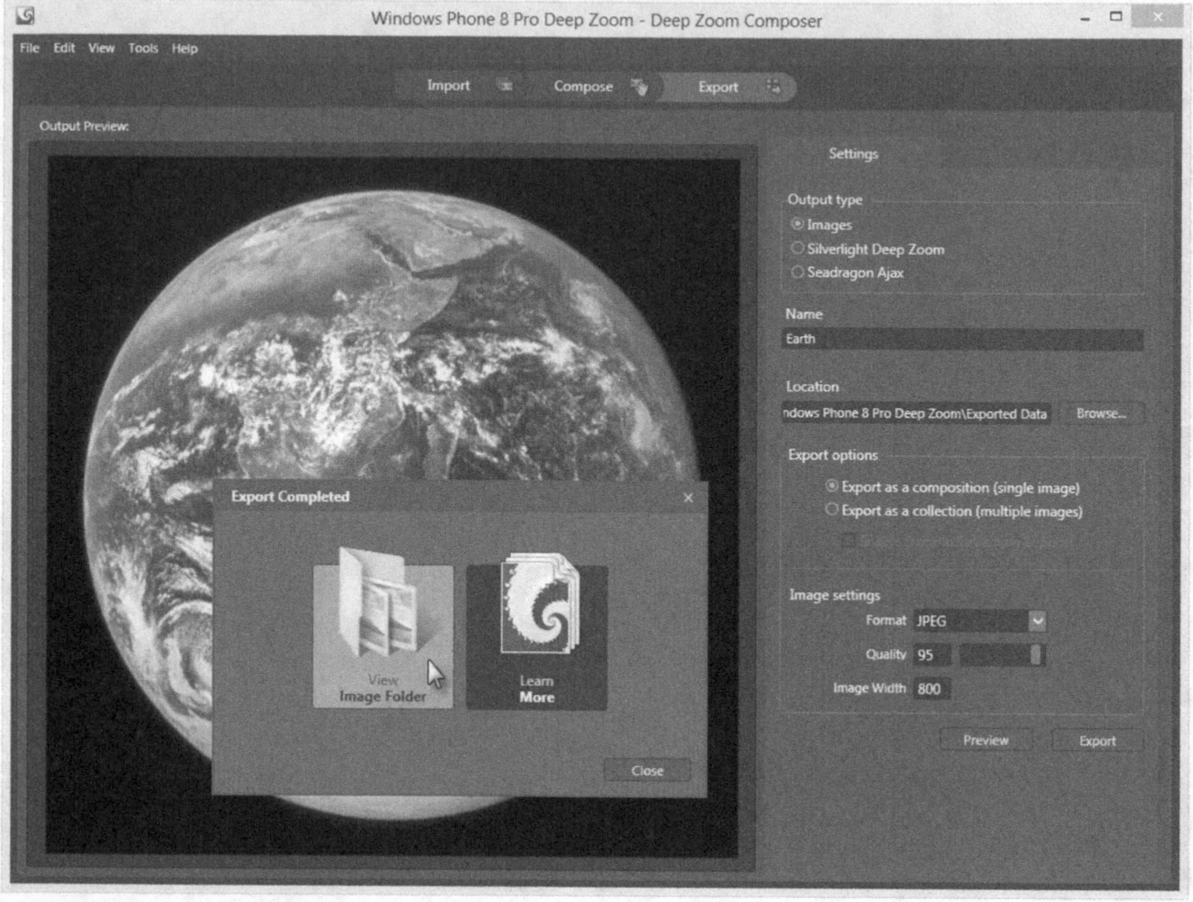

Figure 4-58. *Completed Export*

The key entries you need access to are the `dzc_output.xml` and the `dzc_output_files` folder. Figure 4-59 shows the files that need to be deployed to an external website.

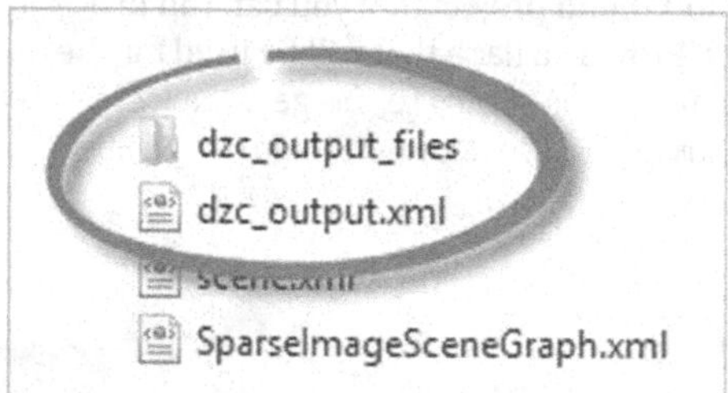

Figure 4-59. *Deep Zoom Composer Exported Files*

Deploy the Deep Zoom Output Files

Copy dzc_output.xml and dzc_output_files to an HTTP accessible website. Because of the large image sizes, these files can't be hosted on the phone device itself. Also avoid hosting on the local machine. Local self-hosting can work if you're running from the emulator and using your local machine's IP address, but the application will fail on the phone if it doesn't have access to that same IP address. It takes a little extra effort to host your files on an external HTTP web site, but hosting in this way will display the images on both the Emulator and on the device.

Assign MultiScaleImage Properties

At minimum, the MultiScaleImage Source property must be assigned the path to the dzc_output.xml file (Listing 4-69).

Listing 4-69. Image with Source and Stretch Properties

```
<MultiScaleImage x:Name="msi"
    Source=http://blog.falafel.com/fictional_location/dzc_output.xml />
```

If the XML file and folders are in the correct format and the network location is accessible, the images should show in the control, even at design-time (Figure 4-60).

Figure 4-60. *MultiScaleImage at Design Time*

■ **Note** You can instead assign the `Source` property to a `DeepZoomImageTileSource` in code:

```
MultiScaleImage1.Source = new DeepZoomImageTileSource(new
System.Uri("http://my_site/dzc_output.xml", UriKind.Absolute));
```

Add Behaviors

Even after `MultiScaleImage` properties are assigned, there is no built-in ability to handle pan or zoom behavior. There is a single method on the `MultiScaleImage` that zooms in on the image:

```
ZoomAboutLogicalPoint(zoomIncrementFactor, zoomCenterLogicalX, zoomCenterLogicalY)
```

The `zoomIncrementFactor` is a number greater than 0, where a value of 1 indicates the image fits the screen exactly. Smaller numbers zoom out, numbers larger than 1 zoom in. The `zoomCenterLogicalX` and `zoomCenterLogicalY` are the points in the `MultiScaleImage` that are zoomed on. `Logical` in this instance indicates a value between 0 and 1. For example, 0.5 is the center of the `MultiScaleImage`. The example in Listing 4-70 shows click event handlers for ApplicationBar buttons. The zoomIncrementFactor is 0.8 to zoom in, 1.2 to zoom out. The last two parameters indicate that the `MultiScaleImage` is centered.

Listing 4-70. MultiScaleImage Zoom

```
private void ZoomOutClick(object sender, EventArgs e)
{
    msi.ZoomAboutLogicalPoint(0.8, 0.5, 0.5);
}

private void ZoomInClick(object sender, EventArgs e)
{
    msi.ZoomAboutLogicalPoint(1.2, 0.5, 0.5);
}
```

The screenshots of the running application in Figure 4-61 show the effect of the `ZoomInClick()` method.

Figure 4-61. *Zooming in*

`MultiScaleImage` has nothing built in to move or pan the view. The position within the larger image is controlled by the `ViewportOrigin` property. By default, `ViewportOrigin` is 0,0 in the upper-lefthand corner of the control. By getting new coordinates from the user through a Tap or other gesture, you can reset the `ViewportOrigin`. The code in Listing 4-71 simplifies the problem by getting the coordinate position of the pointer when the `MultiScaleImage` is tapped. This coordinate is "massaged" to take the screen dimensions into account and to reverse the sign so that the image appears to be drawn towards the pointer.

Listing 4-71. Changing the ViewportOrigin

```
private void msi_Tap(object sender, System.Windows.Input.GestureEventArgs e)
{
    // get the pointer position on the msi element
    var pos = e.GetPosition(msi);

    // offset by half the msi dimensions
    var x = -(pos.X - (msi.ActualWidth / 2));
    var y = -(pos.Y - (msi.ActualHeight / 2));

    // assign the new viewport origin
    msi.ViewportOrigin = msi.ElementToLogicalPoint(new Point(x, y));
}
```

The running application shown in Figure 4-62 shows a zoomed-out image moving towards the pointer at the bottom right of the Emulator.

Figure 4-62. *Setting the ViewportOrigin*

MultiScaleImage Events

When the full image loads, the `MultiScaleImage ImageOpenSucceeded` event fires unless there's a catastrophic error that results in the `ImageOpenFailed` event firing. A third event, `ImageFailed`, is not catastrophic but indicates that one of the image tiles has failed to download or timed out. If `ImageFailed` event fires, the user may still be able to see the image.

The `ViewportChanged` event will fire multiple times when zooming or panning. To make it easier to see all the events, the output for the `ViewportChanged` event in Figure 4-63 has been reduced to just the first and last occurrences. The events are ordered with the newest event on top. When the control has completed zooming and panning, the `MotionFinished` event fires.

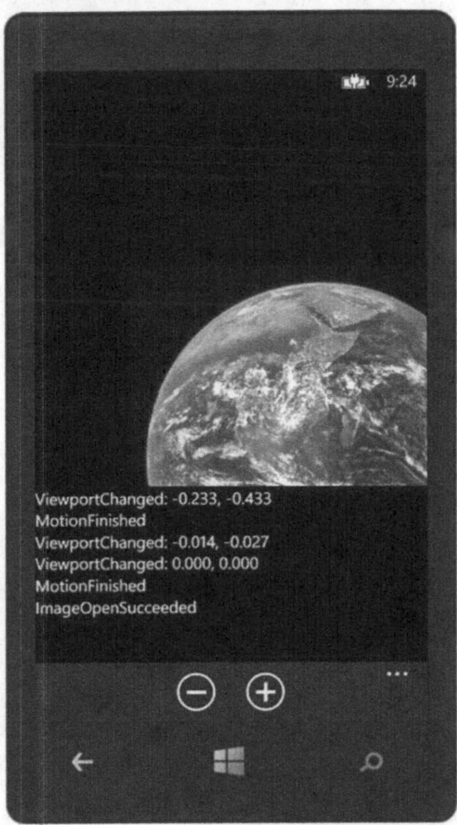

Figure 4-63. *MultiScaleImage Events*

MediaElement

If you don't need to customize the control layout to play media, you can simply use `MediaPlayerLauncher` to add audio or video into your application. See the Windows Phone API chapter, Built-In Tasks section for more information. Listing 4-72 demonstrates using the `MediaPlayerLauncher`.

Listing 4-72. Using MediaPlayerLauncher

```
MediaPlayerLauncher launcher = new MediaPlayerLauncher();
launcher.Media =
    new Uri(
"http://imgsrc.hubblesite.org/hu/gallery/db/video/hm_helix_twist/formats/hm_helix_twist_320x240.wmv");
launcher.Show();
```

The `MediaElement` allows you to tailor how the control will look and respond to events (see Figure 4-64). To use the `MediaElement`, at minimum you need to assign the `Source` property and either call the `Play()` method or set the `AutoPlay` property to `True`. Listing 4-73 simply loads a file `car.wmv` from the `Assets` project folder. `AutoPlay` is set to `True`, so the video starts immediately once the media is loaded.

Listing 4-73. Defining MediaElement

```
<MediaElement VerticalAlignment="Stretch"
    HorizontalAlignment="Stretch"
    Source="Assets/car.wmv"
    AutoPlay="True" />
```

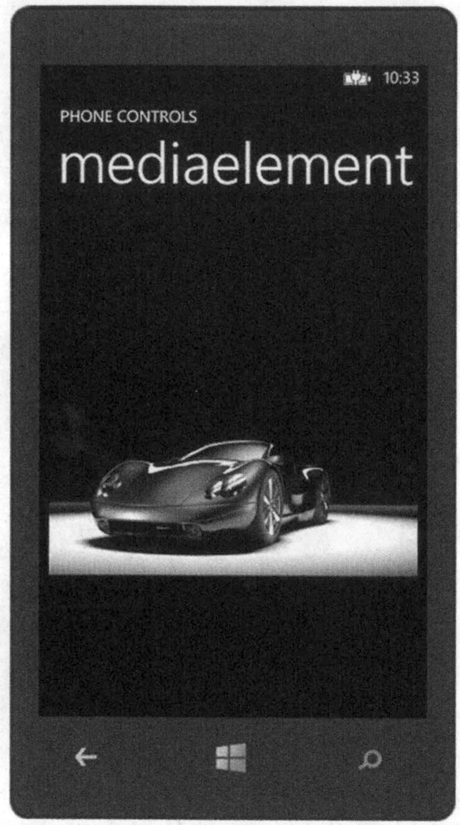

Figure 4-64. *MediaElement Playing*

■ **Caution** One of the big "gotchas" with `MediaElement` is simply getting the correct format content to play. This is not a trivial issue. A format may only be supported in certain scenarios, may have certain maximum capabilities, or a particular format may not play at all in the Emulator. The MSDN article, Supported Media Codecs for Windows Phone, has the details organized in matrix format with columns for Decoder Support, Container (Wav, MP3, MP4, etc.), Possible Audio Combinations, Max Capabilities, and Supported Scenarios.

`http://msdn.microsoft.com/en-us/library/windowsphone/develop/ff462087(v=vs.105).aspx`

MediaElement Operations

Look at any industry standard media player and you will see a common set of controls that include the ability to stop, start, pause, and reposition the video, sound controls for volume, balance, and mute, and some set of indicators for download buffering and current progress.

These basic capabilities are all supported in the `MediaElement` control. Sound is controlled by `Balance`, `Volume`, and `IsMuted` properties. Video is controlled by methods `Play()`, `Pause()`, and `Stop()`. Move the current location in the video using the `Position` property. Position is also a good candidate for binding sliders or progress bars. `CurrentState` is another valuable property used to bind controls so that they automatically reflect the condition of a `MediaElement`. The `MediaElement CurrentState` can be one of the following:

- Closed
- Opening
- Buffering
- Playing
- Stopped
- Individualizing (checking for components related to Digital Rights Management)
- AquiringLicense (obtaining a license required to play DRM protected content)

Properties `CanSeek` (true if able to set `Position` property) and `CanPause` (true if able to call the `Pause` method) are helpful for setting the visual state of your UI controls. You can get extra feedback for your user by displaying the `DownloadProgress`, `BufferingProgress`, and `NaturalDuration` (total playing time, only available after buffering for online sources). These properties have corresponding events that fire when there's a change.

The snippet code below demonstrates how the methods, states, and events are used in conjunction with the `ApplicationBar`. The `ApplicationBar` currently limits commanding, so the code in Listing 4-74 is expressed in code-behind instead of binding.

Listing 4-74. Assigning MediaElement Events

```
void MediaWindow_CurrentStateChanged(object sender, RoutedEventArgs e)
{
    playButton.IsEnabled = MediaWindow.CurrentState != MediaElementState.Playing;
    pauseButton.IsEnabled = MediaWindow.CanPause ?
        MediaWindow.CurrentState != MediaElementState.Paused : false;
}

void MediaWindow_MediaFailed(object sender, ExceptionRoutedEventArgs e)
{
    MessageBox.Show(e.ErrorException.Message);
}

private void RewindButton_Click(object sender, EventArgs e)
{
    MediaWindow.Position = new TimeSpan(0);
}

private void PlayButton_Click(object sender, EventArgs e)
{
    MediaWindow.Play();
}
```

```
private void PauseButton_Click(object sender, EventArgs e)
{
    MediaWindow.Pause();
}

private void FastForwardButton_Click(object sender, EventArgs e)
{
    TimeSpan current = MediaWindow.Position;
    MediaWindow.Position =
        current.Add(new TimeSpan(0, 0, 1));
}
```

In particular, you should handle the `MediaFailed` event. `MediaFailed` provides instant feedback if the video is not supported or some other issue raises its ugly head. If you receive the error AG_E_NETWORK_ERROR, this may indicate that the source is not found or is corrupt. Check the filename and extension. The extension should be of a known type. Play the video in the Windows Media Player to determine if the file is corrupt. If the media file is stored in your project, double-check the `Build Action` and make sure that the syntax of the Source path agrees with the `Build Action` (i.e., if Content should be preceded with a slash and if Resource should not have a preceding slash).

Popups

Popup is an element that contains content in a `Child` property and has an `IsOpen` property that toggles the popup visibility. `VerticalOffset` and `HorizontalOffset` position the popup in the control, as shown in Figure 4-65.

Figure 4-65. *Open Popup*

Listing 4-75 defines a popup with some text and a logo image. A Button click displays the popup and a tap on the popup hides the popup.

Listing 4-75. Defining a Popup

```
<Button Content="Show Popup"
    Click="Button_Click"
    HorizontalAlignment="Left"
    VerticalAlignment="Top" />
<Popup x:Name="MyPopup" VerticalOffset="150"  HorizontalOffset="120">
    <Popup.Child>

        <Border  BorderBrush="Red"  BorderThickness="3">
            <StackPanel Margin="1" Tap="MyPopup_Tap"
                        Orientation="Horizontal" Background="White">
                <Image Margin="5" Source="/Assets/falafel_logo_48px.png" />
                <TextBlock  Margin="5" Text="Text for my popup" Foreground="Black"/>
            </StackPanel>
        </Border>

    </Popup.Child>
</Popup>
```

The code in Listing 4-76 simply toggles the `IsOpen` property.

Listing 4-76. Opening and Closing the Popup

```
private void Button_Click(object sender, RoutedEventArgs e)
{
    MyPopup.IsOpen = true;
}

private void MyPopup_Tap(object sender, System.Windows.Input.GestureEventArgs e)
{
    MyPopup.IsOpen = false;
}
```

LongListSelector with Menus

This section demonstrates using the ApplicationBar menu items to switch between DataContexts. The exercise also shows how to respond to `LongListSelector` using events and through binding commands. Figure 4-66 shows the finished application where ApplicationBar menu items switch the `DataContext` between collections of astronomy, cooking, and language items. The right side of Figure 4-66 shows the tap-and-hold behavior that triggers the context menu.

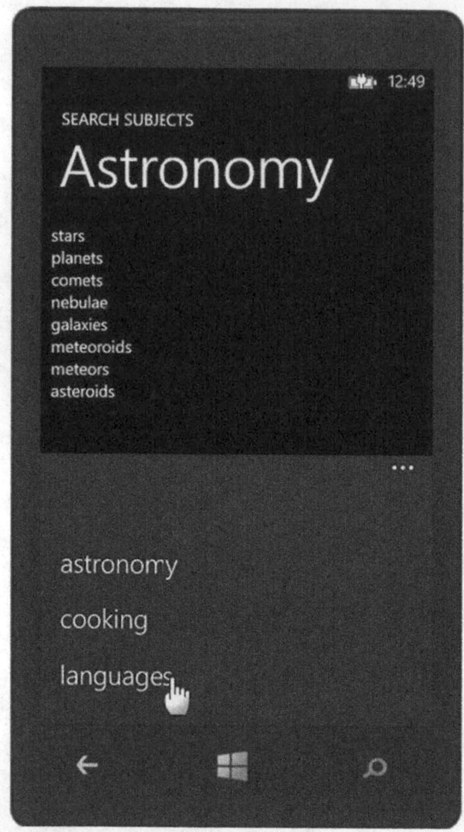

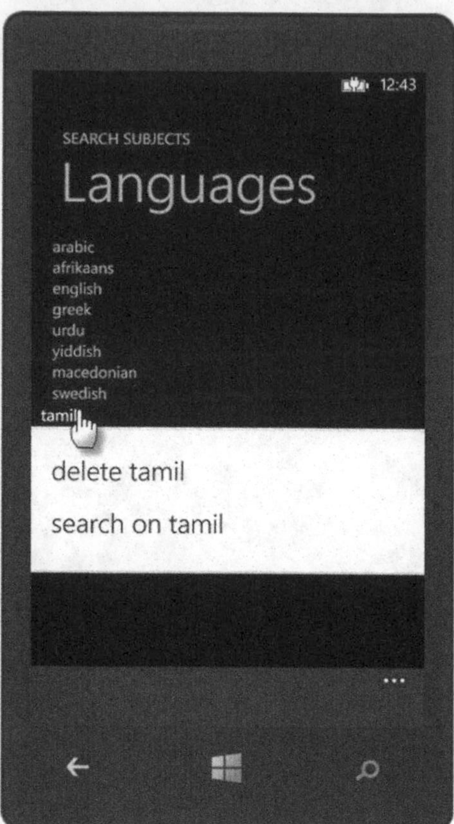

Figure 4-66. *Menu Operations Against the LongListSelector*

Prepare the Project

First prepare your project with the initial folders, images, classes, and packages you will need later.

1. Create a new Windows Phone Application.
2. In the Visual Studio Solution Explorer, create new folders Commands and ViewModels.
3. Copy the Icons folder from <program files>\Microsoft SDKs\Windows Phone\v8.0 directory to the project's Assets folder.

The project folder structure should now look something like Figure 4-67.

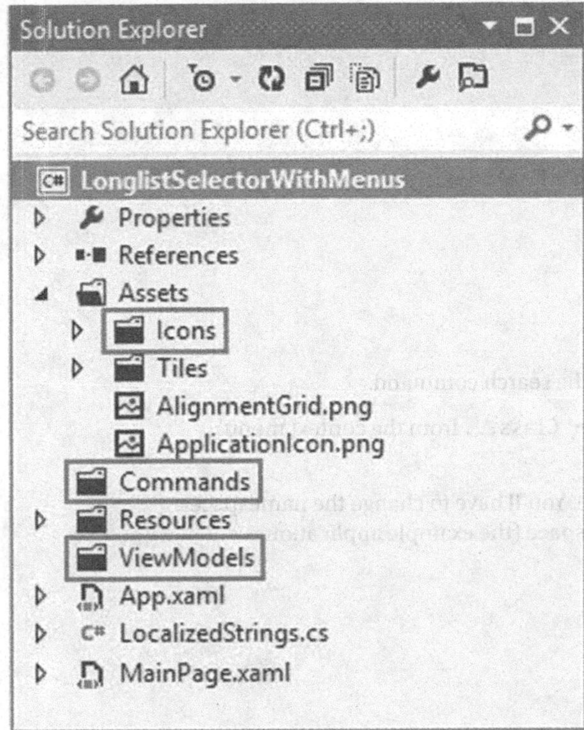

***Figure 4-67.** The Folder Structure*

4. In the Solution Explorer, right-click the References node and select `Manage NuGet Packages...` from the context menu.
5. In the Manage NuGet Packages dialog that displays, select the `Online` ➤ `NuGet official package source` from the outline on the left.
6. In the Search Online box on the right of the dialog, enter "Windows Phone Toolkit."
7. Select the package in the center list and click the `Install` button. When the install completes, close the dialog.
8. Create the Search Command
9. Right-click the `Commands` folder and select `Add` ➤ `Class...` from the context menu. Rename the file `SearchCommand.cs`.
10. Replace the class with the code below. Notice that the `CanExecute()` method returns true if a parameter is passed. That parameter will hold a search string. The `Execute()` method will initiate a `SearchTask` from the `Microsoft.Phone.Tasks` namespace.

```
public class SearchCommand : ICommand
{
    public bool CanExecute(object parameter)
    {
        return parameter != null;
    }
```

```
    public event EventHandler CanExecuteChanged;

    public void Execute(object parameter)
    {
        SearchTask searchTask = new SearchTask();
        searchTask.SearchQuery = parameter as string;
        searchTask.Show();
    }
}
```

Build the SubjectViewModel

Next, build the ViewModel to contain the search subjects and the search command.

1. Right-click the `ViewModels` folder and select `Add` ➤ `Class...` from the context menu. Rename the file `SubjectViewModel.cs`.

2. Add the following namespaces to the "uses" clause. You'll have to change the namespaces for `Commands` so that it uses your application namespace (the example application is named `LonglistSelectorWithMenus`).

```
using System.Collections.Generic;
using System.Collections.ObjectModel;
using System.Linq;
using LonglistSelectorWithMenus.Commands;
```

3. Make the `SubjectViewModel` class public and of a generic type as shown in the code below.

```
public class SubjectViewModel<T>
{

}
```

4. Add public properties for the title that will be shown above the list, the collection of subjects, and the search command.

```
public SearchCommand SearchCommand { get; private set; }
public ObservableCollection<T> Subjects { get; private set;}
public string Title { get; private set; }
```

5. Add a constructor to assign the title, collection, and search command.

```
public SubjectViewModel(string title)
{
    this.Title = title;
    this.SearchCommand = new SearchCommand();
    this.Subjects = new ObservableCollection<T>();
}
```

6. Add a method to include a series of generic objects in the collection.

```
public void AddSubjects(IEnumerable<T> subjects)
{
    foreach (var subject in subjects)
    {
        this.Subjects.Add(subject);
    }
}
```

7. Add a method to delete a single subject based on a string comparison.

```
public void DeleteSubject(string searchOn)
{
    var subject =
        this.Subjects.Single(s => s.ToString().Equals(searchOn));
    this.Subjects.Remove(subject);
}
```

Build the AppViewModel

Create an application-level ViewModel that pulls together the individual subject ViewModels.

1. Right-click the `ViewModels` folder and select Add ➤ `Class...` from the context menu. Rename the file `AppViewModel.cs`.
2. Modify the class to be public and to include three public collection properties.

```
public class AppViewModel
{
    public SubjectViewModel<string> Astronomy { get; private set; }
    public SubjectViewModel<string> Cooking { get; private set; }
    public SubjectViewModel<string> Languages { get; private set; }
}
```

3. Add a constructor to the class that populates each of the `SubjectViewModel` properties with unique titles and subject items.

```
public AppViewModel()
{
    this.Astronomy = new SubjectViewModel<string>("Astronomy");
    this.Astronomy.AddSubjects(new string[] {
        "stars" , "planets", "comets", "nebulae", "galaxies",
        "meteroids", "meteors", "asteroids"
    });

    this.Cooking = new SubjectViewModel<string>("Cooking");
    this.Cooking.AddSubjects(new string[] {
        "baking" , "roasting", "grilling", "searing", "boiling",
        "blanching", "smoking", "simmering", "stewing"
    });
```

```
        this.Languages = new SubjectViewModel<string>("Languages");
        this.Languages.AddSubjects(new string[] {
            "arabic" , "afrikaans", "english","french", "greek",
            "urdu", "yiddish", "macedonian", "swedish", "tamil", "bengali"
        });
    }
```

Build the User Interface

Add the user interface XAML that will list the subjects and display the commands.

1. Add an XML namespace to the toolkit in the phone:PhoneApplicationPage tag.

```
<phone:PhoneApplicationPage
    xmlns:toolkit="clr-namespace:Microsoft.Phone.Controls;assembly=Microsoft.Phone.
Controls.Toolkit" >
```

2. Add a Resources section with a single template that will be assigned to the LongListSelector ItemTemplate. The only item in the DataTemplate is a TextBlock that contains a ContextMenu. We will be binding to a collection of string, so the {Binding} markup refers to one of the strings in the collection. The first menu item in the ContextMenu definition simply calls a Click event handler. The second is bound to the SearchCommand and passes the search string as a parameter.

```
<phone:PhoneApplicationPage.Resources>
    <DataTemplate  x:Key="SubjectItemTemplate" >
        <TextBlock Text="{Binding}" >
            <toolkit:ContextMenuService.ContextMenu >
                <toolkit:ContextMenu Unloaded="ContextMenu_Unloaded_1">

                    <toolkit:MenuItem
                        Click="Delete_Subject"
                        Tag="{Binding}"
                        Header="{Binding StringFormat='delete {0}'}" />

                    <toolkit:MenuItem
                        Command="{Binding ElementName=LayoutRoot,
                            Path=DataContext.SearchCommand}"
                        CommandParameter="{Binding}"
                        Header="{Binding StringFormat='search on {0}'}" />

                </toolkit:ContextMenu>
            </toolkit:ContextMenuService.ContextMenu>
        </TextBlock>
    </DataTemplate>
</phone:PhoneApplicationPage.Resources>
```

3. Modify the TitlePanel stack panel element so that the TextBlock elements are defined. The second TextBlock is bound to the view model's Title property.

```
<StackPanel x:Name="TitlePanel" Grid.Row="0" Margin="12,17,0,28">
    <TextBlock Text="SEARCH SUBJECTS" Style="{StaticResource PhoneTextNormalStyle}"
Margin="12,0"/>
    <TextBlock Text="{Binding Title}" Margin="9,-7,0,0" Style="{StaticResource
PhoneTextTitle1Style}"/>
</StackPanel>
```

4. Inside the ContentPanel grid, add the LongListSelector definition. Assign the SubjectItemTemplate to the ItemTemplate and the ItemsSource to the Subjects collection.

```
<Grid x:Name="ContentPanel" Grid.Row="1" Margin="12,0,12,0" >
    <phone:LongListSelector
        ItemTemplate="{StaticResource SubjectItemTemplate}"
        ItemsSource="{Binding Subjects}" />
</Grid> Code
```

5. Define the ApplicationBar with items for "astronomy", "cooking", and "languages". Each item has a corresponding Click event handler.

```
<phone:PhoneApplicationPage.ApplicationBar>
    <shell:ApplicationBar IsVisible="True" IsMenuEnabled="True">
        <shell:ApplicationBar.MenuItems>
            <shell:ApplicationBarMenuItem Text="astronomy" Click="astronomy_click" />
            <shell:ApplicationBarMenuItem Text="cooking"   Click="cooking_click" />
            <shell:ApplicationBarMenuItem Text="languages" Click="languages_click" />
        </shell:ApplicationBar.MenuItems>
    </shell:ApplicationBar>
</phone:PhoneApplicationPage.ApplicationBar>
```

Code the Main Page

Add code to the main page's code-behind. This code will assign the ViewModels and handle the click events from the ApplicationBar.

1. In the code-behind for the main page, add a private member for the application view model.

```
private AppViewModel _viewModel = new AppViewModel();
```

2. In the MainPage constructor, after the InitializeComponent, assign the DataContext for the LayoutRoot.

```
public MainPage()
{
    InitializeComponent();
    LayoutRoot.DataContext = _viewModel.Astronomy;
}
```

3. Add the event handler for the Delete click of the context menu.

```
private void Delete_Subject(object sender, System.Windows.RoutedEventArgs e)
{
    // get a reference to the SubjectViewModel currently in the DataContext
    var subjectViewModel = LayoutRoot.DataContext as SubjectViewModel<string>;
    // pass the list item text to the view model's DeleteSubject() method
    subjectViewModel.DeleteSubject((sender as MenuItem).Tag as string);
}
```

4. Add handlers for each of the ApplicationBar menu item Click events. Each event handler assigns a different DataContext from the view model.

```
private void astronomy_click(object sender, EventArgs e)
{
    LayoutRoot.DataContext = _viewModel.Astronomy;
}

private void cooking_click(object sender, EventArgs e)
{
    LayoutRoot.DataContext = _viewModel.Cooking;
}

private void languages_click(object sender, EventArgs e)
{
    LayoutRoot.DataContext = _viewModel.Languages;
}
```

5. Add the handler for the ContextMenu Unloaded event. This work-around is intended to prevent unintended side effects of the ContextMenu DataContext being out of sync with the parent item.

```
private void ContextMenu_Unloaded_1(object sender, RoutedEventArgs e)
{
    var contextMenu = sender as ContextMenu;
    contextMenu.ClearValue(FrameworkElement.DataContextProperty);
}
```

Test the Application

Test the application to verify it can perform the actions you coded.

1. Run the application in the Emulator or on a phone device.
2. Verify that you can delete and search from a list of subjects.
3. Verify that you can switch between subjects using the ApplicationBar menu items.
4. Verify that the items maintain their states when switching between subjects (deletions remain deleted).

Summary

Windows Phone 8 has a rich set of controls that play well in the mobile environment. From simple controls like `Buttons` and `TextBox` to more complex controls like the `LongListSelector`, `MultiScaleImage`, and `MediaElement`, your bases are covered. New controls in development are available in the Windows Phone Toolkit and are merged into the main product as the product matures.

You can put these controls to work in the next chapter "Navigation." The Navigation chapter will also introduce the `Panorama` and `Pivot` controls that you can use to provide a native Windows Phone 8 user experience.

CHAPTER 5

Navigation

There are three major paths of travel in Windows Phone 8: within pages, between pages, and to external URIs. Navigation within pages uses controls that present different views such as Panorama and Pivot. Navigation between pages uses the navigation framework.

Navigation between Pages

The relationship of objects used to navigate between pages is shown in Figure 5-1. A single `PhoneApplicationFrame` is created during initialization and assigned to the Application `RootFrame` property. The frame reserves space for the page, application bar, and status bar. The frame also maintains a journal of page visits, lists navigation capabilities, and provides navigation methods/events.

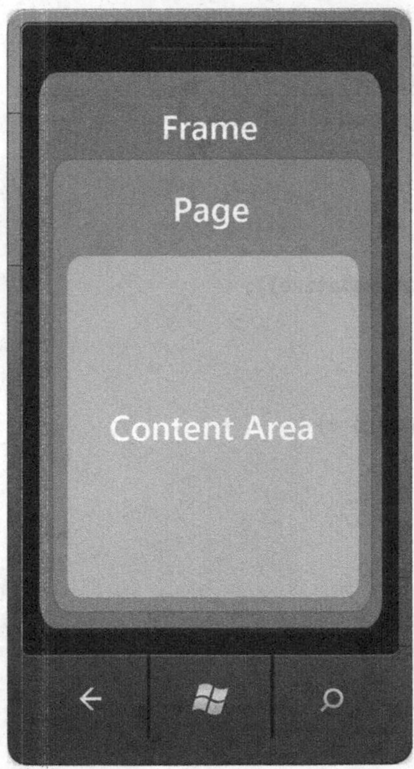

Figure 5-1. *Navigation Hierarchy*

An application has one or more PhoneApplicationPage descendants. Inside the page, the content area is taken up by the LayoutRoot element.

PhoneApplicationFrame

The PhoneApplicationFrame is the outermost container in the hierarchy of controls for a Windows Phone 8 application and the root of the visual tree. PhoneApplicationFrame is actually a ContentControl descendant that supports navigation between pages. Navigation to another page assigns the new page as content of the frame. The code in Listing 5-1 shows how to retrieve the RootFrame and call one of its methods.

Listing 5-1. Navigation Using the Frame

```
private void PhoneAppFrame_Click(object sender, RoutedEventArgs e)
{
    App.RootFrame.Navigate(new Uri("/SecondPage.xaml", UriKind.Relative));
}
```

PhoneApplicationPage

The PhoneApplicationPage is a UserControl descendant that can be navigated to by a frame. The Page's NavigationContext is a dictionary of query strings coming from other pages. The page also surfaces the versatile NavigationService object. Override page events to respond to navigation.

OnFragmentNavigation

A fragment is the part of a URI following a hash mark "#" and is typically used to specify detail within a document. Listing 5-2 shows navigation to a second page and passes the string fragment "detail". Listing 5-3 is the second page's OnFragmentNavigation event handler where the FragmentNavigationEventArgs include the Fragment.

Listing 5-2. Main Page Passes Fragment to Second Page

```
private void PageFragment_Click(object sender, RoutedEventArgs e)
{
    App.RootFrame.Navigate(new Uri("/SecondPage.xaml#detail", UriKind.Relative));
}
```

Listing 5-3. Second Page Receives Fragment

```
protected override void OnFragmentNavigation(FragmentNavigationEventArgs e)
{
    // displays "Fragment: Detail"
    MessageBox.Show("Fragment: " + e.Fragment);
    base.OnFragmentNavigation(e);
}
```

OnNavigatingFrom

OnNavigatingFrom is an opportunity to prevent the user from leaving the page. Listing 5-4 sets the Cancel argument property to true, based on a MessageBox result.

Listing 5-4. Before Navigating From a Page

```
protected override void OnNavigatingFrom(NavigatingCancelEventArgs e)
{
    e.Cancel = MessageBox.Show("You have unsaved data, do you want to exit?", "Unsaved data",
        MessageBoxButton.OKCancel) == MessageBoxResult.Cancel;
    base.OnNavigatingFrom(e);
}
```

OnNavigatedFrom

This method is called when a page is no longer the active page in a frame. The NavigationEventArgs Content property represents the target page. This allows you to pass data from the page you're leaving and send it to the page that is about to display. Listing 5-5 is fired when SecondPage navigates back to MainPage.

Listing 5-5. After Navigating From a Page

```
// Navigated from "SecondPage" back to "MainPage"
protected override void OnNavigatedFrom(NavigationEventArgs e)
{
    MainPage mainPage = e.Content as MainPage;
    if (mainPage != null)
        mainPage.StatusText.Text = "A message from SecondPage OnNavigatedFrom";
    base.OnNavigatedFrom(e);
}
```

OnNavigatedTo

This method is called when a page becomes the active page in a frame. The code in Listing 5-6 overrides the page OnNavigatedTo() method to show the Uri for the active page. NavigationEventArgs also has IsNavigationInitiator to show if the current application is the origin or destination, NavigationMode to show if the navigation is New/Back/Forward/Refresh/Reset, and Content that represents the page.

Listing 5-6. Navigating to a Page

```
protected override void OnNavigatedTo(NavigationEventArgs e)
{
    MessageBox.Show("NavigatedTo: " + e.Uri);
    base.OnNavigatedTo(e);
}
```

NavigationService

The NavigationService is a workhorse that tracks navigation history and provides navigation methods and events. NavigationService is kept as an instance within the Page class. Navigate(Uri) is the most commonly used method:

```
this.NavigationService.Navigate(new Uri("/SecondPage.xaml", UriKind.Relative));
```

You can also travel through navigation history using GoBack(), GoForward(). Use the companion properties CanGoBack and CanGoForward to prevent errors.

```
if (this.NavigationService.CanGoBack)
{
    this.NavigationService.GoBack();
}
```

The BackStack property is an IEnumerable of JournalEntry where each entry contains a URI that the user has visited. Call RemoveBackEntry() to remove the most recent entry from the stack.

Navigation to external URIs

In addition to the HyperlinkButton, you can use the WebBrowserTask or the WebBrowser control to reach external URIs. If you don't need to customize the layout or handle events, you can use the WebBrowserTask to show a stock representation of the browser, as shown in Listing 5-7 and Figure 5-2.

Listing 5-7. Navigating with the WebBrowserTask

```
WebBrowserTask webBrowserTask = new WebBrowserTask();
webBrowserTask.Uri = new Uri("http://www.falafel.com");
webBrowserTask.Show();
```

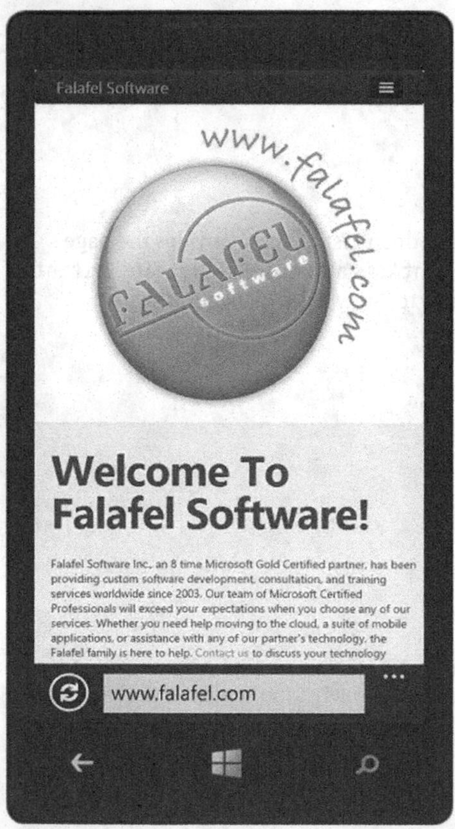

Figure 5-2. *The WebBrowserTask UI*

You may want the browser to appear inside a page, to integrate with other controls, and respond to events. Your best bet is to use the `WebBrowser` control that surfaces events and methods for better control (see Figure 5-3).

Figure 5-3. The WebBrowser Control

The `WebBrowser Navigate()` method overloads can take a URI or a URI with an array of bytes for post data. You can also call `NavigateToString()` if you simply want to pass raw HTML.

If you want to cancel navigation under certain circumstances, subscribe to the `Navigating` event, examine the argument's `Uri` and then decide if you should set `Cancel` to true. You can't cancel the `Navigated` event, but you can scrape the target screen by saving off the `Content` property of the event argument. Finally, the `NavigationFailed` event passes an `Exception` argument to determine the fault cause.

This example in Listing 5-8 navigates to a URL and prints the current status in a `TextBlock` at the base of the browser.

Listing 5-8. Navigating with the WebBrowserTask

```
private void NavigateButton_Click(object sender, RoutedEventArgs e)
{
    Browser.Navigate(new Uri(AddressTextBox.Text));
}

private void Browser_Navigated(object sender,
    System.Windows.Navigation.NavigationEventArgs e)
```

```
{
    StatusText.Text = "Navigated to " + e.Uri.AbsoluteUri;
}

private void Browser_Navigating(object sender, NavigatingEventArgs e)
{
    StatusText.Text = "Navigating to " + e.Uri.AbsoluteUri;
}

private void Browser_NavigationFailed(object sender,
    System.Windows.Navigation.NavigationFailedEventArgs e)
{
    MessageBox.Show("Navigation failed:" + e.Exception.Message);
}
```

Calling JavaScript from the Browser

WebBrowser has two nifty functions that allow the phone to talk with JavaScript in the browser and the JavaScript to send notification back to the application. You might use this ability to help guide the user through entry on a web page before returning to the Windows Phone 8 application (e.g., register on a specific page, then notify the phone that all is well). Here are the pieces that make it work:

1. The web page must have one or more JavaScript functions. If you're not working with a pre-defined web page, you can create one on-the-fly using WebBrowser NavigateToString() and pass raw HTML.
2. The Browser InvokeScript() method passes the name of a JavaScript function, and optionally, a series of parameters.
3. In JavaScript, the window.external.notify() function is called. The notify() function accepts parameters.
4. The Browser ScriptNotify event is triggered and the NotifyEventArgs Value property contains the value passed from the JavaScript notify() call.

The example in Listing 5-9 feeds a simple string of HTML that's fed to the WebBrowser control via the NavigateToString() method. The WebBrowser LoadCompleted event ensures that the document is completely loaded before we try to call script. Inside the LoadCompleted event, the WebBrowser InvokeScript() method calls the custom sendNotify() JavaScript method and passes a string array with a single parameter 'invoked from phone'. The ScriptNotify event handler fires and displays the argument Value, as shown in Figure 5-4.

Listing 5-9. Invoking Script

```
const string html =
        "<html><head>" +
        "<script type='text/javascript'>" +
        "function sendNotify(incoming) " +
        "{ window.external.notify(incoming + ' - sending back to phone'); }" +
        "</script></head><body></body></html>";
```

```
private void JavaScriptButton_Click(object sender, RoutedEventArgs e)
{
    Browser.IsScriptEnabled = true;
    Browser.NavigateToString(html);
}

private void Browser_LoadCompleted(object sender, NavigationEventArgs e)
{
    Browser.InvokeScript("sendNotify", new string[] { "invoked from phone" });
}

private void Browser_ScriptNotify(object sender, NotifyEventArgs e)
{
    MessageBox.Show("ScriptNotify: " + e.Value);
}
```

Figure 5-4. *ScriptNotify Event Fires*

■ Caution It's important to set the `IsScriptEnabled` property to true. Forgetting this step can cause the `InvokeScript()` method to fail with a SystemException, "An unknown error has occurred. Error: 80020006".

Navigation within Pages

`Pivot` and `Panorama` controls are used to navigate within a page and can be used in favor of tabbed interfaces. The presentation of these controls makes it easy to see and navigate your data fluidly. You won't find these controls in desktop or web controls. Both are highly specific to the Windows Phone 8 environment and give your application that "Windows Phone" flavor.

The `Pivot` control slices related data into panels that can be panned (paged horizontally) when the user swipes from one view to another. The data can have multiple views of the same base information (e.g., "movies by rating", "movies by category"), related data (e.g., weather data coming from various web services), or a large set of data filtered in different chunks (e.g., "company directory by department"). The content scrolls over a static background image.

Pivot is virtualized and only loads the current panel and its immediate neighbors to the left and right. Scrolling causes additional panels to be loaded.

The Panorama experience is intended to be bigger than the phone. Panorama follows a "magazine" metaphor where pages of content float over a rich visual background. Think of Panorama as a viewport into a larger canvas. The Panorama shows a small visual trace of the next right side panel as a hint that there is more data. Panning wraps around to the first item, endlessly.

While the Pivot shows closely related data, the Panorama is designed to act as high-level navigation for the user. The Panorama can be used for summary information or as a jumping off point to spelunk into detailed content. Instead of filtering some central store of data, the layout and content of each section in the Panorama can be completely distinct. Expect to build multiple view models under the main application view model where each view model can represent some semantic category.

Both `Panorama` and `Pivot` descend from `TemplatedItemsControl<T>` (an `ItemsControl` descendant) where `T` is either a `PivotItem` or `PanoramaItem`. Both `PivotItem` and `PanoramaItem` are headered ContentControls that can contain other items in the control.

Getting Started with Pivot and Panorama

You can find Pivot and Panorama templates (Figure 5-5) to get started at `File` ➤ `New` ➤ `Project` ➤ `Windows Phone`. From there, choose `Windows Phone Pivot App` or `Windows Phone Panorama App`.

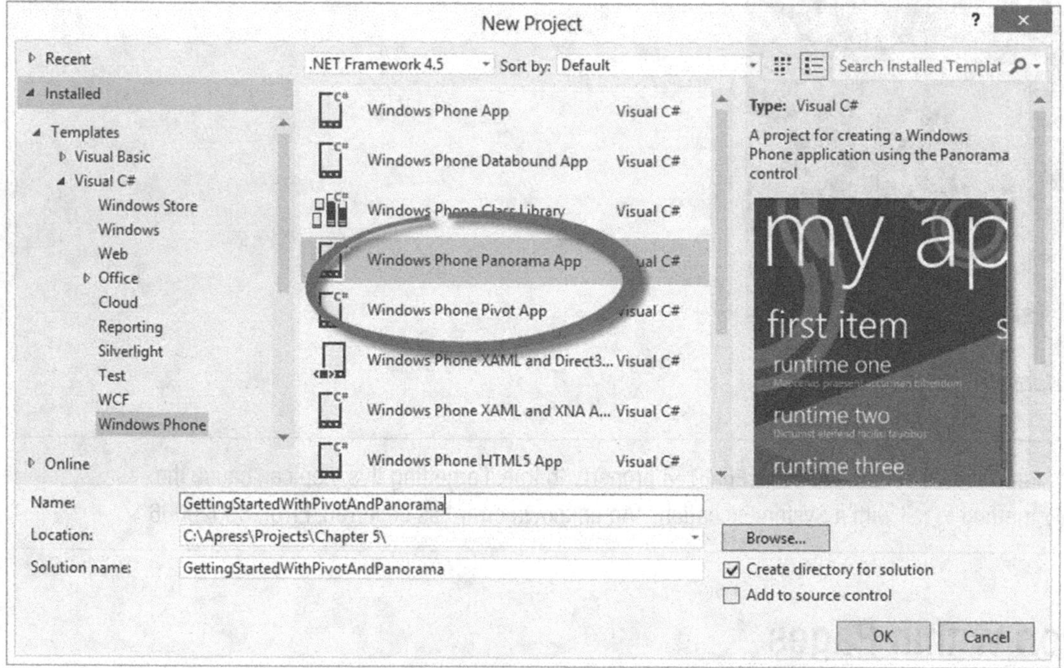

***Figure 5-5.** Templates for Panorama and Pivot*

The templated projects make a great reference and starting point for your own applications. The initial project roughs out the view models and data binding for both design and runtime data. The Panorama project also includes a background image so you can test the scrolling effect. Both templates produce complete running projects.

Your second option is to add Panorama and Pivot controls to existing pages from your Toolbox. Drag the Panorama or Pivot from the Toolbox to the *design surface* where the designer pre-populates the list with a few declarative items. Be aware this only works on the design surface; dragging to the XAML adds a Pivot with no items. Remove the Margin, Width, and Height properties so the Pivot will take up the available screen real estate (see Listing 5-10).

Listing 5-10. The Default Pivot Definition

```
<phone:Pivot HorizontalAlignment="Stretch" Title="pivot" VerticalAlignment="Stretch">
    <phone:PivotItem CacheMode="{x:Null}" Header="item1">
        <Grid/>
    </phone:PivotItem>
    <phone:PivotItem CacheMode="{x:Null}" Header="item2">
        <Grid/>
    </phone:PivotItem>
</phone:Pivot>
```

Only slight differences in layout and behavior differentiate the Pivot from Panorama. The Pivot has three areas of real estate: the `Title` that remains unmoving above the pivot items, the `Header` at the top of each pivot item and the pivot item `Content` (Figure 5-6). Each area can be bound and completely customized using templates.

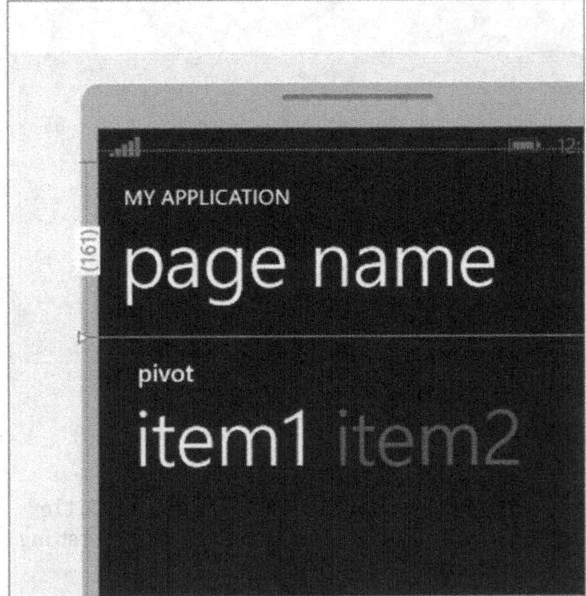

Figure 5-6. *Default Pivot Layout*

While both have the same elements, namely Title, Header, and Content, the Panorama Background, titles, and content will all scroll horizontally, at different rates. The ratio is determined by the number of items. The default background is an abstract 1536 x 1280 image designed to look good while scrolling and wrapping. Photographs are also recommended to provide rich Panorama backgrounds. The background image should allow the font to be easily distinguished from the background (Figure 5-7).

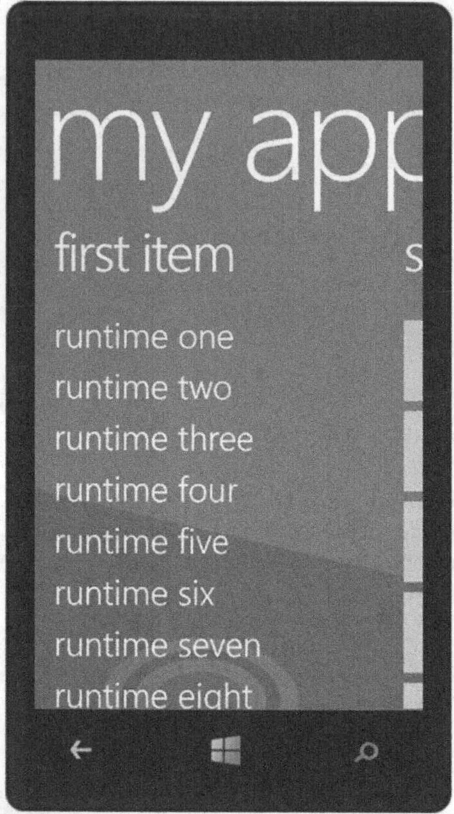

Figure 5-7. *Default Panorama Layout*

Binding Panorama and Pivot

Building `Panorama` and `Pivot` both require similar approaches to binding data and setting up templates.

DataContext

Listing 5-11 defines two simplified objects that represent data the `Pivot` or `Panorama` can hold. `MyData` holds a `Title` and `Subtitle`. `MyItemData` is a generic list of `MyItemData` objects that each has `HeadingText` and a generic list of string `ContentItems`. These objects will feed elements in the `TitleTemplate`, `HeaderTemplate`, and `ItemTemplate`.

Listing 5-11. MyData Definition

```
public class MyItemData
{
   public string HeadingText { get; set; }
   public List<string> ContentItems { get; set; }
}
```

```
public class MyData
{
    public string Title { get; set; }
    public string Subtitle { get; set; }
    public List<MyItemData> ItemData { get; set; }

    public MyData()
    {
        Title = "TITLE";
        Subtitle = "subtitle";
        ItemData = new List<MyItemData>()
        {
            new MyItemData()
            {
                HeadingText = "heading one",
                ContentItems = new List<string>()
                {
                    "Content 1 A", "Content 1 B", "Content 1 C"
                }
            },
            new MyItemData()
            {
                HeadingText = "heading two",
                ContentItems = new List<string>()
                {
                    "Content 2 A", "Content 2 B", "Content 2 C"
                }
            },
            new MyItemData()
            {
                HeadingText = "heading three",
                ContentItems = new List<string>()
                {
                    "Content 3 A", "Content 3 B", "Content 3 C",
                }
            }
        };
    }
}
```

Pivot and Panorama Templates

The `Pivot` in Listing 5-12 is bound via the `DataContext` to the custom `MyData` object. You can assign a new instance of `MyData` in code to the `DataContext` or create a `MyData` static resource. The `Title` is assigned the `{Binding}` markup extension to make sure the `TitleTemplate` is resolved. `ItemsSource` is bound to the "ItemData" collection. `TitleTemplate`, `HeaderTemplate`, and `ItemTemplate` are each bound to `DataTemplate` resources. The background displays an image, but the image will not scroll while paging (Figure 5-8).

Listing 5-12. Pivot Templates Bound with Data

```
<phone:Pivot x:Name="Pivot1"
    Title="{Binding}"
    DataContext="{StaticResource MyData}"
    ItemsSource="{Binding ItemData}"
    TitleTemplate="{StaticResource MyTitleTemplate}"
    HeaderTemplate="{StaticResource MyHeaderTemplate}"
    ItemTemplate="{StaticResource MyItemTemplate}">
    <phone:Pivot.Background>
        <ImageBrush
            ImageSource="/Assets/MyBackground.png" Stretch="UniformToFill" />
    </phone:Pivot.Background>
</phone:Pivot>
```

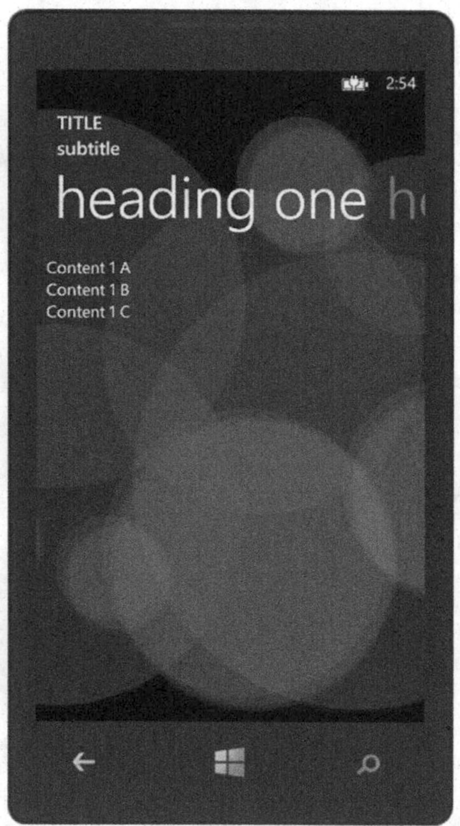

Figure 5-8. *Bound Pivot Title, Header, and Content*

The Panorama has exactly the same property settings as the Pivot (Listing 5-13). Even the templates can be shared between the two.

Listing 5-13. Panorama Using Pivot Property Settings

```
<phone:Panorama x:Name="Panorama1"
    Title="{Binding}"
    DataContext="{StaticResource MyData}"
    ItemsSource="{Binding ItemData}"
    TitleTemplate="{StaticResource MyTitleTemplate}"
    HeaderTemplate="{StaticResource MyHeaderTemplate}"
    ItemTemplate="{StaticResource MyItemTemplate}">
    <phone:Panorama.Background>
        <ImageBrush
            ImageSource="/Assets/MyBackground.png" Stretch="UniformToFill" />
    </phone:Panorama.Background>
</phone:Panorama>
```

When the app is running, the `Panorama` has a different layout from the `Pivot`. The `Background` is scaled differently and scrolls as the user pages (see Figure 5-9).

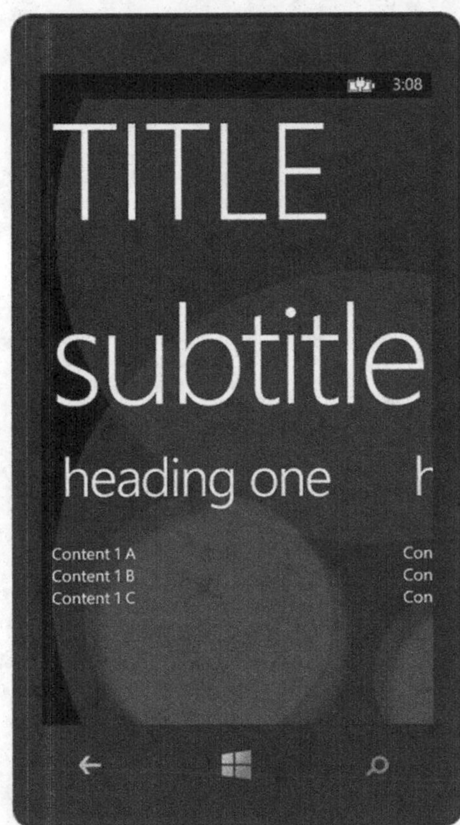

Figure 5-9. *Bound Panorama Title, Header, and Content*

The `TitleTemplate` takes a `DataTemplate` of any arrangement. Listing 5-14 shows the `Title` and `Subtitle` data properties bound to TextBlocks.

Listing 5-14. The TitleTemplate

```
<DataTemplate x:Key="MyTitleTemplate">
    <StackPanel>
        <TextBlock Text="{Binding Title}" />
        <TextBlock Text="{Binding Subtitle}" />
    </StackPanel>
</DataTemplate>
```

The Header takes a simple `TextBlock` bound to the `HeadingText` property, as shown in Listing 5-15.

Listing 5-15. The HeaderTemplate

```
<DataTemplate x:Key="MyHeaderTemplate">
    <TextBlock Text="{Binding HeadingText}" />
</DataTemplate>
```

Each `MyItemData` has a generic List of strings named `ContentItems` that are bound to a `LongListSelector ItemsSource`, as shown in Listing 5-16.

Listing 5-16. The Item Template

```
<DataTemplate x:Key="MyItemTemplate">
    <phone:LongListSelector ItemsSource="{Binding ContentItems}"  >
        <phone:LongListSelector.ItemTemplate>
            <DataTemplate>
                <TextBlock Text="{Binding}" />
            </DataTemplate>
        </phone:LongListSelector.ItemTemplate>
    </phone:LongListSelector>
</DataTemplate>
```

Visual Studio Project Templates

If you create the Pivot or Panorama application from a Visual Studio template, you can run it immediately. The application is setup with MVVM in mind, so bound data will appear in two sample pivot items. The `Pivot` and `Panorama` controls have a `Title` property and a collection of `PivotItem`/`PanoramaItem` objects, where each item is a `ContentControl` with a Header.

Before customizing the data for our own purposes, let's take a tour of what is already in the box. The `ViewModels` directory holds `ItemViewModel`, a simple object with three string properties ("LineOne", "LineTwo", and "LineThree"), as shown in Listing 5-17.

Listing 5-17. The ItemViewModel Definition

```
public class ItemViewModel : INotifyPropertyChanged
{
    private string _lineOne;
    public string LineOne
    {
        get
        {
            return _lineOne;
        }
```

```
        set
        {
            if (value != _lineOne)
            {
                _lineOne = value;
                NotifyPropertyChanged("LineOne");
            }
        }
    }
    ...
```

The ViewModels directory has a second class, MainViewModel, that holds an ObservableCollection of ItemViewModel. MainViewModel also has an IsDataLoaded property and a LoadData() method used by the application to initially populate the collection, as shown in Listing 5-18.

Listing 5-18. The MainViewModel

```
public class MainViewModel : INotifyPropertyChanged
{
    public MainViewModel()
    {
        this.Items = new ObservableCollection<ItemViewModel>();
    }
    public ObservableCollection<ItemViewModel> Items { get; private set; }
    ...
```

The MainViewModelSampleData.xaml file in the SampleData (Figure 5-10) directory defines a MainViewModel and its collection of ItemViewModel. This data is visible during design time.

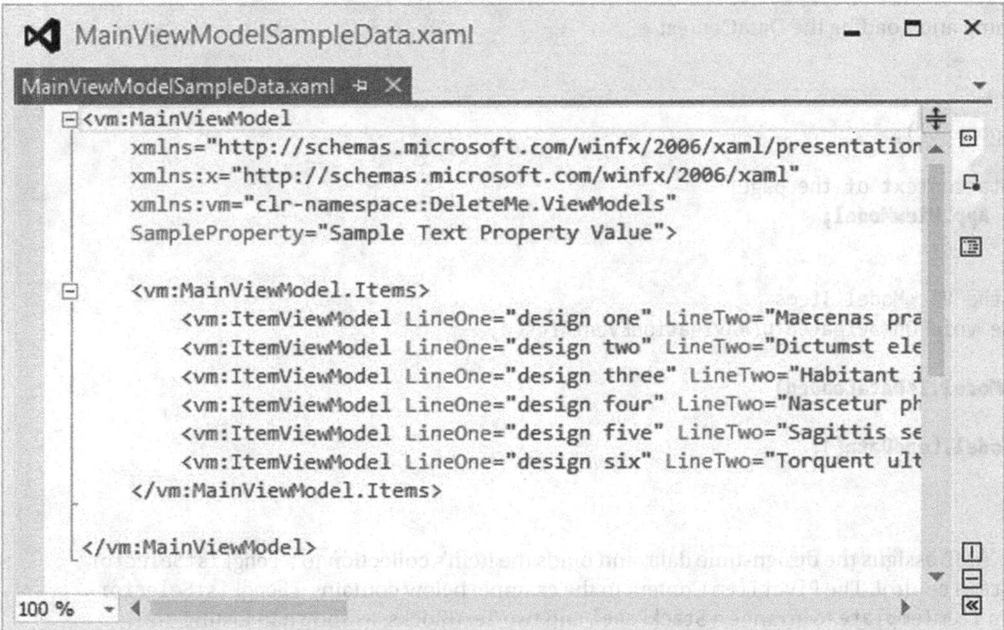

Figure 5-10. *Sample Local Data*

The App.xaml.cs surfaces a static MainViewModel for easy access from any other part of the application, as shown in Listing 5-19.

Listing 5-19. The ViewModel Property

```
public partial class App : Application
{
    private static MainViewModel viewModel = null;

    /// <summary>
    /// A static ViewModel used by the views to bind against.
    /// </summary>
    /// <returns>The MainViewModel object.</returns>
    public static MainViewModel ViewModel
    {
        get
        {
            // Delay creation of the view model until necessary
            if (viewModel == null)
                viewModel = new MainViewModel();

            return viewModel;
        }
    }
```

The `MainPage` constructor assigns the static `App.ViewModel` to the runtime `DataContext` for the page. When the user lands on the page, the view model `IsDataLoaded` flag is checked and `LoadData()` method is called, if necessary. The `LoadData()` method adds a series of `ItemViewModel` objects to the `MainViewModel Items` collection and sets the `IsDataLoaded` flag to true, as shown in Listing 5-20.

Listing 5-20. Assigning and Loading the DataContext

```
public MainPage()
{
    InitializeComponent();

    // Set the data context of the page
    DataContext = App.ViewModel;
}

// Load data for the ViewModel Items
protected override void OnNavigatedTo(NavigationEventArgs e)
{
    if (!App.ViewModel.IsDataLoaded)
    {
        App.ViewModel.LoadData();
    }
}
```

The MainPage XAML assigns the design-time data, and binds the item's collection to a `LongListSelector` in the `Pivot` or `Panorama` control. The `PivotItem` Content in the example below contains a `LongListSelector`, which in turn uses an `ItemTemplate` to arrange a `StackPanel` and two TextBlocks, as shown in Listing 5-21. The TextBlocks are bound to the first and second line properties of the view model.

Listing 5-21. The Pivot Layout

```
<phone:PhoneApplicationPage ...
    d:DataContext="{d:DesignData SampleData/MainViewModelSampleData.xaml}">

    <Grid x:Name="LayoutRoot" Background="Transparent">

        <phone:Pivot Title="MY APPLICATION">
            <!--Pivot item one-->
            <phone:PivotItem Header="first">
                <phone:LongListSelector Margin="0,0,-12,0" ItemsSource="{Binding Items}">
                    <phone:LongListSelector.ItemTemplate>
                        <DataTemplate>
                            <StackPanel Margin="0,0,0,17">
                                <TextBlock Text="{Binding LineOne}" TextWrapping="Wrap"
                                           Style="{StaticResource PhoneTextExtraLargeStyle}"/>
                                <TextBlock Text="{Binding LineTwo}" TextWrapping="Wrap"
                                           Margin="12,-6,12,0"
                                           Style="{StaticResource PhoneTextSubtleStyle}"/>
                            </StackPanel>
                        </DataTemplate>
                    </phone:LongListSelector.ItemTemplate>
                </phone:LongListSelector>
            </phone:PivotItem>

            <!--Pivot item two-->
            <phone:PivotItem Header="second" ... />
        </phone:Pivot>

    </Grid>

</phone:PhoneApplicationPage>
```

Customizing the Visual Studio Project

The generated Visual Studio project makes it easy to swap out the data and leave the infrastructure in place. This next example uses a Pivot and demonstrates creating a "Phonebook" object that simulates a Bing API search on local hotels. The MainViewModel projects the model data into view-model-happy data that can be bound to the view. The data is filtered to show two views, all items and user-rated items (see Figure 5-11).

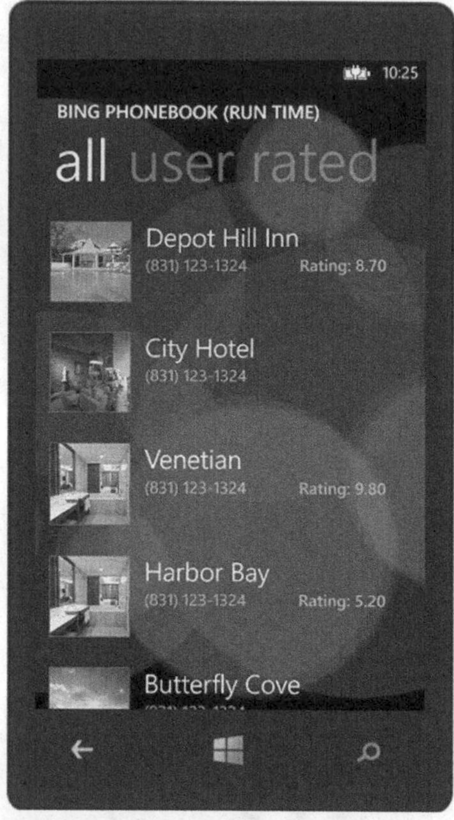

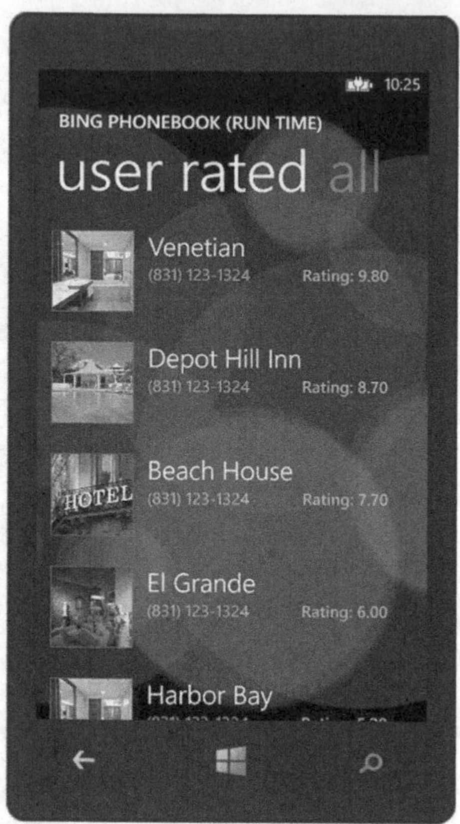

Figure 5-11. *Customized Pivot*

To make the generated project your own, you need to modify the following:

- The Model
- The ViewModel
- The ViewModel Design Data
- The Markup

The Model

The Model in this project is a stand-in for data you might get from a web service or database. The "Phonebook" has a generic list of "PhonebookResult", where each result has a unique id, title, phone number, and user rating, as shown in Listing 5-22. You could replace the Phonebook logic with code to access a REST service, such as the Bing API or any other REST-based API.

See Chapters 11 and 12 for more ways to populate the model.

Listing 5-22. The PhoneBook Object

```
public class PhonebookResult
{
    public string UniqueId { get; set; }
    public string Title { get; set; }
    public string PhoneNumber { get; set; }
    public double? UserRating { get; set; }
}

public class Phonebook
{
    public List<PhonebookResult> Items { get; private set; }

    public Phonebook()
    {
        this.Items = new List<PhonebookResult>()
        {
            new PhonebookResult() { UniqueId = "1", Title = "Depot Hill Inn",
                PhoneNumber = "(831) 123-1324", UserRating = 8.7 },
            new PhonebookResult() { UniqueId = "2", Title = "City Hotel",
                PhoneNumber = "(831) 123-1324"  },
            new PhonebookResult() { UniqueId = "8", Title = "Venetian",
                PhoneNumber = "(831) 123-1324", UserRating = 9.8 },
            new PhonebookResult() { UniqueId = "4", Title = "Harbor Bay",
                PhoneNumber = "(831) 123-1324", UserRating = 5.2 },
            new PhonebookResult() { UniqueId = "5", Title = "Butterfly Cove",
                PhoneNumber = "(831) 123-1324"  },
            new PhonebookResult() { UniqueId = "6", Title = "El Grande",
                PhoneNumber = "(831) 123-1324", UserRating = 6 },
            new PhonebookResult() { UniqueId = "7", Title = "Beach House",
                PhoneNumber = "(831) 123-1324", UserRating = 7.7 },
            new PhonebookResult() { UniqueId = "9", Title = "By the Sea",
                PhoneNumber = "(831) 123-1324" },
            new PhonebookResult() { UniqueId = "3", Title = "Beach Hotel",
                PhoneNumber = "(831) 123-1324" }
        };
    }
}
```

The ViewModel

The `ItemViewModel` properties are changed from `LineOne`, etc., to `UniqueId`, `Title`, `UserRating`, and `PhoneNumber`, as shown in Listing 5-23. These are all string properties except `UserRating` which is a nullable double.

Listing 5-23. The ItemViewModel Definition

```
public class ItemViewModel : INotifyPropertyChanged
{
    private string _uniqueId;
    public string UniqueId
```

```
    {
        get { return _uniqueId; }
        set
        {
            if (value != _uniqueId)
            {
                _uniqueId = value;
                NotifyPropertyChanged("UniqueId");
            }
        }
    }
    //...
}
```

The MainViewModel has two collections, one for all items and another for items that have user rating data, as shown in Listing 5-24. The LoadData() method consumes the Phonebook model data and fills the AllItems collection. AllItems is used as the starting point to fill the RatedItems collection. LINQ is used to select items where UserRating HasValue is true.

Listing 5-24. The MainViewModel Definition

```
public class MainViewModel : INotifyPropertyChanged
{
    public MainViewModel()
    {
        LoadData();
    }

    public ObservableCollection<ItemViewModel> AllItems { get; private set; }
    public ObservableCollection<ItemViewModel> RatedItems { get; private set; }

    private string _sectionTitle = "BING PHONEBOOK (RUN TIME)";
    public string SectionTitle
    {
        get { return _sectionTitle; }
        set
        {
            if (value != _sectionTitle)
            {
                _sectionTitle = value;
                NotifyPropertyChanged("SectionTitle");
            }
        }
    }

    public bool IsDataLoaded
    {
        get;
        private set;
    }
```

```
    public void LoadData()
    {
        Phonebook bingPhoneBook = new Phonebook();
        var allItems = from r in bingPhoneBook.Items
                        select new ItemViewModel()
                        {
                            UniqueId = r.UniqueId,
                            Title = r.Title,
                            PhoneNumber = r.PhoneNumber,
                            UserRating = r.UserRating
                        };

        this.AllItems = new ObservableCollection<ItemViewModel>(allItems);

        var ratedItems = from r in this.AllItems
                            where r.UserRating.HasValue
                            orderby r.UserRating descending
                            select r;

        this.RatedItems = new ObservableCollection<ItemViewModel>(ratedItems);
        this.IsDataLoaded = true;
    }

    public event PropertyChangedEventHandler PropertyChanged;
    private void NotifyPropertyChanged(String propertyName)
    {
        PropertyChangedEventHandler handler = PropertyChanged;
        if (null != handler)
        {
            handler(this, new PropertyChangedEventArgs(propertyName));
        }
    }
}
```

The ViewModel Design Data

The MainViewModel can be declared in its own XAML where the XAML forms the sample data bound to the page DataContext. The MainViewModel defines a SectionTitle property and a collection named "AllItems", as shown in Listing 5-25.

Listing 5-25. MainViewModelSampleData.xaml

```
<vm:MainViewModel
    xmlns="http://schemas.microsoft.com/winfx/2006/xaml/presentation"
    xmlns:x="http://schemas.microsoft.com/winfx/2006/xaml"
    xmlns:vm="clr-namespace:CustomizingTheVisualStudioProject.ViewModels"
    SectionTitle="BING PHONEBOOK (DESIGN TIME)">

    <vm:MainViewModel.AllItems>
        <vm:ItemViewModel UniqueId="1" Title="Depot Hill Inn"
                          PhoneNumber="(831) 123-1324"
                          UserRating="8.7"/>
```

```
        <vm:ItemViewModel UniqueId="2" Title="City Hotel"
                          PhoneNumber="(831) 123-1234" />
        <vm:ItemViewModel UniqueId="3" Title="Venetian"
                          PhoneNumber="(831) 123-1278"
                          UserRating="5.3"/>
        <vm:ItemViewModel UniqueId="4" Title="Harbor Bay"
                          PhoneNumber="(831) 123-6471" />
        <vm:ItemViewModel UniqueId="5" Title="Butterfly Cove"
                          PhoneNumber="(831) 123-0505" />
        <vm:ItemViewModel UniqueId="6" Title="El Grande"
                          PhoneNumber="(831) 123-1295"
                          UserRating="7.77"/>
        <vm:ItemViewModel UniqueId="7" Title="Beach House"
                          PhoneNumber="(831) 123-1295" />
        <vm:ItemViewModel UniqueId="8" Title="By the Sea"
                          PhoneNumber="(831) 123-0607"
                          UserRating="9.1"/>
        <vm:ItemViewModel UniqueId="9" Title="Beach Hotel"
                          PhoneNumber="(831) 123-1707"
                          UserRating="9.8"/>
    </vm:MainViewModel.AllItems>

</vm:MainViewModel>
```

The main page assigns the XAML file to the design-time DataContext using the {d:DesignData} markup.

```
<phone:PhoneApplicationPage ...
    d:DataContext="{d:DesignData SampleData/MainViewModelSampleData.xaml}">
```

As a result of defining the XAML and assigning it to the design-time DataContext, the data is visible in the designer. Notice "(DESIGN TIME)" in the SectionTitle that originates from the sample data.

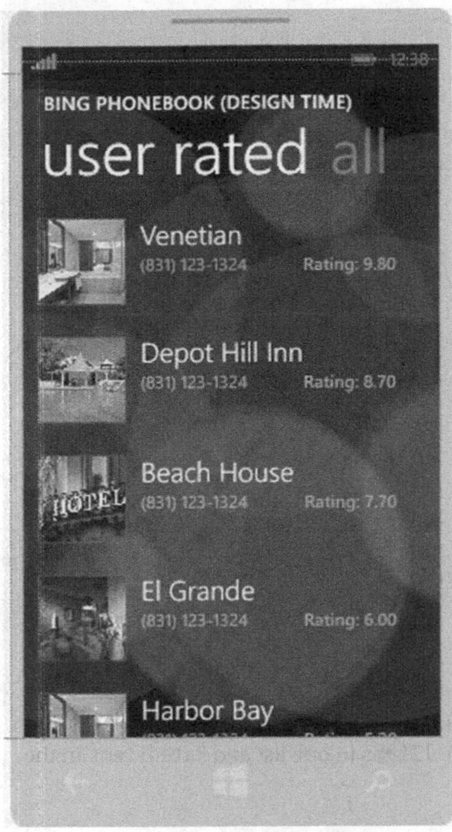

Figure 5-12. The Pivot at Design-Time

The View

The views in the Pivot should not have drastically different layouts, so it makes sense to define one `DataTemplate` and simply filter the data that's piped to the `ItemsSource`. The example in Listing 5-26 sets up three columns and two rows. An `Image` is placed in the upper-left cell and spans two rows. The image names correspond to the `UniqueId` property of each item in the collection. The `Binding StringFormat` builds the path to each image.

Listing 5-26. The ItemTemplate

```
<DataTemplate x:Key="ResultTemplate">

    <Grid Height="120" Width="432" Margin="0,0,0,17" >
        <Grid.ColumnDefinitions>
            <ColumnDefinition Width="110" />
            <ColumnDefinition Width="*" />
            <ColumnDefinition Width="Auto" />
        </Grid.ColumnDefinitions>
```

```
        <Grid.RowDefinitions>
            <RowDefinition Height="Auto" />
            <RowDefinition Height="Auto" />
        </Grid.RowDefinitions>
        <Border x:Name="ImageBorder" BorderThickness="1" BorderBrush="Green"
                Height="100" Width="100" Grid.Column="0" Grid.Row="0"
                Grid.RowSpan="2">
            <Image
                    Stretch="UniformToFill"
                Source="{Binding UniqueId, StringFormat=/Assets/\{0\}.jpg}" />
        </Border>
        <TextBlock Grid.Column="1" Grid.ColumnSpan="2" Grid.Row="0"
            Style="{StaticResource PhoneTextLargeStyle}"
            Text="{Binding Title}" />
        <TextBlock Grid.Column="1" Grid.Row="1"
            Style="{StaticResource PhoneTextSubtleStyle}"
            Text="{Binding PhoneNumber}" />
        <TextBlock Grid.Column="2" Grid.Row="1"
            Style="{StaticResource PhoneTextAccentStyle}"
            Text="{Binding UserRating, StringFormat=Rating: \{0:n\}}" />
    </Grid>

</DataTemplate>
```

Only a few small adjustments are made to `MainPage.xaml` where a background is included, the `ItemTemplate` has been moved into the `App.xaml` as a resource and `ItemsSource` is bound to `AllItems` in one list and `RatedItems` in the second list, as shown in Listing 5-27.

Listing 5-27. Pivot Layout in MainPage.xaml

```
<phone:Pivot
    Title="{Binding SectionTitle}">
    <phone:Pivot.Background>
        <ImageBrush
        ImageSource="/Assets/MyBackground.png" Stretch="UniformToFill" />
    </phone:Pivot.Background>

    <phone:PivotItem
        Header="all">
        <phone:LongListSelector
            ItemsSource="{Binding AllItems}"
            ItemTemplate="{StaticResource ResultTemplate}" />
    </phone:PivotItem>

    <phone:PivotItem
        Header="user rated">
        <phone:LongListSelector
            ItemsSource="{Binding RatedItems}"
            ItemTemplate="{StaticResource ResultTemplate}" />
    </phone:PivotItem>
</phone:Pivot>
```

The Panorama is intended to show different views on each item, so the Pivot's filtering strategy is not really appropriate. Just the same, if the template for `ItemTemplate` is kept in `App.xaml`, you can easily add a Panorama with the same settings as the Pivot. It's a matter of copy and paste from Listing 5-27 and changing the Pivot to Panorama. Notice the section title in Figure 5-13 is stretched across multiple panels.

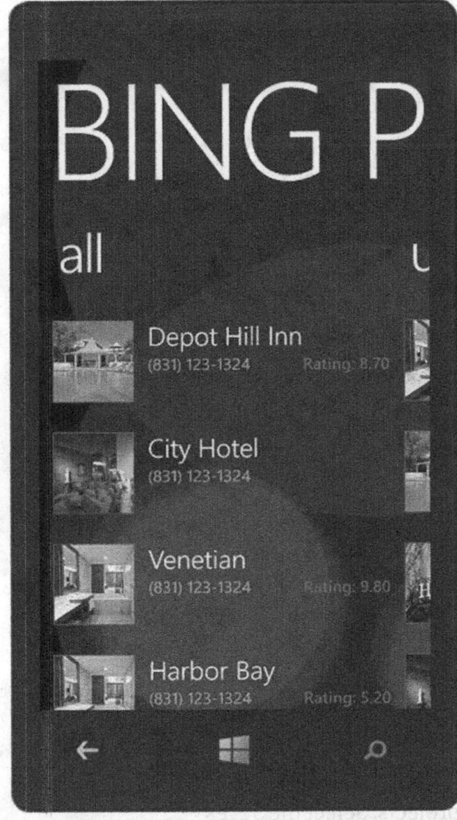

***Figure 5-13.** Custom Data in Panorama*

Design Guidelines

To understand how `Pivot` and `Panorama` controls should be used, check out the online Design Library for Windows Phone. Here are just a few key points extracted from the guidelines:

- Limit the number of pages to avoid confusing the user. The Microsoft guidelines suggest that limiting the number of Panorama views to four or five provides a good user experience. For the Panorama, the objective is to give the user an overview of what they can do in much the same way as a magazine cover provides an overview of its contents. This implies that you shouldn't try to cram lots of detailed information onto the Panorama pages. Panorama elements should be a starting point for more detailed experiences.
- Don't interfere with the default Panorama or Pivot behavior (e.g., animation, scrolling). For example, the Panorama and Pivot are designed to be swiped from side to side. Placing a "doodle" drawing area on one a page would confuse the user as to when they were drawing with their finger on the "doodle" area and when they were swiping the navigation underneath.

- Avoid combining controls so that swiping and panning gestures are ambiguous. The `Pivot` control, for instance, has a well-defined navigation flow where the user expects to pan between pages and then flick up and down to scroll through the data. Adding other controls that change the pre-defined navigation flow is confusing to the user.
- Don't place a `Pivot` control inside a `Panorama` control or another pivot control.
- Don't place a `Map` control inside a `Panorama` or `Pivot` unless it is configured to ignore gestures. Instead, navigate to another page that has the full `Map` functionality.
- Don't use a `Pivot` for task-based navigation, such as a wizard application.

The Design Library for Windows Phone is available at the Windows Phone Dev Center `http://msdn.microsoft.com/en-us/library/windowsphone/design/hh202915(v=vs.105).aspx`. Be sure to follow the "Controls Design Guidelines for Windows Phone" links to Panorama and Pivot Design Guidelines. These guidelines contain extensive detail to help you prepare your application for the Windows Phone Store.

Navigate using the Panorama Example

This next example walks you through building a `Panorama` based application that presents surfing conditions and a list of featured surfing sites.

Prepare the Project

Follow these steps to prepare the project:

1. Create a new Windows Phone application.
2. From the Visual Studio Solution Explorer, right-click the project and select `Add ➤ New Folder` from the context menu. Name the folder `Models`. Repeat this step and create another folder for "ViewModels".
3. Navigate to the `\projects\Images` folder that ships with these projects. Select the `wave.jpg` file and drag it to the `\Assets` folder of your project.
4. Navigate to the `\projects\Images` folder that ships with these projects. Select the `Sites` folder and drag it to the `\Assets` folder of your project.
5. The project in Solution Explorer should look like the example in Figure 5-14.

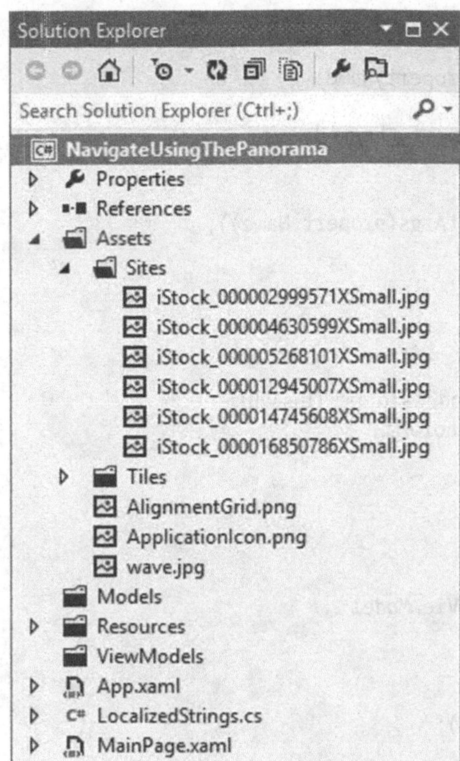

Figure 5-14. *Initial Project Structure*

Create ViewModel Base Classes

Common functionality for the view model is usually packed into a base class. For this example, the view model base class handles the `INotifyPropertyChanged` event, surfaces a `Title`, and tracks data loading.

1. Add `BaseViewModel.cs` to the `ViewModels` folder of the project. Create a base class using the code below.

```
using System;
using System.ComponentModel;

namespace NavigateUsingThePanorama.ViewModels
{
    public abstract class BaseViewModel : INotifyPropertyChanged
    {
        public string Title { get; protected set; }
        public bool IsDataLoaded { get; protected set; }

        public virtual void LoadData()
        {
            this.IsDataLoaded = true;
        }
```

```
        public event PropertyChangedEventHandler PropertyChanged;

        protected void NotifyPropertyChanged(String propertyName)
        {
            PropertyChangedEventHandler handler = PropertyChanged;
            if (null != handler)
            {
                handler(this, new PropertyChangedEventArgs(propertyName));
            }
        }
    }
}
```

2. Add another class named `BaseListViewModel.cs` to the `ViewModels` folder. This will support collections that are displayed on a given page of the `Panorama`.

```
using System.Collections.ObjectModel;

namespace NavigateUsingThePanorama.ViewModels
{
    public abstract class BaseListViewModel<T> : BaseViewModel
    {
        public BaseListViewModel()
        {
            this.Items = new ObservableCollection<T>();
        }

        public ObservableCollection<T> Items { get; set; }
    }
}
```

Add the Surf Conditions Page

The first `Panorama` item will be the "Surf conditions" (see Figure 5-15). The model will represent the conditions for a particular time and will include pressure, swell height, swell direction, and swell period in seconds. This information could be pulled from a web service, but for this example will simply be added directly during the model `Load()` method. The conditions will represent only a single static location during a single time period.

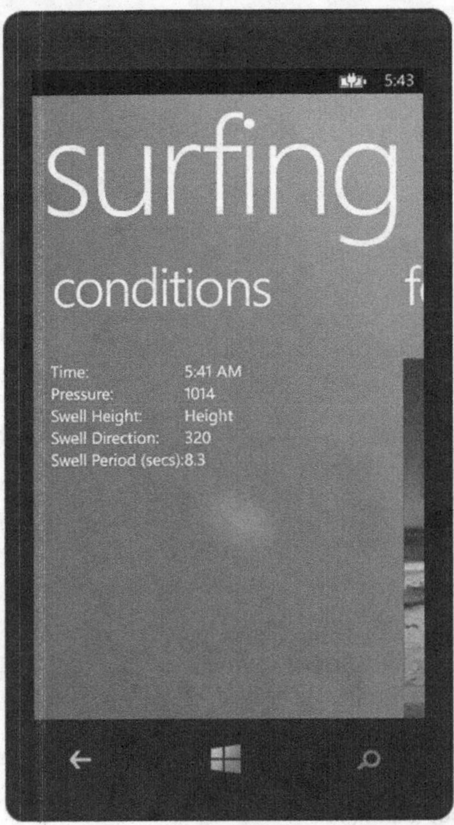

Figure 5-15. The Conditions Panorama Item

3. Add a new class to the `Models` directory and name it `Condition.cs`. Replace the class with the code below.

```
public class Condition
{
    public DateTime Time { get; internal set; }
    public int Pressure { get; internal set; }
    public double SwellHeight { get; internal set; }
    public double SwellDirection { get; internal set; }
    public double SwellPeriodSecs { get; internal set; }
}
```

4. Add a new class to the `Models` directory and name it `Conditions.cs`. Replace the class with the code below. `Conditions` will have a location coordinate and a list of `Condition` objects.

```
using System;
using System.Collections.Generic;
using System.Device.Location;
```

```
namespace NavigateUsingThePanorama.Models
{
    public class Conditions : List<Condition>
    {
        public GeoCoordinate Location { get; private set; }

        public void Load(GeoCoordinate location)
        {
            this.Location = location;
            this.Add(new Condition()
            {
                Time = DateTime.Now,
                Pressure = 1014,
                SwellHeight = 1,
                SwellDirection = 320,
                SwellPeriodSecs = 8.3
            });
        }
    }
}
```

It's cheating the MVVM principle to simply surface the underlying model object. Reusing the model class lets us keep the code a little smaller for demonstration purposes. We will wrap the `Condition` object with a ViewModel that supports `INotifyPropertyChanged`.

5. Add a new class to the `ViewModels` directory and name it `ConditionsViewModel.cs`.

6. Replace the class with the code below. Notice that we're descending from the `BaseListViewmodel`, setting the `Title` in the constructor and populating the `ObservableCollection` of items in the `Load()` method.

```
using System.Device.Location;

namespace NavigateUsingThePanorama.ViewModels
{
    public class ConditionsViewModel : BaseListViewModel<Models.Condition>
    {
        public ConditionsViewModel()
        {
            this.Title = "conditions";
        }

        public void Load(GeoCoordinate location)
        {
            Models.Conditions conditions = new Models.Conditions();
            conditions.Load(location);
            foreach (Models.Condition condition in conditions)
            {
                this.Items.Add(condition);
            }
        }
    }
}
```

7. In the MainPage XAML, add a Panorama control from the Toolbox to the LayoutRoot element of the page. Edit the Panorama to bind the Title property of the Panorama to the Title of the MainViewModel. Set the Panorama Background ImageBrush to the wave.jpg image. The code should look like the example below.

```
<phone:Panorama Title="{Binding Title}">

    <phone:Panorama.Background>
        <ImageBrush ImageSource="/assets/wave.jpg" />
    </phone:Panorama.Background>

</phone:Panorama>
```

8. Add a PanoramaItem to the Panorama. Bind the ConditionsViewModel to the DataContext property of the PanoramaItem. Bind the Header property of the PanoramaItem to the Title of the ConditionsViewModel. The LongListSelector ItemsSource property is bound to the "Items" collection of the ConditionsViewModel. The ItemTemplate points to a ConditionsItemTemplate that still needs to be defined.

```
<phone:PanoramaItem
    Header="{Binding Title}"
    DataContext="{Binding ConditionsViewModel}">
    <phone:LongListSelector
        ItemsSource="{Binding Items}"
        ItemTemplate="{StaticResource ConditionsItemTemplate}" />
</phone:PanoramaItem>
```

9. Add a Resources section to the page and add a new DataTemplate. Define the ConditionsItemTemplate DataTemplate as a Grid with two columns and five rows. Each grid cell should have a TextBlock with literal text in the first column that describes the data, and the second column should have a TextBlock bound to each property in the Condition object.

```
<phone:PhoneApplicationPage.Resources>
    <DataTemplate x:Key="ConditionsItemTemplate">
        <Grid Width="400" Height="400" Margin="10">
            <Grid.ColumnDefinitions>
                <ColumnDefinition Width="Auto" />
                <ColumnDefinition Width="*" />
            </Grid.ColumnDefinitions>
            <Grid.RowDefinitions>
                <RowDefinition Height="Auto" />
                <RowDefinition Height="Auto" />
                <RowDefinition Height="Auto" />
                <RowDefinition Height="Auto" />
                <RowDefinition Height="Auto" />
            </Grid.RowDefinitions>
            <TextBlock Text="Time:" Grid.Column="0" Grid.Row="0" />
            <TextBlock Text="{Binding Time, StringFormat=t}" Grid.Column="1" Grid.Row="0" />
            <TextBlock Text="Pressure:" Grid.Column="0" Grid.Row="1" />
            <TextBlock Text="{Binding Pressure}"  Grid.Column="1" Grid.Row="1" />
```

```
                <TextBlock Text="Swell Height:" Grid.Column="0" Grid.Row="2" />
                <TextBlock Text="Height" Grid.Column="1" Grid.Row="2" />
                <TextBlock Text="Swell Direction:" Grid.Column="0" Grid.Row="3" />
                <TextBlock Text="{Binding SwellDirection}" Grid.Column="1" Grid.Row="3" />
                <TextBlock Text="Swell Period (secs):" Grid.Column="0" Grid.Row="4" />
                <TextBlock Text="{Binding SwellPeriodSecs}" Grid.Column="1" Grid.Row="4" />
            </Grid>
        </DataTemplate>

    </phone:PhoneApplicationPage.Resources>
```

Add the Featured Page

The second Panorama item model shown in Figure 5-16 represents surfing areas and includes Name, Description, a link, an image path, and a Rating. The ViewModel will filter the list to show only "featured" surfing areas, where the rating is greater than "3".

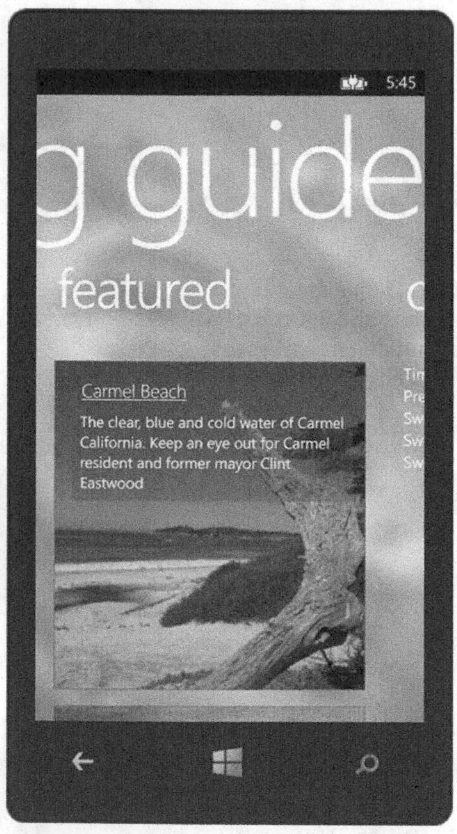

Figure 5-16. *The Features Panorama Item*

1. Add a new class to the `Models` directory and name it `Site.cs`. Replace the class with the code below.

```
using System;
using System.Device.Location;
namespace NavigateUsingThePanorama.Models
{
    public class Site
    {
        public int Id { get; internal set; }
        public string ImageName { get; internal set; }
        public string Name { get; internal set; }
        public string Description { get; internal set; }
        public int Rating { get; internal set; }
        public Uri InfoLink { get; internal set; }
    }
}
```

2. Add the `Sites.cs` class using the code below to the `Models` directory. The `Load()` method will add a number of surf sites with static information.

```
public class Sites : List<Site>
{
    public void Load()
    {
        this.Add(new Site()
        {
            Id = 1,
            Name = "Carmel Beach",
            ImageName = "iStock_000005268101XSmall.jpg",
            Description = "A clear, blue and cold water in Carmel California. " +
        "Keep an eye out for Carmel resident and former mayor Clint Eastwood",
            Rating = 1,
            InfoLink = new
              Uri("http://en.wikipedia.org/wiki/Carmel_River_State_Beach")
        });

        this.Add(new Site()
        {
            Id = 2,
            Name = "Steamers Lane",
            ImageName = "iStock_000016850786XSmall.jpg",
            Description = "A popular surfing on the east side of Santa Cruz,
              California." +
            "A crowded surfing spot and located near the Santa Cruz Surf Museum",
            Rating = 4,
            InfoLink = new Uri("http://en.wikipedia.org/wiki/Steamer_Lane")
        });
```

```
            this.Add(new Site()
            {
                Id = 3,
                Name = "Pleasure Point",
                ImageName = "iStock_000002999571XSmall.jpg",
                Description = "Located on the Monterey Bay in Santa Cruz, California. " +
                "The site for numerous surfing contests",
                Rating = 5,
                InfoLink = new
                  Uri("http://en.wikipedia.org/wiki/Pleasure_Point" +
                  "_Santa_Cruz,_California")
            });

            this.Add(new Site()
            {
                Id = 4,
                Name = "La Jolla Shores",
                ImageName = "iStock_000004630599XSmall.jpg",
                Description = "A mile long stretch in La Jolla, San Diego, California.",
                Rating = 4,
                InfoLink = new Uri("http://en.wikipedia.org/wiki/La_Jolla_Shores")
            });

            this.Add(new Site()
            {
                Id = 5,
                Name = "Mentawai Islands",
                ImageName = "iStock_000014745608XSmall.jpg",
                Description = "A chain of approx 70 islands off the west coast of " +
                "Sumatra, Indonesia. Consistent wave quality year around.",
                Rating = 3,
                InfoLink = new
                  Uri("http://en.wikipedia.org/wiki/Mentawai_Islands_Regency")
            });

            this.Add(new Site()
            {
                Id = 6,
                Name = "Fuerteventura",
                ImageName = "iStock_000012945007XSmall.jpg",
                Description = "Fuerteventura, Spain is in the Canary Islands, " +
                    "located off the coast of Africa in the Atlantic. " +
                    "The best surfing is between October and March. Popular " +
                    "surfing spots: Rocky Point, Harbour Wall, " +
                    "Shooting Gallery, Generosa, Suicides, Mejillonas and Majanicho",
                Rating = 5,
                InfoLink = new Uri("http://en.wikipedia.org/wiki/Fuerteventura")
            });

        }
    }
```

The SitesViewModel is a thin wrapper around the model, with a collection of featured sites.

3. Add a new class to the ViewModels directory and name it SitesViewModel.cs. Replace the class with the code below. Again, we're descending from BaseListViewmodel.

```
using System.Collections.ObjectModel;
using System.Linq;

namespace NavigateUsingThePanorama.ViewModels
{
    public class SitesViewModel : BaseListViewModel<Models.Site>
    {
    }
}
```

4. Add a constructor that sets the Title.

```
public SitesViewModel()
{
    this.Title = "sites";
}
```

5. Add a new read-only property Featured where the accessor filters for Sites where the Rating is greater than "3".

```
public ObservableCollection<Models.Site> Featured
{
    get
    {
        var featured = from Site in this.Items
                       where Site.Rating > 3
                       select Site;
        return new ObservableCollection<Models.Site>(featured);
    }
}
```

6. Add a Load() method that adds Sites to the Models collection. Also notice the call to NotifyPropertyChanged(). The Featured property is bound before the Load() method, so the collection is empty. After loading the collection, call NotifyPropertyChanged() to rebind the Featured collection.

```
public void Load()
{
    Models.Sites sites = new Models.Sites();
    sites.Load();

    foreach (Models.Site site in sites)
    {
        this.Items.Add(site);
    }
    NotifyPropertyChanged("Featured");
}
```

7. In the designer for MainPage.xaml, Add a second PanoramaItem. Bind the SitesViewModel to the DataContext property of the PanoramaItem. Hardcode the Header property of the PanoramaItem to "featured". Bind the LongListSelector ItemsSource property to the Featured collection of the SitesViewModel. The ItemTemplate points to a FeaturedItemTemplate that still needs to be defined.

```
<phone:PanoramaItem
    Header="featured"
    DataContext="{Binding SitesViewModel}">
    <phone:LongListSelector
        ItemsSource="{Binding Featured}"
        ItemTemplate="{StaticResource FeaturedItemTemplate}" />
</phone:PanoramaItem>
```

8. Define the FeaturedItemTemplate DataTemplate as a Grid with a single cell with two elements, an Image and a StackPanel. The Image is bound to the ImageName property of the Site object. The StackPanel displays over the Image and formats the text for the cell. Use a HyperlinkButton as the top element in the StackPanel where the Content is bound to the Site Name property and the NavigateUri is bound to the Site InfoLink. Below the HyperlinkButton, place a TextBlock bound to the Site Description property.

```
<DataTemplate x:Key="FeaturedItemTemplate">
    <Grid Width="400" Height="400" >

        <Image Source="{Binding ImageName, StringFormat='/Assets/Sites/{0}'}"
            Stretch="UniformToFill" />

        <StackPanel
            Background="{StaticResource PhoneSemitransparentBrush}"
            HorizontalAlignment="Stretch" VerticalAlignment="Top"
            Margin="20, 20, 30, 30" >
            <HyperlinkButton
                Content="{Binding Name}"
                FontFamily="{StaticResource PhoneFontFamilyLight}"
                HorizontalAlignment="Left"
                NavigateUri="{Binding InfoLink}"
                TargetName="_blank"
                VerticalAlignment="Top" />
            <TextBlock
                FontSize="{StaticResource PhoneFontSizeSmall}"
                Style="{StaticResource PhoneTextBlockBase}"
                Text="{Binding Description}"
                TextWrapping="Wrap" Margin="10" />
        </StackPanel>
    </Grid>
</DataTemplate>
```

About Phone Resource Styles

Avoiding the built-in brushes and colors in your design may have a cost in flexibility, productivity, and could even cause difficulties submitting your app to the Windows Phone Store.

Why not use your own colors wherever you like? Figure 5-17 shows the effect of a custom brush that paints a semi-transparent background for the text. This is a nice effect where the text is visible, but the background shading is subtle. The snippet below shows the definition of the custom brush.

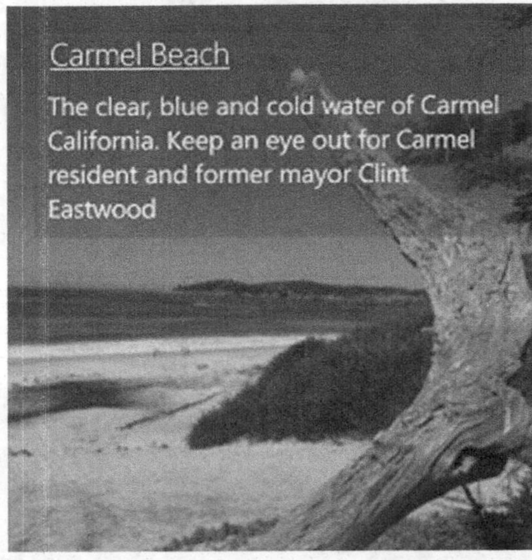

Figure 5-17. *Custom Brush and Dark Theme*

The problem comes into play when you change themes. Using the custom brush when the Light theme is enabled on the device, the text background does not have enough contrast and disappears into the dark portions of the background (see Figure 5-18). Notice the second time the word "Carmel" is used, the word all but disappears into the dark green background.

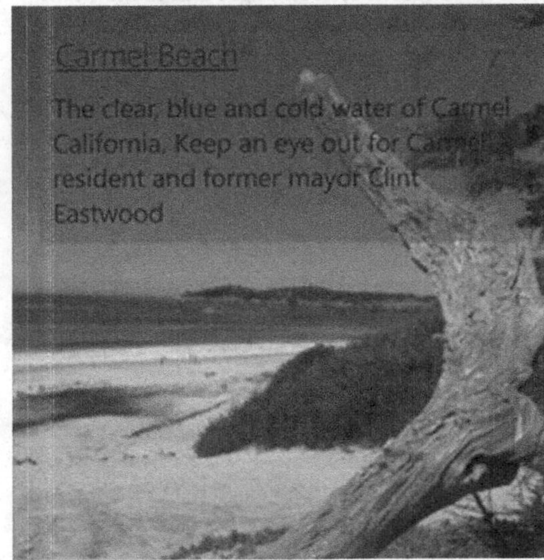

Figure 5-18. *Custom Brush and Light Theme*

The built-in PhoneSemitransparentBrush has plenty of contrast to handle both Light and Dark themes, no matter what the content showing through from the background (see Figure 5-19).

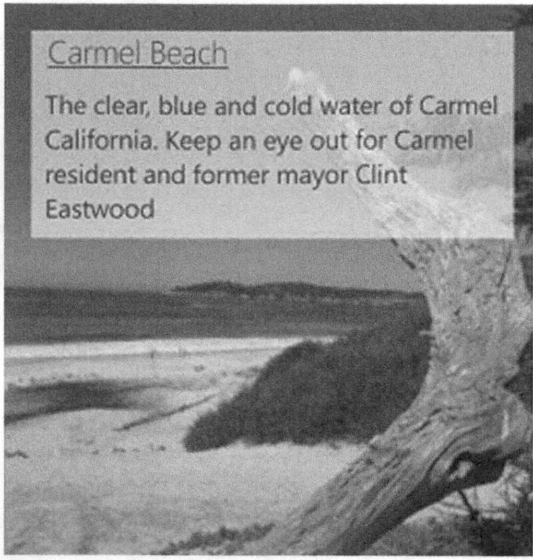

Figure 5-19. PhoneSemitransparentBrush*in in Light and Dark Themes*

Summary

Windows Phone 8 applications navigate within pages, between pages, and to external URIs. Navigation within pages uses the Panorama and Pivot controls to present different views. The PhoneApplicationFrame Navigate() method traverses to relative URLs in the application while PhoneApplicationPage events sense when navigation occurs. The PhoneApplicationPage also supplies the NavigationService object to navigate between pages and to maintain the history backstack. The WebBrowserTask and WebBrowser control are both used to navigate to external URLs.

In the next chapter, "Application Lifecycle," you'll learn how to handle state as you move between pages in your application.

CHAPTER 6

Application Lifecycle

This chapter explains the Windows Phone 8 *application lifecycle*, why the lifecycle is critical, and what you need to do in your applications to work in concert with the lifecycle, including:

- An overview of the application lifecycle, why the lifecycle is structured as it is, key terminology, and the basic flow of events and states in the lifecycle.
- When and where to save and restore your application's state.
- When and where to save and restore your page's state.
- How to use temporary and permanent storage mechanisms.

Understanding the Application Lifecycle

The application's lifecycle is the set of states that the application goes through as the application executes. Small tablet and phone devices must balance multiple tasks, be responsive and have a long battery life. The working conditions of the phone dictate that the lifecycle is more involved than in the desktop world. For example, when leaving a page to take a call, users expect their data to still be on the page when they return. The point to knowing the Windows Phone 8 lifecycle is to know when, where, and how to save and restore state. The application can be in one of three states:

- ***Running***: The application is in the foreground. Only one application is allowed in the foreground at a time.
- ***Dormant***: The application is no longer in the foreground, but the operating system doesn't need the device resources yet. Dormant applications can be reactivated automatically by the operating system without your having to write code to restore state, meaning, the application's objects are still in memory. If the operating system needs resources, dormant applications will be tombstoned and terminated.
- ***Tombstoned***: The application is terminated and the objects of the application are removed from memory. When the application is activated, the user is placed back on the page they left off at, but the objects must be restored from their previous state.

The lifecycle has four events:

- `Application Launching` fires just before the application is running.
- `Application Deactivated` occurs when the application is sent into the background and becomes dormant.

- Application Activated fires when the application is brought into the foreground after being dormant or tombstoned.
- Application Closing fires as the application closes, meaning, the user hits the Back key or powers off the device.

There are two phone application page methods that fire as the application transitions to and from a running state. Whenever the application is about to run, the OnNavigatedTo method is called. The call to the OnNavigateTo() method occurs just after the Application Launching or Activated events. Whenever the application is about to stop running, the OnNavigatedFrom method is called. The call occurs just before the Application Deactivated or Closing events. You can override both of these methods in the page code-behind.

Now that you're aware of the states and events that the application transitions between, you will understand why and where you need to save application data. The next section "Saving and Restoring Application State" will walk you through the application code-behind that corresponds to the application-level events.

Saving and Restoring Application State

In practical terms, you need to know where in the code the state can be saved and restored. The Visual Studio Windows Phone 8 template project hooks up all the application-level event handlers, so you can use them right away. The app.xaml created automatically for each new project (Listing 6-1) defines application-level event handlers for launching, closing, activating, and deactivating.

Listing 6-1. App.xaml

```
<Application.ApplicationLifetimeObjects>
    <!--Required object that handles lifetime events for the application-->
    <shell:PhoneApplicationService
        Launching="Application_Launching" Closing="Application_Closing"
        Activated="Application_Activated" Deactivated="Application_Deactivated"/>
</Application.ApplicationLifetimeObjects>
```

The corresponding event handlers are all roughed in along with comments describing their behavior in the App.xaml.cs (Listing 6-2).

Listing 6-2. App.xaml.cs

```
// Code to execute when the application is launching (eg, from Start)
// This code will not execute when the application is reactivated
private void Application_Launching(object sender, LaunchingEventArgs e)
{
}

// Code to execute when the application is activated (brought to foreground)
// This code will not execute when the application is first launched
private void Application_Activated(object sender, ActivatedEventArgs e)
{
}

// Code to execute when the application is deactivated (sent to background)
// This code will not execute when the application is closing
private void Application_Deactivated(object sender, DeactivatedEventArgs e)
{
}
```

```
// Code to execute when the application is closing (eg, user hit Back)
// This code will not execute when the application is deactivated
private void Application_Closing(object sender, ClosingEventArgs e)
{
}
```

Storing Transient Data

Transient data, that is, information that doesn't need to survive between application launches, is saved to the State property of the PhoneApplicationService. State is a dictionary object indexed with a string key that returns any arbitrary, serializable object. In Listing 6-3, the "LastUpdate" key saves and returns a DateTime.

Listing 6-3. Handling Activated and Deactivated Events

```
private void Application_Activated(object sender, ActivatedEventArgs e)
{
    DateTime lastUpdate =
    (DateTime)PhoneApplicationService.Current.State["LastUpdate"];
    Debug.WriteLine("Application_Activated: LastUpdate=" + lastUpdate.ToLongTimeString());
}

private void Application_Deactivated(object sender, DeactivatedEventArgs e)
{
    Debug.WriteLine("Application_Deactivated: Saving LastUpdate to application state");
    PhoneApplicationService.Current.State["LastUpdate"] = DateTime.Now;
}
```

The Deactivated event fires as other applications come to the foreground. You can replicate this for yourself by hitting the Start button or selecting a chooser. Hitting the Back button reactivates the application and the Activate event is fired. The debug log in the Visual Studio Output window (Figure 6-1) shows that the data is saved, and then re-hydrated from the PhoneApplicationService State property.

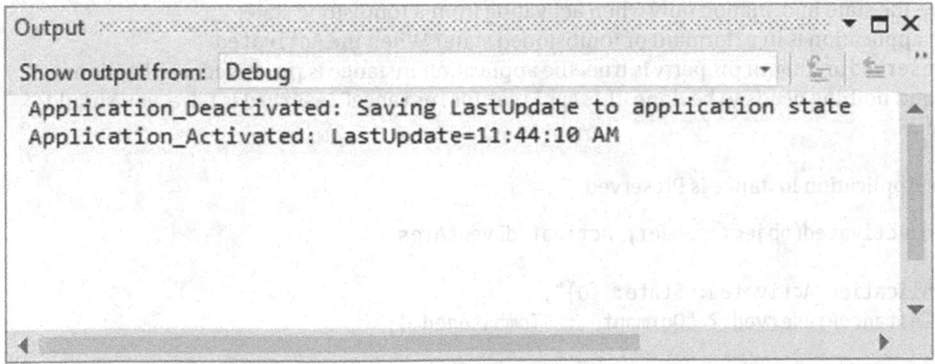

Figure 6-1. *Debug Statements in the Output Window*

The State dictionary can as easily store any object. The custom MyObject defined in Listing 6-4 is stored in the State dictionary when the application is deactivated and restored on activation.

Listing 6-4. Handling Activated and Deactivated Events

```
public class MyObject
{
    public DateTime LastUpdate { get; set; }
}

//...

public MyObject MyObject { get; set; }

private void Application_Deactivated(object sender, DeactivatedEventArgs e)
{
    this.MyObject = new MyObject() { LastUpdate = DateTime.Now };
    // store in dictionary
    PhoneApplicationService.Current.State["MyObject"] = this.MyObject;
    Debug.WriteLine("Application_Deactivated: " + this.MyObject.LastUpdate.ToLongTimeString());
}

private void Application_Activated(object sender, ActivatedEventArgs e)
{
    // restore from dictionary
    this.MyObject = PhoneApplicationService.Current.State["MyObject"] as MyObject;
    Debug.WriteLine("Application_Activated: " + this.MyObject.LastUpdate.ToLongTimeString());
}
```

Tombstoned vs. Dormant

We're missing a trick here for the previous example in Listing 6-5. The Activated event handler always reloads the object. If we're activating from a dormant state, there's no need to restore from the State object to the application's variables. You should restore the state information only when activating from a tombstone state.

How do you know if an application is in a dormant or tombstoned state? When the Activated IsApplicationInstancePreserved argument property is true, the application instance is preserved, application objects are still in memory and nothing needs to be done. If IsApplicationInstancePreserved is false, you should restore the application state.

Listing 6-5. Checking if the Application Instance is Preserved

```
private void Application_Activated(object sender, ActivatedEventArgs e)
{
    Debug.WriteLine("Application_Activated: State: {0}",
        e.IsApplicationInstancePreserved ? "Dormant" : "Tombstoned");

    if (!e.IsApplicationInstancePreserved)
    {
        // restore from tombstone
        this.MyObject = PhoneApplicationService.Current.State["MyObject"] as MyObject;
        Debug.WriteLine("Restored from tombstone");
    }
}
```

■ **Note** There's an exception to the rule where you may have to update your data, even though you are activating from a dormant state. Even if state is preserved, application variables aren't automatically *updated* while dormant. Watch out for scenarios where the data might change during dormancy, such as time or network status changes.

If you're using the emulator to test, the application instance will always be preserved. To debug with `IsApplicationInstancePreserved == false`, right-click the project, navigate to the Debug property page and set the `Tombstone upon deactivation while debugging` checkbox (Figure 6-2). Rerun the application and the "tombstoned" path through the code will run, that is, `IsApplicationInstancePreserved` is true.

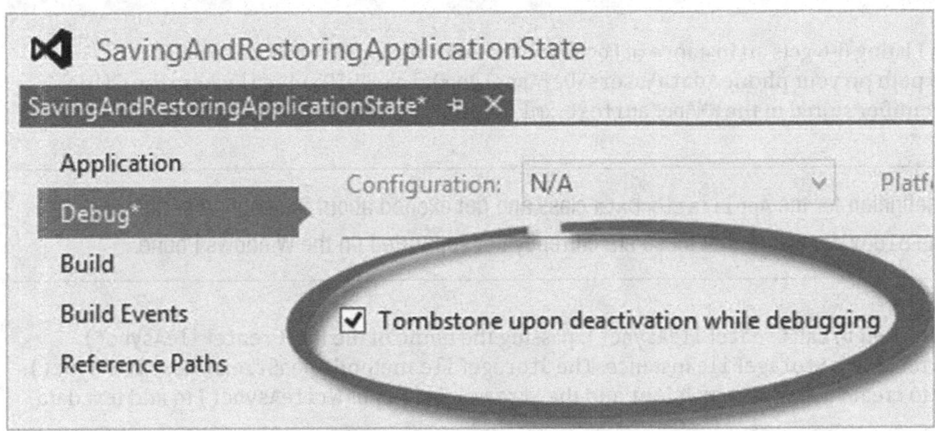

***Figure 6-2.** Enabling Tombstone Debugging*

Storing Persistent Data

If the data needs to survive through the application close and re-launch, you need to save to a persistent data store. Windows Phone Storage provides a sand-boxed area that your application can use as a personal file system and is a good mechanism for persistent data storage. You can also read from external storage devices like SD cards.

Local Storage

The two key classes `StorageFolder` and `StorageFile` support most of the file input/output mechanisms like listing folders and files, creating, loading, saving, copying, renaming, deleting, and moving. The API is heavily focused on asynchronous operations so expect to see the keywords `async` and `await throughout the code`.

Let's look at the minimal code it takes to save text to a file (see Listing 6-6). The first thing to notice about the listing is that the method is marked with the `async` modifier. This is required to use the `await` operation to perform operations that are asynchronous, but allows for a more sequential coding style. See Asynchronous Programming with Async and Await (`http://msdn.microsoft.com/en-us/library/vstudio/hh191443.aspx`) for more information.

Listing 6-6. Writing to a Local File

```
private async void SaveButton_Click_1(object sender, EventArgs e)
{
    // get the instance of the local folder
    StorageFolder localFolder = ApplicationData.Current.LocalFolder;
```

```
    // create a file in the local folder
    StorageFile localFile = await localFolder.CreateFileAsync("MyData");

    // open the file for writing and write to the file
    using (Stream stream = await localFile.OpenStreamForWriteAsync())
    {
        using (StreamWriter writer = new StreamWriter(stream))
        {
            await writer.WriteAsync(DataTextBox.Text);
        }
    }
}
```

The first line of code in Listing 6-6 gets an instance of LocalFolder from the ApplicationData object. LocalFolder represents the path on your phone \data\users\DefApps\AppData\<GUID>\local where the GUID is the unique application identifier stored in the WMAppManifest.xml file.

■ **Note** If you look at the definition for the ApplicationData class and get excited about the cool properties like LocalSettings and RoamingFolder, be aware that these are currently not supported on the Windows Phone.

The LocalFolder is then used to call CreateFileAsync(), passing the name of the file. CreateFileAsync() uses the await operation to retrieve a StorageFile instance. The StorageFile method OpenStreamForWriteAsync() is called, the stream is used to create a new StreamWriter and the StreamWriter calls WriteAsync() to add text data to the file.

To read from the file, call GetFileAsync() and pass the file name. This will return a StorageFile that can call OpenStreamForReadAsync(). The stream is used to construct a StreamReader and the reader's ReadToEndAsync() method returns the file data as a single string. Listing 6-7 shows the code.

Listing 6-7. Reading from a Local File

```
private async void LoadButton_Click_1(object sender, EventArgs e)
{
    StorageFolder localFolder = ApplicationData.Current.LocalFolder;

    try
    {
        StorageFile localFile = await localFolder.GetFileAsync("MyData"); ;
        Stream stream = await localFile.OpenStreamForReadAsync();
        using (StreamReader reader = new StreamReader(stream))
        {
            DataTextBox.Text = await reader.ReadToEndAsync();
        }
    }
    catch (FileNotFoundException ex)
    {
        // handle file not found condition based on your requirements
    }
}
```

■ **Note** Why is there a `try...catch` in Listing 6-7? Isn't throwing exceptions for relatively normal conditions considered bad practice? Couldn't we get the IAsyncInfo back from `GetFileAsync()` and check its ErrorCode? Nope. To discover issues in an asynchronous operation, a `try...catch` is required to report on the problem as it occurs.

Save Settings to Local Storage

Currently, there is no dedicated settings object, but you can create your own using a `StorageFile` in the `LocalFolder`. Most of the logic shown in the preceding Local Storage example is the same here except that we're writing key and value pairs, each on their own line. Listing 6-8 first opens a file in the local folder to contain the settings. `OpenStreamForWriteAsync()` takes a string parameter of the relative path of the file to be opened, and the second parameter, `CreationCollisionOption`, is an enumeration that describes how the method will react if there is already a file with the same name. Then the dictionary is iterated and the `StreamWriter WriteLineAsync()` method places each of the dictionary's Key/Value pairs into the file.

■ **Note** Be aware that `SaveSettings()` will be called from the Application `Closing` event. Because the application is shutting down, this isn't the time to "fire-and-forget" methods through the `await` operator. Instead, you can force a synchronous operation by referencing the `Result` property of `OpenStreamForWriteAsync()`.

Listing 6-8. Saving Settings to a Local File

```
private void SaveSettings(string fileName, Dictionary<string, string> dictionary)
{
    var localFolder = ApplicationData.Current.LocalFolder;
    using (var stream = localFolder.OpenStreamForWriteAsync(fileName,
        CreationCollisionOption.ReplaceExisting).Result)

    using (var writer = new StreamWriter(stream))
    {
        foreach (var item in dictionary)
        {
                writer.WriteLineAsync(item.Key + "|" + item.Value);
        }
    }
}
```

To bring the persisted settings back from the local file and transform them to a dictionary object, you can read the file as a single string, parse the string and use the LINQ `ToDictionary()` method to load the dictionary (see Listing 6-9). You will need to add `System.Linq` to your `using` statements to access the `ToDictionary()` extension method.

Listing 6-9. Loading Settings from a Local File

```
private async Task<Dictionary<string, string>> LoadSettings(string fileName)
{
    var localFolder = ApplicationData.Current.LocalFolder;
    var dictionary = new Dictionary<string, string>();
    try
```

```
    {
        var localFile = await localFolder.GetFileAsync(fileName);
        using (Stream stream = await localFile.OpenStreamForReadAsync())
        {
            using (var reader = new StreamReader(stream))
            {
                string text = await reader.ReadToEndAsync();

                // remove extraneous new lines
                text = text.Replace("\n\n", String.Empty);

                // split text into separate lines
                var arr = text.Split(new string[] { "\r\n" },
                    StringSplitOptions.RemoveEmptyEntries);

                // extract name/value pairs from each line
                dictionary = arr.Select(l => l.Split('|'))
                    .ToDictionary(pair => pair[0], pair => pair[1]);
            }
        }
    }
    catch (FileNotFoundException ex)
    {
        Debug.WriteLine(ex.Message);
    }
    return dictionary;
}
```

Listing 6-10 shows the settings being saved and loaded from a local file during the application Launching and Closing events. Notice that the Application_Closing event handler does not use async or await.

Listing 6-10. Loading and Saving Settings from Application Events

```
private Dictionary<string, string> _settings = new Dictionary<string, string>();

private async void Application_Launching(object sender, LaunchingEventArgs e)
{
    _settings = await LoadSettings("MySettings");
    if (_settings.ContainsKey("LastUpdate"))
    {
        var lastUpdate = _settings["LastUpdate"];
        Debug.WriteLine(lastUpdate);
    }
}

private void Application_Closing(object sender, ClosingEventArgs e)
{
    _settings["LastUpdate"] = DateTime.Now.ToLongTimeString();
    SaveSettings("MySettings", _settings);
}
```

Serialization to Local Storage

The XmlSerializer makes short work of serializing objects with public properties to local storage. You need to add a reference to the System.Xml.Serialization assembly in the References node of the project. Use the XmlSerializer Serialize() and Deserialize() methods to convert and read/write the stream in one step. See Chapter 8 for more serialization techniques.

The examples that follow use a very simple class defined in Listing 6-11 that includes integer, string, and DateTime properties.

Listing 6-11. Simple Object to Serialize

```
public class MyObject
{
    public int Id { get; set; }
    public string Title { get; set; }
    public DateTime LastUpdate { get; set; }
}
```

You can create a generic method to save any kind of object. The custom SaveObject() method in Listing 6-12 takes a file name string and an object of type T to be serialized. After opening the file for writing, create a new XmlSerializer, and call its Serialize() method, passing the file stream and the object to write out. This method is called from the Application_Closing event, so avoid using async and await.

Listing 6-12. Generic Object Serialization

```
private static void SaveObject<T>(string fileName, T obj)
{
    using (var stream = ApplicationData.Current.LocalFolder.OpenStreamForWriteAsync(fileName,
        CreationCollisionOption.ReplaceExisting).Result)
    {
        var serializer = new XmlSerializer(typeof(T));
        serializer.Serialize(stream, obj);
    }
}
```

Loading will occur when the application launches. The LoadObject() method in Listing 6-13 is generic. This method first creates a default object of type T. Once the file is open for streaming (and assuming there's content in the file), the XmlSerializer Deserialize() method uses the stream to re-hydrate the object.

Listing 6-13. Generic Object Deserialization

```
private static async Task<T> LoadObject<T>(string fileName)
{
    T obj = default(T);
    try
    {
        var localFile = await ApplicationData.Current.LocalFolder.GetFileAsync(fileName);
        using (var stream = await localFile.OpenStreamForReadAsync())
        {
            if (stream.Length > 0)
            {
                var serializer = new XmlSerializer(typeof(T));
                obj = (T)serializer.Deserialize(stream);
```

```
            }
        }
    }
    catch (FileNotFoundException)
    {
        Debug.WriteLine(fileName + " not found");
    }
    return obj;
}
```

Usage examples for LoadObject() and SaveObject() are shown in Listing 6-14.

Listing 6-14. Launching and Closing the Application

```
private async void Application_Launching(object sender, LaunchingEventArgs e)
{
    var myObject = await LoadObject<MyObject>("myfile.xml");
    if (myObject != null)
    {
        Debug.WriteLine(myObject.Title + " (" + myObject.Id + ") last updated " +
            myObject.LastUpdate.ToLongTimeString());
    }
}

private void Application_Closing(object sender, ClosingEventArgs e)
{
    var myObject = new MyObject()
    {
        Id = 123,
        Title = "Serialization Example",
        LastUpdate = DateTime.Now
    };
    SaveObject<MyObject>("myfile.xml", myObject);
}
```

Saving and restoring state for the entire application will address situations where the application needs restoration after being tombstoned, dormant, or the phone is shut down. What about the finer-grain scenarios where the user wants to return to a page with the information they entered still in place? For directions on how to handle these situations, read the next section "Saving and Restoring Page State".

Saving and Restoring Page State

If an application hasn't terminated, leaving the page should not erase its data. The user should always return to the page as they left it. If the user enters an address and presses the Start button, the address should still be on the page when they return via the Back button.

Using the Page State Property

As long as the application doesn't terminate, you can use the page State property to store transient information that relates to the page. The PhoneApplicationPage OnNavigatedFrom and OnNavigatedTo events are your opportunities to save and restore (see Listing 6-15).

Listing 6-15. Saving and Restoring Page State

```
protected override void OnNavigatedFrom(System.Windows.Navigation.NavigationEventArgs e)
{
    this.State["Address"] = "123 Pleasant Way";
    base.OnNavigatedFrom(e);
}
protected override void OnNavigatedTo(System.Windows.Navigation.NavigationEventArgs e)
{
    string address = this.State.ContainsKey("Address") ?
        this.State["Address"].ToString() : String.Empty;
    base.OnNavigatedTo(e);
}
```

You can store a ViewModel, or if the ViewModel is too big to be practical, you can store a subset of key values as a starting point to restoring the page state. The following example binds, saves, and restores an object. The object in Listing 6-16 is an INotifyPropertyChanged implementation with a single "Address" property.

Listing 6-16. Minimal ViewModel

```
public class MyPageViewModel : INotifyPropertyChanged
{
    private string _address;
    public string Address
    {
        get { return _address; }
        set
        {
            if (_address != value)
            {
                _address = value;
                NotifyPropertyChanged("Address");
            }
        }
    }

    public event PropertyChangedEventHandler PropertyChanged;
    public void NotifyPropertyChanged(string propertyName)
    {
        if (PropertyChanged != null)
        {
            PropertyChanged(this, new PropertyChangedEventArgs(propertyName));
        }
    }
}
```

Listing 6-17 shows how the view model is saved and restored during page navigation. When the page first displays, the private member _myPageViewModel is assigned a new instance of the "MyPageViewModel" object if the key doesn't exist, or the State dictionary element is retrieved if the key does exist. The retrieved object is assigned to the DataContext for the page. During the OnNavigatedFrom method override, the code-behind for the page saves to the "MyPageViewModel" key of the State dictionary.

Listing 6-17. The Page Class Definition

```
using Microsoft.Phone.Controls;

namespace SavingAndRestoringPageState
{
    public partial class MainPage : PhoneApplicationPage
    {
        private MyPageViewModel _myPageViewModel;

        public MainPage()
        {
            InitializeComponent();
        }

        protected override void OnNavigatedFrom(System.Windows.Navigation.NavigationEventArgs e)
        {
            this.State["MyPageViewModel"] = _myPageViewModel;
            base.OnNavigatedFrom(e);
        }

        protected override void OnNavigatedTo(System.Windows.Navigation.NavigationEventArgs e)
        {
            _myPageViewModel = this.State.ContainsKey("MyPageViewModel") ?
                this.State["MyPageViewModel"] as MyPageViewModel : new MyPageViewModel();
            this.DataContext = _myPageViewModel;
            base.OnNavigatedTo(e);
        }
    }
}
```

The "ContentPanel" holds a TextBox that is bound to the Address property of MyPageViewModel (see Listing 6-18). Notice that the Mode is TwoWay, so the user will update the value on the fly. When the user navigates forward using the Start key or chooser, the TextBox Text value will persist on return.

Listing 6-18. The ContentPanel XAML

```
<Grid x:Name="ContentPanel" Grid.Row="1" Margin="12,0,12,0">
    <StackPanel>
        <TextBlock Text="Address:" />
        <TextBox Text="{Binding Address, Mode=TwoWay}"/>
    </StackPanel>
</Grid>
```

Persisting User Entry Example

This section demonstrates how to persist user entry, even when the user navigates away from the page and returns.

First, you need to prepare the project:

1. Create a new Windows Phone Application.
2. In the Visual Studio Solution Explorer, create a new folder `ViewModels`.

Next, build the ViewModel:

3. Add a new class to the ViewModels folder and name it `UserViewModel.cs`.
4. Open for editing.
5. Mark the class as public scope and implement the `INotifyPropertyChanged` interface as shown in Listing 6-19.

Listing 6-19. Implementing INotifyPropertyChanged

```
public class UserViewModel : INotifyPropertyChanged
{
    public event PropertyChangedEventHandler PropertyChanged;
    public void NotifyPropertyChanged(string propertyName)
    {
        if (PropertyChanged != null)
        {
            PropertyChanged(this, new PropertyChangedEventArgs(propertyName));
        }
    }
}
```

6. Add properties to the class for UserName, Email, and Phone using the code in Listing 6-20.

Listing 6-20. Implementing INotifyPropertyChanged

```
private string _userName;
public string UserName
{
    get { return _userName; }
    set
    {
        if (_userName != value)
        {
            _userName = value;
            NotifyPropertyChanged("UserName");
        }
    }
}

private string _email;
public string Email
{
    get { return _email; }
    set
```

```
        {
            if (_email != value)
            {
                _email = value;
                NotifyPropertyChanged("Email");
            }
        }
    }

    private string _phone;
    public string Phone
    {
        get { return _phone; }
        set
        {
            if (_phone != value)
            {
                _phone = value;
                NotifyPropertyChanged("Phone");
            }
        }
    }
```

Next, handle the page navigation events:

7. Open the `MainPage.xaml.cs` file for editing.
8. Add a private member for the ViewModel (see Listing 6-21).

Listing 6-21. Defining the ViewModel

```
private UserViewModel _vm;
```

9. Override the page `OnNavigatedFrom` event. In the event handler, assign the ViewModel instance to the page `State` (see Listing 6-22).

Listing 6-22. Overriding the OnNavigatedFrom() Method

```
protected override void OnNavigatedFrom(System.Windows.Navigation.NavigationEventArgs e)
{
    this.State["UserViewModel"] = _vm;
    base.OnNavigatedFrom(e);
}
```

10. Override the page `OnNavigatedTo` event. Extract the ViewModel from the page State if it exists and bind the ViewModel to the page `DataContext` (see Listing 6-23).

Listing 6-23. Overriding the OnNavigatedTo() Method

```
protected override void OnNavigatedTo(System.Windows.Navigation.NavigationEventArgs e)
{
    _vm = this.State.ContainsKey("UserViewModel") ?
        this.State["UserViewModel"] as UserViewModel : new UserViewModel();
    this.DataContext = _vm;
    base.OnNavigatedTo(e);
}
```

Now, edit the Main Page XAML:

11. Edit the default "ContentPanel" element to have two columns and three rows as shown in Listing 6-24.

Listing 6-24. Editing the ContentPanel Element

```
<Grid x:Name="ContentPanel" Grid.Row="1" Margin="12,0,12,0">
    <Grid.ColumnDefinitions>
        <ColumnDefinition Width="Auto" />
        <ColumnDefinition Width="*" />
    </Grid.ColumnDefinitions>
    <Grid.RowDefinitions>
        <RowDefinition Height="Auto" />
        <RowDefinition Height="Auto" />
        <RowDefinition Height="Auto" />
    </Grid.RowDefinitions>
</Grid>
```

12. Add three TextBlock instances and three TextBox instances into the ContentPanel element for user entry. Bind the Text property of each TextBox to the ViewModel UserName, Email, and Phone, respectively. The binding Mode should be TwoWay to allow user entries to flow into the ViewModel and to be reflected in the TextBoxes when the ViewModel is restored (see Listing 6-25).

Listing 6-25. Defining Grid Rows and Columns

```
<TextBlock Grid.Column="0" Grid.Row="0" Text="User Name:" />
<TextBox   Grid.Column="1" Grid.Row="0" Text="{Binding UserName, Mode=TwoWay}" />
<TextBlock Grid.Column="0" Grid.Row="1" Text="email:" />
<TextBox   Grid.Column="1" Grid.Row="1" Text="{Binding Email, Mode=TwoWay}" />
<TextBlock Grid.Column="0" Grid.Row="2" Text="phone:" />
<TextBox   Grid.Column="1" Grid.Row="2" Text="{Binding Phone, Mode=TwoWay}" />
```

Before you finish, test the application:

13. Run the application.

14. Enter text into the TextBox controls.

15. Press the Start button.

16. Press the Back button.

17. The text you entered in step #2 should still be displaying in the TextBoxes, as in Figure 6-3.

Figure 6-3. *Form Entry After Start/Back Button Press*

Summary

Windows Phone 8 applications must handle interruptions from phone calls and lock screens, allow jumping to other applications, and remember crucial information when powered off. All this must be provided while preserving a long battery life. Because of the environment that the Windows Phone operates in, understanding the lifecycle is essential to knowing when and how to save state information for individual pages in the application and the application as a whole.

CHAPTER 7

Gestures

Gestures are patterns of movement made by the user interacting with the device: tapping, double-tapping, tap-and-hold, flicking (quick linear movements in one direction), panning (dragging), pinching (multi-touch where two points are dragged together), zooming (multi-touch where two points are dragged apart), and rotating (multi-touch where two points are moved to describe a new angle).

This chapter explores multiple mechanisms used by Windows Phone 8 to recognize gestures:

- The Touch object raises FrameReported events that surface primitive information about what was touched, size, coordinates, and action (up, down, or move). The Touch object won't help interpreting the data to know if the touch was held, is a pinching gesture, or another action. The Touch object will return multiple points in a TouchPointCollection.
- Simple UIElement events Tap, DoubleTap, and Hold are easy to implement, but short on information. Use these events for single-touch input where you want a simple equivalent of a button click.
- Multi-touch UIElement events ManipulationStarted, ManipulationCompleted, and ManipulationDelta provides information about one or two points that are touched, including velocity, if the touch is "inertial" (i.e., touch was still moving when the event fired), scale (size) and translation (position).
- The GestureListener attached property of the GestureService object provides a rich set of events for one or two points including Tap, DoubleTap, Flick, Hold, GestureBegin, GestureCompleted, PinchStarted, PinchDelta, PinchCompleted, DragStarted, DragDelta, and DragCompleted.

The Touch Object

The Touch object from the System.Windows.Input namespace has a single member, the FrameReported event. The Touch code example in Listing 7-1 shows that the FrameReported event certainly returns lots of info, but it's left up to you to make sense of it. The Touch object doesn't tell you if you're pinching, zooming, dragging, rotating, or flicking. It just tells you that you have a set of coordinates that are being touched at any one time.

Listing 7-1. Handling the FrameReported Event

```
public MainPage()
{
    InitializeComponent();

    Touch.FrameReported += new TouchFrameEventHandler(Touch_FrameReported);
}
```

```
void Touch_FrameReported(object sender, TouchFrameEventArgs e)
{
    TouchPointCollection points = e.GetTouchPoints(this);
    TouchPoint point = e.GetPrimaryTouchPoint(this);
    Point position = point.Position;
    Size size = point.Size;
    TouchAction action = point.Action;
    UIElement touchedElement = point.TouchDevice.DirectlyOver;
    this.PageTitle.Text = action.ToString();
}
```

The output of the FrameReported event handler is shown in Figure 7-1. The advantage of the Touch object is that you can work with multiple points of contact against multiple elements. If you need to track more than two points of contact, then the Touch object may be your weapon of choice. For example, if you wanted to allow a three-fingered gesture that would cause the Map control pitch to change angle as the user swiped from top to bottom. But for most common tasks, there are easier alternatives than using the low-level Touch object.

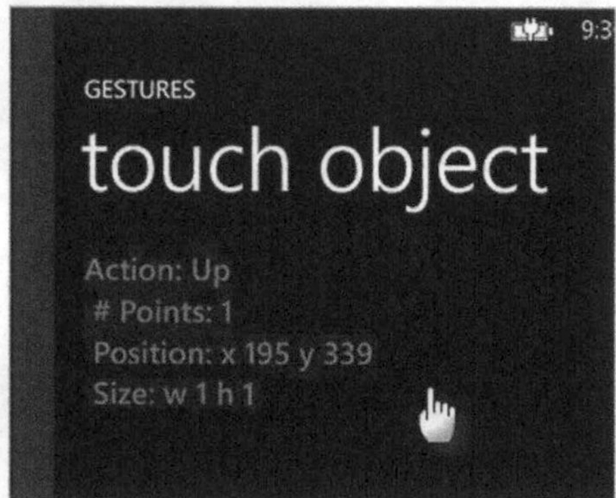

Figure 7-1. *Output from the Touch Object*

UIElement Events

The Tap, DoubleTap, and Hold single touch events can be hooked up to any UIElement descendant. The signatures of all three event handlers are identical. The XAML layout in Listing 7-2 simulates a deck of playing cards. The ContentPanel element is redefined as a Canvas element with a dark green background. An Image of a face-down playing card is placed in the Canvas and is hooked up to the Tap event. The Tap event simulates "dealing" from the deck.

Listing 7-2. Defining the Layout

```
<Canvas x:Name="ContentPanel"
    Background="DarkGreen"
    Grid.Row="1"
    Margin="12,12,12,12">

    <Image Name="ImageCardBack"
        Stretch="Uniform"
        Source="/Assets/Cards/back.png"
```

```
        Height="200"
        Margin="100"
        Tap="ImageCardBack_Tap" />
</Canvas>
```

As the face-down card is tapped, new cards are displayed face-up (see Figure 7-2).

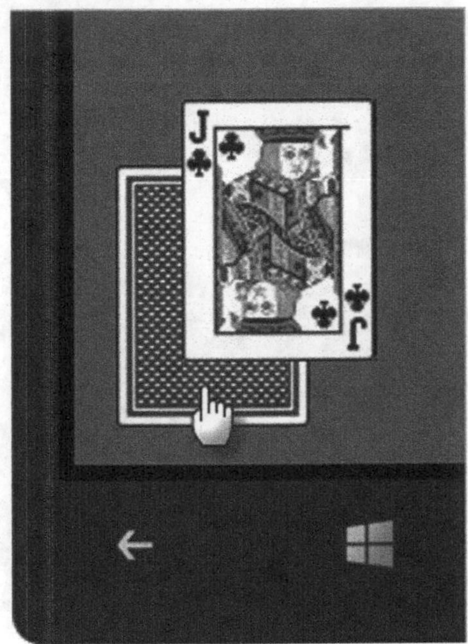

Figure 7-2. *Element Responding to the Tap Event*

The example application defines classes that model a Deck of Card objects. Listing 7-3 first defines SuitType and CardType enumerations that include the possible suit and card value in a deck of cards. The Card object knows its own suit value. The Deck contains an array of all possible cards and the Deck Deal() method returns a random card from the array.

Listing 7-3. Defining Cards

```
public enum SuitType { Clubs, Spades, Hearts, Diamonds }

public enum CardType
{
    Two = 2, Three = 3, Four = 4, Five = 5, Six = 6, Seven = 7,
    Eight = 8, Nine = 9, Ten = 10, Jack = 11, Queen = 12, King = 13, Ace = 14
}

public class Card
{
    public SuitType SuitType { get; internal set; }
    public CardType CardType { get; internal set; }
}
```

```
public class Deck
{
    private Random _random = new Random();
    private List<Card> _cards;

    public Deck()
    {
        // build the array of cards
        _cards =
            (from SuitType suitType in Enum.GetValues(typeof(SuitType))
                from CardType cardType in Enum.GetValues(typeof(CardType))
                select new Card()
                {
                    CardType = cardType,
                    SuitType = suitType
                }).ToList();
    }

    // return a random card from the deck
    public Card Deal()
    {
        Card dealtCard = null;
        if (_cards.Count > 0)
        {
            dealtCard = _cards[_random.Next(0, _cards.Count - 1)];
            _cards.Remove(dealtCard);
        }
        return dealtCard;
    }

    public int Count { get { return _cards.Count; } }
}
```

When the face-down card is tapped, the Deck class dispenses a new Card object from the Deal() method. A custom private method GetCardImage()returns a new Image object and places it slightly up and to the right of the face-down card. Once the Image element is added to the Children collection of the ContentPanel element, the Image becomes visible on the page, as shown in Listing 7-4. If the cards in the Deck are exhausted, the face-down card image is hidden.

Listing 7-4. Handling the Tap Event

```
private Deck _deck = new Deck();

// respond to the face down card tap
private void FaceDownCard_Tap(object sender, System.Windows.Input.GestureEventArgs e)
{
    // get a new random card
    Card card = _deck.Deal();
    // get an image for the new card
    Image cardImage = GetCardImage(card);

    // set the cards position relative to the face down card
    var margin = FaceDownCard.Margin.Left;
    cardImage.Margin = new Thickness(margin + 50, margin - 50, 0, 0);
```

```
    Canvas.SetTop(cardImage, Canvas.GetTop(FaceDownCard));
    Canvas.SetLeft(cardImage, Canvas.GetLeft(FaceDownCard));

    // add the card to the layout
    ContentPanel.Children.Add(cardImage);

    // if done dealing all cards, hide the face-down card
    if (_deck.Count == 1)
    {
        FaceDownCard.Visibility = System.Windows.Visibility.Collapsed;
    }
}

// get the image path based on the card suit and value
private Image GetCardImage(Card card)
{
    const string pathFormat = "/Assets/Cards/{0:d}_{1}.png";
    string path = string.Format(pathFormat, card.CardType, card.SuitType.ToString().ToLower());

    Image cardImage = new Image()
    {
        Source =  new BitmapImage(new Uri(path, UriKind.Relative)),
        Width = ImageCardBack.Width,
        Height = ImageCardBack.Height
    };
    return cardImage;
}
```

You may need to place elements in relation to other elements already on the page, as in the case the "face-down" card within the ContentPanel. Be aware that to get actual dimensions of any element already on the page, you need to wait until the element is available. For example, to get the ActualHeight or ActualWidth from the ContentPanel, wait until the page Loaded event fires. The code in Listing 7-5 waits until the page loads and then places the "face-down" card at the bottom of the ContentPanel.

Listing 7-5. Getting Actual Dimensions During the Loaded Event

```
// when the dimensions are available, place the card at the bottom of the page
private void PageLoaded(object sender, System.Windows.RoutedEventArgs e)
{
    Canvas.SetTop(FaceDownCard, ContentPanel.ActualHeight -
        (FaceDownCard.Height + FaceDownCard.Margin.Bottom + FaceDownCard.Margin.Top));
}
```

Manipulation Events

The preceding "UIElement Events" example has a static, desktop flavor. The user can only single-click stationary elements, but phone applications want natural actions where elements can be moved by simply touching the screen. UIElement has a set of manipulation events that allow elements to be tapped, dragged, flicked, zoomed, pinched, and rotated. A manipulation event is fired whenever one or two fingers touch an element.

Manipulation events also introduce the notion of *inertia* where the element continues to travel a certain distance if touch is removed while the element is still moving. The Manipulation events available for any element are ManipulationStarted, ManipulationDelta, and ManipulationCompleted.

- ManipulationStarted passes a ManipulationContainer object in the arguments that represents the element being manipulated by the user. ManipulationContainer is maintained through the lifetime of the manipulation and can also be assigned. This last point is important if you want to click one element, then create another element and finish the manipulation tracking that new element. For example, if the face-down card image is clicked, but a new card is created and tracked for the remainder of the manipulation operation.
- ManipulationDelta fires multiple times before the manipulation completes. The CumulativeManipulation argument object supplies the total scale and position changes for the element since the manipulation operation started. The DeltaManipulation argument object provides the scale and position since the last delta event. DeltaManipulation is a good choice when you need to scale or position an element relative to the last event.
- ManipulationCompleted fires when the user finishes dragging, rotating, sizing, or other changes. ManipulationCompleted supplies the TotalManipulation scale and position since the operation began. If the IsIntertial property is true, the user was still moving or resizing the element at the end of the operation. In this case you can calculate where the element will come to rest using the FinalVelocities property to determine the LinearVelocity and ExpansionVelocity X and Y coordinates.

Dragging an Element

The example in Figure 7-3 uses manipulation events to emulate a simple drag of an Ellipse element. To demonstrate the start and completion of the manipulation, the outline of the ellipse is highlighted by setting the element's Stroke property.

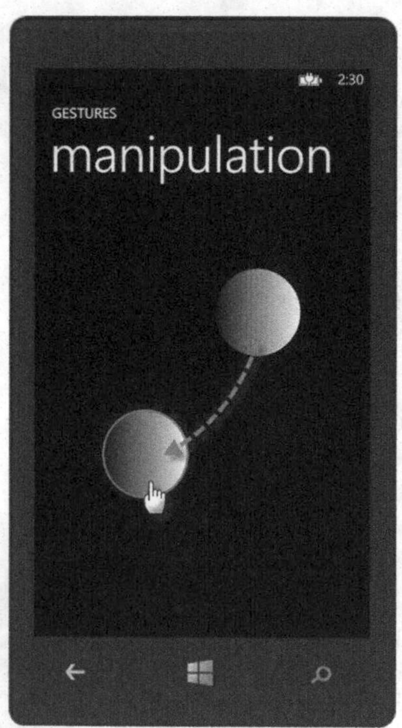

Figure 7-3. Dragging an Element

Manipulation events only let you know about the user gesture, the type of gesture and where the user moved their fingers during the gesture. Moving an element in response to a gesture can be done with a *transformation*. *Transformations* are operations that scale (resize), translate (move), skew (distort), or rotate elements. The RenderTransform property is available from UIElement and is used to contain any Transform object. In the example shown in Listing 7-6, the TranslateTransform is placed inside the RenderTransform element. The TranslateTransform will be used later in the ManipulationDelta event handler to move the element to its new location.

Listing 7-6. The Ellipse Layout

```
<Grid x:Name="ContentPanel" Grid.Row="1" Margin="12,0,12,0">

    <Ellipse Width="125" Height="125" StrokeThickness="3">
        <Ellipse.Fill>
            <LinearGradientBrush EndPoint="1,0.5" StartPoint="0,0.5">
                <GradientStop Color="Black" Offset="0" />
                <GradientStop Color="White" Offset="1" />
            </LinearGradientBrush>
        </Ellipse.Fill>
        <Ellipse.RenderTransform>
            <TranslateTransform />
        </Ellipse.RenderTransform>

    </Ellipse>
</Grid>
```

■ **Note** The RenderTransform can only be assigned a single Transform property. Your options are to add in a single TranslateTransform (to move the element), RotateTransform (to spin the element), SkewTransform (to distort shape by slanting the element along an angle with a new center), and ScaleTransform (to resize the element). If you want to perform multiple operations at once, you can use the TransformGroup or the CompositeTransform. TransformGroup contains multiple transforms in any order you specify. CompositeTransform has the settings for translate, scale, and otherwise alter, but handles the order of operations for you.

The code in Listing 7-7 shows the page constructor hooked up to all three manipulation events. Because manipulation events are defined for UIElement, these events can be defined for any descendant including PhoneApplicationPage, a Grid, or any other element on the page.

Listing 7-7. Assigning the Event Handlers

```
public MainPage()
{
    InitializeComponent();

    // hook up manipulation events
    this.ManipulationStarted += MainPage_ManipulationStarted;
    this.ManipulationDelta += MainPage_ManipulationDelta;
    this.ManipulationCompleted += MainPage_ManipulationCompleted;
}
```

In Listing 7-8, the ManipulationStarted event retrieves the ManipulationContainer and assumes this element is the Ellipse. In production applications, check that the user isn't clicking on the ContentPanel Grid or some other element. These checks are left out of this example so you can see the minimal pieces needed. The ManipulationDelta also gets a reference to the ellipse, and from the ellipse, a reference to the TranslateTransform. From here, you can add the X and Y coordinates of the DeltaManipulation to the TranslateTransform X and Y. Notice that the ManipulationDelta code uses "+=", not simple assignment. ManipulationCompleted simply reverses the action of the ManipulationStarted event by removing the Stroke outline.

Listing 7-8. Handling the Manipulation Events

```
// user has started manipulation, change outline to red
void MainPage_ManipulationStarted(object sender, ManipulationStartedEventArgs e)
{
    Ellipse ellipse = e.ManipulationContainer as Ellipse;
    if (ellipse != null)
    {
        ellipse.Stroke = new SolidColorBrush(Colors.Red);
    }
}

// element is being dragged, provide new translate coordinates
void MainPage_ManipulationDelta(object sender, ManipulationDeltaEventArgs e)
{
    Ellipse ellipse = e.ManipulationContainer as Ellipse;
    if (ellipse != null)
    {
        TranslateTransform transform = ellipse.RenderTransform as TranslateTransform;
        transform.X += e.DeltaManipulation.Translation.X;
        transform.Y += e.DeltaManipulation.Translation.Y;
    }
}

// element is dropped, make the outline transparent
void MainPage_ManipulationCompleted(object sender, ManipulationCompletedEventArgs e)
{
    Ellipse ellipse = e.ManipulationContainer as Ellipse;
    if (ellipse != null)
    {
        ellipse.Stroke = new SolidColorBrush(Colors.Transparent);
    }
}
```

■ **Note** To exclude any element from manipulation events, set the element IsManipulationEnabled property to false.

Flicking an Element

Manipulation events can be used to *flick* an element, that is, dragging and releasing the element so that the element is still moving when the user's touch is removed. Figure 7-4 illustrates "dealing" card image elements by touching a face-down card to create a new card and flicking the new card outward.

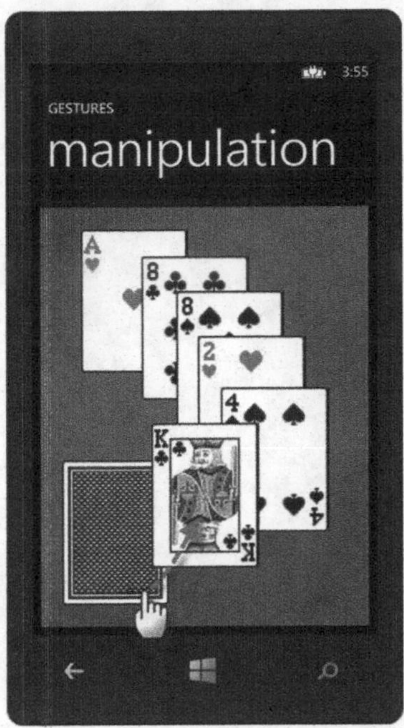

Figure 7-4. *Flicking Elements*

The Deck object and layout from the example in the "UIElement Events" section are reused here. You will need to create the Deck object, code the assignment of the manipulation events and handle each manipulation event. Listing 7-9 demonstrates creating the Deck object and assigning the event handlers. Notice that the event handlers are fired for any manipulation event within and including the ContentPanel Grid.

Listing 7-9. Creating the Deck object and assigning event handlers

```
private Deck _deck = new Deck();

public MainPage()
{
    InitializeComponent();

    ContentPanel.ManipulationStarted += ContentPanel_ManipulationStarted;
    ContentPanel.ManipulationDelta += ContentPanel_ManipulationDelta;
    ContentPanel.ManipulationCompleted += ContentPanel_ManipulationCompleted;
}
```

The ManipulationStarted fires for user interaction anywhere in the ContentPanel Grid element, so the first check makes sure that the ManipulationContainer is an Image named "FaceDownCard" (see Listing 7-10). The Deck object Deal() method creates a new Card object that can be used as raw material. An Image object is created and assigned the Card image. Also notice that the RenderTransform property is assigned a new TranslateTransform object. The transform will be used to move the card around the page. The static Canvas methods SetTop() and SetLeft() place the card image in an initial position on top of the face-down card. If this is the last card in the "Deck", the face-down card is hidden.

Listing 7-10. Handling the ManipulationStarted Event

```
void ContentPanel_ManipulationStarted(object sender, ManipulationStartedEventArgs e)
{
    if ((e.ManipulationContainer is Image) &&
        ((e.ManipulationContainer as Image).Name.Equals("FaceDownCard")))
    {
        Card card = _deck.Deal();
        Image cardImage = GetCardImage(card);

        Canvas.SetTop(cardImage, Canvas.GetTop(FaceDownCard));
        Canvas.SetLeft(cardImage, Canvas.GetLeft(FaceDownCard));

        ContentPanel.Children.Add(cardImage);

        if (_deck.Count == 1)
        {
            FaceDownCard.Visibility = System.Windows.Visibility.Collapsed;
        }

        // track cardImage in delta and completed events
        e.ManipulationContainer = cardImage;
    }
    // suppress other event handlers on this route
    e.Handled = true;
}
```

Initially, the `ManipulationContainer` represents the face-down card tapped by the user. Then, the `ManipulationContainer` is assigned the newly constructed card. In this way, the new card image becomes the element being tracked through subsequent `ManipulationDelta` and `ManipulationCompleted` events.

The `GetCardImage()` method has a few minor but necessary changes (see Listing 7-11). The new card's dimensions and margin both need to match the face-down card. Also, you need to initialize the `RenderTransform` so that it can be retrieved later.

Listing 7-11. Returning the Card Image

```
// get the image path based on the card suit and value
private Image GetCardImage(Card card)
{
    const string pathFormat = "/Assets/Cards/{0:d}_{1}.png";
    string path = string.Format(pathFormat, card.CardType, card.SuitType.ToString().ToLower());

    Image cardImage = new Image()
    {
        Source = new BitmapImage(new Uri(path, UriKind.Relative)),
        Width = FaceDownCard.Width,
        Height = FaceDownCard.Height,
        Margin = FaceDownCard.Margin,
        RenderTransform = new TranslateTransform()
    };
    return cardImage;
}
```

Each time the ManipulationDelta event that fires, the DeltaManipulation Translation object X and Y properties are added to the transformation (see Listing 7-12). The effect is that the card is being dragged to the new X and Y coordinates.

Listing 7-12. Handling the ManipulationDelta Event

```
void ContentPanel_ManipulationDelta(object sender, ManipulationDeltaEventArgs e)
{
    TranslateTransform transform =
        e.ManipulationContainer.RenderTransform as TranslateTransform;
    if (transform != null)
    {
        transform.X += e.DeltaManipulation.Translation.X;
        transform.Y += e.DeltaManipulation.Translation.Y;
    }
    e.Handled = true;
}
```

The ManipulationCompleted handler in Listing 7-13 creates the "inertia" effect, where the card appears to slide slightly past the point of releasing the dragged card. This requires some coding to set up an animation with an "easing" effect to make the card look as if it's sliding slightly.

Listing 7-13. Handling the ManipulationCompleted Event

```
void ContentPanel_ManipulationCompleted(object sender, ManipulationCompletedEventArgs e)
{
    // verify that a flick occurred and the element is intended to have inertia.
    if ((e.IsInertial) && (e.ManipulationContainer is Image))
    {
        // get the RenderTransform property added when the card was
        // created during GetCardImage()
        TranslateTransform transform =
            e.ManipulationContainer.RenderTransform as TranslateTransform;

        // create animations to move the element along X and Y directions
        DoubleAnimation animationX = new DoubleAnimation()
        {
            EasingFunction = new QuinticEase() { EasingMode = EasingMode.EaseOut },
            To = transform.X + (e.FinalVelocities.LinearVelocity.X / 10)
        };
        DoubleAnimation animationY = new DoubleAnimation()
        {
            EasingFunction = new QuinticEase() { EasingMode = EasingMode.EaseOut },
            To = transform.Y + (e.FinalVelocities.LinearVelocity.Y / 10)
        };

        // create a storyboard as a container for the animation
        Storyboard storyBoard = new Storyboard()
        {
            // set the duration for only a quarter of a second
            Duration = new Duration(new System.TimeSpan(0, 0, 0, 0, 250)),
        };
```

```
            // add the animation to the storyboard and hook up the X and Y properties
            // of the Transform to the target, element properties
            storyBoard.Children.Add(animationX);
            Storyboard.SetTarget(animationX, transform);
            Storyboard.SetTargetProperty(animationX, new PropertyPath("X"));

            storyBoard.Children.Add(animationY);
            Storyboard.SetTarget(animationY, transform);
            Storyboard.SetTargetProperty(animationY, new PropertyPath("Y"));

            // animate
            storyBoard.Begin();
        }
        e.Handled = true;
    }
```

After an initial check that IsInertial is true and that the manipulated element is an image, the Image TranslateTransform object (created during ManipulationStarted event) is retrieved. Two Animation objects are created to animate the X and Y transformations. The flicked card slows down in a natural manner due to the EasingFunction that controls the intensity of the property being animated. The To property is assigned the current Transform coordinates plus the FinalVelocities.LinearVelocity X and Y values.

You will need to create a Storyboard object to manage the animations. The Storyboard Duration is a quarter of a second (250 milliseconds). Longer durations look somewhat surreal as the card slides for an abnormally long time. Each animation is added to the Storyboard Children collection. The static Storyboard SetTarget() method hooks up the element's RenderTransform to each animation. The SetTargetProperty points to the property of the Transform that should be animated.

GestureService

GestureService does a great job of packaging gestures into an event model that handles many of the scenarios you're likely to run into. Each gesture has its own event (e.g., GestureBegin, PinchDelta, Flick, etc.) with specialized parameters like the PinchDelta event TotalAngleDelta property that eliminates the calculation of the angle you might have to do otherwise.

This section includes an example that demonstrates dragging an element. This shows a simple replacement of the previous "Dragging an Element" example that uses GestureService in place of manipulation events. A second, more involved example demonstrates how to flick, rotate, and size an element, all at one time. The example allows the user to drag photographs around, resize them with pinch gestures, flick them, and rotate the photos with two fingers.

Using GestureService

The GestureService object can be obtained from the Windows Phone 8 Toolkit. See Chapter 4's "Installing the Windows Phone 8 Toolkit" section for more information on installing the toolkit for a project.

■ Note Newsgroup conversations mention the GestureService was deprecated for Windows Phone 7x. At the time of this writing, GestureService is listed on MSDN as one of the valid ways of handling touch events in Windows Phone 8 (http://msdn.microsoft.com/en-us/library/windowsphone/develop/jj207076(v=vs.105).aspx).

GestureService is a helper class that retrieves GestureListeners for elements. It's the GestureListener that defines the events for each element. The XAML in Listing 7-14 defines an Ellipse, a GestureService, and a GestureListener. Only the GestureBegin, Tap, and GestureCompleted events are defined in this small example.

Listing 7-14. Defining a GestureService and GestureListener

```
<Ellipse x:Name="MyEllipse" Width="75" Height="75">
    <toolkit:GestureService.GestureListener>
        <toolkit:GestureListener
            GestureBegin="GestureListener_GestureBegin"
            GestureCompleted="GestureListener_GestureCompleted"
            Tap="GestureListener_Tap" />
    </toolkit:GestureService.GestureListener>
</Ellipse>
```

The code-behind equivalent uses the GestureService static GetGestureListener() method to pass the element to register the event for, and return a GestureListener. GetGestureListener() will create a new listener if one doesn't exist. You can pass any DependencyObject as the parameter to GetGestureListener(). Use the GestureListener to hook up event handlers for each event as shown in Listing 7-15.

Listing 7-15. Defining GestureListeners in Code

```
GestureListener gestureListener = GestureService.GetGestureListener(MyEllipse);
gestureListener.GestureBegin += gestureListener_GestureBegin;
gestureListener.Tap += gestureListener_Tap;
gestureListener.GestureCompleted += gestureListener_GestureCompleted;
```

GestureListener events are triggered for the common gestures used on a device:

- GestureBegin and GestureCompleted events are called before and after all other gesture events. Gesture events pass GestureEventArgs to their event handlers. The GestureEventArgs OriginalSource property represents the element under the touch point. GestureOrigin and TouchPosition argument properties have coordinates for the initial point where the gesture occurred and where that first touch point is now.
- Tap, DoubleTap, and Hold events are single-touch events that also pass GestureEventArgs to their handlers.
- DragStarted, DragDelta, and DragCompleted pass event argument objects. DragStartedGestureEventArgs only has a Direction property that can be Horizontal or Vertical (the gesture direction determined by the initial drag change). As the drag progresses, the DragDelta event is called repeatedly and the DragDeltaGestureEventArgs supplies the Direction, HorizontalChange (X), and VerticalChange (Y). When the drag operation finishes, DragCompleted fires and passes the DragCompletedGestureEventArgs. DragCompletedGestureEventArgs has the same properties as the DragDeltaGestureEventArgs plus the final HorizontalVelocity (X) and VerticalVelocity (Y) if the drag is inertial.
- Flick fires if the touch point is still moving when released. If we drag and flick an element, the order of events is GestureBegin ➤ DragStarted ➤ DragDelta ➤ Flick ➤ DragCompleted ➤ GestureCompleted. The presence of the Flick event indicates that the gesture is inertial (so the IsInertial property is not needed). FlickGestureEventArgs properties show the Direction, HorizontalVelocity, VerticalVelocity, and Angle of the flick.

- PinchStarted, PinchDelta, and PinchCompleted events fire in response to two points touching an element. The PinchStarted GestureEventArgs includes point properties for the second touch point, called GestureOrigin2 and TouchPosition2. The properties also include an Angle and Distance between the two points. The PinchDelta and PinchCompleted events both pass PinchGestureEventArgs with properties for DistanceRatio and TotalAngleDelta. DistanceRatio is the ratio of the current distance between touch points (PinchDelta event) or the original distance between touch points (PinchCompleted event). The TotalAngleDelta is the difference in angle between the current and original touch positions.

Dragging an Element

The "Manipulation Dragging an Element" example can be refactored to use GestureListener (see Listing 7-16). This example is intended to show the same functionality used by the manipulation events, but using GestureService. This will allow you to explore the minimal code required for basic dragging. The Ellipse element has a GestureListener added with events for the GestureBegin/Completed and for all drag events.

Listing 7-16. Defining the GestureListener

```
<Ellipse x:Name="MyEllipse"  Width="75"  Height="75">
    <toolkit:GestureService.GestureListener>
        <toolkit:GestureListener
            GestureBegin="GestureListener_GestureBegin"
            GestureCompleted="GestureListener_GestureCompleted"
            DragStarted="GestureListener_DragStarted"
            DragDelta="GestureListener_DragDelta"
            DragCompleted="GestureListener_DragCompleted" />
    </toolkit:GestureService.GestureListener>
    <Ellipse.Fill>
        <LinearGradientBrush EndPoint="1,0.5" StartPoint="0,0.5">
            <GradientStop Color="Black" Offset="0" />
            <GradientStop Color="White" Offset="1" />
        </LinearGradientBrush>
    </Ellipse.Fill>
    <Ellipse.RenderTransform>
        <TranslateTransform />
    </Ellipse.RenderTransform>
</Ellipse>
```

The refactored code behind is shown in Listing 7-17. To mark the GestureBegin and GestureComplete events, the Stroke outline color of the Ellipse is set to red and back again to transparent. The DragStarted and DragCompleted events are visualized by setting the Fill Opacity to half strength starting the drag and back to full strength at completion. During the drag, the HorizontalChange and VerticalChange are appended to the TranslationTransform X and Y.

Listing 7-17. The MainPage Code Behind

```
using System.Windows.Media;
using System.Windows.Shapes;
using Microsoft.Phone.Controls;
```

```
namespace GestureService_DraggingExample
{
    public partial class MainPage : PhoneApplicationPage
    {
        public MainPage()
        {
            InitializeComponent();
        }

        private void GestureListener_GestureBegin(object sender,
          Microsoft.Phone.Controls.GestureEventArgs e)
        {
            Ellipse ellipse = e.OriginalSource as Ellipse;
            if (ellipse != null)
            {
                ellipse.Stroke = new SolidColorBrush(Colors.Red);
            }
        }

        private void GestureListener_GestureCompleted(object sender,
          Microsoft.Phone.Controls.GestureEventArgs e)
        {
            Ellipse ellipse = e.OriginalSource as Ellipse;
            if (ellipse != null)
            {
                ellipse.Stroke = new SolidColorBrush(Colors.Transparent);
            }
        }

        private void GestureListener_DragStarted(object sender, DragStartedGestureEventArgs e)
        {
            Ellipse ellipse = e.OriginalSource as Ellipse;
            if (ellipse != null)
            {
                ellipse.Fill.Opacity = 0.5;
            }
        }

        private void GestureListener_DragDelta(object sender, DragDeltaGestureEventArgs e)
        {
            Ellipse ellipse = e.OriginalSource as Ellipse;
            if (ellipse != null)
            {
                TranslateTransform translateTransform =
                    ellipse.RenderTransform as TranslateTransform;
                translateTransform.X += e.HorizontalChange;
                translateTransform.Y += e.VerticalChange;
            }
        }
```

```
        private void GestureListener_DragCompleted(object sender,
          DragCompletedGestureEventArgs e)
        {
            Ellipse ellipse = e.OriginalSource as Ellipse;
            if (ellipse != null)
            {
                ellipse.Fill.Opacity = 1;
            }
        }
    }
}
```

Flicking, Rotating, and Sizing an Element

This next example incorporates a number of new techniques including:

- How to rotate and size an element.
- How to use `CompositeTransform` to allow more than one transformation at a time.
- How to bring touched elements up on top of other elements when elements overlap and the user touches the edge of an element that is "underneath" another element.
- How to prevent overlapped elements being affected by user touch.
- How to enable the capability of accessing photos in the `MediaLibrary` object.
- How to use the `VisualTreeHelper` object to access element parents and children.
- How to bind a list of visual elements to a `Canvas`.

In this next example, a series of photos are arranged on the page. Each image is a `UserControl` that has its own `GestureListener` events. When an image is clicked, the image rises to the top of the pile. Images can be dragged and flicked with one finger or rotated and scaled with two fingers. Figure 7-5 shows the running application with images rotated, sized, and moved through direct user interaction.

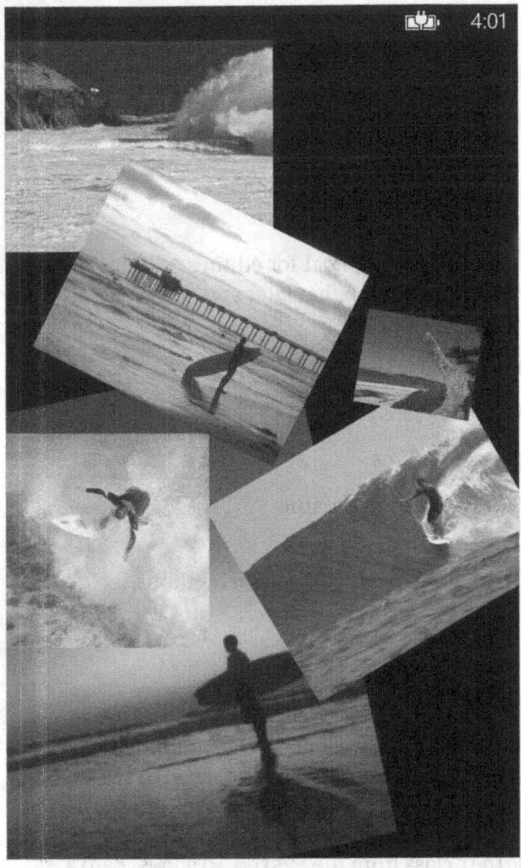

Figure 7-5. Running the Snapshots Application

The example application is a little more complex than some of the earlier examples, so we will need to break the job down into parts. The parts of the application that you will need to modify or create are:

- `WMAppManifest.xml` to add capabilities.
- `DependencyObjectExtensions.cs` to define a set of extension methods that will make it easier to get parents and children of `Snapshot` user controls that are touched by the user. The extension methods will be used in the event handlers of `MainPage.xaml.cs`.
- `PictureViewModel.cs` and `PicturesViewModel.cs` view model classes. These classes allow pictures from the `MediaLibrary` to be bindable.
- `Snapshot.xaml UserControl` to contain an `Image` control.
- `MainPage.xaml` and `MainPage.xaml.cs`. The `MainPage` contains an `ItemsControl` bound to the `PicturesViewModel`. The `ItemsPanelTemplate`, the template for the entire control, is a `Canvas`. The `ItemTemplate` will include the `SnapShot` user control. The `MainPage` will also define the `GestureService`. The `MainPage` code-behind will include `GestureListener` event handlers that transform and animate the contents of the `Snapshot` user control.

Preparing the Project

First, set up your project with the Windows Phone 8 Toolkit, configure the capabilities of the application and define the project structure.

1. Create a new Windows Phone 8 App project.
2. Install the Windows Phone 8 Toolkit. See Chapter 4, "Installing the Windows Phone 8 Toolkit" for more information on installing the toolkit for a project.
3. In the Visual Studio Solution Explorer, open `Properties/WMAppManifest.xml` for editing. In the `Capabilities` tab, check the `ID_CAP_MEDIALIB_PHOTO` capability so that later you will be allowed to access your phone's picture objects.
4. Create new folders in your project named `Extensions` and `ViewModels`.
5. In the new `Extensions` folder, create a class `DependencyObjectExtensions.cs`.
6. In the new `ViewModels` folder create a class file `PicturesViewModel.cs`.
7. In the root of the project, create a new `Windows Phone User Control` and name it `Snapshot.xaml`.

Now that the project is configured, you can build up the project to include helpful extension methods, a ViewModel, and UserControl to represent each photo.

Defining Extension Methods

Extension methods allow you to add new methods to existing classes. For example, we will need a method to retrieve the `Snapshot UserControl` when the user touches any part of the `UserControl`, including the root level `Grid`, the `Image` in the `Grid`, or any other elements you may decide to add later. Rather than bloat our `MainPage` code with logic for traversing the visual elements on a page, we can create extension methods that work for any `DependencyObject`.

The extension methods will make heavy use of the `VisualTreeHelper` class from the `System.Windows.Media` namespace. `VisualTreeHelper` can traverse from a dependency object upward to parent objects and downward through child objects. Unlike `FrameworkElement.Parent`, `VisualTreeHelper` can access parent objects even when the child object is nested within a template.

Define a `Ancestor<T>()` method to climb up the visual tree looking for the first instance of T, and a `Descendants<T>()` method that returns all child objects that are of T:

1. Open `DependencyObjectExtensions.cs` for editing.
2. Create a public static class called `DependencyObjectExtensions`. Overwrite the existing definition with the code in Listing 7-18.

   Listing 7-18. Defining the DependencyObjectExtensions Class

   ```
   public static class DependencyObjectExtensions
   {
   }
   ```

3. Add a method `Ancestor<T>()` to the `DependencyObjectExtensions` class using the code in Listing 7-19. The `Ancestor<T>()` method returns immediately if the `originalSource` parameter is of type `T`. Otherwise the method starts with the visual parent of the `originalSource` property and continues to climb up the visual tree until it can't find a parent or it finds a parent of type `T`. Later we will be able to construct methods like `element.Ancestor<Grid>()` that will return the first ancestor that is a `Grid` type.

Listing 7-19. The Ancestor<T>() Method

```
public static T Ancestor<T>(this DependencyObject originalSource) where T : DependencyObject
{
    if (originalSource is T)
    {
        return originalSource as T;
    }
    DependencyObject element = VisualTreeHelper.GetParent(originalSource) as DependencyObject;
    while (element != null)
    {
        if (element is T)
            return element as T;
        element = VisualTreeHelper.GetParent(element) as DependencyObject;
    }
    return null;
}
```

■ **Note** To be an extension method, the method signature must be marked `public static` and the first parameter must use the keyword `this` to indicate which class will be extended. See the documentation for C# and VB.NET respectively for more information on extension methods: `http://msdn.microsoft.com/en-us/library/vstudio/bb383977.aspx` and `http://msdn.microsoft.com/en-us/library/bb384936.aspx`.

---

4. Add a method `Descendants<T>()` to the `DependencyObjectExtensions` class using the code in Listing 7-20. This method will return all children that are of type T. `Descendants<T>()` uses `VisualTreeHelper` to iterate children of a `DependencyObject`, adds the children of type T to a generic list and then calls itself recursively. If the method finds any children of type T at a particular level of the visual tree, the search is finished.

Listing 7-20. The Descendants<T>() Method

```
public static IEnumerable<T> Descendants<T>(this DependencyObject element) where T :
DependencyObject
{
    List<T> descendants = new List<T>();
    for (int i = 0; i < VisualTreeHelper.GetChildrenCount(element); i++)
    {
        var childElement = VisualTreeHelper.GetChild(element, i) as DependencyObject;
        if (childElement is T)
        {
            descendants.Add(childElement as T);
        }
        // we found child elements of type T, no need to spelunk further
        if (descendants.Count == 0)
        {
            descendants.AddRange(childElement.Descendants<T>());
        }
    }
    return descendants;
}
```

5. Add an Animate() method that can be used to animate a list of properties. The dictionary parameter takes a series of key/value pairs that describe each of the properties to animate. The duration of the animation defaults to half a second but can be overridden by passing in an optional duration value. The *easing function* describes the transition from the old property value to the new property value and is hard-coded in Listing 7-21 for relative simplicity.

Listing 7-21. The Animate() Method

```
public static void Animate(this DependencyObject target, Dictionary<string, double> dictionary,
int duration = 500)
{
    Storyboard storyBoard = new Storyboard()
    {
        Duration = new Duration(new System.TimeSpan(0, 0, 0, 0, duration)),
    };

    foreach (var item in dictionary)
    {
        DoubleAnimation animation = new DoubleAnimation()
        {
            EasingFunction = new QuinticEase() { EasingMode = EasingMode.EaseOut },
            To = item.Value
        };
        Storyboard.SetTarget(animation, target);
        Storyboard.SetTargetProperty(animation, new PropertyPath(item.Key));
        storyBoard.Children.Add(animation);
    }

    storyBoard.Begin();
}
```

Defining the ViewModel

The ViewModel will get a collection of pictures from the MediaLibrary on the phone. By default, this will include any of the sample pictures and any pictures you have taken.

1. Open the \ViewModels\PicturesViewModel.cs file for editing in Visual Studio.
2. Replace the existing using statements and class definitions with those in Listing 7-22. Keep your existing namespace declaration. The PictureViewModel class will store the binary image for each picture in the phone. The PicturesViewModel uses the MediaLibrary Pictures collection to populate a list of PictureViewModel.

Listing 7-22. Defining PicturesViewModel

```
using System.Collections.Generic;
using System.Windows.Media;
using System.Windows.Media.Imaging;
using Microsoft.Xna.Framework.Media;

namespace GestureService_FlickAndRotateElement.ViewModels
{
```

```
    public class PictureViewModel
    {
        public ImageSource PictureSource { get; set; }
    }

    public class PicturesViewModel
    {
        public List<PictureViewModel> Pictures { get; set; }
        public PicturesViewModel()
        {
            Pictures = new List<PictureViewModel>();

            foreach (var picture in new MediaLibrary().Pictures)
            {
                BitmapImage bi = new BitmapImage();
                bi.SetSource(picture.GetImage());
                Pictures.Add(new PictureViewModel() { PictureSource = bi });
            }
        }
    }
}
```

■ **Warning** If you have a large collection of pictures on the phone, it's possible to get a `System.OutOfMemoryException`. To limit the numbers of pictures, you can filter the images to show only those from a particular album (folder) on the phone. For example, you could include only those images stored in the "Sample Pictures" album by adding a check `if (picture.Album.Name.Equals("Sample Pictures"))`.

Defining the User Control

The `UserControl` is used to contain a single picture. Employing a `UserControl` here provides flexibility later if we want to make the layout more complex. To create the `Snapshot UserControl`:

1. Open `Snapshot.xaml` for editing in Visual Studio.
2. Replace the `LayoutRoot Grid` with the XAML in Listing 7-23. `RenderTransformOrigin` is defined as .5 x .5 to allow the element to be rotated around its center. The `Image` element `Source` is bound to our custom `PictureViewModel PictureSource` property. The `Grid` defines a `CompositeTransform` that can be used to move, rotate, and scale in a single operation.

Listing 7-23. Designing the UserControl Layout

```
<Grid RenderTransformOrigin="0.5,0.5">

    <Image x:Name="PictureImage"
           Stretch="UniformToFill"
           Source="{Binding PictureSource}" />
```

```
    <Grid.RenderTransform>
        <CompositeTransform />
    </Grid.RenderTransform>
</Grid>
```

Defining the Main Page Design

The MainPage will contain an ItemsControl where the ItemsPanelTemplate (for the entire control) will be a Canvas and each item will be a Snapshot user control. The ItemsControl will use the PicturesViewModel Pictures collection as its source. The MainPage will also contain a GestureListener and event handlers for each gesture.

1. Add XML namespaces for the local project that contains the Snapshot user control and for the Windows Phone 8 toolkit. See Listing 7-24 for an example of declaring the namespaces. Depending on the name of your application, the paths may be different from the example.

   Listing 7-24. Assigning XML Namespaces in the XAML Markup

   ```
   <phone:PhoneApplicationPage . . .
       xmlns:local="clr-namespace:GestureService_FlickAndRotateElement"
       xmlns:toolkit="clr-namespace:Microsoft.Phone.Controls;assembly= ↵
           Microsoft.Phone.Controls.Toolkit" >
   ```

2. Replace the LayoutRoot Grid with the XAML markup in Listing 7-25. The ItemsSource property is bound to the Pictures collection of the PicturesViewModel. (The ItemsControl DataContext will be assigned in the code-behind.) The ItemsPanelTemplate is the element that will house all of the Snapshot items in the list. The DataTemplate dictates the layout of a single Snapshot. The GestureListener hooks up the events for all the gestures we need to drag, size, rotate, and double-tap each Snapshot element.

   Listing 7-25. Defining the ItemsControl

   ```
   <ItemsControl x:Name="LayoutRoot" ItemsSource="{Binding Path=Pictures}">
       <ItemsControl.ItemsPanel>
           <ItemsPanelTemplate>
               <Canvas />
           </ItemsPanelTemplate>
       </ItemsControl.ItemsPanel>
       <ItemsControl.ItemTemplate>
           <DataTemplate>
               <local:Snapshot Width="250" Height="200"  />
           </DataTemplate>
       </ItemsControl.ItemTemplate>
       <toolkit:GestureService.GestureListener>
           <toolkit:GestureListener
               DragDelta="GestureListener_DragDelta"
               GestureBegin="GestureListener_GestureBegin"
               Flick="GestureListener_Flick"
               PinchDelta="GestureListener_PinchDelta"
           DoubleTap="GestureListener_DoubleTap"
           />
       </toolkit:GestureService.GestureListener>
   </ItemsControl>
   ```

■ **Note** Using the Canvas as the ItemsPanelTemplate is a non-standard and non-intuitive use of the ItemsControl. But this configuration allows us to bind a list of Snapshot items and still arrange them on the canvas at arbitrary locations.

Writing the MainPage Code-Behind

The code-behind for MainPage assigns the ViewModel and handles the GestureListener events.

1. Add using statements for the ViewModels and Extensions namespaces. In particular, you'll need to remember the <project name>.Extensions namespace because you will not get Intellisense, which reminds you. You should also add System.Linq because this namespace also contains extension methods.

2. Override the OnNavigatedTo method as shown in Listing 7-26 to initialize the ItemsControl DataContext.

Listing 7-26. Overriding the OnNavigatedTo Method

```
protected override void OnNavigatedTo(System.Windows.Navigation.NavigationEventArgs e)
{
    base.OnNavigatedTo(e);
    LayoutRoot.DataContext = new PicturesViewModel();
}
```

3. Handle the GestureBegin event as shown in Listing 7-27. This event handler gets the item being touched by the user and gives it the highest z-index, effectively bringing the element to the foreground above the other items. Here we're using the extension method Ancestor<T>()to get the touched element. The Descendants<T>() method retrieves all other items so that we can get the maximum z-index.

Listing 7-27. Handling the GestureBegin Event

```
private void GestureListener_GestureBegin(object sender,
  Microsoft.Phone.Controls.GestureEventArgs e)
{
    // find the ContentPresenter element under the touch
    var touchedElement = (e.OriginalSource as DependencyObject).Ancestor<ContentPresenter>();

    // get all the other content presenter elements.
    // these are the elements hosted by the canvas in the ItemsControl
    var itemElements = this.LayoutRoot.Descendants<ContentPresenter>();
    // get the topmost z-index, increment and assign to the touched element
    var topIndex = itemElements
        .Max(item => Canvas.GetZIndex(item));
    Canvas.SetZIndex(touchedElement, topIndex + 1);
    e.Handled = true;
}
```

■ **Note** The Canvas can only set properties such as ZIndex on its immediate children. In the code of Listing 7-27, we're working with the ContentPresenter that hosts each Snapshot user control instead of the user control itself. The ContentPresenter is the immediate child of the Canvas, not the Snapshot.

---

4. Handle the DragDelta event as shown in Listing 7-28. The Ancestor<T>() method retrieves the Snapshot's Grid that contains a RenderTransform. From there you can get the CompositeTransform and set its TranslateX and TranslateY properties by adding the HorizontalChange and VerticalChange of the arguments passed to the event.

   Listing 7-28. Handling the DragDelta Event

```
private void GestureListener_DragDelta(object sender,
  Microsoft.Phone.Controls.DragDeltaGestureEventArgs e)
{
    // find the element user control being dragged
    var element = (e.OriginalSource as DependencyObject).Ancestor<Grid>();
    if (element != null)
    {
        // get the Snapshot's Transform element and adjust the new coordinates
        CompositeTransform transform =
            element.RenderTransform as CompositeTransform;
        transform.TranslateX += e.HorizontalChange;
        transform.TranslateY += e.VerticalChange;
    }
    // stop handling to prevent all
    // images under touch point from being dragged
    e.Handled = true;
}
```

5. Handle the Flick event as shown in Listing 7-29. The Ancestor<T>() method retrieves the Grid element being touched by the user and gets the Grid's transform. New x and y coordinates are calculated based on the existing TranslateX and TranslateY coordinates combined with the inertia HorizontalVelocity and VerticalVelocity passed in as arguments to the event. The Animate() extension method takes a Dictionary of the properties to be animated. In this case, the new coordinates are applied to the Transform's TranslateX and TranslateY properties.

   Listing 7-29. Handling the Flick Event

```
private void GestureListener_Flick(object sender,
  Microsoft.Phone.Controls.FlickGestureEventArgs e)
{
    // find the element being flicked
    var element = (e.OriginalSource as DependencyObject).Ancestor<Grid>();
    // get the element's Transform and calculate the new coordinates
    CompositeTransform transform =
        element.RenderTransform as CompositeTransform;
    // divide by 10 to tone down the amount of inertia
    var x = transform.TranslateX + (e.HorizontalVelocity / 10);
    var y = transform.TranslateY + (e.VerticalVelocity / 10);
```

```
    // animate the flick
    transform.Animate(new Dictionary<string, double>()
            {
                {"TranslateX", x},
                {"TranslateY", y}
            });
    e.Handled = true;
}
```

6. Handle the `PinchDelta` event as shown in Listing 7-30. Again, the `Ancestor<T>()` method retrieves the element touched by the user, gets the `Transform`, and sets the `Transform's` scaling and rotation. The `DistanceRatio` used to scale the element starts as 1, becomes 0.5 if scaled to half size or 2 if expanded to double size. `TotalDeltaAngle` sets the `Rotation` angle of the element.

Listing 7-30. Handling the PinchDelta Event

```
private void GestureListener_PinchDelta(object sender,
  Microsoft.Phone.Controls.PinchGestureEventArgs e)
{
    // find the element being zoomed or rotated
    var element = (e.OriginalSource as DependencyObject).Ancestor<Grid>();
    // get the element's Transform and adjust to the new scale and rotation
    CompositeTransform transform =
        element.RenderTransform as CompositeTransform;
    transform.ScaleX = e.DistanceRatio;
    transform.ScaleY = e.DistanceRatio;
    transform.Rotation = e.TotalAngleDelta;
    e.Handled = true;
}
```

7. Handle the `DoubleTap` event as shown in Listing 7-31. Double-tapping a `Snapshot` causes the image to center, scale to one and a half its original size, and to rotate upright, all in one smooth animation. The element double-tapped by the user is retrieved, and the `Transform` is extracted. Next, the new left and top coordinates of the `Snapshot` are calculated so that the `SnapShot` is placed in the center of the `Canvas`. Finally, the `Animate()` method moves the `Snapshot` into place.

Listing 7-31. Handling the DoubleTap Event

```
private void GestureListener_DoubleTap(object sender,
  Microsoft.Phone.Controls.GestureEventArgs e)
{
    // find the element being double tapped
    var element = (e.OriginalSource as DependencyObject).Ancestor<Grid>();

    // get the transform of the element
    CompositeTransform transform =
        element.RenderTransform as CompositeTransform;
```

```
        // calculate left and top to place the element in the center.
        var left = (LayoutRoot.ActualWidth - element.ActualWidth) / 2;
        var top = (LayoutRoot.ActualHeight - element.ActualHeight) / 2;

        // animate movement, scale and rotation
        transform.Animate(new Dictionary<string, double>()
        {
            {"TranslateX", left},
            {"TranslateY", top},
            {"ScaleX", 1.5},
            {"ScaleY", 1.5},
            {"Rotation", 0}
        });

        e.Handled = true;
    }
```

Test the Application

To try out all the features, you'll want to run this application on a physical phone device.

1. Make sure your phone is on, connected to the development computer and unlocked.
2. In the Visual Studio Debug Target drop down, select `Device` and run the application.
3. Verify the following:
    a. Images stored on the phone display on the canvas.
    b. Images can be dragged to random locations on the canvas.
    c. Images show on top of the other images when tapped.
    d. You can pinch and stretch an image with two fingers.
    e. You can rotate an image with two fingers.
    f. Double-tapping an image causes it to animate to an upright position in the center of the page.
    g. Tapping, pinching, and dragging the empty areas of the canvas does not cause the application to fail.

Styling the UserControl

Although the UserControl behaves correctly (that is, you can manipulate the photos with two fingers) the presentation is a bit sparse. This next example solves the problem by including a retro, analog snapshot-style border with a slight yellowish tinge of an aged photo. Figure 7-6 shows the running application with the new styling.

Figure 7-6. *The Running Application with Styled Snapshots*

1. Open `Snapshot.xaml` for editing in Visual Studio.
2. Add a `Grid Background` with a gradient brush as shown in Listing 7-32. The `GradientStops` defined here will give the background a yellowed, discolored, and aged background. The result in the designer looks something like Figure 7-7.

Listing 7-32. Defining the Grid Background

```
<Grid.Background>
    <LinearGradientBrush EndPoint="0,1" StartPoint="1,1">
        <GradientStop Color="#FFDADADA" Offset="0" />
        <GradientStop Color="#FFE7E7E7" Offset="1" />
        <GradientStop Color="#FFFFFFE2" Offset="0.238" />
        <GradientStop Color="#FFDDDDCE" Offset="0.783" />
    </LinearGradientBrush>
</Grid.Background>
```

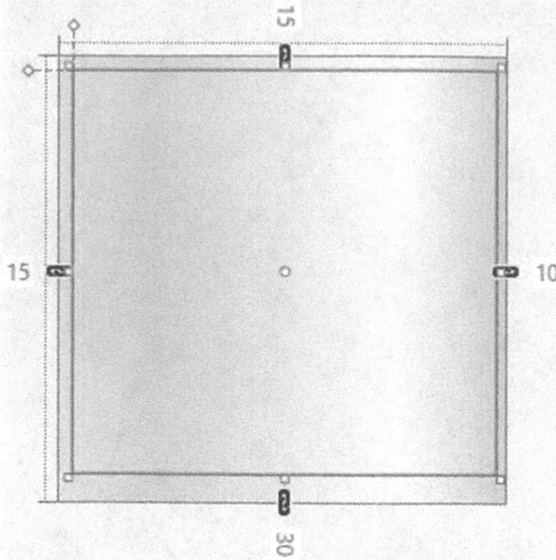

Figure 7-7. *Gradient Background in the Designer*

3. Add a `Rectangle` element below the `Image` as shown in Listing 7-33. The `Rectangle` overlays the image and adds patina to the image surface. Notice that the `Color` values first two digits are the "alpha" channel, that is, the amount of transparency. Values closer to the maximum value of FF will make the images appear more faded, while values closer to 00 will allow the images to look more vivid. See Figure 7-8 to see the result for one of the images.

Listing 7-33. Adding the Rectangle Overlay

```
<Rectangle>
    <Rectangle.Fill>
        <LinearGradientBrush EndPoint="1,1" StartPoint="0,0">
            <GradientStop Color="#55DADADA" Offset="0" />
            <GradientStop Color="#55E7E7E7" Offset="1" />
            <GradientStop Color="#55FFFFE2" Offset="0.238" />
            <GradientStop Color="#55DDDDCE" Offset="0.783" />
        </LinearGradientBrush>
    </Rectangle.Fill>
</Rectangle>
```

Figure 7-8. *The Snapshot with Overlay*

4. Add a `Margin` attribute to the `Image` (see Listing 7-34). This will leave a white border around the image. See Figure 7-9 for the result.

Listing 7-34. Adding the Image Margin

```
<Image x:Name="PictureImage"
    Stretch="UniformToFill"
    Source="{Binding PictureSource}"
    Margin="20,20,20,35" />
```

Figure 7-9. *The Snapshot with Overlay and Margin*

This example that models a stack of old photos combines techniques such as binding, MVVM, styling, and gestures to produce an application that mimics the real world. You can use this application as a starting point or use portions for spare parts in your own work.

Summary

This chapter explored several options for sensing user touch on the phone, each with tradeoffs in complexity and flexibility. We looked very briefly at the ultimately flexible but work-intensive Touch object used when you need complete control for more than two touch points against multiple objects. Then we looked at the simple UIElement events that are convenient to use but are little more than desktop metaphor replacements. The Manipulation events got us closer to a model that handles one and two touches for gestures like flicking and dragging but there were still extraneous calculations to perform. Finally we used the GestureService from the Windows Phone 8 Toolkit with its rich set of events for flicking, pinching, and rotating.

CHAPTER 8

Device Capabilities

Programming a phone is a unique experience compared with using any stationary computing device that has come before. The phone can interact with its environment by knowing where it is in space and its relation with the earth. If the phone is tilted, shaken, or stirred, the phone senses it. The phone is aware of its relation to magnetic north and even its coordinate position on the globe. You can access device capabilities including:

- Querying the capabilities of the device itself.
- Sensors that detect changes in the real world such as accelerometer, gyroscope, and compass.
- The built-in microphone and camera.

Device Support

The first layer of information about the device you're running comes from the `Microsoft.Phone.Info` namespace by using the static `DeviceStatus` class. The `DeviceStatus` static properties tend to be self-documenting and describe some of the limits for the device:

- Device properties: `DeviceName`, `DeviceManufacturer`, `DeviceFirmwareVersion`, `DeviceHardwareVersion`, `DeviceTotalMemory` (physical RAM of the device in bytes) and `DevicePowerSource` (an enumeration that can be `Battery` or `External`).
- Application properties: `ApplicationCurrentMemoryUsage`, `ApplicationMemoryUsageLimit`, `ApplicationPeakMemoryUsage`.
- Keyboard properties: `IsKeyboardDeployed`, `IsKeyboardPresent`.
- Events: `KeyboardDeployedChanged`, `PowerSourceChanged`.

`Microsoft.Phone.Info` also has a `DeviceExtendedProperties` object that you can use to get a unique id for the device. To display these properties, they can be directly assigned in code-behind or gathered under the umbrella of a ViewModel and bound to the user interface. Figure 8-1 shows what the example application will look like running in both the Emulator and on the device.

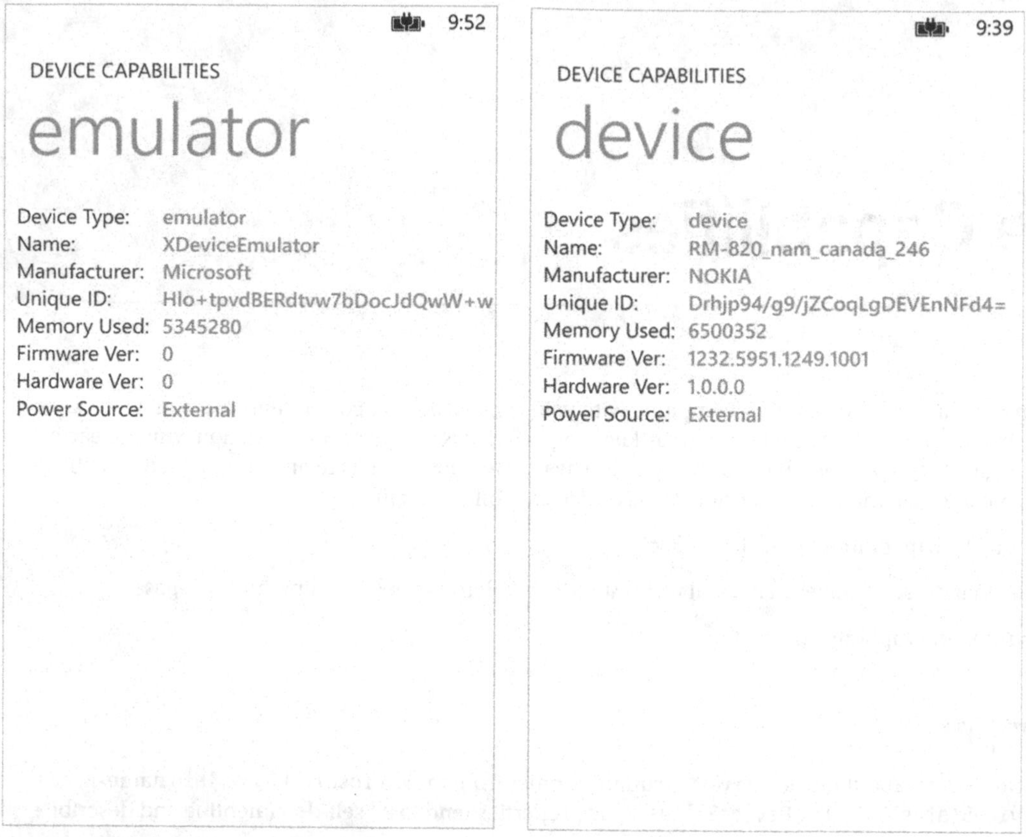

9:52

DEVICE CAPABILITIES

emulator

Device Type: emulator
Name: XDeviceEmulator
Manufacturer: Microsoft
Unique ID: Hlo+tpvdBERdtvw7bDocJdQwW+w
Memory Used: 5345280
Firmware Ver: 0
Hardware Ver: 0
Power Source: External

9:39

DEVICE CAPABILITIES

device

Device Type: device
Name: RM-820_nam_canada_246
Manufacturer: NOKIA
Unique ID: Drhjp94/g9/jZCoqLgDEVEnNFd4=
Memory Used: 6500352
Firmware Ver: 1232.5951.1249.1001
Hardware Ver: 1.0.0.0
Power Source: External

Figure 8-1. *Device Capabilities Listed in the Emulator and on the Device*

■ **Note** To capture the Emulator screen, open the `Additional Tools` dialog, click the `Screenshot` tab, then click the `Capture` button. To capture the screen on a Windows Phone 8 device, click the Start button + the screen lock button. You may have to unhook the phone's USB from the development computer and reattach before you'll be able to see the screenshot in the `\Computer\Windows Phone\Pictures\Screenshots` folder.

To build the application:

1. Create a new Windows Phone 8 App.
2. In the Solution Explorer, open the `\Properties\WMAppManifest.xml` file. Select the `Capabilities` tab, and then check the box next to the `ID_CAP_IDENTITY_DEVICE` capability.
3. Add a folder in the project and name it "ViewModels".
4. Inside the `ViewModels` folder, add a new class `DeviceInformationViewModel.cs`.

5. Open DeviceInformationViewModel.cs for editing and replace the class with the code in Listing 8-1. The ViewModel is a Dictionary keyed by string and may have any type of object as a value. The code uses the DeviceStatus and DeviceExtendedProperties objects from the Microsoft.Phone.Info namespace, and the DeviceType property that comes from Microsoft.Devices.Environment namespace. In particular, notice that the DeviceExtendedProperties GetValue() returns a byte array. Use the System.Convert.ToBase64String() method to convert it to a readable string.

Listing 8-1. Implementing the ViewModel

```
using System.Collections.Generic;
using Microsoft.Devices;
using Microsoft.Phone.Info;

namespace DeviceSupport.ViewModels
{
    public class DeviceInformationViewModel : Dictionary<string, object>
    {
        public DeviceInformationViewModel()
        {
            var id = (byte[])DeviceExtendedProperties.GetValue("DeviceUniqueId");
            var deviceId = System.Convert.ToBase64String(id);

            Add("Device Type", Microsoft.Devices.Environment.DeviceType.ToString().ToLower());
            Add("Name", DeviceStatus.DeviceName);
            Add("Manufacturer", DeviceStatus.DeviceManufacturer);
            Add("Unique ID", deviceId);
            Add("Memory Used", DeviceStatus.ApplicationCurrentMemoryUsage);
            Add("Firmware Ver", DeviceStatus.DeviceFirmwareVersion);
            Add("Hardware Ver", DeviceStatus.DeviceHardwareVersion);
            Add("Power Source", DeviceStatus.PowerSource.ToString());

        }
    }
}
```

6. Open MainPage.xaml.cs for editing in Visual Studio.
7. Add the line of code in Listing 8-2 right after the call to InializeComponent() in the MainPage constructor. This code creates an instance of the ViewModel and assigns it to the MainPage DataContext.

Listing 8-2. Assigning the ViewModel

```
this.DataContext = new DeviceInformationViewModel();
```

8. Redefine the Text property for the two TextBlock elements inside the TitlePanel StackPanel element as shown in Listing 8-3. In particular, you want to bind the Device Type entry of the Dictionary to the second TextBlock. The context for the line of code {Binding [Device Type]} is that the TextBlock is bound to the Dictionary and the [Device Type] indexes into the Dictionary entry with a matching key. This will display "emulator" or "device" in large font.

Listing 8-3. Redefining the TitlePanel

```
<StackPanel x:Name="TitlePanel" Grid.Row="0" Margin="12,17,0,28">
    <TextBlock Text="DEVICE CAPABILITIES"
        Style="{StaticResource PhoneTextNormalStyle}"
        Margin="12,0"/>
    <TextBlock Text="{Binding [Device Type]}"
        Margin="9,-7,0,0"
        Style="{StaticResource PhoneTextTitle1Style}"
        Foreground="{StaticResource PhoneAccentBrush}" />
</StackPanel>
```

9. Add an ItemsControl to the ContentPanel Grid using code from Listing 8-4. Set the Binding Path for the two TextBlock elements inside the ItemTemplate to the Key and Value of the Dictionary, respectively.

Listing 8-4. Redefining the ContentPanel Grid

```
<ItemsControl HorizontalAlignment="Stretch"
                VerticalAlignment="Stretch"
                ItemsSource="{Binding}">
    <ItemsControl.ItemTemplate>
        <DataTemplate>
            <StackPanel Orientation="Horizontal">
                <TextBlock Text="{Binding Path=Key, StringFormat='{}{0}: '}"
                            Width="130" />
                <TextBlock Text="{Binding Path=Value}"
                           Style="{StaticResource PhoneTextAccentStyle}"/>
            </StackPanel>
        </DataTemplate>
    </ItemsControl.ItemTemplate>
</ItemsControl>
```

Sensors

Sensors detect changes to the physical world that affect the phone. In particular, Windows Phone 8 detects orientation and movement in three dimensions using compass, accelerometer, and gyroscope sensors. These sensors are commonly used in games and "augmented reality" applications that overlay data on the device's camera image.

- Accelerometer measures forces caused by movement, gravity, vibration, and tilting the device.
- Gyroscope measures orientation changes with fine accuracy. This sensor is not available on all devices.
- Compass measures magnetic strength and direction relative to magnetic north.

You can find objects for each sensor in the Microsoft.Devices.Sensors namespace. Sensor objects descend from the SensorBase<TSensorReading> class that defines Start()/Stop() methods and a CurrentValueChanged event. Each sensor object also surfaces the static IsSupported property so you can "go to plan B" if a particular feature doesn't exist on the device.

■ **Caution** There is a second namespace `Windows.Devices.Sensors` that has its own set of objects for the sensors. The advantage to the `Microsoft.Devices.Sensors` namespace we're going to work with is that the sensors descend from a common base class, have an `IsSupported` property and have a convenient `Motion` object that returns combined sensor information for one-stop shopping. The point to take away here is to make sure you add `Microsoft.Devices.Sensors` namespace to your `using` statements and make sure that the `Windows.Devices.Sensors` namespace is not used.

Using the Accelerometer Sensor

We can build a very simple application that reports changes from the `Accelerometer`. To build the application, first override the page `OnNavigatedTo()` method to defer using the resource-hungry sensor as late as possible (see Listing 8-5). Check that the sensor is supported, hook up the `CurrentValueChanged` event, then call the `Start()` method. Be aware that `Start()` can fail, so wrap it in a `try...catch` block. Also notice that the `TimeBetweenUpdates` property of the `Accelerometer` is set to return a reading every second.

Listing 8-5. Starting the Accelerometer

```
private Accelerometer _accelerometer;

protected override void OnNavigatedTo(System.Windows.Navigation.NavigationEventArgs e)
{
    base.OnNavigatedTo(e);

    if (Accelerometer.IsSupported)
    {
        _accelerometer = new Accelerometer();
        _accelerometer.TimeBetweenUpdates = new TimeSpan(0, 0, 1);
        _accelerometer.CurrentValueChanged +=
            accelerometer_CurrentValueChanged;
        try
        {
            _accelerometer.Start();
        }
        catch (Exception ex)
        {
            MessageBox.Show(ex.Message, "Unable to start Accelerometer", MessageBoxButton.OK);
        }
    }
}
```

The `CurrentValueChanged` event passes a "reading" event argument appropriate for the sensor type (see Listing 8-6). In this example, an `AccelerometerReading` defines the current X, Y, and Z coordinates. These coordinates correspond exactly to the readings in the `Accelerometer` page in the Emulator.

Listing 8-6. Handling the CurrentValueChanged Event

```
void accelerometer_CurrentValueChanged(object sender,
    SensorReadingEventArgs<AccelerometerReading> e)
{
    Dispatcher.BeginInvoke(() =>
    {
        StatusX.Text = String.Format("X: {0:N4}", e.SensorReading.Acceleration.X);
        StatusY.Text = String.Format("Y: {0:N4}", e.SensorReading.Acceleration.Y);
        StatusZ.Text = String.Format("Z: {0:N4}", e.SensorReading.Acceleration.Z);
    });
}
```

When you're done using the sensor, call the `Stop()` method, unhook the event handlers and dispose of the sensor object (see Listing 8-7). Remove the sensor as early as possible to save resources.

Listing 8-7. Cleaning Up After Using the Sensor

```
protected override void OnNavigatedFrom(
    System.Windows.Navigation.NavigationEventArgs e)
{
    if (Accelerometer.IsSupported)
    {
        _accelerometer.Stop();
        _accelerometer.CurrentValueChanged -= accelerometer_CurrentValueChanged;
        _accelerometer.Dispose();
        _accelerometer = null;
    }
    base.OnNavigatedFrom(e);
}
```

Combined Motion

The `Motion` object wraps all the sensors in a single, convenient package. Like the other sensor objects, `Motion` descends from `SensorBase<TSensorReading>` and works just the same except that the `MotionReading` object passed to the `CurrentValueChanged` event is packed with data from all the other sensors. The `MotionReading` object also handles some of the calculation "heavy lifting" for you. The `MotionReading` properties are:

- `Attitude` reveals the `Yaw`, `Pitch`, and `Roll` of the device (see Figure 8-2). Yaw, Pitch, and Roll are terms borrowed from flight dynamics that define aircraft orientation. If you are sitting in a plane, *Yaw* determines the direction you are heading in. *Pitch* determines if the nose of the plane is pointing up to the sky or down towards the ground. *Roll* determines if the plane is leaning to the left or right. If the Roll is zero, the plane's wings are level.

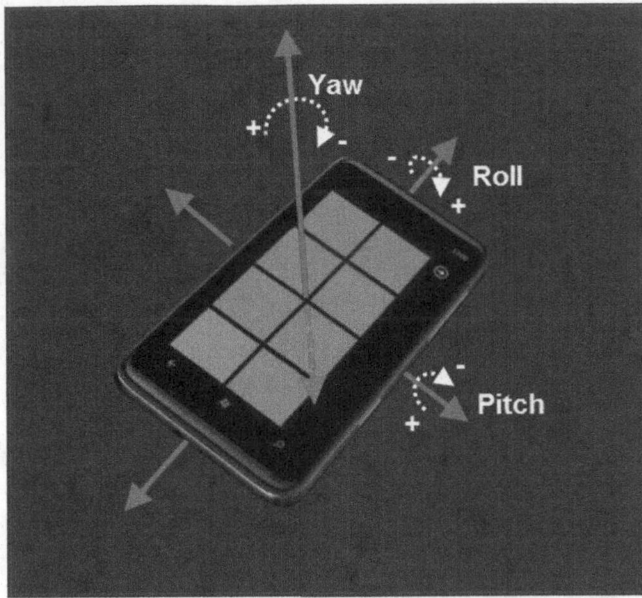

Figure 8-2. *The Attitude of the Phone*

- `DeviceAcceleration` is the linear acceleration of the device, in gravitational units. This is represented as a `Vector3` struct that encapsulates `X` (horizontal location), `Y` (vertical location), and `Z` (depth location) coordinate values.
- `DeviceRotationRate` is the rotational velocity of the device, in radians per second. This is also represented as a `Vector3`.
- `Gravity` is also calculated for you and represented as a `Vector3` type.
- `Timestamp` is the time when the reading was calculated and can be used to correlate readings across sensors to provide additional input for algorithms that process raw sensor data.

Displaying Combined Motion Readings

The following example demonstrates how to display the readings from the `Motion` object using a LongListSelector, where each group represents a sensor (see Figure 8-3 for a screenshot of the application running).

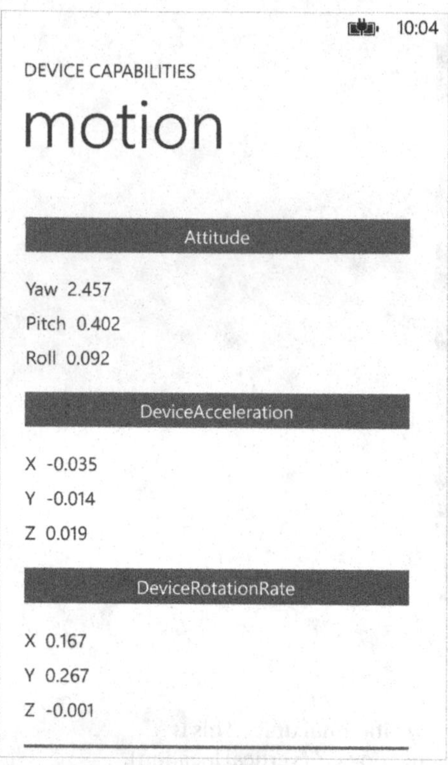

Figure 8-3. *Motion Readings in the LongListSelector*

Preparing the Project

First prepare the project:

1. Create a new project and name the project "CombinedMotion".
2. In the Solution Explorer, open `WMApManifest.xml`, select the `Capabilities` tab and check the `ID_CAP_SENSORS` capability.
3. Add a new `ViewModels` folder to the project.
4. In the `ViewModels` folder, add a series of new class files: `Group.cs`, `MotionViewModel.cs`, `MotionViewModelConsts.cs`, `Reading.cs`, `Readings.cs` and `ViewModelBase.cs`.

Building Supporting ViewModel Classes

Next, implement the classes that support the ViewModel.

1. Open the `ViewModelBase.cs` class file for editing and replace the code with the code in Listing 8-8. The `ViewModelBase` abstract class includes the `INotifyPropertyChanged` implementation.

Listing 8-8. The ViewModelBase Implementation

```
using System.ComponentModel;

namespace CombinedMotion.ViewModels
{
    public abstract class ViewModelBase : INotifyPropertyChanged
    {
        public void OnPropertyChanged(string propertyName)
        {
            if (PropertyChanged != null)
            {
                PropertyChanged(this, new PropertyChangedEventArgs(propertyName));
            }
        }
        public event PropertyChangedEventHandler PropertyChanged;
    }
}
```

2. Open the `Group.cs` file for editing and replace the code in Listing 8-9. The `Group` class is used to organize the data for consumption by the `LongListSelector` control. This is the same class introduced in Chapter 4 in the section "LongListSelector."

Listing 8-9. The Group Class

```
using System.Collections.Generic;

namespace CombinedMotion.ViewModels
{
    public class Group<TKey, T> : List<T>
    {
        public Group(TKey key, IEnumerable<T> items) :
            base(items)
        {
            this.Key = key;
        }
        public TKey Key
        {
            get;
            set;
        }
    }
}
```

3. Open the `MotionViewModelConsts.cs` file for editing and replace the code in Listing 8-10. The `SensorType` enumeration lists the types of sensors wrapped by the `Motion` object. The `SensorType` will be used as the key for our groups.

Listing 8-10. Defining the SensorType Enumeration

```
namespace CombinedMotion.ViewModels
{
    public enum SensorType { Attitude, DeviceAcceleration, DeviceRotationRate, Gravity }
}
```

4. Open the `Reading.cs` file for editing and replace the code in Listing 8-11. The `Reading` class represents a single sensor reading (e.g., for `Accelerometer Pitch`) and descends from `ViewModelBase`. Notice that the `OnPropertyChanged` is only called for the `Value` property because the `Name` and `SensorType` will remain static.

Listing 8-11. The Reading Class

```
namespace CombinedMotion.ViewModels
{
    public class Reading : ViewModelBase
    {
        public SensorType SensorType { get; internal set; }
        public string Name { get; internal set; }

        private double _value;
        public double Value
        {
            get { return _value; }
            set
            {
                if (!_value.Equals(value))
                {
                    _value = value;
                    OnPropertyChanged("Value");
                }
            }
        }
    }
}
```

5. Open the `Readings.cs` file for editing and replace with the code in Listing 8-12. The `Readings` class maintains a list of Reading objects. The constructor takes a flat list of `Reading` objects and does the heavy lifting to populate the `Grouped` property that `LongListSelector` needs to bind to. The indexed `this[]` property allows you to easily index to a property by `SensorType` and property `Name` to update a reading. A Lambda statement is used to get a `Group` instance for a specific `SensorType`. A second Lambda statement looks for a single `Reading` that has a `Name` equal to the name specified in the index.

Listing 8-12. The Readings Class

```
using System.Collections.Generic;
using System.Linq;

namespace CombinedMotion.ViewModels
{
    public class Readings
    {
```

```
        // pass in flat list of Reading, create grouped list
        public Readings(IEnumerable<Reading> readings)
        {
            this.Grouped =
                (from reading in readings
                 group reading by reading.SensorType into grouped
                 select new Group<SensorType, Reading>(grouped.Key, grouped)).ToList();
        }

        // bind presentation ItemsSource against this property
        public IList<Group<SensorType, Reading>> Grouped { get; set; }

        // update against this property
        public Reading this[SensorType sensorType, string name]
        {
            get
            {
                var group = this.Grouped
                    .Where(g => g.Key.Equals(sensorType))
                    .Single();
                return group.Where(r => r.Name.Equals(name)).Single();
            }
        }
    }
}
```

Building the ViewModel

Now that all the supporting classes are built, we can put the ViewModel together:

1. Open `MotionViewModel.cs` for editing.
2. Replace the using statements with the code in Listing 8-13. In particular, make sure you use `Microsoft.Devices.Sensors` instead of `Windows.Devices.Sensors`. The latter does not have a `Motion` object.

   Listing 8-13. The Using Statements

   ```
   using System;
   using System.Collections.Generic;
   using System.Windows.Threading;
   using Microsoft.Devices.Sensors;
   ```

3. Replace the class definition of the ViewModel with the code in Listing 8-14. `MotionViewModel` implements `IDisposable` so there is an opportunity to clean up after the `Motion` object when we navigate away from the page.

   Listing 8-14. Defining the MotionViewModel Class.

   ```
   public class MotionViewModel: IDisposable
   {

   }
   ```

4. Declare properties for the `Motion` (see Listing 8-15).

Listing 8-15. Declaring Properties

```
private Motion _motion;
public Readings Readings { get; private set; }
```

5. Create the constructor using the code in Listing 8-16. The `Readings` property is instantiated and initialized with the set of sensor readings that will be updated by the `Motion CurrentValueChanged` event handler. The `Motion` object is instantiated, hooked up to the `CurrentValueChanged` event and the `Start()` method is called. The `TimeBetweenUpdates` assignment causes readings to be taken once every second.

Listing 8-16. The ViewModel Constructor

```
public MotionViewModel()
{
    if (Motion.IsSupported)
    {
        _motion = new Motion();
        _motion.TimeBetweenUpdates = new System.TimeSpan(0, 0, 1);

        this.Readings = new Readings(
            new List<Reading>()
            {
                new Reading()
                         { SensorType = SensorType.Attitude, Name = "Yaw" },
                new Reading()
                         { SensorType = SensorType.Attitude, Name = "Pitch" },
                new Reading()
                         { SensorType = SensorType.Attitude, Name = "Roll" },
                new Reading()
                         { SensorType = SensorType.DeviceAcceleration, Name = "X" },
                new Reading()
                         { SensorType = SensorType.DeviceAcceleration, Name = "Y" },
                new Reading()
                         { SensorType = SensorType.DeviceAcceleration, Name = "Z" },
                new Reading()
                         { SensorType = SensorType.DeviceRotationRate, Name = "X" },
                new Reading()
                         { SensorType = SensorType.DeviceRotationRate, Name = "Y" },
                new Reading()
                         { SensorType = SensorType.DeviceRotationRate, Name = "Z" },
                new Reading() { SensorType = SensorType.Gravity, Name = "X" },
                new Reading() { SensorType = SensorType.Gravity, Name = "Y" },
                new Reading() { SensorType = SensorType.Gravity, Name = "Z" },
            });

        _motion.CurrentValueChanged += _motion_CurrentValueChanged;
        _motion.Start();
    }
}
```

6. Add the event handler for the Motion object's CurrentValueChanged event (see Listing 8-17). The Readings object this[SensorType, string] indexed property allows us to grab an existing Reading object and update the value.

Listing 8-17. Handling the CurrentValueChanged Event

```
void _motion_CurrentValueChanged(object sender, SensorReadingEventArgs<MotionReading> e)
{
    System.Windows.Deployment.Current.Dispatcher.BeginInvoke(() =>
    {
        this.Readings[SensorType.Attitude, "Yaw"].Value =
            e.SensorReading.Attitude.Yaw;
        this.Readings[SensorType.Attitude, "Pitch"].Value =
            e.SensorReading.Attitude.Pitch;
        this.Readings[SensorType.Attitude, "Roll"].Value =
            e.SensorReading.Attitude.Roll;

        this.Readings[SensorType.DeviceAcceleration, "X"].Value =
          e.SensorReading.DeviceAcceleration.X;
        this.Readings[SensorType.DeviceAcceleration, "Y"].Value =
          e.SensorReading.DeviceAcceleration.Y;
        this.Readings[SensorType.DeviceAcceleration, "Z"].Value =
          e.SensorReading.DeviceAcceleration.Z;

        this.Readings[SensorType.DeviceRotationRate, "X"].Value =
          e.SensorReading.DeviceRotationRate.X;
        this.Readings[SensorType.DeviceRotationRate, "Y"].Value =
          e.SensorReading.DeviceRotationRate.Y;
        this.Readings[SensorType.DeviceRotationRate, "Z"].Value =
          e.SensorReading.DeviceRotationRate.Z;

        this.Readings[SensorType.Gravity, "X"].Value =
            e.SensorReading.Gravity.X;
        this.Readings[SensorType.Gravity, "Y"].Value =
            e.SensorReading.Gravity.Y;
        this.Readings[SensorType.Gravity, "Z"].Value =
            e.SensorReading.Gravity.Z;

    });
}
```

■ **Note** See "Dispatcher and Threads" for more information and why Dispatcher.BeginInvoke( ) is being used.

---

7. Finally, implement the Dispose() method to clean up after the Motion object (see Listing 8-18). This is our chance to make sure the sensor is no longer using the phone's resources.

Listing 8-18. Implementing the Dispose() Method

```
public void Dispose()
{
    if (Motion.IsSupported)
    {
        _motion.Stop();
        _motion.CurrentValueChanged -= _motion_CurrentValueChanged;
        _motion.Dispose();
        _motion = null;
    }
}
```

Building the Main Page

At this point the ViewModel and all the supporting code is built, so we can turn our attention to the MainPage.

1. In the code-behind of `MainPage.cs`, override the `OnNavigatedTo()` and `OnNavigatedFrom()` methods (see Listing 8-19). The idea here is to keep the `MotionViewModel` alive for the shortest amount of time to minimize resource use. In the `OnNavigatedTo()` method, instantiate the `MotionViewModel` and assign it to the MainPage's `DataContext`. In the `OnNavigatedFrom()` method, reference the `MotionViewModel` and call its `Dispose()` method.

Listing 8-19. Implementing the OnNavigatedTo() and OnNavigatedFrom() Events

```
protected override void OnNavigatedTo(NavigationEventArgs e)
{
    base.OnNavigatedTo(e);
    this.DataContext = new MotionViewModel();
}

protected override void OnNavigatedFrom(NavigationEventArgs e)
{
    (this.DataContext as MotionViewModel).Dispose();
    base.OnNavigatedFrom(e);
}
```

2. In the XAML markup of `MainPage. xaml`, add resources that will be used by the `LongListSelector` (see Listing 8-20). The "GroupTile" template displays the key for the group (e.g., "Gravity"). The "Item" template binds the `Name` (e.g., "X") and the `Value`. The `Value` is formatted as a number with three decimal places.

Listing 8-20. Preparing MainPage Resources

```
<phone:PhoneApplicationPage.Resources>

    <phone:JumpListItemBackgroundConverter x:Key="BackgroundConverter"/>
    <phone:JumpListItemForegroundConverter x:Key="ForegroundConverter"/>

    <DataTemplate x:Key="GroupTile">
        <Grid HorizontalAlignment="Stretch"
            Margin="5,20,5,20"
```

```
            Background="{Binding Converter={StaticResource BackgroundConverter}}">
            <TextBlock  HorizontalAlignment="Center" VerticalAlignment="Bottom"
                Text="{Binding Key}"
                Margin="5"
                Style="{StaticResource PhoneTextNormalStyle}"
                Foreground="{Binding Converter={StaticResource ForegroundConverter}}"/>
        </Grid>
    </DataTemplate>

    <DataTemplate x:Key="Item">
        <StackPanel Orientation="Horizontal" HorizontalAlignment="Stretch">
            <TextBlock Text="{Binding Name}"
                Margin="5"
                Style="{StaticResource PhoneTextNormalStyle}" />
            <TextBlock Text="{Binding Value, StringFormat='{}{0:N3}'}"
                Margin="5"
                Style="{StaticResource PhoneTextNormalStyle}" />
        </StackPanel>
    </DataTemplate>

</phone:PhoneApplicationPage.Resources>
```

3. Also in the XAML markup of `MainPage.xaml`, define a `LongListSelector` inside the `ContentPanel` grid as shown in Listing 8-21.

Listing 8-21. Defining the LongListSelector

```
<phone:LongListSelector Padding="10"
    x:Name="longListSelector1"
    HorizontalAlignment="Stretch"
    VerticalAlignment="Stretch"
    ItemsSource="{Binding Readings.Grouped}"
    GroupHeaderTemplate="{StaticResource GroupTile}"
    ItemTemplate="{StaticResource Item}"
    IsGroupingEnabled="true"
    HideEmptyGroups ="true" />
```

DISPATCHER AND THREADS

If you comment out the `Dispatcher.BeginInvoke()` in Listing 8-17 attempting to update the ViewModel properties results in the exception `System.UnauthorizedAccessException: Invalid cross-thread access.` If you place a breakpoint just before this happens we can see how threading is handled with and without the `Dispatcher` (see Figure 8-4).

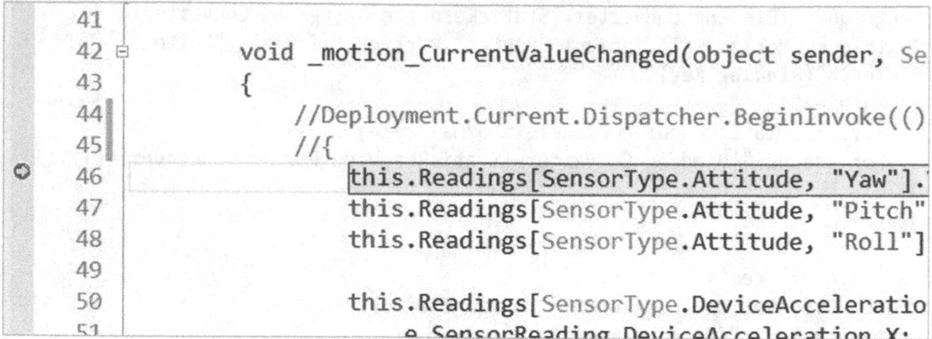

void _motion_CurrentValueChanged(object sender, Se
{
//Deployment.Current.Dispatcher.BeginInvoke(()
//{
this.Readings[SensorType.Attitude, "Yaw"].
this.Readings[SensorType.Attitude, "Pitch"
this.Readings[SensorType.Attitude, "Roll"]
this.Readings[SensorType.DeviceAcceleratio

Figure 8-4. *Break Before Line of Code Fails Without Dispatcher*

When execution stops at the breakpoint, the `Threads` window (`Debug | Windows | Threads or Ctrl-Alt-H`) shows the `CurrentValueChanged` event handler is running in the context of a worker thread, not the main thread (see Figure 8-5).

Threads

Search: ✕ Search Call Stack Group by: Process ID

	ID		Name	Location
Process ID: 2752 (3 threads)				
	3344	1	Main Thread	<not available>
	3212	4	<No Name>	<not available>
⇨	2676	0	<No Name>	CombinedMotion.DLL!CombinedMotion.ViewModels.MotionViewModel._motion_CurrentValueChanged

Figure 8-5. *CurrentValueChanged Event Handler Running in Worker Thread*

Un-commenting the code allows `Dispatcher.BeginInvoke()` to schedule the work for `CurrentValueChanged` on the main thread (see Figure 8-6).

Threads

Search: ✕ Search Call Stack Group by: Process ID

	ID		Name	Location
Process ID: 44 (3 threads)				
⇨	2476	1	Main Thread	CombinedMotion.DLL!CombinedMotion.ViewModels.MotionViewModel._motion_CurrentValueChanged.Anony
	48	4	<No Name>	<not available>
	3340	0	<No Name>	<not available>

Figure 8-6. *CurrentValueChanged Event Handler Running in Main Thread*

Shake Gesture

It's up to you to make sense of raw sensor data. For example, if you're building a contractors "bubble level", the accelerometer sensor might be ok as is. If you want to interpret the data to capture specific "gestures", then you will need to smooth the data, remove "noise" and decipher a series of readings to determine its meaning.

For example, how do I know if the user has "shaken" the device? For that matter, how can I know if they're shaking the device side-to-side, up-and-down, or back-and-forth? Do I care how hard or quickly the user shakes the device to get the reading?

The following demonstrates a simplified Shake object to get you started. The Shake object uses a certain number of Accelerometer readings over a particular threshold to raise its own CurrentValueChanged event. To keep it simple, this only checks the X-axis, side-to-side shaking of the phone. The example application displays a random phrase every time the phone is shaken (see Figure 8-7).

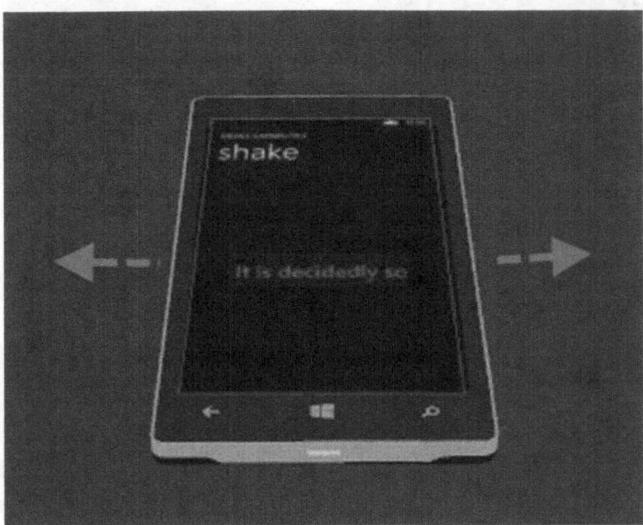

Figure 8-7. *Running the ShakeGesture Application*

Building the Custom Shake Object

The custom Shake object is primarily a wrapper for the Accelerometer. Listing 8-22 shows the initial class definition and its properties. The Shake object is an IDisposable implementation so we can clean up resources after use. The private members include:

- The Accelerometer that we're basing the functionality on.
- AccelerometerReading saves the last reading so that movement can be interpreted between the last and current readings.
- The _shakeCount counts the number of significant movements between readings.
- The ReadingThreshold helps determine if the difference between the previous and current readings is large enough to count.
- The _shakeCount will be compared against the public CountThreshold property to determine if there were enough movements to indicate a "shake".
- The CurrentValueChanged will be fired when the CountThreshold is exceeded.

Listing 8-22. The Shake Object and Properties

```
public class Shake : IDisposable
{
    private Accelerometer _accelerometer;
    private AccelerometerReading _lastReading;
    private int _shakeCount;

    public float ReadingThreshhold { get; set; }
    public int CountThreshold { get; set; }


    public static bool IsSupported
    {
        get { return Accelerometer.IsSupported; }
    }
    public event EventHandler<SensorReadingEventArgs<ShakeReading>> CurrentValueChanged;

    . . .
}
```

The Shake constructor (see Listing 8-23) instantiates the `Acccelerometer` and hooks up to its `CurrentValueChanged` event.

Listing 8-23. The Shake Constructor

```
public Shake()
{
    _accelerometer = new Accelerometer();
    _accelerometer.CurrentValueChanged += _accelerometer_CurrentValueChanged;
}
```

Most of the action happens in the `Accelerometer CurrentValueChanged` event handler (see Listing 8-24). Here we check the difference between the current and previous sensor readings. If the difference is over the `ReadingThreshold`, the `_shakeCount` is bumped. If the `_shakeCount` is over the `CountThreshold`, set the local shaken variable to true and reset the `_shakeCount`. If the phone has been shaken and the `CurrentValueChanged` is subscribed to, the `CurrentValueChanged` event is triggered. The event takes a generic `SensorReadingEventArgs` of a custom type `ShakeReading`. (`ShakeReading` is defined later.)

Listing 8-24. The Accelerometer CurrentValueChanged Event

```
void _accelerometer_CurrentValueChanged(object sender,
  SensorReadingEventArgs<AccelerometerReading> e)
{
    // if the difference between before/now
    // acceleration X values is over the threshold,
    // bump the count.
    if (Math.Abs(_lastReading.Acceleration.X -
       e.SensorReading.Acceleration.X) > ReadingThreshhold)
    {
        _shakeCount++;
    }
```

```
    // if the number of shakes is over the threshold,
    // the device is now officially "shaken"
    bool shaken = false;
    if (_shakeCount > CountThreshold)
    {
        shaken = true;
        _shakeCount = 0; // reset
    }

    // if the phone is shaken and CurrentValueChanged is subscribed to,
    // fire the event handler.
    if (shaken && CurrentValueChanged != null)
    {
        CurrentValueChanged(this,
            new SensorReadingEventArgs<ShakeReading>()
            {
                SensorReading = new ShakeReading()
                {
                    Timestamp = e.SensorReading.Timestamp
                }
            });
    }

    _lastReading = e.SensorReading;
}
```

The Start() and Stop() methods simply wrap the equivalent Accelerometer methods (see Listing 8-25).

Listing 8-25. The Start() and Stop() Methods

```
public void Start()
{
    _accelerometer.Start();
}

public void Stop()
{
    _accelerometer.Stop();
}
```

Finally, the Dispose() method of the Shake object cleans up after the Accelerometer to release device resources (see Listing 8-26).

Listing 8-26. The Dispose() Method

```
public void Dispose()
{
    _accelerometer.Stop();
    _accelerometer.CurrentValueChanged -= _accelerometer_CurrentValueChanged;
    _accelerometer.Dispose();
    _accelerometer = null;
}
```

Building the ShakeReading Object

The ShakeReading object used as an argument to the CurrentValueChanged event is a placeholder that implements ISensorReading (see Listing 8-27). ISensorReading requires a Timestamp property, but you can elaborate on ShakeReading to pass any custom sensor information that suits your purpose.

Listing 8-27. The ShakeReading Object

```
public class ShakeReading : ISensorReading
{
    public DateTimeOffset Timestamp { get; internal set; }
}
```

We can use a simple object to produce random answers to unknown questions. The Answer object in Listing 8-28 returns a random entry from _list when the Ask() method is called. As each question is "asked", the reply is removed from _list to reduce the number of repeats. Once all the replies have been given, _list is replenished from an array of strings.

Listing 8-28. The Answer Object

```
public class Answers
{
    private List<string> _list = new List<string>();
    private string[] _replies =
    {
        "You betcha",
        "It is decidedly so",
        "Outlook good",
        "Ask again later",
        "Don't count on it",
        "Very doubtful",
        "You're kidding, right?"
    };
    private Random _random = new Random();

    public Answers()
    {
        _list.AddRange(_replies);
    }

    public string Ask()
    {
        if (_list.Count.Equals(0))
        {
            _list.AddRange(_replies);
        }
        var index = _random.Next(0, _list.Count - 1);
        var result = _list[index];
        _list.RemoveAt(index);
        return result;
    }
}
```

Building the Main Page

To use the new Shake class, the ContentPanel gets a single new TextBlock to display the answers (see Listing 8-29).

Listing 8-29. The MainPage Markup

```
<Grid x:Name="ContentPanel" Grid.Row="1" Margin="12,0,12,0">
    <TextBlock x:Name="AnswerText"
               HorizontalAlignment="Center"
               VerticalAlignment="Center"
               FontSize="{StaticResource PhoneFontSizeExtraLarge}"
               Style="{StaticResource PhoneTextAccentStyle}" />
</Grid>
```

The code-behind for MainPage.xaml.cs first defines instances of the Shake and Answers objects (see Listing 8-30). The Answers object resource requirements are insignificant and the object is instantiated immediately. The Shake object will be instantiated on the OnNavigatedTo() method and disposed in the OnNavigatedFrom() method.

Listing 8-30. Shake and Answer Objects in MainPage.xaml.cs

```
private Shake _shake;
private Answers _answers = new Answers();
```

The OnNavigatedTo() method (see Listing 8-31) checks the static IsSupported property before creating a new Shake object instance. The constructor is passed the ReadingThreshold and CountThreshold to reduce the sensitivity to random readings. Once the Shake's CurrentValueChanged event handler is hooked up, the Start() method is called. The OnNavigatedFrom() method shuts everything down and cleans up.

Listing 8-31. The OnNavigatedTo and OnNavigatedFrom Methods

```
protected override void OnNavigatedTo(NavigationEventArgs e)
{
    base.OnNavigatedTo(e);
    if (Shake.IsSupported)
    {
        _shake = new Shake() { ReadingThreshhold = 1, CountThreshold = 2 };
        _shake.CurrentValueChanged += _accelerometer_CurrentValueChanged;
        _shake.Start();
    }
}

protected override void OnNavigatedFrom(NavigationEventArgs e)
{
    if (Shake.IsSupported)
    {
        _shake.Stop();
        _shake.CurrentValueChanged -= _accelerometer_CurrentValueChanged;
        _shake.Dispose();
        _shake = null;

    }
    base.OnNavigatedFrom(e);
}
```

The Shake's CurrentValueChanged event handler is fired when enough shake gestures of sufficient magnitude have occurred. The event handler populates the AnswerText BlockText element with a random phrase from the Answer object's Ask() method.

You can test this application on a physical device by shaking the phone from side to side. In this case you can also use the Emulator by opening up the Additional Tools window, selecting the Accelerometer tab and clicking the Recorded Data Play button with the "shake" item selected in the drop-down list.

That's enough for a rudimentary implementation that senses a shake gesture and responds to it. You may also want to search the Windows Phone Dev Center (http://dev.windowsphone.com/en-us/) for other implementations and discussions on shake gestures.

Animating Text

You can extend this project to animate the opacity of the text so that new answers fade-in to the screen. Re-use the DependencyObjectExtensions Animate() method (introduced in Chapter 7 in the "Flicking, Rotating, and Sizing an Element" section) to display the fade-in effect. The listing for the extension method is included here for easy re-use (see Listing 8-32).

Listing 8-32. The DependencyObjectExtensions Object

```
public static void Animate(this DependencyObject target, Dictionary<string, double> dictionary,
    int duration = 500)
{
    Storyboard storyBoard = new Storyboard();

    foreach (var item in dictionary)
    {
        DoubleAnimation animation = new DoubleAnimation()
        {
            EasingFunction = new QuinticEase() { EasingMode = EasingMode.EaseOut },
            Duration = new Duration(new System.TimeSpan(0, 0, 0, 0, duration)),
            To = item.Value
        };
        Storyboard.SetTarget(animation, target);
        Storyboard.SetTargetProperty(animation, new PropertyPath(item.Key));
        storyBoard.Children.Add(animation);
    }

    storyBoard.Begin();
}
```

Then modify the MainPage.xaml.cs code-behind to first set the AnswerText element Opacity to 0 (invisible), then animate the Opacity back to 1 (opaque) (see Listing 8-33). Notice that the optional duration parameter is included to specify a longer animation.

Listing 8-33. Adding the Animation

```
void _shake_CurrentValueChanged(object sender, SensorReadingEventArgs<ShakeReading> e)
{
    this.Dispatcher.BeginInvoke(() =>
    {
        this.AnswerText.Text = _answers.Ask();
        this.AnswerText.Opacity = 0;
```

```
        this.AnswerText.Animate(new Dictionary<string, double>()
        {
            {"Opacity", 1}
        }, 5000);
    });
}
```

Camera

Starting with the PhotoCamera object, you can display a real-time view finder, focus the camera, take images, get thumbnails, and save images to local storage or a library located on the phone. The image preview takes the form of a VideoBrush that can be bound to any element that takes a Brush. The CameraButtons object fires events that respond to the hardware camera shutter button.

Camera Preview

Before you can take a picture, you need to initialize the PhotoCamera and display the preview. To access the camera for preview, first add the ID_CAP_ISV_CAMERA to the WMAppManifest.xml Capabilities.

The two objects you need are PhotoCamera and VideoBrush. Assigning the source of the VideoBrush is required for the PhotoCamera to initialize, even if you don't consume the VideoBrush for any other purpose.

When you navigate to the page, create the PhotoCamera object and hook up the Initialized event as shown in Listing 8-34. Create a new VideoBrush (or reference a VideoBrush defined in the XAML), call SetSource(), and pass the PhotoCamera object. The PhotoCamera constructor can be left without parameters or can take a CameraType enumeration value (Primary or FrontFacing).

Listing 8-34. Initializing the Camera and VideoBrush

```
private PhotoCamera _camera;
private VideoBrush _videoBrush;

protected override void OnNavigatedTo(NavigationEventArgs e)
{
    base.OnNavigatedTo(e);

    _camera = new PhotoCamera(CameraType.Primary);
    _camera.Initialized += _camera_Initialized;

    _videoBrush = new VideoBrush();
    _videoBrush.SetSource(_camera);
}
```

Use the page's OnNavigatedFrom() override to unhook events and dispose of objects as shown in Listing 8-35.

Listing 8-35. Cleaning Up After the Camera and VideoBrush Objects

```
protected override void OnNavigatedFrom(NavigationEventArgs e)
{

    _videoBrush = null;
    _camera.Initialized -= _camera_Initialized;
    _camera = null;

    base.OnNavigatedFrom(e);
}
```

At this point, the orientation of the image for the brush assumes a landscape alignment. To make this assumption work out and at the same time, eliminate the system tray for maximum screen space, set the MainPage.xaml SupportedOrientations and SystemTray.IsVisible as shown in Listing 8-36. Replace the child elements of LayoutRoot with a MediaElement named VideoPlayer.

Listing 8-36. Orientation and System.Tray Settings

```
<phone:PhoneApplicationPage . . .
    SupportedOrientations="Landscape" Orientation="Landscape"
    shell:SystemTray.IsVisible="False">

    <Grid x:Name="LayoutRoot" Background="Transparent">
        <Grid.RowDefinitions>
            <RowDefinition Height="Auto"/>
            <RowDefinition Height="*"/>
        </Grid.RowDefinitions>

        <MediaElement  x:Name="VideoPlayer" Width="800" Height="480"
            Stretch="Fill" />
    </Grid>

</phone:PhoneApplicationPage>
```

When the Camera Initialized event fires, the PhotoCamera is ready and the VideoBrush is ready to paint. We can also set properties on the PhotoCamera object itself (see Listing 8-37). Be aware that the PhotoCamera events do not fire on the main UI thread, so use Dispatcher.BeginInvoke() to interact with the UI. In this example, we're simply assigning the VideoBrush to the LayoutRoot Background. Check the event arguments Succeeded property before using the VideoBrush. Be aware that if the initialization fails, you can check the PhotoCamera Initialized event argument's Exception property for details.

Listing 8-37. Handling the Camera Initialized Event

```
void _camera_Initialized(object sender, CameraOperationCompletedEventArgs e)
{
    if (e.Succeeded)
    {
        var resolution = new Size(2048, 1536);
         if (_camera.AvailableResolutions.Contains(resolution))
         {
             _camera.Resolution = resolution;
         }
        Dispatcher.BeginInvoke(() =>
        {
            this.LayoutRoot.Background = _videoBrush;
        });
    }
}
```

■ **Note** Listing 8-37 includes code to set the PhotoCamera Resolution. What resolutions can you use? Query the PhotoCamera AvailableResolutions collection to get an enumeration of Size with the correct Width and Height pairs that will work for a given device. The smaller sizes like 640 x 480 will provide a lower-resolution image at a memory cost savings while higher sizes like 3264 x 2448 will produce very large files (several MBs).

Capturing an Image

The general steps to retain an image in view when the camera shutter button is pressed are:

- Add the ID_CAP_MEDIALIB_PHOTO capability to the WMAppManifest.xml.
- Hook up the static CameraButtons ShutterKeyPressed event
- Hook up the PhotoCamera CaptureImageAvailable event
- Call the PhotoCamera CaptureImage() method. This will fire the CaptureImageAvailable event and pass the ImageStream property of the event arguments.

We can modify the code from the Camera Preview example in Listing 8-34. In the OnNavigatedTo method override, hook up the PhotoCamera CaptureImageAvailable event and the CameraButtons ShutterKeyPressed event (see Listing 8-38).

Listing 8-38. Subscribing to CaptureImageAvailable and ShutterKeyPressed

```
protected override void OnNavigatedTo(NavigationEventArgs e)
{
    base.OnNavigatedTo(e);

    _camera = new PhotoCamera(CameraType.Primary);
    _camera.Initialized += _camera_Initialized;

    _camera.CaptureImageAvailable += _camera_CaptureImageAvailable;
    CameraButtons.ShutterKeyPressed += CameraButtons_ShutterKeyPressed;

    _videoBrush = new VideoBrush();
    _videoBrush.SetSource(_camera);
}
```

In the OnNavigatedFrom, clean up the new event handlers (see Listing 8-39).

Listing 8-39. Removing the Event Handlers

```
protected override void OnNavigatedFrom(NavigationEventArgs e)
{

    _videoBrush = null;
    _camera.Initialized -= _camera_Initialized;
    _camera.CaptureImageAvailable -= _camera_CaptureImageAvailable;
    _camera = null;

    CameraButtons.ShutterKeyPressed -= CameraButtons_ShutterKeyPressed;

    base.OnNavigatedFrom(e);
}
```

In the ShutterKeyPressed event, call the PhotoCamera CaptureImage() method (see Listing 8-40). You'll find in practice that it's hard to avoid taking an image too soon or you may take too many images in succession. Both of these circumstances will raise an InvalidOperationException where the message will be either *"Cannot be called until capture has completed."* or *"You cannot use this instance until it is fully initialized…"*. To avoid these exceptions during CaptureImage() execution, wrap the call in a try...catch statement. If your exception handler needs to access the main thread, wrap statements inside the catch with a Dispatcher.BeginInvoke().

Listing 8-40. Handling the ShutterKeyPressed Event

```
void CameraButtons_ShutterKeyPressed(object sender, EventArgs e)
{
    try
    {
        _camera.CaptureImage();
    }
    catch (InvalidOperationException ex)
    {
        this.Dispatcher.BeginInvoke(() =>
        {
            MessageBox.Show(ex.Message);
        });
    }
}
```

In the CaptureImageAvailable event handler, the ImageStream property of the event arguments represents the bytes for the image that can be saved to local storage or in the "camera roll" folder on the device. The example in Listing 8-41 constructs a new path for the image and saves the image to the camera roll.

Listing 8-41. The CaptureImageAvailable Event Handler

```
void _camera_CaptureImageAvailable(object sender, ContentReadyEventArgs e)
{

    string path = "picture" + DateTime.Now.ToString("YYYYMMDDHHMMSSmmmm") + ".jpg";

    MediaLibrary library = new MediaLibrary();
    library.SavePictureToCameraRoll(path, e.ImageStream);
}
```

Using the Camera with a ViewModel

Before adding more capabilities to your Camera application, why not create a ViewModel for the camera to reduce and simplify the application code? The following steps demonstrate creating a camera ViewModel and binding the page to the ViewModel.

First, prepare the project:

1. Create a new Windows Phone 8 project.
2. In the Solution Explorer, open the Properties > WMAppManifest.xml > Capabilities and select the ID_CAP_ISV_CAMERA and ID_CAP_MEDIALIB_PHOTO capabilities.
3. Open MainPage.xaml for editing. Reduce the layout markup to show just the LayoutRoot element using the markup in Listing 8-42 as a guide. Change the shell.SystemTray.IsVisible

setting to False and the Orientation properties to Landscape. Removing the SystemTray will provide a little extra real-estate. The Grid Background property should be bound to the Preview property of the ViewModel.

Listing 8-42. Reducing layout markup to show just the LayoutRoot element

```
<phone:PhoneApplicationPage . . .
    SupportedOrientations="Landscape"
    Orientation="Landscape"
    shell:SystemTray.IsVisible="False">

    <Grid x:Name="LayoutRoot" Background="{Binding Preview}"></Grid>

</phone:PhoneApplicationPage>
```

Now create the ViewModel objects that will initialize the camera, capture images and be bound to the page.

1. Add a ViewModels folder to the project.
2. Add a new BaseViewModel class to the ViewModels folder. Replace the code with the code in Listing 8-43. The BaseViewModel will add the property change notification.

Listing 8-43. Defining the BaseViewModel

```
public class BaseViewModel : INotifyPropertyChanged
{
    public void NotifyPropertyChanged(string propertyName)
    {
        if (PropertyChanged != null)
        {
            PropertyChanged(this, new PropertyChangedEventArgs(propertyName));
        }
    }
    public event PropertyChangedEventHandler PropertyChanged;
}
```

3. Add a new class to the ViewModels folder named CameraViewModel.
4. Setup the shell of the CameraViewModel class using the code in Listing 8-44. The ViewModel descends from BaseViewModel to handle property notification and IDisposable to allow resource cleanup. The private properties you'll need later are listed here and the public VideoBrush Preview property is used in the XAML binding.

Listing 8-44. The Shell of CameraViewModel

```
public class CameraViewModel : BaseViewModel, IDisposable
{
    private PhotoCamera _camera;
    private string _captureName;
    private VideoBrush _tempBrush;
    private VideoBrush _preview;
    public VideoBrush Preview
```

```
    {
        get
        {
            return _preview;
        }
        private set
        {
            _preview = value;
            NotifyPropertyChanged("Preview");
        }
    }
}
```

5. Add the code below to the CameraViewModel class for the constructor and Dispose() method as shown in Listing 8-45. The constructor creates the PhotoCamera and hooks up the events. The Dispose() method cleans up the event handlers and objects.

Listing 8-45. The ViewModel Constructor and Dispose

```
public CameraViewModel()
{
    _camera = new PhotoCamera(CameraType.Primary);
    _camera.Initialized += camera_Initialized;
    _camera.CaptureImageAvailable += camera_CaptureImageAvailable;
    _tempBrush = new VideoBrush();
    _tempBrush.SetSource(_camera);
}
public void Dispose()
{
    _camera.Initialized -= camera_Initialized;
    _camera.CaptureImageAvailable -= camera_CaptureImageAvailable;
    _camera.Dispose();
    _camera = null;
    _tempBrush = null;
    this.Preview = null;
}
```

6. Implement the camera's Initialized event handler. If initialization succeeds, assign the initialized _tempBrush to the Preview property (see Listing 8-46). The Preview property will be bound to the LayoutRoot element in the MainPage.

Listing 8-46. Handling the Initialized Event

```
void camera_Initialized(object sender, CameraOperationCompletedEventArgs e)
{
    if (e.Succeeded)
    {
        Deployment.Current.Dispatcher.BeginInvoke(() =>
        {
            this.Preview = _tempBrush;
        });
    }
}
```

7. Create a public Capture() method that builds a file name for the capture and triggers the camera CaptureImage() method (see Listing 8-47). Be sure to catch the InvalidOperationException for images taken too close together, or too soon before initialization.

Listing 8-47. The Public Capture() Method

```
public void Capture(string fileName)
{
    _captureName = fileName;
    try
    {
        _camera.CaptureImage();
    }
    // ignore images taken too close together
    catch (InvalidOperationException) { }
}
```

8. Implement a CaptureImageAvailable event handler that saves the image to the camera roll (see Listing 8-48).

Listing 8-48. Handling the CaptureImageAvailable Event

```
void camera_CaptureImageAvailable(object sender, ContentReadyEventArgs e)
{
    MediaLibrary library = new MediaLibrary();
    library.SavePictureToCameraRoll(_captureName,e.ImageStream);
}
```

Finally, code the page to bind a CameraViewModel instance to the LayoutRoot and to fire camera button events.

1. Add a private member to represent the CameraViewModel (see Listing 8-49). Later you can use this reference to dispose of the object when moving away from the page. Code the OnNavigatedTo method override to create and bind the ViewModel. Also, setup the CameraButtons ShutterKeyPressed event to trigger the capture.

Listing 8-49. Overriding the OnNavigatedTo() Method

```
private CameraViewModel _vm;

protected override void OnNavigatedTo(System.Windows.Navigation.NavigationEventArgs e)
{
    base.OnNavigatedTo(e);

    _vm = new CameraViewModel();
    this.LayoutRoot.DataContext = _vm;

    CameraButtons.ShutterKeyPressed += CameraButtons_ShutterKeyPressed;
}
```

2. Perform cleanup in the OnNavigatedFrom method to override, as shown in Listing 8-50.

Listing 8-50. Overriding the OnNavigatedFrom Method

```
protected override void OnNavigatedFrom(System.Windows.Navigation.NavigationEventArgs e)
{
    this.LayoutRoot.DataContext = null;
    _vm.Dispose();
    _vm = null;

    CameraButtons.ShutterKeyPressed -= CameraButtons_ShutterKeyPressed;

    base.OnNavigatedFrom(e);
}
```

3. Handle the `ShutterKeyPressed` event by first creating a unique name for the capture, then invoking the view model `Capture()` method as shown in Listing 8-51.

Listing 8-51. Handling the ShutterKeyPressed Event

```
void CameraButtons_ShutterKeyPressed(object sender, System.EventArgs e)
{
    string captureName = "picture" +
        DateTime.Now.ToString("yyyyMMddhhmmssfff") + ".jpg";
    _vm.Capture(captureName);
}
```

When you run the application, you should see the entire device client area filled with the moving camera preview image (see Figure 8-8). When you click the hardware shutter button, the image should be retained. You can check the functionality by unhooking the phone from your computer and using File Explorer to open `Windows Phone\Phone\Pictures\Camera Roll`.

Figure 8-8. *New Picture From the Camera Roll*

The user will expect some kind of "Click" feedback when a photo snapshot is taken. The next section demonstrates how to use sound effects for a better user experience.

Adding Sound Effect Feedback

The SoundEffect class can play the sound of an old-school camera shutter clicking as the picture is taken or an error sound if the camera cannot initialize. The SoundEffect class is a "one trick pony" that plays only *.wav files. To get a SoundEffect object complete with the sound data, first use Application.GetResourceStream() to get a StreamResourceInfo from a *.wav file in your project, then use the SoundEffect.FromStream() and pass it the resource's Stream property.

Listing 8-52 shows a minimal code example. The SoundEffect class is from the XNA framework that supports game programming. Notice that the FrameworkDispatcher Update() method must be called to process XNA framework messages.

Listing 8-52. Minimal Code to Play a SoundEffect

```
StreamResourceInfo resource = Application.GetResourceStream(
    new Uri("Assets/Sounds/Windows Critical Stop.wav", UriKind.Relative));
var effect = SoundEffect.FromStream(resource.Stream);
FrameworkDispatcher.Update();
effect.Play();
```

The example that follows creates a wrapper class, SoundEffects, for a set of sounds used in the CameraViewModel. Figure 8-9 shows the project with sound files added to the \Assets directory under \Sounds and a new SoundEffects.cs file under the \ViewModels directory. You can find sound files in the \Windows\Media folder of your Windows 8 installation.

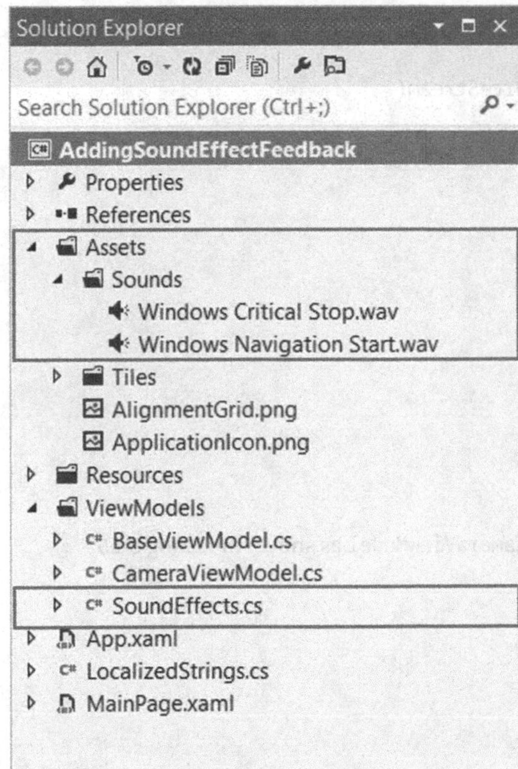

Figure 8-9. *The Project Sound Files*

The custom SoundEffects class first defines an enum of the types of effects it can play (see Listing 8-53).

Listing 8-53. The EffectTypes Enumeration

```
public enum EffectTypes { Click, Error };
```

The SoundEffects class inherits from Dictionary, keyed by the EffectTypes and where each Dictionary entry can return an XNA SoundEffect value (see Listing 8-54). The code from the previous, minimal example in Listing 8-52 is wrapped by the private method LoadSoundEffect(). The SoundEffects constructor adds Dictionary entries by the EffectTypes key and uses LoadSoundEffect() to return the SoundEffect value. The public Play() method takes EffectTypes as a parameter, calls the FrameworkDispatcher Update() method for us and plays the effect.

Listing 8-54. The SoundEffects Class

```
public class SoundEffects : Dictionary<EffectTypes, SoundEffect>
{
    public SoundEffects()
    {
        this.Add(EffectTypes.Click,
          LoadSoundEffect("Windows Navigation Start.wav"));
        this.Add(EffectTypes.Error,
          LoadSoundEffect("Windows Critical Stop.wav"));
    }

    private SoundEffect LoadSoundEffect(string fileName)
    {
        string path = "Assets/Sounds/" + fileName;
        StreamResourceInfo resource = Application.GetResourceStream(
            new Uri(path, UriKind.Relative));
        return SoundEffect.FromStream(resource.Stream);
    }

    public void Play(EffectTypes effectType)
    {
        var effect = this[effectType];
        if (effect != null)
        {
            FrameworkDispatcher.Update();
            effect.Play();
        }
    }
}
```

The SoundEffects class is instantiated and released inside the CameraViewModel as shown in Listing 8-55.

Listing 8-55. Using the SoundEffects class

```
private SoundEffects _effects;

public CameraViewModel()
{
    . . .
    _effects = new SoundEffects();
}
```

```
public void Dispose()
{
    _effects = null;
    . . .
}
```

The SoundEffects Play() method is called from the PhotoCamera Initialized event handler if the initialization fails. The Play() method is also called from the public Capture() method, playing different sounds depending on if the PhotoCamera CaptureImage() method executes without exception (see Listing 8-56).

Listing 8-56. Calling the SoundEffects Play() Method

```
void camera_Initialized(object sender, CameraOperationCompletedEventArgs e)
{
    if (e.Succeeded)
    {
        _camera.Resolution = new Size(2048, 1536);
        Deployment.Current.Dispatcher.BeginInvoke(() =>
        {
            this.Preview = _tempBrush;
        });
    }
    else
    {
        _effects.Play(EffectTypes.Error);
    }
}

public void Capture(string fileName)
{
    _captureName = fileName;
    try
    {
        _camera.CaptureImage();
        _effects.Play(EffectTypes.Click);
    }
    catch (InvalidOperationException)
    {
        _effects.Play(EffectTypes.Error);
    }
}
```

When you run the project with the new sound effects, clicking the phone shutter button plays a "click" sound and if you press the shutter button too quickly in succession, an invalid operation exception is raised and the phone plays a "bong" sound.

You can avoid triggering the invalid operation exception altogether if you track when a capture is under way by handling the PhotoCamera CaptureStarted and CaptureCompleted events (see Listing 8-57).

Listing 8-57. Handling the CaptureStarted and CaptureCompleted Events

```
private bool _isCapturing;

public CameraViewModel()
{
    _camera = new PhotoCamera();
    _camera.Initialized += camera_Initialized;
    _camera.CaptureImageAvailable += camera_CaptureImageAvailable;
    _camera.CaptureStarted += _camera_CaptureStarted;
    _camera.CaptureCompleted += _camera_CaptureCompleted;
    //. . .
}

public void Dispose()
{
    _camera.Initialized -= camera_Initialized;
    _camera.CaptureImageAvailable -= camera_CaptureImageAvailable;
    _camera.CaptureStarted -= _camera_CaptureStarted;
    _camera.CaptureCompleted -= _camera_CaptureCompleted;
    _camera.Dispose();
    _camera = null;
    //. . .
}

void _camera_CaptureCompleted(object sender, CameraOperationCompletedEventArgs e)
{
    _isCapturing = false;
}

void _camera_CaptureStarted(object sender, EventArgs e)
{
    _isCapturing = true;
}

public void Capture(string fileName)
{
    if (!_isCapturing)
    {
        _captureName = fileName;
        _camera.CaptureImage();
        _effects.Play(EffectTypes.Click);
    }
    else
    {
        _effects.Play(EffectTypes.Error);
    }
}
```

Camera Focus

The camera device may support focusing or even focusing at a specific point. Check for allowable operations using the `IsFocusSupported` and `IsFocusAtPointSupported` `PhotoCamera` properties. `PhotoCamera` `Focus()` and `FocusAtPoint()` methods trigger an `AutoFocusCompleted` event that fires when the focus is complete.

The following example adds focus capability triggered when the shutter key is half pressed. A bracket graphic will display in the preview window during the focus. This project extends the preceding "Adding Sound Effect Feedback" example.

First setup new folders to hold images and supporting classes:

1. In the Solution Explorer, add folders `\Converters` and `\Assets\Images`.
2. Add a 48 x 48 pixel image named "focus_bracket.png" to the `\Assets\Images` folder. It's best if the bracket has both light and dark lines for contrast and a transparent background. Figure 8-10 shows the graphic in Windows 8 Paint.

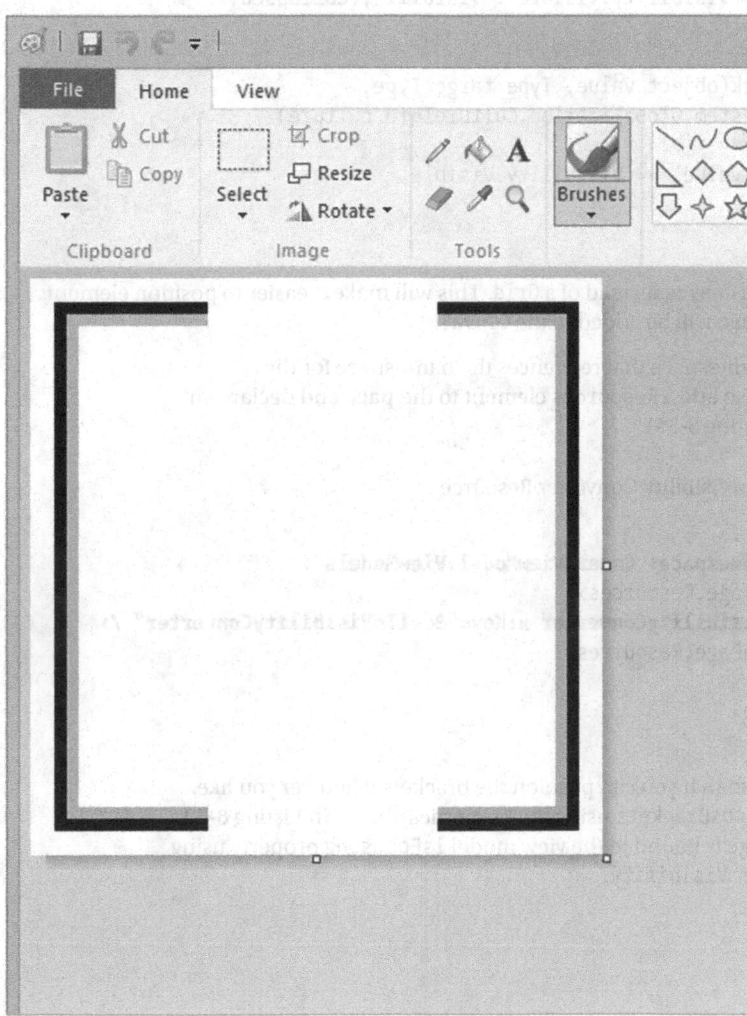

***Figure 8-10.** The Focus Bracket Graphic in Paint*

Next, create an IValueConverter implementation that will make the brackets visible only when focusing the camera:

1. Add a new class to the \Converters directory and name it BoolToVisibilityConverter.cs.
2. Code the Convert method to return Visibility.Visible when true and Visibility.Collapsed when false (see Listing 8-58). The ConvertBack() implementation is included for completeness but not used in this example.

Listing 8-58. Implementing the BoolToVisibilityConverter

```
public class BoolToVisibilityConverter : IValueConverter
{
    public object Convert(object value, Type targetType,
        object parameter, System.Globalization.CultureInfo culture)
    {
        return (bool)value ? Visibility.Visible : Visibility.Collapsed;
    }

    public object ConvertBack(object value, Type targetType,
        object parameter, System.Globalization.CultureInfo culture)
    {
        return ((Visibility)value) == Visibility.Visible;
    }
}
```

The page layout must be changed to be a Canvas instead of a Grid. This will make it easier to position elements anywhere in the space. The focus bracket image will be added to the Canvas:

1. In MainPage.xaml, add an xml namespace that references the namespace for the BoolToVisibilityConverter. Also add a Resources element to the page and declare an instance of the converter (see Listing 8-59).

Listing 8-59. Creating the BoolToVisibility Converter Resource

```
<phone:PhoneApplicationPage . . .
    xmlns:converters="clr-namespace: CameraViewModel.ViewModels">
    <phone:PhoneApplicationPage.Resources>
        <converters:BoolToVisibilityConverter x:Key="BoolToVisibilityConverter" />
    </phone:PhoneApplicationPage.Resources>
. . .
</phone:PhoneApplicationPage>
```

2. Change LayoutRoot to a Canvas so that you can position the brackets wherever you like. Add an Image element named FocusBrackets using the properties shown in Listing 8-60. In particular, notice that the image is bound to the view model IsFocusing property using the BoolToVisibilityConverter Visibility.

Listing 8-60. The LayoutRoot Design

```
<Canvas x:Name="LayoutRoot" Background="{Binding Preview}">
    <Canvas.Children>
        <Image Name="FocusBrackets" Height="150" Width="200" Stretch="Fill"
            Source="/Assets/Images/focus_brackets.png"
            Visibility="{Binding IsFocusing,
                Converter={StaticResource BoolToVisibilityConverter}}">
        </Image>
    </Canvas.Children>
</Canvas>
```

The ViewModel will need support for a new `IsFocusing` property that will be bound to the `Visibility` property of the `Image` element:

1. Add an event handler for the `PhotoCamera AutoFocusCompleted` event and remove the event handler in the `Dispose()` method (see Listing 8-61).

Listing 8-61. Adding and Removing the AutoFocusCompleted Event Handler

```
public CameraViewModel()
{
    . . .
    _camera.AutoFocusCompleted += _camera_AutoFocusCompleted;
}

public void Dispose()
{
    . . .
    _camera.AutoFocusCompleted -= _camera_AutoFocusCompleted;
}
```

2. Add a new `IsFocusing` property to the view model. This property will be bound to the view and needs `INotifyPropertyChanged` support (see Listing 8-62).

Listing 8-62. Adding the Custom IsFocusing Property

```
private bool _isFocusing = false;
public bool IsFocusing
{
    get
    {
        return _isFocusing;
    }
    set
    {
        _isFocusing = value;
        NotifyPropertyChanged("IsFocusing");
    }
}
```

3. Add a new Focus() method to the ViewModel as shown in Listing 8-63. This method checks that focus is supported for this device and that there isn't a capture underway. If all is good, set the custom IsFocusing property to true from within the main thread. When IsFocusing is true, the focus brackets become visible. Finally, call the PhotoCamera Focus() method.

Listing 8-63. Adding the Focus() Method

```
public void Focus()
{
    if ((_camera.IsFocusSupported) && (!_isCapturing))
    {
        Deployment.Current.Dispatcher.BeginInvoke(() =>
        {
            this.IsFocusing = true;
        });
        _camera.Focus();
    }
}
```

4. The PhotoCamera Focus() method triggers the AutoFocusCompleted event. You could check the Succeeded event argument, but in this example, "IsFocusing" should always be turned back off (see Listing 8-64).

Listing 8-64. Handling the AutoFocusCompleted Event

```
void _camera_AutoFocusCompleted(object sender, CameraOperationCompletedEventArgs e)
{
    Deployment.Current.Dispatcher.BeginInvoke(() =>
    {
        this.IsFocusing = false;
    });
}
```

The focus needs to be triggered by some action in the MainPage. The focus bracket graphic also needs to be positioned on the Canvas. In this case, the CameraButtons ShutterKeyHalfPressed event will do the job:

1. Add a CameraButtons ShutterKeyHalfPressed event handler assignment to the OnNavigatedTo() method override and remove the assignment in the OnNavigatedFrom method override (see Listing 8-65).

Listing 8-65. Adding and Removing the ShutterHalfKeyPressed Event

```
protected override void OnNavigatedTo(System.Windows.Navigation.NavigationEventArgs e)
{
    base.OnNavigatedTo(e);

    . . .
    CameraButtons.ShutterKeyHalfPressed += CameraButtons_ShutterKeyHalfPressed;
}
```

```
protected override void OnNavigatedFrom(System.Windows.Navigation.NavigationEventArgs e)
{
    . . .
    CameraButtons.ShutterKeyHalfPressed -= CameraButtons_ShutterKeyHalfPressed;

    base.OnNavigatedFrom(e);
}
```

2. In the ShutterKeyHalfPressed event handler, use the Canvas SetLeft() and SetTop() methods to position the FocusBrackets element in the screen center, and then call the view model Focus() method (see Listing 8-66).

Listing 8-66. Handling the ShutterKeyHalfPressed Event

```
void CameraButtons_ShutterKeyHalfPressed(object sender, EventArgs e)
{
    // place "focus brackets" graphic at screen center.
    Canvas.SetLeft(this.FocusBrackets,
        LayoutRoot.ActualWidth / 2 - (this.FocusBrackets.ActualWidth / 2));
    Canvas.SetTop(this.FocusBrackets,
        LayoutRoot.ActualHeight / 2 - (this.FocusBrackets.ActualHeight / 2));

    _vm.Focus();
}
```

Run the application. When the shutter key is half pressed, the focus bracket element should display over the preview area, you should see some slight focusing activity in the preview, and then the focus brackets should disappear (see Figure 8-11).

Figure 8-11. *The Focus Rectangle Image on Canvas*

You might also consider adding a "tap to focus" feature to your camera by capturing a Tap event from the element displaying the preview. You can display the brackets at the position of the tap and then call the PhotoCamera FocusAtPoint() method. The Tap event handler sets the private _isFocusing to true for later use. Add a Tap event handler to the Layout element replace the event handler with the code in Listing 8-67.

Listing 8-67. Handling the Tap Event

```
private void LayoutRoot_Tap_1(object sender, GestureEventArgs e)
{
    if (!_vm.IsFocusing)
    {
        System.Windows.Point point = e.GetPosition(this.LayoutRoot);
        double x = point.X / this.LayoutRoot.ActualWidth;
        double y = point.Y / this.LayoutRoot.ActualHeight;

        Dispatcher.BeginInvoke(() =>
        {
            Canvas.SetLeft(this.FocusBrackets, point.X - (this.FocusBrackets.ActualWidth / 2));
            Canvas.SetTop(this.FocusBrackets, point.Y - (this.FocusBrackets.ActualHeight / 2));
        });

        _vm.FocusAtPoint(x, y);
    }
}
```

The new ViewModel method FocusAtPoint(x,y) is structurally a copy of the ViewModel Focus() method with the addition of the x and y coordinates except that the method checks the IsFocusAtPointSupported and calls the PhotoCamera FocusAtPoint() method (see Listing 8-68).

Listing 8-68. The Custom FocusAtPoint() Method

```
public void FocusAtPoint(double x, double y)
{
    if ((_camera.IsFocusAtPointSupported) && (!_isCapturing))
    {
        Deployment.Current.Dispatcher.BeginInvoke(() =>
        {
            this.IsFocusing = true;
        });
        _camera.FocusAtPoint(x, y);
    }
}
```

■ **Note** Be aware that the FocusAtPoint() method doesn't take an absolute pixel position, but instead takes a horizontal location in the viewfinder that ranges from 0 (left) to 1 (right). This can be a percentage value reached by taking the location of the tapped point and dividing by the actual width of the tapped element.

Video Capture

Video and Audio captures involve three basic operations:

- Preview, where the "view finder" displays the moving image, but no recording is performed.
- Record, where the audio and image are saved to persistent storage.
- Playback, where the persistent storage is retrieved and displayed.

Preview

Video and Audio capture begin with the `CaptureSource` object from the `System.Windows.Media` namespace. To use `CaptureSource`, first assign `AudioCaptureDevice` and `VideoCaptureDevice` properties. You can get these from the static `CaptureDeviceConfiguration GetDefaultVideoCaptureDevice()` and `GetDefaultAudioCaptureDevice()` methods.

Create a `VideoBrush`, set its source to the `CaptureSource` object and assign the `VideoBrush` to the `Brush` of a visible element. The `CaptureSource Start()` begins collecting audio and visual data. Call the `CaptureSource Stop()` method to end streaming data.

■ **Note** You can also get collections of all available audio and video devices using the `GetAvailableVideoCaptureDevices()` and `GetAvailableAudioCaptureDevices()` methods. Each item in these collections allows you to get a format that the device supports.

The code snippet in Listing 8-69 creates a new `CaptureSource` and assigns the video and audio capture devices using the default values. A `VideoBrush` is created and assigned the `CaptureSource` using the `SetSource()` method. The `VideoBrush` is assigned to the `ContentPanel` Background. Finally, the `CaptureSource Start()` method begins the capture and displays on the background.

Listing 8-69. Using a CaptureSource and VideoBrush

```
// create CaptureSource with default audio and video
CaptureSource captureSource = new CaptureSource();
captureSource.VideoCaptureDevice =
    CaptureDeviceConfiguration.GetDefaultVideoCaptureDevice();
captureSource.AudioCaptureDevice =
    CaptureDeviceConfiguration.GetDefaultAudioCaptureDevice();

// create VideoBrush using CaptureSource as source
VideoBrush videoBrush = new VideoBrush();
videoBrush.SetSource(captureSource);

// assign the VideoBrush to the background and start the capture
this.ContentPanel.Background = videoBrush;
captureSource.Start();
```

Record

Recording uses a `FileSink` object to associate an *isolated storage* file with a `CaptureSource`. *Isolated storage* is a mechanism for storing data to the phone. The steps to setting up the recording are listed below:

1. Stop the `CaptureSource` so it can be used with the `FileSink`.
2. Create a file in isolated storage. No need to do anything with the file yet, just create it using a file name that must end in ".mp4" and close the file.
3. Create the `FileSink` and set the `IsolatedStorageFileName` to the name of the file just created. Set the `FileSink CaptureSource` property to the stopped `CaptureSource`.
4. Finally call the `CaptureSource Start()` method to begin recording to the isolated storage file.

The snippet in Listing 8-70 shows the required code.

Listing 8-70. Recording to Isolated Storage

```
// stop the CaptureSource so we can associate it with a FileSink
captureSource.Stop();

// create a file in isolated storage and close without writing to it
string path = "capture.mp4";
using (IsolatedStorageFile store =
    IsolatedStorageFile.GetUserStoreForApplication())
{
    store.CreateFile(path).Close();
}

// create a FileSink, associate it with the isolated storage file name
// and associate with the CaptureSource
FileSink fileSink = new FileSink();
fileSink.IsolatedStorageFileName = path;
fileSink.CaptureSource = captureSource;

// restart the capture
captureSource.Start();
```

■ **Note** Why was isolated storage used here instead of local storage? Isolated storage has something of a legacy flavor since it works in Windows Phone 7x and Windows Phone 8. The reason for using it here is that the `CaptureSource` allows us to switch easily between recording and previewing. The `CaptureSource` can be directed to isolated storage *or* a `VideoBrush`. The `VideoBrush` provides a nice viewing experience with good performance, right out of the box, without having to manually manipulate buffers of pixel data.

Playback

Use a `MediaElement` to playback the streamed audio and video data sitting in isolated storage. First stop the capture, read the isolated storage file created during recording and set the file as the source of the `MediaElement`. Call the `MediaElement Play()` method to begin playback (see Listing 8-71).

Listing 8-71. Loading the MediaElement from a Stream

```
captureSource.Stop();
string path = "capture.mp4";
IsolatedStorageFileStream isoStream = new IsolatedStorageFileStream(path,
                    FileMode.Open, FileAccess.Read,
                    IsolatedStorageFile.GetUserStoreForApplication());
VideoPlayer.SetSource(isoStream);
VideoPlayer.Play();
```

After the playback is finished you can clean up or notify the user by hooking up the MediaElement MediaEnded event.

Video Capture Example

The fun begins when you try to get these three functions (preview, record, and playback) to play together nicely. The example below is as minimal as possible. The Tap event for the page is used to cycle between the three operations with minimal user interface details. The custom CaptureState enumeration property helps keep track of the current operation.

First open the \Properties\WMAppManifest to the Capabilities tab and make sure that ID_CAP_ISV_CAMERA capability is selected.

Next, layout the page using the key parts defined in Listing 8-72. The page orientation is landscape and the system tray is hidden. Name one of the TextBlock elements "PageTitle" so you can access it in code. The ContentPanel and MediaElement are sized to 800 × 480.

Listing 8-72. The Page Layout

```
<phone:PhoneApplicationPage . . .
    SupportedOrientations="Landscape"
    Orientation="LandscapeLeft"
    shell:SystemTray.IsVisible="False">

    <Grid x:Name="LayoutRoot" Background="Transparent">

        . . .

        <StackPanel x:Name="TitlePanel" Grid.Row="0" Margin="12,17,0,28">
            <TextBlock Text="DEVICE CAPABILITIES" . . . />
            <TextBlock x:Name="PageTitle" Text="" . . . />
        </StackPanel>

        <Grid  x:Name="ContentPanel" Grid.Row="1" Margin="10"
            Width="800" Height="480">
            <MediaElement x:Name="VideoPlayer" Width="800" Height="480" Stretch="Fill"
                          MediaEnded="VideoPlayer_MediaEnded" />
        </Grid>

    </Grid>

</phone:PhoneApplicationPage>
```

Then, set up the shell of the page class using the code in Listing 8-73. This code includes all the members and methods that we will be using on the page.

Listing 8-73. The Page Code Structure

```
public partial class MainPage : PhoneApplicationPage
{
    private const string path = "capture.mp4";

    private enum CaptureState { Preview, Record, Playback };

    private CaptureSource _captureSource;
    private VideoBrush _videoBrush;
    private FileSink _fileSink;
    private CaptureState _captureState;

    protected override void OnNavigatedTo(NavigationEventArgs e)
    {
        base.OnNavigatedTo(e);
    }

    protected override void OnNavigatedFrom(NavigationEventArgs e)
    {
        base.OnNavigatedFrom(e);
    }

    void MainPage_Tap(object sender, GestureEventArgs e) {}
    void VideoPlayer_MediaEnded(object sender, RoutedEventArgs e) { }
    private void RunStateMethod() { }
    private void Preview() { }
    private void Record() { }
    private void Playback() { }
}
```

Populate the `OnNavigatedTo()` method with the code in Listing 8-74. The method creates and initializes the `CaptureSource`, `VideoBrush`, and `FileSink`. The `Tap` event for the page is hooked up, the initial `CaptureState` is set to `Preview` and the `Preview()` method is called.

Listing 8-74. Handling the OnNavigatedFrom() Method

```
protected override void OnNavigatedTo(NavigationEventArgs e)
{
    base.OnNavigatedTo(e);

    _captureSource = new CaptureSource();
    // create CaptureSource with default audio and video
    _captureSource.VideoCaptureDevice =
        CaptureDeviceConfiguration.GetDefaultVideoCaptureDevice();
    _captureSource.AudioCaptureDevice =
        CaptureDeviceConfiguration.GetDefaultAudioCaptureDevice();
    // create VideoBrush using CaptureSource as source
    _videoBrush = new VideoBrush();
    _fileSink = new FileSink();
    _fileSink.IsolatedStorageFileName = path;
```

```
    this.Tap += new EventHandler<GestureEventArgs>(MainPage_Tap);
    _captureState = CaptureState.Preview;

    RunStateMethod();
}
```

Code the OnNavigatedFrom() method to unhook the Tap event handler and clean up after objects used in the project (see Listing 8-75).

Listing 8-75. Overriding the OnNavigatedFrom() Method

```
protected override void OnNavigatedFrom(NavigationEventArgs e)
{
    this.Tap -= new EventHandler<GestureEventArgs>(MainPage_Tap);
    _captureSource = null;
    _videoBrush = null;
    _fileSink = null;

    base.OnNavigatedFrom(e);
}
```

Add code to the Tap handler as defined in Listing 8-76. The handler will bump the CaptureState to the next state in the enumeration. If we're at the last state then CaptureState wraps back around to the Preview state. The custom RunStateMethod() method will call the appropriate method for the corresponding CaptureState.

Listing 8-76. Handling the Tap Event

```
void MainPage_Tap(object sender, GestureEventArgs e)
{
    // bump to the next state
    _captureState = _captureState == CaptureState.Playback ?
        _captureState = CaptureState.Preview :
        ((CaptureState)((int)_captureState) + 1);

    RunStateMethod();
}
```

Next, define the custom RunStateMethod() to set the page title according to the CaptureState and then call the appropriate method (see Listing 8-77).

Listing 8-77. The Custom RunStateMethod()

```
private void RunStateMethod()
{
    // display the state
    this.PageTitle.Text = _captureState.ToString();

    // run the appropriate method
    switch (_captureState)
```

```
    {
        case CaptureState.Preview: { Preview(); break; }
        case CaptureState.Record: { Record(); break; }
        case CaptureState.Playback: { Playback(); break; }
    }
}
```

Add code to the Preview() method to stop the MediaPlayer if it's playing. The CaptureSource should also be stopped and associated with the video brush. Assign the video brush to an element's Brush property (i.e. ContentPanel.Background) and restart CaptureSource (see Listing 8-78).

Listing 8-78. Implementing the Preview() Method

```
private void Preview()
{
    VideoPlayer.Stop();
    VideoPlayer.Source = null;

    // stop any previous captures
    _captureSource.Stop();
    _videoBrush.SetSource(_captureSource);

    // assign the VideoBrush to the background and start the capture
    this.ContentPanel.Background = _videoBrush;

    _captureSource.Start();
}
```

Implement the Record() method as shown in Listing 8-79. The method stops the CaptureSource so that it can be associated with an isolated storage file by way of the FileSink.

Listing 8-79. Implementing the Record() Method

```
private void Record()
{
    // stop the CaptureSource so we can
    // associate it with a FileSink
    _captureSource.Stop();

    // create a file in isolated storage
    // and close without writing to it
    using (IsolatedStorageFile store =
        IsolatedStorageFile.GetUserStoreForApplication())
    {
        store.CreateFile(path).Close();
    }

    // create a FileSink
    // associate it with the isolated storage file name
    // and associate with the CaptureSource
    _fileSink.CaptureSource = _captureSource;
```

```
    // restart the capture
    _captureSource.Start();
}
```

Finally, write the Playback() method as shown in Listing 8-80. The Playback() method reads the recording from an isolated storage file into a stream. The stream is associated with the MediaPlayer. The MediaPlayer Play() method outputs video and audio to the MediaPlayer element. Also notice that the MediaEnded event is hooked up.

Listing 8-80. Implementing the Playback() Method

```
private void Playback()
{
    _captureSource.Stop();

    using (IsolatedStorageFile store =
        IsolatedStorageFile.GetUserStoreForApplication())
    {
        IsolatedStorageFileStream isoStream = new IsolatedStorageFileStream(path,
                FileMode.Open, FileAccess.Read, store);

        VideoPlayer.SetSource(isoStream);
    }

    VideoPlayer.MediaEnded += new RoutedEventHandler(VideoPlayer_MediaEnded);
    VideoPlayer.Play();
}

void VideoPlayer_MediaEnded(object sender, RoutedEventArgs e)
{
    this.PageTitle.Text = "playback ended";
}
```

When you run the application, the preview will be displayed first, as shown in Figure 8-12. Tap the screen to cycle through recording and playing back.

Figure 8-12. *The Running Application*

Summary

This chapter explored some of the unique ways that Windows Phone 8 devices know a lot about themselves. Not just the usual information like operating system and available storage space, but detailed data about the phone's position in space and in relation to the earth. We also used the phone to interact by using the camera for both photo and video capture. Along the way we used XNA to produce sound effects.

Windows Phone 8 devices also know about where they are on the planet. In the next chapter we'll talk about the phone's mapping and geolocation abilities.

CHAPTER 9

Mapping

Windows Phone 8 and mapping are a natural combination that allows users to display locations visually and respond in real time as the user's geographic position changes. This chapter explores Windows Phone 8 mapping mechanisms that include:

- How to use the built-in `Map` control with its ability to add elements such as "pushpins", user location icons and routes. You will also learn how to zoom and position the map to highlight a specific geographic area.
- How to use geocoding services that take some scrap of information such as a street or landmark name and return coordinates that can be displayed on the map.
- How to get the phone's current location.
- How to get directions between two or more locations.

Adding Maps to Your Application

There are two options to include Mapping in your application: launch a built-in `MapTask` or include the `Map` control directly on a page. Both require that you add the `ID_CAP_MAP` capability to the project's `\Properties\WMAppManifest.xml`.

The `MapTask` lives in the `Microsoft.Phone.Tasks` namespace. To use it, instantiate the `MapTask` object and call the `Show()` method (see Figure 9-1 to see the `MapTask` in a running application). There are optional parameters you can use to give the user a head start. `Center` is a `GeoCoordinate` object whose constructor takes `latitude` and `longitude` parameters. `SearchTerm` is a string that the map searches for and displays automatically. `ZoomLevel` can be set from 1 (zoomed all the way out) to 20 (zoomed in).

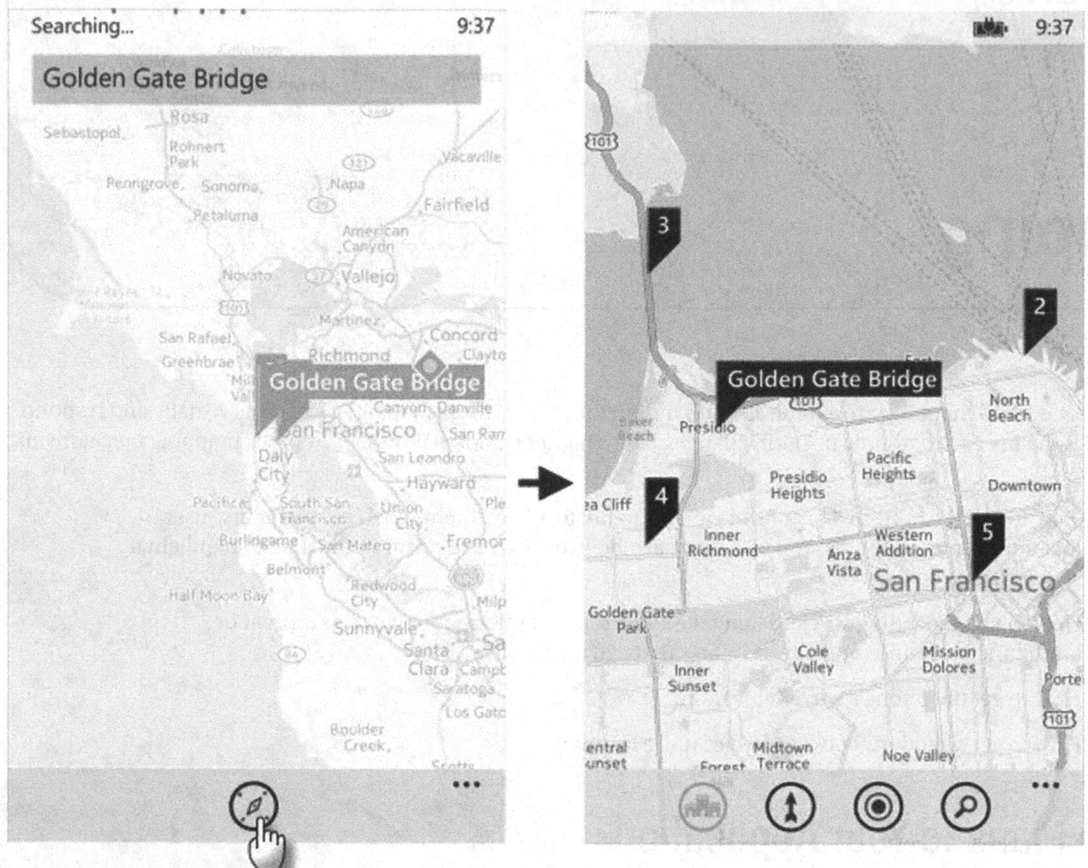

Figure 9-1. *Launching the MapTask*

■ **Note** Although `GeoCoordinate` is often used just to define latitude and longitude, be aware that it has properties for defining location in three-dimensional space, the direction it's headed and how fast it's going. The properties include `Altitude`, `Course` (degrees relative to true north), and `Speed` (meters per second). It also has a nifty `GetDistanceTo()` method that returns the distance (in meters) between the two locations.

The code in Listing 9-1 shows a `MapsTask` instantiated and displayed from an application tool bar button `Click` event.

Listing 9-1. Invoking the MapsTask

```
private void MapClick(object sender, EventArgs e)
{
    var task = new MapsTask();
    var goldenGateBridge = new GeoCoordinate(37.8085880, -122.4770175);
    task.Center = goldenGateBridge;
    task.ZoomLevel = 9;
```

```
    task.SearchTerm = "Golden Gate Bridge";
    task.Show();
}
```

The argument in favor of using the MapTask is that it's a "fire and forget" operation. You don't have any responsibility for the presentation of the UI or managing the map while it's running. The argument against MapTask is that you can't change the UI or manage the map while it's running.

The alternative to MaskTask is to drop a Map control directly on the page in your application. You can use the Map control as-is without setting any properties (see Listing 9-2).

Listing 9-2. Adding the Map Element

```
<Grid x:Name="LayoutRoot" Background="Transparent">
    <Controls:Map x:Name="WorldMap" />
</Grid>
```

The initial view is zoomed out and shows the world as one big road map (see Figure 9-2).

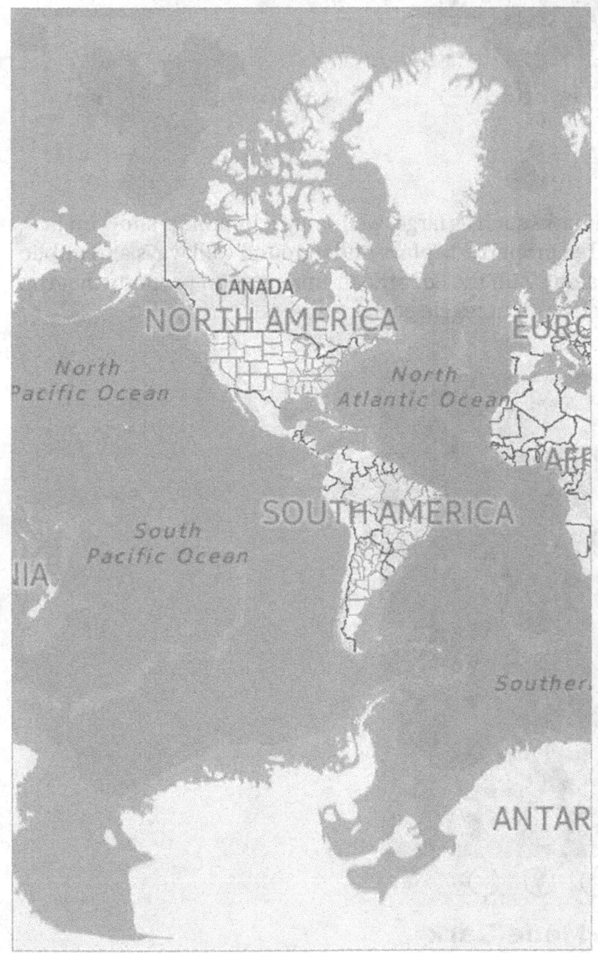

Figure 9-2. *Default Map View*

The CartographicMode enumeration determines the style of map display. Figure 9-2 shows the default Road mode. Figure 9-3 shows a comparison of the CartographicMode settings in the Map. The Aerial mode setting shows a satellite overhead view without location labels. The Hybrid is a combination of the Aerial map with the Road location labels. The Terrain map shows the topography of the location graphically.

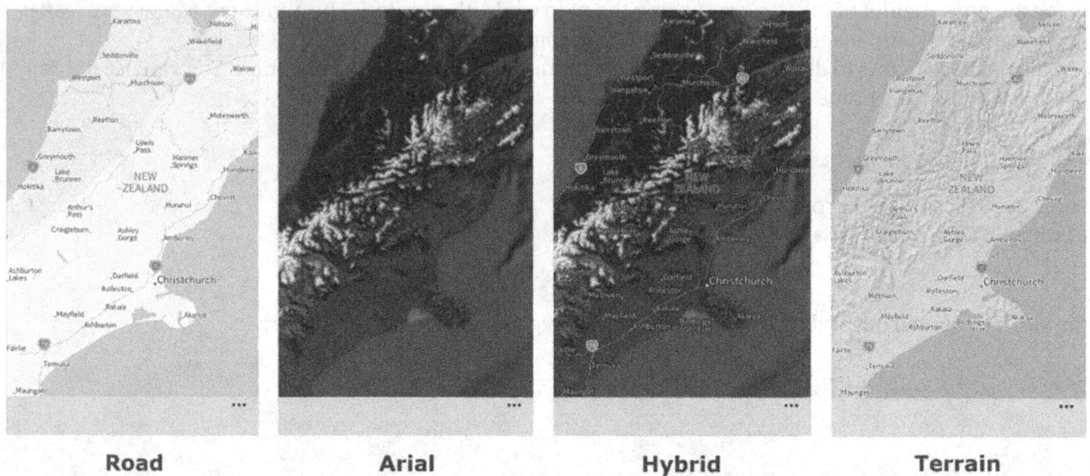

Figure 9-3. *CartographicModes in the Map Display*

When the LandmarksEnabled property is turned on, landmarks such as large, well-known buildings show up in three dimensions on the map. The PedestrianFeaturesEnabled property displays underground walkways and public stairs. See Figure 9-4 to see both of these properties enabled, along with the ColorMode enumeration property that can be Light or Dark. The example shows custom application bar icons that toggle each feature.

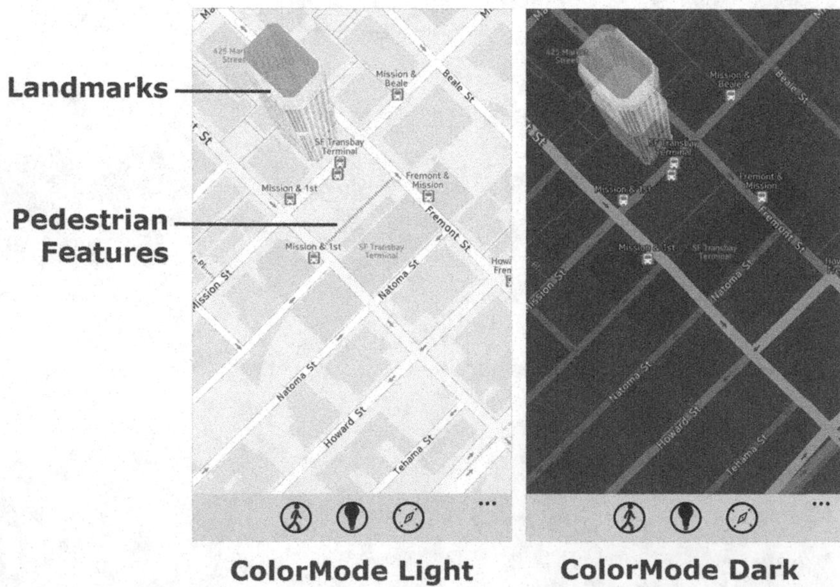

Figure 9-4. *PedestrianFeaturesEnabled, LandmarksEnabled, and ColorMode Properties*

The XAML markup to build the application bar is included in Listing 9-3.

Listing 9-3. The Application Bar Definition

```
<phone:PhoneApplicationPage.ApplicationBar>
    <shell:ApplicationBar>
        <shell:ApplicationBar.Buttons>
            <shell:ApplicationBarIconButton
                IconUri="Assets/Icons/pedestrian.png"
                Text="Features"
                Click="PedestrianFeaturesClick" />
            <shell:ApplicationBarIconButton
                IconUri="Assets/Icons/lightbulb.png"
                Text="Color Mode"
                Click="ColorModeClick" />
            <shell:ApplicationBarIconButton
                IconUri="Assets/Icons/compass.png"
                Text="Landmarks"
                Click="LandmarksClick" />
        </shell:ApplicationBar.Buttons>
        <shell:ApplicationBar.MenuItems>
            <shell:ApplicationBarMenuItem Text="Road"    Click="CartographicModeClick" />
            <shell:ApplicationBarMenuItem Text="Aerial"  Click="CartographicModeClick" />
            <shell:ApplicationBarMenuItem Text="Hybrid"  Click="CartographicModeClick" />
            <shell:ApplicationBarMenuItem Text="Terrain" Click="CartographicModeClick" />
        </shell:ApplicationBar.MenuItems>
    </shell:ApplicationBar>
</phone:PhoneApplicationPage.ApplicationBar>
```

The code for the event handlers is included in Listing 9-4. The event handler simply toggles Boolean properties and assigns enumeration values.

Listing 9-4. Event Handlers for the Application Bar

```
private void CartographicModeClick(object sender, EventArgs e)
{
    var menuItem = sender as ApplicationBarMenuItem;
    var cartographicMode =
        (MapCartographicMode)Enum.Parse(typeof(MapCartographicMode), menuItem.Text);
    this.WorldMap.CartographicMode = cartographicMode;
}

private void ColorModeClick(object sender, EventArgs e)
{
    this.WorldMap.ColorMode = this.WorldMap.ColorMode.Equals(MapColorMode.Light) ?
        MapColorMode.Dark :  MapColorMode.Light;
}

private void PedestrianFeaturesClick(object sender, EventArgs e)
{
    this.WorldMap.PedestrianFeaturesEnabled = !this.WorldMap.PedestrianFeaturesEnabled;
}
```

```
private void LandmarksClick(object sender, EventArgs e)
{
    this.WorldMap.LandmarksEnabled = !this.WorldMap.LandmarksEnabled;
}
```

Positioning the Map

Rather than making the user start with the whole world and have to pinch-and-zoom to an area of the map, you can position them automatically using the Map SetView() method. The code in Listing 9-5 creates a new GeoCoordinate with Latitude and Longitude properties that place it at the San Francisco Golden Gate Bridge. This GeoCoordinate parameter defines the center of the view. The second parameter to the SetView() method is the zoomLevel (1 = zoomed out, 20 = zoomed in).

Listing 9-5. Positioning the Map

```
GeoCoordinate GoldenGateBridge =
    new GeoCoordinate(37.8085880, -122.4770175);
SanFranciscoMap.SetView(GoldenGateBridge, 15);
```

If you have several related points of interest to show at the same time, you don't have to calculate the zoom yourself. SetView() takes a LocationRectangle, i.e., a set of GeoCoordinate that describe the view area. The static CreateBoundingRectangle()method takes a collection or array of GeoCoordinate.SetView() automatically zooms the view to include all the coordinates. The example in Listing 9-6 defines three well-known San Francisco landmarks as coordinates, creates a LocationRectangle from these coordinates and finally sets the view to include all three.

Listing 9-6. Setting the View to a LocationRectangle

```
private void WorldMap_Loaded(object sender, System.Windows.RoutedEventArgs e)
{
    // define coordinates
    GeoCoordinate GoldenGateBridge = new GeoCoordinate(37.8085880, -122.4770175);
    GeoCoordinate GoldenGatePark = new GeoCoordinate(37.7716645, -122.4545772);
    GeoCoordinate FishermansWharf = new GeoCoordinate(37.8085636, -122.4097141);

    // make an array of all coordinates
    var coordinates = new GeoCoordinate[]
    {
        GoldenGateBridge,
        GoldenGatePark,
        FishermansWharf
    };

    // zoom to include all coordinates in array
    var locationRectangle = LocationRectangle.CreateBoundingRectangle(coordinates);
    this.WorldMap.SetView(locationRectangle);
}
```

Figure 9-5 shows the zoom level that includes all three points. The problem here is, "what three points?" The next section will solve this problem by adding "pushpins" to describe each location visually.

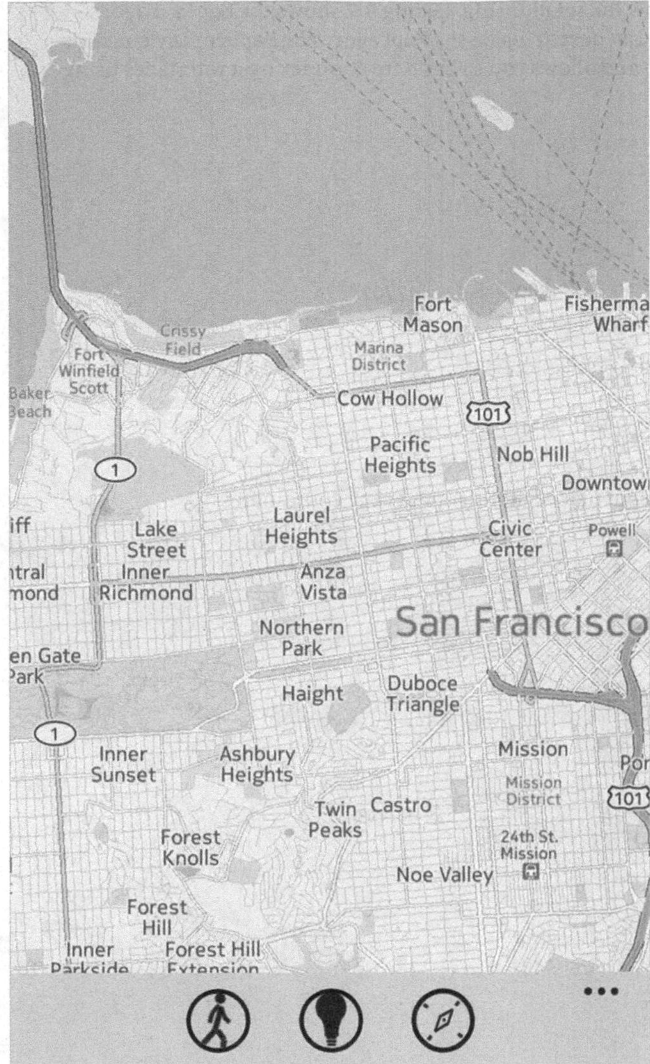

Figure 9-5. *Map Positioned on Multiple Coordinates*

Adding Pushpins

A *pushpin* is simply an element that has both content and a location. Rather than have a dedicated pushpin control, the `Map` control allows you to add any `UIElement` to the map.

The three objects that allow adding elements to the map are:

- `UIElement` can be any `UIElement` descendant, including a layout container such as a `Grid`, `StackPanel`, or `Canvas`.
- `MapOverlay` has both a `GeoCoordinate` and `Content` properties. The `UIElement` is assigned to the `Content` property and placed at the `GeoCoordinate` location.
- `MapLayer` is a collection of `MapOverlay`. You can add as many overlays as you like.

A working minimal example in XAML will help show the relationship. Listing 9-7 shows the `Map's Layers` collection, a single `MapLayer`, and then a single `MapOverlay` nested inside the `MapLayer`. The `MapOverlay` contains a `TextBlock` element. This arrangement is quite flexible and allows you to build up complex user interfaces using standard XAML parts off the shelf.

Listing 9-7. Adding a Map Layer

```
<Controls:Map>
    <Controls:Map.Layers>
        <Controls:MapLayer>
            <Controls:MapOverlay GeoCoordinate="37.8085880,  -122.4770175">
                <TextBlock Text="Golden Gate Bridge" />
            </Controls:MapOverlay>
        </Controls:MapLayer>
    </Controls:Map.Layers>
</Controls:Map>
```

Figure 9-6 shows the result with the `TextBlock` content placed at the `MapOverlay` coordinates.

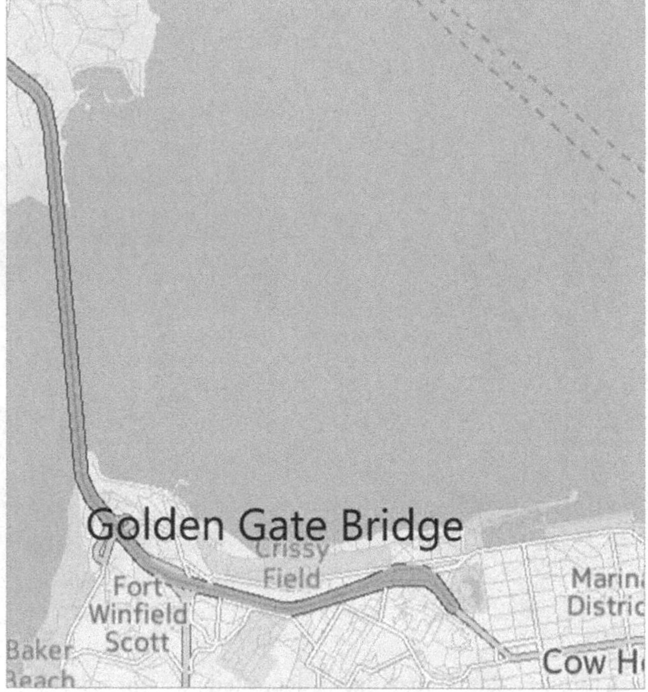

Figure 9-6. *The MapLayer, MapOverlay, and TextBlock*

Starting with the basic structure of `MapLayer` - `MapOverlay` - `UIElement`, you can style the elements so they stand out from the map. For example, you can place the `TextBlock` within a border. The example in Listing 9-8 styles a border with a semi-transparent background and accent colored border. There are three `MapLayer` elements defined, one for each location.

Listing 9-8. Multiple MapLayer Elements

```
<Controls:Map x:Name="WorldMap" Loaded="WorldMap_Loaded" >
    <Controls:Map.Resources>
        <Style x:Name="MapElementBorder" TargetType="Border">
            <Setter Property="Background" Value="{StaticResource PhoneSemitransparentBrush}" />
            <Setter Property="BorderBrush" Value="{StaticResource PhoneAccentBrush}" />
            <Setter Property="BorderThickness" Value="1" />
            <Setter Property="Padding" Value="10" />
        </Style>
    </Controls:Map.Resources>
    <Controls:Map.Layers>
        <Controls:MapLayer>
            <Controls:MapOverlay GeoCoordinate="37.8085880, -122.4770175">
                <Border Style="{StaticResource MapElementBorder}" >
                    <TextBlock Text="Golden Gate Bridge"
                      Style="{StaticResource PhoneTextAccentStyle}" />
                </Border>
            </Controls:MapOverlay>
            <Controls:MapOverlay GeoCoordinate="37.7716645, -122.4545772">
                <Border Style="{StaticResource MapElementBorder}" >
                    <TextBlock Text="Golden Gate Park"
                      Style="{StaticResource PhoneTextAccentStyle}" />
                </Border>
            </Controls:MapOverlay>
            <Controls:MapOverlay GeoCoordinate="37.8085636, -122.4097141">
                <Border Style="{StaticResource MapElementBorder}" >
                    <TextBlock Text="Golden Gate Park"
                      Style="{StaticResource PhoneTextAccentStyle}" />
                </Border>
            </Controls:MapOverlay>
        </Controls:MapLayer>
    </Controls:Map.Layers>
</Controls:Map>
```

The running application in Figure 9-7 shows all three `MapOverlay` elements at their assigned coordinates and `TextBlock` contents.

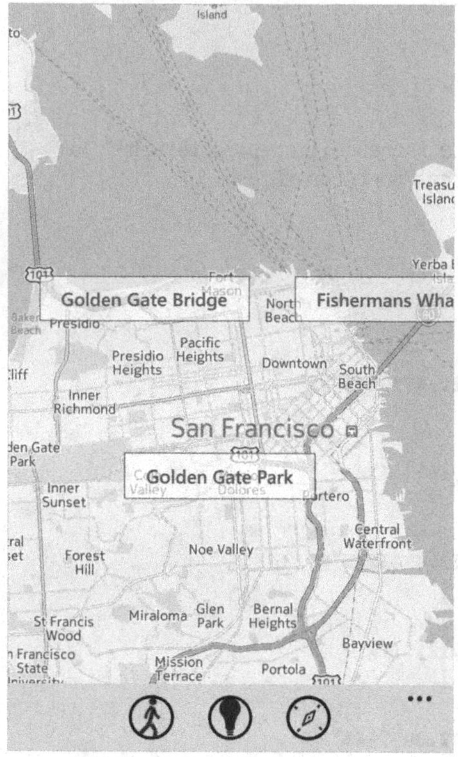

Figure 9-7. The Running Application with MapOverlay Elements

The equivalent to adding a map layer in XAML is shown in the code Listing 9-9. The process of translating the XAML to code consists of starting with the innermost elements, i.e., the `TextBlock` followed by the `Border`, and working outward to the `Map Layers` collection. The second issue is how to assign `Style` properties in code. Assign resources in code by indexing into the `Resources` property of the `FrameworkElement` that contains the resource in question. Be sure to cast the resource to the type you expect to get out of the dictionary, e.g., `Style`.

Listing 9-9. Adding Map Layers in Code

```
// build this by starting with the innermost element and
// walking back to the Map Layers
var textBlock = new TextBlock()
{
    Text = "Golden Gate Bridge",
    Style = (Style)this.Resources["PhoneTextAccentStyle"]
};

var border = new Border()
{
    Child = textBlock,
    Style = (Style)WorldMap.Resources["MapElementBorder"]
};
```

```
WorldMap.Layers.Add(new MapLayer() {
    new MapOverlay()
        {
            GeoCoordinate = new GeoCoordinate(37.8085880,  -122.4770175),
            Content = border
        }
});
```

Binding Pushpins to the Map

While the MapLayer and MapOverlay objects are flexible for use in XAML or direct code, what if you want to bind a ViewModel? The Map doesn't provide a straightforward way to bind data to MapLayer and MapOverlay. Fortunately the Windows Phone 8 Toolkit provides a set of objects to bridge the gap. See the Chapter 4 section "Installing the Windows Phone 8 Toolkit" for step-by-step directions on installing the toolkit to your solution.

To use the toolkit in XAML, add a XML namespace for the Microsoft.Phone.Maps.Toolkit assembly. The toolkit introduces key map objects:

- MapExtensions with a Children property that can contain one or more elements. In XAML markup, the MapExtensions tag is put just inside the Map tag.
- MapItemsControl acts like an ItemsControl within the context of a Map and has ItemsSource and ItemTemplate properties. You add the MapItemsControl within the MapExtensions tag in XAML.
- MapChildControl is a ContentControl descendant that has a GeoCoordinate property. If you don't want built-in styling, you can use MapChildControl directly within the MapItemsControl ItemTemplate. If you want the control styled to look like a standard Windows Phone 8 pushpin or "current location" marker, use the Pushpin or UserLocationMarker descendants of MapChildControl.

Before building a full ViewModel example, first look at the minimal example of a single Toolkit Pushpin (see Listing 9-10). Here, all the elements are hard-coded with the Map containing the MapExtensions.Children and the Pushpin being the only child element. The Pushpin defines a GeoCoordinate centered on London and the Content is plain text.

Listing 9-10. A Single Toolkit Pushpin

```
<Controls:Map>
    <Toolkit:MapExtensions.Children>
        <Toolkit:Pushpin
            Content="London"
            GeoCoordinate="51.499493,-0.124753" />
    </Toolkit:MapExtensions.Children>
</Controls:Map>
```

Figure 9-8 shows the result in the map. The "London" label is styled as a standard Windows Phone 8 pushpin.

Figure 9-8. The Toolkit Pushpin

Instead of placing the Pushpin directly in the MapExtensions Children collection, add a MapItemsControl instead (see Listing 9-11). The Pushpin will be moved into the ItemTemplate and ItemsSource will be assigned the ViewModel.

Listing 9-11. Adding the MapItemsControl

```
<Controls:Map x:Name="WorldMap" >
    <Toolkit:MapExtensions.Children>
        <Toolkit:MapItemsControl
            ItemTemplate="{StaticResource MapItemTemplate}"
            ItemsSource="{Binding
                Source={StaticResource LocationViewModel}, Path=Locations}" />
            </Toolkit:MapExtensions.Children>
</Controls:Map>
```

The ViewModel in Listing 9-12 consists of an ObservableCollection of custom Location objects. Each Location has Title and GeoCoordinate properties. Notice that the GeoCoordinate is decorated with the TypeConverter attribute so that it can be assigned from a string directly in XAML.

Listing 9-12. The ViewModel

```
public class Location
{
    public string Title { get; set; }
    [TypeConverter(typeof(GeoCoordinateConverter))]
    public GeoCoordinate GeoCoordinate { get; set; }
}
```

```
public class LocationViewModel
{
    public ObservableCollection<Location> Locations { get; set; }

    public LocationViewModel()
    {
        Locations = new ObservableCollection<Location>();
    }
}
```

The resources for the page declare the ViewModel and several Location objects (see Listing 9-13). The GeoCoordinate can be assigned right in the XAML because of the TypeConverter that decorates the property. Leaving out the GeoCoordinateConverter in Listing 9-12 would generate an XMLParseError at runtime. The DataTemplate named "MapItemTemplate" (used in the ItemTemplate of the MapItemsControl) contains a Pushpin control bound to the GeoCoordinate and Title properties of the ViewModel.

Listing 9-13. Declaring the ViewModel

```
<phone:PhoneApplicationPage.Resources>
    <vm:LocationViewModel x:Key="LocationViewModel" >
        <vm:LocationViewModel.Locations>
            <vm:Location Title="London" GeoCoordinate="51.499493,-0.124753" />
            <vm:Location Title="Paris" GeoCoordinate="48.858222,2.2945" />
            <vm:Location Title="Rome" GeoCoordinate="41.890268,12.492315" />
        </vm:LocationViewModel.Locations>

    </vm:LocationViewModel>

    <DataTemplate x:Name="MapItemTemplate">
        <Toolkit:Pushpin GeoCoordinate="{Binding GeoCoordinate}"
                         Content="{Binding Title}" />
    </DataTemplate>

</phone:PhoneApplicationPage.Resources>
```

Figure 9-9 shows the resulting application with the ViewModel bound to the ItemsSource and the ItemsTemplate populated with a bound Pushpin.

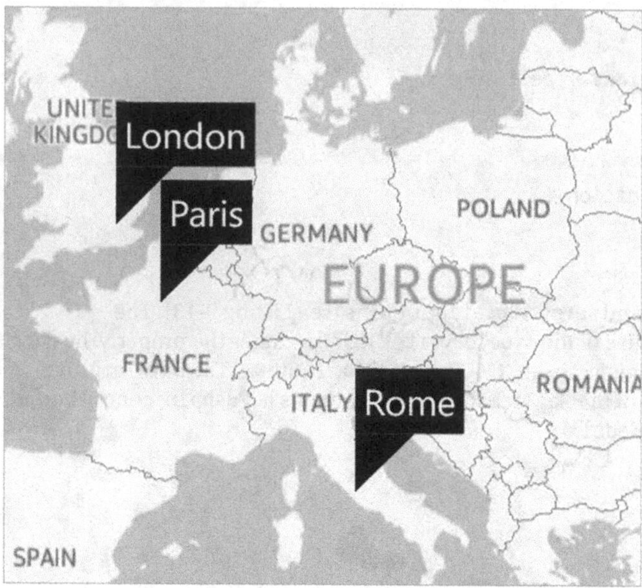

***Figure 9-9.** The Running Application with Multiple Pushpins*

Styling Pushpins

Define the `ControlTemplate` for the `Pushpin` to fully style the layout and content. The minimal example in Listing 9-14 adds a `ControlTemplate` with a single `TextBlock` bound to the view model `Title`.

Listing 9-14. Defining the Pushpin ControlTemplate

```
<DataTemplate x:Name="MapItemTemplate">
    <Toolkit:Pushpin GeoCoordinate="{Binding GeoCoordinate}" >
        <Toolkit:Pushpin.Template>
            <ControlTemplate>
                <TextBlock Text="{Binding Title}"
                    Style="{StaticResource PhoneTextAccentStyle}" />
            </ControlTemplate>
        </Toolkit:Pushpin.Template>
    </Toolkit:Pushpin>
</DataTemplate>
```

The running example in Figure 9-10 shows the `TextBlock` elements displayed in `PhoneTextAccentStyle` at their correct coordinate locations.

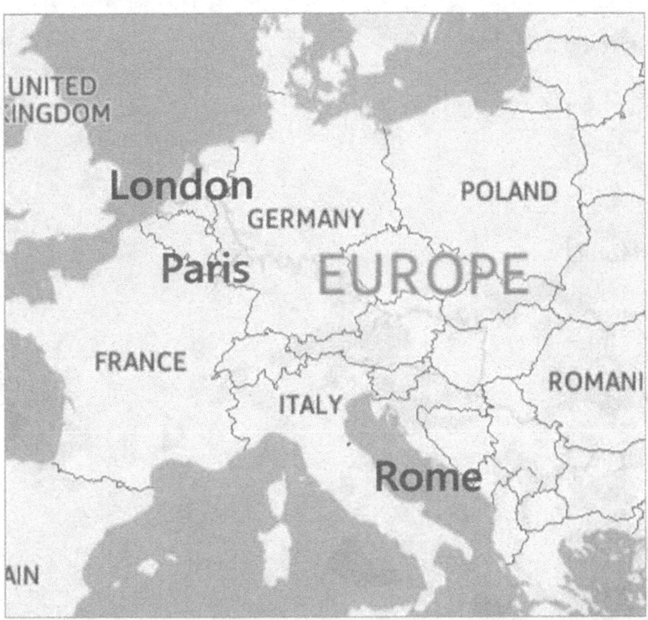

Figure 9-10. *The Running Application with Templated Pushpins*

The map in Figure 9-10 is missing some indication of where the exact point is for each bound item. To position the `Pushpin`, first set the `PositionOrigin` to a point value ranging between 0,0 and 1,1. By default, the `PositionOrigin` is set to 0,1 where the `Pushpin` is aligned with the bottom left edge at the `Pushpin's GeoCoordinate`. You can also move the relative position of the items in the `Pushpin` template to account for each element's dimensions.

The example in Figure 9-11 displays photographs pinned to locations on the map. The "pin" is a user control that appears to hold up a photographic image. The ViewModel `Title` property is displayed in the lower right of the image in two colors and slightly offset to provide contrast against the background. All these elements are displayed on a `Canvas` inside the `ItemTemplate`.

Figure 9-11. *Styled Pushpins*

The major change here is that only the `Pushpin` template is redefined (see Listing 9-15) while the ViewModel binding remains unchanged. The `Pushpin GeoCoordinate` is bound to the `GeoCoordinate` property of the ViewModel. `PositionOrigin` is left undefined, so the `Pushpin` is aligned to the default "0,1" at the bottom left. The `Image` is bound using the `Title` property of the ViewModel. A set of images in the project's `assets/images` folder are named "London.jpeg", "Rome.jpeg", and "Paris.jpeg". The `Source` binding uses the `StringFormat` attribute to build the path to the image. To adjust each element relative to the `Pushpin PositionOrigin` and to each other, the `Canvas Left` and `Top` attached properties are assigned. The `Pin` user control is in the XML namespace defined as `local` (the XML namespace definition is not shown in this listing).

Listing 9-15. Defining the Pushpin Template

```
<Toolkit:Pushpin GeoCoordinate="{Binding GeoCoordinate}" >
    <Toolkit:Pushpin.Template>
        <ControlTemplate>

            <Canvas>
                <Image
                    Source="{Binding Title, StringFormat='{}assets/images/{0}.jpeg'}"
                    Stretch="UniformToFill"
                    Width="120" Height="90"
                    Canvas.Left="-110" Canvas.Top="-20" />
                <local:Pin
                    Width="24" Height="45"
                    Canvas.Top="-45" Canvas.Left="-12" />
```

```
            <TextBlock
                Text="{Binding Title}"
                Width="100" TextAlignment="Right"
                Canvas.Left="-109" Canvas.Top="39"
                Style="{StaticResource PhoneTextNormalStyle }"  />
            <TextBlock
                Text="{Binding Title}"
                Width="100" TextAlignment="Right"
                Canvas.Left="-110" Canvas.Top="40"
                Style="{StaticResource PhoneTextContrastStyle }"  />
        </Canvas>

    </ControlTemplate>
  </Toolkit:Pushpin.Template>
</Toolkit:Pushpin>
```

BUILDING THE PIN USERCONTROL

The push pin user control was designed in Expression Blend (see Figure 9-12). It was created using simple `Ellipse` and `Rectangle` elements. The control consists of:

- A red pin head represented by an `Ellipse` painted with gradient fill to shade the upper right portion.
- Another `Ellipse` for the shine on the lower left of the pin head.
- The "shiny metal" part of the pin is represented by a `Rectangle` rotated slightly to the right.
- A final `Ellipse` at the foot of the pin simulates shadow.

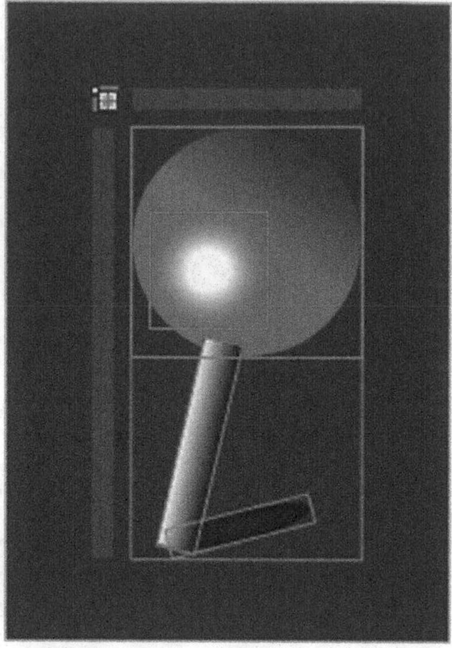

Figure 9-12. Pin User Control in Expression Blend

The full listing of the user control is included in Listing 9-16.

Listing 9-16. The Pin User Control Definition

```
<UserControl x:Class="StylingPushpins.Pin"
     xmlns="http://schemas.microsoft.com/winfx/2006/xaml/presentation"
     xmlns:x="http://schemas.microsoft.com/winfx/2006/xaml"
     xmlns:d="http://schemas.microsoft.com/expression/blend/2008"
     xmlns:mc="http://schemas.openxmlformats.org/markup-compatibility/2006"
     mc:Ignorable="d"
     d:DesignWidth="24" d:DesignHeight="45">

    <Grid x:Name="LayoutRoot" Background="Transparent">
        <Ellipse Height="3" Margin="3.833,0,5.167,1.833" StrokeThickness="4"
                 VerticalAlignment="Bottom" RenderTransformOrigin="0.5,0.5"
                 UseLayoutRounding="False" d:LayoutRounding="Auto">
            <Ellipse.RenderTransform>
                <CompositeTransform Rotation="-14.532"/>
            </Ellipse.RenderTransform>
            <Ellipse.Fill>
                <RadialGradientBrush>
                    <GradientStop Color="Black" Offset="1"/>
                    <GradientStop Color="#AD2D1111"/>
                </RadialGradientBrush>
            </Ellipse.Fill>
        </Ellipse>
```

```
            <Ellipse Margin="0,0,0,21" >
                <Ellipse.Fill>
                    <LinearGradientBrush EndPoint="0.221,0.915" StartPoint="0.779,0.085">
                        <GradientStop Color="#FF581B1B"/>
                        <GradientStop Color="#FFFB0202" Offset="0.488"/>
                    </LinearGradientBrush>
                </Ellipse.Fill>
            </Ellipse>
            <Ellipse Height="12" Margin="2,9,10,0" VerticalAlignment="Top"
                     RenderTransformOrigin="0.5,0">
                <Ellipse.Fill>
                    <RadialGradientBrush>
                        <GradientStop Color="#FFFDFDFD" Offset="0.375"/>
                        <GradientStop Color="#19E5BBB7" Offset="1"/>
                    </RadialGradientBrush>
                </Ellipse.Fill>
            </Ellipse>
            <Rectangle Margin="5.125,22.25,0,0.75" StrokeThickness="0"
                       RenderTransformOrigin="0.5,0.5" HorizontalAlignment="Left"
                       UseLayoutRounding="False" Width="4" d:LayoutRounding="Auto">
                <Rectangle.RenderTransform>
                    <CompositeTransform Rotation="12.99"/>
                </Rectangle.RenderTransform>
                <Rectangle.Fill>
                    <LinearGradientBrush EndPoint="0,0.5" StartPoint="1,0.5">
                        <GradientStop Color="Black" Offset="0"/>
                        <GradientStop Color="White" Offset="1"/>
                    </LinearGradientBrush>
                </Rectangle.Fill>
            </Rectangle>
        </Grid>
    </UserControl>
```

Geocoding

Geocoding is the process of retrieving a location from a description of the location. For example, if I pass "Golden Gate Bridge" to a geocoding service, I receive a latitude and longitude in return. *Reverse geocoding* takes the latitude and longitude, and then returns descriptive information about the location such as address, label, country, city, postal code, and so on.

Geocode Queries

The `Microsoft.Phone.Maps.Services` namespace includes `GeocodeQuery` and `ReverseGeocodeQuery` objects. To use the `GeocodeQuery`, create a new instance and assign the `SearchTerm` string property. Then assign a `QueryCompleted` event handler and call `QueryAsync()` (see Listing 9-17). The search term should be some location that can be found on the map, e.g., some part of an address or a place name like "Golden Gate Bridge", "Eiffel Tower", "Beijing", etc. The `GeoCoordinate` property must not be null, even if the property isn't used in a search.

Listing 9-17. Using the GeocodeQuery

```
var geocodeQuery = new GeocodeQuery()
{
    GeoCoordinate = new GeoCoordinate(),
    SearchTerm = "Capitola, California"
};
geocodeQuery.QueryCompleted += queryCompleted;
geocodeQuery.QueryAsync();
```

The QueryCompleted event handler passes back a Result property in the arguments parameter. The Result is an IList of MapLocation that can be iterated for address information. Listing 9-18 shows a stub QueryCompleted event handler that checks that the argument Error parameter is empty and that there are results to iterate over.

Listing 9-18. Handling the QueryCompleted Event

```
void queryCompleted (object sender, QueryCompletedEventArgs<IList<MapLocation>> e)
{
    if ((e.Error == null) && (e.Result.Count > 0))
    {
        foreach (var location in e.Result)
        {
          // do something with each address
        }
    }
}
```

The query results aren't worth much unless we make the map respond visually in some way. You can place pushpins at each found location and then zoom the map view to include just those locations. Start with a Map containing a MapItemsControl from the Windows Phone 8 Toolkit (see Listing 9-19).

Listing 9-19. The Map XAML

```
<Controls:Map x:Name="Worldmap" >
    <Toolkit:MapExtensions.Children>
        <Toolkit:MapItemsControl />
    </Toolkit:MapExtensions.Children>
</Controls:Map
```

Listing 9-20 shows an example that creates Pushpin objects and adds them to the map. The handler first gets the instance of an empty MapItemsControl that already exists in the Map XAML using LINQ (add System.Linq to the using statements to get the where() method extension). While iterating the results, Pushpins are created. Each Pushpin is assigned the GeoCoordinate of the query result and a caption using the information in the location's Information.Address object. A custom method GetAddressCaption() parses the information in the Address object.

Listing 9-20. Creating Pushpins using Geocode Information

```
void queryCompleted (object sender, QueryCompletedEventArgs<IList<MapLocation>> e)
{
    if ((e.Error == null) && (e.Result.Count > 0))
    {
        var mapItemsControl = MapExtensions.GetChildren(this.Worldmap)
            .Where(c => c is MapItemsControl).Single() as MapItemsControl;
```

```
        foreach (var location in e.Result)
        {
            var pushpin = new Pushpin()
            {
                GeoCoordinate = location.GeoCoordinate,
                Content = GetAddressCaption(location.Information.Address)
            };
            mapItemsControl.Items.Add(pushpin);
        }
    }
}
```

The running application is shown in Figure 9-13 with the Pushpin displaying address information.

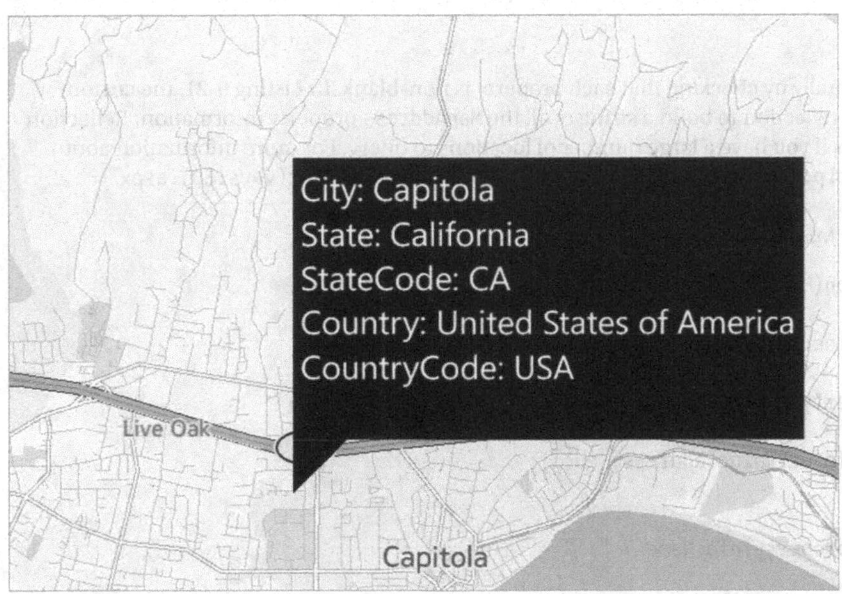

***Figure 9-13.** The Pushpin with MapAddress Property Values*

The `Address` is a `MapAddress` object type that has a simple list of 18 public string properties for `Continent`, `Country`, `City`, `State`, `BuildingName`, and so on (see Figure 9-14).

```
namespace Microsoft.Phone.Maps.Services
{
    public class MapAddress
    {
        public string BuildingFloor { get; internal set; }
        public string BuildingName { get; internal set; }
        public string BuildingRoom { get; internal set; }
        public string BuildingZone { get; internal set; }
        public string City { get; internal set; }
        public string Continent { get; internal set; }
        public string Country { get; internal set; }
```

Figure 9-14. *The MapAddress Class*

You could build this string manually by checking that each property is non-blank. In Listing 9-21, the custom `GetAddressCaption()` method uses reflection to build a string of all the `MapAddress` property information. Reflection is known to be slow, so don't use this if you have a large number of locations to query. For more information about reflection see the MSDN article at `http://msdn.microsoft.com/en-us/library/ms173183(v=vs.80).aspx`.

Listing 9-21. Building a String from MapAddress Properties

```
private string GetAddressCaption(MapAddress address)
{
    var result = new StringBuilder();

    foreach (PropertyInfo propertyInfo in typeof(MapAddress).GetProperties())
    {
        var value = propertyInfo.GetValue(address, null);
        if (value != "")
        {
            result.AppendLine(propertyInfo.Name + ": " + value);
        }
    }
    return result.ToString();
}
```

Reverse Geocode Queries

The reverse geocode lookup, i.e., starting from a coordinate and getting the address, follows the same pattern as the geocode query. The `ReverseGeocodeQuery` in Listing 9-22 uses a hard-coded coordinate (of London, House of Parliament), hooks up the `QueryCompleted` event handler and calls `QueryAsync()`. In fact, the `QueryCompleted` event handler is identical to that used by the `GeocodeQuery`, so `GeocodeQuery` and `ReverseGeocodeQuery` can share the same `QueryCompleted` event handler.

Listing 9-22. The Reverse Geocode Query

```
private void ReverseGeocode()
{
    var reverseGeocodeQuery = new ReverseGeocodeQuery()
    {
        GeoCoordinate = new GeoCoordinate(51.499493,-0.124753)
    };
    reverseGeocodeQuery.QueryCompleted += queryCompleted;
    reverseGeocodeQuery.QueryAsync();
}
```

Using gestures, we should be able to touch the map with a finger and get a pushpin at that location. Fortunately, the Map object has two utility methods that convert between the screen X and Y positions and GeoCoordinate locations:

- ***ConvertViewportPointToGeoCoordinate*** takes a System.Windows.Point with X and Y screen coordinates and returns a GeoCoordinate.
- ***ConvertGeoCoordinateToViewportPoint*** takes a GeoCoordinate and returns a System.Windows.Point that describes where that GeoCoordinate is in screen coordinates on the Map control.

By adding a Hold event handler to the map, we can get the X and Y position of the touch from the GestureEventArgs. See the example code in Listing 9-23 that handles the Hold event, calls the GestureEventArgs GetPosition() method, and gets a Point in return. The Map's ConvertViewportPointToGeoCoordinate() method takes the Point and returns the corresponding GeoCoordinate. Now we have the GeoCoordinate corresponding to where we touched the map that can be passed to ReverseGeocodeQuery. The code for handling QueryCompleted and adding the Pushpins is identical to the example in the "Geocode Queries" section and is not listed here. (For more information on assigning Tap and Hold gestures, please see Chapter 7.)

Listing 9-23. Handling the Map Hold Event

```
private void Worldmap_Hold_1(object sender, System.Windows.Input.GestureEventArgs e)
{
    GeoCoordinate coordinate =
        Worldmap.ConvertViewportPointToGeoCoordinate(e.GetPosition(Worldmap));
    var reverseGeocodeQuery = new ReverseGeocodeQuery()
    {
        GeoCoordinate = coordinate
    };
    reverseGeocodeQuery.QueryCompleted += queryCompleted;
    reverseGeocodeQuery.QueryAsync();
}
```

Running the new code, we can touch multiple places on the map and create pushpins at all these locations (see Figure 9-15).

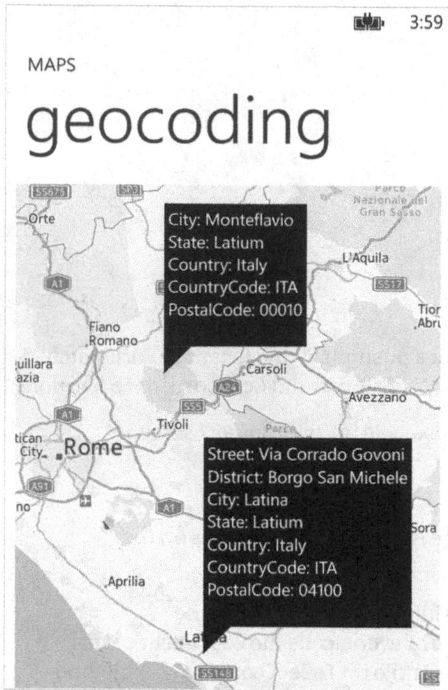

Figure 9-15. Pushpins from Hold Gesture

Setting the View on Results

After populating the Map with Pushpin objects, you should adjust the view to see all the pushpins easily. Use LINQ to select just the GeoCoordinate property from the results (see Listing 9-24). If there is one result, you need only zoom the map to approximately city level (zoom = 13). If you have multiple results, CreateBoundingRectangle() can transform the list of GeoCoordinate into a LocationRectangle.

Listing 9-24. Setting the View

```
var coordinates = locations.Select(l => l.GeoCoordinate);
if (coordinates.Count() == 1)
{
    Worldmap.SetView(coordinates.Single(), 13);
}
else
{
    var locationRectangle =
        LocationRectangle.CreateBoundingRectangle(coordinates);
    Worldmap.SetView(locationRectangle);
}
```

Getting Your Location

Windows Phone 8 can answer the question "where am I" with a good degree of accuracy by providing a GeoCoordinate you can use on the map. The Windows Phone 8 Toolkit also provides a special marker that denotes your current location.

The Geolocator from the Windows.Devices.Geolocation namespace returns your current position and lets you specify the conditions that trigger a reading. To use the Geolocator, you will need to enable ID_CAP_LOCATION in the \properties\WMAppManifest.xml, Capabilities tab. You can take a single snapshot of your position by calling the GetGeopositionAsync() method. This technique has the smallest resource footprint.

The examples in this section use the XAML defined in Listing 9-25. Notice the UserLocationMarker in the MapExtensions Children. UserLocationMarker is a Windows Phone 8 Toolkit object, and is a descendant of MapChildControl, like the Pushpin. The UserLocationMarker Visibility is Collapsed until we're ready to move it to a location on the map and display it.

Listing 9-25. The Map and UserLocationMarker XAML

```
Grid x:Name="ContentPanel" Grid.Row="1" Margin="12,0,12,0">
    <Controls:Map x:Name="WorldMap">
        <Toolkit:MapExtensions.Children>
            <Toolkit:UserLocationMarker x:Name="locationMarker"
                Visibility="Collapsed" />
        </Toolkit:MapExtensions.Children>
    </Controls:Map>
</Grid>
```

The code in Listing 9-26 demonstrates how Geolocator obtains your current position. The example code uses a Click event from a button in the toolbar. Call the GetGeopositionAsync() method to return a Geoposition object. GetGeopositionAsync is awaitable, so add async to the calling method and use the await keyword to get the returned value. Geoposition contains a Coordinate that is incompatible with the GeoCoordinate we're using for the map. Fortunately the Toolkit provides an extension method ToGeoCoordinate() that translates to GeoCoordinate automatically. The code example next gets a reference to the UserLocationMarker, makes it visible, and sets its new GeoCoordinate. Finally, the Map SetView() method is called to center the view on the new position.

Listing 9-26. Using GeoLocator

```
private async void WhereAmIButton_Click_1(object sender, EventArgs e)
{
    // get the current location
    var geoLocator = new Geolocator();
    var position = await geoLocator.GetGeopositionAsync();
    // use toolkit extension ToGeoCoordinate get usable type
    var geoCoordinate = position.Coordinate.ToGeoCoordinate();
    // get the UserLocationMarker element, make visible and position
    var locationMarker = this.FindName("locationMarker") as UserLocationMarker;
    locationMarker.Visibility = System.Windows.Visibility.Visible;
    locationMarker.GeoCoordinate = geoCoordinate;
    // center the map on the coordinate
    WorldMap.SetView(geoCoordinate, 13);
}
```

When the user clicks the button in the application toolbar, the UserLocationMarker is displayed in the correct spot on the map (see Figure 9-16).

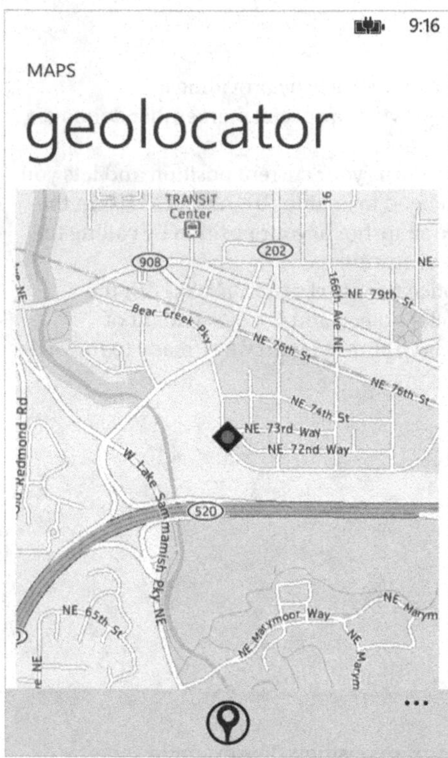

Figure 9-16. *Displaying the UserLocationMarker*

If you need constant polling, hook up to the `PositionChanged` event. `Geolocator` does not have specific start and stop methods, but instead relies on assigning the `PositionChanged` event and later removing the `PositionChanged` event handler when no longer needed.

When does the `PositionChanged` event fire? You can set the `ReportInterval` in milliseconds between events *or* set a `MovementThreshold` for the number of meters to move before the event fires. To set accuracy you can use the `DesiredAccuracy` enumeration (`Default`, `High`) or you can set `DesiredAccuracyInMeters`.

The example in Listing 9-27 shows the `Geolocator` setup during the `OnNavigatedTo()` method override. The `PositionChanged` event should fire every 5 seconds with accuracy to the single meter.

Listing 9-27. Setting up the Geolocator

```
private Geolocator _locator;
protected override void OnNavigatedTo(NavigationEventArgs e)
{
    base.OnNavigatedTo(e);

    _locator = new Geolocator()
    {
        // set either ReportInterval (milliseconds) or MovementThreshold (meters)
        ReportInterval = 5000,
```

```
        //DesiredAccuracy = PositionAccuracy.High
        DesiredAccuracyInMeters = 1
    };
    _locator.PositionChanged += _locator_PositionChanged;
}
```

Unhook the PositionedChanged event as soon as possible to save resources as shown in Listing 9-28.

Listing 9-28. Tearing Down the Geolocator

```
protected override void OnNavigatedFrom(NavigationEventArgs e)
{
    _locator.PositionChanged -= _locator_PositionChanged;
    _locator = null;
    base.OnNavigatedFrom(e);
}
```

Location changes are reported in the PositionedChanged event handler (see Listing 9-29). The argument parameter passed to the handler has the Position.Coordinate. Again, this needs to be translated into a GeoCoordinate type the Map can work with by using the ToGeoCoordinate() extension method. The code example then gets a reference to the UserLocationMarker and sets its GeoCoordinate property.

Listing 9-29. Handling the PositionChanged Event

```
void _locator_PositionChanged(Geolocator sender, PositionChangedEventArgs args)
{
    this.Dispatcher.BeginInvoke(() =>
        {
            var geoCoordinate = args.Position.Coordinate.ToGeoCoordinate();
            var locationMarker = this.FindName("locationMarker") as UserLocationMarker;
            if (locationMarker != null)
            {
                locationMarker.Visibility = System.Windows.Visibility.Visible;
                locationMarker.GeoCoordinate = geoCoordinate;
                WorldMap.SetView(geoCoordinate, 15);
            }
        });
}
```

You may want to respond to Geolocator status changes to make your application more robust. Listing 9-30 shows a minimal StatusChanged event handler that sets text to the current PositionStatus value.

Listing 9-30. Handling the StatusChanged Event

```
void _locator_StatusChanged(Geolocator sender, StatusChangedEventArgs args)
{
    this.Dispatcher.BeginInvoke(() =>
        {
            var textBlock = this.FindName("StatusText") as TextBlock;
            textBlock.Text = "Status: " + args.Status.ToString();
        });
}
```

The possible values of the PositionStatus enumeration from the inline comments are:

- ***Ready***: Location data is available.
- ***Initializing***: The location provider is initializing. This is the status if a GPS is the source of location data and the GPS receiver does not yet have the required number of satellites in view to obtain an accurate position.
- ***NoData***: No location data is available from any location provider. `LocationStatus` will have this value if the application calls `GetGeopositionAsync` or registers an event handler for the `PositionChanged` event, before data is available from a location sensor. Once data is available LocationStatus transitions to the `Ready` state.
- ***Disabled***: The location provider is disabled. This status indicates that the user has not granted the application permission to access location.
- ***NotInitialized***: An operation to retrieve location has not yet been initialized. `LocationStatus` will have this value if the application has not yet called `GetGeopositionAsync` or registered an event handler for the `PositionChanged` event.
- ***NotAvailable***: The Windows Sensor and Location Platform are not available on this version of Windows.

Directions

The Windows Phone 8 API makes it easy to add step-by-step route directions to your application. You can use a task to display directions if you don't need any special presentation and only have a single start and end point (see Figure 9-17).

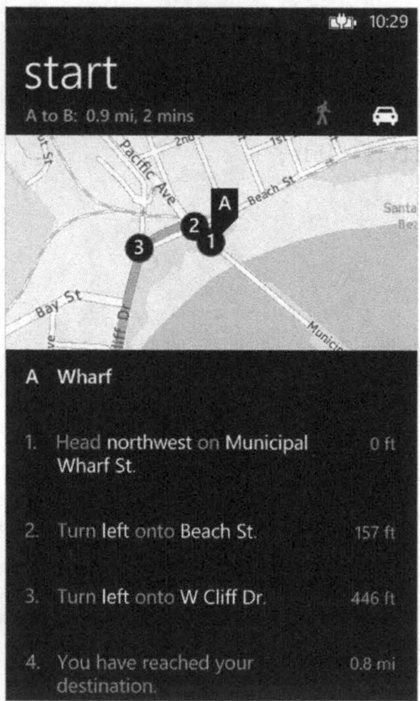

Figure 9-17. *The MapsDirectionTask*

Listing 9-31 demonstrates invoking a MapsDirectionsTask that lists directions between two points on the map. The task takes two LabeledMapLocation objects that each contain a Label and a Location GeoCoordinate. Assign these two objects to the Start and End properties of the MapsDirectionsTask and then call the Show() method.

Listing 9-31. Using the MapsDirectionsTask

```
var wharf = new LabeledMapLocation()
{
    Label = "Wharf",
    Location = new GeoCoordinate(36.96252, -122.023372)
};

var park = new LabeledMapLocation()
{
    Label = "Lighthouse Park",
    Location = new GeoCoordinate(36.95172, -122.026783)
};

var task = new MapsDirectionsTask() { Start = wharf, End = park };
task.Show();
```

The second approach uses a RouteQuery service from the Microsoft.Phone.Maps.Services namespace. The query produces a Route object that can be added to the Map. The Map knows how to draw the Route automatically so you won't need to worry about trying to draw it yourself on an overlay.

If you want to document the route as a set of text directions, the Route's Legs collection has information about each part of the journey including:

- EstimatedDuration as a TimeSpan. Use the TimeSpan ToMinutes() method to get a human readable string that can be added to the text directions.
- Maneuvers is a collection of RouteManeuver where each element has readable InstructionText (e.g., "Head southeast on Municipal Wharf St."), an InstructionKind enumeration value (e.g., Start or TurnLeft), LengthInMeters, and StartGeoCoordinate.
- Geometry is a collection of GeoCoordinate that lists each individual change in direction.

To code a RouteQuery, first define the GeoCoordinate instances that the route must arrive at. You could look these up manually online (there are several map services that will give you latitude and longitude for locations on the map), use the geocoding service, or get the coordinates from the map using ConvertViewportPointToGeoCoordinate(). Whatever you decide, GeoCoordinates are used to populate the Waypoints property. Once the Waypoints are defined, refine the query by setting the InitialHeadingInDegrees, RouteOptimization (MinimizeTime or MinimizeDistance) and TravelMode (Driving or Walking). Listing 9-32 puts all the pieces together by defining three GeoCoordinates and assigning them to the Waypoints property of a new RouteQuery. The RouteOptimization is set for minimal distance and the TravelMode is set to Driving.

Listing 9-32. Setting Up the RouteQuery

```
var wharf = new GeoCoordinate(36.96252, -122.023372);
var park = new GeoCoordinate(36.95172, -122.026783);
var lagoon = new GeoCoordinate(36.963365, -122.031932);

var routeQuery = new RouteQuery()
{
```

```
    Waypoints = new List<GeoCoordinate>() { wharf, park, lagoon },
    RouteOptimization = RouteOptimization.MinimizeDistance,
    TravelMode = TravelMode.Driving
};
routeQuery.QueryCompleted += routeQuery_QueryCompleted;
routeQuery.QueryAsync();
```

To handle the QueryCompleted event, first check the argument's Error property, and then get the argument's Result. The Result is a Route object. Feed the Result to a MapRoute constructor. MapRoute adds visual properties to the Route like the line Color. The example code in Listing 9-33 shows a minimal implementation of adding a Route. You will want to zoom in on the route to display it properly. The handy BoundingBox property of the Route can be passed directly to the SetView() method.

Listing 9-33. Handling the QueryCompleted Event

```
void routeQuery_QueryCompleted(object sender, QueryCompletedEventArgs<Route> e)
{
    if (e.Error == null)
    {
        this.WorldMap.AddRoute(new MapRoute( e.Result));
        this.WorldMap.SetView(e.Result.BoundingBox);
    }
}
```

Figure 9-18 shows the added route. It has all three legs of the route and is displayed with the default properties.

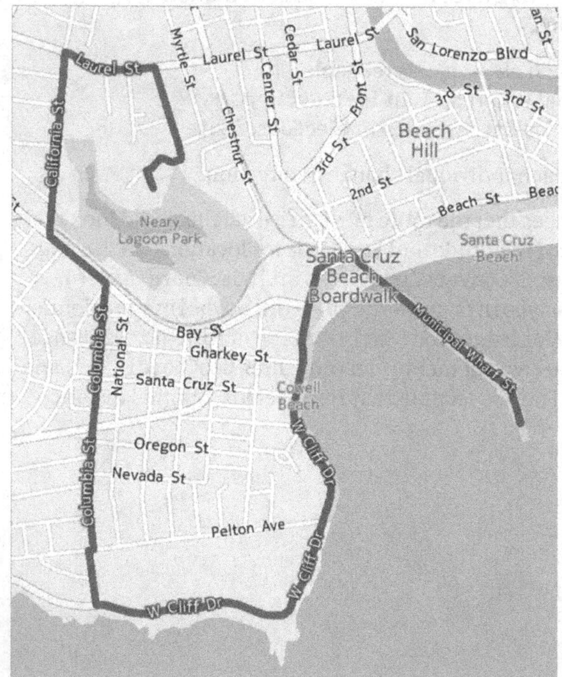

Figure 9-18. *The Map with Added Route*

The MapRoute RouteViewKind property automatically determines the color of the route drawing if the enumeration value is Primary or Secondary. Set RouteViewKind to UserDefined if you want to set the Color to a custom value (see Listing 9-34).

Listing 9-34. Setting UserDefined MapRoute Color

```
var mapRoute = new MapRoute(e.Result)
{
    Color = Colors.Red,
    RouteViewKind = RouteViewKind.UserDefined
};
this.WorldMap.AddRoute(mapRoute)
```

To build a list of readable text directions, iterate the Route Legs property. There is information you can use to build the directions at the Route level, for each Leg and each Maneuver (see Listing 9-35).

Listing 9-35. Building the Text Directions

```
var sb = new StringBuilder();
var i = 0;

sb.AppendFormat("Estimated time: {0} minutes\n",
    e.Result.EstimatedDuration.TotalMinutes.ToString());
foreach (var leg in e.Result.Legs)
{
    foreach (var maneuver in leg.Maneuvers)
    {
        sb.AppendFormat("{0}. {1}: {2}\n",
            ++i, maneuver.InstructionKind.ToString(), maneuver.InstructionText);
    }
}
MessageBox.Show(sb.ToString());
```

Figure 9-19 shows the text directions in a MessageBox.

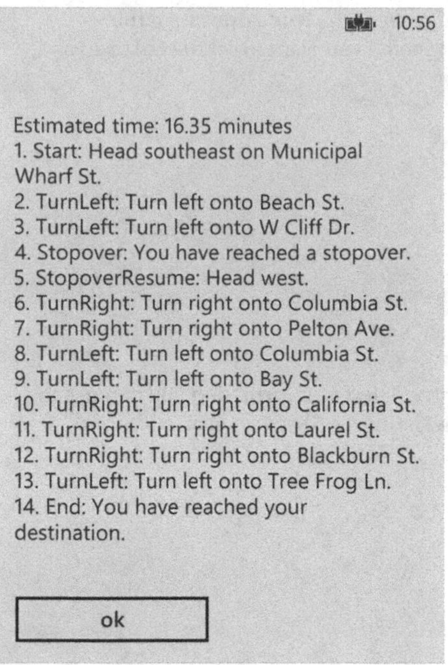

Figure 9-19. *The List of directions*

Summary

The Windows Phone's powerful mapping controls, tasks, and services magnify the usefulness of your application by integrating your data onto a visual graphic representation. This chapter explored the techniques to display the `Map` control, position/zoom the map, and add visual elements. Geocoding and reverse geocoding were used to perform lookups between fragments of address information and geographic coordinates. The `Geolocator` was used to return the phone's current position. The `RouteQuery` was able to take multiple sets of coordinates and create a route that could be displayed or used to create a set of written directions.

CHAPTER 10

Live Tiles and Notifications

This chapter explores the ways your application can communicate with the user, even when the application is not running, by means of live tiles, notifications, and by customizing the lock screen. Live tiles and notifications establish a conversation with the user that is dynamic but unobtrusive. A live tile on the Start screen is the store front to your application, inviting people to use the application and giving a peek to what's featured inside (see Figure 10-1). Notifications update the user with critical information displayed in the tile, as a toast in the system tray or as raw information sent directly to your application. When the screen is locked and the live tiles are not available, the lock screen allows you to notify the user of status changes.

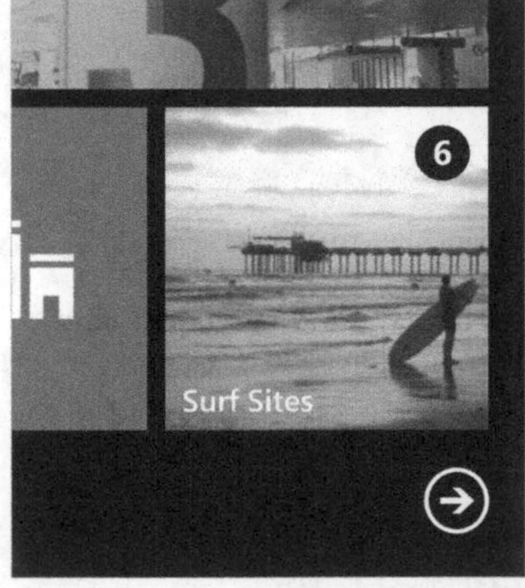

Figure 10-1. *Live Tile on the Start Screen*

Live Tiles

Live tiles display on the Start screen and provide an immediate, at-a-glance, synopsis of your application state. The live tile displays a graphic along with a title and text messages. The contents of the live tile can change dynamically to show new images and text. This allows you to signal the user that fresh content is available, encouraging the user to click on the tile and reenter the application.

Introducing Live Tiles

The live tile is created by the user tapping-and-holding the application and then clicking the `Pin to Start` option from the context menu (see Figure 10-2).

***Figure 10-2.** Pinning an Application to the Start Screen*

The tile created by the user is the primary tile and cannot be deleted programmatically. Additional secondary tiles can be created and removed programmatically.

Tiles come in small, medium, and large sizes. Users can press-and-hold a tile to display the arrow graphic that appears at the tile's corner (see Figure 10-3). Clicking the arrow toggles through small, medium, and large tiles. Clicking the arrow for the large tile wraps back to the medium tile again.

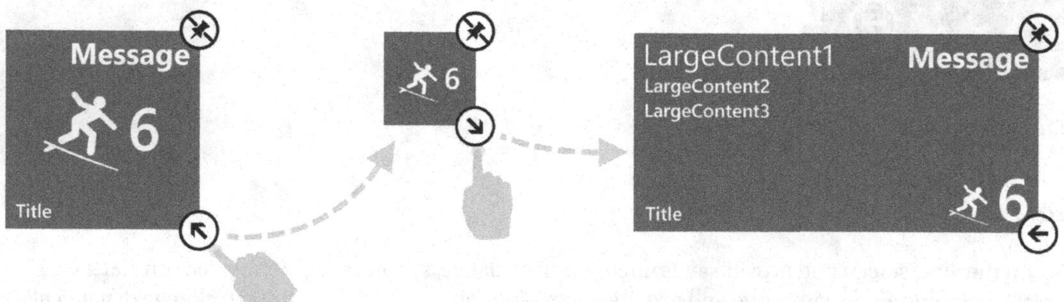

***Figure 10-3.** Sizing the Live Tile*

Creating Tiles in XML

Tiles are arranged within one of three possible templates. All three options have a `Title` and `Count`. All three have a small tile represented with an image that does not animate.

- ***Flip***: Medium and large size tiles show an eye-catching flip animation at random intervals. The front of the tile displays primary information and any secondary information is shown on the back side.
- ***Iconic***: The iconic tile displays icon images that follow Windows Phone Design Principles, namely, clean, easy-to-read images much like the symbols you might see used on airport signage. The large tile also shows an additional message and three lines of context text.
- ***Cycle***: This tile runs through a set of up to nine images. The image is subtly animated between changes.

The quickest way to initially define the tile template type you want to use is to open the `WMAppManifest.xml` by double-clicking the file in Solution Explorer. In the `Application UI` tab of the `WMAppManifest.xml`, select a `Tile Template` from the drop-down list (see Figure 10-4). The area below the drop-down list will change to reflect your choice. Provide a `Tile Title` and select `Tile Images`.

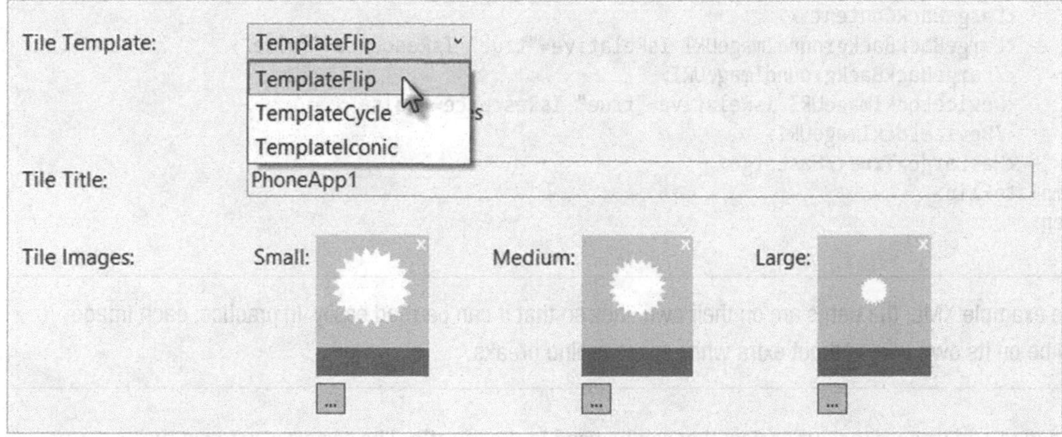

***Figure 10-4.** Configuring the Tile Template*

Once you have selected a template, title, and images, the `Application UI` tab is all done giving you help, yet the task is not complete. There are still properties that need to be assigned, like the title and images for the flip side of the icon. From here on, you'll have to "rough it" by editing the XML file directly. To do this, right-click the `WMAppManifest.xml` file and select `View Code` from the context menu. Because the file is already opened in the designer, you'll be prompted to close it. Click the `Yes` button to close the designer view of the file and open the XML. The XML has the full set of elements that can be defined for the template. The template is defined inside another element named `<PrimaryToken>`. See Listing 10-1 for an example of the resulting XML. The template element name will be `<TemplateFlip>`, `<TemplateCycle>`, or `<TemplateIconic>`. Notice that the tile's back elements are not yet defined. You don't need to define the `DeviceLockImageURI` element as it relates to the lock screen (see the "Customizing the Lock Screen" section coming up next).

Listing 10-1. The Resulting XML

```
<PrimaryToken TokenID="LiveTilesToken" TaskName="_default">
        <TemplateFlip>
                <SmallImageURI IsRelative="true" IsResource="false">
                        Assets\Tiles\FlipCycleTileSmall.png
                </SmallImageURI>
                <Count>0</Count>
                <BackgroundImageURI IsRelative="true" IsResource="false">
                        Assets\Tiles\FlipCycleTileMedium.png
                </BackgroundImageURI>
                <Title>My Title</Title>
                <BackContent></BackContent>
                <BackBackgroundImageURI IsRelative="true" IsResource="false">
                </BackBackgroundImageURI>
                <BackTitle></BackTitle>
                <LargeBackgroundImageURI IsRelative="true" IsResource="false">
                        Assets\Tiles\FlipCycleTileLarge.png
                </LargeBackgroundImageURI>
                <LargeBackContent />
                <LargeBackBackgroundImageURI IsRelative="true" IsResource="false">
                </LargeBackBackgroundImageURI>
                <DeviceLockImageURI IsRelative="true" IsResource="false">
                </DeviceLockImageURI>
                <HasLarge>True</HasLarge>
        </TemplateFlip>
</PrimaryToken>
```

■ **Note** In the example XML, the paths are on their own lines so that it can be read easily. In practice, each image element should be on its own line, without extra white space or line breaks.

You will need to add images to your project that can be used in the live tile. The easiest way to get the recommended dimensions of each tile is to start with the default tiles already supplied in the project under `\Assets\Tiles` (see Figure 10-5). The `FlipCycle...` images can be used for both Flip and Cyclic style icons. The iconic images have a single "MediumLarge" tile that works for both medium and large sizes because the icon is resized to fit the larger area. You can use the Visual Studio Graphics Designer to edit images directly using the tools provided or paste in existing graphics. You can also use the drawing tool of your choice to create the images.

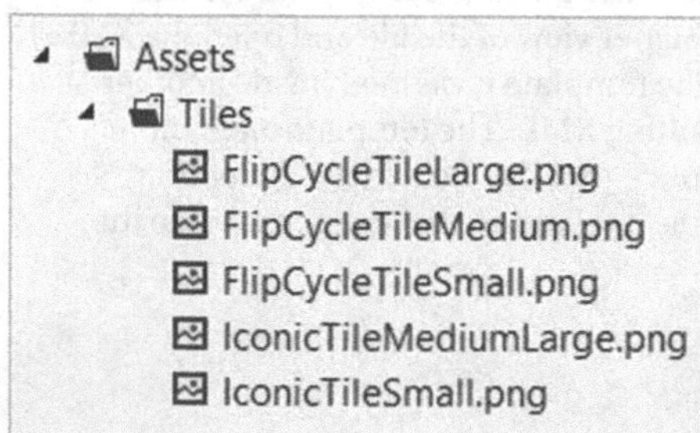

Figure 10-5. *The Default Tiles*

Creating Tiles in Code

The pattern to create a tile in code is to first create and populate one of the specialized `ShellTileData` descendants: `FlipTileData`, `IconicTileData`, or `CycleTileData`. The `ShellTile` object has methods to create and update tiles using the tile data. Each tile is associated with a navigation URI parameter that it is created with. Each tile's navigation URI must be a relative path.

The essential code looks something like the stripped down example in Listing 10-2. Notice the line where `ShellTile.Actives.FirstOrDefault()` is used to determine the existence of the tile. The `ShellTile` object lists all tiles that are pinned to the Start screen.

If the tile doesn't exist in this list, the `ShellTile.Create()` method uses tile data to create it. The `Create()` method takes a navigation URI that will be the destination when a user clicks the tile, the tile data and a Boolean that indicates wide tile support if true.

If the tile does exist, the `ShellTile` instance returned from `FirstOrDefault()` calls its own `Update()` method, passing the tile data. Attempting to create a tile where one already exists with the same URI throws an `InvalidOperationException`.

Listing 10-2. Code to Create or Update a Tile

```
var tileData = new IconicTileData()
{
    Title = "Surf Sites",
    SmallIconImage = new Uri("Assets/Tiles/IconicTileSmall.png", UriKind.Relative),
    IconImage = new Uri("Assets/Tiles/IconicTileMediumLarge.png", UriKind.Relative),
    Count = 6
};

Uri uri = new Uri("/SecondPage.xaml", UriKind.Relative);
var tile = ShellTile.ActiveTiles.FirstOrDefault(t => t.NavigationUri.Equals(uri));
if (tile == null)
{
    ShellTile.Create(uri, tileData, true);
}
else
{
    tile.Update(tileData);
};
```

Once the tile is created, only update the tile with the same tile data type. For example, if after creating a tile with `FileTileData` you attempt to update the tile with `IconTileData`, an argument exception will be generated:

```
Template type mismatch. You can only update the tile using the same template it was created with.
```

Iconic

The iconic tile displays an image on a background color that you choose. There are text elements for the `Title` shown at the bottom of the tile, a `Message` shown upper right, and a `Count`. The large tile also shows `LargeContent1`, `LargeContent2`, and `LargeContent3` (see Figure 10-6). Though the naming convention "content" suggests that you can place any collection of elements inside, these three content elements are strings. Watch out for the `BackColor` property. This should be a hexadecimal string in the form of "#RRGGBB". At the time of this writing, the format "#AARRGGBB" does not work, nor does using a standard color name like "Blue." In these two cases, the tile is displayed in the theme background color.

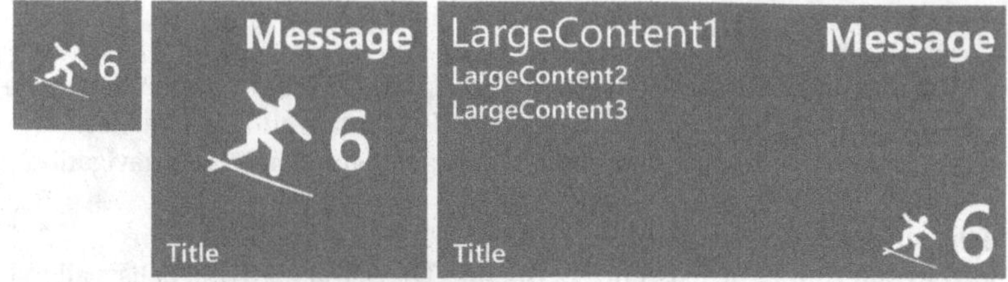

***Figure 10-6.** The Iconic Tile in Small, Medium, and Large Sizes*

The XML definition that produced the tiles in Figure 10-6 is shown in Listing 10-3. The image paths ending in URI are intended to be placed on a single line with no extra spaces. Also notice the formatting of the BackgroundColor as a six-digit hexadecimal number.

Listing 10-3. Defining TemplateIconic

```
<TemplateIconic>
    <SmallImageURI IsRelative="true" IsResource="false">
        Assets\Tiles\IconicTileSmall.png
    </SmallImageURI>
    <Count>6</Count>
    <IconImageURI IsRelative="true" IsResource="false">
        Assets\Tiles\IconicTileMediumLarge.png
    </IconImageURI>
    <Title>Title</Title>
    <Message>Message</Message>
    <BackgroundColor>#5A7594</BackgroundColor>
    <HasLarge>True</HasLarge>
    <LargeContent1>LargeContent1</LargeContent1>
    <LargeContent2>LargeContent2</LargeContent2>
    <LargeContent3>LargeContent3</LargeContent3>
    <DeviceLockImageURI></DeviceLockImageURI>
</TemplateIconic>
```

You can create a secondary tile in code by populating an IconicTileData object and calling the static ShellTitle.Create() method (see Listing 10-4).

Listing 10-4. Creating an Iconic Tile

```
Uri uri = new Uri("/SecondPage.xaml", UriKind.Relative);

var tileData = new IconicTileData()
{
    Title = "Surf Sites",
    SmallIconImage = new Uri("Assets/Tiles/IconicTileSmall.png", UriKind.Relative),
    IconImage = new Uri("Assets/Tiles/IconicTileMediumLarge.png", UriKind.Relative),
    Count = 6,
    BackgroundColor = Color.FromArgb(255, 90, 117, 148),
    WideContent1 = "LargeContent1",
```

```
    WideContent2 = "LargeContent2",
    WideContent3 = "LargeContent3",
};

ShellTile.Create(uri, tileData, true);
```

■ **Note** In the example from Listing 10-4, `BackgroundColor` is assigned from the static `Color.FromArgb()` method from the `System.Windows.Media` namespace. There are `Color` objects from several namespaces, so be sure to add `System.Windows.Media` to your `using` statements. Make sure the alpha channel of the color, that is, the transparency value from 0...255 in the first parameter, is always 255. Anything less will cause the tile to display the theme color. You can also use `Colors.<standard color name>`, such as `Colors.Blue`.

As of this writing, there are a few minor differences between the XML and code versions of the iconic tile. The `Message` element is not represented in the `IconicTileData` object. The `LargeContent1...LargeContent3` are represented as `WideContent1...WideContent3` properties in the `IconicTileData` object. It may be just as well that `Message` is left out because `WideContent1` text can be wide enough to overrun the space occupied by `Message`. Content that is too wide for the three content properties does not wrap and is simply truncated by the edge of the tile.

Flip

The flip template works well for applications that have some secondary information to display on the reverse side of the tile. For example, a pet adoption application could display a "Critter of the day" title on the flip side or a surfing application could show weather advisories.

The flip template should have five images (see Figure 10-7). One for the `SmallImageURI` (the small tile does not flip, so only one image is required), and two more front-and-back image sets for the medium and large sizes (`BackgroundImageURI`, `BackBackgroundImageURI`, `LargeBackgroundImageURI`, and `LargeBackBackgroundImageURI` respectively).

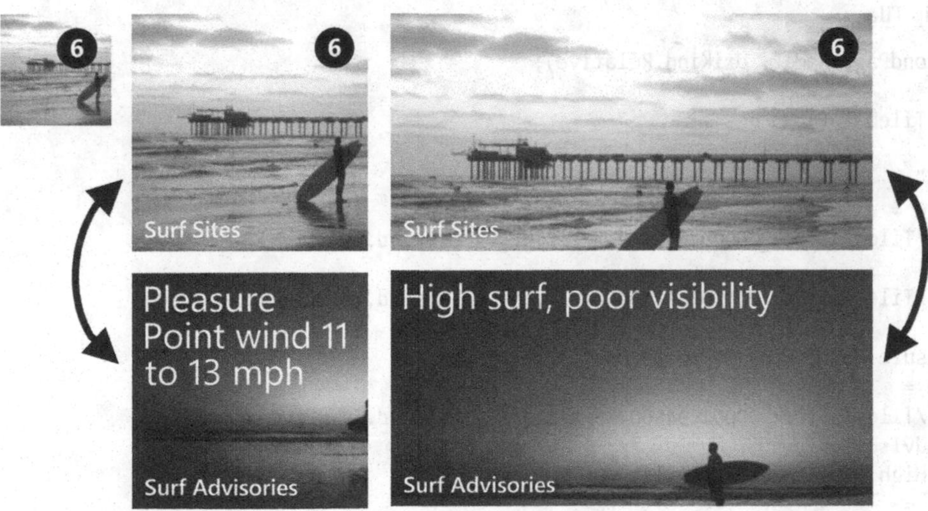

***Figure 10-7.** The Flip Tile in Small, Medium, and Large Sizes*

The front displays a `Title`, `Count`, and `BackgroundImage`. The back displays `BackTitle` in the tile's lower-left corner and `BackContent` displays above the `BackTitle`. The XML to define the template is shown in Listing 10-5.

Listing 10-5. Defining TemplateFlip

```
<TemplateFlip>
        <SmallImageURI IsRelative="true" IsResource="false">
                Assets\Tiles\iStock_000004630599XSmall.jpg
        </SmallImageURI>
        <Count>6</Count>
        <BackgroundImageURI IsRelative="true" IsResource="false">
                Assets\Tiles\iStock_000004630599XSmall.jpg
        </BackgroundImageURI>
        <Title>Surf Sites</Title>
        <BackContent>Pleasure Point wind 11 to 13 mph</BackContent>
        <BackBackgroundImageURI IsRelative="true" IsResource="false">
                Assets\Tiles\iStock_000012945007XSmall.jpg
        </BackBackgroundImageURI>
        <BackTitle>Surf Advisories</BackTitle>
        <LargeBackgroundImageURI IsRelative="true" IsResource="false">
                Assets\Tiles\iStock_000004630599XSmall.jpg
        </LargeBackgroundImageURI>
        <LargeBackContent>High surf, poor visibility</LargeBackContent>
        <LargeBackBackgroundImageURI IsRelative="true" IsResource="false">
                Assets\Tiles\iStock_000012945007XSmall.jpg
        </LargeBackBackgroundImageURI>
        <DeviceLockImageURI IsRelative="true" IsResource="false"></DeviceLockImageURI>
        <HasLarge>True</HasLarge>
</TemplateFlip>
```

In code, the flip tile is built by creating a `FlipTileData` object and passing it to the static `ShellTitle.Create()` method (see Listing 10-6).

Listing 10-6. Creating a Flip Tile

```
Uri uri = new Uri("/SecondPage.xaml", UriKind.Relative);

var tileData = new FlipTileData()
{
    Title = "Surf Sites",
    SmallBackgroundImage =
        new Uri("Assets/Tiles/iStock_000004630599XSmall.jpg", UriKind.Relative),
    BackgroundImage =
        new Uri("Assets/Tiles/iStock_000004630599XSmall.jpg", UriKind.Relative),
    Count = 6,
    BackContent = "Pleasure Point wind 11 to 13 mph",
    BackBackgroundImage =
        new Uri("Assets/Tiles/iStock_000012945007XSmall.jpg", UriKind.Relative),
    BackTitle = "Surf Advisories",
    WideBackContent = "High surf, poor visibility",
    WideBackgroundImage =
        new Uri("Assets/Tiles/iStock_000004630599XSmall.jpg", UriKind.Relative),
```

```
    WideBackBackgroundImage =
        new Uri("Assets/Tiles/iStock_000012945007XSmall.jpg", UriKind.Relative)
};

ShellTile.Create(uri, tileData, true);
```

Cyclic

The cycle template displays up to nine images in succession. Each image shows briefly, and then scrolls slowly upward while the next image scrolls into place (see Figure 10-8). This style of template works nicely for applications that have a series of choices represented by images, such as photo galleries, travel destinations, or product choices.

Figure 10-8. *The Cycle Tile Transitioning Between Images*

The cycle template has one SmallImageURI that does not scroll and a set of image path properties Photo01ImageURI through Photo09ImageURI that are displayed in medium and large tiles (see Listing 10-7). Title is displayed on the lower left of the tile for medium and large tiles and Count is shown upper right on all three tile sizes.

Listing 10-7. Defining TemplateCycle

```
<TemplateCycle>
        <SmallImageURI IsRelative="true" IsResource="false">
                Assets\Tiles\iStock_000002999571XSmall.jpg
        </SmallImageURI>
        <Title>Surf Sites</Title>
        <Photo01ImageURI IsRelative="true" IsResource="false">
                Assets\Tiles\iStock_000002999571XSmall.jpg
        </Photo01ImageURI>
        <Photo02ImageURI IsRelative="true" IsResource="false">
                Assets\Tiles\iStock_000004630599XSmall.jpg
        </Photo02ImageURI>
        <Photo03ImageURI IsRelative="true" IsResource="false">
                Assets\Tiles\iStock_000005268101XSmall.jpg
        </Photo03ImageURI>
        <Photo04ImageURI IsRelative="true" IsResource="false">
                Assets\Tiles\iStock_000012945007XSmall.jpg
        </Photo04ImageURI>
        <Photo05ImageURI IsRelative="true" IsResource="false">
                Assets\Tiles\iStock_000014745608XSmall.jpg
        </Photo05ImageURI>
        <Photo06ImageURI IsRelative="true" IsResource="false">
                Assets\Tiles\iStock_000016850786XSmall.jpg
        </Photo06ImageURI>
```

```
        <Photo07ImageURI IsRelative="true" IsResource="false">
        </Photo07ImageURI>
        <Photo08ImageURI IsRelative="true" IsResource="false">
        </Photo08ImageURI>
        <Photo09ImageURI IsRelative="true" IsResource="false">
        </Photo09ImageURI>
        <Count>6</Count>
        <HasLarge>True</HasLarge>
        <DeviceLockImageURI IsRelative="true" IsResource="false">
        </DeviceLockImageURI>
</TemplateCycle>
```

In code, the cycle tile is built by creating a CycleTileData object and passing it to the static ShellTitle.Create() method (see Listing 10-8). The CycleImages is an IEnumerable of Uri, but cannot have more than nine elements without throwing an ArgumentException.

Listing 10-8. Creating the Cycle Tile

```
Uri uri = new Uri("/CycleTarget.xaml", UriKind.Relative);

var tileData = new CycleTileData()
{
    Title = "Surf Sites",
    SmallBackgroundImage =
        new Uri("Assets/Tiles/iStock_000004630599XSmall.jpg", UriKind.Relative),
    Count = 6,
    CycleImages = new List<Uri>()
    {
            new Uri("Assets/Tiles/iStock_000002999571XSmall.jpg", UriKind.Relative),
            new Uri("Assets/Tiles/iStock_000004630599XSmall.jpg", UriKind.Relative),
            new Uri("Assets/Tiles/iStock_000005268101XSmall.jpg", UriKind.Relative),
            new Uri("Assets/Tiles/iStock_000012945007XSmall.jpg", UriKind.Relative),
            new Uri("Assets/Tiles/iStock_000014745608XSmall.jpg", UriKind.Relative),
            new Uri("Assets/Tiles/iStock_000016850786XSmall.jpg", UriKind.Relative)
    }
};

ShellTile.Create(uri, tileData, true);
```

Updating Tiles

The beauty of live tiles is that they are not static. While flipping tiles and cycling through images is great eye candy, you will still want to update your tiles with fresh data. The ShellTileSchedule object from the Microsoft.Phone.Shell namespace updates the tile image a single time or on a regular schedule (see Figure 10-9).

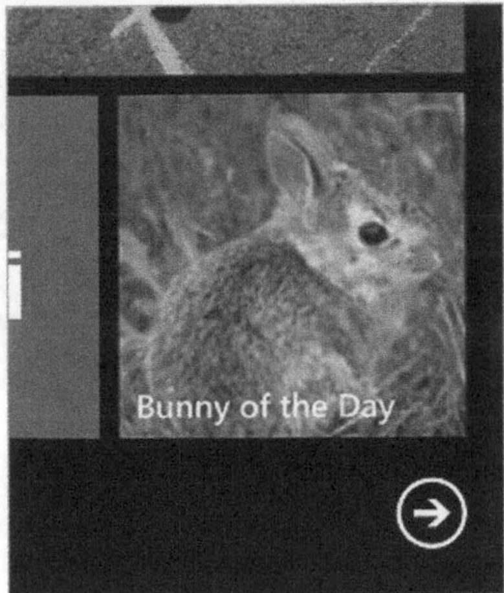

Figure 10-9. Updated Tile

To update your primary tile, create a new ShellTileSchedule instance, assign the RemoteImageUri with an absolute path to an external image, set the StartTime to a DateTime, set the Recurrence (OneTime or Interval) and call the Start() method (see Listing 10-9). One hour is the shortest update interval. To stop the ShellTileSchedule you will need to start it again. You can do that either by creating an empty ShellTileSchedule or keep an instance of the ShellTileSchedule. Notice the ShellTileSchedule constructor that takes both ShellTile and ShellTileData parameters.

Listing 10-9. Starting and Stopping the Tile Schedule

```
private void ScheduleButton_Click_1(object sender, EventArgs e)
{
    var tileSchedule = new ShellTileSchedule();
    tileSchedule.StartTime = DateTime.Now;
    tileSchedule.Recurrence = UpdateRecurrence.Interval;
    tileSchedule.Interval = UpdateInterval.EveryHour;
    tileSchedule.RemoteImageUri = remoteUri;
    tileSchedule.Start();
}

private void StopButton_Click_1(object sender, EventArgs e)
{
    var primaryTile = ShellTile.ActiveTiles.FirstOrDefault();
    if (primaryTile != null)
    {
        var shellTileSchedule = new ShellTileSchedule(primaryTile, new FlipTileData());
        shellTileSchedule.Start();
        shellTileSchedule.Stop();
    }
}
```

Right away we're running into limitations of the ShellTileSchedule. What if we want to use local images or populate the small and wide icons? What if you want to update the secondary tile and not the primary tile? You can use the ShellTileSchedule constructor that takes both ShellTile and ShellTileData parameters so you can get any live tile instance and update with any of the specialized ShellTileData descendent properties.

Figure 10-10 shows a secondary tile updated from a local image for the wide tile that also includes a new title and content. This example also updates the back title, images, and content.

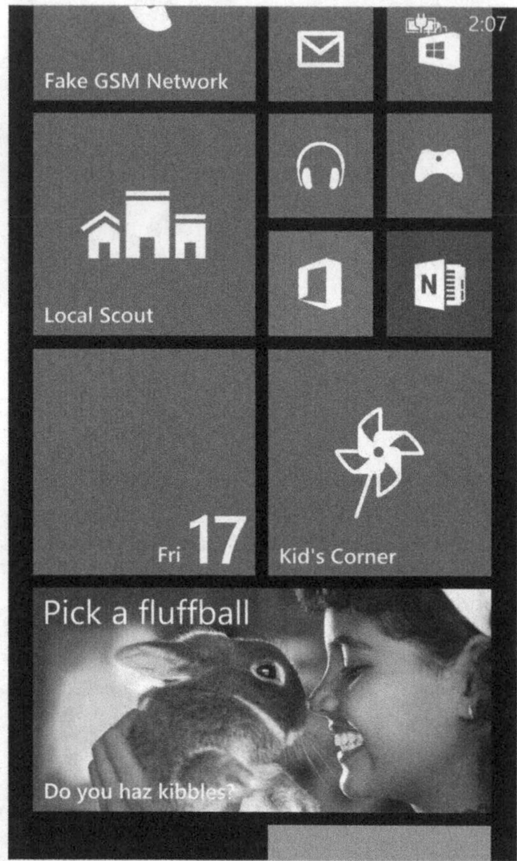

Figure 10-10. *Wide Secondary Tile*

Listing 10-10 shows how it's done. First, filter the static `ShellTile.ActiveTiles` collection with a LINQ `Where()` method (you'll need `System.Linq` in your `using` statements) to get a specific `ShellTile` instance. Create your `ShellTileData` descendant instance (i.e., `FlipTileData`, `IconicTileData`, or `CycleTileData`) and load its properties as you would if you were creating an entirely new tile. Finally, in the `ShellTileSchedule` constructor, pass both the `ShellTile` instance along with the `ShellTileData` instance. The `URI` fields point to local images in the `\assets\tiles` folder (the code that declares these URIs are not shown here).

Listing 10-10. Updating a Secondary Tile

```
var secondaryTile = ShellTile.ActiveTiles
    .Where(t => t.NavigationUri.Equals(secondaryUri));
var tile = secondaryTile.SingleOrDefault();

if (tile != null)
{
    var tileData = new FlipTileData()
```

```
    {
        Title = "We're no trouble",
        BackContent = "Adopt me!",
        SmallBackgroundImage = smallBunnyUri,
        BackgroundImage = mediumBunnyUri,
        WideBackgroundImage = largeBunnyUri,
        Count = 6,

        BackTitle = "Do you haz kibbles?",
        WideBackContent = "Pick a fluffball",
        BackBackgroundImage = mediumBunnyUri,
        WideBackBackgroundImage = largeBunnyUri
    };

    var tileSchedule = new ShellTileSchedule(tile, tileData);
    tileSchedule.StartTime = DateTime.Now;
    tileSchedule.Recurrence = UpdateRecurrence.Onetime;
    tileSchedule.Start();
}
```

■ **Note** "I've set the tile to update every hour, but sometimes the tile takes 1.5 hours to refresh. Is this expected?" Yes. The online help for `ShellTileSchedule` mentions that the timing may be altered to optimize for battery life or use of the radio. You may not see the update for "up to two times the chosen interval." You may not see the update at all if the image download fails.

This next section will show more techniques to notify the user that conditions have changed, that new content is available or that some action needs to be taken.

Notifications

How do you know if a tornado is brewing nearby, a friend is in town or a stock price dips below a certain level? Windows Phone 8 notifications allow you to update tiles, create "toasts" that display in the system tray at the top of the page, and show popup alarms/reminders. Notifications can be sent from your background tasks or pushed externally from a service in the cloud.

Background Agents

Background agents can execute code even when your application is not in the foreground. There are numerous types of Windows Phone 8 background agents that perform background processing such as audio streaming, wallet change notification, or task scheduling. The agent object is essentially a wrapper that is registered in the manifest and has methods for notifying the operating system when work is either complete or aborted.

In particular, we're interested in the `ScheduledTaskAgent` that adds an abstract `OnInvoke()` method. `OnInvoke(ScheduledTask task)` is called automatically by the operating system and is where you put code to perform the background task. When you're done with `OnInvoke()`, the `ScheduledTaskAgent NotifyComplete()` method indicates that the test is done or, the `Abort() method` signals that the agent was unable to complete its intended task. Scheduled tasks come in two flavors:

- Resource-intensive tasks run for relatively long periods when the phone isn't being actively used and are encapsulated in the `ResourceIntensiveTask` object.
- Periodic tasks have short recurring routines such as updating tiles. These tasks are encapsulated in the `PeriodicTask` object.

Our focus will be on using the `PeriodicTask` to update tiles.

The Game Plan

A task doesn't live in a vacuum. It has to be scheduled for execution. The `ScheduledActionService` schedules tasks using static methods `Find()`, `Remove()`, and `Add()`. It also has a special method `LaunchForTest()` that allows you to add a task and get a response immediately without having to wait the typical half hour required in production.

The basic steps to update tiles using a scheduled task agent are:

1. Create a new `Windows Phone App`.
2. Add a `Windows Phone Scheduled Task Agent` project to your solution.
3. Code the agent's `OnInvoke()` method.
4. In the main project that houses `MainPage.xaml`, include a reference from the main application to the agent project.
5. In the main project that houses `MainPage.xaml`, configure `WMAppManifest.xml` to include the agent.
6. In the main application `MainPage.xaml.cs`, write code to schedule the task.

Implementing a Background Task

Now that we have a roadmap for how we're going to implement a background task, let's build it step-by-step.

Preparing the Solution

First, prepare the solution to include tile images and add a second page to act as a landing page for the notification.

1. First, create a new `Windows Phone App`. Later, we'll add code to `MainPage.xml.cs`, but for now, we only need the project to exist. Name the project `BackgroundAgents`.
2. Optionally, you can modify the images in `Assets\Tiles` for `FlipCycleTileLarge.png`, `FlipCycleTileMedium.png` and `FlipCycleTileSmall.png`. You can use your favorite drawing utility or double-click the image in Visual Studio to activate the built-in image editor. The example uses custom photographs and icons (see Figure 10-11). The new images are the same dimensions as the default images.

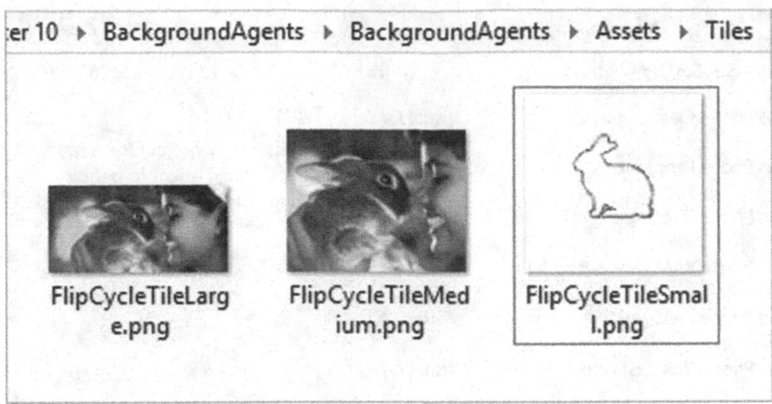

Figure 10-11. *New Icon Images*

Building the Background Agent

Now that the main project that houses `MainPage.xaml` is ready, build the background agent.

1. From the Visual Studio menu select `File` ➤ `New` ➤ `Project...`; select the `Windows Phone Scheduled Task Agent` from the list of Windows Phone templates. Name the project `UpdateTilesAgent`. Select `Add to solution` from the `Solution` drop down. Click the `OK` button to close the dialog (see Figure 10-12). When prompted to choose a `Windows Phone Platform OS Version`, select `Windows Phone OS 8.0`, then click the `OK` button to add the new project to your solution.

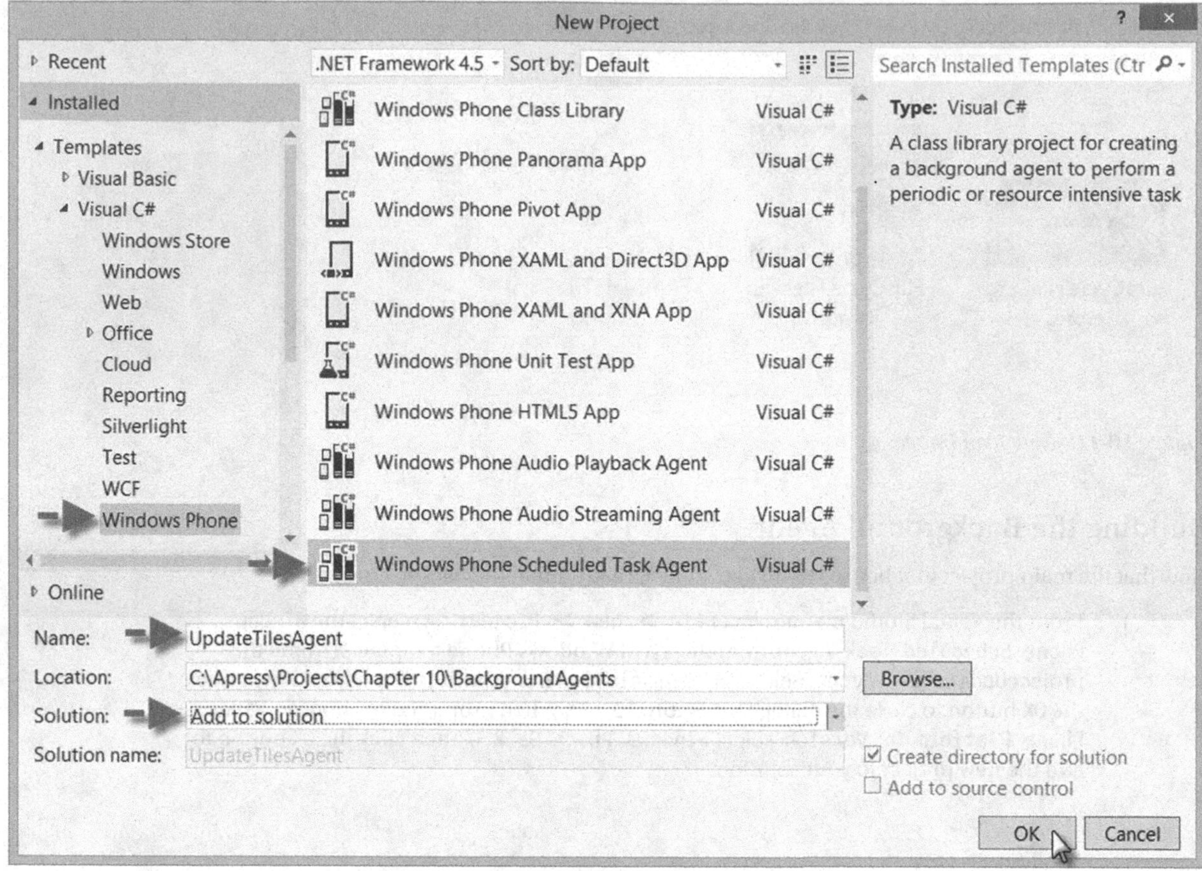

Figure 10-12. *Adding the Windows Phone Scheduled Task Agent*

2. In the `UpdateTilesAgent` project, a class file named `ScheduledAgent.cs` should already be open. If not, open the file for editing.

3. In `ScheduledAgent.cs`, find the `OnInvoke()` method override. Visual Studio will have already created a shell implementation (see Listing 10-11).

Listing 10-11. Overriding the OnInvoke() Method

```
protected override void OnInvoke(ScheduledTask task)
{
    //TODO: Add code to perform your task in background

    NotifyComplete();
}
```

4. At the top of the `OnInvoke()` method, add code to define tile and page URIs (see Listing 10-12). Even though we're in the `UpdateTilesAgent` project, the paths are relative to the main, user interface project.

Listing 10-12. Adding URIs to the OnInvoke() method

```
protected override void OnInvoke(ScheduledTask task)
{
    var pageUri = new Uri("/", UriKind.Relative);
    var smalUri = new Uri("Assets/Tiles/FlipCycleTileSmall.png", UriKind.Relative);
    var mediumUri = new Uri("Assets/Tiles/FlipCycleTileMedium.png", UriKind.Relative);
    var largeUri = new Uri("Assets/Tiles/FlipCycleTileLarge.png", UriKind.Relative);
    . . .
```

5. Next, add code to get the tile if it is running in the Start screen (see Listing 10-13). You will need to add a reference to `System.Linq` in your `using` statements to make this line of code work.

Listing 10-13. Getting the Tile

```
var tile = ShellTile.ActiveTiles
    .Where(t => t.NavigationUri.Equals(pageUri))
    .SingleOrDefault();
```

6. Add code to populate `FlipTileData` if the tile is running in the Start screen and then update the tile with the tile data (see Listing 10-14). Notice that the call to `NotifyComplete()` comes right after all the work is done.

Listing 10-14. Updating the Tile

```
if (tile != null)
{

    var tileData = new FlipTileData()
    {
        Title = "We're no trouble",
        BackContent = "Adopt me!",
        SmallBackgroundImage = smalUri,
        BackgroundImage = mediumUri,
        WideBackgroundImage = largeUri,
        Count = 6,
        BackTitle = "Do you haz kibbles?",
        WideBackContent = "Pick a fluffball",
        BackBackgroundImage = mediumUri,
        WideBackBackgroundImage = largeUri
    };

    tile.Update(tileData);
}
NotifyComplete();
```

Configuring the Main Project to use the Background Agent

Next, you'll need to configure the main project to use the background agent:

1. Back in the main project that houses `MainPage.xaml`, add a reference to `UpdateTilesAgent` (see Figure 10-13).

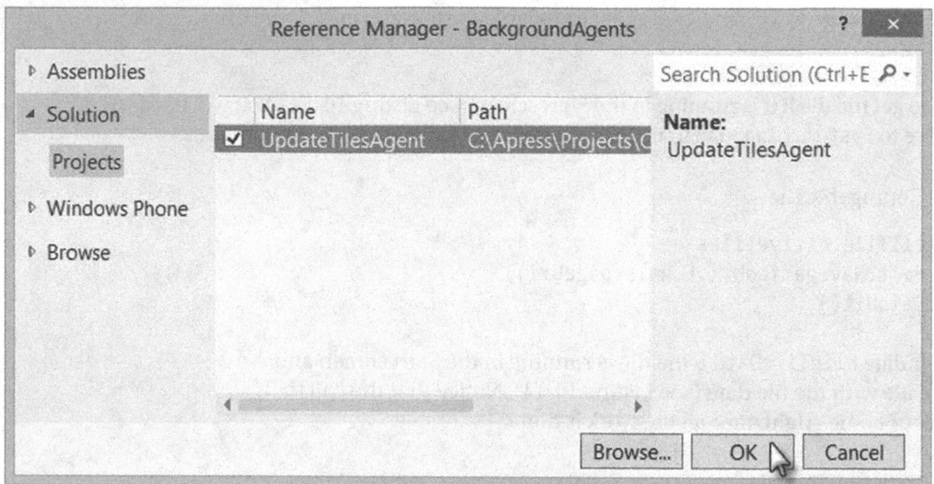

Figure 10-13. *Adding a Reference to the Background Agent*

2. Open the project's `\properties.WMAppManifest.xml` file for editing by right-clicking and selecting `View Code` from the context menu.
3. Under the `Tasks` element, add an `ExtendedTask` element that describes the `BackgroundServiceAgent` (see Listing 10-15). The `BackgroundServiceAgent Specifier` is an enumeration that includes `ScheduledTaskAgent`. There can only be one `ScheduledTaskAgent` for this project. `Name` is the name of the assembly that holds the background agent. `Source` is the name of the source file for the background agent assembly. `Type` is the full class name of the background agent; that is, the `ScheduledAgent` class in the `UpdateTilesAgent` namespace.

Listing 10-15. Adding the BackgroundServiceAgent

```
<Tasks>
        <DefaultTask Name="_default" NavigationPage="MainPage.xaml" />
        <ExtendedTask Name="BackgroundTask">
                <BackgroundServiceAgent
                        Specifier="ScheduledTaskAgent"
                        Name="UpdateTilesAgent"
                        Source="UpdateTilesAgent"
                        Type="UpdateTilesAgent.ScheduledAgent" />
        </ExtendedTask>
</Tasks>
```

Next, set up the MainPage.xaml user interface with an application bar button that will invoke the code to trigger the agent.

1. Open MainPage.xaml for editing.
2. Add an ApplicationBar to the page. Add a single ApplicationBarIconButton element with Text "background" and a Click event handler as shown in Listing 10-16.

Listing 10-16. Adding the ApplicationBar

```
...
<phone:PhoneApplicationPage.ApplicationBar>
    <shell:ApplicationBar>
        <shell:ApplicationBarIconButton
            x:Name="BackgroundButton"
            Text="background"
            IconUri="/Assets/AppBar/feature.alarm.png"
            Click="BackgroundButton_Click" />
    </shell:ApplicationBar>
</phone:PhoneApplicationPage.ApplicationBar>

</phone:PhoneApplicationPage>
```

3. In MainPage.xaml, place your cursor in the ApplicationBarIconButton element. In the Visual Studio Properties window, drop down the list for the IconUri property. Select the Alarm icon from the feature icons section of the list (see Figure 10-14).

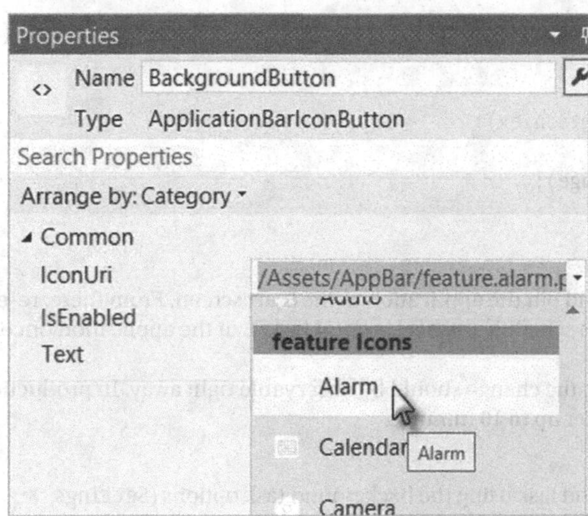

Figure 10-14. *Selecting the Alarm Icon Image*

4. Right-click the Click event handler name BackgroundButton_Click and select Navigate to Event Handler from the context menu. This will place you in the code-behind for the main page inside the BackgroundButton_Click event handler.

5. Replace the event handler with the code in Listing 10-17. The code first looks for an existing task named "AdoptionTask." This name is arbitrary and does not relate to any of the names in the manifest or in the background agent class. If the task exists, the task must be removed before re-adding it. Next, a new `PeriodicTask` is created, configured, and added using the `ScheduledActionService` static `Add()` method. Notice the `try...catch` that traps for the `InvalidOperationException`. This can easily happen if the user has disallowed background tasks for the application in the background tasks options (`Settings` ➤ `application` ➤ `background tasks`). Also notice that `LaunchForTest()` is called and will allow the task to run much more quickly than the purely production version (this should only be called during testing).

Listing 10-17. Scheduling the Background Agent

```
private void BackgroundButton_Click(object sender, EventArgs e)
{
    const string taskName = "AdoptionTask";
    var task = ScheduledActionService.Find(taskName) as PeriodicTask;
    if (task != null)
    {
        ScheduledActionService.Remove(taskName);
    }
    task = new PeriodicTask(taskName);
    task.Description = "Update bunny adoptions tiles";
    try
    {
        ScheduledActionService.Add(task);
        #if DEBUG
            ScheduledActionService.LaunchForTest(taskName, TimeSpan.FromSeconds(1));
        #endif
    }
    catch (InvalidOperationException ex)
    {
        Debug.WriteLine(ex.Message);
    }
}
```

To test the application, exit the application and pin the application to the Start screen. From there, re-enter the application and click the application bar button to schedule the background task. Exit the application once again and observe the live tile on the Start screen.

If you're using the `LaunchForTest()` method, the change should be observable right away. In production, the task will typically run every 30 minutes, but may wander up to 10 minutes.

So what could possibly go wrong?

- The user could disallow the background task using the background task options (`Settings` ➤ `application` ➤ `background tasks`). Battery-saving mode may prevent execution. Depending on the device, you may exceed a limit to the number of periodic agents that can run. For these issues, wrap the `ScheduledActionService.Add()` in a `try...catch(InvalidOperationException)`.

- If the background agent fails to run the task and calls `Abort()`, the operating system will set the task's `IsScheduled` property to false.

You can also place a breakpoint in the background agent's `OnInvoke()` method to see if the tile is being updated.

Alarms and Reminders

`Alarm` and `Reminder` notifications can be scheduled by `ScheduledActionService`. `Alarms` are simple notifications that show string `Content` and can optionally play a custom sound. A `Reminder` has a `Title`, `Content`, and a `NavigationUri`. `Alarms` and `Reminders` appear as popups along with a sound (see Figure 10-15). The `Alarm` can be snoozed or dismissed by the user pressing the buttons in the popup. A `Reminder` has an additional wrinkle. If the user touches outside the buttons, they are navigated to the page specified in the `NavigationUri`.

Figure 10-15. *A Reminder*

To create an alarm, call the `Alarm` constructor and pass a unique name. The example in Listing 10-18 uses `Guid.NewGuid()` for this purpose. Set the `BeginTime` to a `DateTime` value, set the `Content` to a string. If you want a custom sound to play, assign the `Sound` parameter the URI to a sound file (the default will play if you don't assign a `Sound`). Use the `ScheduledActionService Add()` method to schedule the alarm. Be sure to trap for `InvalidOperationException`. The exception can be thrown for a number of reasons including if "the action's start time has passed when trying to create/update the request."

Listing 10-18. Creating and Scheduling the Alarm

```
var uniqueName = Guid.NewGuid().ToString();
var alarm = new Alarm(uniqueName)
{
    BeginTime = DateTime.Now.AddSeconds(20),
    Content = "Gather tax documents",
    Sound = new Uri(@"assets\sounds\windows notify.wav", UriKind.Relative)
};

try
{
    ScheduledActionService.Add(alarm);
}
catch (InvalidOperationException ex)
{
    Debug.WriteLine(ex.Message);
}
```

■ **Note** `Alarm` has a `Title` property that it inherits from `ScheduledNotification`, but it is not supported. Attempting to use it will throw a `NotSupportedException`.

The `Reminder` is handled very much like the `Alarm`. The difference is that it does not have a custom `Sound` property; it supports the `Title` property and has a `NavigationUri` property. The `NavigationUri` can include query string parameters that you can retrieve from the page by overriding the `OnNavigatedTo()` method and checking the page's `NavigationContext.QueryString`. The example in Listing 10-19 creates a new `Reminder` with a `NavigationUri` that points to a second page in the project.

Listing 10-19. Creating and Scheduling the Reminder

```
var uniqueName = Guid.NewGuid().ToString();
var reminder = new Reminder(uniqueName)
{
    BeginTime = DateTime.Now.AddSeconds(20),
    Title = "Taxes",
    Content = "View tax check list",
    NavigationUri = new Uri("/TaxChecklist.xaml", UriKind.Relative)
};
try
{
    ScheduledActionService.Add(reminder);
}
catch (InvalidOperationException ex)
{
    Debug.WriteLine(ex.Message);
}
```

Toasts

Toasts show users relevant and time-critical information when they're not actually running your application. Toasts appear in the system tray showing the application icon, a title in bold font, and content in regular font (see Figure 10-16). When the user clicks the toast, they're navigated to the application.

Figure 10-16. *Notification in the System Tray*

Toasts can be sent locally, from within the application, or pushed from a server (see the "Push Notifications" section). "Local" notification is something of a misnomer because toasts are designed for delivery outside of the application. For example, it makes perfect sense to be notified of e-mail delivery when you're on the Start screen, but not if you are already viewing your inbox. Local toasts are actually sent from background agents and viewable outside the application only.

To send a toast, create a `ShellToast` instance inside the background agent's `OnInvoke()` method and assign strings to the `Title` and `Content` properties, then call the `Show()` method. The icon will be the application icon assigned in the `Application UI` tab of `WMAppManifest.xml`. This icon cannot be changed programmatically after the application starts running. Listing 10-20 shows the `ShellToast` being configured and shown inside a background agent's `OnInvoke()` method. See the "Background Agents" section for directions on setting up a background agent. The only part that changes between a background agent used to update tiles and a toast notification is the `OnInvoke()` code.

Listing 10-20. Sending a Toast

```
protected override void OnInvoke(ScheduledTask task)
{
    var toast = new ShellToast()
    {
        Title = "Bunny Adoption",
        Content = "Meet Harvey"
    };
    toast.Show();

    NotifyComplete();
}
```

By default, when the user touches the toast in the system tray, they navigate to the main page of the application. `ShellToast` has a `NavigationUri` property that will allow you to "deep link" from the toast to any URI within the application. This next example shows a "Bunny Adoption" toast that deep links to a new page named `DailyBunny.xaml` in the main project. Listing 10-21 shows the `NavigationUri` being populated and that the path to the page includes a custom query parameter named `NavigatedFrom`.

Listing 10-21. Adding NavigationUri

```
protected override void OnInvoke(ScheduledTask task)
{
    const string path = "/DailyBunny.xaml?NavigatedFrom=Toast Notification";

    var toast = new ShellToast()
    {
        Title = "Bunny Adoption",
        Content = "Meet Harvey",
        NavigationUri = new Uri(path, UriKind.Relative)
    };
    toast.Show();

    NotifyComplete();
}
```

The `DailyBunny.xaml` page is just image content and some text (see Listing 10-22 for the `ContentPanel` XAML layout). The bottom of the page has a `TextBlock` named "Origin" that will show where the page navigated from.

Listing 10-22. The ContentPanel XAML for DailyBunny.xaml

```
<StackPanel x:Name="ContentPanel"
    Grid.Row="1" Margin="12,0,12,0">
    <TextBlock Style="{StaticResource PhoneTextTitle3Style}"
        HorizontalAlignment="Center"
        Text="Meet Harvey the Party Lagomorph" />
    <Border BorderBrush="{StaticResource PhoneAccentBrush}"
        BorderThickness="1" Margin="5">
        <Image Source="/Assets/Images/bunny.jpg" />
    </Border>
    <TextBlock Style="{StaticResource PhoneTextSmallStyle}"
        Foreground="{StaticResource PhoneAccentBrush}"
        Text="Harvey is herbivorous, likes to be scratched between the ears, enjoys rearranging↵
        things and throwing things around. He particularly loves tunnels, especially cardboard↵
        tunnels he can chew on. Adopt Harvey today at the Lagomorph Protection Society, contact↵
        http://www.lagomorphh.net/"
        TextWrapping="Wrap" />
    <Border Height="100">
        <TextBlock x:Name="Origin"
            Text="Navigated From:"
            TextAlignment="Right"
            VerticalAlignment="Bottom"/>
    </Border>
</StackPanel>
```

The `DailyBunny.xaml.cs` code-behind in Listing 10-23 overrides the `OnNavigatedTo()` method, parses out the `NavigatedFrom` query string parameter and displays it in the `Origin TextBlock`.

Listing 10-23. Overriding the OnNavigatedTo() Method

```
protected override void OnNavigatedTo(NavigationEventArgs e)
{
    base.OnNavigatedTo(e);

    string navigatedFrom;
    if (NavigationContext.QueryString.TryGetValue("NavigatedFrom", out navigatedFrom))
    {
        this.Origin.Text = "Navigated from: " + navigatedFrom;
    }
}
```

When the user touches the toast, they navigate directly to the `DailyBunny.xaml` page and the string "Toast Notification" is displayed (see Figure 10-17).

12:31
LIVE TILES AND NOTIFICATIONS
daily bunny
Meet Harvey the Party Lagomorph
Harvey is herbivorous, likes to be scratched between the ears, enjoys rearranging things and throwing things around. He particularly loves tunnels, especially cardboard tunnels he can chew on. Adopt Harvey today at the Lagomorph Protection Society, contact http://www.lagomorphh.net/
Navigated from: Toast Notification

Figure 10-17. *Deep Linked Page*

Push Notifications

Push notifications are announcements that come from outside your application and show up as toasts, tile changes, or events in your application. Notifications have three basic components:

- The ***client Windows Phone 8 application*** that receives notifications. Your application opens a channel to the Microsoft Push Notification Service and gets a unique URI on which to continue the conversation.
- The ***Microsoft Push Notification Service***. This server acts as a middle layer between your phone application and a server you build to send notifications. The Microsoft Push Notification Service receives notifications from a custom service that you build and sends them on to your client application.
- A custom service that you build using any platform that can send HTTP requests, such as ASP.NET, Web API, WCF services, and WPF. The custom service application sends an HTTP request to the Microsoft Push Notification Service using the URI retrieved by the client application as the target address.

The steps required to complete a push notification are shown in Figure 10-18. A unique URI is retrieved from the Microsoft Push Notification Service and used to identify the communication in all the steps that follow.

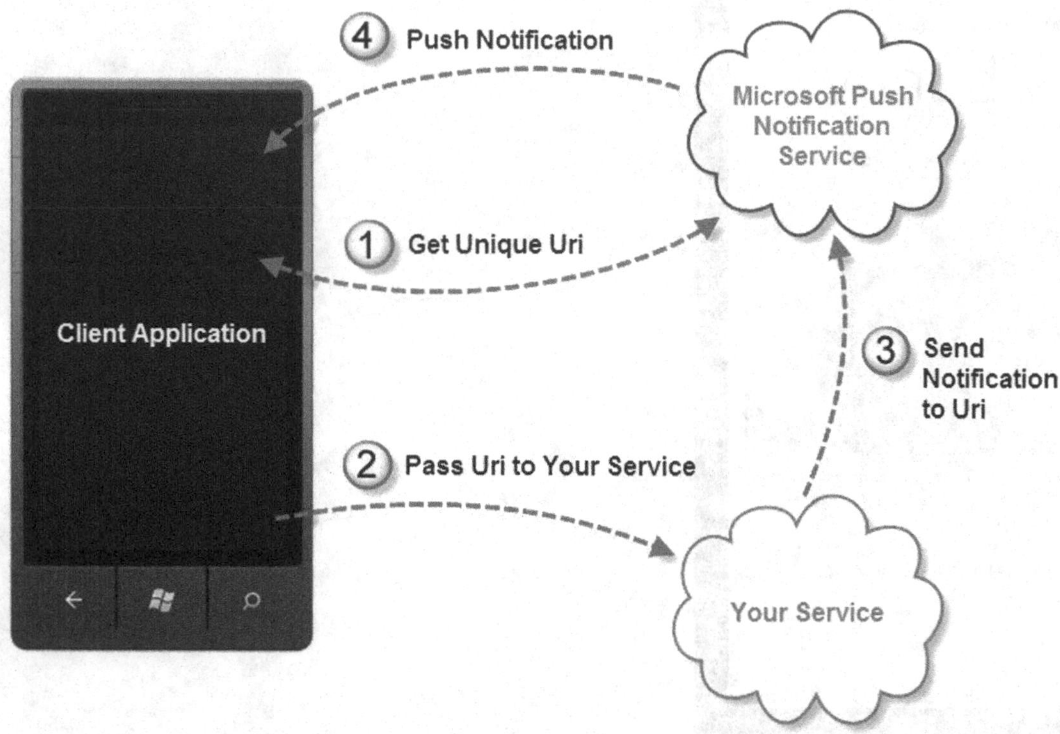

Figure 10-18. *The Push Notification Sequence of Events*

The sequence of events shown in Figure 10-18 is:

1. The client application opens a channel to the Microsoft Push Notification Service and receives a unique URI. This URI is used for all communications going forward.
2. The URI is passed from the Client Application to the custom service.
3. The custom service sends an HTTP Request to the unique URI. The body of the message is specific to the type of message you're sending (i.e., toast, tile, or raw).
4. Microsoft Push Notification Service pushes the notification to the device running the client application.

Sending Toast Notifications

To keep the example simple, we're actually going to physically copy the URI from the debug window of the client application and paste it in to a text box for the custom service application. In production, you would typically build a web service with a method for registering Windows Phone 8 clients. The web service method would then pass the URI from the client to the custom service. For our purposes, we will keep the code base as small as possible.

Building the Notification Client Application

The first step is to build the notification client application. The notification client is a Windows Phone 8 application that receives the URI from the Microsoft Push Notification Service. The `HttpNotificationChannel` is the key object that opens a channel to the Microsoft Push Notification Service, and then hooks up `ChannelUriUpdated` and `ErrorOccurred` events (see Listing 10-24).

Listing 10-24. Getting the Channel URI

```
using System.Diagnostics;
using Microsoft.Phone.Controls;
using Microsoft.Phone.Notification;

namespace PushNotificationClient
{
    public partial class MainPage : PhoneApplicationPage
    {
        public MainPage()
        {
            InitializeComponent();

            // unique name for the channel
            const string channelName = "AdoptABunny";

            // get existing channel or create a channel if it doesn't exist
            var channel = HttpNotificationChannel.Find(channelName) ??
                                                new HttpNotificationChannel(channelName);

            // hook up event handlers to know what the channel Uri is
            // and report any exceptions
            channel.ChannelUriUpdated += channel_ChannelUriUpdated;
            channel.ErrorOccurred += channel_ErrorOccurred;

            // open the channel
            if (channel.ChannelUri == null)
            {
                channel.Open();
            }
            else
            {
                Dispatcher.BeginInvoke(() =>
                    Debug.WriteLine(channel.ChannelUri.ToString()));
            }

            if (!channel.IsShellToastBound)
            {
                channel.BindToShellToast();
            }
        }
```

```
        void channel_ErrorOccurred(object sender, NotificationChannelErrorEventArgs e)
        {
            Dispatcher.BeginInvoke(() => Debug.WriteLine("A push error occurred: " +
                e.Message));
        }

        void channel_ChannelUriUpdated(object sender, NotificationChannelUriEventArgs e)
        {
            Dispatcher.BeginInvoke(() =>
                Debug.WriteLine(e.ChannelUri.ToString()));
        }
    }
}
```

Before starting the coding, enable the `ID_CAP_PUSH_NOTIFICATION` capability to the `WMAppManifest.xml`. Forgetting this step will cause a `UnauthorizedAccessException` to be thrown when you try to create an `HttpNotificationChannel` object.

If you are pushing a toast notification, check the channel `IsShellToastBound` property and if it is not bound, call the channel `BindToShellToast()` method. Likewise, to update tiles with a notification, check the `IsShellTileBound` property and call the `BindToShellTile()` method if it is not true.

Building the Custom Service

Next, you need to build a custom service that will take the URI of the channel and post an HTTP message to the Microsoft Push Notification Service. You can use any type of application that can perform an HTTP `POST` method.

The ASP.NET example in Listing 10-25 has a `TextBox` and a `Button` that triggers building the HTTP request. To set up for this code, first build a simple ASP.NET Empty Web Application and add a single Web Form to it. Add a `Button` and a `TextBox` to the web page.

Listing 10-25. Pushing a Toast Notification

```
protected void ToastButton_Click(object sender, EventArgs e)
{
    // create the web request out to the unique Uri
    // obtained from the MS Push Notification Service
    var request = WebRequest.Create(UriTextBox.Text);
    request.Method = "POST";

    // the format expected by the MS Push Notification Service
    const string messageFormat = "<?xml version=\"1.0\" encoding=\"utf-8\"?>" +
                                 "<wp:Notification xmlns:wp=\"WPNotification\">" +
                                 "<wp:Toast>" +
                                 "<wp:Text1>{0}</wp:Text1>" +
                                 "<wp:Text2>{1}</wp:Text2>" +
                                 "<wp:Param>{2}</wp:Param>" +
                                 "</wp:Toast> " +
                                 "</wp:Notification>";

    // message to be written out the request stream
    var message = String.Format(messageFormat, "Bunny Adoption", "Meet Harvey",
            "/DailyBunny.xaml?NavigatedFrom=Push Toast Notification");
```

```
    // convert the xml to an array of bytes
    byte[] bytes = Encoding.Default.GetBytes(message);

    // configure the request to match the content
    request.ContentLength = bytes.Length;
    request.ContentType = "text/xml";
    request.Headers.Add("X-WindowsPhone-Target", "toast");
    request.Headers.Add("X-NotificationClass", "2");

    // make the request
    using (var stream = request.GetRequestStream())
    {
        stream.Write(bytes, 0, bytes.Length);
    }

    // get the response from the Microsoft Push Notification Server
    // . . .
}
```

The expected format sent to the Microsoft Push Notification Service for toast notifications is shown in Listing 10-25 as `messageFormat`. The format expects `Text1` and `Text2` elements, that is, the title and sub-title of the toast. In this example, the title is "Bunny Adoption" and the sub-title is "Meet Harvey". Notice the `ContentType` and `Headers` for the message. The `X-WindowsPhone-Target` header indicates that this is a toast notification. The `X-NotificationClass` header defines how quickly this notification is delivered.

X-NOTIFICATIONCLASS SETTINGS

`X-NotificationClass` takes a value that determines how quickly the notification is delivered. Often you'll want near-immediate delivery. You can also choose to deliver the message within 7.5 minutes or 15 minutes.

Tile	Toast	Raw	Delivery Interval
1	2	3	Immediate delivery.
11	12	13	Delivered within 450 seconds.
21	22	34	Delivered within 900 seconds.

The end of Listing 10-25 needs a check on how the request was received. To do this, call the request `GetResponse()` method and look at the response headers. If there are no problems, you can expect to see `NotificationStatus Received`, `SubscriptionStatus Active`, and `DeviceConnectionStatus Connected`. Listing 10-26 shows how response headers sent back from the Microsoft Push Notification Server are retrieved. This example simply prints status headers to the Visual Studio Output window. You can come up with your own business rules regarding if messages are re-queued, logged, or another outcome. The full set of response codes and their meanings can be found in the MSDN article "Push Notification Service response codes for Windows Phone" (`http://msdn.microsoft.com/en-us/library/windowsphone/develop/ff941100(v=vs.105).aspx`).

Listing 10-26. Getting the Response

```
var response = request.GetResponse();
string status = response.Headers["X-NotificationStatus"];
string channelStatus = response.Headers["X-SubscriptionStatus"];
string connectionStatus = response.Headers["X-DeviceConnectionStatus"];
Debug.WriteLine("{0}:{1}:{2}", status, channelStatus, connectionStatus);
```

The possible status header code values are:

- `X-NotificationStatus` will tell you if the request was `Received`, `Dropped`, or if the queue was full (`QueueFull`).
- `X-DeviceConnectionStatus` indicates if the connection is `Connected`, `InActive`, `Disconnected`, or `TempDisconnected`. The `TempDisconnected` state can have many reasons including: the user disabled the data connection while roaming, an unreliable data connection, or the battery saver is enabled.
- `X-SubscriptionStatus` will be either `Active` or `Expired`.

To test a simple toast notification, first run the client application. The page constructor will run, open up a channel to the Microsoft Push Notification Service, the `ChannelUriUpdated` event will fire and output the URI. Copy the URI from the Output window (see Figure 10-19).

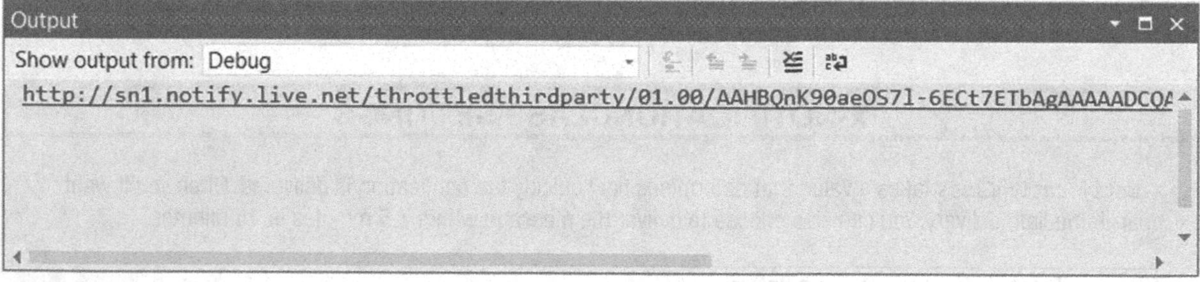

Figure 10-19. *URI in the Output Window*

Exit the client application. Then run the custom service, paste the URI in the text box, and click the button to send the notification (see Figure 10-20).

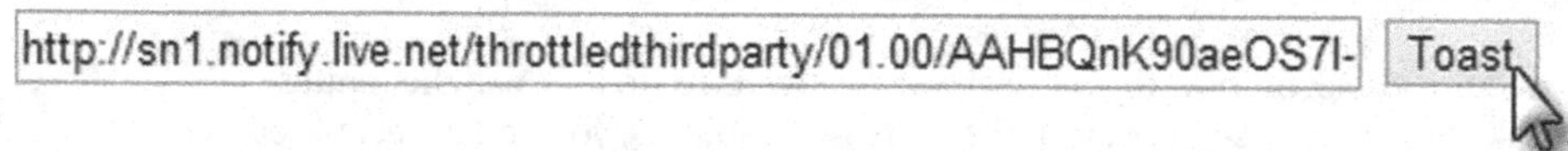

Figure 10-20. *Sending to the Microsoft Push Notification Service*

The emulator or device will show the toast in the system tray. The application icon will display at the left side of the toast, `Text1` will show in bold font, and `Text2` will display in regular font. Clicking the toast will navigate you to the page of the client application specified by the `<wp:Param>` element of the XML payload.

If you're running the client application, the toast will not display. Similarly, you can respond to the toast in the application by subscribing to the `ShellToastNotificationReceived` event of the `HttpNotificationChannel` object. The event arguments `Collection` property is a dictionary of name value pairs (see Listing 10-27).

Listing 10-27. Listing the Collection Contents

```
channel.ShellToastNotificationReceived += ChannelShellToastNotificationReceived;

// . . .

private void ChannelShellToastNotificationReceived(object sender, NotificationEventArgs e)
{
    foreach (var pair in e.Collection)
    {
        Debug.WriteLine(pair.Key + ": " + pair.Value);
    }
}
```

The dump of the collection contents is shown in the output window (see Figure 10-21).

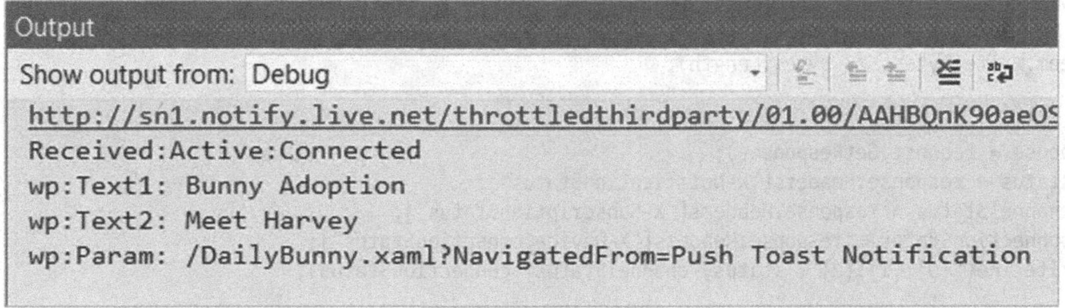

Figure 10-21. *Listing the Collection Contents*

Sending Tile Notifications

Sending a tile notification from a custom service has a similar pattern to the toast example except that the XML payload sent via HTTP POST describes tile properties and the request headers are slightly different (see Listing 10-28).

Listing 10-28. Pushing a Tile Notification

```
protected void TileButton_Click(object sender, EventArgs e)
{
    var request = WebRequest.Create(UriTextBox.Text);
    request.Method = "POST";

    const string messageFormat =
        "<?xml version=\"1.0\" encoding=\"utf-8\"?>" +
        "<wp:Notification xmlns:wp=\"WPNotification\">" +
        "<wp:Tile>" +
        "<wp:BackgroundImage>{0}</wp:BackgroundImage>" +
        "<wp:Count>{1}</wp:Count>" +
        "<wp:Title>{2}</wp:Title>" +
        "<wp:BackBackgroundImage>{3}</wp:BackBackgroundImage>" +
        "<wp:BackContent>{4}</wp:BackContent>" +
```

```
        "<wp:BackTitle>{5}</wp:BackTitle>" +
        "</wp:Tile> " +
        "</wp:Notification>";

    var message = String.Format(messageFormat,
        "assets/images/tile.png", "7", "New Adoptions",
        "assets/images/tileback.png", "u haz kibbles?", "waiting adoption");
    Debug.WriteLine(message);

    byte[] bytes = Encoding.Default.GetBytes(message);

    request.ContentLength = bytes.Length;
    request.ContentType = "text/xml";
    request.Headers.Add("X-WindowsPhone-Target", "token");
    request.Headers.Add("X-NotificationClass", "1");

    using (var stream = request.GetRequestStream())
    {
        stream.Write(bytes, 0, bytes.Length);
    }

    var response = request.GetResponse();
    string status = response.Headers["X-NotificationStatus"];
    string channelStatus = response.Headers["X-SubscriptionStatus"];
    string connectionStatus = response.Headers["X-DeviceConnectionStatus"];
    Debug.WriteLine("{0}:{1}:{2}", status, channelStatus, connectionStatus);
}
```

When the custom service sends the HTTP request, the tile changes. The results are shown in Figure 10-22.

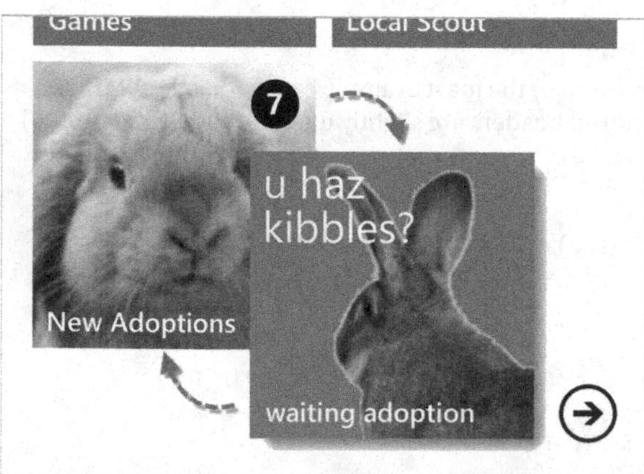

Figure 10-22. *Tile Changed by Notification*

Sending Raw Binary Notifications

In addition to toasts and tile notifications, you can send raw binary data directly to the client application. The custom service writes arbitrary binary data to the request stream (see Listing 10-29). Again, the difference from the toast and tile examples is in the data payload sent in the request, the request content type, and some tweaks to the request headers. To make the code in Listing 10-29 work, you will need to include `System`, `System.Drawing`, `System.Drawing.Imaging`, `System.IO`, and `System.Net` in your using statements.

Listing 10-29. Sending Raw Binary Data

```
protected void RawButton_Click(object sender, EventArgs e)
{
    // get an image from the project, make it into a smaller thumbnail
    // and convert it to an array of bytes
    var image = Image.FromFile(Server.MapPath("tile.png"));
    var thumbnail = image.GetThumbnailImage(100, 100, null, (IntPtr)null);
    var imageStream = new MemoryStream();
    thumbnail.Save(imageStream, ImageFormat.Jpeg);
    byte[] bytes = imageStream.ToArray();

    // create the web request out to the unique Uri
    // obtained from the MS Push Notification Service
    var request = WebRequest.Create(UriTextBox.Text);
    request.Method = "POST";

    // configure the request to match the content
    request.ContentLength = bytes.Length;
    request.ContentType = "image/jpeg";
    request.Headers.Add("X-NotificationClass", "3");

    // make the request
    using (var stream = request.GetRequestStream())
    {
        stream.Write(bytes, 0, bytes.Length);
    }
}
```

To receive raw data in the client application, handle the channel's `HttpNotificationReceived` event. The example code in Listing 10-30 retrieves the data from the arguments' `Notification.Body` property, a stream that is converted to a `WriteableBitmap` and assigned to the `Image Source` property. The `PictureDecoder` class (from the `Microsoft.Phone` namespace), is a one-method pony that only knows how to take a stream containing image data and turn it into a `WriteableBitmap`. The example uses an `Image` control on the page named `RawImage`. The `WriteableBitmap` is assigned to the `Source` property of `RawImage`.

Listing 10-30. Handling the `HttpNotificationReceived` Event

```
void channel_HttpNotificationReceived(object sender, HttpNotificationEventArgs e)
{
    Dispatcher.BeginInvoke(() =>
    {
        Debug.WriteLine("Http notification received: " +
                        e.Notification.Channel.ToString());
        RawImage.Source = PictureDecoder.DecodeJpeg(e.Notification.Body);
    });
}
```

Customizing the Lock Screen

When the user hits the hardware lock button or when the phone times out, the user is locked out of the phone. When they click the hardware button a second time, the lock screen appears. You can make your application a provider of lock screen content including: the lock screen background, detailed status, and quick status icon, and count (see Figure 10-23). Any content you add to the lock screen should be lightweight, such as brief notifications the user might need immediately.

Figure 10-23. *The Lock Screen*

To make your application into a lock screen provider, there are a number of tasks to perform in disparate parts of the application including in the WMAppManifest and in code. Also, the user must manually grant access and configure lock screen settings. The general steps are:

- Add lock screen images to your project, one for the lock screen and another small image for the icon in the quick status area.
- Add extensions to `WMAppManifest.xml` that identify areas of the application you're trying to extend. In this case we want to extend the lock screen background, icon count, and notification text field. This step will involve adding some boiler-plate, predefined XML to the manifest.

- Also in `WMAppManifest.xml`, configure the live tile sections to include text and images you want shown on the lock screen.
- Add code to request the application become a lock screen provider.
- Optionally, provide a direct link to the lock screen settings from your application.
- The user must explicitly grant access to the lock screen either when requested through the application or directly in the lock screen settings.

Adding Lock Screen Images

Add an image for the lock screen and a second image for the quick status area. Images can be placed in a folder of the project or placed in isolated storage. In the example that follows, we will place the images in a project folder.

■ **Note** If you want to display images from remote locations on the internet in the lock screen, you'll have to first save them to isolated storage.

You can add lock screen images of any size to your project. Images larger than the dimensions of the phone's resolution will be cropped from the center and smaller images will be stretched. The quick status image should be 38 × 38 white pixels. Pixels can have varying degrees of transparency.

This example happens to use a 425 × 282 image file named `LockScreen.jpg` that is stored in the `\assets` folder. The image file name is arbitrary. Figure 10-24 shows the image in the Visual Studio Graphics Designer.

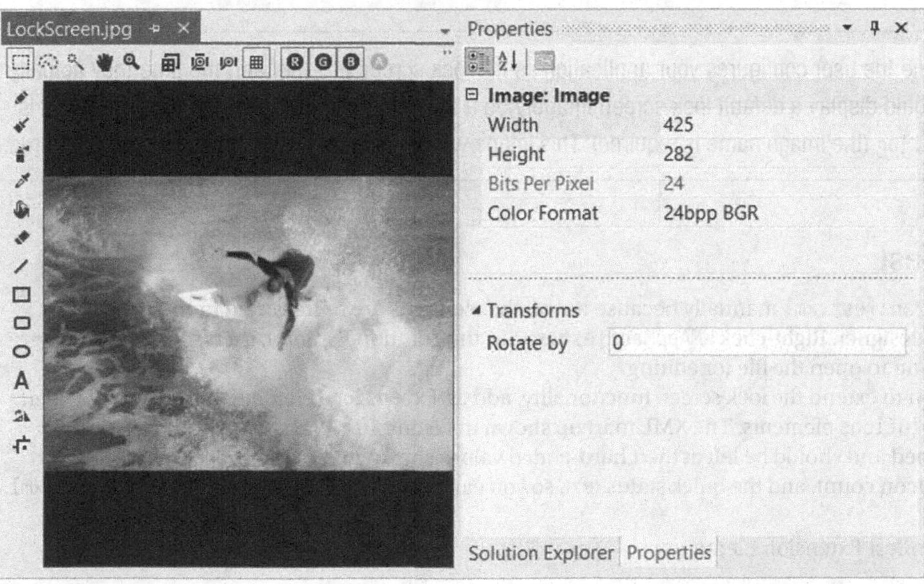

Figure 10-24. *The Lock Screen Image*

The quick status icon image is a 36 × 38 pixel icon of someone on a surfboard (see Figure 10-25). The image file name is `surfer.png` and is stored in the `\assets` folder. The `Build Action` for these image files should be `Content` (`Content` is the default when images are added to the project).

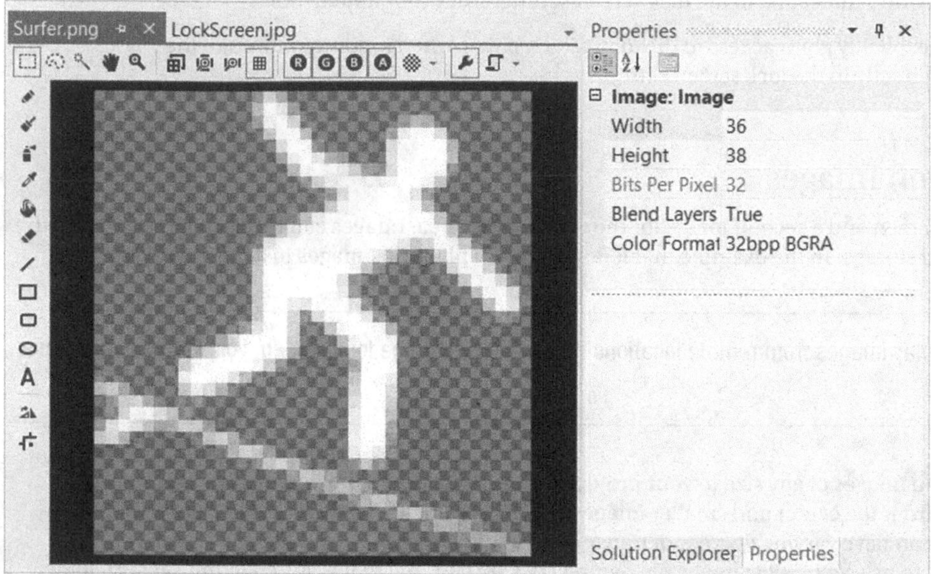

Figure 10-25. The Quick Status Icon

■ **Note** In between the time the user configures your application as the lock screen provider and the time they actually run your application, you should display a default lock screen image. Add a default image to the root of your drive that is named `DefaultLockScreen.jpg` (the image name is required). This image will be used until your application is able to run.

Editing the Manifest

You will need to edit `WMAppManifest.xml` manually because not all the elements are represented in the `WMAppManifest.xml` visual designer. Right-click `WMAppManifest.xml` in the Solution Explorer, then select `View Code` option from the context menu to open the file for editing.

To declare our intention to extend the lock screen functionality, add an `Extensions` element to the XML between the `Tokens` and `ScreenResolutions` elements. The XML markup shown in Listing 10-31 is boiler plate. That is, the names and ids are pre-defined and should be left at their hard-coded values shown in the listing. We want to support the background image, the icon count, and the quick status text, so you can paste this XML as-is to `WMAppManifest.xml`.

Listing 10-31. WMAppManifest Extension Elements

```
<Extensions>
      <Extension ExtensionName="LockScreen_Background"
                          ConsumerID="{111DFF24-AA15-4A96-8006-2BFF8122084F}"
                          TaskID="_default" />
      <Extension ExtensionName="LockScreen_Notification_IconCount"
```

```
                              ConsumerID="{111DFF24-AA15-4A96-8006-2BFF8122084F}"
                              TaskID="_default" />
    <Extension ExtensionName="LockScreen_Notification_TextField"
                              ConsumerID="{111DFF24-AA15-4A96-8006-2BFF8122084F}"
                              TaskID="_default" />
</Extensions>
```

The lock screen notification detail status (the text you add to the lock screen) comes from the live tile `Title` element. If the `BackTitle` is defined in `WMAppManifest.xml`, then that is used instead. The quick status count comes from the live tile `Count` element. The path to the small 38 × 38 image is defined in the `DeviceLockImageURI` element. In this example we're using the flip style of live tile. Listing 10-32 shows the key properties.

Listing 10-32. Live Tile Properties that feed the Lock Screen

```
<TemplateFlip>
    . . .
    <Count>6</Count>
    <Title>Surf Sites</Title>
    <BackContent>Pleasure Point: Santa Cruz, Ca</BackContent>
    <BackTitle>Surf Advisories</BackTitle>
    <LargeBackContent>
        Pleasure Point: high wind advisory through Wednesday afternoon
    </LargeBackContent>
    <DeviceLockImageURI IsRelative="true" IsResource="false">
        Assets\surfer.png
    </DeviceLockImageURI>
    . . .
</TemplateFlip>
```

■ **Note** In Listing 10-32, `LargeBackContent` and `DeviceLockImageURI` are on multiple lines in order to be visible in this book. You should edit this listing so that each starting and ending element is on a single line with no extra spaces.

Requesting Access to the Lock Screen from Code

You need to make sure you have access to the lock screen. Request access if necessary and set the lock screen background. The code depends on the objects in the `Windows.Phone.System.UserProfile` namespace, namely the `LockScreenManager` that manages access and the `LockScreen` object that assigns the current lock screen image. Listing 10-33 uses the `LockScreenManager` to see if access has already been granted. If not, the `LockScreenManager` requests access from the user.

Listing 10-33. Configuring the Lock Screen in Code

```
protected async override void OnNavigatedTo(NavigationEventArgs e)
{
    base.OnNavigatedTo(e);

    var isLockscreenProvider =
        LockScreenManager.IsProvidedByCurrentApplication;
```

```
    // if the app is already a provider, carry on,
    // otherwise, request access from the user.
    if (!isLockscreenProvider)
    {
        var access = await LockScreenManager.RequestAccessAsync();
        isLockscreenProvider = access == LockScreenRequestResult.Granted;
    }

    // the user has granted access at some point
    // so create a path to the image for the lockscreen and set it.
    if (isLockscreenProvider)
    {
        // Note:
        // "ms-appx:///" is the prefix used for content in the project
        // "ms-appdata:///Local/" is the prefix for isolated storage

        var uri = new Uri("ms-appx:///assets/lockscreen.jpg",
            UriKind.Absolute);
        LockScreen.SetImageUri(uri);
    }
}
```

The request displays the dialog shown in Figure 10-26. This is an awaitable operation, so the method call is proceeded with await and the calling method is marked with async. Once access has been granted, create a URI to the lock screen image and call the LockScreen SetImageUri() method. In particular, notice how the path is constructed for the URI. ms-appx:/// is a path to files in the project. In this case the path is to the lockscreen.jpg file that resides in the \assets folder. If you decide to use isolated storage, the path will be preceded with ms-appdata:///Local/. At the time of this writing, these are the only two options.

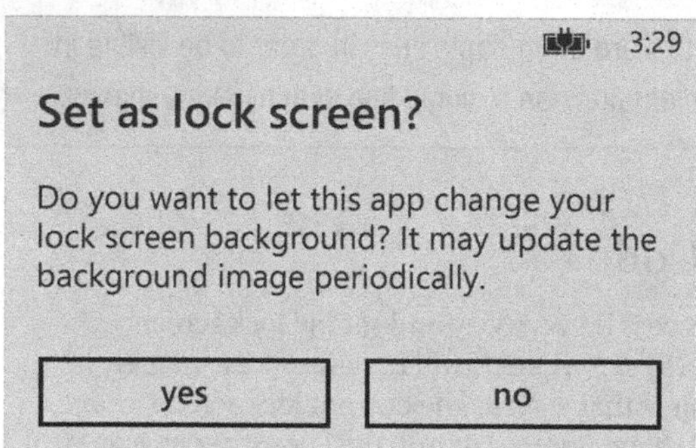

Figure 10-26. *The LockScreenManager Request*

Configuring Access to the Lock Screen

If the user answers yes to the Set as lock screen? prompt, the lock screen settings will be set automatically to include your application as the provider for the background (see Figure 10-27).

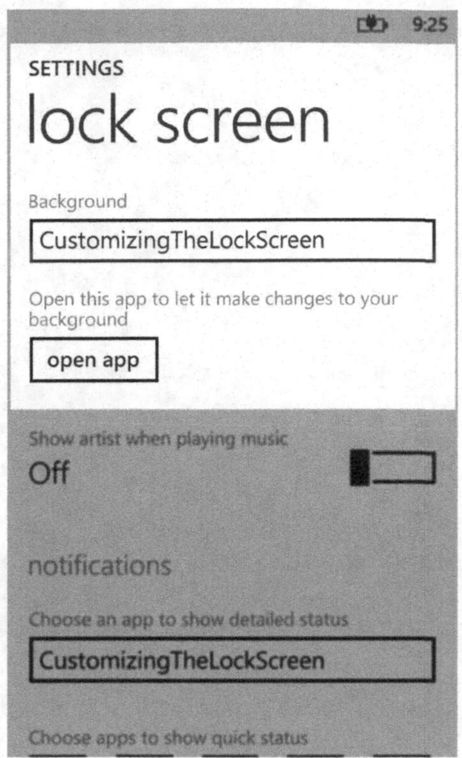

Figure 10-27. *Configuring the Lock Screen Background*

That gets us as far as setting the lock screen background. To set the notifications' detailed status text, the user will need to click the `Choose an app to show detailed status` option and select your application.

The quick status icon and count shown at the bottom of the lock screen are configured in the same lock screen settings page. There are slots for up to five applications to display in the quick status area. The small 38 × 38 icon defined in the `DeviceLockImageURI` element will display alongside the `Count`. In Figure 10-28, the demo application `CustomizingTheLockScreen` is selected to show detailed status and the first quick status selection on the left shows the surfing icon.

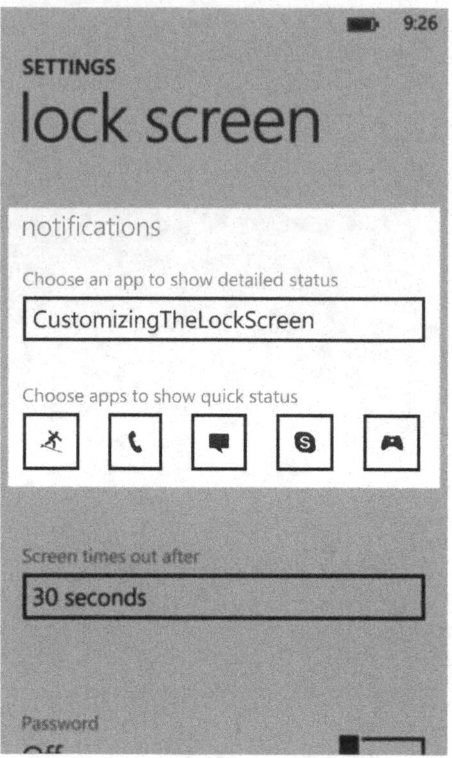

Figure 10-28. *The Lock Screen Notification Settings*

Providing Access to Lock Screen Settings

It's a one-liner to access the lock screen settings from your application. For example, you could add an `ApplicationBar` button and implement the `Click` event as shown in Listing 10-34.

Listing 10-34. Invoking Lock Screen Settings

```
private async void SettingsButton_Click_1(object sender, EventArgs e)
{
    await Windows.System.Launcher.LaunchUriAsync(
        new Uri("ms-settings-lock:"));
}
```

Once the user arrives in the lock screen settings page, they could navigate right back to your application by clicking the `open app` button (see Figure 10-27). When the user navigates through this path, a query string with the key `WallpaperSettings` is passed back. If that `QueryString` element is present, you know they got there via the lock screen settings page. The code in Listing 10-35 shows stub code that decides if you're coming from the lock screen status page. From there you can navigate to a settings page that you create in your own application. This page could contain settings that choose the images displayed on the lock screen background. Your application settings page could also determine what and how items are counted that show up in the quick status portion of the lock screen.

Listing 10-35. Getting the WallpaperSettings QueryString Value

```
protected async override void OnNavigatedTo(NavigationEventArgs e)
{
    base.OnNavigatedTo(e);

    string value = String.Empty;

    if (NavigationContext.QueryString.TryGetValue("WallpaperSettings", out value))
    {
        // navigate to a settings page in your application.
    }
    //. . .
}
```

Summary

Your applications can maintain a dynamic conversation with the user through Windows Phone 8 live tiles and notifications. Fresh live tile content grabs attention and draws your audience back in. Toasts display new, relevant information when the user is outside your application, allowing the user to dive back into your app for more detailed information or to respond to the current situation. Even when the screen is locked, your application can have a presence on the screen showing custom background images, status text, and count information.

CHAPTER 11

Data Sources

The core usefulness of an application is in its information. Slick presentation, innovative new device capabilities, gestures, and beautiful controls, all serve the main task of capturing, manipulating, and storing data. Windows Phone 8 connects to data from all over the world through a number of data sources and data types. And if you were looking for a full relational database right on your phone, Windows Phone 8 makes that possible too.

Consuming XML

Some of the data you work with comes to the phone in XML form. Before this raw XML data can become nice usable objects you must first:

- Load the data into your application from wherever the data is located. The XML can be located in the assembly (`Build Action` = `Resource`), outside the assembly (`Build Action` = `Content`), or somewhere on the web reachable from a URI.
- Convert the XML from its format of elements and attributes to an object form easily consumed in your application. The `System.Xml.Linq` assembly is well stocked with extension methods that slice-and-dice XML and place data into objects.

This section explains how to use the `XDocument` object to load XML as a file from inside your project, how to parse XML into an object format usable by your application and how to deal with XML namespace issues that are sure to come up.

Loading and Parsing XML Project Files

There are multiple methods to load and parse XML. In this next set of examples we will focus on the `XDocument` object from the `System.Xml.Linq` namespace. The `Tweets.xml` file in Listing 11-1 contains simplified XML content that we can start with.

Listing 11-1. Tweets.xml File Contents

```
<?xml version="1.0" encoding="utf-8" ?>
<Tweets>
  <Tweet>
    <Author>Bary Nusz</Author>
    <Content>Wildfire at Lake Texoma http://twitpic.com/5kpxtf</Content>
    <Notes>Lack of rain dropped Lake Texoma by 6 ft</Notes>
  </Tweet>
```

```
  <Tweet>
    <Author>Matt Kurvin</Author>
    <Content>Golden afternoon! http://www.surfline.com/surf-news/big-wave-coverage-from-➥
             mavericks_61122/ http://fb.me/wuSH467z</Content>
    <Notes>Surfing at Mavericks, solid 15 ft with a couple 18, 20 ft sets</Notes>
  </Tweet>
  <Tweet>
    <Author>J Tower</Author>
    <Content>Beautiful day! The perfect weather to ride my bike to the office.</Content>
    <Notes>Been on the Hart-Montague Trail State Park bike trail?</Notes>
  </Tweet>
  <Tweet>
    <Author>Conan O'Brien</Author>
    <Content>A publisher just asked me to write my autobiography, but they want it to be about➥
             Johnny Depp.</Content>
    <Notes>Funny guy!</Notes>
  </Tweet>
</Tweets>
```

XML files with the `Build Action` property marked `Content` are accessed through a simple path in your project. `Tweets.xml` is located in a folder named `Data` in the project. The `XDocument Load()` method in Listing 11-2 reads the data and returns an `XDocument` object.

Listing 11-2. Loading the XML Data Content

```
var document = XDocument.Load("Data/Tweets.xml");
```

From there, use the `Element()` and `Elements()` methods to drill down to the XML data you want to display (see Listing 11-3). Be aware that the code here is simplified to be as brief as possible. In production code you will need to check for null references from each method.

Listing 11-3. Using the Elements() and Element() Methods

```
var tweetElements = document.Element("Tweets").Elements("Tweet");
```

Use Linq syntax to project XML data elements into .NET objects. This example demonstrates populating a collection of simple `Tweet` objects. Each `Tweet` object has only `Author` and `Content` properties. The collection is then bound to the `DataContext` of a `ListBox` (see Listing 11-4).

Listing 11-4. Projecting XML Data Elements to .NET Objects

```
var tweets = tweetElements
    .Select(t => new Tweet()
    {
        Author = t.Element("Author").Value,
        Content = t.Element("Content").Value,
    });

TweetListBox.DataContext = tweets;
```

All the code for `MainPage.xaml.cs` is shown together in Listing 11-5.

Listing 11-5. Transforming XML Data to Objects

```
using System.Linq;
using System.Xml.Linq;
using Microsoft.Phone.Controls;
using XMLAsContent.Classes;

namespace XMLAsContent
{
    public partial class MainPage : PhoneApplicationPage
    {
        public MainPage()
        {
            InitializeComponent();

            var document = XDocument.Load("Data/Tweets.xml", LoadOptions.None);

            var tweetElements = document.Element("Tweets").Elements("Tweet");

            var tweets = tweetElements
                .Select(t => new Tweet()
                {
                    Author = t.Element("Author").Value,
                    Content = t.Element("Content").Value
                });
            TweetListBox.DataContext = tweets;
        }
    }
}
```

Listing 11-6 shows the simple `Tweet` class with properties for `Author` and `Content`.

Listing 11-6. The Tweet Class

```
public class Tweet
{
    public string Author { get; set; }
    public string Content { get; set; }
}
```

Finally, the layout for the example uses a `ListBox` with two `TextBlock` elements to display the `Author` and `Content` data (see Listing 11-7).

Listing 11-7. The MainPage.xaml Layout

```
<Grid x:Name="ContentPanel" Grid.Row="1" Margin="12,0,12,0">
    <ListBox x:Name="TweetListBox"
        ItemsSource="{Binding}"
        HorizontalAlignment="Stretch"
        VerticalAlignment="Stretch">
        <ListBox.ItemTemplate>
            <DataTemplate>
```

```
                <StackPanel>
                    <TextBlock Text="{Binding Author}"
                        HorizontalAlignment="Stretch"
                        Style="{StaticResource PhoneTextAccentStyle}" />
                    <TextBlock Text="{Binding Content}"
                        TextWrapping="Wrap"
                        HorizontalAlignment="Stretch" />
                </StackPanel>
            </DataTemplate>
        </ListBox.ItemTemplate>
    </ListBox>
</Grid>
```

The running application loads up the XML file, parses the elements to a collection of objects and binds the collection to the ListBox (see Figure 11-1).

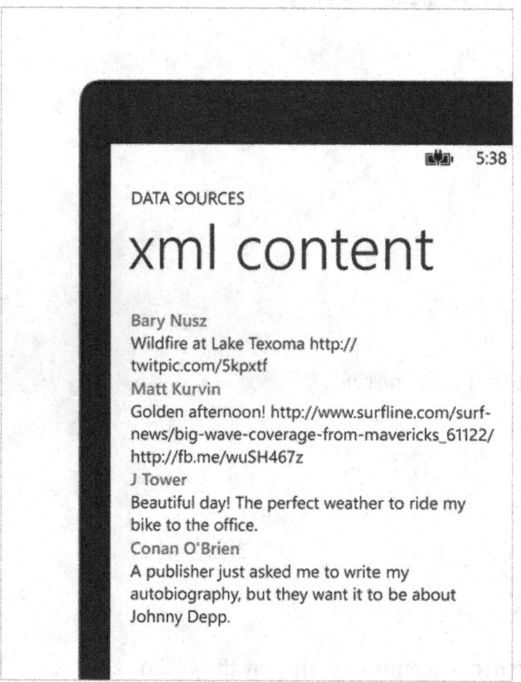

Figure 11-1. *The Running Application*

Loading XML from a Resource

If the XML file Build Action property is marked Resource, use the Application.GetResourceStream() method to retrieve the data as a stream. The path for the URI passed to the GetResourceStream() method should follow the pattern:

```
/your_project_name;component/your path to xml
```

Notice the semicolon that separates the project name and the literal word `component`. After the word `component` comes the path to the resource. The `XDocument Load()` overloaded methods can handle streams, paths, and readers. Listing 11-8 shows the `Tweets.xml` file on the exact same path as the earlier example, but in this case the `Tweets.xml` file is marked as a resource.

Listing 11-8. Loading a Resource File

```
// Use this syntax for Build-Action = Resource
var resourceStream =
    Application.GetResourceStream(
        new Uri("/ConsumingXML;component/Data/Tweets.xml", UriKind.Relative));
var document = XDocument.Load(resourceStream.Stream);
```

Handling XML Namespace Issues

Production data is typically a good deal more complex than our simple Twitter XML file. In the wild, you may run into a "null reference" error where an element isn't found, even though you can clearly see the element in the XML. This is likely because the element is marked with an XML namespace that needs to be handled differently in code.

Listing 11-9 shows a snippet of XML that includes an XML namespace with alias `falafel` that references `http://www.falafel.com/`. This namespace has been added to the `<Tweets>` element and used to qualify a new `<falafel:Notes>` element.

Listing 11-9. XML with XML Namespace

```
<?xml version="1.0" encoding="utf-8" ?>
<Tweets xmlns:falafel="http://www.falafel.com/">
  <Tweet>
    <Author>Bary Nusz</Author>
    <Content>Wildfire at Lake Texoma http://twitpic.com/5kpxtf</Content>
    <falafel:Notes>Lack of rain dropped Lake Texoma by 6 ft</falafel:Notes>
  </Tweet>
  . . .
  </Tweet>
</Tweets>
```

The URI after the `xmlns:falafel` is purely an identifier. The URI may actually point at some online resource or it may not. Its purpose in the XML is to identify an element name uniquely. If at some time in the future, a new `<Notes>` element is added, `<falafel:Notes>` will still be unique. In Listing 11-9, `Notes` is specifically marked as being in the `falafel` namespace.

To deal with the namespace in code, create an `XNamespace` that corresponds exactly to the namespace defined in the XML (see Listing 11-10). Notice how the Notes element within the `Tweets` element is qualified with the namespace. Forgetting the `XNamespace` will trigger a `NullReferenceException` when the element is accessed. A `Notes` property is added to the `Tweet` object and the Linq `Select()` method populates the new property.

Listing 11-10. Using the XML Namespace

```
var resourceStream =
    Application.GetResourceStream(
        new Uri("/ConsumingXML;component/Data/Tweets.xml", UriKind.Relative));
var document = XDocument.Load(resourceStream.Stream);
```

```
XNamespace ns = @"http://www.falafel.com/";

var tweetElements = document.Element("Tweets").Elements("Tweet");

var tweets = tweetElements
    .Select(t => new Tweet()
    {
        Author = t.Element("Author").Value,
        Content = t.Element("Content").Value,
        Notes = t.Element(ns + "Notes").Value
    });
TweetListBox.DataContext = tweets;
```

The running application in Figure 11-2 shows the new Notes field bound to an additional TextBlock.

Figure 11-2. *Running Application with Notes*

If the XML namespace doesn't have a specific name, then the assigned value is the default namespace and applies to all elements. In the XML snippet shown in Listing 11-11, the Tweets element and everything inside it is part of the http://www.falafel.com/ namespace.

Listing 11-11. XML with Default Namespace

```
<?xml version="1.0" encoding="utf-8" ?>
<Tweets xmlns="http://www.falafel.com/">
  <Tweet>
    <Author>Bary Nusz</Author>
    <Content>Wildfire at Lake Texoma http://twitpic.com/5kpxtf</Content>
    <Notes>Lack of rain dropped Lake Texoma by 6 ft</Notes>
  </Tweet>
. . .
```

In code, you'll need to reference the namespace on every element from the Tweets element down (see Listing 11-12).

Listing 11-12. Qualifying the Default Namespace in Code

```
var document = XDocument.Load("Data/Tweets.xml");

XNamespace ns = @"http://www.falafel.com/";

var tweetElements = document.Element(ns + "Tweets").Elements(ns + "Tweet");

var tweets = tweetElements
    .Select(t => new Tweet()
    {
        Author = t.Element(ns + "Author").Value,
        Content = t.Element(ns + "Content").Value,
        Notes = t.Element(ns + "Notes").Value
    });
TweetListBox.DataContext = tweets;
```

Serializing Objects

For our purposes, *serialization* is the process of transforming object instances to a format that can be easily sent across a network or stored in a database. The serialized format is typically a string representation of the object in XML or JSON (JavaScript Object Notation). Some of the out-of-the-box objects that can perform serialization are:

- `XMLSerializer` was introduced with .NET 1.0 and provides full control over the serialization format. `XmlSerializer` can only serialize public properties that include a "get" and "set". Use `XmlSerializer` if you need control over the XML output to construct small payloads.
- `DataContractSerializer` was introduced with .NET 3.0 to work with Windows Communication Foundation (WCF). `DataContractSerializer` works on an "opt in" design where only classes and members marked with attributes are included. Members of any access level (need not be public) can be serialized, but the serialization format (except for member name and order) is controlled by `DataContractSerializer`. The fact that `DataContractSerializer` knows the format in advance allows for optimizations that make serialization faster than with `XmlSerializer`. Use `DataContractSerializer` when serialization format isn't important, but you need better serialization performance.
- `DataContractJsonSerializer` serializes JSON (JavaScript Object Notation). Many web services return data in JSON format or at least offer the option along with XML. JSON has a very simple structure where curly braces indicate objects, square braces enclose arrays, and properties take the form of name and value pairs separated by a colon. Where XML requires all data to be surrounded by tags using angle brackets, such as `<data>some data</data>`, JSON can leave out tags and other meta-data and is lighter weight as a result. The JSON format's smaller size is a good match for the resource constraints of the phone, and `DataContractJsonSerializer` makes it convenient to translate between JSON in string form to objects that can be used directly.

XMLSerializer

The `XmlSerializer` class takes care of serializing objects into XML, then re-hydrating the XML back into object form. The serialized objects can be saved to the database, local storage, or passed to some other process. To use `XmlSerializer`, add the `System.Xml.Serialization` assembly to the `References` node of your project.

The Save button in this next example creates a simple Person object with FirstName and LastName properties, serializes the object, and displays the XML in a TextBox (see Figure 11-3). The XML can be edited by hand. When the Restore button is clicked, the XML is consumed again by the XmlSerializer and the Person object is recreated with the new data.

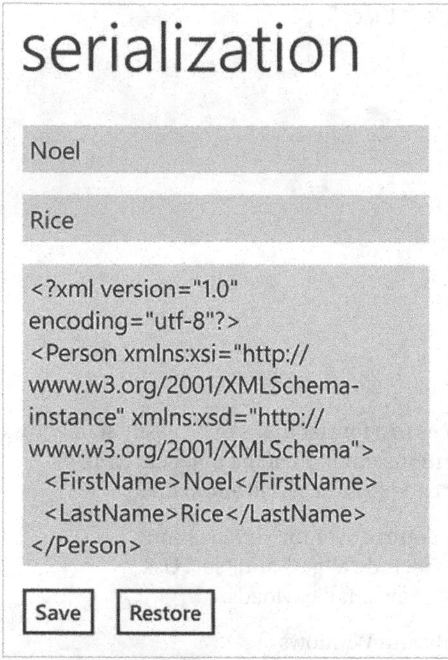

Figure 11-3. *The Serialized Object*

In Listing 11-13, the Save button click creates the Person object using the data entered in the text boxes. The XmlSerializer constructor takes the Person type and then serializes the Person object to a stream. Finally, the stream contents are displayed in a third text box.

Listing 11-13. Serializing the Person Object

```
private void SaveButton_Click(object sender, RoutedEventArgs e)
{
    // Create the Person object with user data
    var person =
        new Person()
        {
            FirstName = FirstNameTextbox.Text,
            LastName = LastNameTextbox.Text
        };

    // create an XmlSerializer for the Person type
    var serializer = new XmlSerializer(typeof(Person));
    // serialize the Person object to XML stored in a stream
    var stream = new MemoryStream();
    serializer.Serialize(stream, person);
```

```
    // extract the XML and display in the textbox
    stream.Position = 0;
    var reader = new StreamReader(stream);
    XmlTextBox.Text = reader.ReadToEnd();
}
```

In Listing 11-14, the Restore button reverses the process by converting the XML text back into a Person object and displaying the object contents.

Listing 11-14. Deserializing the Person Object

```
private void RestoreButton_Click(object sender, RoutedEventArgs e)
{
    // create the XmlSerializer for the Person type
    var serializer = new XmlSerializer(typeof(Person));
    // place the XML text into a stream
    var stream = new MemoryStream(Encoding.UTF8.GetBytes(XmlTextBox.Text));
    // deserialize the stream containing XML to the Person object
    var person = serializer.Deserialize(stream) as Person;
    // Display the reconstituded object in the text boxes
    FirstNameTextbox.Text = person.FirstName;
    LastNameTextbox.Text = person.LastName;
}
```

DataContractSerializer

DataContractSerializer is faster than XmlSerializer, but has fewer options for tweaking the XML output. If you don't need control over the XML format, DataContractSerializer can be swapped for XmlSerializer with only a few changes.

You must mark classes and members to be serialized with attributes from the System.Runtime.Serialization namespace. The ContractPerson class in Listing 11-15 is marked with the DataContract attribute and the properties are marked with the DataMember attribute.

Listing 11-15. The Person Object Marked with DataContract and DataMember Attributes

```
[DataContract]
public class ContractPerson
{
    [DataMember]
    public string FirstName { get; set; }
    [DataMember]
    public string LastName { get; set; }
}
```

Listing 11-16 shows that the DataContractSerializer is used in substantially the same way as XmlSerializer except that DataContractSerializer replaces ReadObject() and WriteObject() methods with XmlSerializer Serialize() and Deserialize().

Listing 11-16. Serializing with DataContractSerializer

```
private void SerializeWith_DataContractSerializer()
{
    // Create the Person object with user data
    var person =
        new ContractPerson()
        {
            FirstName = FirstNameTextbox.Text,
            LastName = LastNameTextbox.Text
        };

    // create an DataContractSerializer( for the Person type
    var serializer = new DataContractSerializer(typeof(ContractPerson));
    // serialize the Person object to XML stored in a stream
    var stream = new MemoryStream();
    serializer.WriteObject(stream, person);
    // extract the XML and display in the textbox
    stream.Position = 0;
    var reader = new StreamReader(stream);
    XmlTextBox.Text = reader.ReadToEnd();
}

private void DeserializeWith_DataContractSerializer()
{
    // create the DataContractSerializer for the Person type
    var serializer = new DataContractSerializer(typeof(ContractPerson));
    // place the XML text into a stream
    var stream = new MemoryStream(Encoding.UTF8.GetBytes(XmlTextBox.Text));
    // deserialize the stream containing XML to the Person object
    var person = serializer.ReadObject(stream) as ContractPerson;
    // Display the reconstituded object in the text boxes
    FirstNameTextbox.Text = person.FirstName;
    LastNameTextbox.Text = person.LastName;
}
```

DataContractJsonSerializer

JavaScript Object Notation (JSON) is the other big player in the data serialization space. Its simplicity and lighter weight makes it a pervasive choice among web services.

JSON serialization is like the previous XML serialization examples except that `DataContractJsonSerializer` from the `System.Runtime.Serialization.Json` namespace performs the heavy lifting. Figure 11-4 shows the deserialized `Person` object in a `TextBox`.

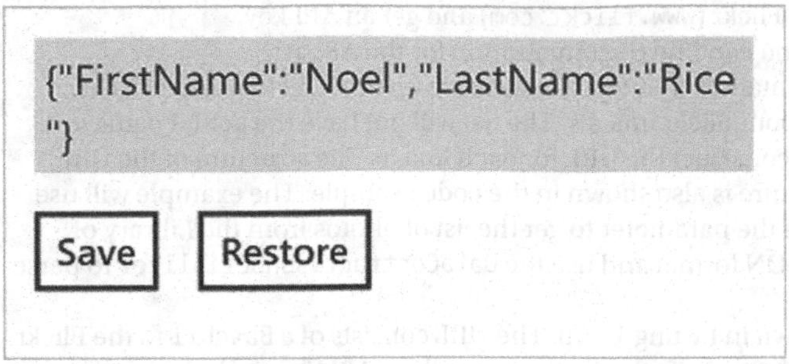

{"FirstName":"Noel","LastName":"Rice
"}

Save Restore

Figure 11-4. Serialized JSON Data

Instead of calling `Serialize()` and `Deserialize()` methods, `DataContractJsonSerializer` uses `WriteObject()` to serialize and `ReadObject()` to de-serialize (see Listing 11-17).

Listing 11-17. Serializing Using DataContractJsonSerializer

```
// Create the Person object with user data
Person person = new Person()
{
    FirstName = FirstNameTextbox.Text,
    LastName = LastNameTextbox.Text
};

// serialize the object to Json form
var serializer = new DataContractJsonSerializer(typeof(Person));
var stream = new MemoryStream();
serializer.WriteObject(stream, person);

// write the Json out to a textbox
stream.Position = 0;
var reader = new StreamReader(stream);
JsonTextBox.Text = reader.ReadToEnd();
```

Consuming Web Resources

`WebClient` and `HttpRequest` objects retrieve XML or JSON data from remote locations on the web, RSS feeds, and web services. `WebClient` is the simpler of the two to use and is handy for one time access to web services or for downloading remote resources. `HttpRequest` is slightly more complex but designed for greater control over content type, headers, cookies and credentials.

WebClient

Use the `WebClient` method `DownloadStringAsync()` to bring down a string of text or `OpenReadAsync()` to retrieve a stream of binary data. In both cases, set up a handler for the completion of the operation and call the appropriate asynchronous method. Before we can call either method, we need to set up the objects and methods that will parse and store the data. In the example that follows, we will pull data from the Flickr API.

To use the Flickr API, you will need to sign up with Flickr (www.flickr.com) and get an API key (http://www.flickr.com/services/apps/create/). You can find documentation for the API at http://www.flickr.com/services/api/. The documentation shows you how to set up the URL for each API call.

The example will pull down a list of information about Flickr images. The list will not have the actual paths to the images, but will include the information needed to construct the URL for each image. The structure of the URL is included in the Flickr documentation. The URL structure is also shown in the code example. The example will use the Flickr getPublicPhotos API method and hard-code the parameter to get the list of photos from the Library of Congress. We will request that the data come back in JSON format and use the DataContractJsonSerializer to parse the data.

The first step is to build the URL for the API as shown in Listing 11-18. The URL consists of a BaseUrl to the Flickr API REST service, followed by a series of query strings that specify the method to call, an API key, and a key to the user that we want photos for. You will need to obtain your API key and insert it into the YourApiKey constant for this example to run correctly.

Listing 11-18. Forming the getPublicPhotos Url

```
private const string BaseUrl = "http://ycpi.api.flickr.com/services/rest/";
private const string QueryStrings =
    "?method={0}&api_key={1}&user_id={2}&format=json&nojsoncallback=1";
private const string FlickrMethod = "flickr.people.getPublicPhotos";
private const string YourApiKey = "<replace with api key here>";
private const string LibraryOfCongressKey = "8623220@N02";
private string FlickrPhotosUrl = BaseUrl +
    String.Format(QueryStrings, FlickrMethod, YourApiKey, LibraryOfCongressKey);
```

The URL returns a JSON string that looks something like Listing 11-19. You can paste the URL into a browser and the browser will return the JSON. You will need this sample of the JSON to work out the next task.

Listing 11-19. A Partial JSON String from the Flickr API

```
{
   "photos":{
      "page":1,
      "pages":193,
      "perpage":100,
      "total":"19222",
      "photo":[
         {
            "id":"9319237625",
            "owner":"8623220@N02",
            "secret":"e0d73d680b",
            "server":"5537",
            "farm":6,. . .
```

The next task is to make C# objects that the DataContractJsonSerializer can populate. You could do this by hand, but fortunately, web sites like json2csharp.com make short work of translating from JSON to C# objects. Navigate to json2csharp.com, paste the JSON in the text box provided, and click the Generate button. A second text box will have a series of C# class definitions. Create a new class named Photo.cs and paste the C# class definitions in the class file. The definition will look something like Listing 11-20. You should generate your own in case the JSON format changes. Notice the top level object named RootObject. DataContractJsonSerializer will use RootObject as the container to deserialize into.

Listing 11-20. The Generated Photo Classes

```
using System.Collections.Generic;

namespace ConsumingXML.Classes
{
    public class Photo
    {
        public string id { get; set; }
        public string owner { get; set; }
        public string secret { get; set; }
        public string server { get; set; }
        public int farm { get; set; }
        public string title { get; set; }
        public int ispublic { get; set; }
        public int isfriend { get; set; }
        public int isfamily { get; set; }
    }

    public class Photos
    {
        public int page { get; set; }
        public int pages { get; set; }
        public int perpage { get; set; }
        public string total { get; set; }
        public List<Photo> photo { get; set; }
    }

    public class RootObject
    {
        public Photos photos { get; set; }
        public string stat { get; set; }
    }
}
```

The classes generated by `json2csharp.com` will have more information than you need and will also not contain the URL to each photo. You will need to create one more class to contain the data that will be bound to a `ListBox` on the page. Listing 11-21 shows the `FlickrPhoto` class that has only the `Title` and `Uri` needed for binding.

Listing 11-21. The FlickrPhoto Class

```
public class FlickrPhoto
{
    public string Title { get; set; }
    public Uri Uri { get; set; }
}
```

Make a method in your main form that returns a List of `FlickrPhoto` objects that can be bound to the main page. Listing 11-22 takes a string of JSON and uses a `DataContractJsonSerializer ReadObject` method to place the data for the entire JSON string into the `RootObject`. Using LINQ statements, you can drill down and get the `RootObject` list of photos and project them into a `List` of `FlickrPhoto`. Notice how the `FlickrPhoto Uri` property is populated with the full URI of each image.

Listing 11-22. Returning a List of FlickrPhoto

```
private static List<FlickrPhoto> GetFlickrPhotos(string json)
{
    const string baseUrl =
        "http://farm{0}.staticflickr.com/{1}/{2}_{3}_s.jpg";

    List<FlickrPhoto> FlickrPhotos = null;
    var serializer = new DataContractJsonSerializer(typeof(RootObject));
    using (var stream = new MemoryStream(Encoding.UTF8.GetBytes(json)))
    {
        var root = serializer.ReadObject(stream) as RootObject;
        FlickrPhotos = (from photo in root.photos.photo
                        select new FlickrPhoto
                        {
                            Title = photo.title,
                            Uri = new Uri(String.Format(baseUrl,
                                photo.farm, photo.server, photo.id, photo.secret))
                        }).ToList();
    }
    return FlickrPhotos;
}
```

The code in Listing 11-23 downloads JSON text using the Flickr API. The `DownloadStringCompleted` event handler is called inline. `Dispatcher.BeginInvoke()` is called inside the event handler to avoid cross thread exceptions while updating the user interface.

Listing 11-23. Using WebClient to Download a String

```
private void UseWebClient()
{
    var uri = new Uri(FlickrPhotosUrl);

    var client = new WebClient();
    client.DownloadStringCompleted += (sender, e) =>
    {
        var photos = GetFlickrPhotos(e.Result);
        Dispatcher.BeginInvoke(() =>
        {
            FlickrListBox.DataContext = photos;
        });
    };
    client.DownloadStringAsync(uri);
}
```

You will need to add a call to `UseWebClient()` from the constructor of `MainPage.xaml.cs`.

The layout for the main page in Listing 11-24 shows the binding of the `Title` property to a `TextBlock` and the `Uri` property to the `Image control's Source` property.

Listing 11-24. The XAML for the Main Page

```
<Grid x:Name="LayoutRoot" >
    <ListBox x:Name="FlickrListBox"
        ItemsSource="{Binding}">
        <ListBox.ItemTemplate>
            <DataTemplate>
                <StackPanel Orientation="Horizontal">
                    <Image Stretch="UniformToFill" Width="100" Height="100"
                        Source="{Binding Uri}" />
                    <TextBlock Grid.Column="1" Margin="10,0,0,0"
                        Text="{Binding Title}"
                        HorizontalAlignment="Stretch" />
                </StackPanel>
            </DataTemplate>
        </ListBox.ItemTemplate>
    </ListBox>
</Grid>
```

The running application shows images from the Library of Congress in the ListBox as shown in Figure 11-5.

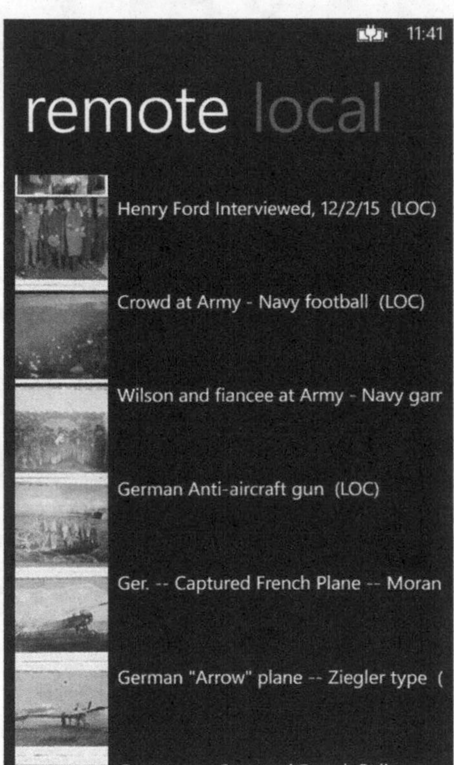

Figure 11-5. *The Listbox Populated with JSON Data*

HttpWebRequest

For conversations involving a resource over HTTP, use the `HttpWebRequest` object. The code in Listing 11-25 calls the static `WebRequest Create()` method. and casts the result to an `HttpWebRequest`. The `HttpWebRequest` object calls the `BeginGetResponse()` method The first parameter is a method with an `AsyncCallback` signature that triggers when the request finishes. The request itself is passed in the second, `state`, parameter of the call.

Listing 11-25. Setting Up the HttpWebRequest

```
var uri = new Uri(FlickrPhotosUrl);
var request = (HttpWebRequest)WebRequest.Create(uri);
request.BeginGetResponse(new AsyncCallback(HandleRequest), request);
```

The handler for `BeginGetResponse()` passes an `AsyncResult`. The `HttpWebRequest` is contained in the `IAsyncResult AsyncState` parameter (see Listing 11-26). Using the `HttpWebRequest`, call the `EndGetResponse()` method. The `HttpWebResponse GetResponseStream()` method brings back the data you requested. In this example we're using a `StreamReader` to get the request data back as a JSON string. Finally, the JSON is again translated into a list of custom `FlickrPhoto` objects.

Listing 11-26. Handling the Request

```
private void HandleRequest(IAsyncResult asyncResult)
{
    var request = asyncResult.AsyncState as HttpWebRequest;
    using (var response =
            (HttpWebResponse)request.EndGetResponse(asyncResult))
    {
        string json = new StreamReader(response.GetResponseStream()).ReadToEnd();
        var photos = GetFlickrPhotos(json);

        Dispatcher.BeginInvoke(() =>
        {
            FlickrListBox.DataContext = photos;
        });
    }
}
```

So how is `HttpWebRequest` a better choice than `WebClient`? If you want to alter the request headers, `HttpWebRequest` properties cover all the standard HTTP headers like `ContentType`, `Accept`, and so on. Some services change their output type based on the HTTP header values instead of query string parameters. Listing 11-27 shows a request to a database service that modifies the `Accept` header to request JSON data.

Listing 11-27. Modifying the Headers

```
var uri =
    new Uri("http://services.odata.org/Northwind/Northwind.svc/Categories");
var request = (HttpWebRequest)WebRequest.Create(uri);
request.Accept = "application/json";
request.BeginGetResponse(new AsyncCallback(HandleRequest), request);
```

Consuming OData

Open Data Protocol (OData) is an HTTP based protocol for querying and updating data. OData services are accessed with simple HTTP, even directly from a browser. The OData standard is published at `www.odata.org`. Sample OData services are at the OData Ecosystem page (`www.odata.org/ecosystem`) on the `Producers` tab. Click the `Browse...` link to navigate the browser to the root URL of the service (see Figure 11-6). The examples in this section will use Stack Overflow, a web site for questions, and answers on programming topics.

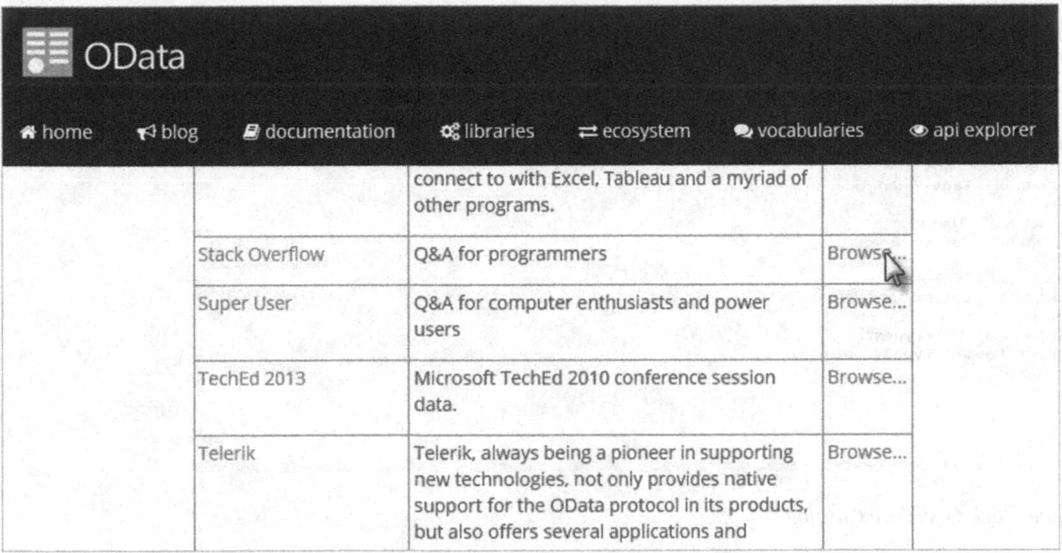

***Figure 11-6.** Browsing an OData Catalog*

After clicking the `Browse...` button, the root URI for Stack Overflow at `data.stackexchange.com/stackoverflow/atom` displays. The web page lists a catalog of collections you can access, such as `Tags`, `Users`, `Posts`, and so on (see Figure 11-7).

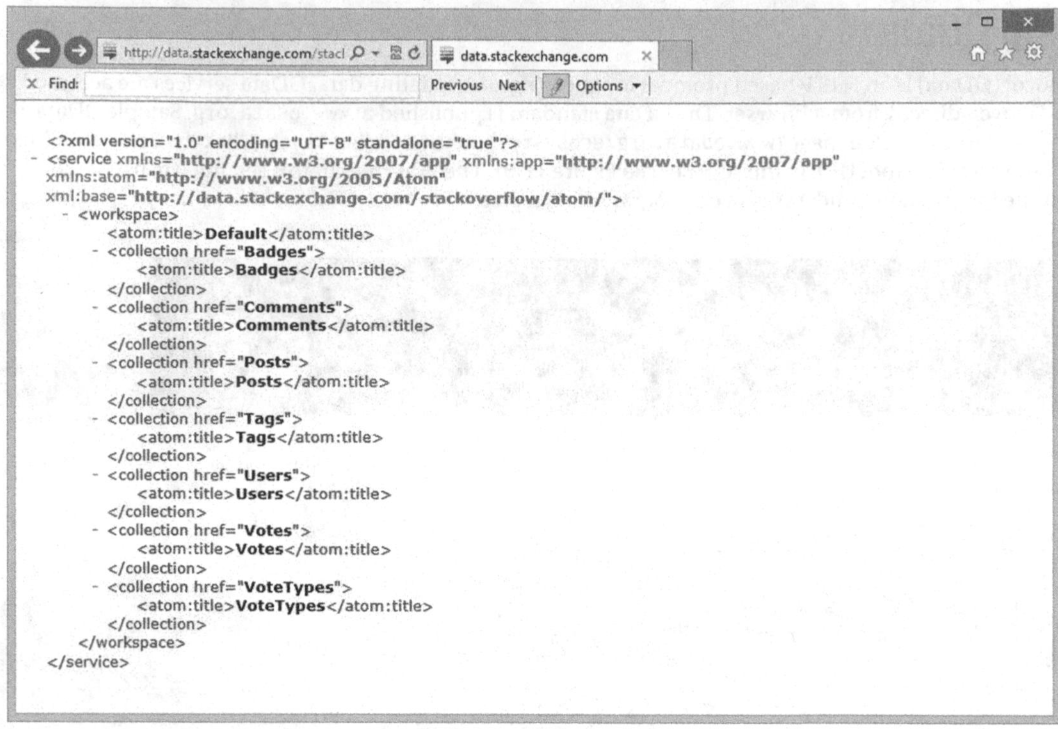

Figure 11-7. *The Stack Overflow Catalog*

Adding a collection name to the root URI pulls back the corresponding data. In this case, appending `Users` to the root URI returns entries for people registered with the service (see Figure 11-8).

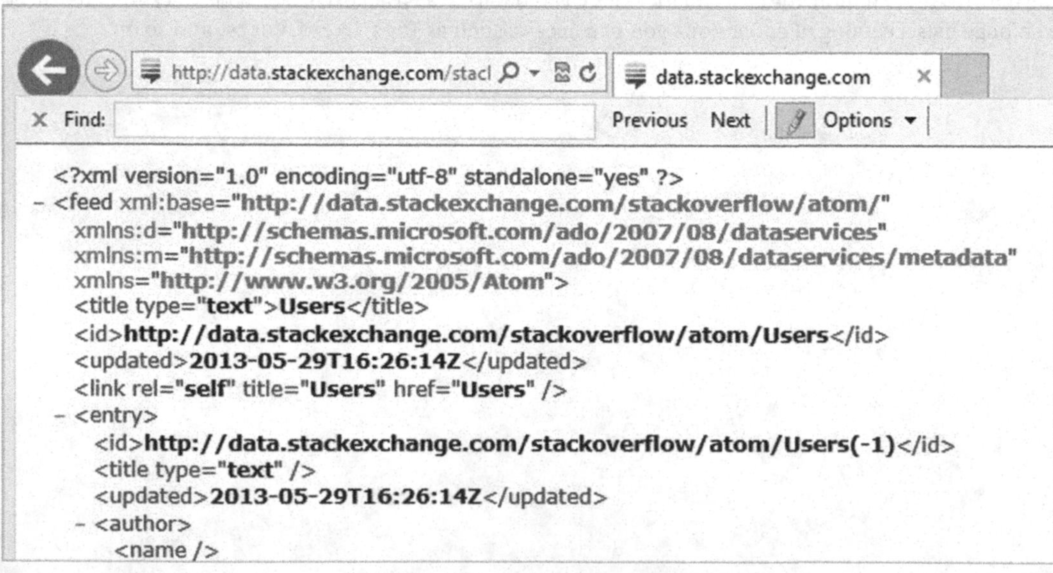

Figure 11-8. *The Users Collection*

Generating a Proxy Class

You could use HttpRequest to bring OData service content back and then use DataContractJsonSerializer to create the objects. In this scenario you would need to create the .NET classes manually. The easier option is to download the OData Client Tools for Windows Phone Apps (www.microsoft.com/en-us/download/details.aspx?id=35461). The installation adds support for adding OData service references in Solution Explorer.

Once the OData Client Tools are installed, right-click the References node in the Solution Explorer and select Add Service Reference... from the context menu. In the Add Service Reference dialog that displays, enter the Address of the service and click the Go button (see Figure 11-9). If the OData Client Tools are installed and the address is valid, you should see a list of Services. To create the proxy class, enter a unique Namespace, and then click the OK button.

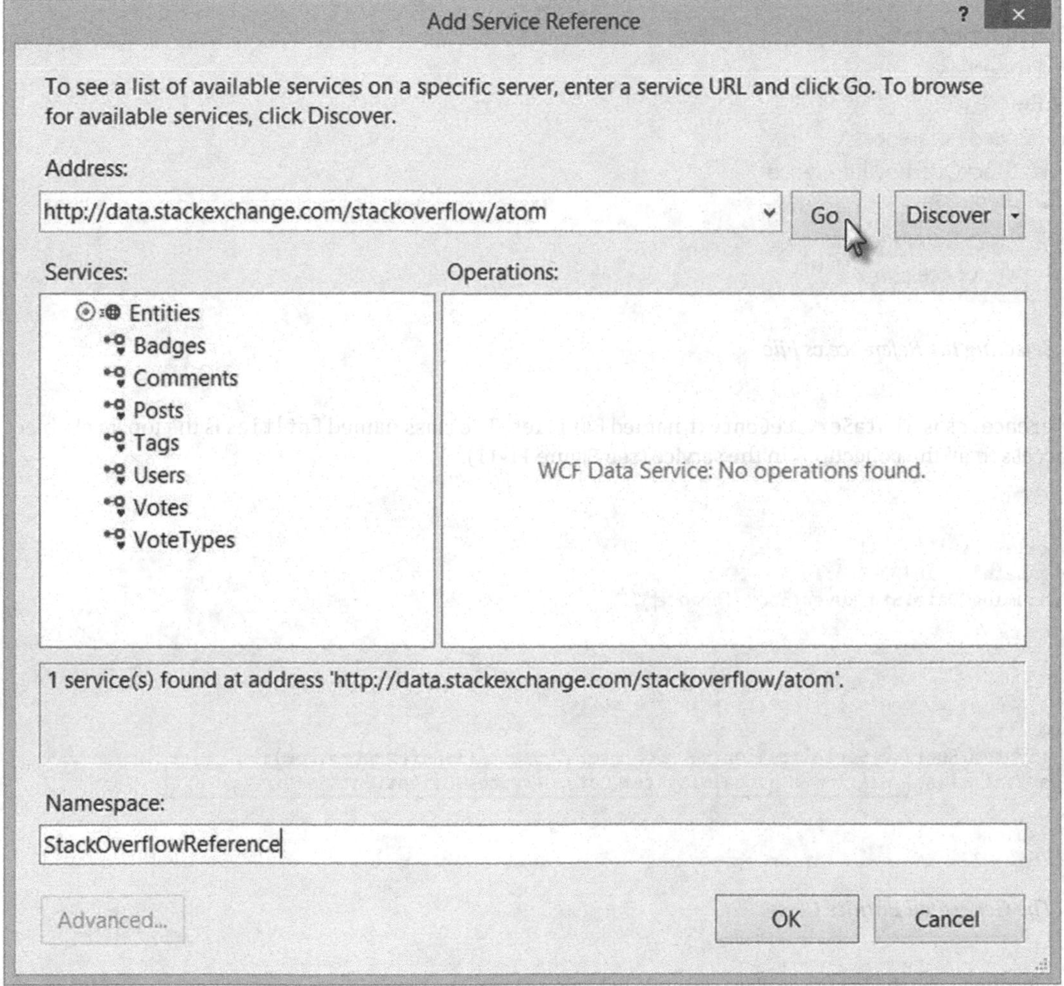

Figure 11-9. *Defining the OData Service Reference*

The class file is generated but you won't be able to see it immediately in the Solution Explorer. Instead, you'll find a new `Service References` node that contains a node with the namespace of the service. To see the generated class file, click the `Show All Files` button in the toolbar of the Solution Explorer. You should now be able to drill down into the namespace node and find a file named `Reference.cs` (see Figure 11-10).

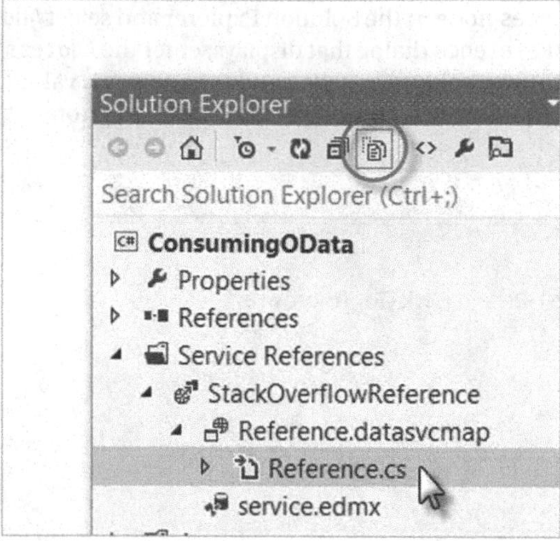

Figure 11-10. *Selecting the Reference.cs File*

Inside `Reference.cs` is a `DataServiceContext` named `Entities`. The class named `Entities` is the top level object that provides access to all the collections in the service (see Figure 11-11).

```
// Original file name:
// Generation date: 5/28/2013 4:10:54 PM
namespace ConsumingOData.StackOverflowReference
{

    /// <summary>
    /// There are no comments for Entities in the schema.
    /// </summary>
    [global::System.Runtime.Serialization.DataContractAttribute(IsReference=true)]
    public partial class Entities : global::System.Data.Services.Client.DataServiceContext
    {
        /// <summary>
        /// Initialize a new Entities object
```

Figure 11-11. *The Generated Entities Class*

The essential code to use the `Entities` class is shown in Listing 11-28. The `Entities` constructor requires a URI to the service. From there you can reach any of the collections from `Entities` instance. In this example, we need a list from the `Users` collection. `Entities.Users` is a `DataServiceQuery`, an implementation of `IQueryable`. As such, `Users` is not populated until the `EndExecute()` method is called with usable results. Also notice the call to `Dispatcher.BeginInvoke()` that places the assignment to the page `DataContext` in the main thread.

Listing 11-28. Using the Entity Class

```
protected override void OnNavigatedTo(NavigationEventArgs e)
{
    base.OnNavigatedTo(e);
    var uri = new Uri("http://data.stackexchange.com/stackoverflow/atom",
        UriKind.Absolute);
    var entities = new Entities(uri);
    entities.Users.BeginExecute((asyncResult) =>
    {
        var query = asyncResult.AsyncState as DataServiceQuery<User>;
        Dispatcher.BeginInvoke(() =>
            {
                this.DataContext = query.EndExecute(asyncResult).ToList();
            });
    }, entities.Users);
}
```

The `Entities` class contains everything you need to display the list of users on the page and acts as a ViewModel. The properties for the individual entities, such as `User`, already have change notification hooked up with implementations of `INotifyPropertyChanging` and `INotifyPropertyChanged`.

At some point you will need to extend `Entities` or one the generated files classes. For example avatars for the Stack Overflow site are stored at a separate site, `www.gravatar.com`. To get the path to the user's avatar, you need to meld the URI with the `User EmailHash` property. You could wrap the `Entities` class in your ViewModel class and hustle all the values over into your own collections. Instead, `Entities` is a partial class that can be extended using a minimal amount of code. The key is to use the ***exact same namespace*** as the generated `Entities` class. Listing 11-29 shows a new `IconPath` property added to the `User` class. The namespace `ConsumingOData.StackOverflowReference` is copied directly from `Reference.cs`.

Listing 11-29. Extending the Partial Class

```
using System;

namespace ConsumingOData.StackOverflowReference
{
    public partial class User : global::System.ComponentModel.INotifyPropertyChanged
    {
        const string path = "http://www.gravatar.com/avatar/{0}?d=identicon&s=64";

        public string IconPath
        {
            get { return String.Format(path, this.EmailHash); }
        }
    }
}
```

Building an OData Client

This example displays a list of users from the Stack Overflow OData service. You need to install the OData Client Tools for Windows Phone Apps (see the preceding "Generating a Proxy Class" section of this chapter for more information) before performing the following steps.

1. Create a new Windows Phone App and name it `ConsumingOData`.
2. Add two 32 × 32 images named `UpArrow.png` and `DownArrow.png` to the `\Assets` directory of the project. These images don't need to be terribly fancy and can be drawn in any paint or drawing program.

■ **Note:** You'll get the best look if the image background is transparent.

---

3. In the Solution Explorer, right-click the `References` node and select `Add Services Reference...` from the context menu.
4. In the `Add Service Reference` dialog, enter the following address: `http://data.stackexchange.com/stackoverflow/atom`. Change the `Namespace` to `StackOverflowReference`. Click the `OK` button.
5. Add a new class named `User.cs` to the project. Edit the class file and add the code in Listing 11-30.

Listing 11-30. Extending the User Class

```
using System;

namespace ConsumingOData.StackOverflowReference
{
    public partial class User : global::System.ComponentModel.INotifyPropertyChanged
    {
        const string iconPath = "http://www.gravatar.com/avatar/{0}?d=identicon&s=64";

        public string IconPath
        {
            get { return String.Format(iconPath, this.EmailHash); }
        }
    }
}
```

■ **Note** If you decide to name the project something other than `ConsumingOData`, the generated `Entities` class name space will be different than the steps described here. If that's the case, click the `Show All Files` button, navigate to the `Reference.cs` file, and copy the namespace. Use this same namespace as the namespace for the `User` partial class. See the "Generating a Proxy Class" section of this chapter for more information.

---

6. In the code-behind for `MainPage.xaml.cs`, include the `using` statements from Listing 11-31.

Listing 11-31. Including Using Statements

```
using System;
using System.Data.Services.Client;
using System.Linq;
using System.Windows;
using System.Windows.Navigation;
using ConsumingOData.StackOverflowReference;
using Microsoft.Phone.Controls;
```

7. In the code-behind for `MainPage.xaml.cs`, override the `OnNavigatedTo()` method using the code in Listing 11-32.

Listing 11-32. Overriding the OnNavigatedTo() Method

```
protected override void OnNavigatedTo(NavigationEventArgs e)
{
    base.OnNavigatedTo(e);

    var uri = new Uri("http://data.stackexchange.com/stackoverflow/atom",
       UriKind.Absolute);
    var entities = new Entities(uri);
    entities.Users.BeginExecute((asyncResult) =>
    {
        Deployment.Current.Dispatcher.BeginInvoke(() =>
        {
            var query = asyncResult.AsyncState as DataServiceQuery<User>;
            this.DataContext = query.EndExecute(asyncResult)
                .ToList();
        });
    }, entities.Users);
}
```

8. In the XAML view of `MainPage.xaml`, add a `Resources` element inside the `Grid` named `ContentPanel` as shown in Listing 11-33.

Listing 11-33. Adding Resources to ContentPanel

```
<Grid x:Name="ContentPanel" Grid.Row="1" Margin="12,0,12,0">
    <Grid.Resources>

    </Grid.Resources>
</Grid>
```

9. Inside the `Resources` tag, add a resource that defines the `DataTemplate` named `UserRowTemplate` as shown in Listing 11-34.

Listing 11-34. Defining the DataTemplate

```
<DataTemplate x:Key="UserRowTemplate">
    <Grid>
        <Grid.ColumnDefinitions>
            <ColumnDefinition Width="Auto"  />
            <ColumnDefinition Width="Auto"  />
```

```
                <ColumnDefinition Width="Auto"  />
                <ColumnDefinition Width="Auto"  />
                <ColumnDefinition Width="Auto"  />
                <ColumnDefinition Width="Auto" />
            </Grid.ColumnDefinitions>
            <Grid.RowDefinitions>
                <RowDefinition Height="*" />
                <RowDefinition Height="*" />
            </Grid.RowDefinitions>
            <Image Stretch="UniformToFill" Source="{Binding IconPath}"
                    Width="64" Height="64" Grid.RowSpan="2"
                    Margin="0,10,20,10" VerticalAlignment="Center" />
            <TextBlock Text="{Binding DisplayName}" Margin="0,10,0,0"
                    Grid.Column="1" Grid.ColumnSpan="5"
                    Style="{StaticResource PhoneTextAccentStyle}"/>
            <TextBlock Text="{Binding Views, StringFormat=Views: \{0\}}"
                    Grid.Row="2" Grid.Column="1" Margin="0,0,5,0"
                    VerticalAlignment="Top" />
            <Image Stretch="UniformToFill"  Width="32" Height="32"
                    Source="/Assets/UpArrow.png" Grid.Row="2" Grid.Column="2"
                    VerticalAlignment="Top" />
            <TextBlock Text="{Binding UpVotes}" Grid.Row="2" Grid.Column="3"
                    Margin="0,0,5,0"  VerticalAlignment="Top"/>
            <Image Stretch="UniformToFill" Width="32" Height="32"
                    Source="/Assets/DownArrow.png" Grid.Row="2" Grid.Column="4"
                    VerticalAlignment="Top" />
            <TextBlock Text="{Binding DownVotes}" Grid.Row="2" Grid.Column="5"
                    Margin="0,0,5,0" VerticalAlignment="Top" />
        </Grid>
    </DataTemplate>
```

10. Add a LongListSelector from the Toolbox to the Grid just below the Resources declaration as shown in Listing 11-35. {Binding} is assigned to the ItemsSource property to make the List of User objects available to the LongListSelector. ItemTemplate is assigned a resource named UserRowTemplate.

Listing 11-35. Binding the LongListSelector

```
<phone:LongListSelector ItemsSource="{Binding}"
                        ItemTemplate="{StaticResource UserRowTemplate}"/>
```

Figure 11-12 shows the running application with the bound Entities User data from the References.cs class file.

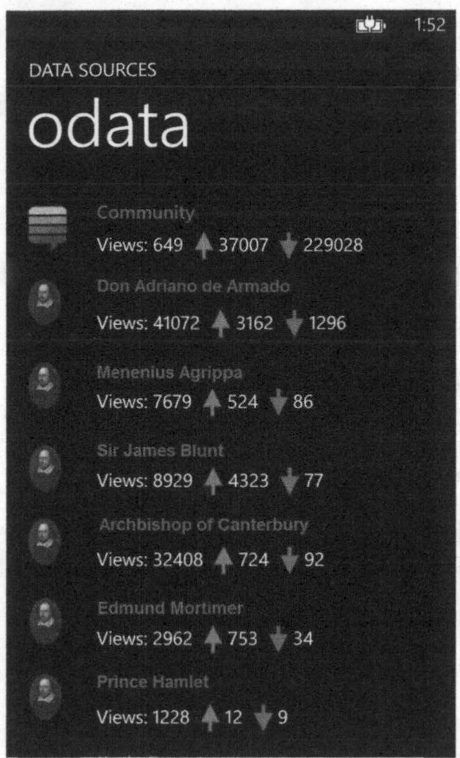

Figure 11-12. *The Running OData Application*

Using a Local Database

Not all scenarios fit well with remote services, serialized objects, or local storage with simple files. A local SQL database makes better sense for complex schema, simple schema with large amounts of data or local caching of structured data.

In Windows Phone 8, the local database is based on Microsoft SQL Server Compact edition (SQL CE) and accessed through LINQ to SQL. Instead of directly executing SQL statements such as `INSERT INTO MYTABLE`, you get to work with plain old .NET objects—LINQ to SQL provides the plumbing back to the database. The key tasks to building a database and performing operations on data include:

1. Build data model objects and decorate these with attributes from the `System.Data.Linq.Mapping` namespace. This step describes the tables and columns in the database.
2. Create a data context object that represents the database. This object connects to the actual database in local storage and is responsible for performing all database operations.
3. Create the database if it doesn't exist. This happens as the application is constructed. Your application can include code to version the database or migrate the data.
4. Perform CRUD (Create, Read, Update, and Delete) operations on the data.

Building a Data Model

You can start working with LINQ to SQL using a single class or "entity" that corresponds to a table in the database. Listing 11-36 defines a simple Juice class with Id and Name properties.

Listing 11-36. Defining the Juice Class

```
public class Juice
{
    public int Id { get; set; }
    public string Name { get; set; }
}
```

To prepare the Juice class to participate in LINQ to SQL operations, you must decorate it with the Table attribute from the System.Data.Linq.Mapping namespace (see Listing 11-37). Also, mark each property you want to persist to the database with the Column attribute. Notice how the Column parameters for the Id property describe how the field should be treated by the database, namely, that Id is a primary key, generated by the database and is a non-null identity field.

Listing 11-37. Decorating the Juice Class

```
[Table]
public class Juice
{
    [Column(IsPrimaryKey = true,
        IsDbGenerated = true,
        DbType = "INT NOT NULL Identity",
        CanBeNull = false)]
    public int Id { get; set; }
    [Column]
    public string Name { get; set; }
    [Column]
    public string Description { get; set; }
}
```

Creating a Data Context

DataContext from the System.Data.Linq namespace (not to be confused with the DataContext property of FrameworkElement) handles database creation, deletion, and pushing changes out to the database. The act of constructing this object creates the actual database as a file with an sdf extension in isolated storage. The root of the data source path is either isostore (located in isolated storage) or appdata (located in the installation folder).

The DataContext tracks one or more data model objects. In Listing 11-38, the Juices table property is part of the JuiceDataContext. Objects must be "in context" to be updated by the database. From your programming perspective, the Juices table is a collection that you can insert items to, delete items from, and bind to elements in the user interface.

Listing 11-38. Defining the DataContext

```
public class JuiceDataContext : DataContext
{
    public const string ConnectionString = @"Data Source=isostore:/Juice.sdf";

    public JuiceDataContext(string connectionString)
        : base(connectionString) { }

    public Table<Juice> Juices;
}
```

Creating the Database

Now that you have the basic database infrastructure in place, you need to create the database for the first time. In the constructor of the application, create an instance of the `DataContext`, passing the connection string in the constructor (see Listing 11-39). The first time the application runs, the database doesn't exist and is created.

Listing 11-39. Creating the Database

```
using (var context = new JuiceDataContext(JuiceDataContext.ConnectionString))
{
    if (!context.DatabaseExists())
    {
        context.CreateDatabase();
    }
}
```

Performing CRUD Operations

CRUD (Create, Read, Update, and Delete) operations follow a common pattern:

1. Get a `DataContext` instance.
2. Insert or delete objects from a collection in the data context. Updates are handled by changing object properties.
3. Call `SubmitChanges()` to push changes to the underlying database.

To insert a new object, for example, create the object and populate its properties, call the collection's `InsertOnSubmit()` method, and finally call `SubmitChanges()` to persist your changes to the database (see Listing 11-40).

Listing 11-40. Inserting a New Object

```
using (var context =  new JuiceDataContext(JuiceDataContext.ConnectionString))
{
    // create the object
    var juice = new Juice()
      {
        Name = "Mango Tango Infusion"
      };
    // place the object in pending insert state
    context.Juices.InsertOnSubmit(juice);
    // commit the changes to the database
    context.SubmitChanges();
}
```

The Table collection supports the IEnumerable interface, so listing the objects from one of the tables is a matter of binding the collection to an ItemsSource (see Listing 11-41).

Listing 11-41. Binding the Table Collection

```
using (var context = new JuiceDataContext(
    JuiceDataContext.ConnectionString))
{
    JuiceListBox.ItemsSource = context.Juices;
    JuiceListBox.DisplayMemberPath = "Name";
}
```

Figure 11-13 shows a ListBox bound to the Table<Juice> collection.

Figure 11-13. *Table Collection Items in a ListBox*

To update the data, simply change the object properties and call the DataContext SubmitChanges() method (see Listing 11-42).

Listing 11-42. Updating Items in the Table Collection

```
using (var context = new JuiceDataContext(JuiceDataContext.ConnectionString))
{
    var mangoFlavors = context.Juices
        .Where(j => j.Name.ToLower().Contains("mango"))
        .Select(j => j);
    foreach (Juice juice in mangoFlavors)
        juice.Name = "Bombay Mango";
    context.SubmitChanges();
}
```

To delete an object, pass the object to the DeleteOnSubmit() method of the Table, then call the SubmitChanges() method. The example in Listing 11-43 gets the name of the currently selected object in the ListBox and then locates the object in the corresponding Table of the DataContext. The collection's DeleteOnSubmit() method is called, followed by the call to the data context SubmitChanges() method. Finally, the Juice object instance is removed from the collection.

Listing 11-43. Deleting an Item from the Table

```
if (JuiceListBox.SelectedItem != null)
{
    // get the selected object
    var juice = JuiceListBox.SelectedItem as Juice;

    using (var context = new JuiceDataContext(JuiceDataContext.ConnectionString))
    {
        // place in pending delete state
        var juiceToDelete = context.Juices
            .Where(j => j.Id.Equals(juice.Id))
            .Single() as Juice;
        context.Juices.DeleteOnSubmit(juiceToDelete);

        // commit the changes to the database
        context.SubmitChanges();

        // sync object to the observable collection
        (JuiceListBox.ItemsSource as ObservableCollection<Juice>).Remove(juice);
    }
}
```

Building a Local Database Application

The example that follows builds an application that lists blended juice drinks. This data is stored and retrieved from the local database.

1. Create a new Windows Phone 8 App.
2. Install the Windows Phone Toolkit. See the section "Installing the Windows Phone 8 Toolkit" in Chapter 4 for more information on installing the toolkit for a project.
3. In Solution Explorer, add a directory named `Classes`.
4. Add a new class file to the `Classes` directory named `Juice.cs`. Define the class with properties for `Id` and `Name` and decorated with `Table` and `Column` attributes as shown in Listing 11-44.

    Listing 11-44. Decorating the Juice Class

    ```
    [Table]
    public class Juice
    {
        [Column(IsPrimaryKey = true,
            IsDbGenerated = true,
            DbType = "INT NOT NULL Identity",
            CanBeNull = false)]
        public int Id { get; set; }
        [Column]
        public string Name { get; set; }
    }
    ```

5. Add a new class file named `JuiceDataContext.cs` to the `Classes` directory and define the class as shown in Listing 11-45.

Listing 11-45. Defining the DataContext

```
public class JuiceDataContext : DataContext
{
    public const string ConnectionString = @"Data Source=isostore:/Juice.sdf";

    public JuiceDataContext(string connectionString)
        : base(connectionString) { }

    public Table<Juice> Juices;
}
```

6. Add the code in Listing 11-46 to the `App.xaml.cs` file to the end of the `App` class constructor.

Listing 11-46. Creating the Database

```
using (var context = new JuiceDataContext(JuiceDataContext.ConnectionString))
{
    if (!context.DatabaseExists())
    {
        context.CreateDatabase();
    }
}
```

7. Open `Main.xaml` for editing and replace the `Grid` named `ContentPanel` with the XAML in Listing 11-47. Note that you can use a `PhoneTextBox` from the Windows Phone Toolkit or just a standard `TextBox` control. See the section "Installing the Windows Phone 8 Toolkit" in Chapter 4 for more information on installing the toolkit for a project. The `PhoneTextBox` just adds the `Hint` property.

Listing 11-47. Defining the ContentPanel Grid

```
<Grid x:Name="ContentPanel" Grid.Row="1" Margin="12,0,12,0">
    <Grid.RowDefinitions>
        <RowDefinition Height="Auto" />
        <RowDefinition Height="Auto" />
        <RowDefinition Height="*" />
    </Grid.RowDefinitions>
    <toolkit:PhoneTextBox x:Name="JuiceNameTextBox"
        Grid.Row="0" Hint="Enter Juice Name" />

    <ListBox x:Name="JuiceListBox" Grid.Row="2" >
        <ListBox.ItemTemplate>
            <DataTemplate>
                <StackPanel>
                    <TextBlock Text="{Binding Name}" />
                </StackPanel>
            </DataTemplate>
        </ListBox.ItemTemplate>
    </ListBox>
</Grid>
```

8. At the end of the page, inside the PhoneApplicationPage tag, add the markup shown in Listing 11-48 to define the application bar.

Listing 11-48. Adding the Application Bar

```
<phone:PhoneApplicationPage.ApplicationBar>
    <shell:ApplicationBar IsVisible="True" IsMenuEnabled="True">
        <shell:ApplicationBarIconButton
            IconUri="/Assets/AppBar/add.png"
            Text="Add"
            Click="AddClick" />
        <shell:ApplicationBarIconButton
            IconUri="/Assets/AppBar/delete.png"
            Text="Delete"
            Click="DeleteClick" />
    </shell:ApplicationBar>
</phone:PhoneApplicationPage.ApplicationBar>
```

9. The images referenced in Listing 11-48 don't exist yet, so place the cursor in the XAML for the first button, navigate to the Properties window, and select add.png from the IconUri property drop-down list selector. Repeat this step for the second button and select the delete.png image. Both images should now be created in the /Assets/AppBar directory.

10. In the code-behind for MainPage.xaml.cs, add the namespaces from Listing 11-49 to your using statements.

Listing 11-49. Adding Using Statements

```
using System;
using System.Collections.ObjectModel;
using System.Linq;
using LocalDatabase.Classes;
using Microsoft.Phone.Controls;
```

11. Add private members for the data context and an observable collection of Juice objects as shown in Listing 11-50.

Listing 11-50. Declaring the Data Context and Collection

```
private JuiceDataContext _context;
private ObservableCollection<Juice> _juices;
```

12. Override the page OnNavigatedTo() method as shown in Listing 11-51. This step will initialize the data context, retrieve the Juices table collection and assign the collection to the ListBox ItemsSource property.

Listing 11-51. Overriding the OnNavigatedTo() Method

```
protected override void OnNavigatedTo(System.Windows.Navigation.NavigationEventArgs e)
{
    base.OnNavigatedTo(e);

    // create the DataContext to manage database
    _context = new JuiceDataContext(JuiceDataContext.ConnectionString);
```

```
        // create observable collection to display in UI
        _juices = new ObservableCollection<Juice>(
            _context.Juices);
        JuiceListBox.ItemsSource = _juices;
    }
```

13. Override the page `OnNavigatedFrom()` method as shown in Listing 11-52. This step will clean up after the data context.

Listing 11-52. Overriding the OnNavigatedFrom( ) Method

```
protected override void OnNavigatedFrom(System.Windows.Navigation.NavigationEventArgs e)
{
    // cleanup after the DataContext
    _context.Dispose();
    _context = null;

    base.OnNavigatedFrom(e);
}
```

14. Implement the `AddClick()` method of the application toolbar as shown in Listing 11-53.

Listing 11-53. Implementing the AddClick( ) Method

```
private void AddClick(object sender, EventArgs e)
{
    // avoid added the same name twice
    bool juiceExists = _juices
        .Any(j => j.Name.Equals(JuiceNameTextBox.Text));

    if (!juiceExists)
    {
        // create the object
        var juice = new Juice()
        {
            Name = JuiceNameTextBox.Text,
        };
        // place the object in pending insert state
        _context.Juices.InsertOnSubmit(juice);
        // commit the changes to the database
        _context.SubmitChanges();

        // sync object to the observable collection
        _juices.Add(juice);
        JuiceNameTextBox.Text = String.Empty;
    }
}
```

15. Implement the DeleteClick() method of the application toolbar as shown in Listing 11-54.

Listing 11-54. Implementing the DeleteClick( ) Method

```
private void DeleteClick(object sender, EventArgs e)
{
    if (JuiceListBox.SelectedItem != null)
    {
        // get the selected object
        var juice = JuiceListBox.SelectedItem as Juice;

        if (!_context.Juices.Any(j => j.Equals(juice)))
        {
            // associate the object with the context
            _context.Juices.Attach(juice);
        }

        // place in pending delete state
        _context.Juices.DeleteOnSubmit(juice);
        // commit the changes to the database
        _context.SubmitChanges();

        // sync object to the observable collection
        _juices.Remove(juice);
    }
}
```

Run the application. You should be able to enter new names into the text box at the top of the page and click the plus button to add them (see Figure 11-14). You should be able to quit and restart the application to view the items persisted in the local database. You should also be able to select items and click the delete icon to remove them.

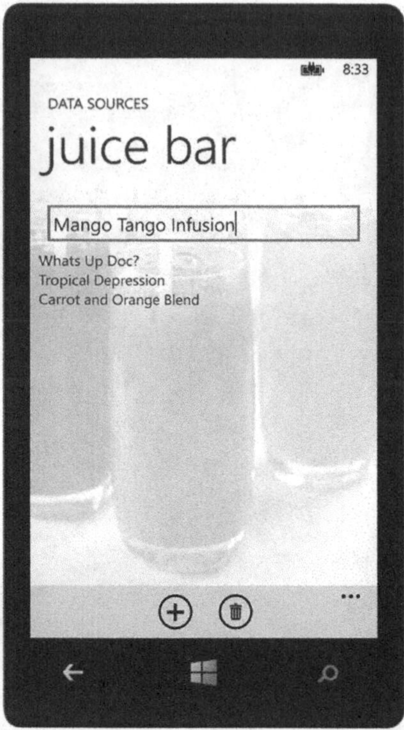

Figure 11-14. *Running the Local Database Application*

If you use the Emulator to test, be aware that if you completely close the Emulator application (not just the local database application), that will erase any local database you've created.

The running application shows an image faintly in the background. This effect is achieved by adding an `ImageBrush` to the `Grid` Background, using a jpg as the background image and setting the `Opacity` property to 20% to make the image very faint (see Listing 11-55).

Listing 11-55. Painting the Background

```
<Grid x:Name="LayoutRoot" >
    <Grid.Background>
        <ImageBrush Opacity="0.2"
            ImageSource="/Assets/drinks.jpg"
            Stretch="UniformToFill" />
    </Grid.Background>
    . . .
```

Versioning the Database

The shining moment comes when new columns are added to the data model and version 2.0 rolls off the line. New downloads of the application are no problem, because the database is created fresh along with new tables and columns. Existing database installations are another issue altogether because the new column needs to be tucked in without disturbing user data.

When you need to alter existing databases, use the `DatabaseSchemaUpdater` class to add tables, columns, indexes, and associations to the database, and to update the database version.

In this next example we're adding a new Description column to the Juice table. Listing 11-56 shows a JuiceDB class with a single static InitializeLocalDatabase() method that modifies and versions the database. If the database doesn't exist, it's created. The DataContext CreateDatabaseSchemaUpdater() method retrieves an instance of the DatabaseSchemaUpdater. The DatabaseSchemaVersion property is checked to verify it's the latest version. If the version is prior to v.2, then the updater object AddColumn() method creates the new Description column in the database. The new Description property must already exist in the model object and the Column attribute for the new property must allow null (this is the default setting).

Listing 11-56. The JuiceDB Class Definition

```
public class JuiceDB
{
    private const int DatabaseVersion = 2;

    public static void InitializeLocalDatabase()
    {
        using (JuiceDataContext context = new
            JuiceDataContext(JuiceDataContext.ConnectionString))
        {
            if (!context.DatabaseExists())
            {
                context.CreateDatabase();

                // set version here, still works when
                // a new database is created with a later version
                var updater = context.CreateDatabaseSchemaUpdater();
                updater.DatabaseSchemaVersion = DatabaseVersion;
                updater.Execute();
            }
            else
            {
                var updater = context.CreateDatabaseSchemaUpdater();

                if (updater.DatabaseSchemaVersion < 2)
                {
                    updater.AddColumn<Juice>("JuiceDescription");
                }
                updater.DatabaseSchemaVersion = DatabaseVersion;
                updater.Execute();
            }
        }
    }
}
```

Once you're done adding schema changes using the updater, set the DatabaseSchemaVersion and call Execute() to submit all schema changes to the database in a single transaction.

Summary

Windows Phone 8 works with a variety of data sources and data types. In particular, we looked at serializing XML and JSON data, consuming web resources at a variety of levels including raw requests of files and RSS feeds. With the help of OData Client Tools for Windows Phone Apps, we were able to interact with an OData service through a proxy client object. LINQ to SQL allowed us to build a local database and perform CRUD operations.

CHAPTER 12

Using Data in the Cloud

Unless you live out in the sticks, you probably buy electricity from a power company rather than run your own generator. Likewise, the "Cloud" delivers computing infrastructure as a service rather than a product. The physical servers, storage, connectivity, IT staff, planning, provisioning, and management infrastructure all live somewhere else but are controlled by you.

Why is that good for your organization? Isn't buying better than renting?

Let's say you are about to deliver a groundbreaking application, "Slightly Incensed Fowl", to the market. You estimate server traffic patterns, order servers, hire IT staff, build a support website, and get ready for the deluge of "SIF" downloads. Due to a parts shortage, the servers arrive two weeks late and a competitor brings "Mildly Perturbed Penguins" to market a week before your debut. Initial interest is low, your IT staff has nothing to do and the servers sit idle. A month later Lady Gargle declares she's addicted to the game, traffic spikes and now you're scrambling again.

Slow time to market, slow reaction to change, over provisioning, and under provisioning all cost your organization and can be mitigated with Cloud services.

The Microsoft Windows Azure Platform cloud services promises that you can "deploy in your own data center" and... "build, host and scale applications in Microsoft data centers with no up-front expenses and pay only for the resources you use."

Windows Azure Mobile in particular has lots of Windows Phone 8 developer goodies for hosting services in the cloud where your customers can reach them anytime, anywhere in the world. This chapter will focus on using Windows Azure Mobile Services to work with tables and to provide push notifications, all from the cloud.

Getting Started With Windows Azure

You will need a Windows Azure account to create Azure databases and mobile services.Windows Azure has a free, one-month trial at `www.windowsazure.com/en-us/pricing/free-trial/` (at the time of this writing). Once you're logged in to your account, you can navigate to the Windows Azure dashboard (`https://manage.windowsazure.com/#Workspaces/All/dashboard`) where you can create and manage services and data in the cloud (see Figure 12-1).

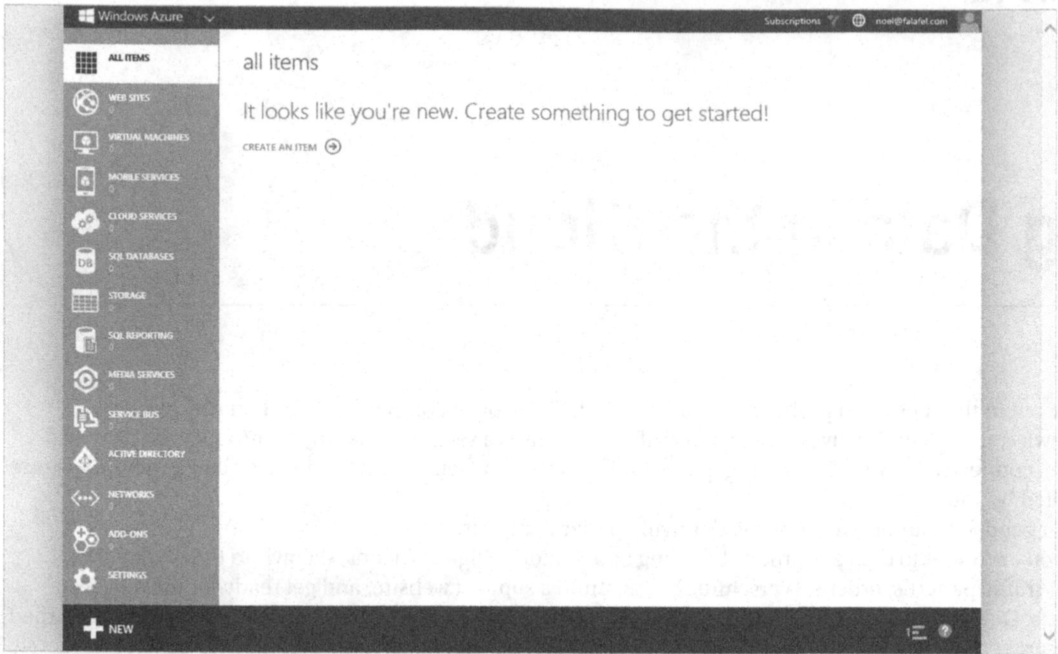

Figure 12-1. *The Azure Dashboard*

Mobile Serviceshas a nice feature where you can create a quick example SQL Server database with a "To Do" list table, a mobile service that knows how to talk with the database and also generates a Windows Phone 8 solution that you can download. This feature gets you up-and-running in a short time with a sample table and code to access the table.

1. Navigate your browser to the Windows Azure dashboard at `https://manage.windowsazure.com/#Workspaces/All/dashboard`.
2. Click the `Mobile Services` node (see Figure 12-2).

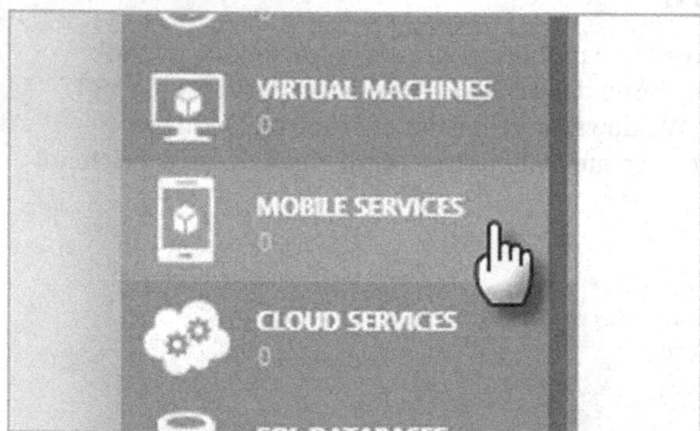

Figure 12-2. *Selecting the Mobile Services Dashboard Option*

3. Click the `CREATE A NEW MOBILE SERVICE` link (see Figure 12-3). This will display the `NEW Mobile Service` dialog.

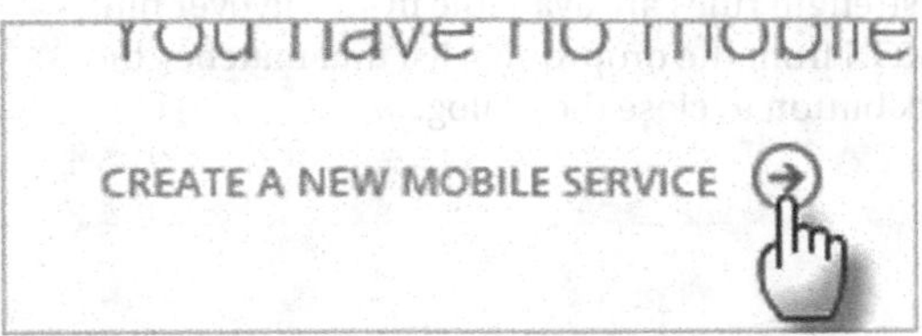

Figure 12-3. *Creating the New Mobile Service*

4. On the `Create aMobile Service` page, enter a unique URL. In this example (see Figure 12-4), the URL is `ApressProject`. The name forms the domain portion of a URL that is created automatically by Azure. Choose a `DATABASE` option from the drop-down list. Select your SUBSCRIPTION from the drop-down list (this will vary depending on if you are using the trial subscription, `Pay-As-You-Go` or one of the other Azure account payment plans). Finally, choose the `REGION` where your service will be hosted. Click the right-arrow button to continue.

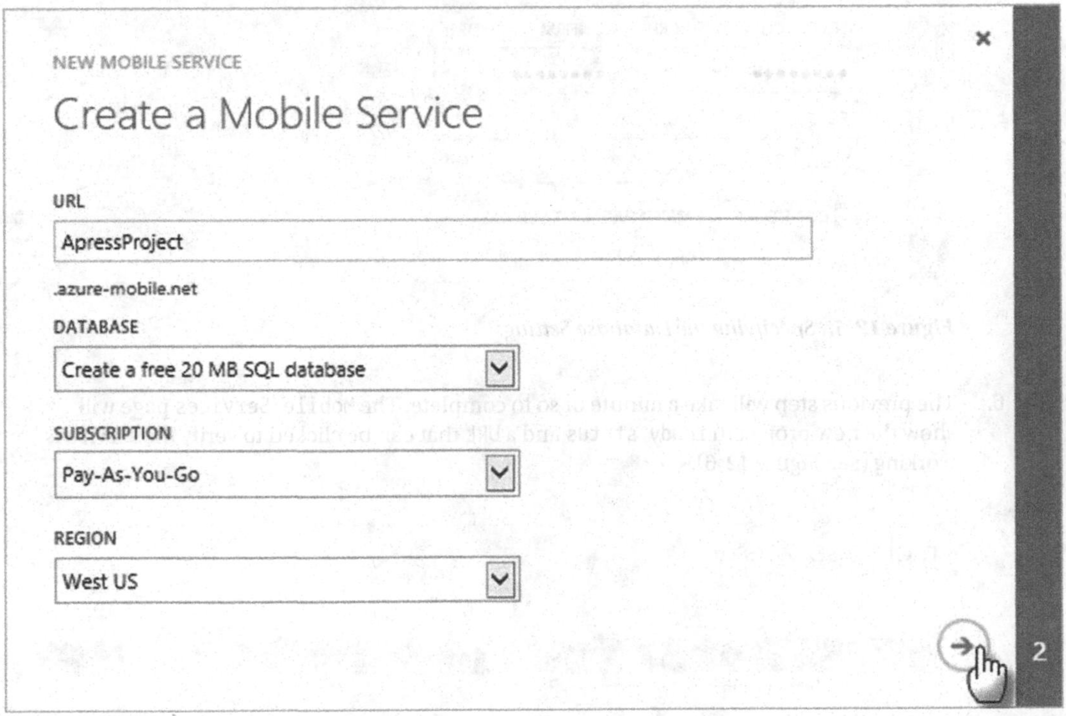

Figure 12-4. *The New Mobile Service Dialog*

5. In the `Specify database settings` page of the dialog (see Figure 12-5), leave the `NAME` at its default setting. Select `New SQL database server` from the `SERVER` drop-down list. Provide the `SERVER LOGIN NAME` that you want to use, and then enter a `SERVER LOGIN PASSWORD` and confirmation. The password strength rules are available from a flyover hint when there is an error. Finally, select a REGION from the drop-down list that matches the region for your service. Click the check mark button to close the dialog.

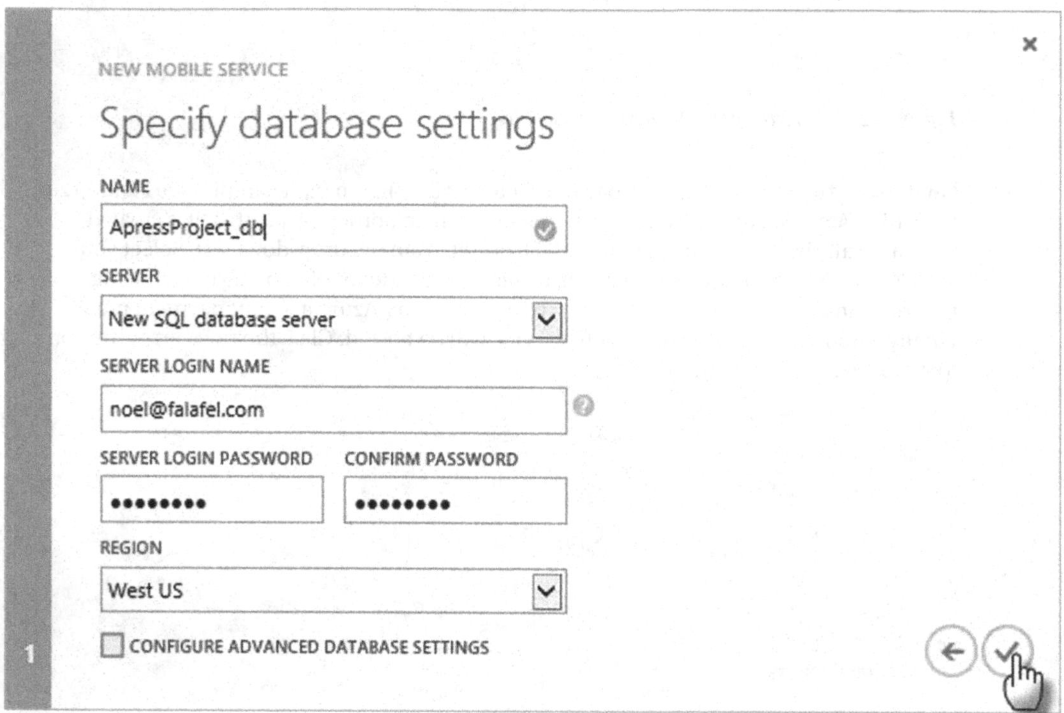

Figure 12-5. *Specifying the Database Settings*

6. The previous step will take a minute or so to complete. The `Mobile Services` page will show the new project in `ready status` and a `URL` that can be clicked to verify the service is working (see Figure 12-6).

mobile services PREVIEW

NAME	STATUS	SUBSCRIPTION	URL
ApressProject	Ready	Pay-As-You-Go	https://apressproject.azure-mobile.net/

Figure 12-6. *The New Mobile Service*

7. Still on the `Mobile Services` page, click the project link in the NAME column. This will take you to a quick start page where you can generate a new sample Windows Phone 8 application.

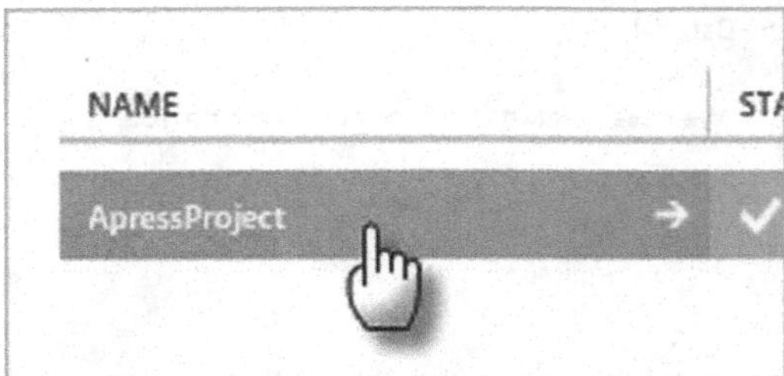

Figure 12-7. *Selecting the Mobile Service*

8. On the quick start page of the mobile service, select the `Windows Phone 8` platform button, and then click the `CREATE A NEW WINDOWS PHONE 8 APP` link (see Figure 12-8).

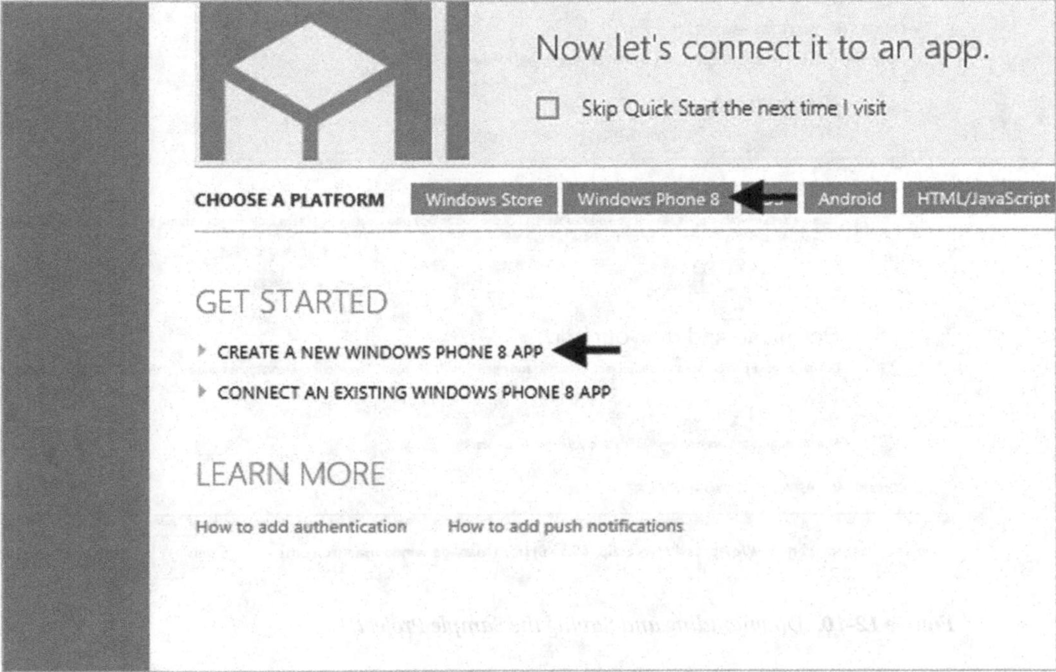

Figure 12-8. *Creating a New Windows Phone 8 App*

9. A list of three steps should now be displayed below the `CREATE A NEW WINDOWS PHONE 8 APP` link. You can skip the first step called `Get the tools`, assuming you already have Visual Studio 2012 installed. In step 2, `Create a Table`, click the `Create TodoItem Table` button (see Figure 12-9).

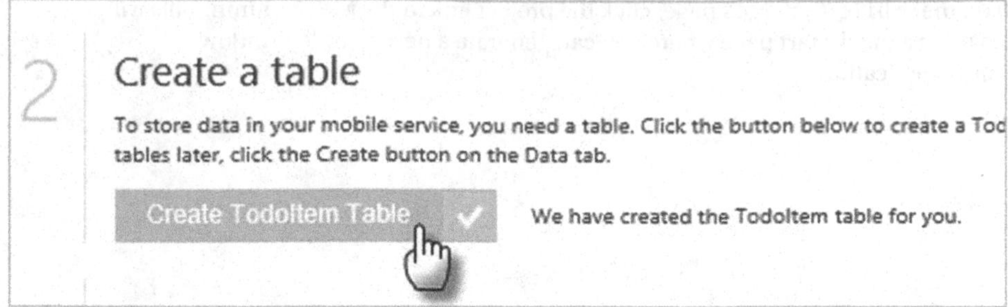

Figure 12-9. *Creating the Table*

10. In step 3, `Download and run your app`, click the `Download` button (see Figure 12-10). A Visual Studio solution that knows how to talk to the service and the database will be downloaded in zip format to your PC.Save and unzip this file on your PC.

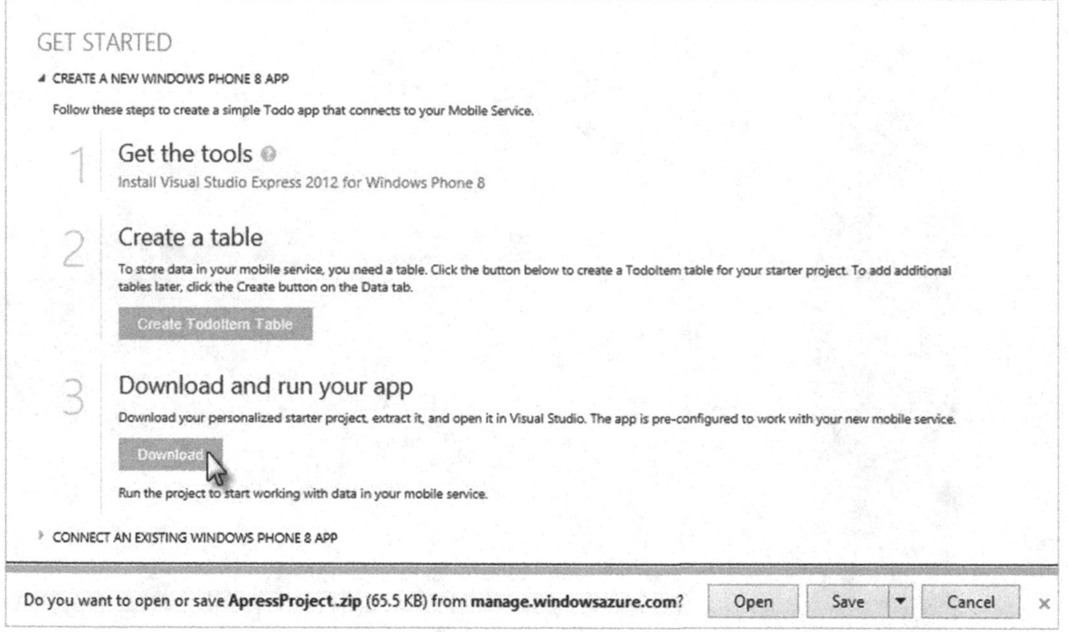

Figure 12-10. *Downloading and Saving the Sample Project*

11. Open the unzipped folder created in the previous step. You will find the Visual Studio Solution, project folder, and NuGet packages that contain the Windows Azure Mobile Services SDK.

12. Open the solution in Visual Studio.

13. From the main Visual Studio menu open `Options` ➤ `Tools`. Select the `Package Manager` node and make sure that the `Allow NuGet to download missing packages during build` check box is selected.

14. Make sure you have an internet connectionon the Emulator or physical device. You can run Internet Explorer to verify this.

15. Press F5 to run the application. The running application will allow you to add new items and to check them off (see Figure 12-11).

***Figure 12-11.** The Running Azure Client Application*

A Closer Look

What did we learnfrom the sample project that we can reuse? First, that the NuGet package `Windows Azure Mobile Services` supplies the client library that lets us connect to the mobile service. To check that the NuGet package is installed, right-click the `References` node in the Solution Explorer and select `Manage NuGet Packages...` Search for `Windows Azure Mobile Services` in the `NuGet official package source` (see Figure 12-12).

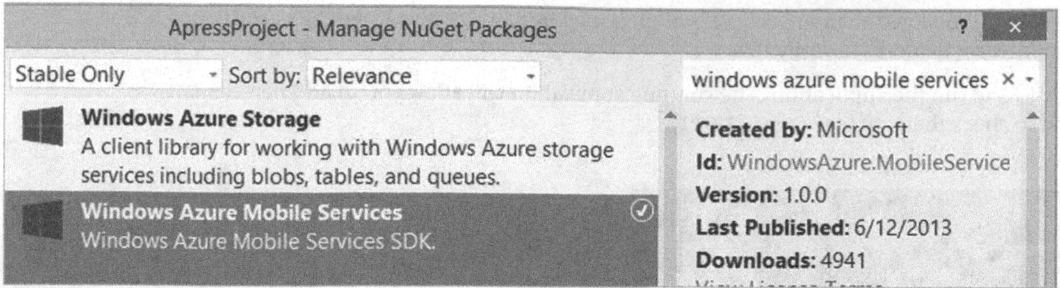

Figure 12-12. *The Windows Azure Mobile Services NuGet Package*

The client library includes a `MobileServiceClient` object that connects to the service and retrieves Azure tables. The client is instantiated as a public property of the Appobject as shown in Figure 12-13. The constructor for the `MobileServiceClient` takes the URL created by Azure for the mobile service and an application key. Both parameters are supplied automatically in the generated code.

```
public partial class App : Application
{
    /// <summary>
    /// Provides easy access to the root frame of the Phone Application.
    /// </summary>
    /// <returns>The root frame of the Phone Application.</returns>
    public static PhoneApplicationFrame RootFrame { get; private set; }

    public static MobileServiceClient MobileService = new MobileServiceClient(
        "https://apressproject.azure-mobile.net/",
        "VixMNeAxpUMjcZeRMVmtUDWeCjfNih24"
        );
```

Figure 12-13. *The MobileServiceClient*

`MainPage.xaml.cs` defines a `TodoItem` class that includes `Id`, `Text` and `Complete` properties as shown in Listing 12-1.

Listing 12-1. The TodoItem Class Definition

```
public class TodoItem
{
    public int Id { get; set; }

    [JsonProperty(PropertyName = "text")]
    public string Text { get; set; }

    [JsonProperty(PropertyName = "complete")]
    public bool Complete { get; set; }
}
```

The MainPage class uses the App.MobileService to retrieve an object representing the table and also defines a collection of TodoItem objects that are bound to a LongListSelector in the MainPageuser interface (see Listing 12-2).

Listing 12-2. Retrieving the TodoItem Table

```
private IMobileServiceTable<TodoItem> todoTable = App.MobileService.GetTable<TodoItem>();

private MobileServiceCollection<TodoItem, TodoItem> items;
```

IMobileServiceTable methods perform all the usual CRUD methods: InsertAsync(), ReadAsync(), UpdateAsync(), and DeleteAsync(). The RefreshAsync() method pulls in the latest values from the database and the Where() method filters on a custom expression.

The MainPage RefreshTodoItems() method is called when the page displays and whenever the user clicks the Refresh button. Notice that Where() statement in Listing 12-3 filters out complete items.Items are populated using the ToCollectionAsync() extension method and assigned to the ItemsSource of the LongListSelector.

Listing 12-3. Populating the Collection of TodoItem

```
private async void RefreshTodoItems()
{
    try
    {
        items = await todoTable
            .Where(todoItem => todoItem.Complete == false)
            .ToCollectionAsync();
    }
    catch (MobileServiceInvalidOperationException e)
    {
        MessageBox.Show(e.Message, "Error loading items", MessageBoxButton.OK);
    }

    ListItems.ItemsSource = items;
}
```

The InsertTodoItem() and UpdateCheckedTodoItem() methods accept a TodoItem instance and keep the todoTable and items collection in sync (see Listing 12-4). Before InsertTodoItem() is called, the item's Id property is zero. When the method is complete, the Id is assigned with a non-zero number. The item is then added to the items collection and will be visible in the bound LongListSelector. UpdateCheckedTodoItem() assumes that the TodoItem parameter Complete property will be true. The item is updated in the database, removed from the collection and disappears from view in the LongListSelector.

Listing 12-4. Inserting and Updating Items

```
private async void InsertTodoItem(TodoItem todoItem)
{
    await todoTable.InsertAsync(todoItem);
    items.Add(todoItem);
}

private async void UpdateCheckedTodoItem(TodoItem item)
{
    await todoTable.UpdateAsync(item);
    items.Remove(item);
}
```

The other methods in the MainPage class respond to events in the user interface. For example, the Save button creates a new TodoItem instance and calls the InsertTodoItem() method as shown in Listing 12-5.

Listing 12-5. Handling the ButtonSave_Click() Event

```
private void ButtonSave_Click(object sender, RoutedEventArgs e)
{
    var todoItem = new TodoItem { Text = TodoInput.Text };
    InsertTodoItem(todoItem);
}
```

Building a Mobile Service Application from Scratch

The Azure quick start page held our hand by building the Azure table, adding the client library package, and generating the code, complete with correct application key. For production use, you'll want to know how to build a Mobile Services application from the ground up in order to customize the application to your specifications.

This next example will record the user's current location to a table. This general patterncan be used for tracking where youparked your car, lost pet sightings, or justabout anything that requires marking alocation. In this example, we'll do somethinguseful by tracking "Bigfoot" (otherwise known as the "Yeti") sightings (see Figure 12-14).

Figure 12-14. *The Running Yeti Detector Application*

Create the Azure Service and Table

The first task is to create the Azure service and a single table named `Sighting`. It may seem odd if you're accustomed to manually creating tables and mapping object properties to table columns, but you don't need to configure table columns at all. Columns are created automatically when you insert a record by virtue of an Azure configuration setting called `dynamic schema`that is turned on by default.

1. Navigate your browser to the Windows Azure dashboard at `https://manage.windowsazure.com/#Workspaces/All/dashboard`.
2. Click the `MOBILE SERVICES` node.
3. Click the `CREATE A NEW MOBILE SERVICE` link. This will display the `NEW MOBILE SERVICE` dialog.
4. In the `NEW MOBILE SERVICE` dialog, enter a unique URL. In this example, the URL is `YetiDetector`. Choose a `DATABASE` option from the drop-down list: `Use an existing SQL database` is the easiest choice that minimizes configuration later on. Select your SUBSCRIPTION from the drop-down list. Finally, choose the `REGION` where your service will be hosted. Click the right-arrow button to continue.
5. In the `Database Settings` page of the dialog, enter a `LOGIN PASSWORD`. Click the check mark button to close the dialog.
6. Wait until the STATUS column for the YetiDetector service displays Ready as shown in Figure 12-15.

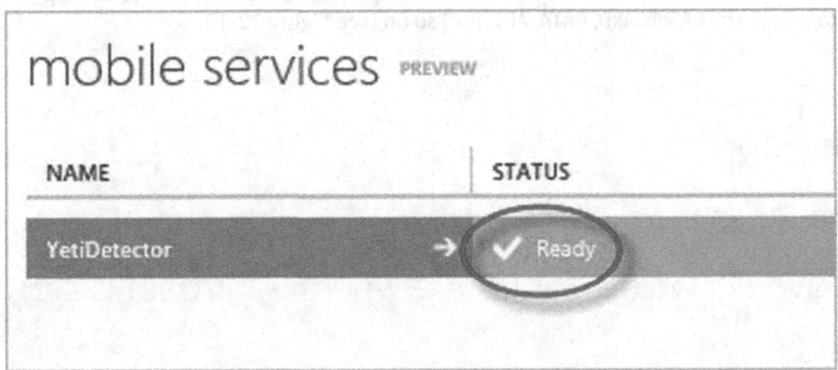

Figure 12-15. *The Mobile Service in Ready Status*

7. Click the `MANAGE KEYS` button at the bottom of the page. This will display the `Manage Access Keys` dialog. It will take a moment to generate the keys. Click the copy button next to the APPLICATION KEY (see Figure 12-16) and store the key for later use when you instantiate the mobile client. Click the check mark button to close the dialog.

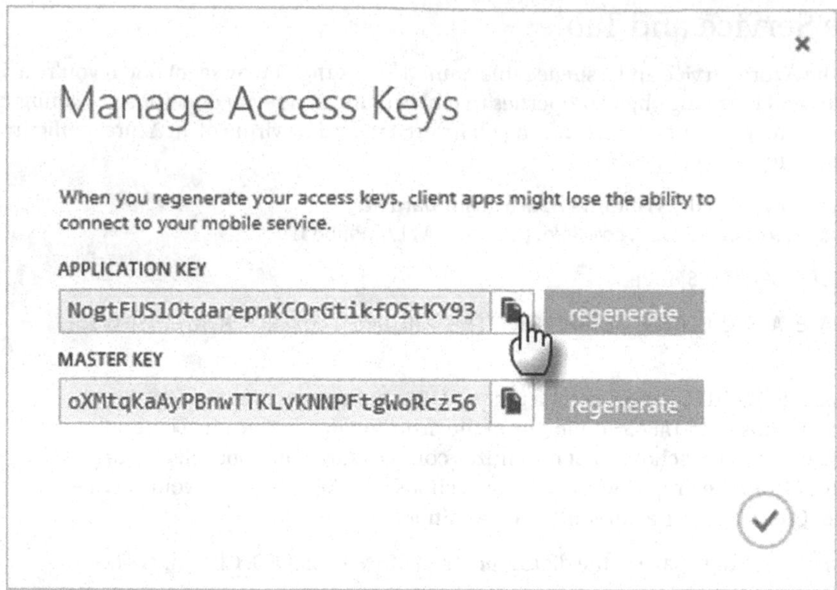

Figure 12-16. *Copying the Application Key*

8. Click the mobile service in the `NAME` column. This will display menu options across the top of the page to access the `DASHBOARD`, `DATA`, `API`, and so on (see Figure 12-17).

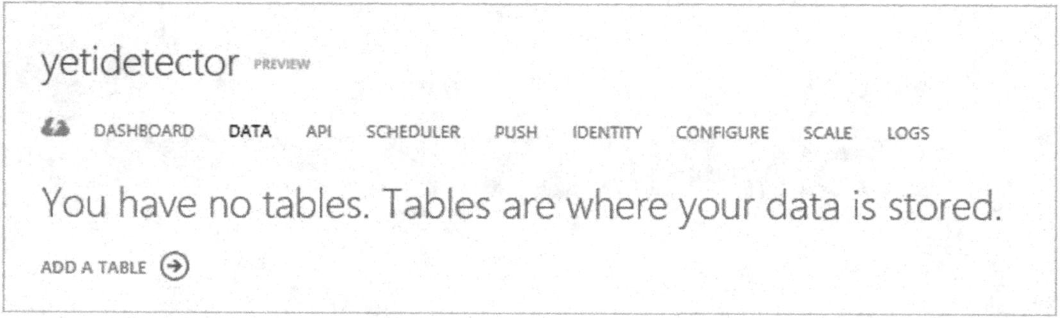

Figure 12-17. *The Mobile Service Menu Options*

9. Click the `DATA` menu option.
10. Click the `ADD A TABLE` link.
11. In the `MOBILE SERVICES DATA` dialog that displays, enter `Sighting` as the table name. Leave the permissions at their default values and click the checkmark button to close the dialog.

MOBILE SERVICES: DATA

Create New Table

TABLE NAME

Sighting

You can set a permission level against each operation for your table.

INSERT PERMISSION

Anybody with the Application Key

Figure 12-18. *Creating the New Sighting Table*

Build the Windows Phone 8 Application

Now we need to build a Windows Phone 8 application that connects to the Azure service and can write records to the `Sighting` table.

1. Create a new Windows Phone 8 application.
2. In the Solution Explorer, right-click the `References` node and select `Manage NuGet Packages...` from the context menu.
3. In the Manage NuGet Packages dialog, select `NuGet official package source` from the left-hand outline under the `Online` node. In the `Search Online` textbox, enter `Windows Azure Mobile Services`. Select `Windows Azure Mobile Services` in the list and click the `Install` button.
4. In the Solution Explorer, open the `Properties` node and then double-click `WMAppManifest.xml` to open it. Navigate to the `Capabilities` tab and enable `ID_CAP_LOCATION`.
5. Open `App.xaml.cs` for editing.
6. Add a public `MobileService` property to the `App` class as shown in Listing 12-6. Replace `"<your app key here>"` with the key you obtained from the `MANAGE ACCESS KEYS` dialog.

   Listing 12-6. Adding the MobileService Property

   ```
   public static MobileServiceClient MobileService = new MobileServiceClient(
       "https://yetidetector.azure-mobile.net/",
       "<your app key here>"
       );
   ```

7. Open `MainPage.xaml` for editing.
8. Replace the existing Layout Root grid with the XAML in Listing 12-7.

Listing 12-7. The MainPage Xaml

```
<Grid x:Name="LayoutRoot" Background="Transparent">
<Grid.RowDefinitions>
<RowDefinition Height="Auto" />
<RowDefinition Height="*" />
</Grid.RowDefinitions>

<StackPanel x:Name="TitlePanel" Grid.Row="0" Margin="12,17,0,28">
<TextBlock x:Name="ApplicationTitle" Text="CLOUD"
                    Style="{StaticResource PhoneTextNormalStyle}" />
<TextBlock x:Name="PageTitle" Text="yeti detector"
                    Margin="9,-7,0,0"
                    Style="{StaticResource PhoneTextTitle1Style}" />
</StackPanel>

<Grid x:Name="ContentPanel" Grid.Row="1" Margin="14,0,10,0"
        Background="{StaticResource PhoneAccentBrush}">
<Grid.OpacityMask>
<ImageBrush Stretch="Fill"
                ImageSource="/Assets/bigfoot.png" />
</Grid.OpacityMask>
</Grid>
<Border Margin="179,56,69,338"
            BorderThickness="0"
            BorderBrush="{StaticResource PhoneForegroundBrush}" Grid.Row="1">
<TextBlockx:Name="YetiButton" Text="I seen 'em"
            Style="{StaticResource PhoneTextExtraLargeStyle}"
            TextWrapping="Wrap"  VerticalAlignment="Center"
            FontSize="64" FontWeight="Bold"
            Tap="CritterSpottedTap" />
</Border>
</Grid>
```

9. Add an image named `bigfoot.png` to the `Assets` folder. If you can't obtain such an image, you can comment out the `ImageBrush` from `MainPage.xaml`. Note that the image consists of a black silhouette against a transparent background as shown in Figure 12-19. The Grid's `OpacityMask` in Listing 12-7 contains an `ImageBrush` that has the effect of "cutting out" the image to show the Grid's background color.

Figure 12-19. The Bigfoot.png Image

10. Right-click the project and select `Add` ➤ `Class...` from the context menu. Name the class `Sighting.cs`. Add `Newtonsoft.Json` to the `using` statements. Replace the class definition with the code in Listing 12-8.

Listing 12-8. The Sighting Class

```
public class Sighting
{
    public int Id { get; set; }

    [JsonProperty(PropertyName = "latitude")]
    public double Latitude { get; set; }

    [JsonProperty(PropertyName = "longitude")]
    public double Longitude { get; set; }

    [JsonProperty(PropertyName = "lastseen")]
    public DateTimeOffset LastSeen { get; set; }
}
```

11. Open MainPage.xaml.cs for editing. Add references to Microsoft.WindowsAzure.MobileServices and Windows.Devices.Geolocation in your using statements.

12. Add a private IMobileServiceTable<Sighting> property to the MainPage class and assign the table using application's MobileService.GetTable() method as shown in Listing 12-9.

    Listing 12-9. The IMobileServiceTable property

```
private IMobileServiceTable<Sighting> sightingTable =
App.MobileService.GetTable<Sighting>();
```

13. Add a Tap event handler to the MainPage class as shown in Listing 12-10. The event handler will get the current location of the phone, create a new Sighting instance and add that instance to the table using the InsertAsync() method.

    Listing 12-10. Handling the Tap Event

```
private async void CritterSpottedTap(object sender, System.Windows.Input.GestureEventArgs e)
{
    var position = await new Geolocator().GetGeopositionAsync();
    var sighting = new Sighting()
                    {
                        Latitude = position.Coordinate.Latitude,
                        Longitude = position.Coordinate.Longitude,
                        LastSeen = position.Coordinate.Timestamp
                    };
    await sightingTable.InsertAsync(sighting);
}
```

14. Press F5 to run the application. Click the "I seen 'em" text to trigger the record insertion. If the call to InsertAsync() fails with message "Error: Unauthorized", double-check that the application key you pass when initializing the App.MobileService property matches the APPLICATION KEY in the Manage Access Keys dialog.

15. Now, check your data. In the browser, navigate to https://manage.windowsazure.com/#Workspaces/All/dashboard.

16. Click the MOBILE SERVICES node, and then click the YetiDetector mobile service in the NAME column as shown in Figure 12-20.

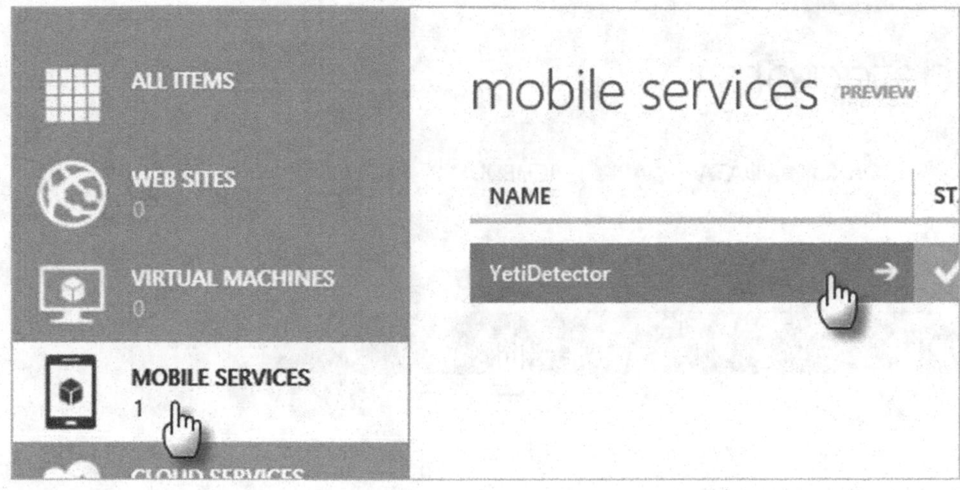

Figure 12-20. *Selecting the Mobile Service*

17. Finally, click the `DATA` menu item as shown in Figure 12-21.

Figure 12-21. *Selecting the Mobile Service Data Menu Item*

18. You should see the `Sighting` table listed. Click `Sighting` in the `TABLE` column as shown in Figure 12-22.

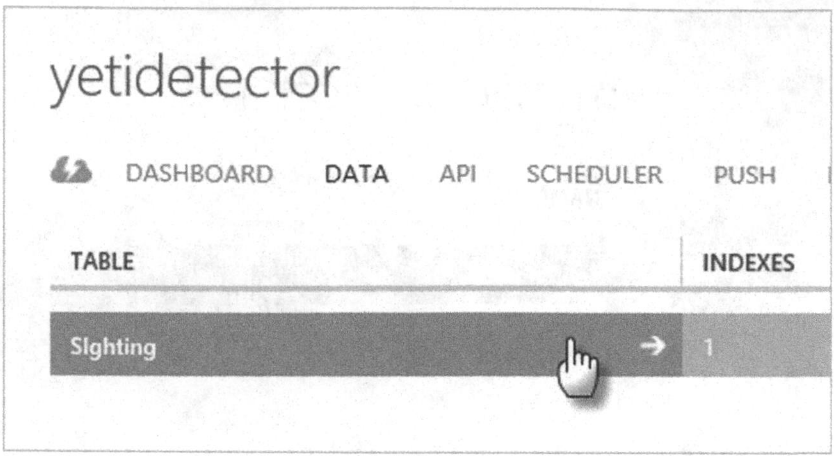

Figure 12-22. *Selecting the Sighting Table*

The table shows the record that was added from the application, recording the position and timestamp (Figure 12-23). Notice that the column names reflect the lower-case convention defined in the `Sighting` class using the `JsonProperty` attribute. The `JsonProperty PropertyName` parameter defines the name used to serialize the property. The mobile service receives the lowercase property names and dynamically creates the columns using those names.

sighting

BROWSE SCRIPT COLUMNS PERMISSIONS

id	latitude	longitude	lastseen
1	47.64324	-122.14196	2013-06-25T15:14:25.828+00:00

Figure 12-23. *The Sighting Table*

Push Notifications from Azure

Your mobile service can send push notifications in response to CRUD (create, read, update, and delete) operations on tables. The fun part is how Azure makes these operations extensible. Each CRUD operation is executed through server-side JavaScript. The default methods are already implemented for you (see Figure 12-24). You can see these by navigating to the table's SCRIPT menu item. The `OPERATION` drop-down includes Insert, Read, Update, and Delete. The function bodies for each operation execute its default behavior and are simply coded as `request.execute()`.

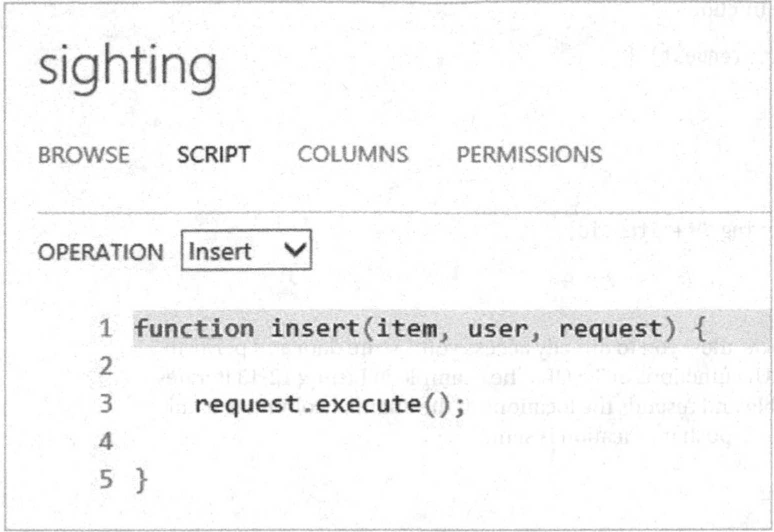

Figure 12-24. *The Mobile Services Scripting Interface*

You can add your own code to any of these functions using the server-side API. The API goes beyond the basic user, request, and response objects used in CRUD functions but also includes a bag full of intriguing goodies:

- The push object allows push notification through Microsoft Push Notification Service (MPNS), Windows Notification Services (WNS) for communicating with Windows Store apps, Google Cloud Messaging (GCM) for communicating with Android apps, and Apple Push Notification Service (APNS) for talking to iOS apps. The `push.mpns` object in particular has methods `sendFlipTile()`, `sendTile()`, `sendToast()`, and `sendRaw()`. The example in Listing 12-11 passes a callback function to the `execute()` function. If the `insert()` is successful, a standard 200 response is sent. Finally, the `push.mpns` object calls `sendFlipTile()` using the data in the current row to populate the channel and payload parameters.

  Listing 12-11. Using the Push Server-Side Object

```
function insert(item, user, request) {
// insert the record
    request.execute({
        success: function() {
            // send standard response
            request.respond();
            // push flip tile message using data in the current row item
push.mpns.sendFlipTile(item.channel, {
                title: "Yeti at " + item.latitude.toFixed(2) + "," + item.longitude.toFixed(2)
            });
        }
    });
}
```

- `console` is used to write to the Windows Azure Mobile Services log. Log entries are accessible through the mobile service `LOGS` menu item. See Listing 12-12 for an example that logs the id of the inserted record.

Listing 12-12. Using the Log Function

```
function insert(item, user, request) {
// insert the record
    request.execute({
success: function() {
// send standard response
request.respond();
console.log("inserted sighting " + item.id);
    }})
}
```

- tables, table, and query objects allow you to directly access your Azure data and perform further operations through CRUD functions or T-SQL. The example in Listing 12-13 iterates the records of the Sighting table and resends the locations. If the channel column is blank, the record is deleted, otherwise, a push notification is sent.

Listing 12-13. Iterating a Table

```
function resend() {
    var sightingTable = tables.getTable("sighting");
    sightingTable
        .read({ success: function(results) {
            if (results.length > 0) {
                for (var i = 0; i < results.length; i++) {
                    var item = results[i];
                    if (results.channel === "")
                    {
                        sightingTable.del(item.id);
                    } else {
                        push.mpns.sendFlipTile(item.channel, {
                                title: "Yeti at " +
                                    item.latitude.toFixed(2) + "," +
                                    item.longitude.toFixed(2)})
                        }
                    }
                }
            }
        }
    )
}
```

To view the whole bag of goodies, see the Mobile Services server script reference at `http://msdn.microsoft.com/en-us/library/windowsazure/jj554226.aspx`.

To make the Windows Phone 8 client application work with the push notifications, you will need to do the following:

- Add the capability ID_CAP_PUSH_NOTIFICATION.
- Create a channel to receive the notification, either through binding to tiles or through Http notification.
- Record the application's channel in an Azure table where the channel string can be picked up by the server-side JavaScript. The channel can be retrieved through the application object: `App.CurrentChannel.ChannelUri.ToString()`.

Building the Push Notification Application

If you actually see a Yeti, you'll of course want to tell everyone. This next example sends a raw notification to anyone with the Windows Phone 8 application. The example will create a separate `Channel` table to record the application's `ChannelUri`. The notification will be pushed to everyone in the `Channel` table whenever a Sighting record is inserted. The example Windows Phone 8 application will receive the raw notification as a JSON string, deserialize the JSON to a `Sighting` object and then change the "I seen' em" text to the Sighting object's coordinates.

Records in the `Channel` table should have unique URI's. The Azure server-side code for the `Channel` table insert will only add unique records. Also, a channel's subscription status can expire and cause an error when attempting to send a push notification from server-side code. This error needs to be handled and the expired channel removed from the table.

Create the Azure Service and Tables

First, create the Azure service, tables and code the `insert()` server-side methods:

1. Navigate your browser to the Windows Azure dashboard at `https://manage.windowsazure.com/#Workspaces/All/dashboard`.
2. Click the `MOBILE SERVICES` node.
3. Click the `CREATE A NEW MOBILE SERVICE` link.
4. In the `NEW MOBILE SERVICE` dialog, enter a unique URL. In this example, the URL is `YetiDetector2`. Choose `Use an existing SQL database as theDATABASE` option from the drop-down list. Select your SUBSCRIPTION from the drop-down list. Finally, choose the `REGION` where your service will be hosted. Click the right-arrow button to continue.
5. In the `Database Settings` page of the dialog, enter a `LOGIN PASSWORD`. Click the check mark button to close the dialog.
6. Wait until the STATUS column for the `YetiDetector2` service displays Ready.
7. Select the `YetiDetector2` service in the list and click the `MANAGE KEYS` button at the bottom of the page. This will display the `Manage Access Keys` dialog. It will take a moment to generate the keys. Click the copy button next to the `APPLICATION KEY` and store the key for later use when you instantiate the mobile client. Click the check mark button to close the dialog.
8. Click the mobile service in the `NAME` column.
9. Click the `DATA` menu option.
10. Click the `ADD A TABLE` link.
11. In the `MOBILE SERVICES DATA` dialog that displays, enter `Sighting` as the table name. Leave the default values and click the checkmark button to close the dialog.
12. Click on `Sighting` in the `TABLE` column as shown in Figure 12-25.

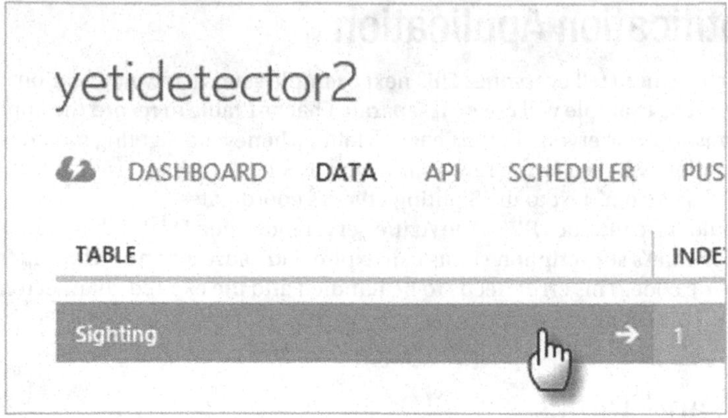

Figure 12-25. *Selecting the Sighting Table*

13. Click the `SCRIPT` menu item as shown in Figure 12-26.

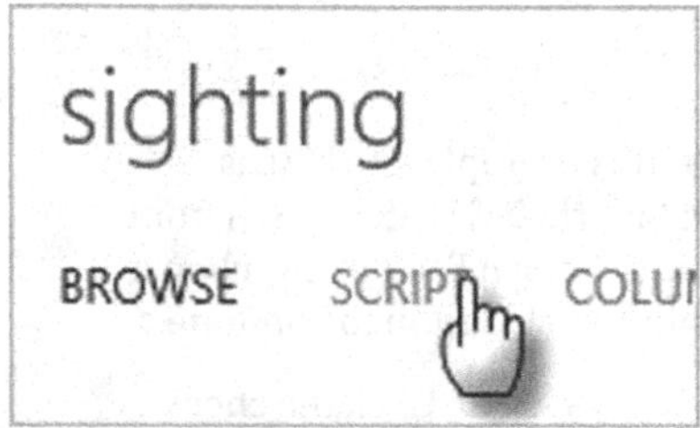

Figure 12-26. *Selecting the Script Menu Item*

14. The `OPERATION` drop-down should already have `Insert` selected. If not, select `Insert` from the drop-down list now.

15. Add the code in Listing 12-14 below the `insert()` function. These will be assigned to the success and error properties of the `sendRaw()` function.

Listing 12-14. Adding the Success and Error Handlers

```
function successHandler(payload) {
    return function () {
        console.log("sent payload:" + payload);
    };
}

function errorHandler(channelTable, item) {
    return function (error) {
        if (error.subscriptionStatus == "Expired"){
            console.log(item.id + " is expired");
            channelTable.del(item.id);
        }
    };
}
```

16. Add the code in Listing 12-15 below the `insert()` function. The function expects a serialized `Sighting` in JSON format. The function first gets a reference to the `Channel` table and reads all the channel records. If the `read()` function is successful, the records are iterated. If the `channeluri` for each record is non-blank, a raw notification is sent via the `sendRaw()` function, passing the `channeluri` and the serialized `Sighting`.

Listing 12-15. Sending Notification to All

```
function sendToAll(sighting) {
    var channelTable = tables.getTable("Channel");
    channelTable.read({
        success: function(results) {
            for (var i = 0; i < results.length; i++) {
                var item = results[i];

                if (item.channeluri !== ""){
                    push.mpns.sendRaw(item.channeluri, { payload: sighting },
                    {
                        success: successHandler(sighting),
                        error: errorHandler(channelTable, item)
                    })
                }
            }
        }
    })
}
```

17. Replace the `insert()` function with the code in Listing 12-16. If the `insert()` is successful, a standard response is return, the `Sighting` object is deserialized using the built-in `JSON.stringify()` function. Finally, `sendToAll()` is called to send the sighting data to all URIs listed in the `Channel` table.

Listing 12-16. Replacing the Insert Function

```
function insert(item, user, request) {
// insert the record
    request.execute({
      success: function() {
        // send standard response
        request.respond();

        var sighting = JSON.stringify(item);
        sendToAll(sighting);
    }})
}
```

■ **Tip** So what was the purpose of the `successHandler()` and `errorHandler()` functions in Listing 12-14? Trying to code the success and error properties of the `sendRaw()` function by directly assigning a function inline ends up with some very strange results. For example, only the last item in the Channel table is recognized. Why? JavaScript functions are objects. JavaScript will create a new function/object on every iteration of the loop. Each function/object is assigned to the success or error property, and with each over-writing the previous. For this reason, a syntax error will be flagged in the source code with a message to not place functions inside of loops.

The fix is to move your function out of the loop and return it from inside a wrapping function. Take a second look at Listing 12-14 where the `successHandler()` and `errorHandler()` functions actually return the handlers used by the `success` and error properties.

18. Click the Save button to save changes to the `Insert` script.
19. Navigate back to the `DATA` page of the mobile service.
20. Click the `CREATE` button at the bottom of the `DATA` page as shown in Figure 12-27.

***Figure 12-27.** Creating a Second Table*

21. In the `MOBILE SERVICES DATA` dialog, set the `TABLE NAME` to `Channel`, leave the default permissions and click the check mark button to close the dialog (see Figure 12-28).

MOBILE SERVICES: DATA

Create New Table

TABLE NAME

Channel

You can set a permission level against each operation for your table.

INSERT PERMISSION

Anybody with the Application Key

UPDATE PERMISSION

Anybody with the Application Key

DELETE PERMISSION

Anybody with the Application Key

READ PERMISSION

Anybody with the Application Key

Figure 12-28. *Creating the Channel Table*

22. Select `Channel` in the `TABLE` column.
23. Click the SCRIPT menu item.
24. Replace the `insert()` function with the code in Listing 12-17. The additional code ensures that the `Channel` object passed in does not have a `channeluri` that matches an existing record. If there's no match, the default `request.execute()` behavior fires. Otherwise, an OK status is passed back.

Listing 12-17. Coding the Insert Function

```
function insert(item, user, request) {

    var channelTable = tables.getTable("Channel");
    channelTable.where({ channeluri: item.channeluri }).read({
        success: function(results){
            if (results.length === 0){
                request.execute();
            }
```

```
                else {
                    request.respond(statusCodes.OK, results[0])
                }
            }
        });
    }
```

25. Click the Save button to retain the Insert script changes.

Build the Windows Phone 8 Application

The Windows Phone 8 application extends the example in "Building a Mobile Service Application from Scratch".

1. In the Solution Explorer, open the `Propertiesnode and then double-click` `WMAppManifest.xml` to open it. On the `Capabilities` tab, make sure that `ID_CAP_LOCATION` and `ID_CAP_PUSH_NOTIFICATION` are enabled.

2. Open `App.xaml.cs`, locate the `MobileService` property and replace the `MobileServiceClient` constructor application URL and key.

3. In `App.xaml.cs`, add a public property to hold the current HTTP notification channel as shown in Listing 12-18.

   Listing 12-18. Declaring the CurrentChannel Property

   ```
   public static HttpNotificationChannel CurrentChannel { get; private set; }
   ```

4. Also in `App.xaml.cs`, replace the code for the `Application_Launching` event with the code in Listing 12-19. This code establishes an HTTP notification channel that can receive push notifications from the Azure mobile service.

   Listing 12-19. Handling the Application_Launching Event

   ```
   private void Application_Launching(object sender, LaunchingEventArgs e)
   {
       const string channelName = "YetiChannel";
       CurrentChannel = HttpNotificationChannel.Find(channelName);

       if (CurrentChannel == null)
       {
           CurrentChannel = new HttpNotificationChannel(channelName);
           CurrentChannel.Open();
       }
   }
   ```

5. In the Solution Explorer, right-click the project and select `Add` ➤ `Class...` from the context menu. Name the class file `Channel.cs`. Inside the class, add `Newtonsoft.Json` to the `using` statements. Replace the class with the code in Listing 12-20.

Listing 12-20. Defining the Channel Class

```
public class Channel
{
    public int Id { get; set; }

    [JsonProperty(PropertyName = "channeluri")]
    public string ChannelUri { get; set; }
}
```

6. Open `MainPage.xaml.cs` for editing.

7. Add `System.IO` and `Newtonsoft.Json` to the `using` statements.

8. Inside the `MainPage` class definition, add an `IMobileServiceTable` as shown in Listing 12-21.

Listing 12-21. Adding the ChannelTable Property

```
private IMobileServiceTable<Channel> channelTable = App.MobileService.GetTable<Channel>();
```

9. Inside the `MainPage` constructor, assign the `HttpNotificationReceived` event handler as shown in Listing 12-22.

Listing 12-22. Assigning the HttpNotificationReceived Event Handler

```
App.CurrentChannel.HttpNotificationReceived +=
    CurrentChannel_HttpNotificationReceived;
```

10. Below the `MainPage` constructor, add the `HttpNotificationReceived` event handler as shown in Listing 12-23. This event responds to the raw push notification. The event args contain a `Notification.Body` property that is a stream containing the serialized `Sighting` object from the mobile service. The `Newtonsoft.Json` library supports a `JsonConvert.DeserializeObject()` method that loads a `Sighting` object from a JSON string. The newly loaded `Sighting` object is used to format the content for the main text on the page.

Listing 12-23. Handling the HttpNotificationReceived Event

```
void CurrentChannel_HttpNotificationReceived(object sender,
    Microsoft.Phone.Notification.HttpNotificationEventArgs e)
{
    var json = new StreamReader(e.Notification.Body).ReadToEnd();
    var sighting = JsonConvert.DeserializeObject<Sighting>(json);
    Dispatcher.BeginInvoke(() =>
    {
        YetiButton.Text = sighting.Latitude.ToString("0.00") + "," +
            sighting.Longitude.ToString("0.00");
    });
}
```

11. In the `CritterSpottedTap()` event handler, above the call to `Geolocator().GetGeopositionAsync()`, add the code from Listing 12-24.

Listing 12-24. Adding the Channel Insert

```
private async void CritterSpottedTap(object sender,
    System.Windows.Input.GestureEventArgs e)
{
    var channel = new Channel()
    {
        ChannelUri = App.CurrentChannel.ChannelUri.ToString()
    };
    await channelTable.InsertAsync(channel);

    // . . .
}
```

12. Press F5 to run the application. Press the "I seen' em" text and wait for the text to change to the coordinates from the push notification.

13. In the browser, open the Azure dashboard at `https://manage.windowsazure.com/#Workspaces/All/dashboard`. Navigate to your `YetiDetector2` mobile service. Check out the records in the `Sighting` and `Channel` tables. Also, click the `LOGS` menu item for the mobile service. The logging should include the JSON payload sent to the `Sighting` table `insert()` function (see Figure 12-29).

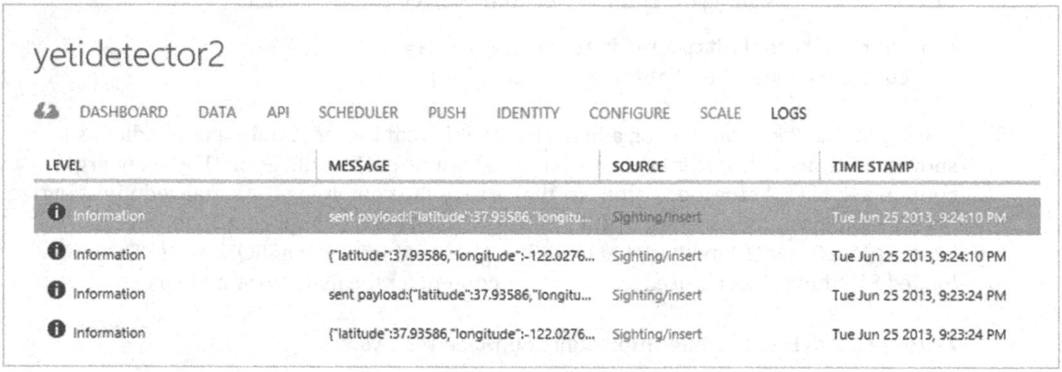

yetidetector2

DASHBOARD DATA API SCHEDULER PUSH IDENTITY CONFIGURE SCALE LOGS

LEVEL	MESSAGE	SOURCE	TIME STAMP
Information	sent payload:{"latitude":37.93586,"longitu...	Sighting/insert	Tue Jun 25 2013, 9:24:10 PM
Information	{"latitude":37.93586,"longitude":-122.0276...	Sighting/insert	Tue Jun 25 2013, 9:24:10 PM
Information	sent payload:{"latitude":37.93586,"longitu...	Sighting/insert	Tue Jun 25 2013, 9:23:24 PM
Information	{"latitude":37.93586,"longitude":-122.0276...	Sighting/insert	Tue Jun 25 2013, 9:23:24 PM

Figure 12-29. *Viewing the Mobile Service Logs*

The running application makes the full round trip by communicating with the Azure service, writing to the Azure tables, and using the SQL insert to push notifications back to the application.

Summary

Windows Azure Mobile Services places your server infrastructure in the cloud with a minimum of work on your part, but still with a great deal of control. Earlier incarnations of Windows Azure required that you build web services and deploy them to the cloud before they could be used by a Windows Phone client application. Windows Azure Mobile Services now allows you to build the back-end completely in the cloud, all from the Windows Azure dashboard.

In this chapter, we initially used the Get Started functionality built into the mobile service to create tables and even to build an example project. Then we created our own tables, built a mobile service from scratch, and created a Windows Phone 8 application that could insert records to the Azure table. Finally, we built a mobile service and Windows Phone 8 combination that could push notifications to multiple phones.

CHAPTER 13

Designing In Blend

To say that Blend for Visual Studio 2012 is an interactive design tool for XAML misses the power of the product.It's like comparing Notepad to Visual Studio. In theory, you could get everything done in Notepad, but in reality you would get bogged down almost immediately. Or, as someone once said, "In theory, there is no difference between theory and practice. In practice, there is" (multiple attributions).

Working in Blend is a fluid experience. You can certainly build your pages interactively with the graphically oriented tools, but you can also animate elements, react to state changes, customize templates visually, trigger actions, add effects and bind elements.

This chapter is a guide to getting started designing Windows Phone 8 pages using Blend. It describes how Blend works together with Visual Studio and how to get around in the Blend user interface. You'll learn some of the key techniques for building custom controls, user controls and working with templates.

Introducing Blend

The choice between Visual Studio and Blend at any moment may depend on the toolset for each environment, your personal style or your organization's standards.

Use Blend when you need to make extensive changes to your application's user interface. You will be particularly glad to have Blend when complex styles need to be overhauled, when user actions should trigger changes in the user interface or if elements need to be animated in any way. Blend currently works on Windows Store apps (HTML and XAML), Windows Phone, WPF (Windows Presentation Foundation) and Silverlight applications.

By contrast, Visual Studio is more "code-centric" and can deal with a larger palette of application types. These application types include those that Blend can handle but also embrace WCF (Windows Communication Foundation), web applications such as ASP.NET or MVC, Windows forms applications, reporting, and many others.

At the end of the day, it's not a case of "Blend or Visual Studio." The two are designed to be used together. Both environments are aware of project changes and stay in sync without any configuration changes on your part.

Getting Started

To get started with Blend, first download and install `Blend + SketchFlow Preview for Microsoft Visual Studio 2012` from the Microsoft Download Center, currently located at `www.microsoft.com/en-us/download/confirmation.aspx?id=30702`. We won't be using the Sketch Flow prototyping tool, but it is included in the download.

The following example demonstrates the smooth interaction between Visual Studio and Blend. Instead of starting immediately in Blend, let's start our Windows Phone 8 project in Visual Studio and move to Blend from there:

1. Create a new Windows Phone 8 application.
2. Open `MainPage.xaml.cs` for editing.

3. In the design view, select the `TextBlock` with text "MY APPLICATION" and change the `Text` property to "BLEND DEMO".

4. Select the `TextBlock` with text "page name" and change the `Text` property to "designing". The page in the designer should look like the screenshot in Figure 13-1.

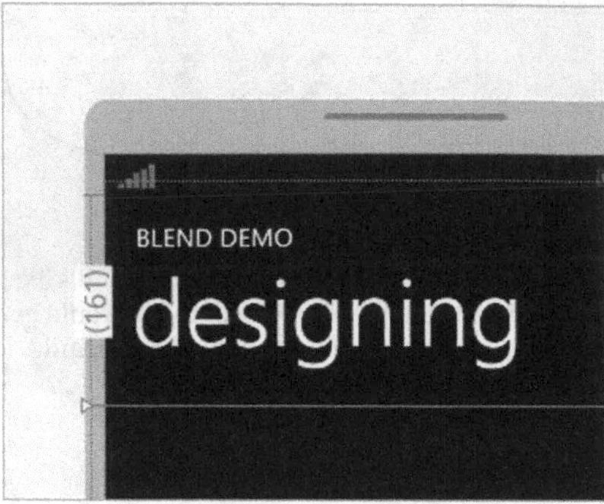

***Figure 13-1.** Designing in Visual Studio*

5. In the Visual Studio Solution Explorer, right-click the project and select `Open in Blend...` from the context menu (see Figure 13-2). If you're prompted to save changes, do so. Do not close Visual Studio.

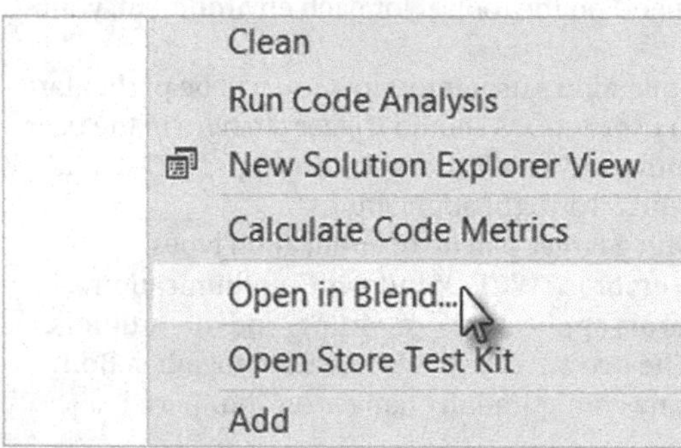

***Figure 13-2.** Opening in Blend*

Blend will run and display the project (see Figure 13-3).

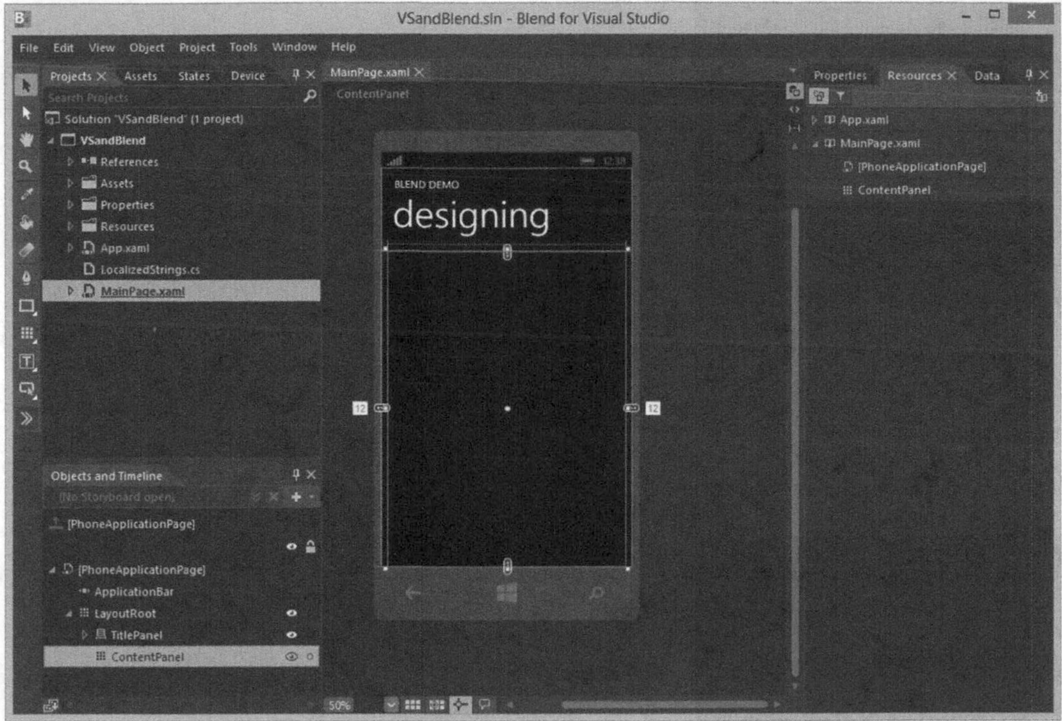

Figure 13-3. *The Project in Blend*

6. Click on the `ContentPanel` element (below the titling) to select it (see Figure 13-4).

Figure 13-4. *Selecting the ContentPanel*

7. From the tools on left hand side of the screen, double-click the button tool (see Figure 13-5). This action will create a `Button` element in the `ContentPanel`.

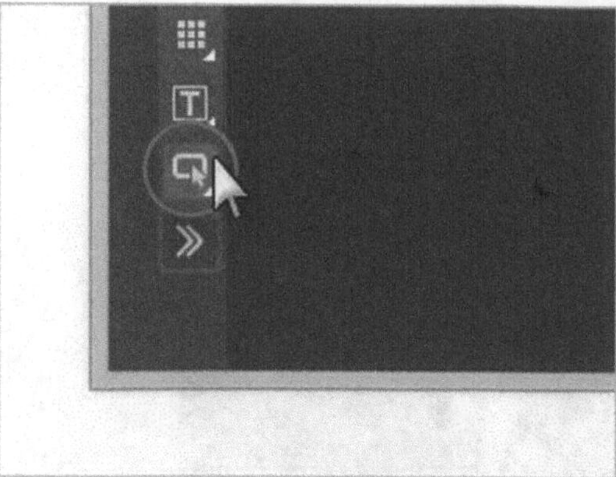

Figure 13-5. *Adding a Button*

The page should now look like the screenshot in Figure 13-6.

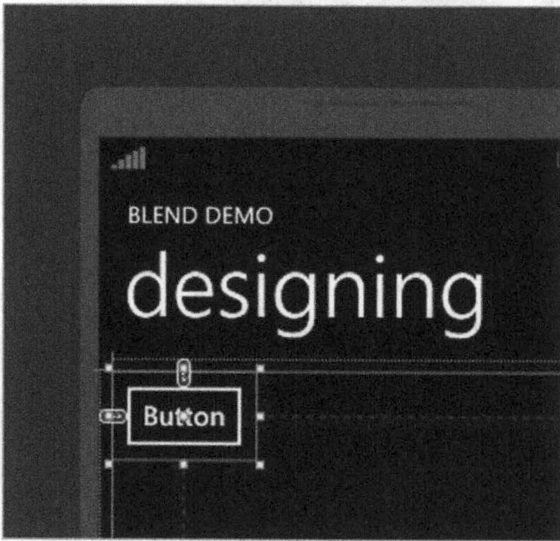

Figure 13-6. *The Page Design*

8. Double-click the button to allow the `Content` property of the `Button` to be edited directly as shown in Figure 13-7.

Figure 13-7. *Editing the Button Content*

9. Enter new text "Say Howdy!"and then click outside of the button to see the results (see Figure 13-8).

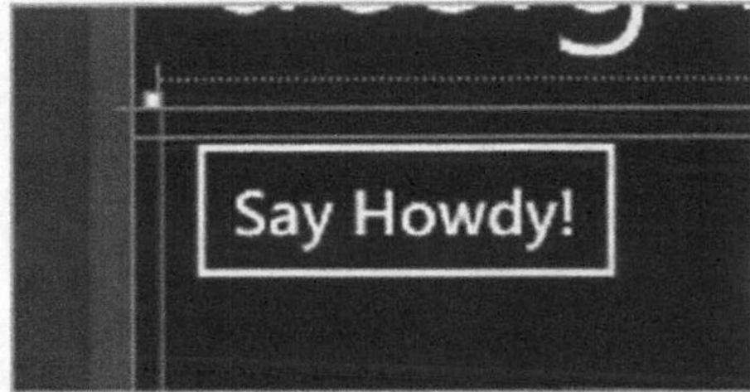

Figure 13-8. New Button Content

10. From the Blend menu, select `Project` ➤ `Run Project`. By default, this will run the project in the Emulator as shown in Figure 13-9. The button doesn't have a `Click` event handler yet, so the page is display only.

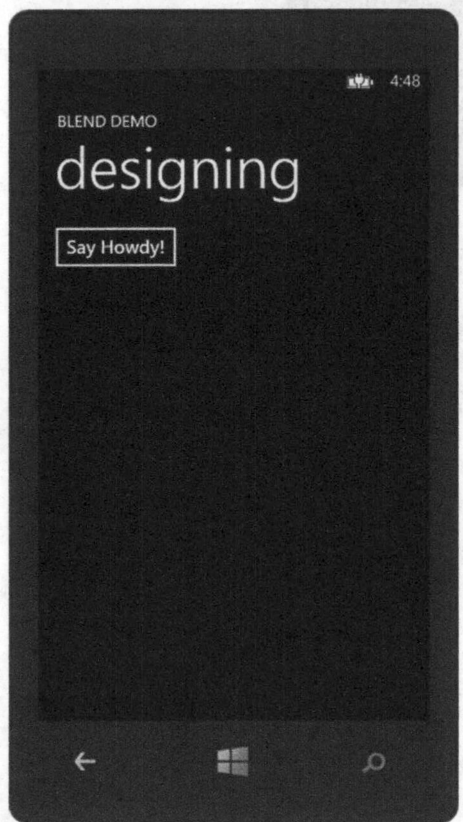

Figure 13-9. Project Running in the Emulator

11. In the upper left hand corner of Blend, locate the `Projects` tab. Right-click the `Solution` node and select `Edit in Visual Studio` from the context menu as shown in Figure 13-10.

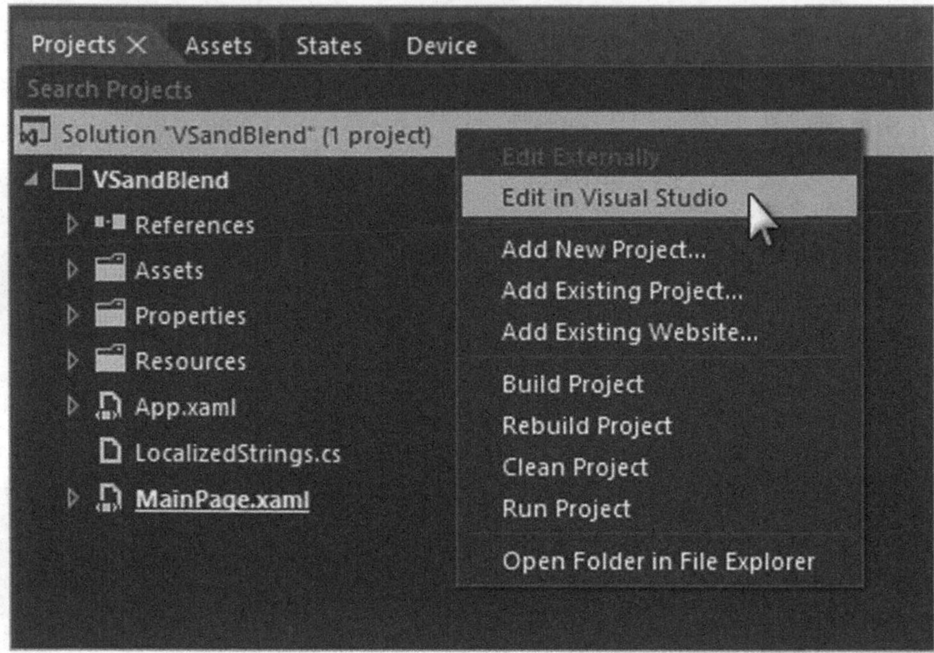

Figure 13-10. *Using the Edit in Visual Studio Option*

12. Bring Visual Studio to the foreground. A dialog will display a "This file has been modified..." message. Click the Yes button as shown in Figure 13-11.

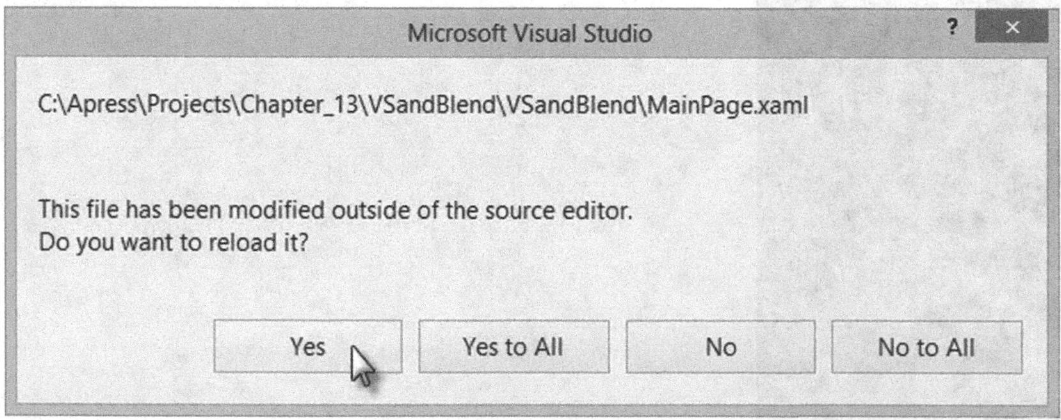

Figure 13-11. *The File Has Been Modified Dialog*

13. In the Visual Studio Design surface, double-click the "Say Howdy" button. This will create a button `Click` event handler. Add the code in Listing 13-1 to the `Click` event handler.

Listing 13-1. Handling the Click Event

```
private void Button_Click(object sender, RoutedEventArgs e)
{
    MessageBox.Show("Howdy");
}
```

14. From the Visual Studio main menu bar, select `File` ➤ `Save All`.
15. In the Visual Studio Solution Explorer, right-click the project and select `Open in Blend...` from the context menu.
16. A warning that the file has been modified outside of Blend appears (see Figure 13-12). Click the Yes button.

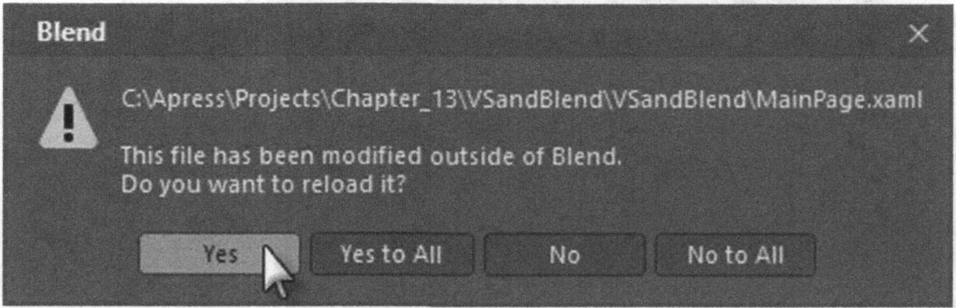

Figure 13-12. *Closing the File Modification Warning*

17. From the Blend menu, select `Project` ➤ `Run Project`. Click the "Say Howdy" button. The ok message displays as shown in Figure 13-13.

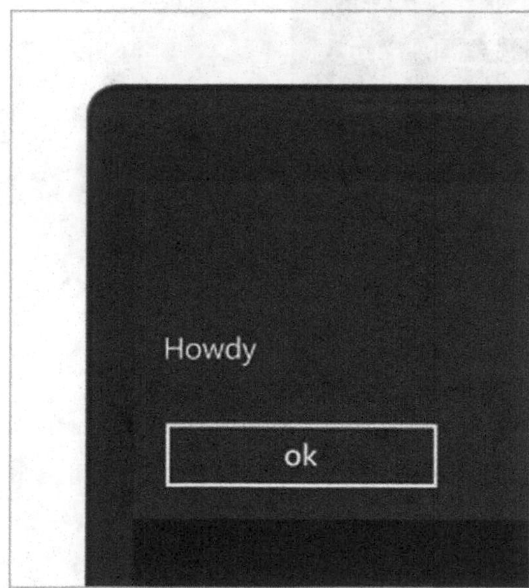

Figure 13-13. *Testing the Button Click*

This example demonstrated the smooth interaction between Visual Studio and Blend. The rest of the chapter will show many of the unique features that differentiate Blend from Visual Studio.

Blend Project Types

New Blend projects produce the same project structure and page layout as their Visual Studio counterparts. Create new Windows Phone projects from the Blend New Project dialog shown in Figure 13-14 (`File` ➤ `New Project...`).

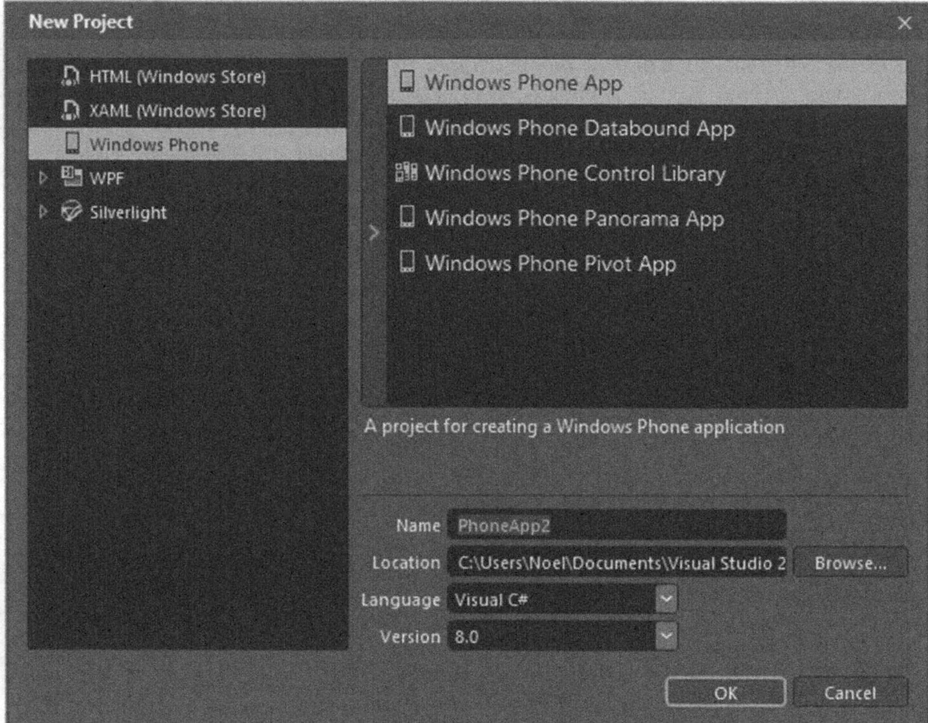

Figure 13-14. *Viewing Blend Project Types*

The project types you can create in Blend include:

- `Windows Phone App` with application title, page title and content panel. This is a no-frills project you can use to build your app from the ground up.
- `Windows Phone Databound App` with basic framework for loose coupling between View and View Model. The predefined View displays sample data in a `LongListSelector`. The View Model has a few sample properties and property change notification built in. This project type is a good choice for displaying data in a list.
- `Windows Phone Control Library` provides a minimal assembly framework with a single `UserControl`. This project type can be used to create a `UserControl` that can be included in other projects. See the "Make into UserControl" topic for more on `UserControls`.

- `Windows Phone Panorama App` uses the `Panorama` control in a data bound project. This project type is structured like the Windows Phone Data bound App type, but the `LongListSelector` is displayed inside multiple `Panorama` items. See Chapter 5 for more on the `Panorama` control.
- `Windows Phone Pivot App` uses the `Pivot` control in a data bound project. This project type is structured like the Windows Phone Data bound App type, but the `LongListSelector` is displayed inside multiple `Pivot` items. See Chapter 5 for more on the `Pivot` control.

Simplifying the Blend User Interface

Blend has a hectic user interface that seems busy at first glance (see Figure 13-15). Fortunately, you cansimplify the UI to show just the windows of interest.

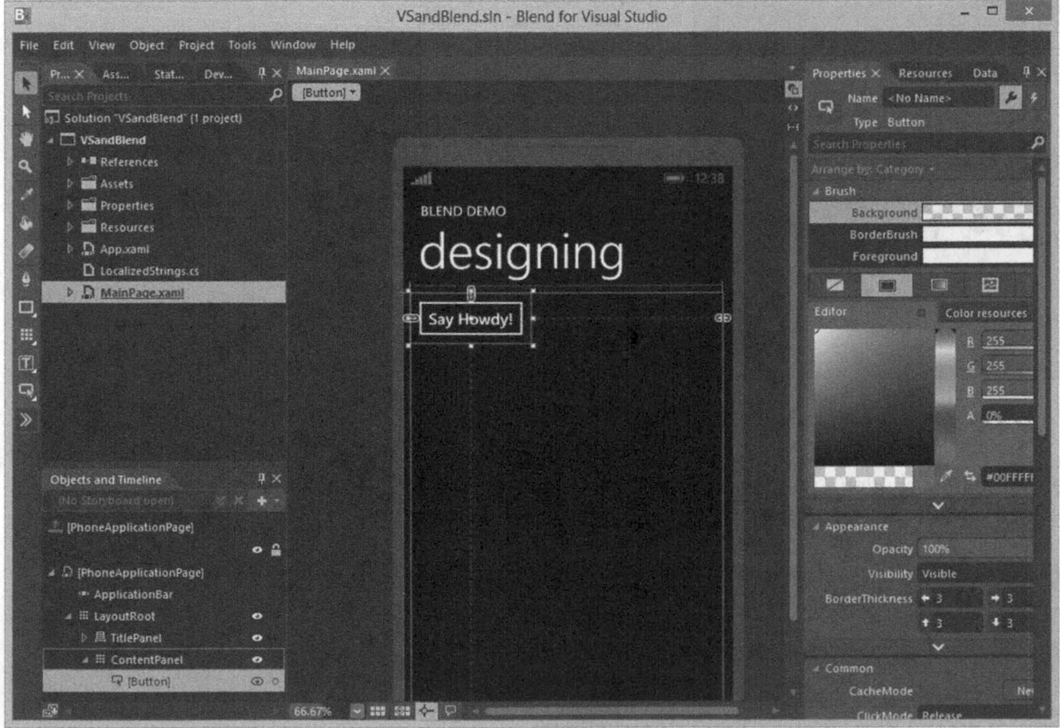

Figure 13-15. The Blend User Interface

Use the `Window` menu to hide panels you're not using. You can start with just the items shown selected in Figure 13-16.

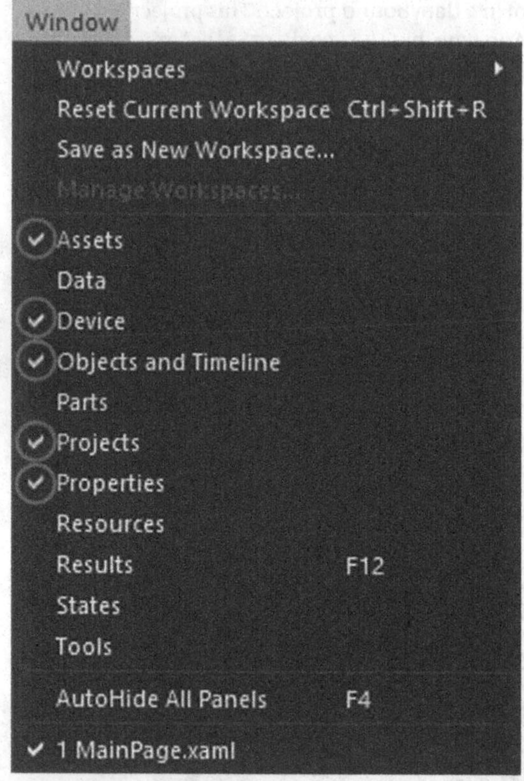

Figure 13-16. *The Window Menu Options*

To save your simplified windows arrangement, click the `Window` ➤ `Saveas New Workspace...` menu option. Provide a name for the workspace and click the `OK` button as shown in Figure 13-17.

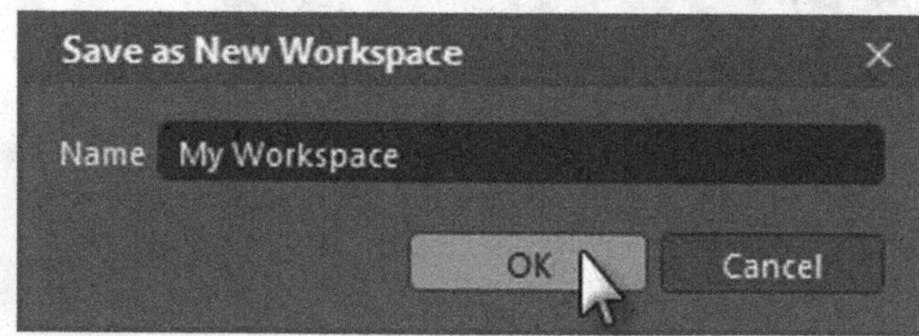

Figure 13-17. *Saving a Custom Workspace*

Now you can select your workspace from the `Window` ➤ `Workspaces` submenu or choose from the built-in `Design` or `Animation` layouts (see Figure 13-18). You can also press `Ctrl-F11` to toggle through all three workspaces.

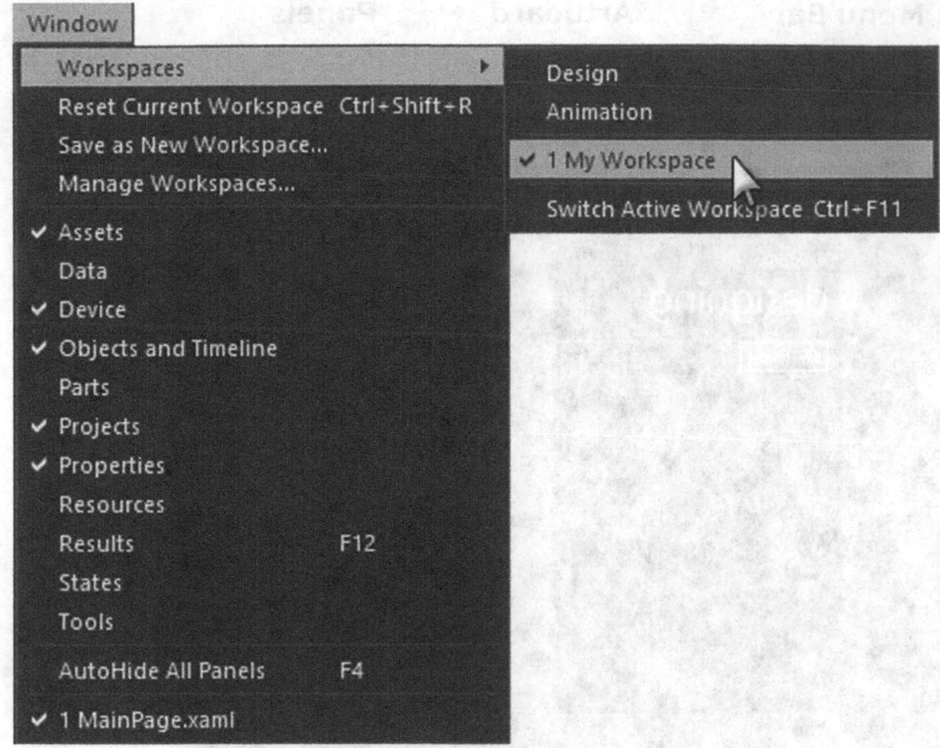

Figure 13-18. *Selecting Workspaces*

Blend User Interface

Starting with the panels enabled in the simplified user interface, here is the top level of the Blend user interface shown in Figure 13-19. The heart of the interface is the Artboard, where you visually design your Windows Phone 8 page interface. The main menu bar and panels work in relation to the elements selected in the Artboard.

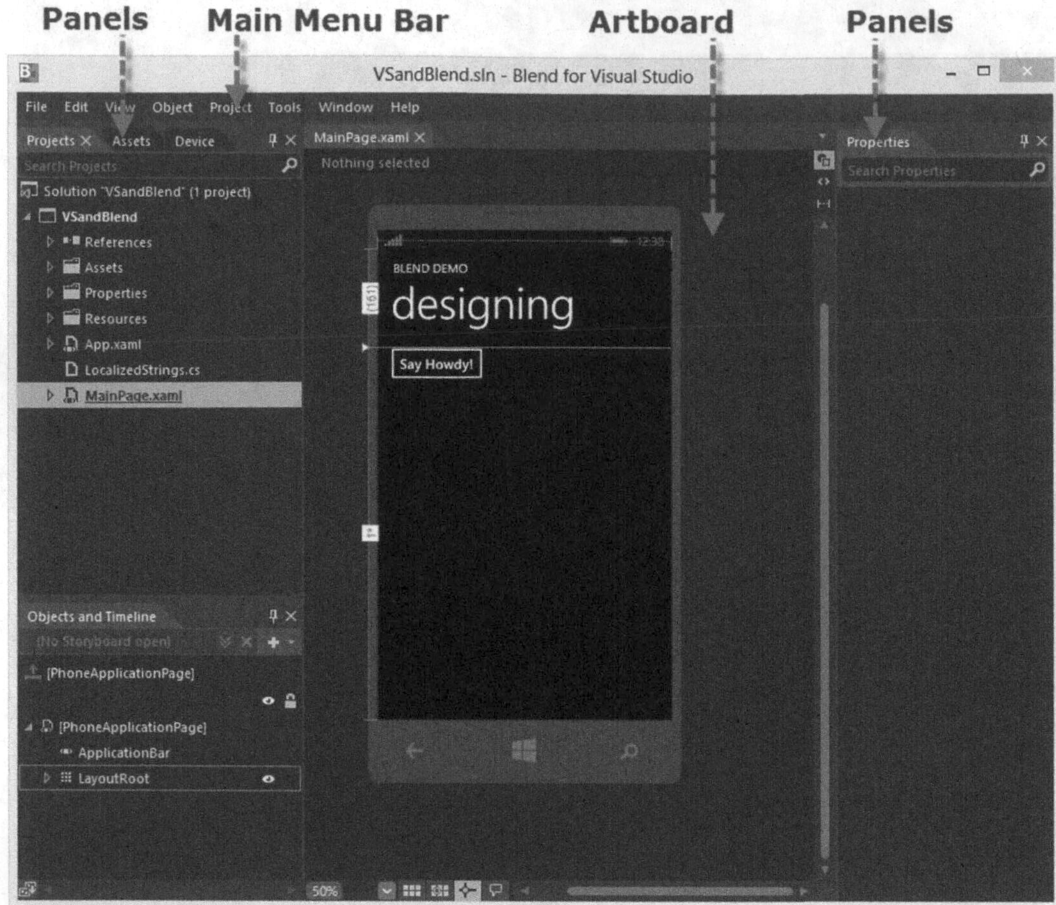

Figure 13-19. The Blend User Interface Layout

Now that you've seen the overall layout, let's take a closer look atthe tools and capabilities for each panel in the Blend user interface.

Projects

The Projects panel serves the same function as the Visual Studio Solution Explorer (see Figure 13-20). Right-clicking the solution node has options for adding, building and running projects. The project node menu has options for referencing adding items and folders. Also notice the Startup Project option. Each XAML file has a Startup option as well.

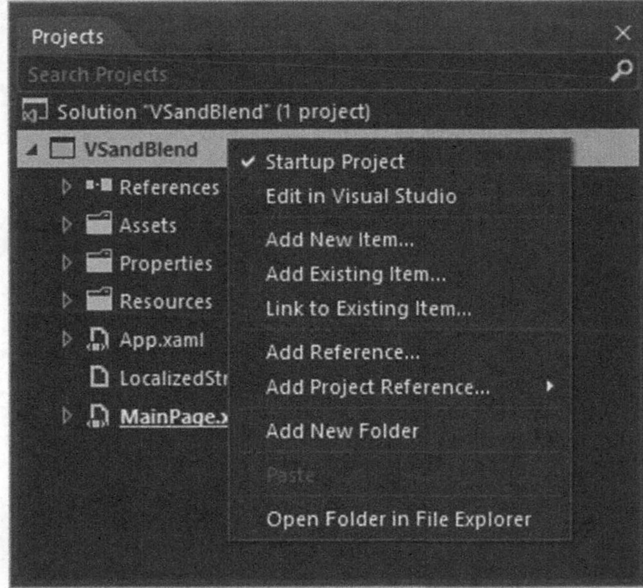

Figure 13-20. *The Projects Panel*

Assets

The `Assets` panel is like the Visual Studio Toolbox, but a good deal more powerful (see Figure 13-21). The `Assets` panel has all the Windows Phone 8 `controls` you would expect but also has assets unique to Blend that don't show up in the Visual Studio Toolbox. The top level categories are:

- *Project*: shows assets defined by the current project including the `MainPage` object and styles defined in the application.
- *Controls*: contains a full list of common controls such as buttons, borders, text boxes, shapes, grids and so on.
- *Styles*: includes any styles you have defined in your app and all the system defined styles.
- *Behaviors*: can be dropped on an element to make the element respond in some way without having to write code. For example, the `MouseDragElementBehavior` allows an element to be dragged and dropped.
- *Shapes*: contain primitive and business-related shapes like rectangles, ellipses, arrows, and stars.
- *Media*: lists all the images, audio, video and other object files in the project.
- *Categories*: are groupings created by the control developer.
- *Locations*: list all assets for a selected DLL.

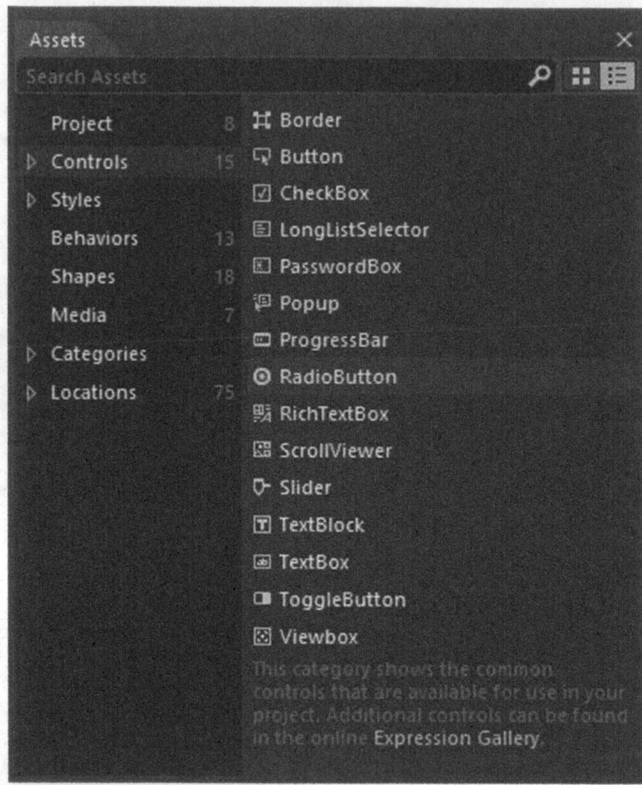

***Figure 13-21.** The Assets Panel*

Individual assets can show up under more than one category in the list. The `Search` capability makes it easy to narrow down the list in realtime as you type.

Properties

The `Properties` panel is analogous to its Visual Studio cousin but is easier to design with (see Figure 13-22). Wherever possible, the Blend design team has added visual cues and tools to make creating your user interface more like painting and less like writing a shopping list. Properties are grouped into functional areas with "corner case" property groups collapsed out of the way. Note that as the tools mature, you will see more overlap and merging of functionality. For example, the `Brush` property editor shown in the screenshot is now incorporated into Visual Studio.

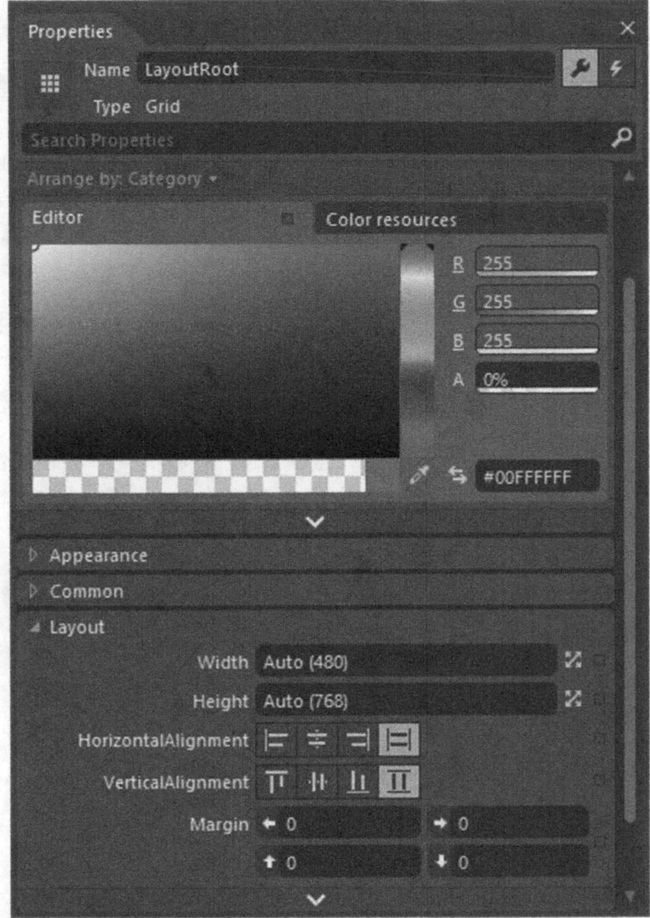

Figure 13-22. *The Properties Panel*

Objects and Timeline

The `Objects and Timeline` panel organizes all page elements in a tree view (see Figure 13-23). You can add assets to this outline directly or to the `Artboard`. Visual cues let you know where elements are being dropped (handy in complex layouts). You can lock elements from being moved accidentally or hide them temporarily.

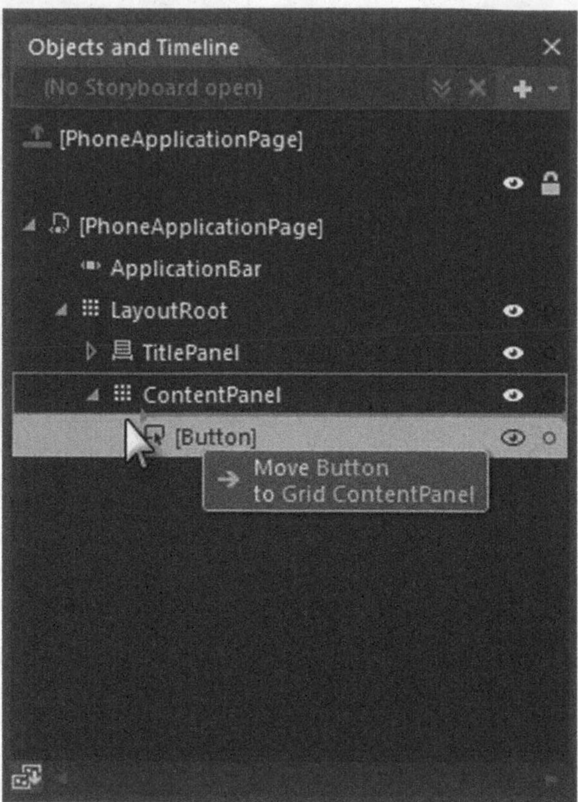

***Figure 13-23.** The Objects and Timeline Panel*

The `Objects and Timeline` panel has a second purpose as a container for animation. The `Timeline` portion of the panel presents a series of dots that represent property changes at different points of time (see Figure 13-24).

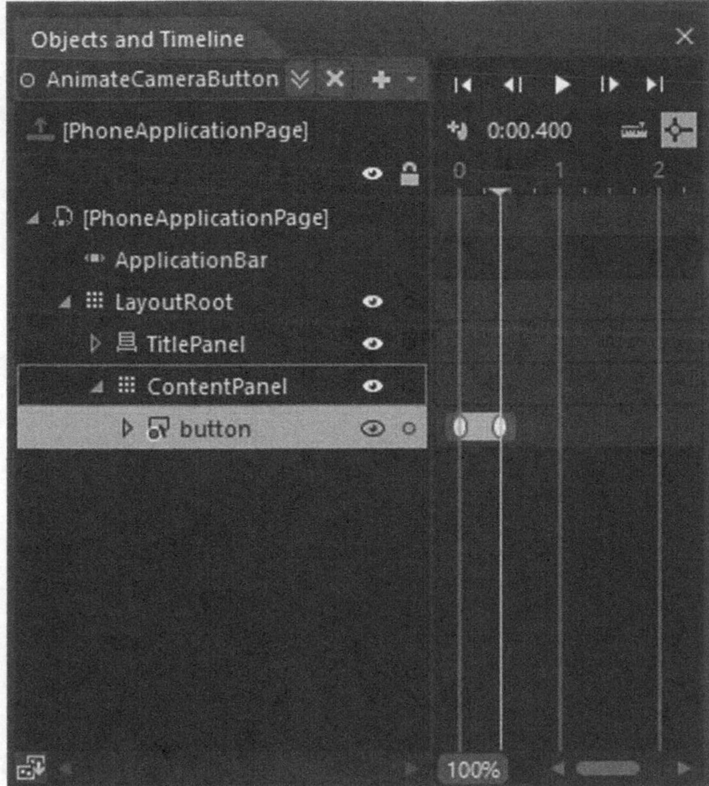

Figure 13-24. The Objects and Timeline Storyboard Timeline

Device

The `Device` panel configures landscape and portrait `Orientation`, `Display` resolutions, light and dark `Theme`, and `Accent` colors for the design view (see Figure 13-25). Like Visual Studio, the `Deploy Target` drop down lets you switch between running on the Windows Phone Device and several different resolutions of the Emulator. You can also toggle whether to `Show chrome` in the design view.

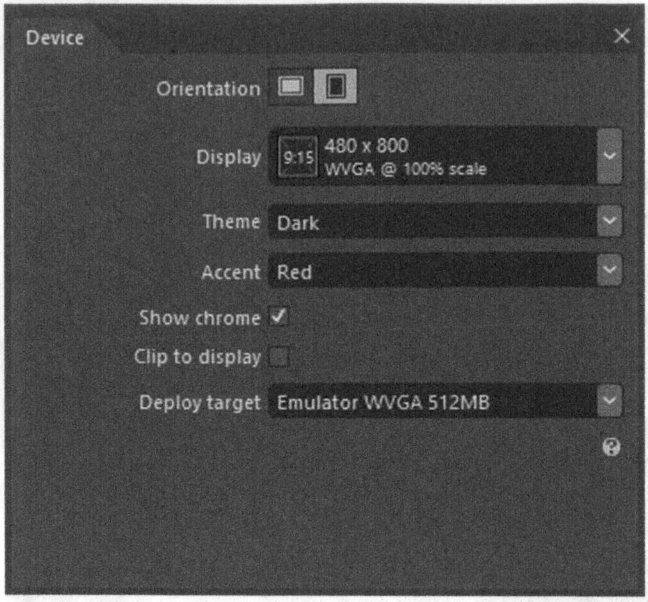

Figure 13-25. *The Device Panel*

Tools

You may also want to enable the `Tools` panel (see Figure 13-26), particularly for the `Selection` tool at the top of the panel.

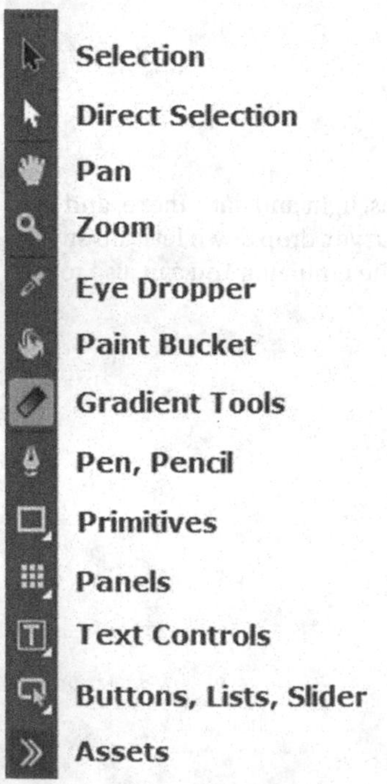

Figure 13-26. *The Toolbar*

Selection down through Paint Bucket are individual tools that can be used directly.

- The Selection tool is the default and used to select, size and move elements on the page.
- Direct Selection is a special-purpose tool that allows you to work on the internals of an element, such as points in a path or sub items in a ContentControl. Pan and Zoom move and resize the Artboard. Double-clicking restores the default position and zoom level. Alt-click the Artboard to zoom out.
- The Eye Dropper selects a color from anywhere in the Artboard for use in the current drawing operation. The Eye Dropper can be used to pick colors out of an organization's logo or some aspect of the visual design you want to coordinate with.
- Use the Paint Bucket to copy fills, patterns and brushes. Paint Bucket is typically used with the Eye Dropper to first pick out a color from the UI and then apply the brush somewhere else with the Paint Bucket.

The remaining tools below the Paint Bucket have multiple options and are described in more detail.

Gradient Tools

The Gradient Tool displays an arrow graphic that applies a gradient brush (see Figure 13-27). The arrow can be sized and rotated to adjust the gradient. You can also add and adjust gradient stops to define individual colors along the gradient. Figure 13-27 shows the Gradient Tool over a Rectangle element. Be aware that this tool only shows as part of the design in the Artboard. When the tool is dropped on an element in the Artboard, nothing is added to the XAML.

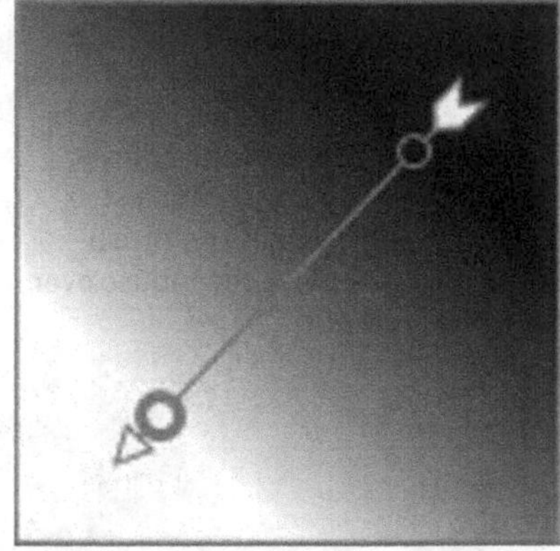

***Figure 13-27.** The Gradient Tool Used on a Rectangle*

The right-diagonal arrow next to the Gradient Tool indicates other related tools available by way of right-click. Figure 13-28 shows the Gradient Tool and the Brush Transform.

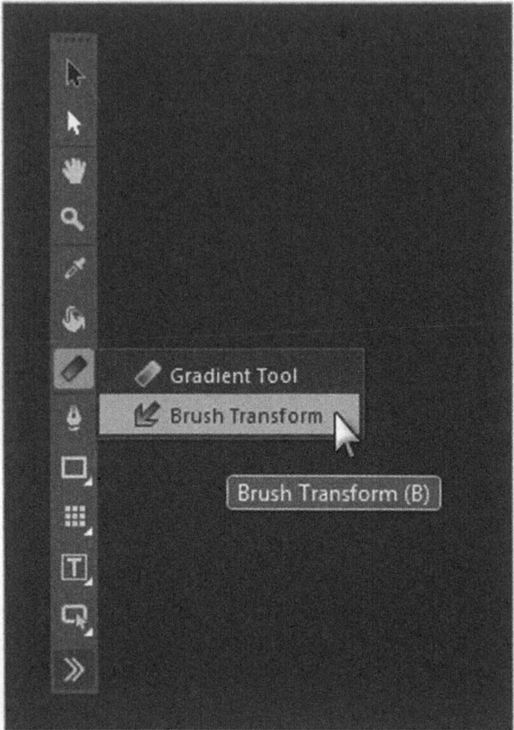

Figure 13-28. *Selecting the Brush Transform*

Like the `Gradient Tool`, the `Brush Transform` also tweaks the gradient but uses a rectangular tool that allows you to move, size, rotate and skew the gradient. Figure 13-29 shows the gradient being skewed. To use the tool, start by adding the Gradient Tool; then, with the Gradient Tool still selected, click the Brush Transform tool. The Brush Transform tool will appear in place of the Gradient Tool as a bounding box. From there you can move the mouse over, looking for visual cues of the mouse cursor where you can size, move, rotate and skew the gradient.

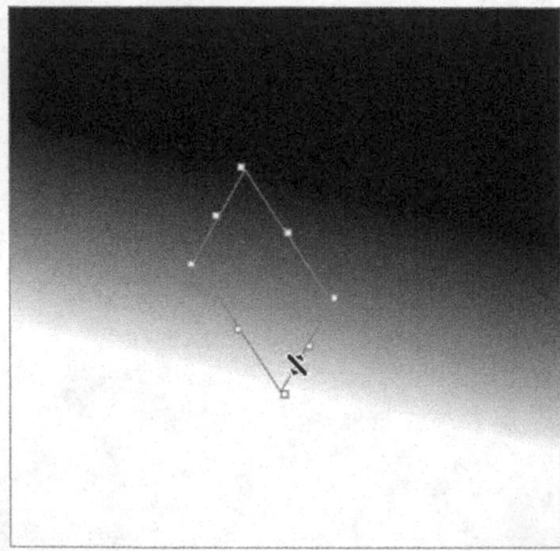

Figure 13-29. *Using the Brush Transform*

Drawing

Use the Pen tool to drop points in the Artboard. Blend "connects the dots" to create ashape with the current fill as shown in Figure 13-30.

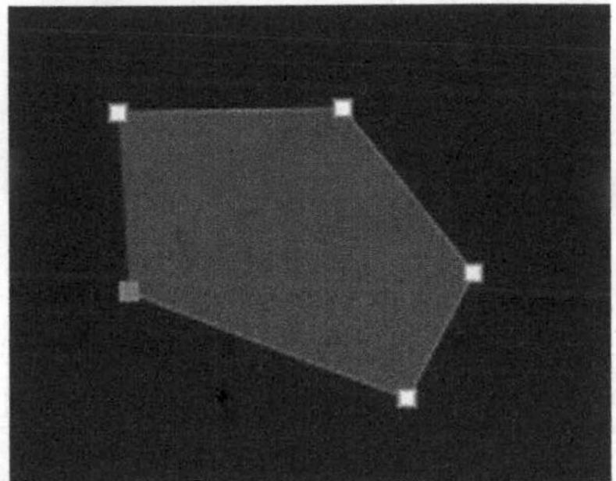

Figure 13-30. *Using the Pen Tool*

This is where the Direct Selection tool starts to make sense. By clicking the Direct Selection tool, you can drag any of the points independently to adjust the shape or to select points for deletion. Figure 13-31 shows one of the points being dragged.

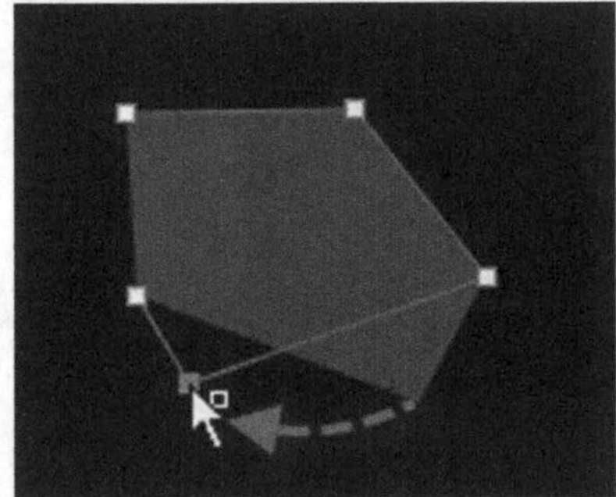

Figure 13-31. *Using the Direct Selection Tool*

The shape is represented in XAML as a Path where each individual point is recorded in the Data property (see Listing 13-2). The work is done for you by simply moving the drag anchors.

Listing 13-2. The Path XAML

```
<Path
    Data="M149.33333,447 L271.33368,461 L196.00026,523.66656 L81.999641,511.66696
L77.999619,467.66678"
    Fill="#FF7100FF"
    Height="77.667"
    Margin="77.5,0,184.167,82.833"
    Stretch="Fill"
    Stroke="Black"
    UseLayoutRounding="False"
    VerticalAlignment="Bottom" />
```

You can start combining tools to create more complex effects. The `Gradient Tool` is used in Figure 13-32 to give depth of field to the shape and the background.

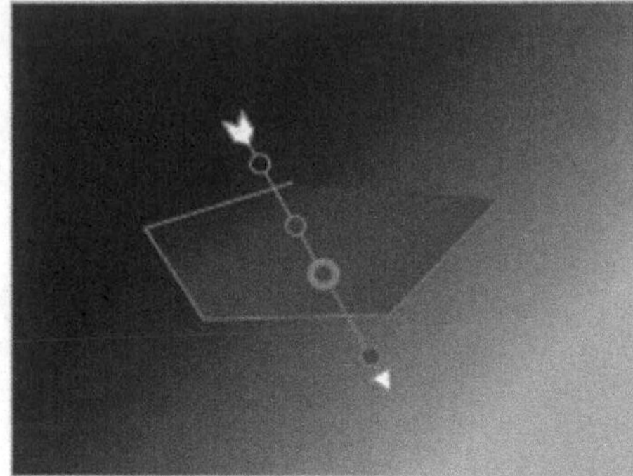

Figure 13-32. *Combining Tool Effects*

Instead of simply dropping points with the `Pen` tool, you can create curves by dragging points (see Figure 13-33). As you drag away from the point, a secondary line displays showing the angle and amplitude of the curve. The farther you drag away from the established point, the more the curve increases.

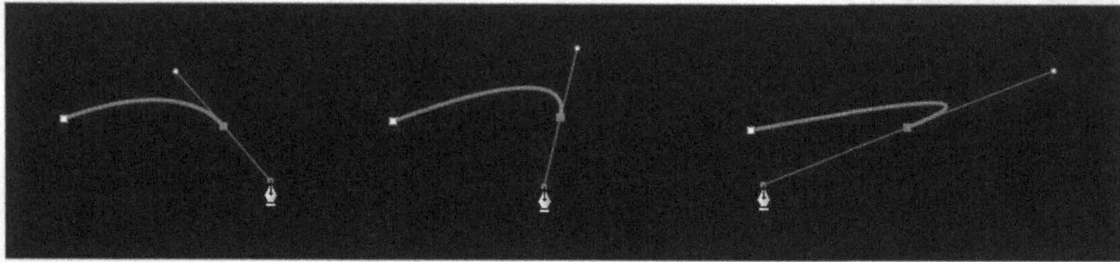

Figure 13-33. *Dragging to Curve Lines*

The `Pencil` tool, by contrast, is used for freehand drawing. Like the `Pen` tool, when you let up on the mouse, the shape takes on the current fill (see Figure 13-34). Be aware that the `Pencil` tool produces substantially more points in its XAML Data points collection.

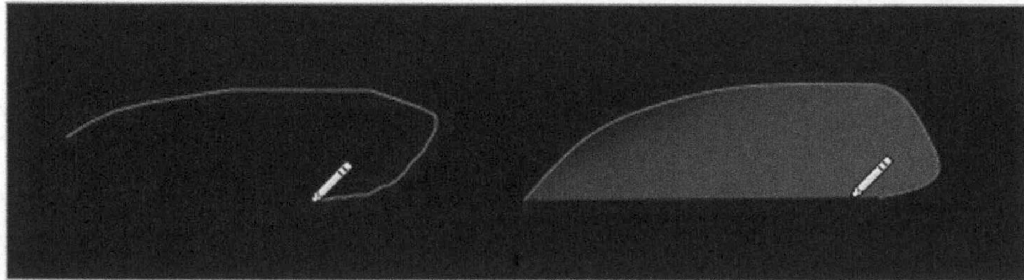

Figure 13-34. *Using the Pencil Tool*

Primitive shape tools include the Rectangle, Ellipse and Line (see Figure 13-35). You can alter the Fill and Stroke brushes, StrokeThickness and Opacity for effect. There are additional primitivesnot found in the Tools panel that you can findin Assets ➤ Shapes.

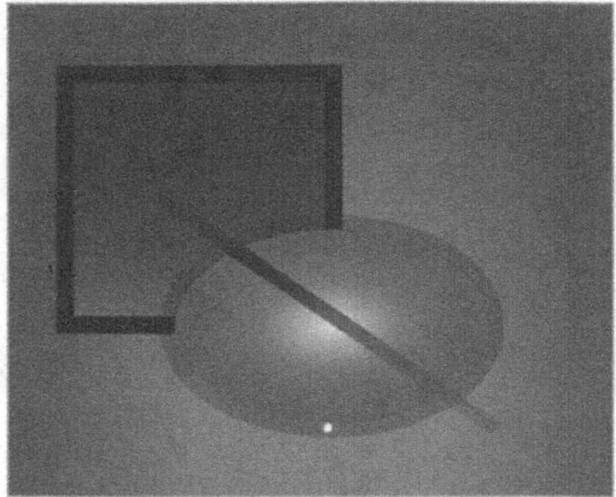

Figure 13-35. Using Primitives from the Tools Panel

Panels

You can find all the usual Panel objects used for layout control: Canvas, StackPanel, Grid, Border, ScrollViewer and Viewbox (see Figure 13-36). You can also select a number of elements on the Artboard, right-click and select Group Into from the context menu. This will create the panel and place the child controls within the panel.

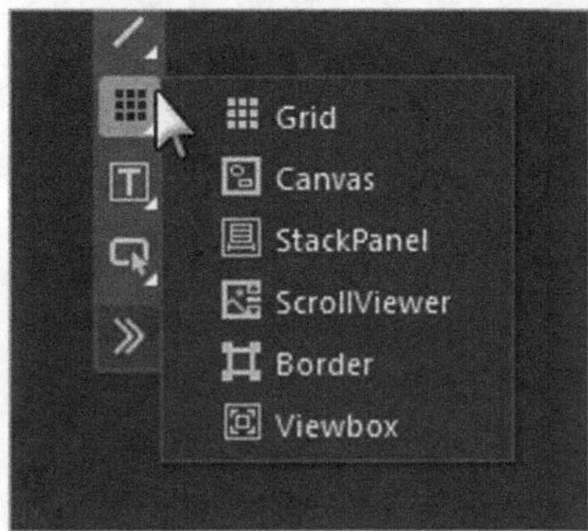

Figure 13-36. The Layout Panel Tools

Text Controls

The Text tools from the Tools panel provide easy access to TextBlock, TextBox, RichTextBox and PasswordBox (see Figure 13-37). Once the text control is in the designer, edit the text content directly by double-clicking the control or press F2. To exit text-editing mode, press the Esc key or click somewhere else on the Artboard.

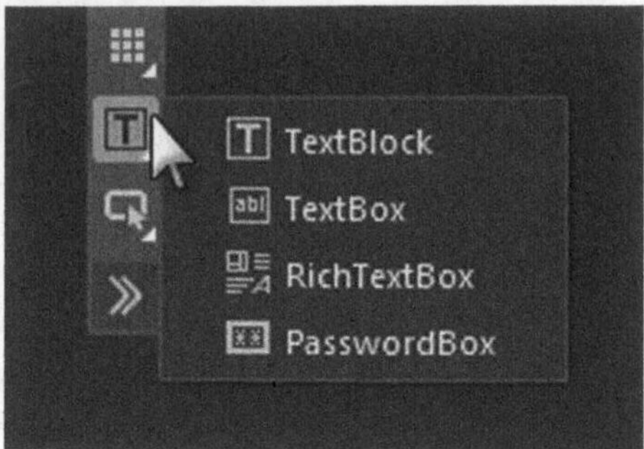

Figure 13-37. The Text Controls

Controls

This set of tools access commonly used controls for selection and input (see Figure 13-38). To get the full set of possible controls, use the `Assets` button.

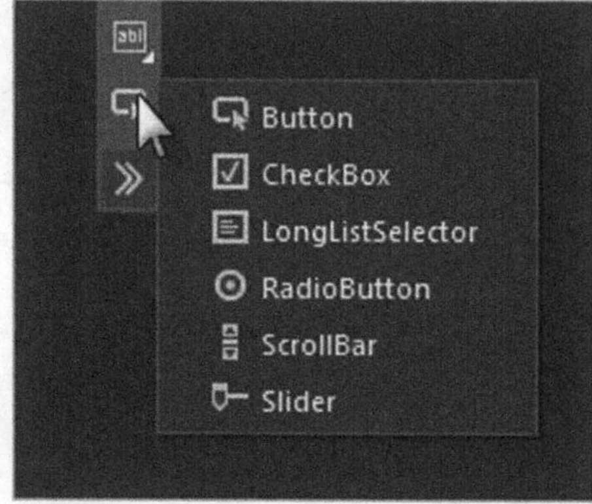

Figure 13-38. Commonly Used Controls

Assets

This double angle brackets "➤➤" button displays a pop out`Assets` window for easy access to all controls and resources (see Figure 13-39). Use the search box at the top to quickly filter on just the controls you're interested in. The left side of the Assets panel lists the possible categories of assets with a count of individual items in each category.

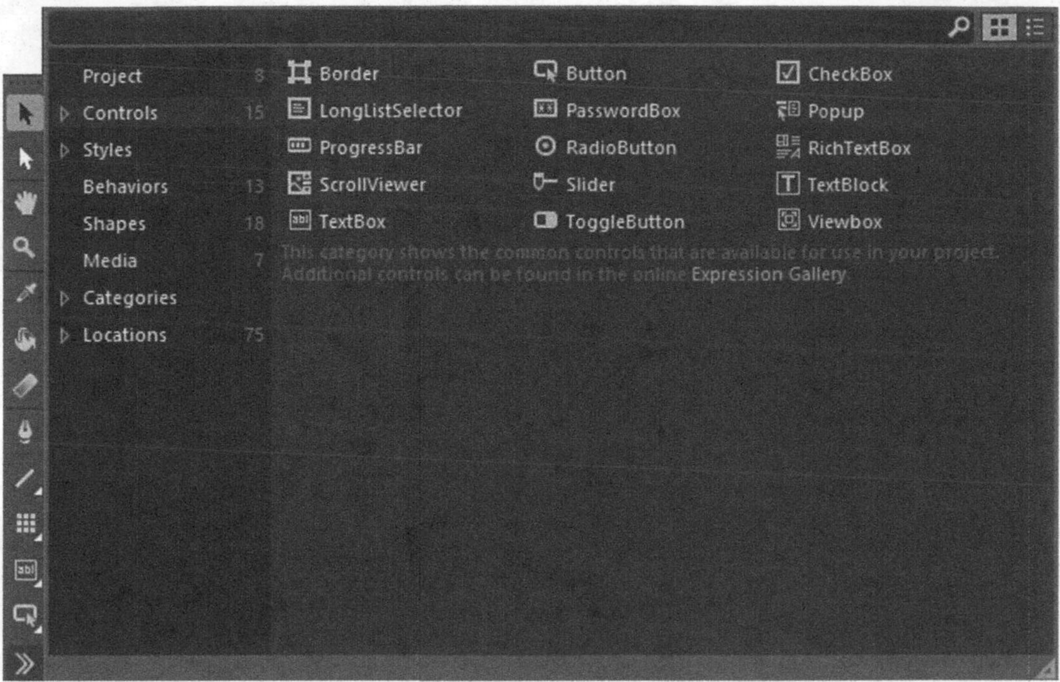

Figure 13-39. *The Popup Assets Panel*

The Artboard

Your application's visual interface is painted on the `Artboard` (see Figure 13-40). One or more files can be open in the file tabs along the top of the `Artboard`. The breadcrumb trail just below the file tabs synchronize with the `Objects` and `Timeline` panel. The breadcrumb trail also has a drop-down button with options for template editing. The top-right side of the `Artboard` has a drop-down file list with all files being edited. The active document view toggles between the design mode (shown below), XAML and a split between XAML and design.

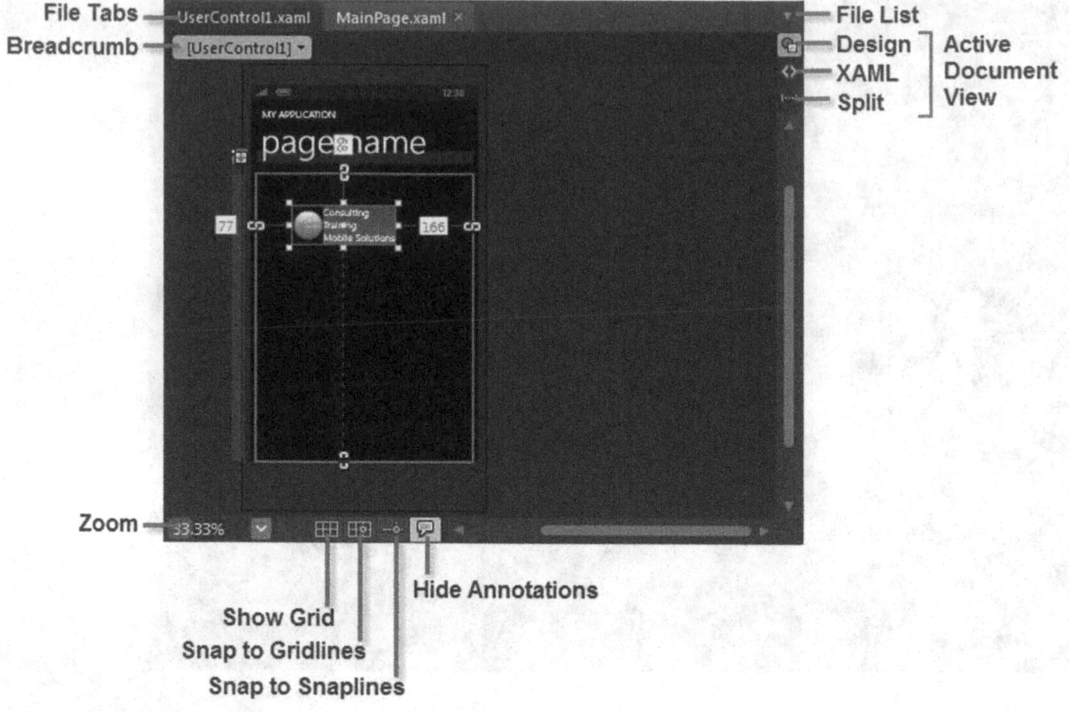

Figure 13-40. *The Artboard Layout*

The zoom control at the foot of the Artboard can take entry of an arbitrary zoom level or you can drop down to choose a preset zoom level. The buttons next to the zoom toggle effect visibility, show a grid overlay, toggle snap to grid lines, snap to snap lines (alignment guides between elements) and toggle annotations visibility.

How the Artboard handles the arrangement of elements on a page depends on the layout type, for example, using a layout type of `StackPanel`, `Canvas` or `Border`. One of the most flexible and powerful layout types is the `Grid` layout.

Grid Layout

Like most tasks in Blend, layout can be handled visually. This is great for grids because you can quickly define rows and columns visually without having to look at the XAML.

Resting the mouse over the top or left margins of a `Grid` element displays a divider arrow. Clicking the arrow places the divider at its current location. Figure 13-41 shows a divider in yellow as it's dragged along the top of the grid. Placing a divider establishes new columns. The right side of Figure 13-41 shows that you can change the proportions of the column by dragging the divider. Adding dividers along the left side of the grid creates new rows. To resize the columns or rows, drag the column or row divider.

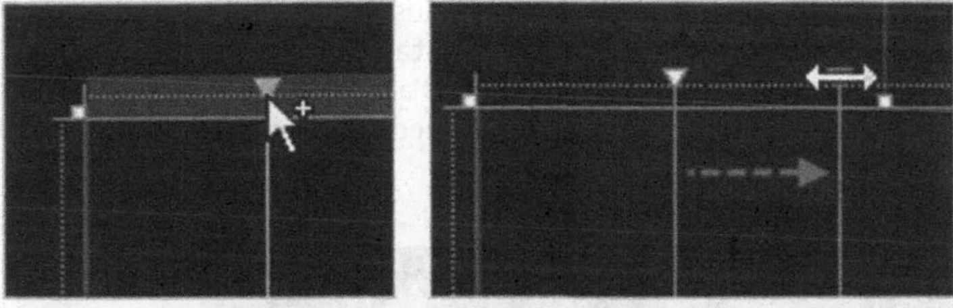

Figure 13-41. Placing and Dragging Columns

Dragging elements onto columns or rows automatically sets the `Grid.Row` and `Grid.Column` properties in the XAML (see Figure 13-42). Selecting an element in a `Grid` displays margin adorners to show up on all four sides of the `Grid`. The margin adorner indicates if a margin is set. The margin settings are displayed next to each margin adorner. Click a margin adorner to unset the margin for that edge.

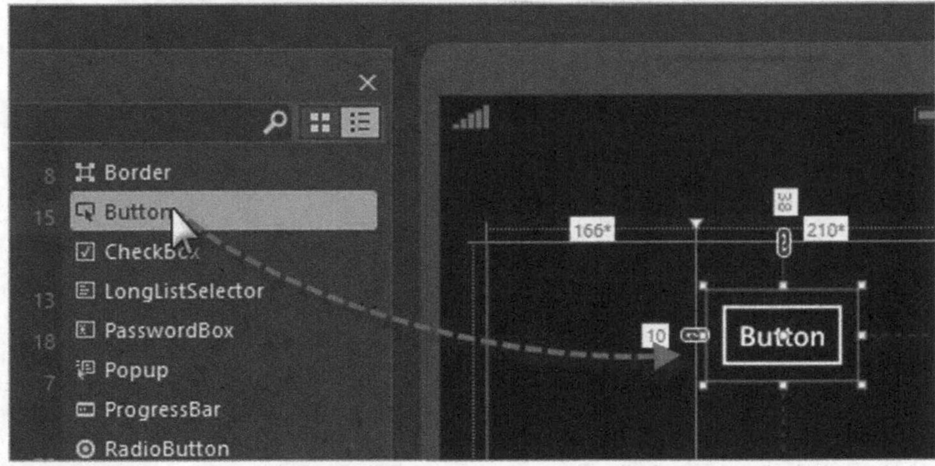

Figure 13-42. Dropping an Element on a Column

Also know that unsetting a margin may change other properties of the element such as the `Width`, `HorizontalAlignment` or `Vertical` alignment. To see how this works, click the `Split` button on the upper right of the `Artboard` so you can see both the `Design` and `Code` views are visible (see Figure 13-43).

Figure 13-43. Setting the Split View

Now click the margin adorners and view the effect on the elements in the column. Just before the screenshot for Figure 13-44 was taken, the Button `Margin` on the right was set to 97 and the `HorizontalAlignment` and `Width` properties were not assigned. Once the margin adorner on the right side was unset, the `Margin` on the right was set to zero, and because there was no right margin, the `HorizontalAlignment` and `Width` needed to be set to maintain the Button's position in the column.

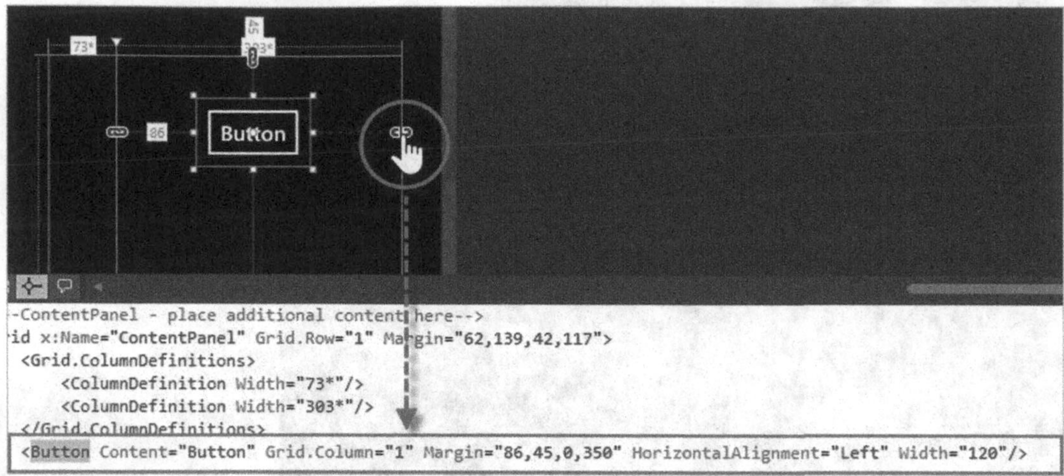

Figure 13-44. *Unsetting the Margin Adorner*

You may want to spend some time working with both the `Designer` and `Code` views present so you can begin to predict how the designer will edit your XAML.

Changing the Layout Type

Layout elements such as `Grid` or `StackPanel` can be switched to other types by right-clicking the element, selecting `Change Layout Type` from the context menu, and then picking an alternative layout from the sub menu. The context menu is available from the `Objects and Timeline` panel and directly in the `Artboard`. This is a welcome improvement over working directly in the XAML. Figure 13-45 shows changing the layout type to a `StackPanel`.

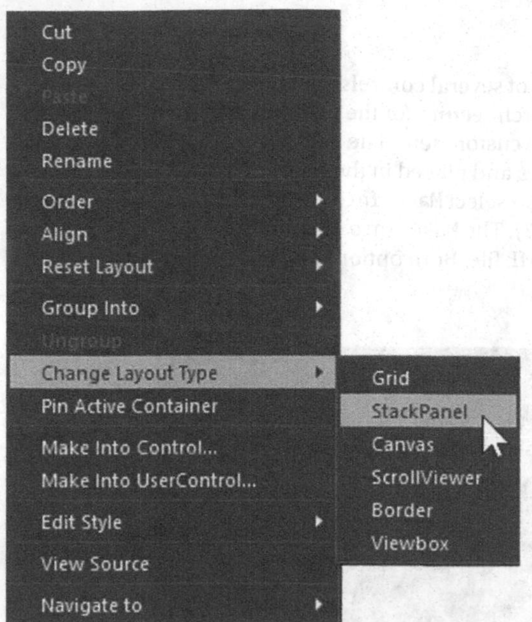

Figure 13-45. *Changing the Layout Type*

In related news, you can right-click an element or multiple elements and select one of the `Group Into` sub menu options. This option automatically creates the selected layout and plops the selected elements right inside it. Figure 13-46 shows three selected buttons being grouped into a Grid.

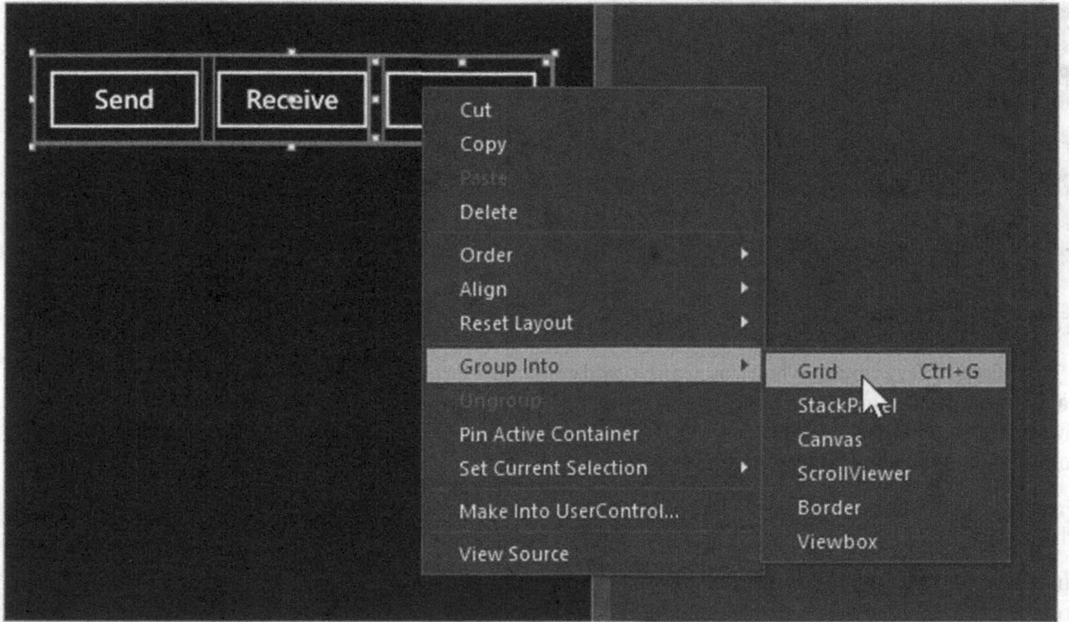

Figure 13-46. *Grouping Elements Into a Grid*

Creating Controls

Back in the day, if you wanted a customized control or a composite of several controls working as a unit, you needed to start with code and thorough understanding of the component architecture for the platform. The Blend approach is to work with existing elements in the `Artboard` and convert them to custom template controls or user controls.

Elements can be converted by Blend into different control types and placed in the same page XAML or as a `UserControl` in another file. Right-click any element on the page and select `Make Into Control...` to transform that element into a completely different type of control (see Figure 13-47). The `Make Into UserControl...`option converts the selected element into a new `UserControl` placed in its own XAML file. Both options open the door for customizing existing controls and code reuse.

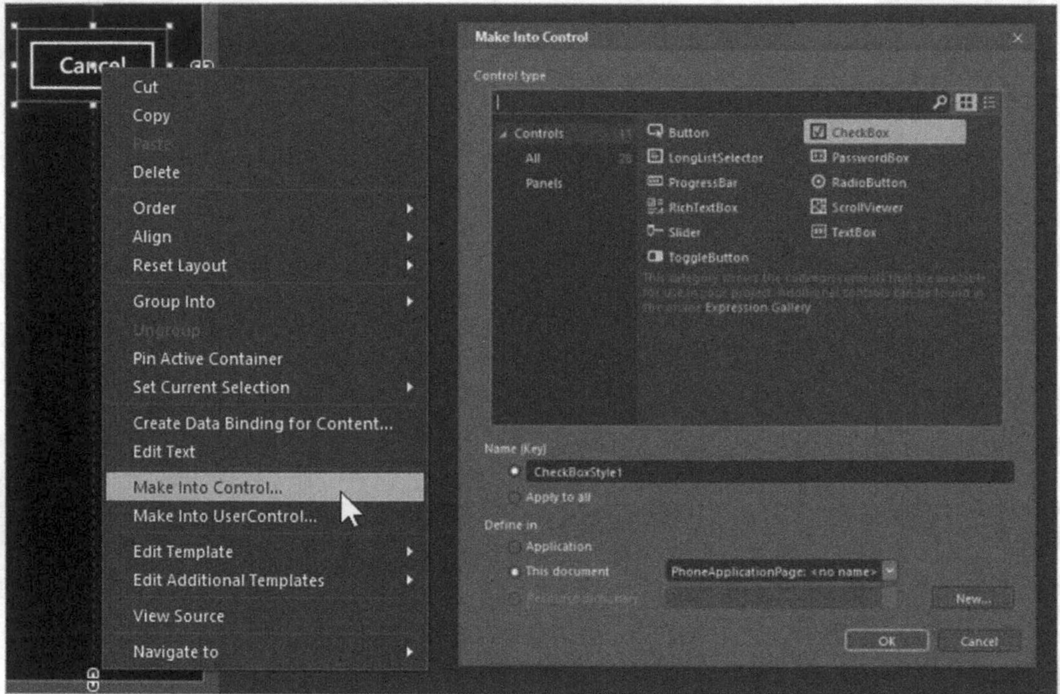

Figure 13-47. *Converting an Element Into Another Control Type*

Make Into Control

Use the `Make Into Control...` option when you want to add capabilities to a single element. This option converts the element into a new control type and uses templates to retain the original appearance of the element.

The following example takes an `Image` control that displays a coffee cup image and converts it into a `Button`. The control will continue to look like an image but will now act like a `Button`.

1. From the Blend main menu bar, select `File` ➤ `New Project` and create a new `Windows Phone App`.
2. In the `Projects` panel, select the `\Assets` folder. Then, drag a file named `coffeecup.png` from the Windows Explorer to the `\Assets` folder. This example image of a coffee cup has a transparent background, but you can use your own image for this. Blend creates an `Image` element and sets the `Source` property of the `Image` to point to the `coffeecup.png` file.

3. Drag the `coffeecup.png` image file from `Projects` panelonto the `ContentPanel` of the page. You can drag the image file directly onto the `Artboard`. Once the image file is dragged to the Artboard, Blend creates an `Image` object.

■ **Note** The `Objects and Timeline` panel will highlight the `ContentPanel` when you have the dragged image over the correct portion of the Artboard.

---

4. In the `Properties` panel, find the `Layout` category of properties, find the `Margin` property and click the white button located on the right. Click the `Reset` button from the context menu as shown in Figure 13-48.

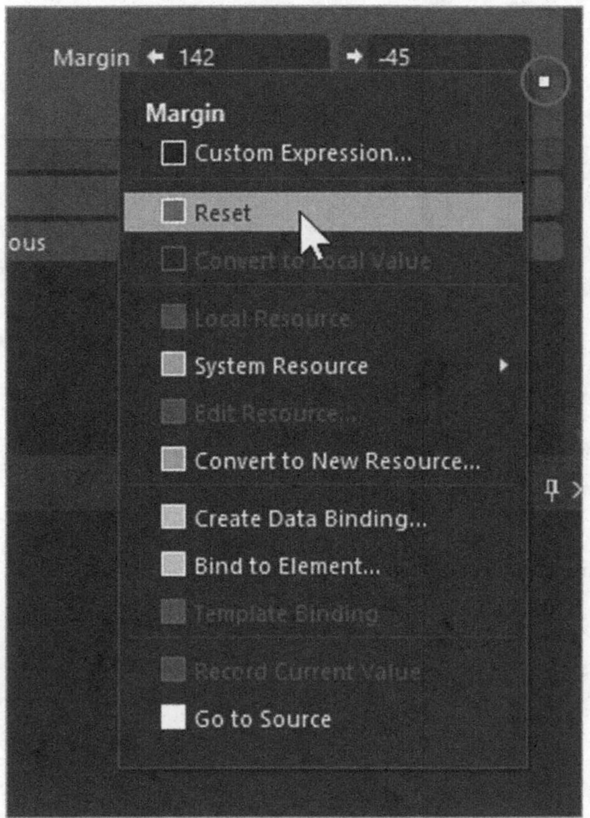

***Figure 13-48.** Resetting the Margin Property*

At this point, the element is still an `Image` (see Figure 13-49).

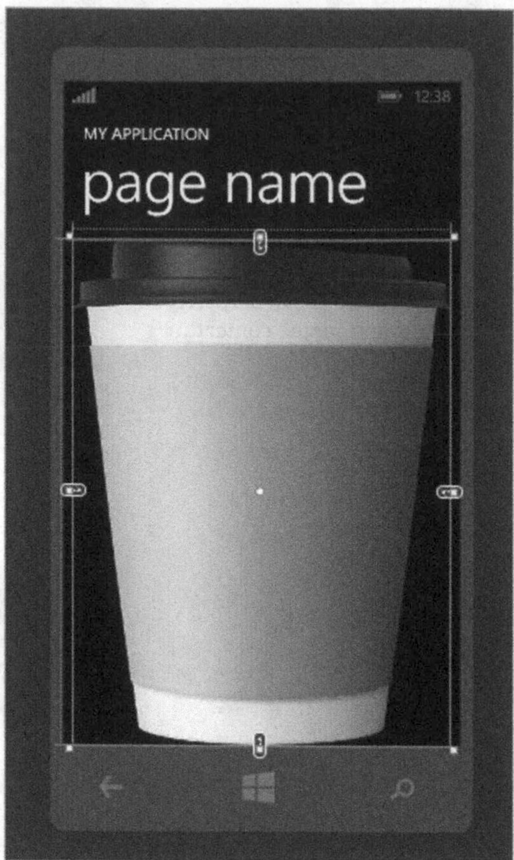

Figure 13-49. *The Image Control in the Designer*

5. Right-click the image to bring up the context menu and select the `Make Into Control...` option as shown in Figure 13-50.

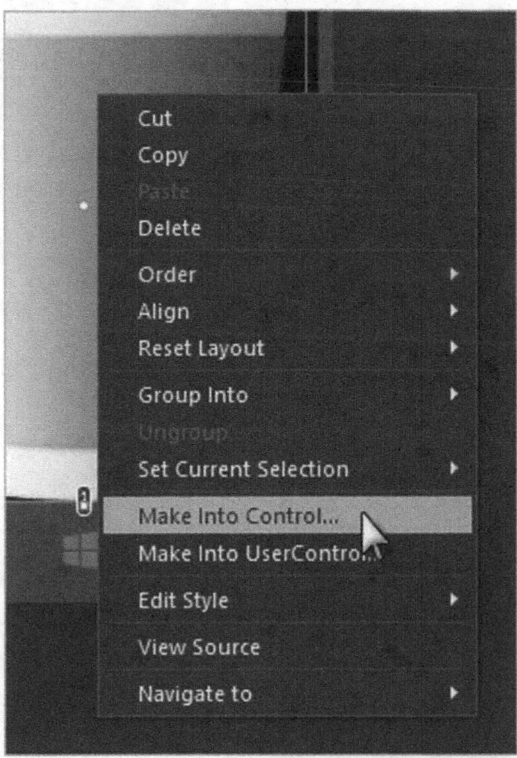

***Figure 13-50.** Selecting the `Make Into Control` option*

6. In the `Make Into Control` dialog, choose the `Button` control type and set the `Name` to `BaristaButtonStyle` as shown in Figure 13-51. Click the `OK` button.

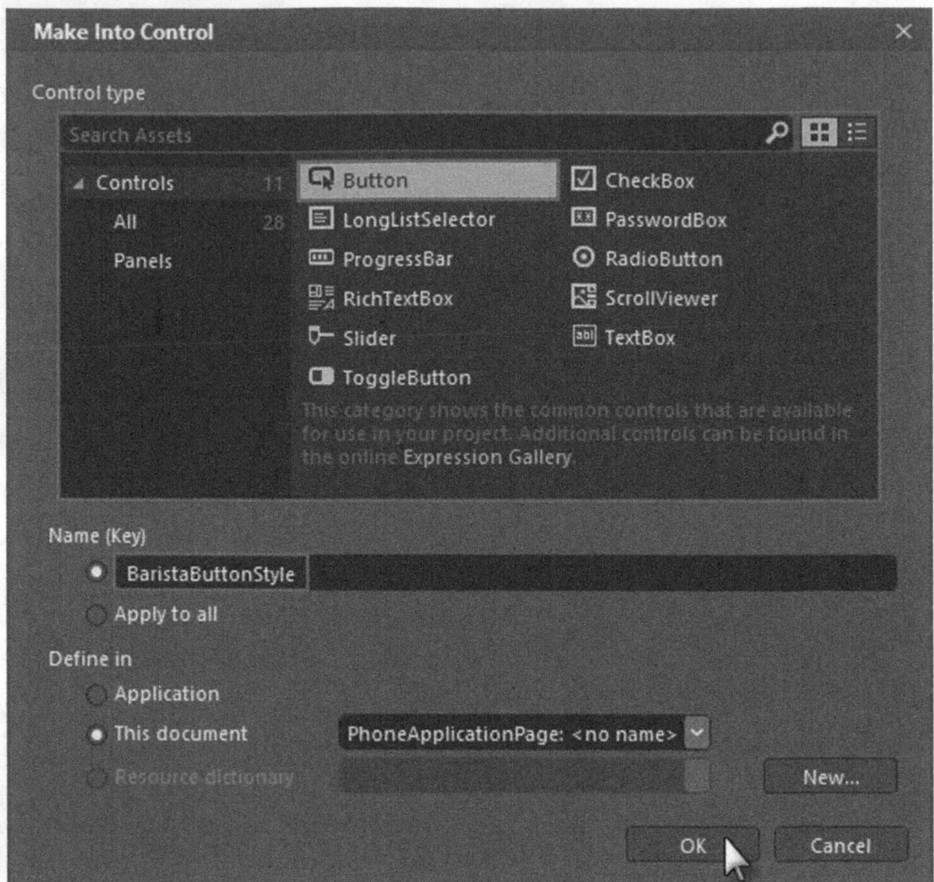

Figure 13-51. *Assigning the Initial Control Properties*

7. In the `Artboard`, switch to the XAML view and find the `ContentPanel` element.

A quick look at the resulting XAML (see Listing 13-3) tells us that the `Image` was turned into a `Button` and the `BaristaButtonStyle` makes the button look very much like the image we started with. The former image now has all the functionality of a button. The new events, methods and behavior are all there. The `Content`property has been assigned the default "Button" value that displays in the new control.

Listing 13-3. The New Button Control

```
<Grid x:Name="ContentPanel" Grid.Row="1" Margin="12,0,12,0">
<Button Content="Button" Style="{StaticResource BaristaButtonStyle}"/>
</Grid>
```

8. In the XAML, locate the `BaristaButtonStyle Style` definition (see Listing 13-4). The style creates a new `ControlTemplate` with a `Grid` that contains both the `Image` and a `ContentPresenter`. The `ContentPresenter` acts as a placeholder to display whatever `Content` is assigned.

Listing 13-4. Defining the BaristaButtonStyle

```
<Style x:Key="BaristaButtonStyle" TargetType="Button">
<Setter Property="Template">
<Setter.Value>
<ControlTemplate TargetType="Button">
        <Grid>
        <Image Source="Assets/coffeecup.png" Stretch="Fill"/>
        <ContentPresenter
HorizontalAlignment="{TemplateBinding HorizontalContentAlignment}"
        VerticalAlignment="{TemplateBinding VerticalContentAlignment}"/>
        </Grid>
</ControlTemplate>
</Setter.Value>
</Setter>
</Style>
```

The `Make Into Control` option has converted the `Image` control into another type of control, namely a `Button`. The styling makes the `Button` look like the original `Image` control but have the behaviors of a `Button`. This option works well for a single element that doesn't need additional code-behind logic. If you need to composite multiple controls or need custom code-behind logic for a control, consider the `Make Into UserControl` option.

Make Into UserControl

Use the `Make Into UserControl...` option when you want to composite multiple elements together as a single control or when you need to add code-behind logic to the control.

This example will create a control that contains several elements and responds to its own events and code-behind. The example control responds to taps by the user and displays coffee drink suggestions on the side of the coffee cup (see Figure 13-52).

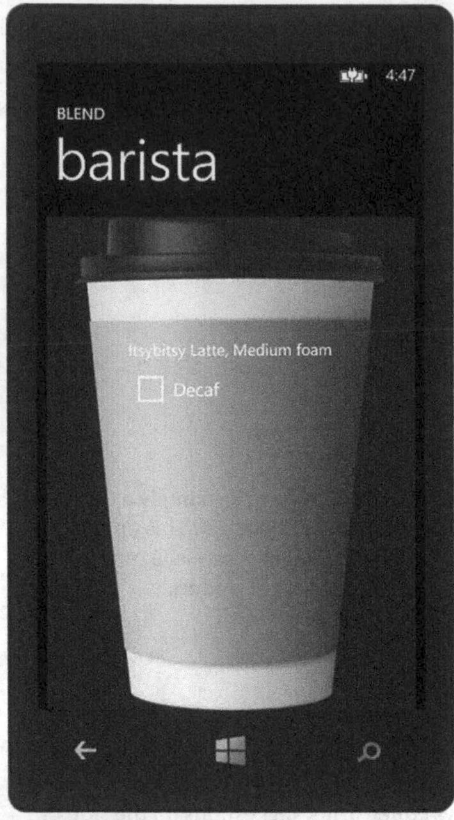

Figure 13-52. *The Barista Application*

Setting Up the Project

First, setup the project with an image file and an Image control.

1. From the Blend main menu bar, select File ➤ New Project and create a new Windows Phone App.
2. In the Projects panel, select the \Assets folder. Then, drag a file named coffeecup.png from the Windows Explorer to the \Assets folder. This example image of a coffee cup has a transparent background, but you can use your own image for this.
3. Drag the coffeecup.png image file from Projects panel onto the ContentPanel of the page.
4. In the Properties panel, find the Layout category of properties, find the Margin property and click the white button located on the right. Click the Reset button from the context menu. From the Common Properties group, find Stretch and reset that property as well (see Figure 13-53).

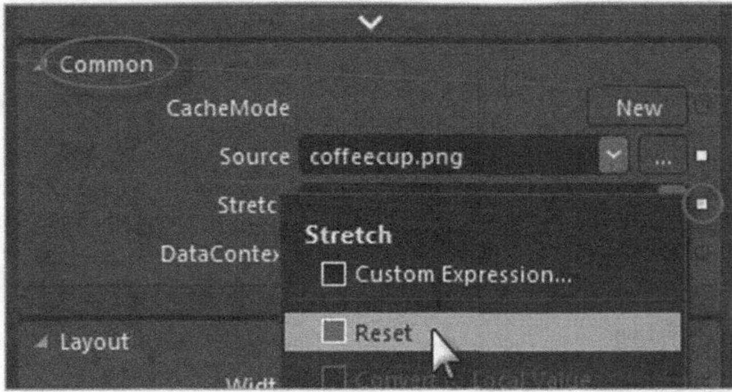

***Figure 13-53.** Resetting the Image Stretch Property*

5. At this point, the Image should take up most of the client area. Switch to the XAML view and verify that the XAML has no extra properties set. The XAML for `ContentPanel` should look like the example in Listing 13-5.

   Listing 13-5. The ContentPanel XAML

```
<Grid x:Name="ContentPanel" Grid.Row="1" Margin="12,0,12,0">
        <Image Source="Assets/coffeecup.png"/>
</Grid>
```

Creating the UserControl

Next, convert the `Image` into a `UserControl`and design the layout for the new control.

1. In the Blend design view, right-click the `Image`.
2. Select `Make Into UserControl...` from the context menu. Name the control `BaristaControl` and then click the `OK` button as shown in Figure 13-54.

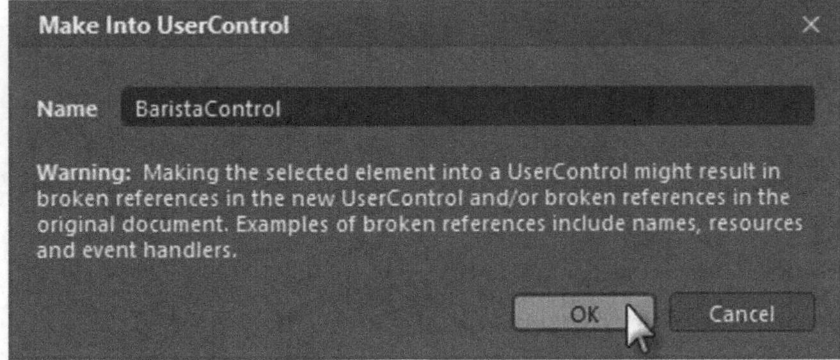

***Figure 13-54.** Naming the UserControl*

■ **Tip** Notice the warning "Making the selected element into a UserControl might result in broken references…" Quite right. You should create the user control as early as possible, before you've added logic or resources.

Notice that new files are created: `BaristaControl.xaml` and `BaristaControl.xaml.cs`. `BaristaControl.xaml`is showing in the `Artboard` and the `Objects and Timeline` panel (see Figure 13-55).

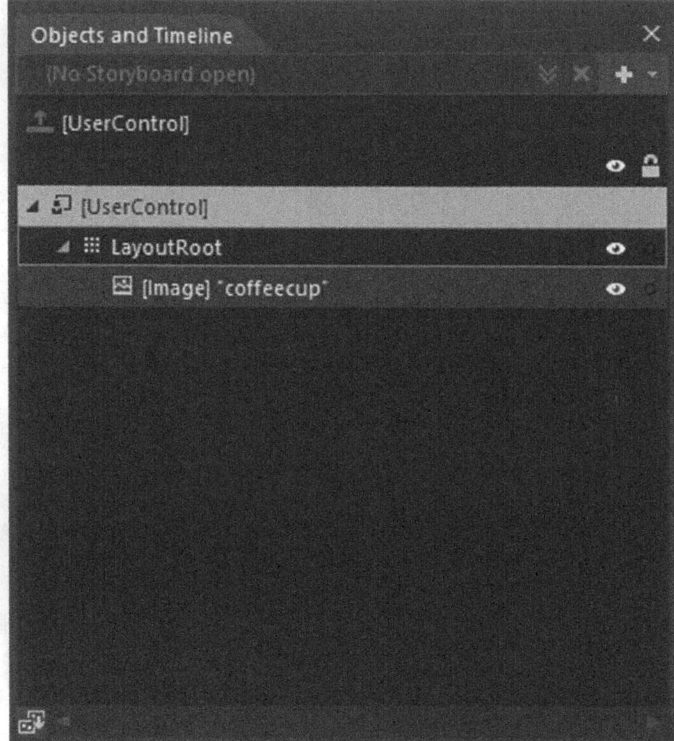

***Figure 13-55.** The UserControl in the Objects and Timeline Panel*

3. Now double-click `MainPage.xaml` in the `Projects` panel to open the file. Navigate to the XAML view and notice the reference to the `BaristaControl` and that the `Image` control is no longer there (see Listing 13-6).

   Listing 13-6. The MainPage ContentPanel UserControl Reference

   ```
   <Grid x:Name="ContentPanel" Grid.Row="1" Margin="12,0,12,0">
           <local:BaristaControl/>
   </Grid>
   ```

4. Double-click `BaristaControl.xaml` in the `Projects` panel.

5. In the Objects and Timeline panel, select the LayoutRoot element. In the Assets panel, select Controls ➤ Panels, then double-click Grid.
6. In the Properties panel, set the following properties as shown in Figure 13-56:
    a. Set the Name property to CoffeeSleeveGrid.
    b. In the Layout property group, reset the Width and Height properties by clicking the small white square, then selecting Reset from the context menu.
    c. Reset the HorizontalAlignment and VerticalAlignment properties.
    d. Set the Margin 100 from the left, 75 from the right and 150 from the top and 50 from the bottom.

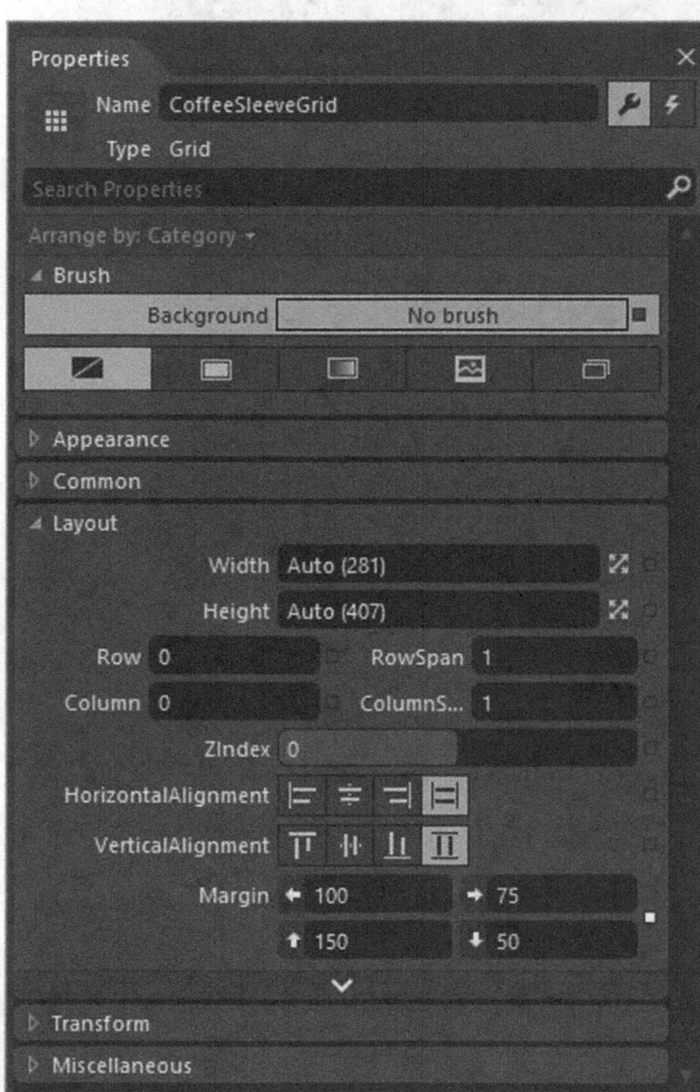

Figure 13-56. *The CoffeeSleeveGrid Properties*

7. Click the downward arrow at the bottom of the Layout group to show advanced properties. Click the ellipses next to the RowDefinitions collection property.

8. In the RowDefinition Collection Editor dialog that displays, click the Add button twice to create two row definitions. Select each RowDefinition in the list and set the Layout Height to Auto as shown in Figure 13-57. Click the OK button to close the dialog.

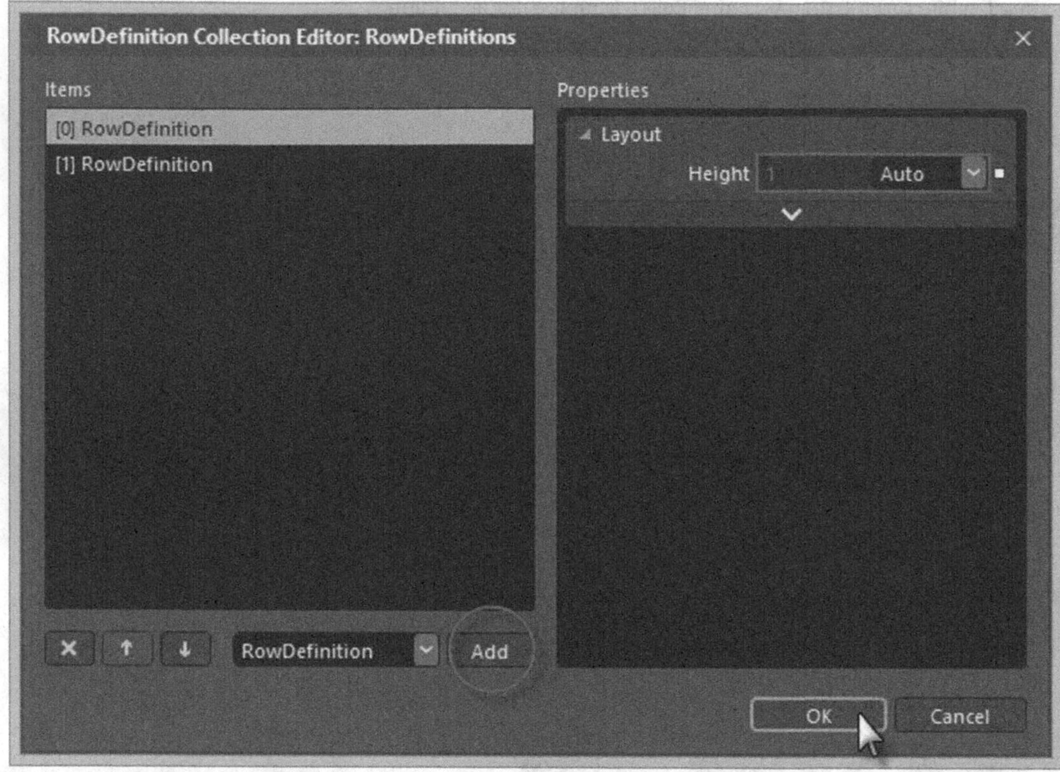

***Figure 13-57.** Adding and Configuring Grid RowDefinitions*

9. In the Objects and Timeline panel, make sure the CoffeeSleeveGrid element is selected. In the Assets panel, select Styles ➤ System Styles, then double-click PhoneTextNormalStyle. This will create a styled TextBlock inside the grid.

10. With the TextBlock still selected, reset the Properties ➤ Layout HorizontalAlignment and VerticalAlignment properties.

11. In the Objects and Timelinepanel, re-select the CoffeeSleeveGridelement. In the Assets panel, select Controls, then double-click CheckBox.

12. With the Checkbox still selected, set the Properties ➤ Layout ➤ Row property to 1. Reset the HorizontalAlignment and VerticalAlignment properties. Set the Common ➤ Content property to "Decaf" (see Figure 13-58).

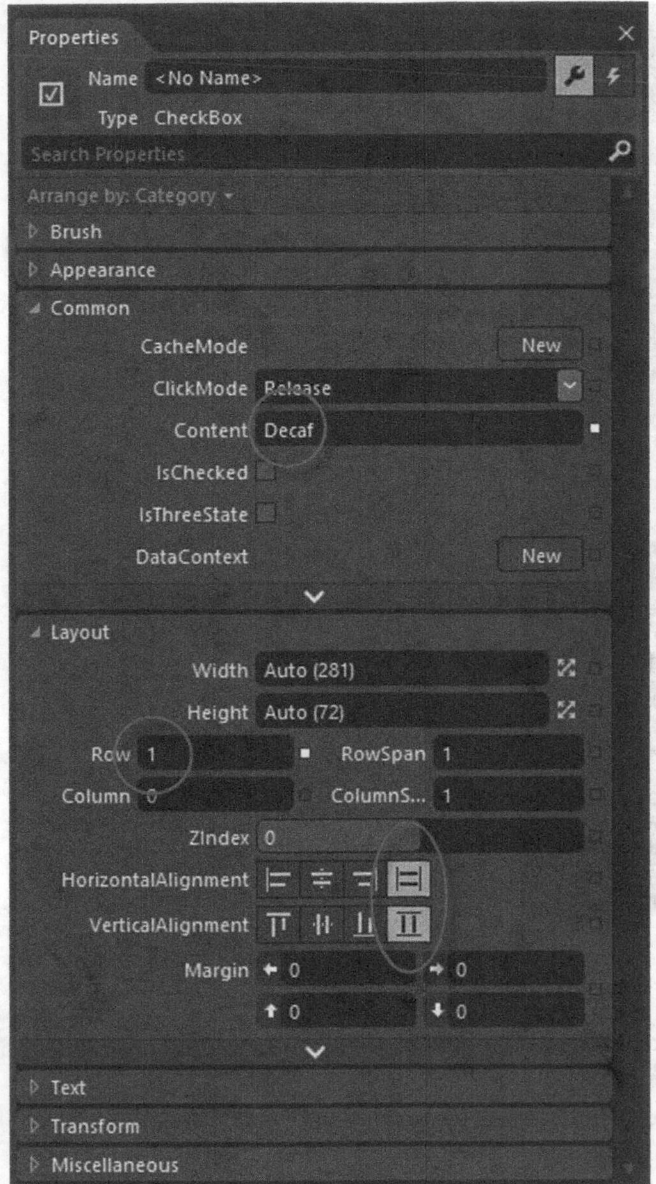

***Figure 13-58.** Assigning the Checkbox Properties*

13. Double-check that the layout for the `UserControl` looks something like figure 13-59.

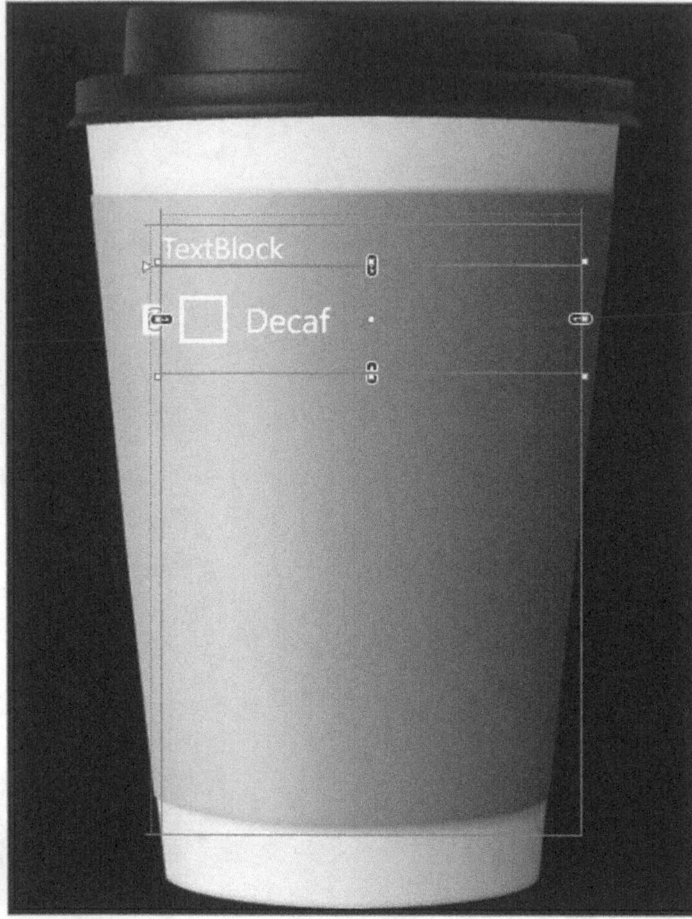

Figure 13-59. *The UserControl layout*

14. In the Artboard, double-click the TextBlock that reads "MY APPLICATION" and enter "BLEND" in its place.

15. Also in the Artboard, double-click the TextBlock that reads "page name" and enter "barista" in its place.

Creating the ViewModel

Next, setup a ViewModel that will represent drink suggestions with randomized sizes, drinks, amount of foam and so on.

1. In the Projects panel, right-click the project and select Add New Item...

2. In the New Item dialog, select Class and set the Name to BaristaEnums.cs. Replace the BaristaEnums class with the code in Listing 13-7.

Listing 13-7. Defining the Enumerations

```
public enum Sizes
{
Itsybitsy, Wee, Diminutive, Tiny, Small, Medium, Large, Huge, Colossal, Planatoid
};

public enum Drink
{
Coffee, Latte, Mocha, Mochachino, Americano, Cappuccino, Espresso
};

public enum Foam
{
Light, Medium, Heavy
}
```

3. Create another class named `Order.cs` and populate with the code in Listing 13-8.

Listing 13-8. Defining the Order Class

```
public class Order
{
    public Sizes Size { get; set; }
    public Drink Drink { get; set; }
    public Foam Foam { get; set; }
    public bool Decaf { get; set; }

    public string Description
    {
        get { return String.Format("{0} {1}, {2} foam", Size, Drink, Foam); }
    }
}
```

4. Create a third class named `Barista.cs` and populate with the code in Listing 13-9. Add a reference to `System.ComponentModel` to the `using` statements. The `MakeSuggestion()` method creates a new `CurrentOrder` with random values. The `Barista` class supports `INotifyPropertyChanged`, so when `CurrentOrder` is assigned, the binding updates, and we will see the new order description displayed on the coffee cup in the user interface.

Listing 13-9. Defining the Barista Class

```
public class Barista : INotifyPropertyChanged
{
    public Barista()
    {
        MakeSuggestion();
    }

    private Order _order;
    public Order CurrentOrder
    {
        get { return _order; }
```

```
            set
            {
                _order = value;
                if (PropertyChanged != null)
                {
                    PropertyChanged(this, new PropertyChangedEventArgs("CurrentOrder"));
                }
            }
        }

        // Create a new Order with random settings and assign to the
        // CurrentOrder property
        public void MakeSuggestion()
        {
            var random = new Random();

            CurrentOrder = new Order()
                         {
                             Size = (Sizes)random.Next(9),
                             Drink = (Drink)random.Next(7),
                             Foam = (Foam)random.Next(2),
                             Decaf = random.Next(2) == 1
                         };
        }
        public event PropertyChangedEventHandler PropertyChanged;
    }
```

Binding the ViewModel

These next steps attach the ViewModel to the user interface. All these steps can be performed without having to work with the XAML.

1. From the Blend main menu bar, select `Window` ➤ `Data` to display the `Data` panel.
2. In the `Project` panel, double-click `BaristaControl.xaml`.
3. In the `Data` panel, hover the mouse over the tool bar until you find the `Create Data Source` button on the far right side. Click the downward-pointing arrow and select `Create Object Data Source` from the context menu as shown in Figure 13-60.

***Figure 13-60.** Displaying the Create Object Data Source dialog*

4. In the `Create Object Data Source` dialog that displays, select `Barista` and click the `OK` button as shown in Figure 13-61.

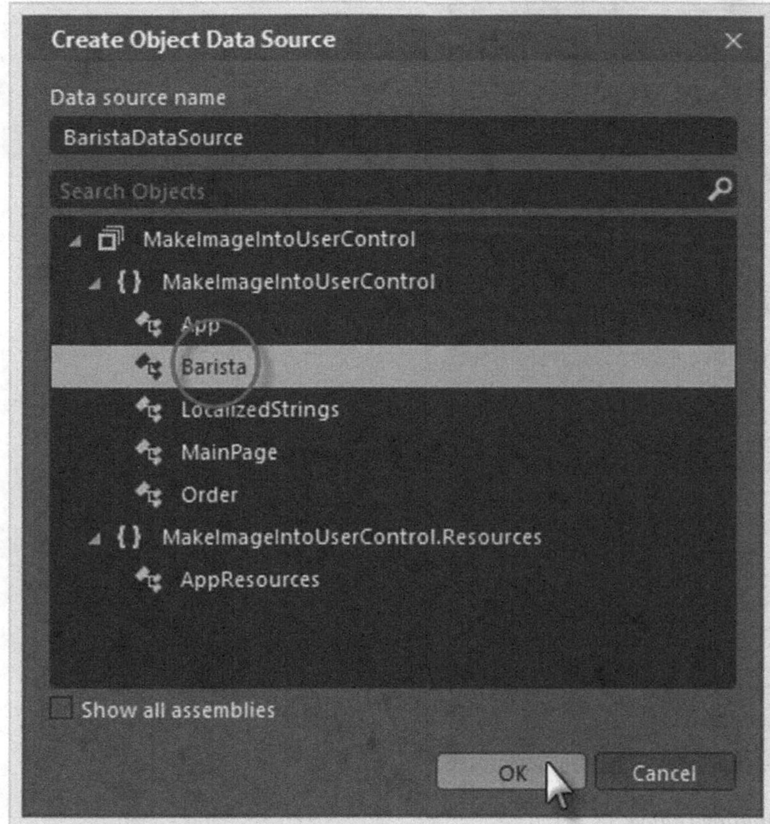

Figure 13-61. *Creating the BaristDataSource*

5. In the `Project` panel, double-click `BaristaControl.xaml`.
6. In the `Objects and Timeline` panel, select the `TextBlock`. In the Properties panel, locate the`Common ➤ Text` property. Click the small white button to the right of the property for advanced options and select `Create Data Binding...` from the context menu as shown in Figure 13-62. This will display the `Create Data Binding` dialog.

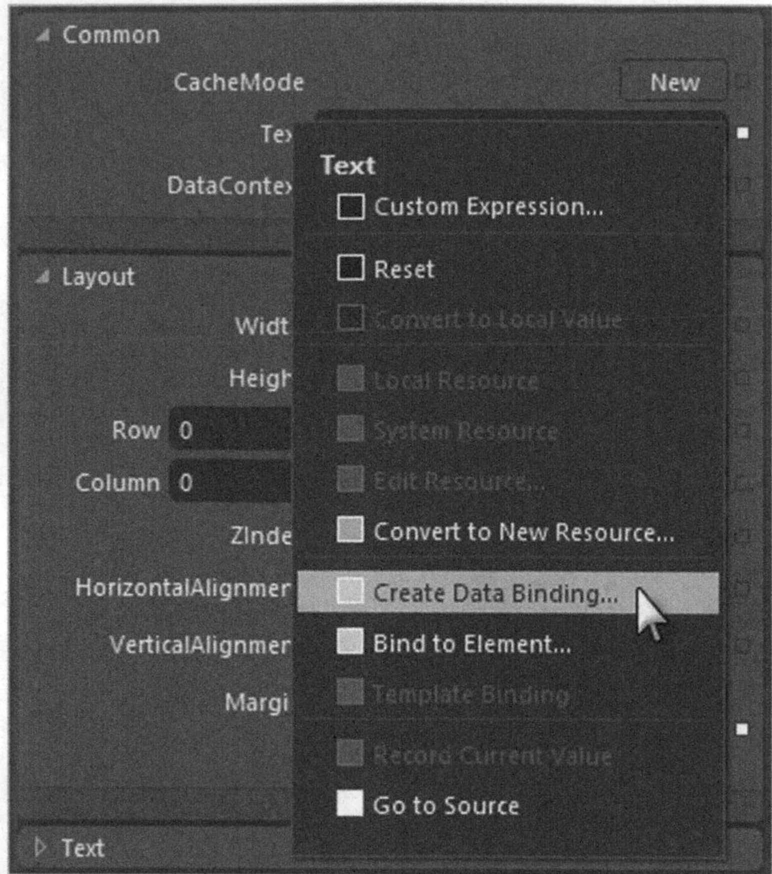

Figure 13-62. *Displaying the Create Data Binding Dialog*

7. In the `Data source` list, select `BaristaDataSource`. In the `Path` list, select the `CurrentOrder` ➤ `Description` property. Click `OK` to create the binding and close the dialog. The `TextBlock` is now bound, and you will see design time data in the `Artboard` as shown in Figure 13-63.

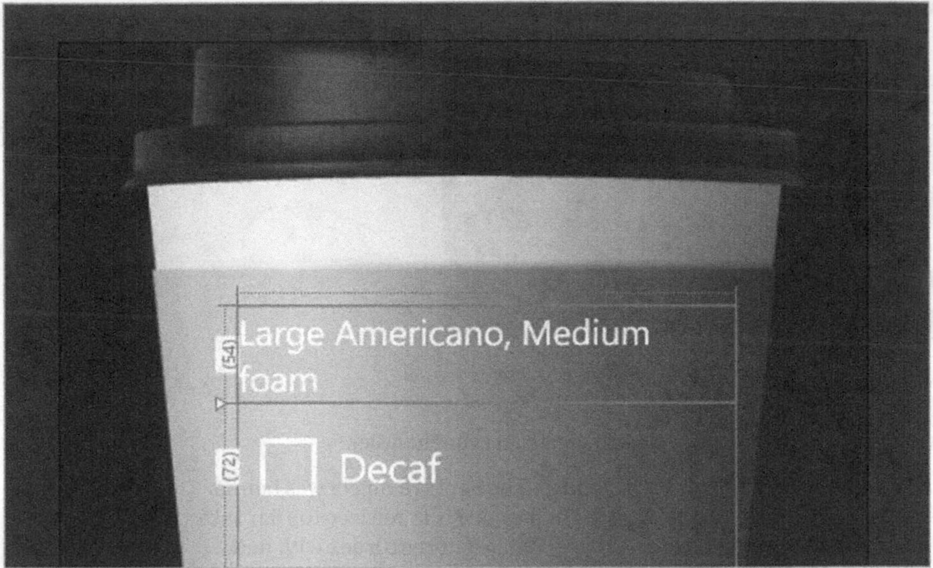

Figure 13-63. *Bound Textblock with Data*

8. In the Objects and Timeline panel, select the `CheckBox` and locate the `Properties` ➤ `Common` ➤ `IsChecked` property. Click the small button to the right of the property and select `Create Data Binding...` from the popup menu. This will display the `Create Data Binding` dialog.

9. In the `Create Data Binding` dialog, in the `Path` list, select `Barista` ➤ `CurrentOrder` ➤ `Decaf`. Also in the `Create Data Binding` dialog, open the `More settings` area. Set the `Binding Direction` to `OneWay` in the drop-down list. Click the `OK` button to create the binding and close the dialog.

Coding the Page

The last step is to hook up events and code so the user can tap the cup and the text will change.

1. In the `Projects` panel, double-click `BaristaControl.xaml` to open the design view in the `Artboard`.

2. In the `Objects and Timeline` panel, select the `LayoutRoot` element.

3. In the `Properties` panel click the `Events` button as shown in Figure 13-64.

Figure 13-64. *Selecting Event Properties*

4. Find the `Tap` event in the list and double-click to create an event handler.
5. Add the code in Listing 13-10 to the `Tap` event handler. The `Barista` object was bound to the `DataContext` of `LayoutRoot`, so the first step in the code is to retrieve the `Barista` object. The `MakeSuggestion()` method is called to populate `CurrentOrder` with new random settings. `CurrentOrder` is hooked up to the `NotifyPropertyChanged` event, so the new data will be displayed in the `UserControl`.

Listing 13-10. Handling the Tap Event

```
private void LayoutRoot_Tap(object sender, System.Windows.Input.GestureEventArgs e)
{
        Barista barista = (sender as FrameworkElement).DataContext as Barista;
        barista.MakeSuggestion();
}
```

6. Press `F5` to run the application (see Figure 13-65).

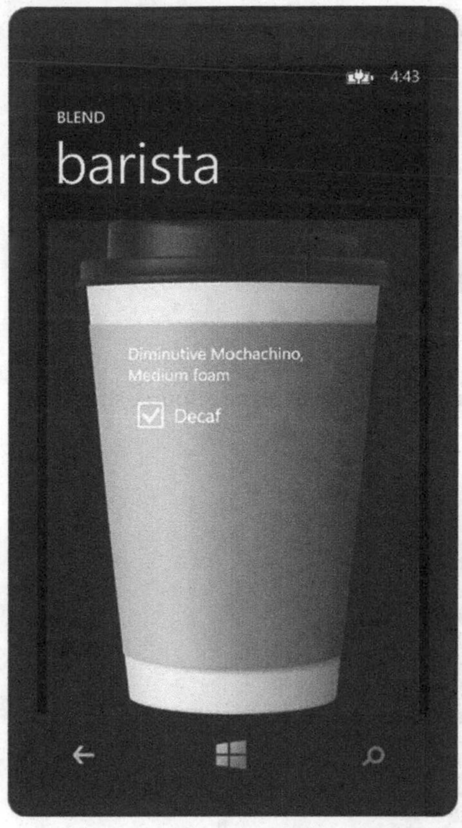

Figure 13-65. The Running Barista Application

Custom Templates

Chapter 3 introduced `ControlTemplates` and `DataTemplates`, working directly in the XAML for the most part. Blend lets you tweak the appearance of data templates and entire controls without having to write your own XAML.

Custom Templates Tour

Templates can be created completely from scratch or by using an existing template as a starting point. Let's try both and compare the results.

Starting with a new Windows Phone App with a single `Button` on the page as a guinea pig, right-click the `Button` and select `Edit Template ➤ Create Empty...`(see Figure 13-66).

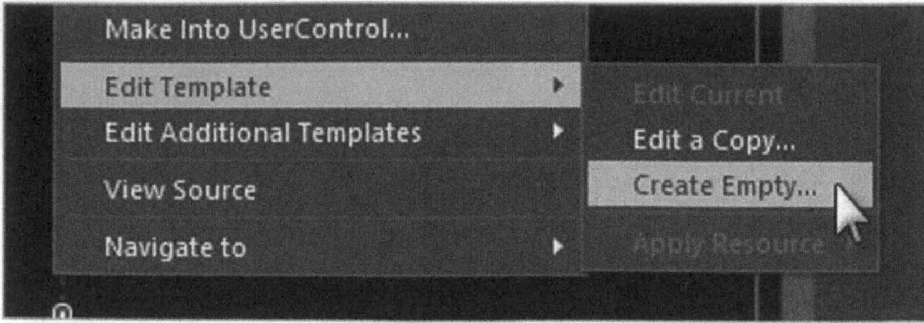

Figure 13-66. *Creating an Empty Template*

The `Create ControlTemplate Resource` dialog allows you to `Name` and `Define in` where the resource should be placed (see Figure 13-67). Take the defaults and click the `OK` button.

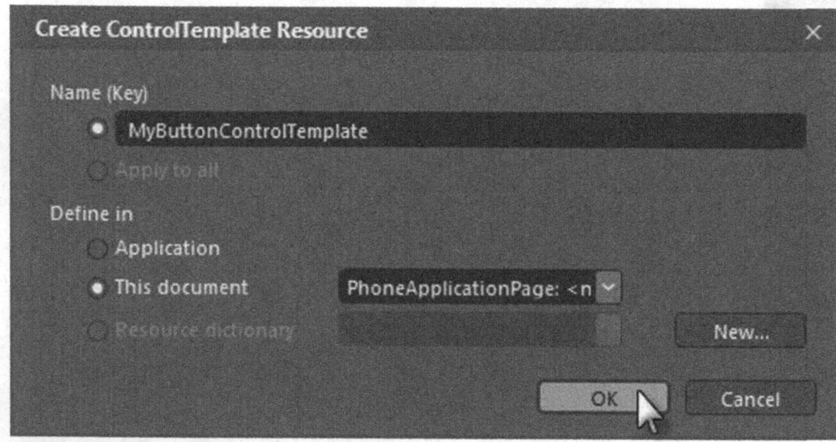

Figure 13-67. *Assigning the Name and Location of the ControlTemplate*

Blend creates a resource with a control template and references the template from the button (see Listing 13-11). It's left up to you to figure out what goes in the template. Without knowing more about what should go in the template, this is going to be one very blank, non-functional button.

Listing 13-11. The Generated ControlTemplate XAML

```
<phone:PhoneApplicationPage.Resources>
        <ControlTemplate x:Key="MyButtonControlTemplate" TargetType="Button">
                <Grid/>
        </ControlTemplate>
</phone:PhoneApplicationPage.Resources>

...

<Button Content="Button" HorizontalAlignment="Left" Margin="59,66,0,0" VerticalAlignment="Top"
        Template="{StaticResource MyButtonControlTemplate}"/>
```

Blend provides a better way by giving you a `ControlTemplate` with a copy of the default style. Let's start over and try again, this time selecting the `Edit a Copy...` menu option. The option displays the Create Style Resource dialog as shown in Figure 13-68.

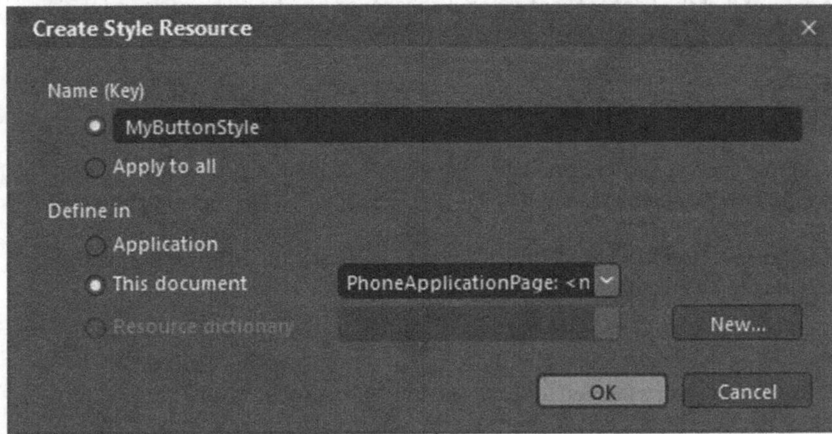

Figure 13-68. *Creating the Style Resource*

The button on the page looks the same, but you can "pop the hood" and get at all the visual aspects of the control. Figure 13-69 shows a small sampling of the XAML that's produced in the page's `Resources` tag.

```
<phone:PhoneApplicationPage.Resources>
    <Style x:Key="MyButtonStyle" TargetType="Button">
        <Setter Property="Background" Value="Transparent"/>
        <Setter Property="BorderBrush" Value="{StaticResource PhoneForegroundBrush}"/>
        <Setter Property="Foreground" Value="{StaticResource PhoneForegroundBrush}"/>
        <Setter Property="BorderThickness" Value="{StaticResource PhoneBorderThickness}"/>
        <Setter Property="FontFamily" Value="{StaticResource PhoneFontFamilySemiBold}"/>
        <Setter Property="FontSize" Value="{StaticResource PhoneFontSizeMedium}"/>
        <Setter Property="Padding" Value="10,5,10,6"/>
        <Setter Property="Template">
            <Setter.Value>
                <ControlTemplate TargetType="Button">
                    <Grid Background="Transparent">
                        <VisualStateManager.VisualStateGroups>
                            <VisualStateGroup x:Name="CommonStates">
                                <VisualState x:Name="Normal"/>
                                <VisualState x:Name="MouseOver"/>
                                <VisualState x:Name="Pressed">
                                    <Storyboard>
```

Figure 13-69. *Sample of Generated Resources*

Take a moment to browse MainPage in Blend Code view. The ControlTemplate includes a Grid, a Border inside the Grid and a ContentControl inside the Border. Even more intriguing is the VisualStateManager.VisualStateGroups section that defines visual states for the control, for example, MouseOver, Pressed, and so on. Also notice the Storyboard collections of animations that execute when the control transitions into a particular state. For example, the Disabled state defines that the ContentContainer Foreground brush will be assigned the PhoneDisabledBrush resource.

Styling a Control with Templates

A typical use of custom templates is to simply change a color, round an edge or hide an element, all with the intent to making the control mingle sociably with the other elements on the page. Perhaps you need a control to fit your organization logo color scheme.

Restyling a control is an exploration process. You need to identify the visual aspects of the control that can be changed. To demonstrate, let's style a Slider to an image for the thumb portion that slides along the track.

1. In Blend, create a new Windows Phone 8 application and add a 48 x 48 monochrome image to the \assets folder. Any of the icons used for application bar buttons will do. The application bar buttons are 76 x 76, so you will need to resize the images manually to 48 x 48. Icons can be found in the Windows Phone 8 SDK at \Program Files (x86)\Microsoft SDKs\Windows Phone\v8.0\Icons. This example will use an icon named surf.png (see Figure 13-70).

***Figure 13-70.** The Surf Icon*

2. Locate the ContentPanel in the Objects and Timeline panel and select it.
3. In the Assets panel, locate and double-click the Slider. This will add the Slider to the upper left corner of the ContentPanel.
4. In the Properties panel, with the Slider still selected, reset theLayout ➤ HorizontalAlignment property (this will cause the HorizontalAlignment to revert to Stretch).
5. Right-click the Slider and select Edit Template ➤ Edit a Copy from the context menu. This will display the Create Style Resource dialog.
6. Name the resource SurferSliderStyle and click the OK button as shown in Figure 13-71.

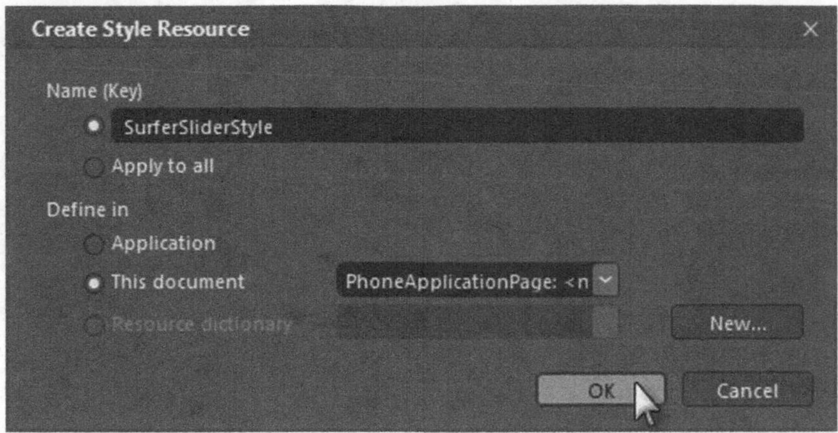

Figure 13-71. *Creating the SurferSliderStyle Resource*

■ **Note** If you enter a specific key Name in the `Create Style Resource` dialog, the resource must be bound to each element to be styled using the `{StaticResource}` XAML extension syntax. If you choose `Apply to all`, then you are defining an implicit style automatically applied to all elements with a given `TargetType`. The `Define in` section of the dialog places the resource XAML inside `Resources` section in `App.xaml`, orthe current document (`MainPage.xaml`), by adding the resource to the `Resources` section of the control selected in the drop down, or a separate `Resource dictionary` file.

---

7. Take a moment to get oriented in Blend and notice the `Objects and Timeline` panel and the bread crumb trail at the top of the `Artboard`. The icon in the middle of the breadcrumbs trail indicates that we're working inside a style and that the style contains a template(see Figure 13-72).

Figure 13-72. *The Breadcrumb Trail Above the Artboard*

8. The `Objects and Timeline` panel tells us we're working on the slider template inside the style. Also notice the button at the top left of the `Objects and Timeline` panel. This button returns to the next level up in scope, that is, the `PhoneApplicationPage`. You can rest the mouse over the icon to display a hint on the icon's use (see Figure 13-73).

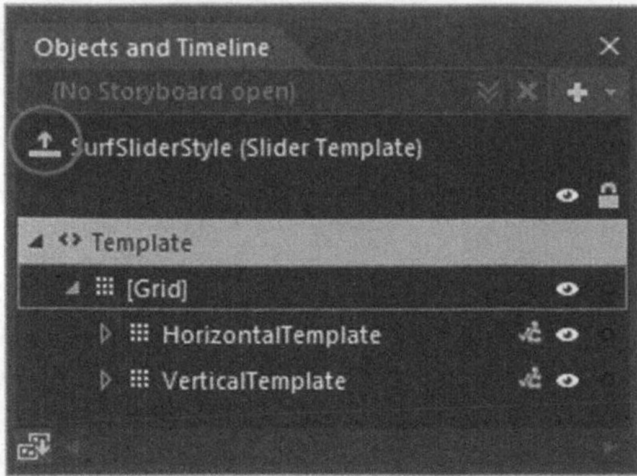

Figure 13-73. *The Objects and Timeline Panel when Editing the Slider Template*

The `Objects and Timeline` panel actually contains two templates, `HorizontalTemplate` and `VerticalTemplate`. These templates are visible depending on the `Orientation` property of the `Slider` control.

9. In the `Objects and Timeline` panel, open the `HorizontalTemplate` node. Here you can see that the `HorizontalTemplate` is made up of a fill, the `HorizontalTrack` that the thumb slides along, the `HorizontalFill` inside the track and the `HorizontalCenterElement`, that is, the thumb itself (see Figure 13-74).

Figure 13-74. *The HorizontalTemplate Elements*

10. In the `Objects and Timeline` panel, select the `HorizontalCenterElement`.

11. In the `Properties` panel, set the `Layout` ➤ `Widthproperty` to 48 and the `Layout` ➤ `Height` property to 48. This will change the thumb to an icon-sized square as shown in Figure 13-75.

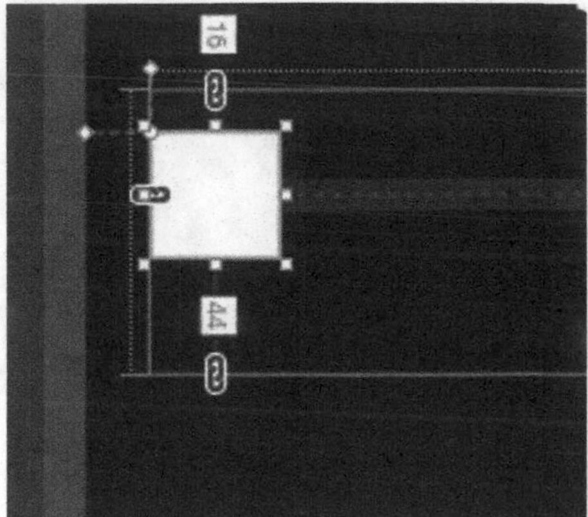

Figure 13-75. The 48 x 48 Thumb Named HorizontalCenterElement

12. In `Properties` ➤ Appearance, click the downward arrow to show advanced properties as shown in Figure 13-76.

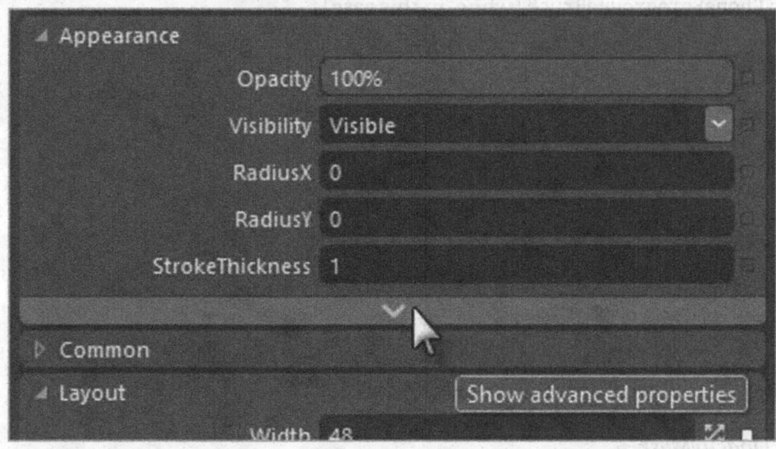

Figure 13-76. Expanding the Advanced Properties

13. Click the area to the right of the `OpacityMask` property, and then select the `Tile` brush from the tools that drop down as shown in Figure 13-77.

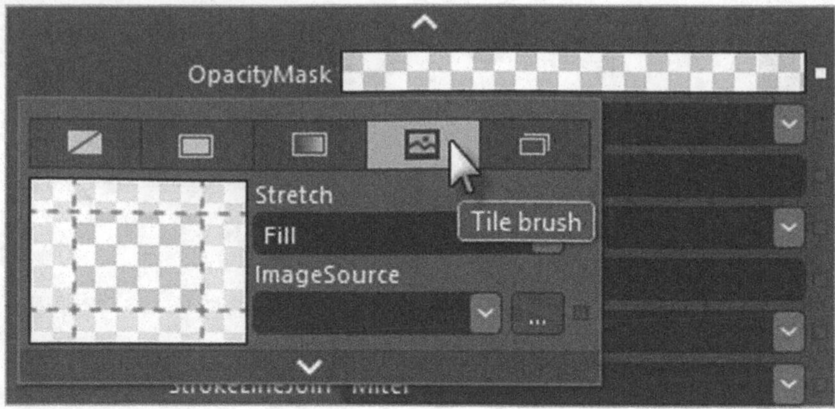

Figure 13-77. Selecting the Tile Brush

14. Select `surf.png` from the drop-down `ImageSource` list. Now the slider should look something like the Figure 13-78. Notice that because `surf.png` has a transparent background, the `OpacityMask` carves out the silhouette in the fill color of the thumb rectangle, which happens to be `PhoneForegroundBrush` (white, in this case).

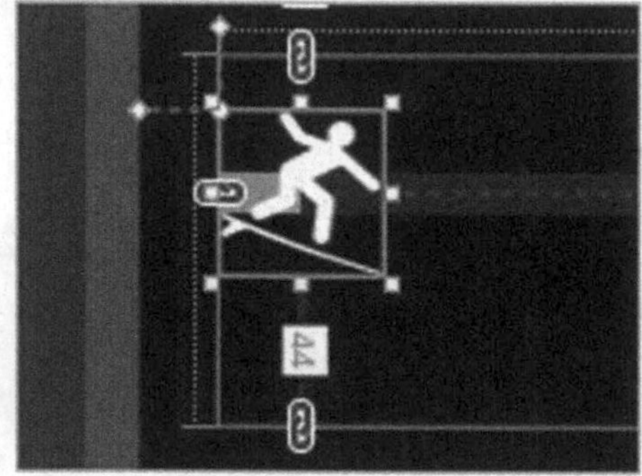

Figure 13-78. The Slider Style Showing the OpacityMask

15. Select the `HorizontalTrack` element. This is the area of the track to the right of the thumb, and the `Fill` is bound to the `Background`. In the `Properties` panel, click the button to the right of the `Fill` brush and select `Reset` from the drop-down menu.

16. Select the gradient brush as shown in Figure 13-79.

Figure 13-79. Selecting Gradient Brush for the HorizontalTrack Fill

17. Select the left-side gradient stop as shown in Figure 13-80.

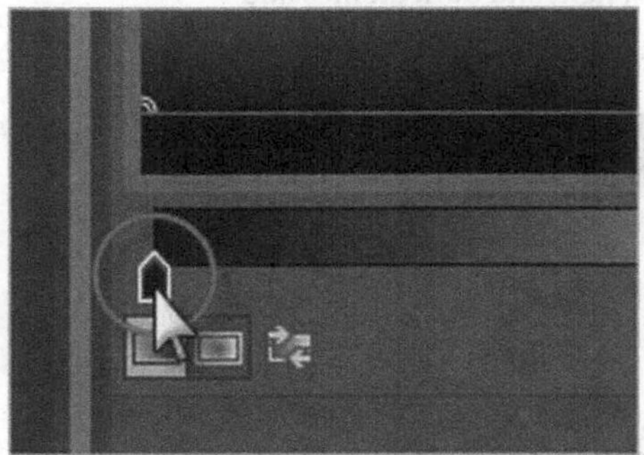

Figure 13-80. Selecting the Left Gradient Stop

18. Select the `Color Resources` tab and then select the `PhoneAccentColor` from the list as shown in Figure 13-81.

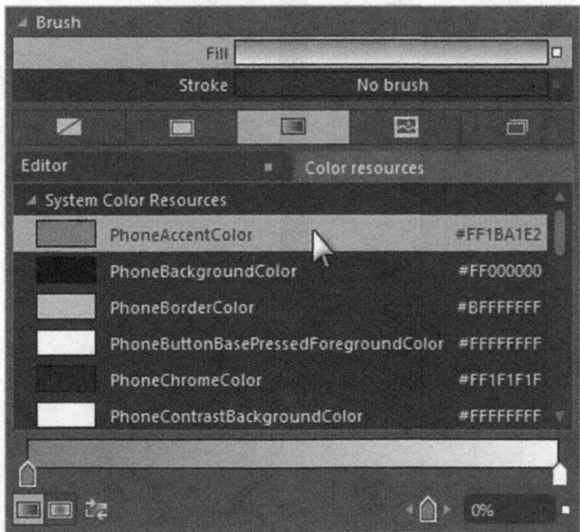

Figure 13-81. Selecting the PhoneAccentColor

19. Click the downward arrow on the `Brush` category to open the advanced properties. Set the `StartPoint` to 0, 0.5 and the `EndPoint` to 1, 0.5 as shown in Figure 13-82. This will make the gradient go from left to right, not top to bottom.

***Figure 13-82.** Setting the Gradient StartPoint and EndPoint Properties*

20. Press `F5` to run the application (see Figure 13-83). The styled slider thumb travels along the track as it's dragged by the user. Test the application against light and dark themes and using different colors.

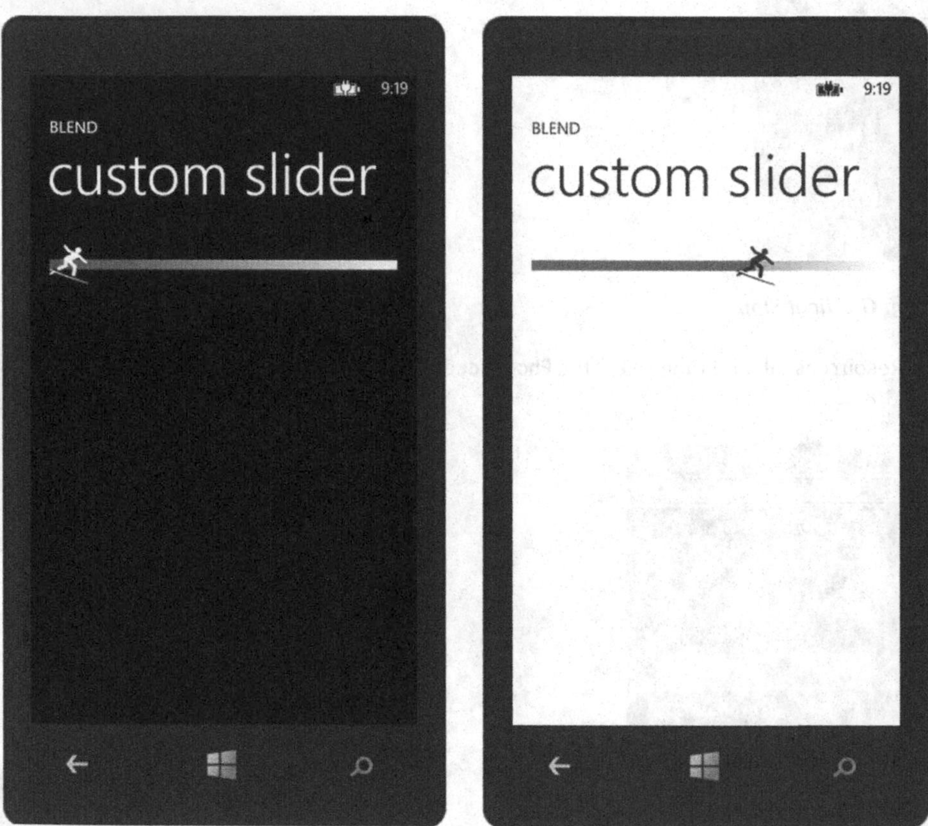

***Figure 13-83.** The Running Application With Custom-Styled Slider*

Animation

From a Blend perspective, *animation* is the process of setting properties incrementally over time. In Blend, you define a time (1 second, for example) and then change the properties for that point in time. These property changes can be mapped over a time line using a `Storyboard`, or transitions can be shaped for you automatically using predefined *easing functions*.

Animations can be triggered directly in code or triggered by changes in the control's state (in response to the control's being focused, for example). Behaviors can be used to make a control event (such as the `Tap` event), to trigger a state change. These interactive animation techniques are flexible enough to handle typical scenarios and can frequently be combined to produce unique and creative effects.

Storyboarding

Storyboards are named animation sequences managed in the `Objects and Timeline` panel. The timeline portion appears to the right of the objects outline and has a time graph that stretches out to the right. You can define points on the `Timeline` and then change properties of anything on the `Artboard` to the values that they should be for that point in time.

1. In Blend, create a new `Windows Phone App` project.
2. To create a storyboard, we'll start with an image that should fade-in and become larger over a period of two seconds (see Figure 13-84). You can use any image you have on hand.

Figure 13-84. *The Image to be Animated*

3. In the `Properties` panel, set the `ImageAppearance` ➤ `Opacity` to 50%.
4. The top of the `Objects and Timeline` panel will show the message `No Storyboard open`. Click the plus + button to the right to create a new storyboard as shown in Figure 13-85.

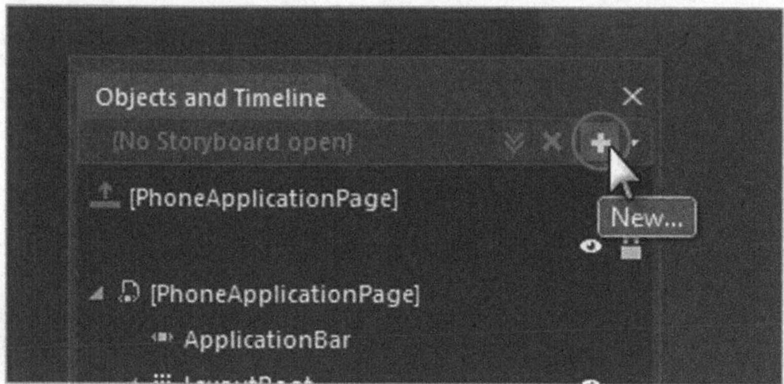

Figure 13-85. *Creating a new Storyboard*

5. In the `Create Storyboard Resource` dialog that displays, enter the `Name` as `FadeInAndEnlarge` and click the `OK` button to create the Storyboard and close the dialog (see Figure 13-86).

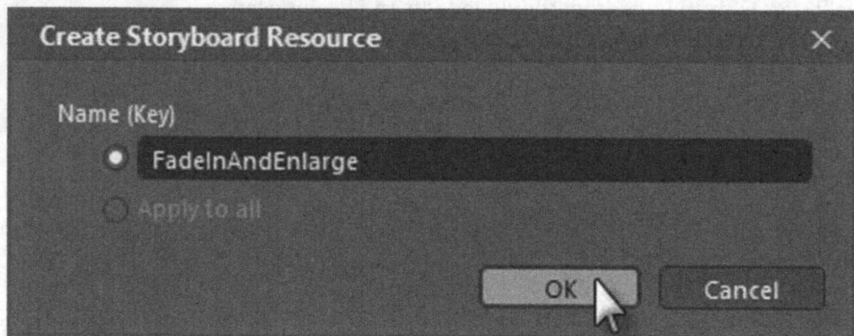

Figure 13-86. *Creating the Storyboard*

Two changes will happen to the Blend user interface after creating the storyboard. First, the `Objects and Timelinepanel` will open up on the right to show the `Timeline` portion (see Figure 13-87). Notice that the storyboard is labeled `FadeInAndEnlarge`, with a red dot to the left of the title indicating that the storyboard is in the process of recording.

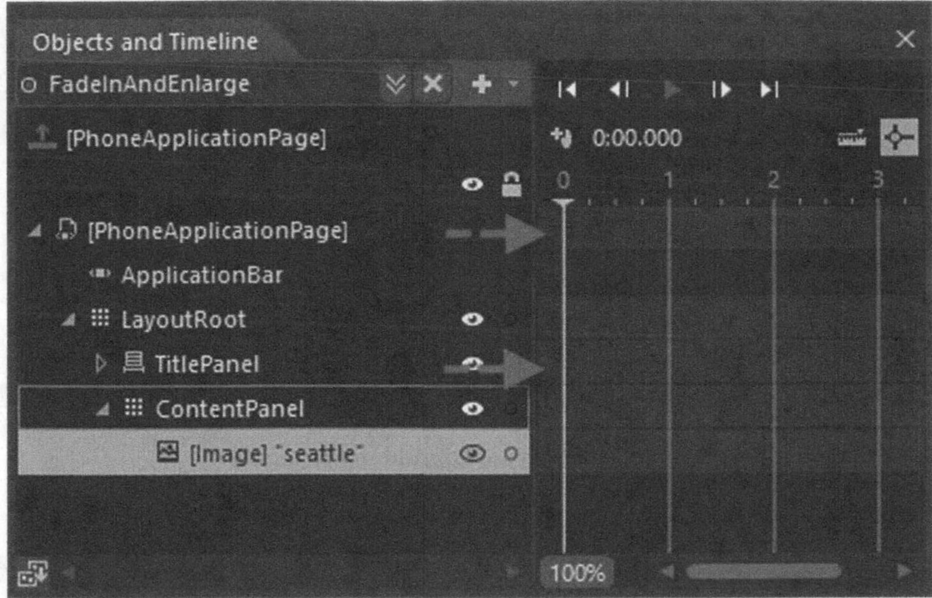

Figure 13-87. *The Timeline*

The second change is that the `Artboard` indicates that recording for the storyboard's timeline is turned on (see Figure 13-88). This means that any property changes to elements on the `Artboard` will be recorded on the timeline.

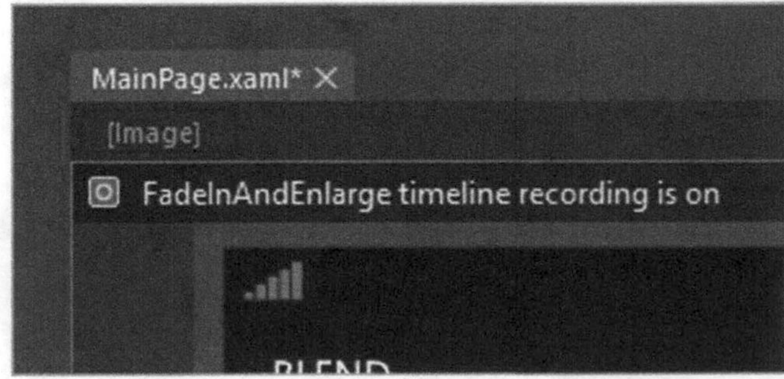

Figure 13-88. *The Artboard with Timeline Recording On*

6. In the timeline, drag the yellow time marker to approximately the one-quarter second mark as shown in Figure 13-89.

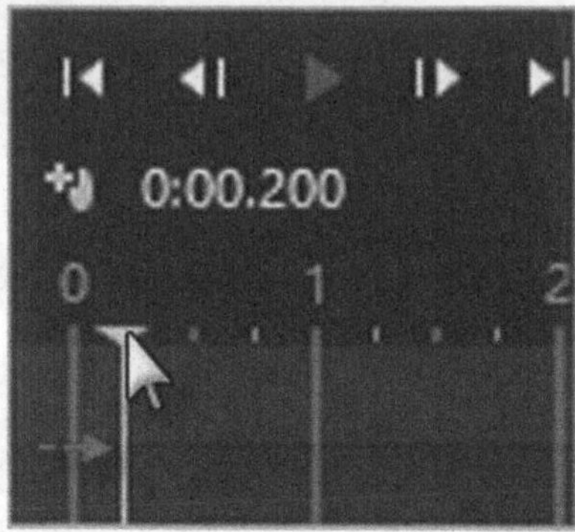

Figure 13-89. *Moving the Time Marker*

7. In the `Properties` panel, set the `Appearance` ➤ `Opacity` to 62%. Add approximately 10 pixels to the `Layout` ➤ `Width` and `Layout` ➤ `Height` properties. The `Objects` and `Timeline` panel should show marks for each property changed (see Figure 13-90).

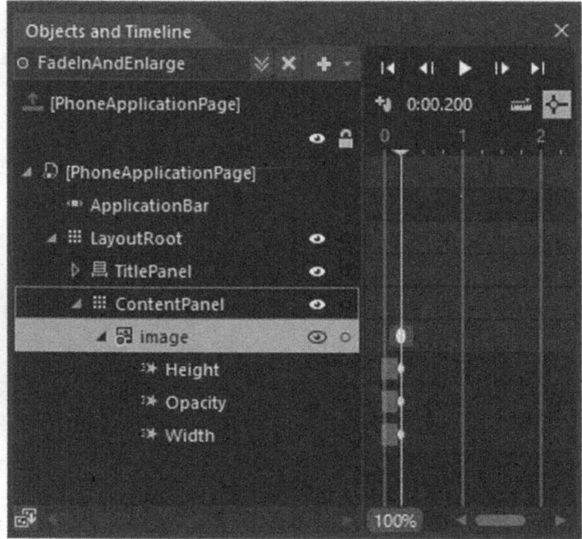

Figure 13-90. *Property Changes on the Timeline*

8. In the timeline, drag the yellow time marker to approximately midway between 0 and 1. In the `Properties` panel, set the `Appearance` ➤ `Opacity` to 75%. Add approximately 10 pixels to the `Layout` ➤ `Width` and `Layout` ➤ `Height` properties.

9. In the timeline, drag the yellow time marker to approximately three-quarters of the way between 0 and 1. In the `Properties` panel, set the `Appearance` ➤ `Opacity` to 87%. Add approximately 10 pixels to the `Layout` ➤ `Width` and `Layout` ➤ `Height` properties.

10. In the timeline, drag the yellow time marker to approximately the 1 second mark. In the `Properties` panel, set the `Appearance` ➤ `Opacity` to 100%. Add approximately 10 pixels to the `Layout` ➤ `Width` and `Layout` ➤ `Height` properties. The Objects and Timeline panel should look something like Figure 13-91.

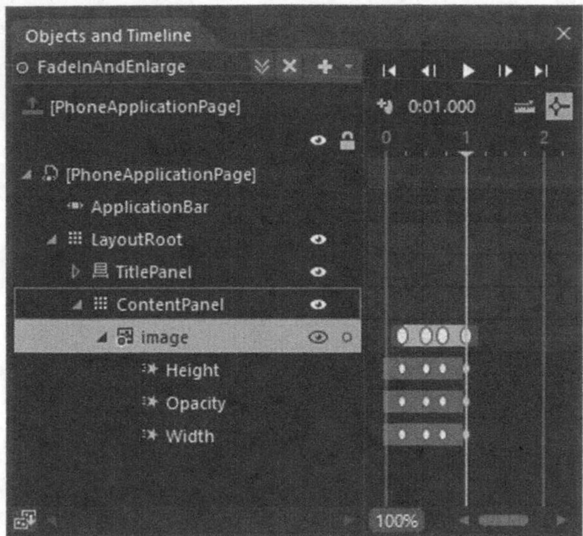

***Figure 13-91.** The Timeline at the One Second Mark*

11. Click the `Play` button at the top of the timeline as shown in Figure 13-92.

***Figure 13-92.** Playing the Animation*

When the animation plays, the image gradually enlarges and becomes more opaque as shown in Figure 13-93.

***Figure 13-93.** Stages in the Animation*

Now we want to trigger this storyboard to animate when the image is pressed. We could use code to call the `Storyboard`, but Blend can make this happen cleanly and without code using `Behaviors`.

1. Click the red target button in the upper left of the `Artboard` to shut off recording (see Figure 13-94). This prevents adding unintended properties to the animation.

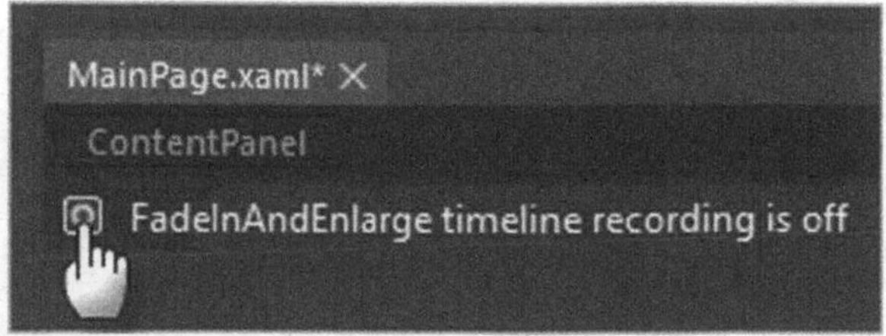

***Figure 13-94.** Turning off Timeline Recording*

2. In the `Objects and Timeline` panel, select the `Image` element.
3. In the `Assets` panel, select the `Behaviors` group on the left, and then double-click the `ControlStoryBoardAction` item. This will add the `ControlStoryBoardAction` as a child of the `Image`.
4. The `Properties` panel for the `ControlStoryBoardAction` manages the trigger that causes an action to fire. Select `MouseLeftButtonDown` from the drop-down list for the `Trigger ➤ EventName` property. Select `FadeInAndEnlarge` from the drop-down list in `Common ➤ Storyboard`.
5. Press `F5` to run the application. Tap the image to watch the animation.

Handling Visual State

States in Blend are a named collection of visual properties. A `Button`, for example, has pre-defined states for `Normal`, `Disabled`, and `Pressed` as shown in Figure 13-95. All the internal wiring is taken care of for you to fire each state in response to user actions.

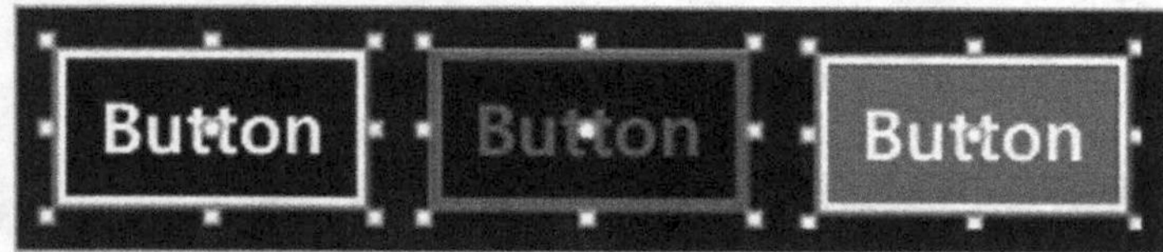

***Figure 13-95.** Button in Normal, Disabled and Pressed States in the Artboard*

To access `Button` predefined states, you need to edit a copy of the `Button` style template.

1. Add a default `Button` from the toolbox on the page
2. Right-click the button and select `Edit Template ➤ Edit a Copy` from the context menu. Give the style any name and press `OK` to create the style.
3. Select the `States` tab to see the predefined states as shown in Figure 13-96.

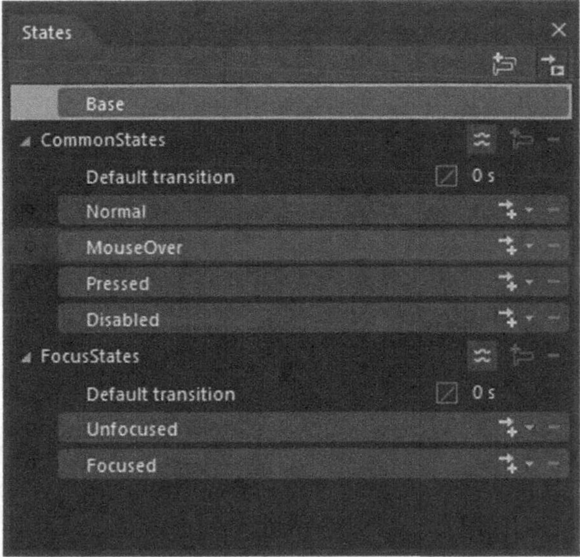

Figure 13-96. *The States for a Button Style*

4. Click `Pressed` in the `States` panel list. Notice that the button properties change and the button background in the `Artboard` turns red.
5. Click between the states and notice the difference in appearance and values that change in the `Properties` panel.

What if we want the border to be thicker when the button is pressed? Again, we need to select a state, and change the `Border` property.

1. Select the `Pressed` item in the `States` panel and notice that state recording is turned on in the `Artboard`.
2. Select the `ButtonBackground` in the `Objects and Timeline` panel, then reset the `Appearance` ➤ `BorderThickness` property.
3. Select `Normal` in the `States` panel, and then set the `Border`property of each edge to 3.
4. For the `Pressed` state, set the border for each edge to 10.
5. Now click back and forth between the `Normal` and `Pressed` states and verify that the border changes in the `Artboard`.
6. Run the application, press the button and watch the response to the state changes.

Custom Visual States

You aren't restricted to predefined states. You can create your own control, add custom states and then trigger those states from events on the control. This next example starts with an ellipse that has an image background. A custom `pressed` state will allow us to change its appearance in response to the user.

1. In Blend, create a new `Windows Phone App`.
2. Add an image to the `Assets` folder. Any image will do. This example will use an image of the Seattle skyline.

3. Add an `Ellipse` from the `Assets` panel to the `Content Panel`.
4. Select the `Ellipse` in the `Objects and Timeline` panel.
5. In the `Properties` panel, select `Brush` ➤ `Tilebrush` (from the row of icons). Select the image from the `Brush` ➤ `ImageSource` drop-down list. Set the `Brush` ➤ `Stretch` property to `UniformToFill`. The example looks like Figure 13-97.

Figure 13-97. *The Ellipse With Background*

6. Set the `Appearance` ➤ `Opacity` property of the `Ellipse` to `50%`.
7. In the `States` panel, click the `Add state group` button as shown in Figure 13-98. This adds a group named `VisualStateGroup` with a `Default transition`.

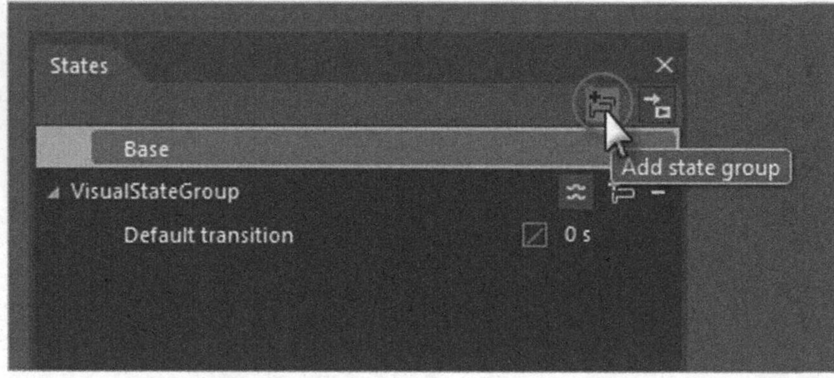

Figure 13-98. *Adding a State Group*

8. From the buttons to the right of the `VisualStateGroup`, add a `State` as shown in Figure 13-99. Once the state is added, the recording for the state will be turned on automatically.

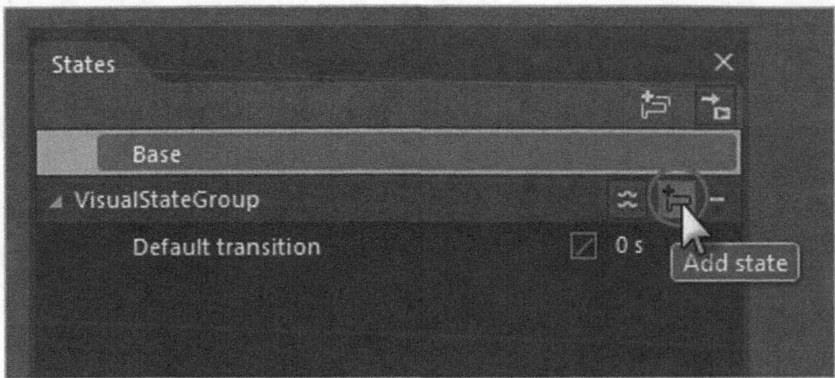

Figure 13-99. Adding a State

9. Name the new visual state Pressed as shown in Figure 13-100.

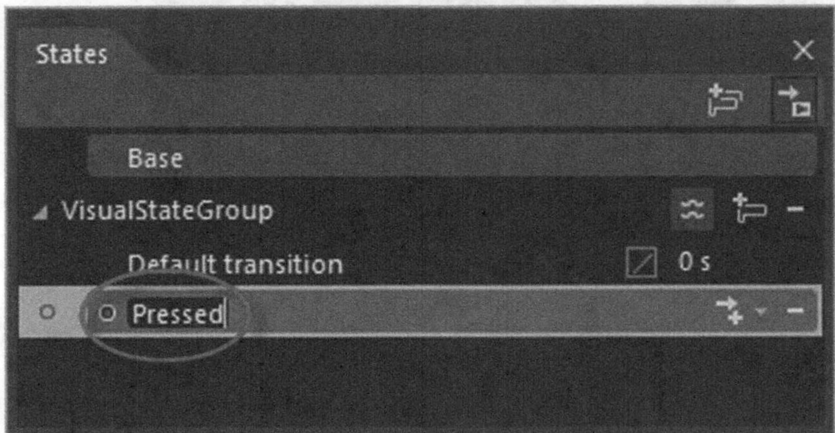

Figure 13-100. Renaming the State

10. Set the Opacity property to 100%. Set the Layout ➤ Width and Layout ➤ Height properties to 150.

11. From the buttons to the right of the Pressed state, click the drop-down arrow with the hint Add Transition. Select the * ➤ Pressed option from the drop-down list as shown in Figure 13-101. Then select the Pressed ➤* option from the drop-down list.

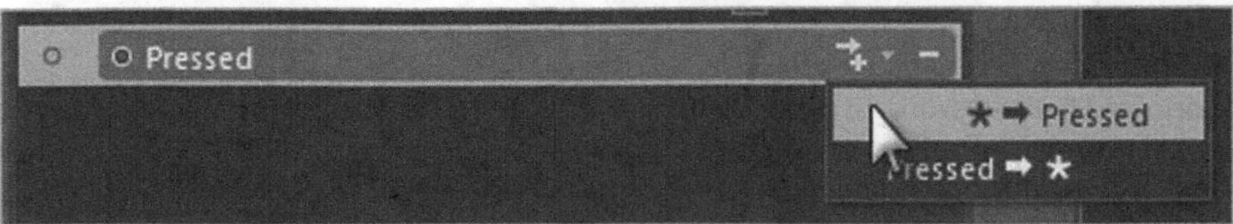

Figure 13-101. Adding a Transition

Transitions map how the changes between properties will take place. The transition specifies the animation duration in seconds. You can also control the intensity of the property changes over time using *Easing functions (see* Figure 13-102).

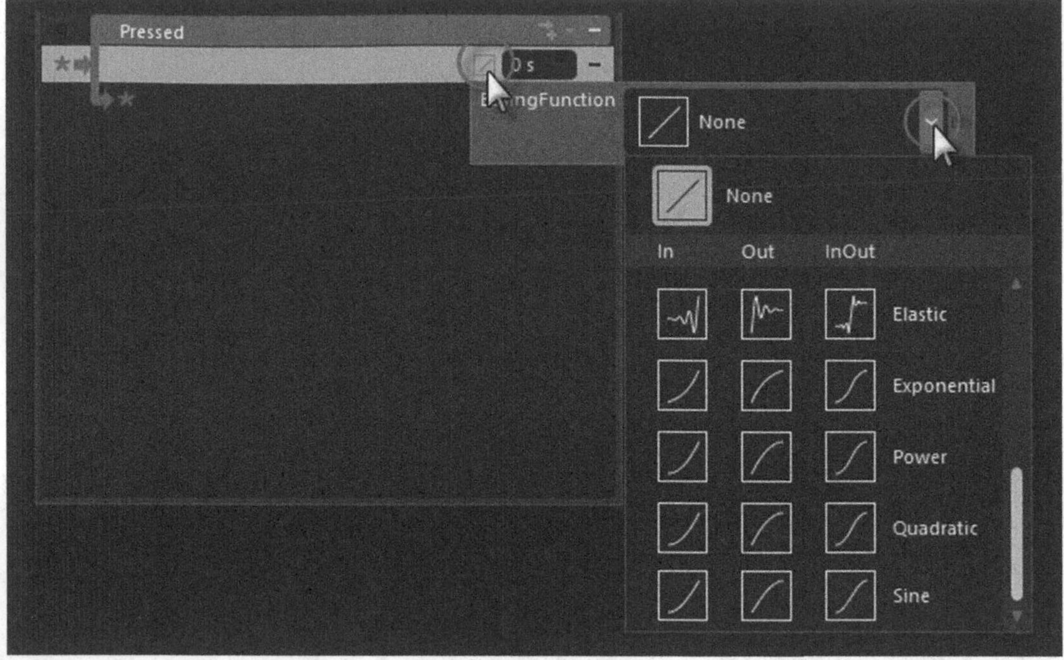

Figure 13-102. *Selecting the Transition Easing Function*

12. Add a second state and name it `Unpressed`.
13. To fire the state change, select the `Ellipse` in the `Objects and Timeline`, then add a `GoToStateAction` from the `Assets` panel under the `Behaviors` node.
14. With the `GoToStateAction` selected in the `Objects and Timeline`panel, set the `Common` ➤ `StateName` property to `Pressed`. Make sure that the `EventName` is `MouseLeftButtonDown`.
15. Add a second `GoToStateAction` and set the `Common`➤`StateName` to `Unpressed`. Set the `EventName` to `MouseLeftButtonUp`.
16. Press `F5` to run the application. When the ellipse is pressed, the image becomes larger and more opaque. When the ellipse is no longer pressed, the image returns to a smaller size and becomes partly transparent.

Summary

Blend is a powerful graphics-oriented tool that works in concert with Visual Studio. With Blend we can delve deeply into the styling and behavior of the controls or build new controls from scratch.

This chapter was a guide to getting started designing Windows Phone 8 pages using Blend. It described how Blend works together with Visual Studio and how to get around in the Blend user interface. This chapter explored some of the key techniques for building custom controls, user controls, working with templates, animation and state handling.

CHAPTER 14

Taking Your App to Market

Writing the application is only one of the many jobs performed during the lifetime of a product. This chapter looks at some of the key tasks to be completed to get the application to the Windows Phone Store, including satisfying certification requirements, testing your application using the Store Test Kit, and the process for submitting your application.

Certification Requirements for Windows Phone Store

Certification requirements verify that your application is ready to roll into the Windows Phone Store. The goal of certification is to make sure that your application is reliable, makes efficient use of resources, doesn't mess with phone functionality, and is free of malicious software.

The App certification requirements for Windows Phone have been iterated since their introduction and are pretty much to the point. You can find the requirements listed at the App certification requirements for Windows Phonepage(`msdn.microsoft.com/en-us/library/windowsphone/develop/hh184843(v=vs.105).aspx`). Each requirement is designed to be clear, objective, and testable. The general categories in the document are:

- ***App policies for Windows Phone*** (`http://msdn.microsoft.com/en-us/library/windowsphone/develop/hh184841(v=vs.105).aspx`) helps make sure the application supports the user's purposes rather than just the developer's. These rules govern how the application handles issues like location awareness, user's personal information, chat facilities, advertising, and notifications. A few examples:
    - "If your app includes or displays advertising... must have distinct, substantial and legitimate content and purpose other than the display of advertising."
    - "Your app must provide in-app settings that allow the user to enable and disable your app's access to and use of location from the Location Service API."
    - "Your app must be fully functional when acquired from the Windows Phone Store and it must provide functionality other than launching a webpage."
- ***Content policies for Windows Phone*** (`http://msdn.microsoft.com/en-us/library/windowsphone/develop/hh184842(v=vs.105).aspx`) block various types of illegal subject matter including unlicensed copyrighted material, threatening or slanderous content, adult material, violence, or excessive profanity.
- ***App submission requirements for Windows Phone*** (`http://msdn.microsoft.com/en-us/library/windowsphone/develop/hh184844(v=vs.105).aspx`) covers how the application is described and packaged for the Windows Phone Store. This includes checking that the application code base is using the proper, documented API calls and that the application's icons and screenshots conform to prescribed sizes and types.

- ***Technical certification requirements for Windows Phone*** (`http://msdn.microsoft.com/-en-us/library/windowsphone/develop/hh184840(v=vs.105).aspx`) verify that your application is reliable, performs well, and doesn't hog resources. Test Steps are included to help you verify these requirements. A few excerpts:
  - "The app must render the first screen within 5 seconds after launch."
  - "Pressing the Back button from the first screen of an app must close the app."
  - "The app must not stop responding or close unexpectedly when there is an incoming phone call, SMS message, or MMS message."
- **Additional requirements for specific app types for Windows Phone** (`http://msdn.microsoft.com/en-us/library/windowsphone/develop/hh184838(v=vs.105).aspx`) cover rules for particular Windows Phone 8 aspects such as location awareness, push notifications, music and video, background processing, and applications running under a locked screen.

Using the Store Test Kit

The `Store Test Kit` is a convenient way to pre-qualify that your application will pass the certification requirements. Be aware that the `Store Test Kit` is merely a smoke test to reveal no-brainer issues that could stop your application from being accepted by the store. It won't reveal deeper issues with the application covered by the certification requirements. In the Visual Studio Solution Explorer, right-click the project node to execute the `Open Store Test Kit` option from the context menu (see Figure 14-1).

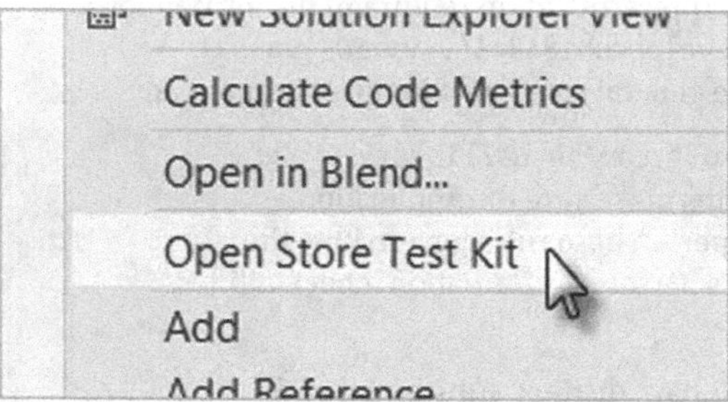

Figure 14-1. *Running the Open Store Test Kit Option*

Running the `Open Store Test Kit` option opens a set of property pages that you can fill out top-to-bottom to help make your application ready for the store.

- The `Application Details` tab lets you define the path to your release-compiled application package and to store images. Your application could be rejected if the application was compiled in Debug mode or if any of the required images are missing (see Figure 14-2). Notice the Application Package at the top of the page contains the path to the XAP file that you will ultimately send to the store.

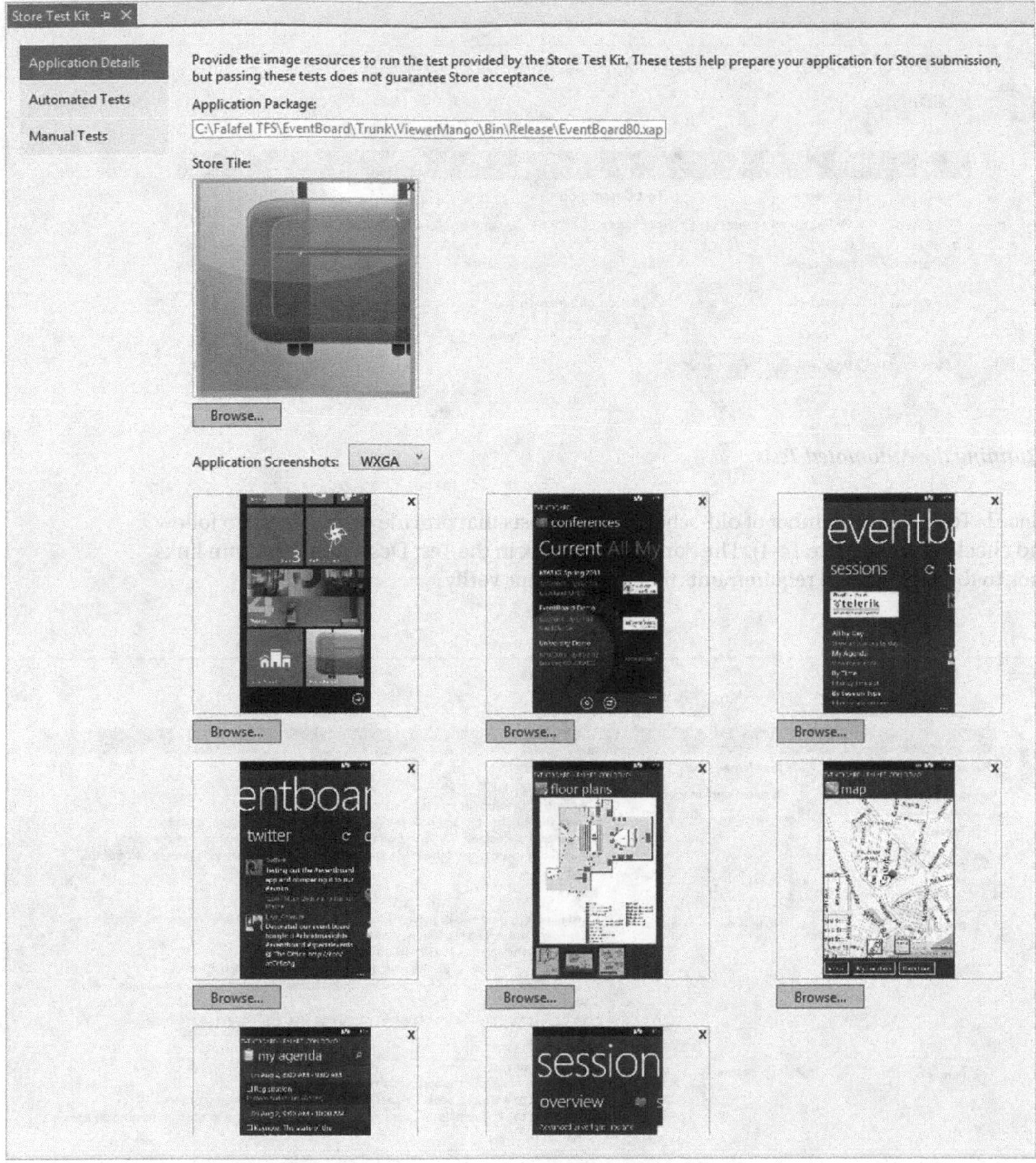

Figure 14-2. Opening the Application Details Tab

- `Automated Tests` verify XAP package requirements, capabilities, icons, and screenshots as shown in Figure 14-3.

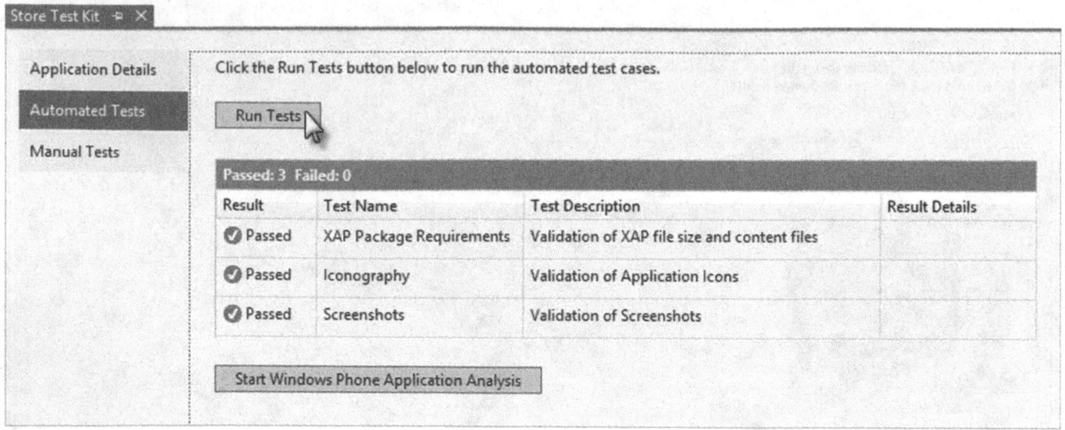

***Figure 14-3.** Running the Automated Tests*

- `Manual Tests` lists a number of old-school manual tests that provide steps for you to follow and check off (see Figure 14-4). The `More info...` link in the Test Description column links back to the certification requirements that the test steps verify.

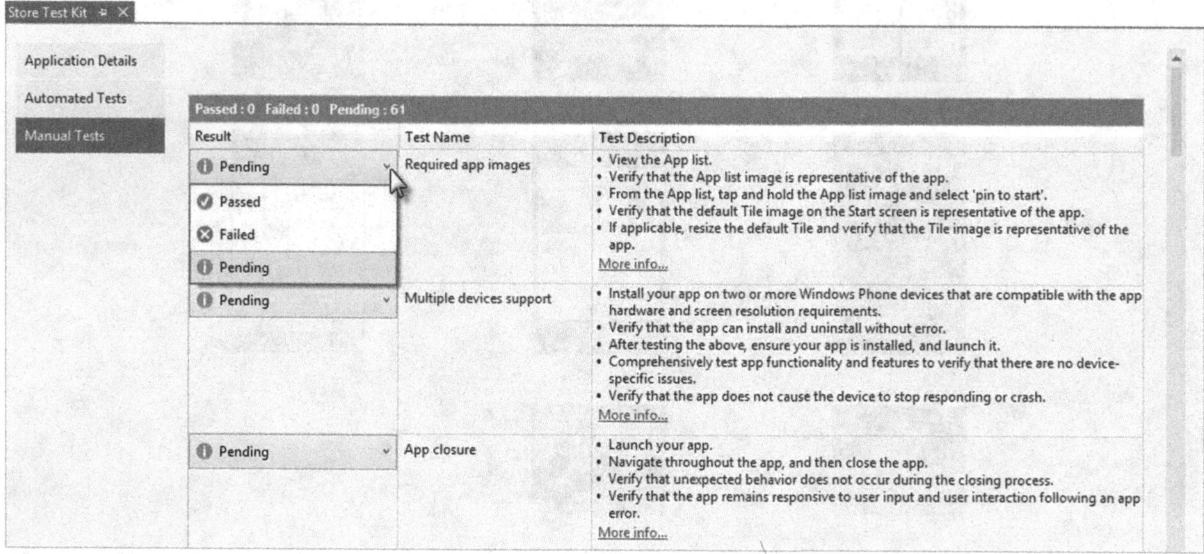

***Figure 14-4.** Running the Manual Tests*

Submitting Your App to the Windows Phone Store

The initial submission process can take a little time and effort, but subsequent updates are much easier. Before submitting your application to the store, be sure you have your XAP file ready. You can get the file path from `Store Test Kit` ➤ `Application Details` ➤ `Application Package`. Also be sure to have images for the tile that represent your application in the Windows Phone Store, any optional background images you want displayed in the store, and at least one screenshot. Be aware that you can have up to eight screenshots per resolution and language combination.

1. In your browser, navigate to the Windows Phone Dev Center (`https://dev.windowsphone.com/en-us/develop`) and then click the `SUBMIT APP` link. If you have a Dev Center account, you will navigate to the `Submit App` page (`https://dev.windowsphone.com/en-us/AppSubmission/Hub`).

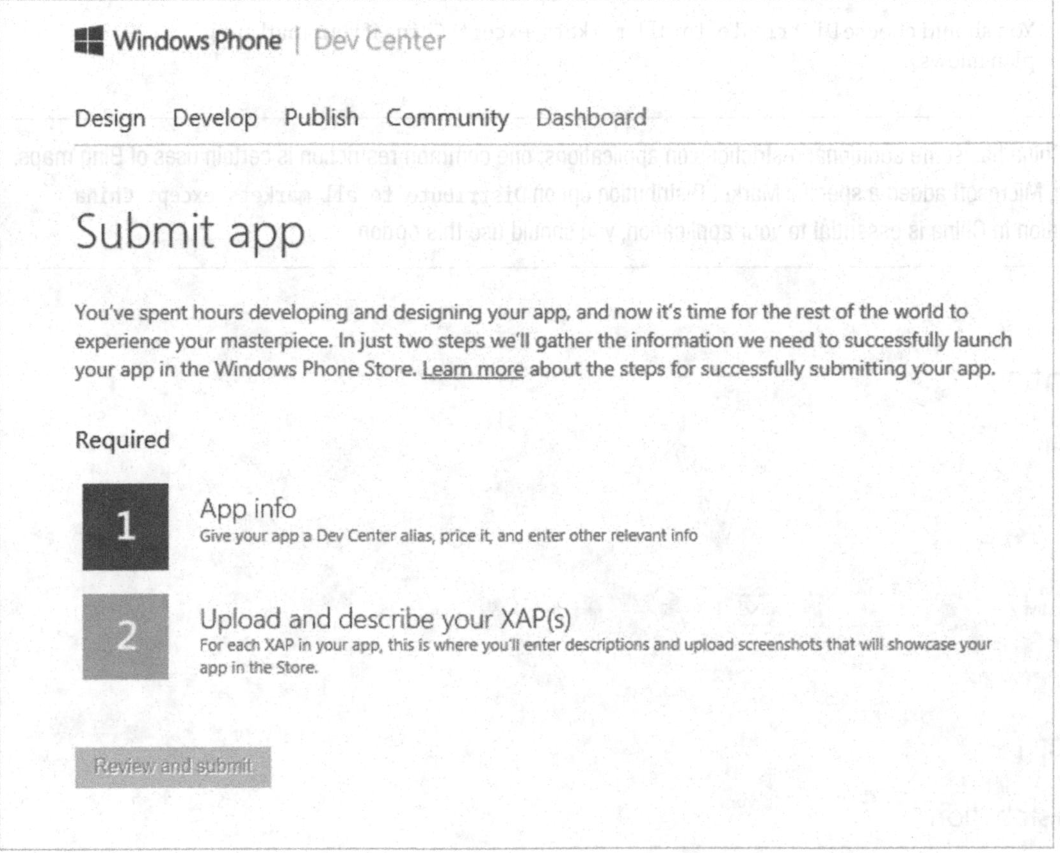

***Figure 14-5.** The Submit App Page*

■ **Note** If you don't have a Dev Center account, you will see directions on joining. Be aware that you can be signed in with a valid Microsoft login, but still not be registered with Dev Center.

---

2. First, click the `App info` link. The App info page shown in Figure 14-6 is a simplified view of the page with key entry fields.
3. Complete the following options:
   a. The `App alias` entry takes the name that the application will be referred to in the Dev Center (the name that the user sees is taken from the XAP file).
   b. Pick a `Category` you think best describes your application from the drop-down list. Some categories, such as "Games", will have a sub category drop-down (not shown).
   c. If you want to directly monetize your application, select a `Base Price` from the drop-down list.
   d. The `Market distribution` option directly affects how easily your application will pass certification.
   e. You should choose `Distribute to all markets except China` if your marketing plan allows.

■ **Caution** China has some additional restrictions on applications; one common restriction is certain uses of Bing maps. For this reason, Microsoft added a specific Market Distribution option `Distribute to all markets except China`. Unless distribution in China is essential to your application, you should use this option.

Figure 14-6. *Filling out the App Info Page*

4. Click the `More options` link to show the `Distribution channels` and `Publish` options (see Figure 14-7).

   a. The `Distribution channels` option lets you control who sees the application by placing it in the `Public Store` or into a `Beta` where only people in the email list can participate. Also notice the checkbox under `Public Store` that allows you to hide the application from browsing and searching.

   b. The `Publish` option is typically set to `Automatically, as soon as certified`, but you can choose to do this `Manually` if you need to publish at a specific time.

   c. The Microsoft Push Notification Service (MPNS) drop-down list is populated only if you have uploaded certifications (`https://dev.windowsphone.com/en-us/Account/Certificates`) to allow authenticated notifications. Without a certification, push notifications are limited to 500 per subscription, per day and take place over standard HTTP.

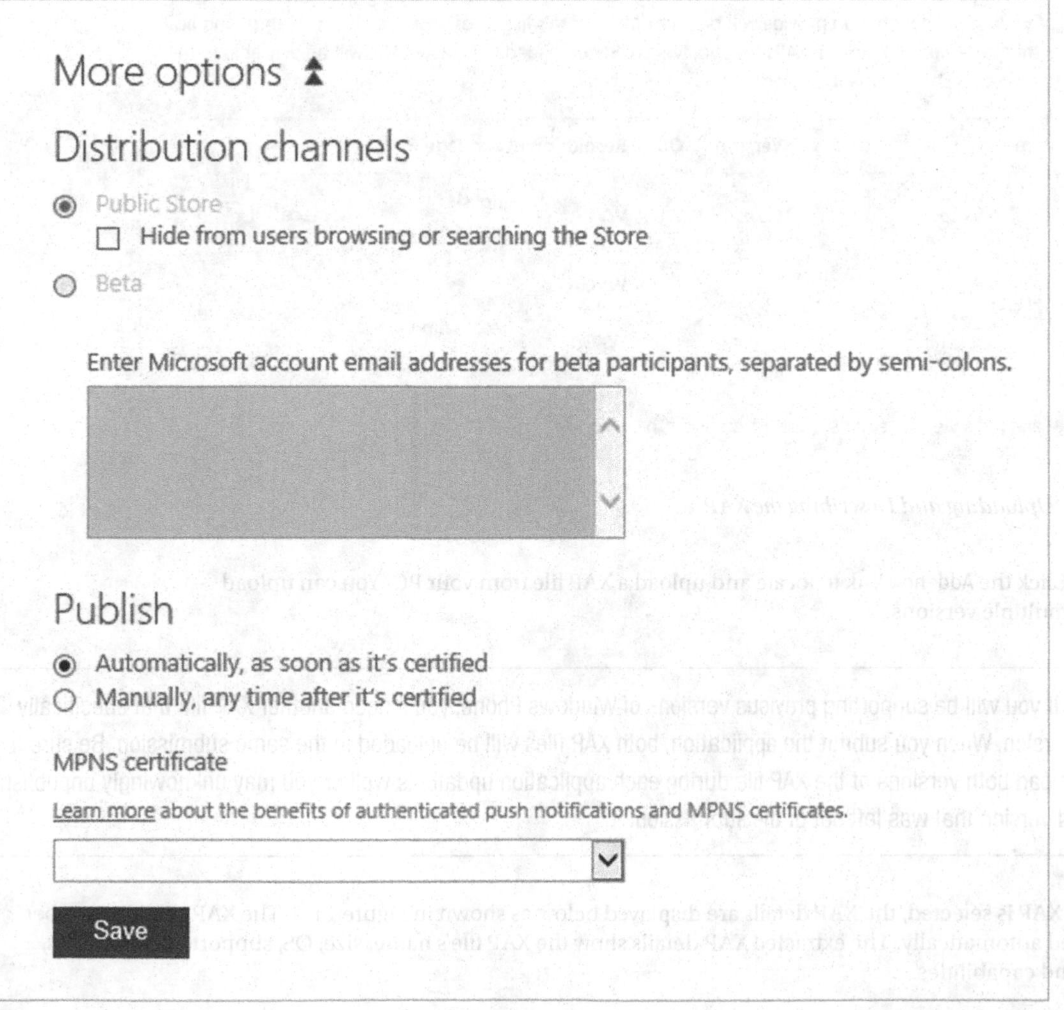

***Figure 14-7.** The More Options Section of the App Info*

5. Once you have the `App info` filled in, click the Save button to retain your changes.
6. Upon returning to the `Submit App` page, click the link for the second step `Upload and describe your XAP` (see Figure 14-8). Much of the information will come straight from your XAP file when it's uploaded. The list shows the XAP name, XAP version, OS, supported resolutions, and languages.

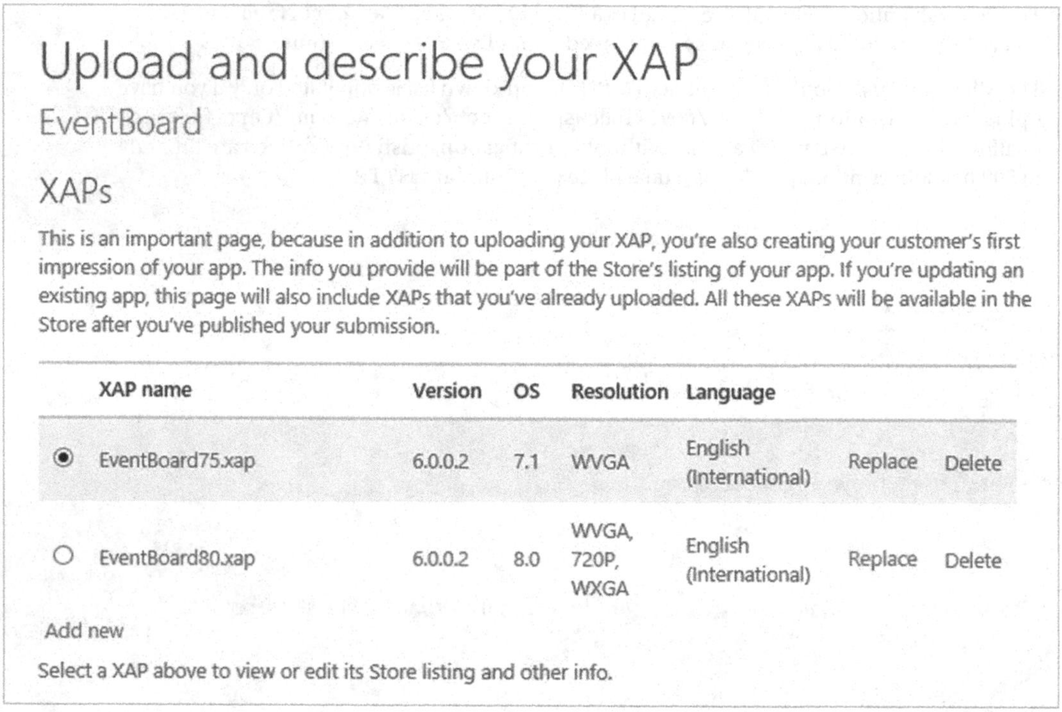

Upload and describe your XAP

EventBoard

XAPs

This is an important page, because in addition to uploading your XAP, you're also creating your customer's first impression of your app. The info you provide will be part of the Store's listing of your app. If you're updating an existing app, this page will also include XAPs that you've already uploaded. All these XAPs will be available in the Store after you've published your submission.

	XAP name	Version	OS	Resolution	Language		
◉	EventBoard75.xap	6.0.0.2	7.1	WVGA	English (International)	Replace	Delete
○	EventBoard80.xap	6.0.0.2	8.0	WVGA, 720P, WXGA	English (International)	Replace	Delete

Add new

Select a XAP above to view or edit its Store listing and other info.

Figure 14-8. *Uploading and Describing the XAP*

7. Click the `Add new` link to locate and upload a XAP file from your PC. You can upload multiple versions.

■ **Caution** If you will be supporting previous versions of Windows Phone, you'll need another XAP file that specifically targets that version. When you submit the application, both XAP files will be uploaded in the same submission. Be sure to create and upload both versions of the XAP file during each application update as well or you may unknowingly unpublish the supported version that was left out of the submission.

When a XAP is selected, the XAP details are displayed below as shown in Figure 14-9. The XAP version number is not updated automatically. The extracted XAP details show the XAP file's name, size, OS, supported resolutions, languages, and capabilities.

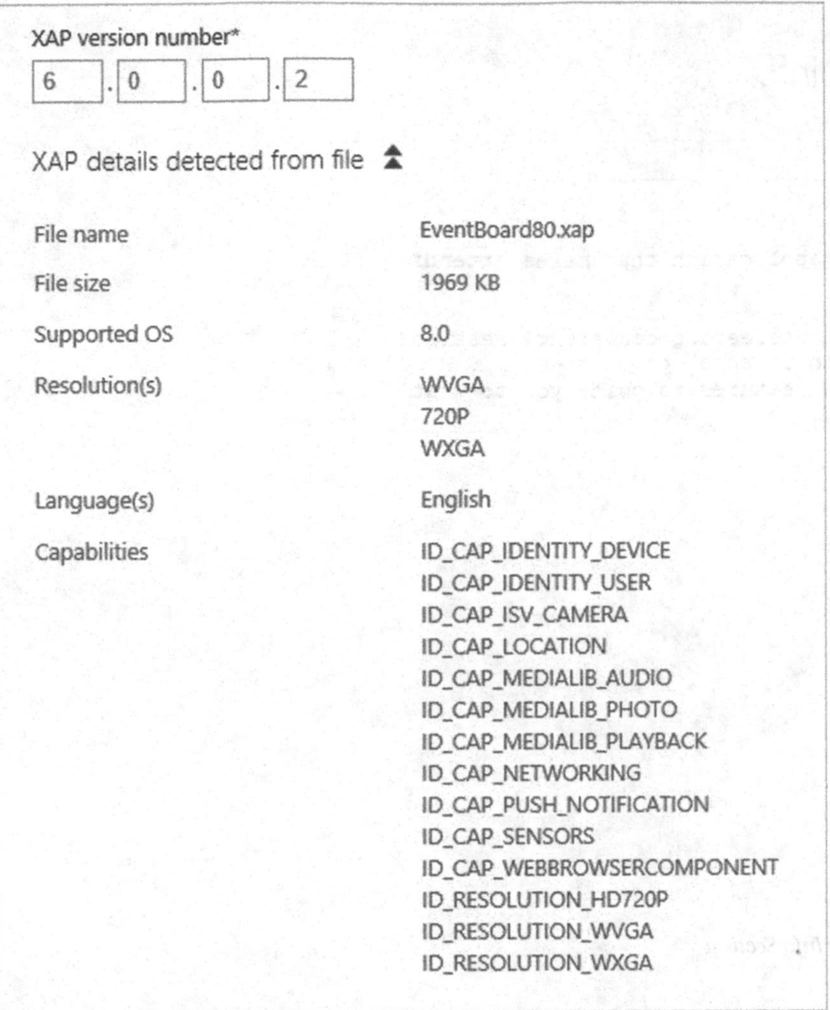

Figure 14-9. *The XAP Details Page*

8. Scroll past the XAP details to find the `XAP's Store listing info` (see Figure 14-10) and set the following options:

   a. If the XAP supports more than one language, the language drop-down will allow you to add specific store listing information for each language.

   b. The `Description for the Store` entry is your chance to make a case for your application and what it will do for your users.

   c. The `Specify keywords` section takes words or phrases that people can use to find your application in the store.

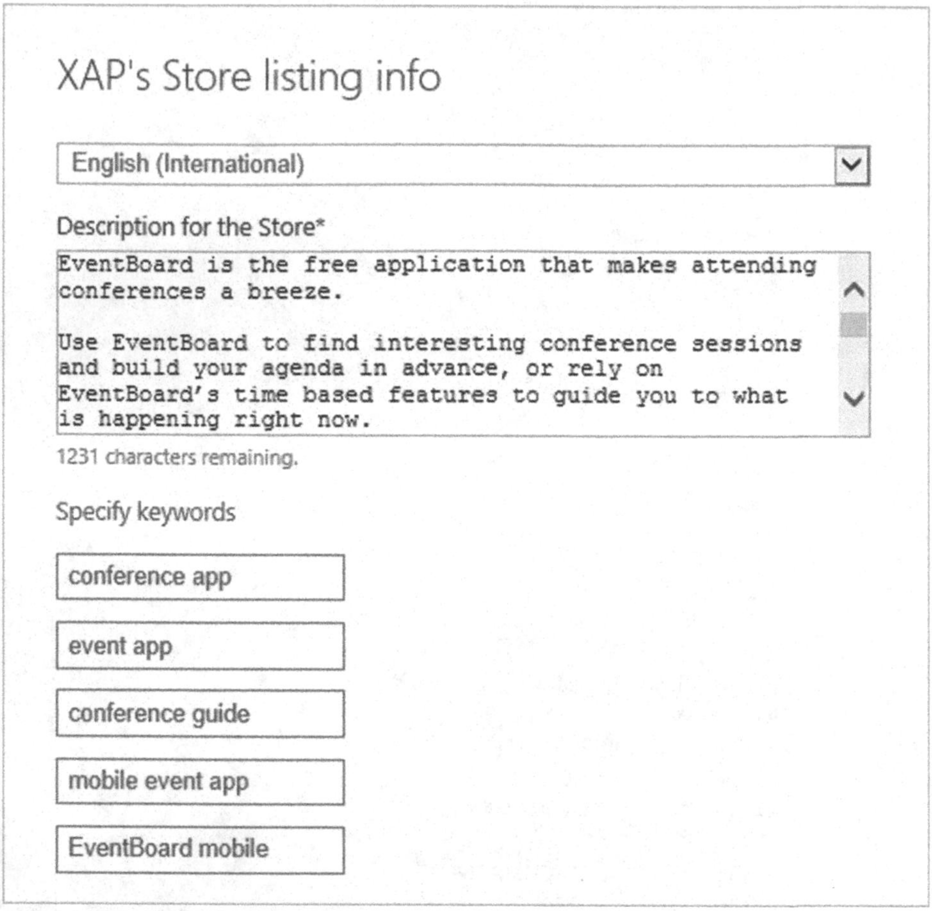

XAP's Store listing info

English (International)

Description for the Store*

EventBoard is the free application that makes attending conferences a breeze.

Use EventBoard to find interesting conference sessions and build your agenda in advance, or rely on EventBoard's time based features to guide you to what is happening right now.

1231 characters remaining.

Specify keywords

conference app

event app

conference guide

mobile event app

EventBoard mobile

Figure 14-10. *The XAP Store Listing Info Section*

9. Below the keywords you should add images to represent the `App tile icon`, `Background image` and screenshots for each resolution. Here are a few tips on creating these images:

   - The expected dimensions are listed by each image.
   - You can add up to 8 screenshots for each resolution.
   - The checkbox option `Automatically create lower resolution screenshots from WXGA` allows you to only upload one set of images, but you will get higher quality if you create screenshots for each resolution.
   - To create screenshots, use either the `Screenshot` tab from the `Emulator's Additional Tools` or click `Lock` + `Start` on the phone to save the current screen to the `screenshots` album.

■ **Note** For more information on creating screenshots for the store, see `msdn.microsoft.com/en-us/library/windowsphone/develop/gg442300(v=vs.105).aspx`.

Figure 14-11. Uploading Images for the Store

When you complete the `Upload and describe your XAP` page, click the Save button to retain your changes.

■ **Note** Before sending your application to the store you can also specify optional information for in-app advertising, define custom pricing,and get a map service application ID and token.

Back on the `Submit app` page, click the `Review and submit` button to send your application to the Windows Phone Store. Submission times vary. It may take up to 5 days for your application to be approved. If your application has a hard deadline, be sure to plan for this delay in availability.

After the Windows Phone Store

Getting your application to the store is a great start, but if you want to ensure the longevity and success of your newly minted creation, you will want to do your own marketing outside of the Windows Phone Store. A website, social media campaign, and more can encourage adoption. Blog and contribute meaningful content that pertains to the market you're selling in.

If your application's audience includes bigger customers, introduce yourself and demo the product to them. Explain how your app is positioned, where it excels and why. Develop a product road map to help maintain the application's position in the market.

Many applications don't have big customers per se, just people looking for a solution to a problem they hope your application can solve.

In today's market, everyone is an expert. All of your customers have a voice in your application's store rating. If you put out something that doesn't work, you're going to hear about it quickly (usually in ego-deflating terms). If you were to go around the room and ask people if they've downloaded something with a one-star rating, no one will have. The app can be very simple, but it must work.

Summary

Marketing covers a wide swath of activity that includes researching your market, building a useful application with great content, testing, creating Windows Phone Store collateral, submitting your app to the Windows Phone Store, and listening to customer feedback. In this chapter we talked about some of the straight-forward mechanics of getting your application past the certification requirements for Windows Phone and discussed some of the ephemeral aspects of making your app successful in the marketplace.

Special thanks to Mike Dugan, VP of Products at Falafel Software, for his assistance on this chapter.

Index

A

B

C

■ D

E, F

G

■ H

■ I

■ J, K

■ L

M

■ N

O

P, Q, R

■ S, T

■ U

■ V

■ W

X

■ Y, Z